BERNARD FREYBERG, VC

Soldier of Two Nations

Paul Freyberg

Hodder & Stoughton

LONDON SYDNEY AUCKLAND TORONTO

For Ivry, Annabel, and all
who have contributed to this book

British Library Cataloguing in Publication Data

Freyberg, Paul
  Bernard Freyberg, VC: soldier of two nations.
  1. Great Britain. Armies
  I. Title
  355.33109

  ISBN 0-340-39693-8

Published by Hodder and Stoughton,
a division of Hodder and Stoughton Ltd,
Mill Road, Dunton Green, Sevenoaks, Kent TN13 2YA.
Editorial Office: 47 Bedford Square, London WC1B 3DP.

Photoset by Rowland Phototypesetting Ltd,
Bury St Edmunds, Suffolk
Printed in Great Britain by
St Edmundsbury Press Ltd,
Bury St Edmunds, Suffolk

Contents

CONTENTS

Note on the Illustrations

The photographs in this book appear in four groups of eight pages: between pages 52–3, 148–9, 308–9, and 468–9. The pictures all come from the author's personal collection except where they are specifically acknowledged to copyright holders in the captions.

The frontispiece reproduces a sketch of General Freyberg in the Western Desert in 1941. It is by Peter McIntyre, the official artist to the New Zealand Forces in the Second World War, and is taken from his book *The Painted Years*. It was made for a later formal portrait.

List of Maps

Author's Acknowledgments

In the Author's Introduction, in the Note on unpublished sources, and in the Notes and Sources for each chapter I have given the provenance of the information on which this biography is based. I would like also to express my appreciation of the special help I have received over different parts of the book.

First, my thanks are due to Her Majesty the Queen for her gracious permission to reproduce her letter to my mother of 7 October 1947, written when she was Princess Elizabeth.

I would like to make special mention of all the help I have received from Sir John White, who was my father's PA during most of the Second World War, and from Lieutenant-General Sir Leonard Thornton. They gave me a great deal of their time over a period of years in checking and commenting on the World War II chapters. In particular, the daily Diary kept by Sir John White at NZ Division HQ between 1941–45 was an invaluable aide-memoire. In addition, many of the photographs in the book were taken by Sir John during his time as my father's PA.

I wish to thank Mr G. W. G. Munnery for his researches into the early history of the Freyberg family; and Mrs Kitty Freyberg and the late Captain Geoffrey Freyberg, RN, for passing on their knowledge of the family during the nineteenth century, and photographs. I owe a debt to Brigadier J. Ferris Fuller for tracking down information about my father's time as a dentist in New Zealand, and to Mr George Kaye for providing some of the facts there at the turn of the century.

I remain extremely grateful to the late Lady Violet Bonham Carter for all that she told me personally about my father in the First World War; and also to Mr Joseph Murray, one of the last survivors of the Royal Naval Division, who likewise recounted to me much about Gallipoli and the battle of the Ancre. I wish to acknowledge the courtesy of Coutts Bank in allowing me to see my father's accounts from 1914 to his marriage in 1922, which provided a great deal of hitherto unknown background material.

Author's Acknowledgments

For the inter-war years I have the late Major-General Sir Allan Adair to thank for his description of my father in his early time as a Grenadier, and also the late General Sir James Marshall-Cornwall for his account of the course at Versailles which he, the late Field Marshal Viscount Wavell and my father attended in 1934.

I would like to thank the late Sir John Colville for his help over my father's visits to Downing Street and Chequers in the summer of 1940. Three of my father's Intelligence Officers have been of great assistance. Sir Geoffrey Cox provided first-hand knowledge of the campaigns and has allowed me to quote extensively from his books; while the late Dan Davin also gave the biography much sympathetic support and encouragement. Also the late Robin Bell for his information about Crete. I am grateful to the late Major-General Sir Guy Salisbury-Jones for his help over the Greek and Crete chapters; and to Sir Charles Mott-Radclyffe for his unrivalled knowledge of the background to the Greek campaign. My father's ADC, Jack Griffiths, gave me my first intimation of how the ULTRA information reached my father in Crete. Sir Harry Hinsley, Mr Martin Gilbert, and Major-General Sir Digby Raeburn also helped me with information that enabled me eventually to solve what had remained a mystery for so long.

General Sir Charles Richardson's comments on the later North African chapters were extremely helpful. I acknowledge too using the books on the North African and Italian campaigns by Brigadier J. T. Burrows and the late Major-General W. G. Stevens, and Robert de Stacpoole kindly sent me the book about Father Dolly. I am also grateful to General Sir David Fraser for his constructive suggestions on the sections dealing with both World Wars. In addition Lord Wigram commented very usefully on the first Governor-General chapter.

Mr Eugene Fleury has drawn a most comprehensive set of maps. Many of the photographs (often originally taken by Sir John White) have come from family scrapbooks, and have been transposed for the book by Mr James Graham. Lord Neidpath has kindly given permission for the use of a photograph of Lady Cynthia Charteris (Asquith), and the Hon. Mrs Mary Rous has supplied a portrait of her father, Brigadier-General Arthur Asquith.

I am grateful also to Mr Michael King, of the Alexander Turnbull Library in Wellington, and to Mr Nigel Steele of the Imperial War Museum in London, for all their assistance. I should also like to mention the help I have had over the early New Zealand chapter from the late Dr Macdonald Wilson, Mr Tim and Mr Dick Hegglum,

Author's Acknowledgments

Dr J. S. Munro, Sir Vincent Meredith, Mrs Lesbia Paine, Mr J. D. C. Neill and Sir Stephen Allen.

I am particularly grateful to Mrs Julia Woodington for her skill and patience in typing successive drafts of the book; and to my eldest daughter Annabel for helping me on the editorial side, including offering many ideas and suggestions for improving the text. Finally I would like to record my sense of great gratitude to the publishers' editor, Mr John Bright-Holmes. Without his encouragement, professionalism and expertise this book would not have been completed in its present form.

Finally I should add that, despite all my indebtedness, the responsibility for how the information at my disposal has been presented and interpreted is entirely my own.

Author's Introduction

It had been my father's intention to write his memoirs as soon as he could find the time after the Second World War. He took a great deal of trouble to preserve his Second World War records, which he kept in a number of tin trunks. Although he gave the official New Zealand historians access to most of his papers, he kept back some of the more sensitive documents, particularly those that related to arguments with commanders-in-chief and other senior officers who were still alive. Above all, my father was very careful to preserve the ULTRA secret during his lifetime.

The New Zealand government set up a War Histories Branch in 1945 under the overall control of General Sir Howard Kippenberger, 'Kip' as he was universally called. When, in June 1946, my father arrived in New Zealand as Governor-General, he found himself drawn into discussions with Kip and other historians about what had happened to the New Zealand Division at various stages of the war. He started work on his own memoirs soon after his arrival in Wellington, and managed to write a number of chapters during the next six years; but his output was limited because of the constant interruptions of the Governor-General's job, as well as the time he spent helping with the official histories.

Yet he had an eventful story to tell. Since he was born in 1889 he was old enough to fight throughout the First World War but not too old to be a senior commander in the second. In 1914 in the Great War he started as a Lieutenant RNVR in the Royal Naval Division at its formation. Two and a half years later he was a Brigadier-General, a VC, and had been wounded nine times. In the Second World War he commanded 2 New Zealand Division from October 1939 until October 1945. The NZ Division saw as much fighting as any Allied formation, if not more; this included Greece in 1941 and Crete immediately afterwards, where he was made Commander-in-Chief at Winston Churchill's instigation. He played a major role in the relief of Tobruk in November 1941, at Alam Halfa in 1942 and at El Alamein,

[1]

where Montgomery put him in charge of 'Supercharge', the operation that led to the final defeat of the Germans in North Africa. Thereafter he commanded the NZ Division throughout the Italian campaign right up to the capture of Trieste, which, but for the Division's speed of advance, would have fallen behind the Iron Curtain. And yet this was a soldier whom army doctors had declared unfit in the 1930s; who, before he left New Zealand in 1914, had trained as a dentist; and who also attempted twice to swim the English Channel.

When Freyberg returned to England in the autumn of 1952 he hoped to resume work on his memoirs, but for various family and accommodation reasons it was not until 1955 that he was able to return to them. However he then found himself troubled by not being able to discover precisely what had happened in Crete or about the contradictory orders he had received on its defence. ULTRA remained a highly classified secret for the remainder of his life; it could not even be mentioned let alone discussed.

During these years, however, my father kept in close and constant touch with Kip in New Zealand about other aspects of the war; but on 5 May 1957 Kip died. The news was a body-blow to my father. He was devoted to Kip as a personal friend, and as the officer closest to him in the New Zealand Division during the six war years.

Now that Kip was gone there was no one with whom he could share this interest on quite the same level. It was at this time that he first suggested to me that I might like to consider writing his biography after his death. Besides the ULTRA problem over Crete there was another reason why my father decided not to continue with his memoirs himself – he was becoming bored. On several occasions he said to me that the war and its aftermath had been going on for too long; for nearly twenty years in fact. This feeling was noticeable as the production of the final New Zealand war history volumes continued. His copies of the volumes published before 1957 were well-thumbed and contained many comments written in the margins. The later volumes sent to him after Kip's death were uncut, unmarked and obviously unread.

I took some time before coming to a decision about writing my father's biography, but in the end I told him I would be happy to undertake it, especially as he had asked me to do so. I also told him that I did not think I would have the time for the research that would be needed as long as I was still in the army. At the time I was in his old regiment, the Grenadier Guards, in my early thirties, and at the Joint Services Staff College at Latimer. My father appeared to be in good health, and it all seemed to be a distant prospect.

My father regarded his biography as a very personal matter, and one

[2]

which he much preferred should be kept within the family. He did not want it to be written by a professional who, however competent, would not have known him personally. There was a further reason. My father had spent almost exactly half his life in England, and the other half in New Zealand or in the service of New Zealand. Few in England knew much about his New Zealand life, and fewer New Zealanders were aware of his English background. Only members of his family knew about both.

Once I had agreed my father told me where I could best find out about his early life. My mother had met many of his friends and companions from before the First World War while she was in New Zealand. He also reminded me that he had written a 230-page account of his activities in the First World War, from 1916 onwards, called 'A Linesman in Picardy', which Sir James Barrie had persuaded him to write.

Much of the account in this book of my father's career in the Second World War comes from my own observation and recollections. I joined the New Zealand Army in August 1940, and took part in the campaign in Greece in April 1941 as a private soldier in 23 Infantry Battalion of the NZ Division. After my father was appointed Commander-in-Chief in Crete I saw him several times, and stayed with him on the night of 5 May at his headquarters outside Canea. After the Crete battle I met him in Cairo on a number of occasions while I was at the Officer Cadet Training Unit (OCTU) at Kasr el Nil Barracks. At the time he told me little that was not already public knowledge, but I was able to observe the atmosphere in which he was working, and sense some of the pressures he was under.

In early September 1941 I joined the Long Range Desert Group (LRDG), and spent the next nine months with its New Zealand Patrol in the Western Desert, until the end of May 1942. I saw my father on several occasions, both before and after the battle for the relief of Tobruk. Then I returned to England to join the Grenadiers and did not see him for a year; but we linked up again in Tunisia in May 1943 at the end of the campaign in North Africa, by which time I was serving in 5 Battalion Grenadier Guards, with the British First Army. During the two years in Italy between 1943 and 1945 I not only saw him frequently, but by then I was twenty-one and the needs of security were less important than in the early part of the war. Consequently he talked to me much more frankly than he had done before.

When the war was over he began to tell me more about what had happened in Crete, but it was not until the year before he died that he told me about ULTRA and the part it had played in the events leading up to the German invasion. Before he did so he made me promise not to tell anyone about his disclosure until the ULTRA secret was declassified. Now that most things to do with ULTRA have been published it is often forgotten what a closely guarded secret it was, not only during the war but for nearly thirty years afterwards.

My father finally told me all that he knew at Easter 1962. There were two reasons why he chose that particular moment: he had begun to suspect that he was not much longer for this world and did not want to take his version of events with him to the grave; and he had just been criticised yet again over his defence of the island. This had come in a book called *The Fall of Crete* by Alan Clark, who in 1990 is the Minister of State for Defence Procurement. It was published in 1962, twelve years before ULTRA was declassified, and so contains no knowledge of the information ULTRA provided or the operational restrictions that governed its use. Nevertheless the account upset my father, who described the book as inaccurate and its comments as unfair. He was, however, unable to defend himself because of the security rules that still applied to everything to do with ULTRA.

These restrictions continued in force until the ULTRA secret was declassified in 1974. By that time the three principal actors in the Crete drama were dead. Wavell, who had been C-in-C in Cairo, had died in 1950; Freyberg, in command on Crete itself, died in 1963; while Churchill, in charge at the London end, followed in 1965. As far as is known none of them left any written account of the influence ULTRA had had on the events leading up to the airborne attack, which was in accordance with the security rules that were then in force.

After it became possible to write about ULTRA in the second half of the 1970s, a number of articles and books appeared purporting to show how ULTRA had affected the Crete battle. Among them were two by Ronald Lewin, a military historian of repute who, in *ULTRA Goes to War* (1978) and *The Chief* (1980), discusses some of the intelligence that Wavell and Freyberg received from ULTRA. Lewin described how the British commanders had apparently failed to make use of the unprecedented amount of information made available to them about the German plan of attack, and concluded that the defence of Crete had therefore been badly mishandled. But Lewin, and others writing during this period, still did not appreciate fully the security constraints that governed the use to which intelligence derived from ULTRA could be put. The severity and significance of these restrictions only became apparent later.

Crete had become an obsession for my father in his last years, since he was never able to discover what had gone wrong in London or Cairo.

[4]

That is why he handed over the task to me, in the hope that in the fullness of time I would be able to discover what had always eluded him. Before he died he gave me detailed information to show what I had to look for. I found the facts well concealed and difficult to uncover, but eventually the pieces of the jigsaw fell into place. The story given in the Crete chapters of this book is what eventually emerged.

December 1990   PAUL FREYBERG

1

The Family Background

The Freyberg family originally came from the north-east cantons of Switzerland, where there are records of Freybergs from the time of Charlemagne to the Habsburgs (AD 809–1439).[1] To the north of Grisons, in the canton of Glarus, are the Freiburg mountains, which form part of the Glarus Alpen. The name Freyberg is of German origin, originally adapted from the Latin *de libero monte*. This can be translated literally as 'from a free mountain', or more colloquially as 'free man of the mountain'. The name has been spelt in various ways, such as Freiburg, Freyburg and even Freidberg.

During the fourteenth century a branch of the Freyberg family moved to south Germany and established themselves in Schloss Hohenaschau in the principality of Württemberg (Swabia) near the border with Austria. They lived there for the next five hundred years. In about 1480 a Freiherr Pancraz von Freyberg had a magnificent suit of armour and horse armour made for him, which is now in the Wallace Collection in London.[2] The Freybergs were friends of Martin Luther (1483–1546), who stayed at Schloss Hohenaschau. Some members of the family were closely involved with the Reformation movement, while others appear to have remained true to the Catholic faith.

For much of the time between the fifteenth century and the end of the Napoleonic wars the Freybergs were soldiers of fortune. In the days before standing armies, the employment of mercenaries was an economical way for rulers of states on the continent to resort temporarily to military force. Even though the word 'mercenary' has since become a pejorative term, during the sixteenth and seventeenth centuries the

[7]

profession was regarded in Europe as an honourable calling in much the same way as the armed forces are today.

One of the few continental records to survive in the English branch of the family is a coat of arms produced in Milan in the seventeenth century.[3] This incorporates the Turkish crescent at the top of the shield and was made for a Freyberg who fought in John Sobieski's Polish Army which raised the siege of Vienna by the Turks in 1683.

A branch of the Freyberg family moved from the mainly Catholic south of Germany to the Protestant north in about 1700, possibly because of religious persecution. Certainly from the eighteenth century onwards the Freybergs of Bernard's branch have been Protestants. They settled in Saxony, around Dresden, and from there Bernard's great-grandfather moved to Russia where he joined the Russian infantry in the last decades of the eighteenth century. He had several sons, three of whom later joined the cavalry in about 1806, after Napoleon's victory at Austerlitz. Father and sons all fought against Napoleon's invasion of Russia in 1812. Two of the sons were killed in Marshal Ney's attack on Smolensk. The father then took part in the battle of Borodino, where casualties of about 40,000 on each side were incurred in just two days. The fighting was at its most intense in three areas – Raevski's Redoubt, Bagration's Flèches and Semonovskaya village. It was in the last-named that the father, Ivan Petrovitch Friberg, and his battalion faced the French onslaught directed by Napoleon in person. After a tremendous struggle the Russian line was broken and the road to Moscow forced open, but Borodino proved a pyrrhic victory for the French. It was followed by the catastrophic retreat from Moscow and the virtual destruction of Napoleon's Grande Armée.

Ivan Petrovitch Friberg, a major of the Astrakhan Grenadier Regiment,[4] is also sometimes referred to as Johan Freidberg.[5] He commanded a composite Grenadier battalion of 2 Grenadier Division at Borodino, and was wounded; afterwards he was decorated with the Order of St George, 4th Class. Later he commanded the Astrakhan Regiment with the rank of Colonel until 1818, and from 1819 to 1828 was Commandant of the Imperial General Headquarters, first of Alexander I (who reigned 1801–25) and then of Nicholas I (Tsar, 1825–55).

Peter, the surviving son of Ivan Petrovitch (and Bernard Freyberg's grandfather), was present at the destruction of Moscow as a twenty-five-year-old officer in the Russian Army.[6] Four or five years later Peter married an Englishwoman, Ann Elkins, and came to live in England. Ann, born in Odiham in Hampshire on 11 February 1797, was the seventh child of George Elkins of Farnham and Mary Mulford of Odiham, two families who were of prosperous yeoman stock. One of their forebears was Sir Christopher Milton (1615–93), a Baron of the Exchequer and a younger brother of the poet, John Milton.[7]

When or where Peter Freyberg and Ann Elkins met is uncertain. Ann's family had business connections in the Baltic, and after the end of the Napoleonic wars there was a flourishing British community in St Petersburg. Although she may have met Peter Freyberg in Russia, Bernard has stated that 'Peter Freyberg was fighting until 1814, when, being at the occupation of Paris he came to England'.[8] Certainly Peter's prospects in the Russian Army at the end of the long Napoleonic wars would not have been promising. According to an obituary of James Freyberg, Peter's son and Bernard Freyberg's father, Peter came to England 'in the suite of the Emperor Nicholas'; but if Peter Freyberg came to England on the informal tour Nicholas made in November 1816, the latter was still a Grand Duke, for Nicholas did not become Emperor till 1825. At all events, when Nicholas visited England in 1844 Peter was invited to meet him and was asked where his family's Cross of St George was; Peter replied that he had never received it, whereupon Nicholas took off his gold watch and chain and handed them to him. The watch was later inscribed 'From the Emperor of All the Russias to Peter Freyberg 1844'.[9]

Peter and Ann were in London on 13 June 1819 when their first child, George Frederick, was christened. The date of birth, however, was given as 17 October 1817, some twenty months earlier. When their second child was born on 25 January 1821 the christening took place the more usual four months afterwards. It seems likely, therefore, that the first child was born while the parents were abroad, presumably in Russia. Altogether Peter and Ann had eight children, of whom Bernard's father James, born in 1827, was the fifth.[7]

James Freyberg, who married twice, brought up two separate families. His first wife Jane Wood, whom he married in 1852 when he was twenty-five, bore him five children and died in 1877. Three years later James married Julia Hamilton, a twenty-eight-year-old Scotswoman from Argyllshire. They had five more children, this time all boys and all born in the 1880s: Oscar, Paul, Cuthbert, Claud, and Bernard. The youngest, Bernard Cyril, was born at 8 Dynevor Road, Richmond, Surrey on 21 March, the first day of spring 1889 (see Appendix II).

James appears to have tried his hand at many different professions. In census returns between 1840 and 1880 he is described variously as decorator, estate agent, auctioneer and surveyor. During his first marriage he lived at various addresses in Belgravia: 35 Chester Square West; 11 Grosvenor Street; 41 Chester Square; and 31 Western

Street, Eaton Square.[9] But early on during his second marriage James's finances took a turn for the worse, and he and his family moved to less expensive areas further from central London, first in Earl's Court Road and then in Dynevor Road in Richmond. He was in partnership with a colleague who went bankrupt – in those days a particularly traumatic and harrowing experience for all associated with it – and in 1885 he began to make enquiries about starting a new life overseas. Julia was most reluctant to leave Britain, however, and she flatly refused to consider going anywhere in Africa, but in the end agreed that a fresh start overseas would give the young boys better educational opportunities than if they remained in England. James corresponded with one George Flux, who had emigrated to New Zealand in 1885, and after receiving favourable reports from him New Zealand was decided on.[7]

On 17 October 1891 all seven Freybergs of James's second family embarked at Plymouth on the RMS *Aorangi*, bound for Wellington. On 2 December 1891 the shipping column of the *New Zealand Times* carried the news of the arrival in Wellington the day before of the RMS *Aorangi* from London via Plymouth, Tenerife, Cape Town and Hobart, and listed among the passengers disembarking Mr and Mrs Freyberg and five children.[10] Bernard, then aged two and a half, remembered only one thing about the voyage – a noisy quarrel between the couple in the next-door cabin.

2

New Zealand

The family went to live in Hawker Street, a road on the western slopes of Mount Victoria branching off from Majoribanks Street and running to the top of FitzGerald Point which overlooks Wellington Harbour. In the 1890s the now closely-populated area of Hataitai (the eastern slopes of Mount Victoria) was not yet built, but consisted mainly of scrub and manuka (tea tree), surrounded by hills and valleys – an outdoor playground for all.[1] Nearby were the Te Aro Baths (which later became a focal point in Bernard's life), Wellington Harbour and the boat sheds.

The Freybergs lived first at 40 Hawker Street, then in 1895 moved to no. 62. This was one of twenty houses at the top of the hill which were burnt down in the Hawker Street fire of 1901, in which the Freyberg family lost all its records and photographs of earlier generations. After the fire they moved to no. 27, where they lived until 1908, and this house (now no. 43) stands today much as it did in the early 1900s.[1]

There were several families with boys of the same age as the Freybergs living in Hawker Street in the 1890s. Dr Macdonald Wilson, a contemporary and neighbour of Bernard's, recalls that there were six Forbes boys, three McLeans and three Wilsons, as well as 'a number of Macintyres'. They formed their own football and cricket teams and 'issued challenges to other youngsters in neighbouring streets . . . The Freybergs as a family, however, never showed any special interest in either soccer or cricket, their passion being the sea – either swimming or yachting.'

The boys grew up in an open-air environment with many opportunities not only for playing games but also for roaming the hills and

[11]

valleys nearby on camping expeditions, building 'whares' (huts; a whare being a Maori word for a house), hunting wild pigs and goats, and fishing in lakes and streams.[1]

The personalities and characters of the Freybergs differed greatly. James, the father, was a martinet. A member of his first family, all of whom were over thirty when he set off for New Zealand (and of whose existence the second family was for many years unaware), described him as 'a very difficult old man' who lost all interest in them. James must have had considerable vitality, however, even an iron streak, to be prepared to leave England at the age of sixty-four and, with little income to speak of, begin a new life in a strange country. After arriving in New Zealand he cabled to his two sons by his first marriage to ask for financial help, but they were both hard up too and only sent him £5 each! His profession in New Zealand was described as a timber adviser to the NZ government (until, apparently, he quarrelled with Mr Seddon, the Prime Minister), and surveyor and land agent. He had a quick and sometimes violent temper.

James Freyberg – who like many businessmen in those days always dressed in a frock-coat and top hat – made a strong, even stark impression on Dr Wilson as a child in the 1890s:

> . . . a tall fresh complexioned man of distinguished appearance. His height was increased by the fact that he always wore an old-fashioned 'tile' hat, tall and almost brimless. While the hat caused us youngsters some amusement, it was evidently also a source of amusement to the younger members of his own family. Even 'Tiny' [Bernard] from behind a fence would call out to his Dad in passing 'Dad, in your old tarpot'. Mr Freyberg always seemed to us youngsters very stern and distant. We boys knew him and he knew us, so in passing we would always raise our caps, but never expected nor got the slightest acknowledgement in return.[1]

Another Hawker Street neighbour, Alec Forbes, claimed to have got a friendly greeting once from James Freyberg. It was at the end of the Boer war: 'I met Mr Freyberg coming up the street with Oscar and Paul on each side of him and both in NZ South African "Rough Rider" uniform. "You see, Alec," said Mr Freyberg, "I have got both my boys home again."'

Julia Freyberg was much loved by her sons. An educated woman, she had received university education in Scotland or England but, as this was in the mid-1870s, before women were allowed to take degrees or be recognised at university, there is no record of her attending one. Neighbours said she had an 'air of the old country about her', and was tall, good-looking and sympathetic. In later life she is depicted as a gentle, somewhat retiring figure, but in the early days in New Zealand she clearly had an uphill struggle on little money to bring up, feed and clothe her family of five growing boys, whom she also insisted on schooling at home.

In the 1890s and early 1900s the five Freyberg boys formed a striking and tightly-knit group who 'were all big men of powerful physique, with perhaps Paul and Bernard outgrowing their brothers by a small margin,' wrote Dick Hegglum, a friend of Bernard's. 'With the exception of Claud, who was a somewhat reserved youth, the other four boys were good athletes, particularly at swimming, and possessed a devil-may-care character that appeared to drive any fear whatsoever from their souls.'[2] Like their mother they retained, according to Dr Wilson, the traits and manners of their English upbringing.

Bernard's eldest brother Oscar, born in 1881, was the daredevil of the family, constantly in trouble for reckless behaviour; but his high spirits and enterprise had a great influence on Bernard at an impressionable age. One day Dick Hegglum and the Freyberg brothers were out sailing and a 10-foot shark began to hover alongside their boat:

Someone dared Oscar to dive on it. Whether Oscar detected any glint of kindness in that shark's eye, he didn't reveal, but overboard he went, clothes and all, on top of the shark, and to this day, I'm not too sure who received the greatest fright, the shark or us, but it certainly wasn't Oscar.[2]

In 1900 Oscar and Paul went as private soldiers to the South African war; later they both joined the Volunteer Naval Brigade in Wellington, holding commissioned rank for several years. Oscar trained as a lawyer, and in the early 1900s edited the yachting pages in a magazine called *Progress*, but seemed unable to stick at any job for long. When war broke out in 1914 he joined the Collingwood Battalion of the Royal Naval Division.

Bernard's favourite brother was Paul Milton (after whom he named his own son). Born in 1883, he was a more gentle and stable character than Oscar, and possessed a quietly humorous attitude to life which he revealed in the *NZ Yachtsman*, to which he used to contribute under the pen-name of 'Boat 'Arbour Bill'. Paul was trained as a law clerk and also used to write verses.

The next in age, Cuthbert, born in 1886, was the least complicated member of the family, with a good record in the First World War. He returned to New Zealand afterwards and became a solicitor, got married and had a family. Nearest in age to Bernard was Claud

(1888–1963) who was less physically robust than his brothers. Consequently he received a particular measure of protection from his mother and, in order that one member of the family should remain with her, did not join up in the First World War. He became a civil servant.

The name 'Tiny' was given to Bernard as a boy, no doubt because he was the youngest – and at one stage the smallest – of a tall family; it stuck to him as he became a tall youth of six foot one and a half; and he continued to be referred to as 'Tiny' by New Zealanders, even as a General on the battlefields of the Second World War.

Julia refused to allow her children to attend the state primary school, Clyde Quay School, insisting on educating them herself at home until they were old enough to go to secondary school at Wellington College. There were two reasons for this. The first was what Dr Wilson called 'an English mistrust of State education', the second her belief that she could give her sons a better grounding in the basic subjects than they would get elsewhere.

Not long after their arrival in New Zealand the older Freyberg boys acquired a boat, which was succeeded by a series of sailing yachts of increasing size and range in which to explore the waters in and around Wellington harbour. The 14-foot *Kura* was followed by the *Mapu* and the *Ariel*, which in turn were replaced by the 14-foot *Bluey* and then the *Siren*. On one occasion when four of the brothers – Oscar, Paul, Claud and Bernard – won a race in *Bluey*, during one of Wellington's none too gentle zephyrs, the press report commented that the ability of *Bluey* to avoid capsizing was 'the 24 feet of Freyberg hanging out to windward!' Their ultimate boat was the *Viking*, whose size and seaworthiness matched the brothers' increasing ambitions. They were not content to remain within the confines of Wellington Harbour for long, and their sights soon began to focus across the treacherous Cook Strait to the waters of the South Island.[3]

Viking was a 33-foot keeler built in Auckland with kauri (a native New Zealand wood) timbers and planks, and purchased in the late 1890s. She became a familiar sight along the Wellington coast and Marlborough Sound. A favourite jaunt was to head out across Cook Strait for The Brothers rock, near the northern entrance to Queen Charlotte Sound, and then steer for Endeavour Inlet, a long arm of the Sound where Captain Cook and his ship *Endeavour* took refuge in 1770. Frequently their crossings of the Cook Strait were made in gale conditions when no other boats would go out; all on board would be soaked to the skin, and any food not washed overboard was saturated with salt water. Once in the calmer waters of the Sound the *Viking* would head for one of several refuges to dry out, stock up with food and

[14]

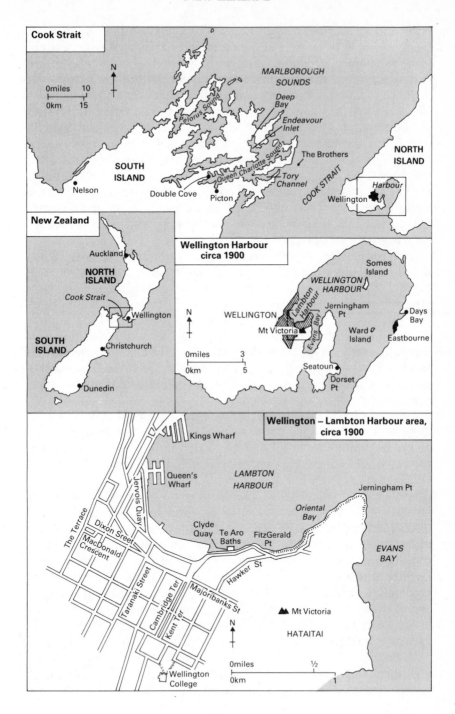

Cook Strait

0miles 10
0km 15

N

MARLBOROUGH
SOUNDS

Deep
Bay

Endeavour
Inlet

Pelorus Sound

The Brothers

NORTH
ISLAND

SOUTH
ISLAND

Queen Charlotte Sound

Tory
Channel

Harbour

COOK STRAIT

Nelson

Double Cove

Picton

Wellington

New Zealand

Auckland

NORTH
ISLAND

Cook Strait

Wellington

SOUTH
ISLAND

Christchurch

Dunedin

**Wellington Harbour
circa 1900**

Somes
Island

WELLINGTON
HARBOUR

Lambton Harbour

WELLINGTON

Jerningham
Pt

Days
Bay

N

Mt Victoria

Evans Bay

Ward
Island

Eastbourne

0miles 3
0km 5

Seatoun

Dorset
Pt

**Wellington – Lambton Harbour area,
circa 1900**

Kings Wharf

Queen's
Wharf

LAMBTON
HARBOUR

Jerningham Pt

Jervois Quay

Oriental
Bay

The Terrace

Dixon Sreet

MacDonald
Crescent

Clyde
Quay

Te Aro
Baths

FitzGerald
Pt

EVANS
BAY

Hawker St

Taranaki Street

Cambridge Ter

Kent Ter

Majoribanks St

Mt Victoria

N

HATAITAI

Wellington
College

0miles ½
0km 1

[15]

water and resume the voyage. Often the brothers and their friends were made welcome by farmers and their families at isolated farmsteads in Endeavour Inlet or Double Cove.[2]

Their ultimate destination was usually Picton, the small seaport at the head of Queen Charlotte Sound, where they would anchor about a hundred yards off shore. A constant problem was how to get to dry land in the absence of a dinghy. Sometimes the brothers managed to persuade a passing boat to give them a lift, but often the only way was to swim. Once ashore they would head for the nearest local for a meal and a night out, before embarking for the return journey – sometimes being chased by incensed youths after heated discussions about 'some sporting fixture or other topic of no importance'; they would dive into the sea and hang their sodden clothes on the rigging to dry while they went about their sailing tasks quite naked.[2]

This routine took place several times a year during the early 1900s; but at other times the brothers would go fishing on the east or west coast of North Island, or explore further down South Island. Bernard was particularly enamoured of the story of 'Pelorus Jack', the grey Risso's dolphin, who for more than twenty years from 1888 used to meet and escort ships on the run between Nelson and Wellington over a certain stretch of water off Pelorus Sound. This dolphin became so much a part of the Wellington scene that an Order in Council was proclaimed in 1904 protecting it – thought to be the first time that such a preservation order was enacted.

Until 1897, when he was eight, Bernard was taught at home by his mother. Then he joined the first form at Wellington College. 'I was lucky,' he wrote, 'because I had four elder brothers who advised and protected me in the early days of my school life.' The headmaster of Wellington College was J. P. Firth, one of the great headmasters of the period. Large, tall, with a commanding presence and universally known as 'The Boss', he was renowned throughout New Zealand as a disciplinarian. But what he excelled at was developing the personalities of his charges. He taught his pupils that they must lead honest and truthful lives, be completely straight in all their dealings, loyal to their families and friends, and kind to each other. Although Firth valued academic excellence he considered that this was only one element among many other factors in producing a well-rounded individual. His influence in the moulding of Bernard's character at an impressionable age was a strong and lasting one.[4]

Bernard did not excel academically at any period of his school career. His life at this time was dominated by his passion for swimming. A contemporary at Wellington College, Dr J. S. Monro, describes

Bernard as having an easy-going manner and being most at home in the swimming baths, where 'his movements were seal-like, in fact he reminded one very much of that animal. Rather clumsy and awkward on land, but given a few feet of water, immediately transformed into a body of grace and vital activity and flowing movement.'[5]

Bernard used frequently to swim in Wellington harbour, and also across to Eastbourne, some ten kilometres away. Between 1900 and 1911 he won fourteen gold and nine silver medals in swimming competitions, mostly from the New Zealand Amateur Swimming Association Championships, for distances varying from 25 yards to 1 mile (Appendix III). In 1906 he became Swimming Champion of New Zealand. He was also 'a dashing centre forward' and 'prolific scorer' in the water polo team of Swift's Swimming Club, which won the NZ water polo championships in 1907.[6]

At the end of November 1905, when he was sixteen, Bernard went to Australia to represent New Zealand in the Australasian swimming championships. It was the first time he had been out of New Zealand since the family arrived there, and he was up against the best Australian swimmers who, in those days, held many of the world championship titles and records. At Sydney on 29 November in the 250-yard race, he came third to two of the Australian star performers, Kieran and McKelvie. At Brisbane, on 7 December, he was beaten into third place a second time in another 250-yard race and again in the mile on 9 December. The *Sydney Morning Herald* of 11 December 1905 records that on the last of these occasions 'the New Zealander was swimming with a long steady stroke, rolling porpoise-like through the water'.

Bernard's performance in the Australasian championships was, according to Dick Hegglum, below his normal standard:

Tiny had an easy style, swimming on top of the water, appearing to glide along without effort. Barney Kieran was the world swimming champion at the time, and his style of swimming was one of rolling low in the water, and so it was that Tiny was put under George Farmer, a well-known Australian swimming coach who was Kieran's tutor and also custodian of the baths they trained at. The inevitable happened; Farmer tried to make a second Kieran of Tiny by changing his style to the roll, something which I consider was wrong and very poor judgement on Farmer's part. On his return to New Zealand, Tiny retained the Kieran style of swimming and performed with no greater significance than he did in Australia.[2]

Some time later Tiny reverted to his original style, and this helped him to win the 1906 New Zealand swimming championships, as W. T. Churchward described:

[17]

In 1906 I trained him for these championships and he won four out of five. In the fifth, the 440 yards, he was second. He should have won it, as it was his best distance, and he held the New Zealand record for the distance. He was leading in the race at the last turn, when after turning he collided with someone who had swum across his path. The swimmer behind him was 10 yards ahead when Tiny got going again, and using his famous crawl stroke, he gradually caught up on his opponent over the last 40 yards, but he could not quite make up the gap and so was second a yard behind. Morally he was a winner.[6]

His most stirring race was in the 1910 New Zealand championships. According to Dick Hegglum, 'Tiny brought to their feet the throng that packed Albert Street Baths when he staved off the efforts of O'Hare and Champion to win the most meritorious and exciting contest ever witnessed for the 100 yards Championship of New Zealand.'[2]

When the Freyberg family arrived in Wellington in 1891 New Zealand had been a British colony for just fifty-one years. The total population of the country was between 500,000 and 750,000 and that of Wellington, the capital, 31,000. But it was growing rapidly, and by 1911, twenty years later, the population had more than doubled to 71,000.[7]

In 1891 many roads were still composed of gravel, and transport, other than the town trams, was entirely horse-drawn. Dr Macdonald Wilson recalls how, in Hawker Street:

... we youngsters did not enter one another's homes very much, and mothers who had large families did not encourage their children to bring additional youngsters into the house. Consequently we boys tended to play either in the yard, the street, or on the open hills. In those days apart from the odd butcher's or baker's cart that came along we had the street to ourselves for playgrounds.[1]

The first cars in New Zealand, two Benzes, arrived in Wellington in 1898. The railways were then beginning to connect the cities, but the final section of line between Wellington and Auckland was not completed until 1908. Much inter-city traffic was still by sea. The Union Steam Ship Company of New Zealand had 53 steamers engaged in coastal work in the North and South Islands, as well as in the fast-expanding trade in primary products, such as wool and meat, which were being exported to England and elsewhere.[7]

Anthony Alpers, in his biography of Katherine Mansfield (1888–1923), describes the vagaries of the climate to be found in the exposed capital city:

Its loveliness on a calm clear day, with that sheer of brilliant blue before it and the bush-clad hills beyond, would take the breath away. But the calm days were so rare. There was always the wind – the irritable northerly, rattling windows, making people clutch their hats, the drenching southerly, straight from the Antarctic; or the beclouded westerly, howling through the strait outside. The incessant wind, and the lack of the comfort of flat ground (steep hills came crowding to the water's edge, on every side), made Wellington a restless place for the colonists, as well as very unlike 'home'.[8]

Katherine Mansfield, who was a year older than Bernard and lived there during the same period, parodied Wellington in her stories as 'Philistia', but could also be more affectionate about her childhood town when describing it from far away, as in her story 'The Scholarship' (1918):

He saw the town below him – the red-roofed houses set in plumy, waving gardens, the absurd little city-quarter, 'built in American style', the wharves, the tarred wharf-sheds, and behind these black masses two cranes, that looked somehow, from this distance, like two gigantic pairs of scissors stuck on end. And then the deep, brimming harbour, shaped like a crater, in a curving brim of hills, just broked in the jagged place to let the big ships through.[9]

In December 1904, three months short of his sixteenth birthday, and only in the fourth form, Bernard abruptly left Wellington College.

The reason for this early termination of his schooling, before he had obtained any proper qualifications, can only be explained by his father's authoritarian character and the family's weak finances. In making arrangements for his sons' future careers, James did not seem to be influenced either by what was most appropriate for them or by what they themselves wanted. In later life Claud used to relate how Oscar was prevented from joining the merchant marine, and he claimed that he too had not been permitted to follow the career of his choice but was forced into a profession, the civil service, which his father chose against his wishes. James Freyberg, now in his late seventies, seems to have been motivated entirely by the desire to reduce his own financial commitments by pushing his children into careers that involved little training or outlay for him.

Bernard originally wanted to be a doctor[10] but in order to become a doctor, he would have had to possess qualifications and perform academic work for which he may not then have been suited. The nearest and cheapest alternative for James was to apprentice Bernard to a dentist, and it so happened that a well-known Wellington dentist, J. S. Fairchild, lived in Hawker Street. At the age of fifteen Bernard was in no position to know what was best for him or where his aptitudes might lie; but from the day he was apprenticed to Mr Fairchild in December 1904, and until he left Wellington nine years later, Bernard was a member of the dental profession in New Zealand.

Until the early 1900s all that was required to gain entry to the dental profession was to be apprenticed to an accredited dentist for several years for a fee of £100 or so (then a considerable sum), pass a board of three dentists and three doctors in an oral examination, and thereby obtain permission to register and practise as a dentist. Such a system was clearly outdated and ripe for change, and it came in the form of the New Zealand Dental Act of 1904.

The main provision of this Act was to establish a proper framework to regulate the profession. For the first time a Chair of Dentistry was established at Dunedin's Otago University, and a four-year degree course of training instituted, which was henceforth to be organised by standards reached through written examinations set by the university. There was to be a transitional period, expiring at the end of 1908, before the rules came into full force (and before the first course at the university began), which were nevertheless to be applied to those who became apprentices after 1 January 1905. The Act was passed in November 1904, to come into force on 1 January 1905, and since nothing was said in the Act about the position of those who were dental apprentices before the end of 1904 it was assumed that the old rules of entry would continue to apply to them, together with the old method of examination when they came to qualify. This was almost certainly the reason why James removed Bernard so abruptly from Wellington College in December 1904, one month after the Act was passed but one month before it came into force. If his apprenticeship had been left until after the New Year James would have had to maintain Bernard over a four-year period of training, which would have cost far more than a one-off payment.

Bernard acquiesced in these arrangements for quite different reasons. Never much interested in academic work, he lived principally for swimming races and aquatic life in general. The apprenticeship allowed him to carry on living at home, near to the Te Aro Baths,* and

---

* The Te Aro Baths have since been rebuilt. In October 1963 they were reopened as the Freyberg Tepid Pool.

gave him ample time to train for competitions, play water polo and sail. In the midst of his swimming excitements he was quite content to be apprenticed to Mr Fairchild. Later Bernard was under the pupillage of another prominent Wellington dental practitioner of the time, Arthur Hoby; and the three men he went on to work for after he qualified – Arthur L. Yule, Robert D. Elliott and Stuart Mackenzie, were all ex-students of Hoby's.[11]

From 1905 to 1907 Bernard continued to live at home with his parents, enjoy his swimming triumphs and work at his new profession. After leaving school, where he had been in the Cadet Corps, he was keen enough on military matters to join the Corps Volunteers. Sir Vincent Meredith, QC, remembered Bernard being in 'D' Battery in Wellington at the time he, Meredith, commanded the naval detachments which manned the forts at Seatoun, at the entrance to Wellington Harbour. They both served under a regular soldier, Major George Richardson, who was to play a crucial role in Bernard's career at the beginning of the Great War.[12]

In 1908 Bernard's father retired and the family moved from Hawker Street to Macdonald Crescent. In the absence of contemporary records there are no means of knowing exactly what happened between 1907 and 1910; but some time in 1907, after two and a half years of apprenticeship, Bernard and one Percy Walter Staples (who had been apprenticed to Fairchild since 21 November 1904 and was therefore at the same stage as Bernard) discovered that they only had until 10 January 1908 to pass the board examination. After that date they would be unable to qualify as dentists in the way for which they had been trained.

They later told how they had been apprenticed 'in complete ignorance of the passing of the Dental Act, and that their employer, in common with other practising dentists, was also unaware of the change in the law'. When they did realise their predicament they looked for other apprentices in the same position (and found eight or so). They then presented a petition to Parliament in 1907 asking for an amendment to the Dental Act to enable them to sit an examination under the old Dental Board rules. The petition was favourably received. Freyberg and Staples were interviewed by T. K. Sidney, MP for Dunedin South and in charge of establishing the dental school, and the Hon. G. W. Fowlds, Minister of Public Health. In July 1908 Fowlds wrote to Freyberg and Staples (in response to another letter from them) telling them he had instructed an amendment to the Dental Act to be drafted. However, 'excess of business' in Parliament that session prevented the amendment from being introduced. Sidney, by this stage

[21]

reluctant to amend his Act, was afraid it might be compromised. He suggested instead that the petitioners should – for a specific and limited period – attend the new dental school at Otago University in Dunedin, which would enable them to sit the new examination.

The regulations of the university were specially modified so that the petitioners could attend the course, on the one condition that they first passed the physics and chemistry section of the university entrance examination. Freyberg – who gave up competitive swimming for 1909 to concentrate on his dentistry and to fight his case through Parliament – easily exceeded the average pass mark of 47.5 per cent, with scores of 78.5 per cent for physics and 70 per cent for chemistry.[13]

In 1910, some time between March (the start of the first term) and 2 May (the beginning of the winter term), the four successful candidates – Freyberg, Staples, Ryan and Quinn – attended the course at the dental school.[14] It was a very unhappy period for Bernard. At the age of twenty his future career was in jeopardy as a result of not being told of the time-bar to the old rules. According to Lesbia Wilson (who knew him a few years later when they were both living in Levin) Bernard had ten shillings a week to live on, and could not afford any form of digs in the city.[15] He therefore stayed in a 'bach' (a New Zealand word for a small beach house or hut) behind St Clair Beach, along the coast from Dunedin, and walked the four and a half miles to the university each day. The only meat he ate – he had a shotgun – was rabbit. Bernard later told Lesbia, 'I will never look a rabbit in the face again.'[15]

After attending lectures for several weeks Bernard realised he did not have enough time to pass under the new rules. By then attitudes had hardened. The dental establishment considered that the unfortunates who had fallen between the old and new systems ought to have taken steps to pass under the old rules while there was still time. But those adversely affected pointed out that no one whose duty it was to frame the regulations had warned them of the time limit. Bernard left Dunedin and returned to Wellington to reconsider his position.

Brigadier J. Ferris Fuller, an internationally distinguished dentist, has recounted in the *New Zealand Dental Journal* what happened next:

> Bernard Freyberg was not a man to be beaten – ever. He then, along with Percy Walter Staples, petitioned Parliament in August 1910 for the Act to be amended to enable those who had been apprenticed up to the time of the 1904 Act coming into operation to be admitted . . .
>
> Professor Pickerill, the Dean of the fledgling Dental School, had an axe to grind. He was fighting to establish his school as the sole dental educational centre. This is commendable and understandable. But he

[22]

made a submission to the Public Petitions Committee in which he cast doubts on Bernard Freyberg's intelligence, a statement which did his cause no good at all. Later he tried to deny and explain it away . . .

The upshot of Bernard Freyberg's lobbying was that the Dentists' Act was amended forthwith in 1910; he completed the requirements, sat and passed the prescribed Dental Board Examination, and was admitted to the Dentists' Register on 22 May 1911 under Section 2 of the Dental Amendment Act 1910 where his name remained until 30 July 1936, when it was removed 'at request'. Bernard Freyberg had won his first battle against formidable odds. What scars remained we shall never know because he was essentially a private man who rarely spoke of the past to any of us.[11]

The scars which the episode left on Bernard never healed completely. I was always able to discuss most subjects with my father, but there were two exceptions. He would never talk about his relationship with his own father James, and he would never discuss his time as a dentist.

The successful outcome of Bernard's appeal brought many changes in his way of life. He left home and, except for brief visits, never again lived under the parental roof. He took up his first post after qualifying as an assistant and locum tenens to Arthur L. Yule at Morrinsville, a small town about 90 miles south-east of Auckland.

Away from the training facilities of Wellington Bernard was unable to continue competitive swimming; but he often swam in the Waihou river, sometimes starting at dawn and carrying on till dusk, and completed a swim in it from Te Aroha to Paeroa, which the NZ Swimming Association recorded as a distance of 35 miles covered in 10 hours – although on the map the distance appears to be somewhat shorter.[16] He also trained energetically in other sports, and was more or less teetotal and a non-smoker.

A significant development was that on 20 November 1911, while in Morrinsville, he was gazetted a Second Lieutenant in 6 Hauraki Regiment, one of the newly-raised Territorial Units. The TA Unit in the Morrinsville–Hamilton area was started from scratch by Colonel Sir Stephen Allen (as he later became) and Bernard was the only subaltern.[17] A telegram on Bernard's personal army file from a Major Braithwaite to 'Freyberg, 6th Hauraki Regt, Hamilton, dated 5 March 1912' indicates how seriously he took his work in the Territorial Army: 'Saw General Godley about you yesterday. He much regrets that he can give no more direct commissions into New Zealand Staff Corps.

Am writing.'[18] This reveals that less than a year after being registered as a dentist Bernard was contemplating a totally different career.

Bernard worked for Arthur Yule for just under a year and during the last few months managed a branch for him in nearby Hamilton. Afterwards he moved to Levin, then a town of 1,700 people about 70 miles north of Wellington. He was employed in the surgery of Stuart Mackenzie, whose dental practice took in a large area of the surrounding district. Bernard spent nearly two years in Levin. In addition to his strenuous swimming (both in the lake and in the sea, where he would swim out of sight for hours at a time, and then sprint on the beach) he also played golf and tennis, roller-skated in the old Cosmos Theatre, and turned out for the local Rugby football club.

Towards the end of 1912 the news came through of the disaster that had befallen Captain Robert Falcon Scott and his expedition in the Antarctic. The expedition, of course, used New Zealand as a base and, late in 1910, its ship *Terra Nova* had spent a month at Lyttelton while the expedition completed its preparations. To Bernard this was an epic tale of heroism and tragedy which had a powerful effect on him, and made him feel, as Helen Wilson (Lesbia Wilson's mother) relates, that 'he had missed the opportunity of a lifetime in not being a member of it. He knew the name of every man on both ships and why they had secured a berth.' She adds that for a time Bernard could talk of nothing else.[15] This story has a sequel. In England in 1916, Bernard sought out Lady Scott to tell her of his admiration for her husband.

The other main event that took place while Bernard was in Levin was the dock and shipping strike of 1913. This was the first big national labour dispute in New Zealand between employers and unions, and when it erupted on the Wellington waterfront and spread nationwide the government was forced to intervene in order to maintain law and order and keep essential supplies moving. The Minister in charge of strike arrangements, Mr Herdman, called for volunteers from the Manawatu and Wairarapa districts to act as mounted special constables, and armed them with batons. Bernard decided to enrol as a Special and travelled to Wellington with others who had volunteered; although, apparently, he had never been on a horse before. A story from that time relates that when the Specials were lined up on Jervois Quay at the wharf gate Bernard lost control of his mount, which bolted into the mob of strikers massed opposite. He charged right through them, and the sight of him hanging on for grim life, arms and legs flying, was apparently so hilarious that it helped to dissolve the growing tension.

The main dispute in Wellington was eventually settled, but some of the seamen remained on strike. The government amended the Shipping and Seamen's Act, which required specific qualifications to man ships, and called for volunteers to work the boats to Sydney. Bernard went as a stoker on the *Maunganui* and did the Wellington to Sydney trip several times, often working double shifts so that he could qualify for a stoker's certificate. Sir Vincent Meredith relates how on one occasion:

> . . . volunteer firemen had their meals in the saloon. The stewards were not on strike. Tiny was having a late dinner when he came off duty and the steward addressed him as a 'bloody scab' asking him what he would have. Tiny got up and hit him and by the blow coinciding with the roll of the ship knocked the steward from one end of the saloon to the other. He received better service after that.[12]

One of the main organisers of the strike which Bernard was brought in to break was Peter Fraser, who had come to New Zealand from Scotland in 1910. In 1939 he would be Acting Prime Minister of New Zealand and the man chiefly responsible for choosing Bernard as GOC New Zealand Expeditionary Force.

The strike and its aftermath were welcome diversions for Bernard's energies, but they only accentuated his growing restlessness. He was approaching his mid-twenties and feeling frustrated by the kind of life available to him. An old swimming friend, J. O. C. Neill, after living in the United States for seven years returned to New Zealand, bought a farm near Levin and, as he wrote, found Tiny working as an assistant dentist:

> He used to come out to our home quite often and we were always glad to see him. As an older and more experienced man I became somewhat worried about him. He was so obviously chafing at the limitations of his job and of the small town environment, that I strongly urged him to do as I had done – cut adrift and find his feet in a wider world. He did not take much urging.[19]

Bernard acted on Neill's advice. He handed in his notice to Mackenzie and prepared for the first stage of his journey to America. Shortly before he left his father died in Wellington on 22 January 1914, aged eighty-seven. Bernard attended the funeral along with other members of his family; but he did not change his plans. The *Horowhenua Chronicle* records that 'Mr Freyberg was about to leave Levin for Philadelphia via San Francisco to pursue further studies in dentistry'.[14] Bernard, however, had other ideas.

On 27 March 1914 Bernard boarded the Royal Mail Steamer

[25]

(RMS) *Tahiti* at the Wellington docks, and began the three and a half week journey across the Pacific. He was just turned twenty-five years of age, six foot one and a half inches tall, strong, good-looking and superbly fit. He possessed few material assets, but like many young men before and since he wanted to see the world and find out what it had to offer.

3

A Price on his Head?

Of the five months from the last week of March 1914 when Bernard left Wellington until his arrival in Liverpool towards the end of August, very little was known during his lifetime even by his family. Bernard arrived in San Francisco on 20 April. He wrote a number of letters to relatives and friends from California, but these ceased at the end of May and there was silence until he arrived in England. During the Great War, however, he gave several people, of whom my mother was one, an account of his activities during these months, which included a visit to Mexico, where he was staying when war broke out. In later life he said little about this time beyond that he had gone there to see what it was like. But, although unwilling to discuss Mexico, on one exceptional occasion in 1961 he told his newly-married daughter-in-law that he had been there at the beginning of the war and had left the country with a price on his head. After he died this was confirmed when various books were published by and about people Bernard had known in the early days of the First World War.

One day in 1976, however, a brown paper parcel arrived at our home from Bermuda. It contained some dozen letters in Bernard's distinctive handwriting, mostly written while he was in the United States in the summer of 1914, together with a small scrapbook and some American newspaper clippings. The parcel came from the estate of a Miss Queenie Penboss, and inside was a covering letter from her to Bernard's executors saying that she had noticed from previous accounts of his life that little seemed to be known about the period immediately before the First World War, and that therefore it might be of interest for them to have this information. One of Miss Penboss's trustees in Bermuda was Sir Gilbert Cooper, who told me later that year that the Penbosses had come originally from Australia. Queenie Penboss's father was a surgeon who had gone on ahead of his family to set up practice in New York; his wife Lucinda, and Queenie, their only child, then aged sixteen, were travelling to America to join him. They sailed from Australia on the *Tahiti*, which called at Wellington where Bernard boarded the ship. Queenie later moved to Bermuda in 1936, where she became a successful businesswoman until her death in February 1976.[1] She never married.

The small scrapbook describes in pictures their three and a half week journey across the Pacific on the *Tahiti*. There are photographs of Bernard and the Penboss mother and daughter, some taken on board, others on visits to Rarotonga and to the island of Tahiti itself. It tells the story of a leisurely journey through the South Seas in a comfortable ship of some 7,500 tons. There are accounts of excursions to banana and coconut plantations, of drives by car through tropical forests and high volcanic hills; further descriptions and photographs depict yachts in harbour, native fishing boats of the Tahiti pearling fleet and unbelievably beautiful sunsets. During the long run between Tahiti and San Francisco they passed and took photographs of great sailing ships becalmed in the doldrums. The social highlight of the voyage was a fancy-dress ball for which Queenie dressed as a mermaid, with other characters in equally exotic disguise. In short, the scrapbook is a record of an idyllic voyage across the Pacific.

The photographs were developed in San Francisco after the *Tahiti*'s arrival on 20 April 1914, and the scrapbook was written up by Bernard over the next six weeks. On the flyleaf is written:

Mama and The Infant
This little Volume is dedicated by
B Freyberg June 2nd 1914

'Mama' and 'the Infant' are the names used for Lucinda and Queenie Penboss in Bernard's letters from California. Mother and daughter went on by train to New York where they joined Mr Penboss at his temporary address, before moving to 200 West 79th Street, New York.

Meanwhile Bernard remained in the San Francisco area trying to decide what to do next. The nominal reason for his journey to America had been to continue his studies in dentistry, but it was no more than a vague, unspecified plan and his heart was no longer, if it ever had been, in that profession. His letters to Mrs Penboss and her daughter make it clear that he was toying with a number of other ideas. He was greatly

[28]

stimulated by America, and in one of his letters he describes the excitement of riding from San Francisco to Sacramento and then up into the lumber camps. In another letter he mentions a possible visit to Alaska.

Bernard also contemplated enrolment at university, and wrote to J. P. Firth, his old headmaster at Wellington College, who mentioned in the school magazine: 'I got a letter from B. C. Freyberg from San Francisco asking if I would send his school record, because he wished to go to Leland Stanford University. I looked up the record and sent it to the Dean.'[2]

On 28 April 1914 Bernard wrote to Mrs Penboss from 1129 Leavenworth Street, San Francisco, saying that he was able to start a course at Stanford University in September; but four weeks later, on 24 May, he was still dithering: 'I am still trying to make up my mind on whether to take a three year course at the university and then take a degree or not – I am waiting for mail from New Zealand.'

He was also lonely. In a letter from France in 1918 he recalled 'being in the San Joaquin Valley, South California, and walking twelve miles to speak to an Australian sheepshearer who lived at a place called Fresno. His Sydney twang sounded as sweet as any music I had heard.'[3]

For some time before Bernard arrived in America Mexico had been in the throes of civil war; the military President Porfirio Diaz had fled the country in 1911 after thirty years of dictatorship, and the turmoil and unrest that ensued persisted well into the 1920s, with fierce, often brutal fighting between opposing factions. Hostilities between rival groups were often as bitter as against their 'official' opposition. The President in 1913–14 – and therefore for part of the time Bernard was in America – was General Huerta, but he was unpopular with the influential USA, who preferred his rival Carranza, and he was forced to flee Mexico on 17 July 1914.[4] Provisions and services from California to Mexico were threatened by attack from rebels and bandits and had to be escorted by armed guards. There were numerous advertisements in San Francisco asking for volunteers, and they obviously attracted Bernard in his desire for adventure.

The first indication of what Bernard was contemplating came in another part of his 28 April letter to Mrs Penboss:

Last week I gave my name in to go to Mexico, only to be told that they did not require anybody other than those they had, and if they required any volunteers I would be written to. Since then I have heard of a way I may be able to work. A private crowd are going to the front for a big picture

[29]

combine; I have offered to go and help them in any capacity they like, and may get away with them. I hope so. If I do I will write and tell you before I start. It must be a fairly large undertaking as it has to carry its own supplies and travels with the enemy's column as well as with the American – not at the same time, of course, but when it suits.

Nothing more seems to have happened for a month, and then in the undated letter he sent with the scrapbook (which itself was finished at the beginning of June 1914) Bernard stated: 'I am penning this from Bakersfield. I am going down to Mexico to look for a job of any description as I think I would like to see a bit of that part of this continent. I leave at the end of this week.'

To Lesbia Wilson he wrote: 'I have signed up as an armed guard looking after the National Film Unit, which is going to the Mexican War to take pictures of the war.'[5]

And his old headmaster recorded in *The Wellingtonian*: 'Then I received a letter from Freyberg saying he was very sorry he had bothered me, but he was not going to the University. He was going to Mexico.'[2]

There are no more letters to the Penboss family or to anyone else during the months of June and July 1914. This is not surprising, as Bernard would have had little time for writing in Mexico, and it seems improbable that the postal services were functioning properly during the civil war. Whether he made the journey to Mexico with a film unit or with some other organisation, there can be no doubt that he went; and there is certainly no trace of him in California or anywhere else for the next two months.

After Bernard's death some of the books published which referred to him included letters and diary accounts from 1914 and 1915. Violet Asquith (later Lady Violet Bonham Carter), for example, who met Bernard in February 1915 in England, states that 'His passion for fighting led him to leave New Zealand for Mexico where Civil War was going on between two Generals', and she expands on this somewhat misleading description after a visit to her brother Oc Asquith in Alexandria in June 1915, where he and Bernard were recovering from wounds received at Gallipoli. She records:

Freyberg asked me to go for a drive with him next day before he sailed, and called for me in the morning in a Goz. As we drove round and round, he told me all about his life. He had been wandering since he was fifteen, and knew the South Sea Islands well . . . Just before the war he had gone to Mexico, where civil war was raging, and offered his services first to Huerta and then to [Pancho] Villa – who accepted them. He was fighting as a mercenary for

[30]

Villa when he heard of the outbreak of war in Europe. He deserted with a blood-price on his head, walked and hitch-hiked some three hundred miles.[6]

During the same period in Egypt Bernard met a New Zealand acquaintance, A. E. M. Rhind, who wrote in his diary: 'Sunday 23 May 1915. Met Freyberg at 12.00. He was interesting as he had fought in the Mexican Rebellion and deserted from there when this war broke out . . .'[7]

In Rupert Brooke's letters at the end of 1914 there are several references to the same story. In December 1914 Brooke tells Russell Loines: 'Among the officers in this Division are two young Asquiths, an Australian professional pianist who twice won the Diamond Sculls, a New Zealander who was fighting in Mexico and walked three hundred miles to get a boat when he heard of the war.'[8]

There is also independent evidence of Bernard's presence in Mexico at the time of the outbreak of the Great War, in *Reminiscences of the Mexican Revolution* by Patrick O'Hea, who was acting as British Consul in Mexico in 1914:

> Several men of military age and medically fit were passed along by me to Tampico after the outbreak of the European War, for transatlantic transport by tankers of the Mexican Eagle Oil Company. One such, whose name I never kept but of whom I recall the youthful twenties, his height above the average, the neat blue suit spared from his service in the Villa army and of fair complexion and blonding hair, said he was a dentist by profession who had worked his passage from New Zealand to San Francisco; and thence, for lack of suitable employment or for lust of battle, had moved southwards and enlisted as a mercenary in the Villa army, from which I was instrumental in extricating him for his departure for Tampico and the War.[9]

Francisco 'Pancho' Villa (1878–1922) was an almost legendary figure, who, prior to the civil war, had thrived as an outlaw with a dubious reputation as champion of the poor. He was a territorial leader in the north of Mexico, and at one stage commanded more than 30,000 men; he also supported Carranza for a while. At this time he was at the peak of his military and political career. In his book about the Mexican Revolution, *Pancho Villa and John Reed* (1984), Jim Tuck confirms that Bernard probably served under Villa, and suggests that he may well have been present at the decisive engagement of the revolution's campaign at Zacatecas on 23–4 June 1914, when Villa sealed Huerta's doom.[4] Indeed it is the only action in which he could have participated when he was in the country, for it seems probable that Bernard entered

Mexico at El Paso in early June 1914, and likely that this was as a guard of some sort – either for a bank payroll or a mining company, or even for a film company. The attack on Zacatecas began on 23 June and the city fell on 24 June.[4] It would have been possible for Bernard to have reached Zacatecas before then. He could only have been involved in the fighting for a couple of weeks, however, because, as Jim Tuck relates, 'the villistas, owing to Villa's quarrel with Carranza, took no part in the July drive on Mexico City, and by early August Freyberg was on his way to England'. Zacatecas is about 300 miles from the port of Tampico, which ties in with Bernard's story about walking and hitchhiking for 300 miles to catch a boat out of Mexico as soon as he heard of the outbreak of the Great War.

Tuck wonders what Freyberg's duties were while fighting with the villistas, and reports that one Emil Michner, an enthusiast for Mexican history, was told by Lieutenant-Colonel Eduardo Angeles Meras, head of the villista veterans' organisation, that 'Freyberg was attached to the staff of his cousin General Felipe Angeles. General Angeles was Villa's highly talented artillery commander.' J. O. C. Neill of New Zealand claims that Bernard rose to be the officer in charge of transport, and that Villa, who had a 'foreign legion' of supporters, strongly objected to his going. Maybe it was Villa who put a price on Bernard's head. At all events, Patrick O'Hea recalls that Bernard borrowed $100 from him to cover his passage money from Tampico to New York.

The First World War started at midnight on 4 August 1914, London time, and Bernard probably heard the news early on 5 August Mexico time. On his military file in Wellington there is an incomplete signal dated 7 August 1914, signed by the Consul in San Francisco, saying, 'Lieutenant Freyberg reports that left for England to be attached.'[10] This telegram could well have been sent by Bernard from Tampico, or even when he was already at sea, to San Francisco, and probably dates his departure from Mexico. Shipping records in the London Guildhall Library show that there were a large number of sailings from Tampico to the United States in August 1914, especially by the Mexican Eagle Oil Fleet (later taken over by Shell), and that there were frequent tanker movements across the Gulf of Mexico to New Orleans, a distance of about 700 miles, taking two or three days in transit. Such a voyage could have been followed by a fast railway journey to New York; equally Bernard may have gone direct by sea to New York. If his departure from Tampico took place on 7 August he would have reached New York by 11 or 12 August. Once there he went to the house of the Penboss family.

In 1917, after he had won his VC in France, an article about Bernard appeared in a New York newspaper, the date and name of which was not included in the cutting which Queenie Penboss kept. This not only describes how he left Mexico at the outbreak of war in Europe, when, it claims, Bernard was fighting under General Carranza, but offers a colourful version of how he financed his journey from New York to Liverpool:

> The news reached the Carranza army and Carranza lost an extremely promising Captain simultaneously. The pay of his rank was by no means capitalistic, but he stretched it a bit and a few days later crawled off a tramp steamer in New York, his first questions being as to the location of the British Consulate. Now at that time Great Britain had made no provision for the return of her men who wanted to fight and could do little for the young man Freyberg except tell him to come back in a day or so and they would see what could be done. He hasn't been back yet, but a few nights later at a fight club somewhere in Harlem a dark brown, rangy looking youth who was introduced as 'Kid Comptyomph' or something like that, the middleweight champion of Chihuahua, walloped the everlasting daylights and nightlights out of a certain Jewish gentleman called Young McGuffey, who had been thought considerable of as a mauler up to those moments.
>
> A night or so after that same Mexican box fighter played an identical trick upon a scrapper who, it may be observed, was not Young McGuffey, and then a day after that Capt. Freyberg, late of the Carranzistas, boarded a steamer for Liverpool with no great amount of surplus wealth about him, but still enough to make a go of it.

A friend from New Zealand recalls 'Tiny' knocking down the New Zealand lightweight boxer Tim Tracey in 1904 when challenged to punch him as hard as he could in the solar plexus, but whether he proved his boxing prowess in America in the way the article suggests, cannot be ascertained. However the newspaper account was certainly accurate about the steamer bound for Liverpool. The ship concerned was the 20,000-ton White Star liner *Cedric*, which sailed from New York on 14 August 1914 with Bernard on board. There are two letters in the Penboss package written on White Star Line writing paper, with the address 'On board SS *Cedric*'. One of these was sent to Mrs Penboss and was obviously written in great haste. It reads:

> Dear Mama
> I want to thank you for all you did for me. I will not forget it. I am putting this on with the pilot.
> > Yrs Bernard Freyberg.

The second was a much longer letter to Queenie Penboss written on 23 August and posted in Liverpool, describing incidents that occurred on board and speculating about what might happen on arrival. The first and last paragraphs state:

> We have had a great trip – only men on board, all going back to join; we have had a happy crowd . . .
> I will write to you from time to time when I get the opportunity. It was very sweet of you to come and see me depart – Goodbye. Best of love to all,
> Bernard Freyberg.

The SS *Cedric* was a slow boat. After calling at Queenstown in Ireland she reached Liverpool late on Sunday evening, 24 August 1914.[11] Early on Monday, 25 August Bernard caught the 'Territorial Special' to London.

That week was to change the whole of Bernard's life.

4

The Royal Naval Division and the 'Argonauts'

The First World War had been in progress for three weeks when Bernard Freyberg arrived in England. In that time the British Expeditionary Force (BEF) had been moved to France, and was already in action against the German Army at Mons. The Royal Navy had been mobilised and was at battle stations; but for many thousands of naval reservists who had been called up there were no vacant berths in any of the ships at sea. The Committee of Imperial Defence had foreseen this situation long before the war, and proposed that surplus reservists, rather than be kept mobilised without suitable employment, should be formed into two naval brigades. These new brigades, plus the regular brigade of Royal Marines, were to form the Royal Naval Division (RND).

The First Lord of the Admiralty, Winston Churchill, was the leading spirit behind the RND's formation, having played a prominent part in raising and organising it. Indeed he had an understanding with Lord Kitchener, Minister for War, that in certain circumstances he was to resign as First Lord and be given the rank of Lieutenant-General in order to lead the RND in the field.[1] When the crisis broke at the beginning of October 1914 Kitchener, during the Cabinet meeting on 4 October, offered to commission Churchill as a Lieutenant-General immediately if H. H. Asquith, the Prime Minister, consented to release him.[2] Asquith rejected any such arrangement, but that it existed at all

[35]

demonstrates the close personal interest which Churchill took in everything to do with the RND.

Orders to form the two naval brigades were issued by the Admiralty on 16 August 1914, and the reservists began arriving at camps at Walmer and Betteshanger in Kent for 1 and 2 Naval Brigades respectively in the last ten days of August. On 16 August Churchill had minuted the First and Second Sea Lords as follows:

> The two naval brigades will consist of four battalions, each, if possible, of 880 men, organised in sixteen double companies of 220 . . . The officers commanding companies and battalions must be appointed forthwith. The first essential is to get the men drilling together in brigades; and the deficiencies of various ranks in the battalions can be filled up later . . . All the men, whether sailors or marines, while training in the three brigades will be available if required for service afloat, and it must be distinctly understood that this is the paramount claim upon them; but in the meanwhile they will be left to be organised for land service.[1]

There were relatively few opportunites for volunteers to get into active units quickly at the beginning of the war. The BEF in France was mostly composed of regulars, or reservists who had been recalled to the colours. Kitchener's New Armies existed only on paper, and recruiting for them lay in the future. Consequently the RND was one of the few formations in which there was a prospect of seeing early active service and Churchill found himself inundated with applicants seeking to enlist. Many of the first junior officer appointments to the RND were arranged on a personal basis by Edward Marsh, Churchill's private secretary.

The senior officers of the new naval battalions – which were named after famous admirals of the Royal Navy, such as Collingwood, Nelson and Hood – were mainly regular soldiers who had recently retired from the Brigade of Guards; together with Warrant Officers from the Royal Marines and Chief Petty Officers from the Royal Navy, they formed the professional backbone of the units. The element missing from this mixture of mature senior and young junior officers was the middle-piece company commander with some experience of soldiering.

Freyberg arrived in London on the morning of Monday, 25 August 1914. He called early on G. H. Scholefield, a New Zealand press representative whose Fleet Street office was a rendezvous for New Zealanders, and he and Freyberg discussed ways of getting into the fighting forces. Scholefield wrote: 'I was able to tell him that Major

[36]

G. S. Richardson, the New Zealand staff officer in London, was then acting on the staff of the Royal Naval Division.'[3]

This was an extraordinary piece of luck, for it was the same Major Richardson from Wellington whom Freyberg had encountered in the Corps Volunteers and Territorials. Six days before Freyberg's arrival in London, Churchill had sent for Richardson, one of the last graduates of the 1913 Staff College Course not already in a war appointment, and asked him to join the administrative staff of the Royal Naval Division.[4]

Churchill has been credited with giving Freyberg a commission in the RND, and Bernard did approach him with just this aim in mind. Their first meeting is described in Churchill's Second World War memoirs, not altogether accurately:

> Bernard Freyberg and I had been friends for many years. When as a young volunteer from New Zealand in the First World War he had made his way through many difficulties to England, he had an introduction to me, and met me one day in the Admiralty in September 1914 and asked for a commission.[5]

Their meeting took place, in fact, on the Horse Guards Parade when Churchill was walking between the Admiralty and Downing Street. In the days before bodyguards were required for politicians Freyberg was able to approach the First Lord of the Admiralty, who at first tried to 'brush him aside'.[6] But he was faced with a very determined young man, and eventually had to stop and listen to his request, as Lady Violet Bonham Carter confirms in *Winston Churchill As I Knew Him*: 'I asked Winston in December 1960 through whom Freyberg made contact with the RND. He told me that Freyberg had accosted him one day on the Horse Guards Parade and asked him if he might apply to serve in it, which Winston encouraged him to do.'[7]

Freyberg immediately applied to join the RND. Major Richardson, now on its administrative staff, was also NZ Liaison Officer attached to New Zealand House in London, and as a previous member of the NZ Permanent Staff Corps in Wellington he was well aware of Freyberg's military service. Freyberg therefore was at once commissioned into the Hood Battalion of the RND. He was gazetted as a temporary Lieutenant in the Royal Naval Volunteer Reserve (RNVR). This appeared in the *London Gazette* of 8 September 1914 though his seniority dated back to the end of August.[8]

It was the turning point of Freyberg's life.

In 1914 there were plenty of young men of nineteen or twenty who were eager to serve but lacked training or any knowledge of the army.

[37]

Freyberg was twenty-five, he had held a territorial commission and had seen some fighting in Mexico. He *was* that rare commodity, the 'middle-piece' officer. Indeed almost immediately after joining the Hood Battalion he was given command of 'A' Company, one of the 'double companies' of 220 men.

The day of Freyberg's arrival at Betteshanger Camp in Kent was remembered by Richard Henry Tobin, a Petty Officer from the Mersey Division of the RNVR, who later in the war became Freyberg's Chief Petty Officer:

> All of the Hood officers and ratings were in 'blues'. The new draft of Sub-Lieutenants caused the greatest interest, because they were in khaki. One giant who arrived caused great excitement and amusement. He wore a real naval uniform, that is a double-breasted reefer jacket – but in khaki – with two rings and the curl on his sleeve. The troops at once christened him 'Khaki Jack'.[9]

'Khaki Jack' was fortunate in having as his first Commanding Officer Lieutenant-Colonel Arnold Quilter, an ex-Grenadier who came from an old Suffolk family. He was an experienced professional soldier who, in the midst of trying to forge a team of nearly 1,000 naval reservists and north-country recruits into a fighting infantry unit, managed to instil into the Hood Battalion an *esprit de corps*. He also practised a traditional method of soldiering that somehow withstood the terrible casualties and survived four years of war, even though he himself was killed in 1915.

From Betteshanger Freyberg sent two letters to the Penboss family. The first, written soon after arrival, was a very short one addressed to 'Mama', to say where he was. A longer one to Queenie towards the end of September reveals that:

> I have been given a very important command in the Naval Brigade which is to land at Ostend with 4.7 guns. I am very hard worked and do not know which way to turn but love every hour of it. I am in charge of a Company (220 strong) RN Stokers who are a burly lot. I am in this with all my heart and have never been so keen in my life. I must go now to mount guard.[10]

The war on the Western Front had been growing progressively worse for the Allies. The BEF and the French armies had been in full retreat for most of September, and the Germans were beginning to threaten Paris as well as the ports of the Low Countries and the English Channel. All the British regular divisions were already in France, and even the Royal Marine Brigade had been sent to Dunkirk by the end of September. One of the few formed bodies of troops still in England were the two Naval Brigades, and these had been in existence for only six weeks.

When the crisis broke and the Naval Brigades were required to go into action, not only had they had virtually no training but they lacked almost all the supply units and administrative services necessary to maintain them in the field. There were no signals, artillery, engineers, field ambulances, divisional headquarters or administrative staffs. Battalions had few vehicles, and the troops could only be moved by ship, train or their own feet. But in spite of all these deficiencies, such was the emergency caused by the collapse of the Allied lines in Belgium (which threatened Antwerp – and ultimately the Channel ports) that the order for them to embark for Antwerp was given none the less. It reached Walmer and Betteshanger early in the morning of 2 October 1914 for immediate implementation.

The Hood was one of the four battalions – the others were named Howe, Anson and Nelson – of 2 Naval Brigade under the command of Commodore Backhouse. Oliver Backhouse commanded the brigade with distinction for nearly a year, until it was disbanded in Gallipoli in July 1915 because of extremely severe casualties. He then went back to the fleet, and commanded HMS *Orion* at the Battle of Jutland. He kept a detailed private diary of what happened to his brigade, first at Antwerp and then at Gallipoli, which has never been published.[11] This diary, written in a notebook in pencil, gives a much more personal account than the official histories of what happened at Antwerp during the extraordinary fortnight of the first half of October 1914.

Backhouse was woken at 4 a.m. on Sunday, 2 October with orders for 2 Naval Brigade to be ready to embark at Dover at 2 p.m. that day. He describes the pandemonium in the camps as they packed up to go to war with only ten hours warning, of having to recall battalions which were out on training, of issuing five days' rationing and two million rounds of ammunition to all units, and the numerous other preparations all being made 'against the clock'.

On arrival at Dover Backhouse found that the transport ships were not expected before 4 p.m., and they finally arrived between 6 p.m. and 8 p.m. For the next few hours the battalions' stores were loaded, and the ships eventually sailed at 11.30 p.m. They were bound for Dunkirk, and anchored just outside at 5 a.m. on Monday, 3 October. They entered the harbour at noon, where they found orders to disembark and proceed by rail to Antwerp. General Sir Henry Rawlinson, who had been sent by Kitchener to command the force intended for the relief of Antwerp, warned that there was a possibility that the trains might not get through.

In the event they did get through, and at first light on Tuesday, 4 October the troops were received with warm cheers by the inhabitants of Antwerp. At 7.30 a.m. Backhouse was met off the train by Major Richardson and, after two changes of plan, given orders to proceed to the inner line of forts covering the southern and eastern approaches to Antwerp itself. Backhouse decided to deploy the Howe Battalion between the Vieux Dieu Road and Fort 5; Hood Battalion between Forts 5 and 6; Anson Battalion between Forts 6 and 7; and Nelson Battalion behind them in reserve near his headquarters in Wilrych. These positions were taken up early on Wednesday, 5 October, and the troops started digging in with entrenching tools borrowed from the retreating Belgians. The men were well fed, and the weather warm and dry.[12]

In the meantime the Germans were starting to close up to the positions held by the RND, particularly those of 1 Naval Brigade which was occupying the line of forts to the north of 2 Naval Brigade.

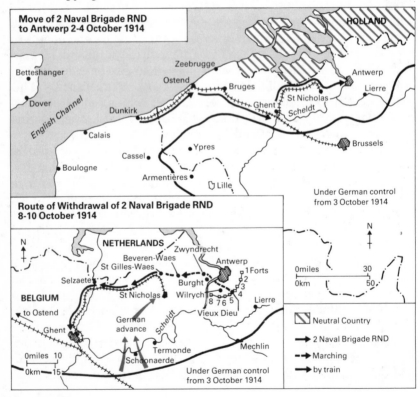

Considerable shelling of all the positions began, and German patrols were also in evidence. Neither of these developments was unexpected nor particularly ominous, and this situation continued for the next two days. What was more alarming to General Paris, the Divisional Commander, were developments elsewhere.

On the evening of 7 October the Germans secured a footing on the north bank of the river Scheldt at Schoonaerde. By next morning they had increased their bridgehead to more than a brigade. This posed a direct threat to the road and rail communications Ostend–Ghent–Antwerp on which the RND depended for all its supplies, and there were no reserves available to contain it. Unless the RND was quickly evacuated from Antwerp, therefore, it was in grave danger of being cut off from its base. At 5 p.m. on 8 October General Paris decided on evacuation, and the Admiralty and military headquarters in France were so informed.

Freyberg, reconnoitring a withdrawal route for his company, put his hand on barbed wire that, unknown to anyone, had been electrified by the Belgians. The current glued his right hand to the wire, and it was some time before the electric switch could be found and turned off. This was the first of the many injuries he sustained. According to the Naval 'Certificate of Wounds and Hurts' signed by Colonel Quilter on 28 November 1914, there were lacerated wounds on 'the palmar aspects' of his hands and fingers, and the scars stayed with him for the rest of his life.[8]

In his diary entry for 8 October Backhouse describes the retreat, detailing the precise movements of his troops, the shells exploding in burning oil vats beside the roads, the equipment and stores that had to be left behind, the roads crowded with troops and refugees, the false alarms, the waiting, forced marches in the middle of the night and so on:

> Reached St Gillies Waes station at 7 a.m. having covered 20 miles from Fort 5 since 8.30 p.m. Five special trains waiting for our men – took them to Selzaete close to Dutch frontier to avoid German troops. Drove to Selzaete with Maxwell [the Brigade Major]. Pitiful to see all the refugees retreating to Dutch frontier. Reached Selzaete at 9 – had a shave – bought vaseline for feet. Everyone movingly warm welcome and refusing payment for goods bought. Met our troop trains and got them food. Drove on at 12 to Bruges.[11]

By midday on 9 October, 2 Naval Brigade was well clear of the area threatened by the advancing German troops. 1 Naval Brigade was not so fortunate. Because of a series of mishaps – orders to withdraw not received in time, and the urgency not understood – part of the Brigade started their withdrawal too late and were cut off by the German advance: 1,479 officers and men crossed over into Holland and were interned; and 936 fell into the hands of the enemy.[12]

In spite of the extremely painful wound to his hand Freyberg remained in command of 'A' Company throughout the withdrawal. Only when they reached Ostend on 10 October did he go into the British hospital there, and the next day he sent a shakily written postcard to Queenie Penboss to say, 'Am in hospital – got wounded at Antwerp in the right arm. Cheerio, BF.' The postcard had on its other side a photograph of Bernard taken in Ostend, wearing his double-breasted khaki naval jacket.[10] Shortly afterwards he returned to England.

While the expedition to Antwerp cannot be described other than as a failure, in that it did not save the city from capture, it did, in the words of the Commander-in-Chief, BEF, 'delay the enemy for a considerable time, and assisted the Belgian Army to regain its value as a fighting force'.[13]

The Naval Brigades were the first non-regular troops to see action in the Great War. After its initial skirmish and withdrawal 2 Naval Brigade embarked in three ships at Ostend, and sailed for Dover on 12 and 13 October, with orders to return to camp at Betteshanger. Four days later, on 17 October, Freyberg lunched with Winston Churchill at the Admiralty, and met Edward Marsh, Churchill's private secretary, for the first time.[14] The following evening Marsh and Freyberg dined with Mrs Guest, the mother of Johnny Dodge, a young officer then in the Anson Battalion but shortly to transfer to the Hood. Mrs Guest's first marriage had been to Charles Dodge, of Dodge cars. After their divorce she married the Hon. Lionel Guest, so that Johnny, although American by birth, was brought up in England from the age of nine. The next day Mrs Guest took Freyberg to Coutts and introduced him to the bank, where he kept his personal account for the rest of his life.[15]

During November 1914 the Royal Naval Division moved from its tented accommodation at Walmer and Betteshanger to a hutted camp at Blandford, some four miles from Blandford Forum in Dorset. After the shake-up and losses at Antwerp all units were in for major reorganisation and the officer composition of the Hood Battalion began to change. In addition, clashes of personality in other battalions had meant that a number of officers requested transfers, and many of the more lively and spirited of them came to the Hood. The main reason for this was the personality of the Commanding Officer, Arnold Quilter. Once a few of the 'brighter sparks' had joined they attracted others, and so before long some of the *crème de la crème* of Oxford and Cambridge found their way into the battalion. Many of them were personal friends of Winston Churchill and 'Eddie' Marsh, who subsequently referred to them as the 'Argonauts'.[14] Thus Freyberg found himself in the centre of a group of officers who were both an intellectual and a social élite.

Perhaps the most notable of the Argonauts was Arthur (Oc) Asquith, the third son of the Prime Minister. At thirty and as a junior officer he was older than many of his contemporaries in the battalion, but his relative maturity, combined with a natural gift for soldiering and a strong personality, resulted in a wartime career in which, like Freyberg, he rose from Lieutenant RNVR to Brigadier-General in three years and was awarded the DSO three times. His father is credited with saying that 'two of my children are *formidable*', one being Arthur and the other Violet.[16] He was Freyberg's greatest friend in the First World War and during the inter-war years. The RND historian Douglas Jerrold portrayed him in his *Georgian Adventure* as:

> ... the finest of all our amateur soldiers, and the most respected. He was from Winchester and New College but he had long ago escaped into the world and had no illusions about old school ties. His dominating gift was a quiet, patient and inquiring mind inspired by a profound humility to go on learning ... In the first two years of the war he had learnt more than some generals learn in a long professional career.[17]

Cleg Kelly, an Australian by birth, was a music scholar at Balliol. He was one of the most talented musicians of the day, as well as three times winner of the Diamond Sculls at Henley. He was not an enthusiastic soldier, but a very conscientious one nevertheless. He spent most of his leisure composing music and reading books, but he was also contentious and loved argument; fascinated by the psychology of his friends he was both highly critical of them and warmheartedly loyal. He was also devoted to cats, and later on in France collected a number of kittens from deserted villages. When the battalion moved each of his company officers carried a kitten in a sandbag slung over his shoulder.[18]

Denis Browne was a long-standing Rugby friend of Rupert Brooke, who called him 'one of the best young English musicians and an extremely brilliant critic'.[19] It was Denis Browne who sat at Rupert Brooke's bedside as he lay dying in the French hospital ship *Duguay-Trouin*, and it was he and Oc Asquith who had to decide immediately afterwards to bury him on the island of Skyros, in view of the imminent departure of the RND for Gallipoli.[19] Denis was killed on 4 June 1915 in trench fighting at Helles. A few days earlier he had written to Edward Marsh: 'I've gone now too: not too badly I hope. I'm luckier than Rupert, because I've fought. But there's no one to bury me as I buried him, so perhaps he's best off in the long run.'[20]

Johnny Dodge too was one of the group who helped to dig Rupert Brooke's grave on Skyros. Brooke describes him as 'a very charming and beautiful American youth, infinitely industrious'. He survived Gallipoli and the rest of the war, in spite of being in the thick of the fighting throughout, winning the DSO, DSC and MC.

Rupert Brooke was already a legendary figure who had crammed much into his twenty-seven years. At first sight his and Bernard Freyberg's was an improbable friendship, since they came from such different backgrounds, experiences and interests. Violet Asquith records that what brought them together initially was a mutual love of the South Sea Islands. Rupert had gone there in the autumn of 1913 intending only a short visit; he was still in the South Seas many months later. On 20 November 1913 he wrote from Fiji to Denis Browne:

> I've been cruising about these islands, Samoan, Fijian, and the rest, for some time. It is mere heaven. One passes from Paradise to Paradise. The natives are incredibly beautiful, and very kindly. Life is one long picnic. I have been living in native villages and roaming from place to place . . . You will not know me, when – if ever – I return.[20]

On 7 February 1914, two months before Freyberg landed in Tahiti, Rupert wrote to his actress friend Cathleen Nesbitt of a scene beside 'a wide verandah over a blue lagoon':

> Everyone has a white flower behind their ear – Tuatamata has given me one. Do you know the significance of a white flower worn over the ear?
>
> > A white flower over the right ear means
> > I am looking for a sweetheart.
> > A white flower over the left ear means
> > I have one sweetheart and am looking for another,
>
> A white flower over each ear, my dear, is dreadfully the most fashionable way of adorning yourself in Tahiti.[20]

There was probably no one else in the Naval Division who had seen and could talk about such South Sea phenomena, except Bernard Freyberg, who had visited Rarotonga and Tahiti even more recently than Rupert, and whose interpretation of white-flower wearing was somewhat different: 'The way to tell a married Tahitian woman from an unmarried is to look at their ears; if married they wear a white flower in their right ear.'

Rupert Brooke had started his soldiering with the Anson Battalion at Betteshanger, where he composed his most famous poem, 'If I should die think only this of me . . .'. He is thought to have taken the original manuscript with him to Antwerp, where it disappeared with the rest of his baggage during the evacuation. He later described how his transfer to the Hood came about in a letter to his friend Dudley Ward:

> I'm really writing to tell you that the worst suddenly turned best. What happened, I gather, (this is England), is that Papa Asquith who had been dimly amused by the whole thing, suddenly took the idea that his son had been insulted and ill-used (as he had), sent for Winston, cussed him, and told him to put it right. So Winston damned an Admiral, who made blue Hell for the GOC Marines, who wiped the floor with X, who – and finally two Sub-Lieutenants Browne and Brooke were wired to, to join the Hood, where Asquith was. So here I am: for good, I trust.[20]

On 5 December Brooke wrote to Cathleen Nesbitt from Blandford Camp:

> I'm rather happy, really, in this new Battalion. Oc is about, and I'm in a company with rather a good lot of officers. At the head, a New Zealand youth who was fighting in Mexico, heard the news in August, walked 300 miles to the coast, got a boat, turned up here. He is also an Olympic Swimmer: and knows the South Seas.[20]

As a result of the timing of his arrival at Betteshanger in September 1914, and his participation with the Hood in the defence of Antwerp a month later, Freyberg was a founder-member of the battalion; even Oc Asquith, whose name later became so closely associated with the Hood, began his soldiering with the Anson. This seniority of membership gave Freyberg an advantage when the otherwise dauntingly brilliant young officers started to fill up the battalion.

Another of the company, Charles Lister, the son of Lord and Lady Ribblesdale, was a fine scholar, of great linguistic ability, with an innate love of Greek and Latin poetry, myth and history. After Eton and Balliol he went into the Foreign Office, serving in Rome and in Constantinople. Patrick Shaw-Stewart, another of the Argonauts, describes how Charles Lister joined the Hood Battalion:

> At Port Said Charles introduced himself by most subterranean methods into the Hood. He pulled as many strings to get off the Staff as others to get

[45]

on to it – and in about three days he had a platoon . . . It became a very jolly family party on board ship.[19]

The noise of the combination was described by Rupert Brooke after the RND arrived in Egypt in a letter to Violet Asquith (9 April 1915):

> Imagine what an extraordinary, an unprecedented conglomeration of sound Oc and I and Denis Browne put up with, when you learn that Patrick with his loud titter, Cleg Kelly with his whinny, and Charles with his great neighs, are all in the same tent. The sound from it frights the Egyptian night, and sends the ghost of Antony and the gypsy scudding away across the sands.[21]

This gathering of junior officers was christened 'the Latin Table' by their shipmates. Its membership was a feature of the *Grantully Castle* from 29 February 1915 when the boat left the Avonmouth Docks, and reached its apogee with the arrival of Charles Lister. It was renowned throughout the ship for its high-spirited gaiety, wit and *joie de vivre*, though it only existed for a few weeks. Sir Patrick Duff – later private secretary to Stanley Baldwin and British High Commissioner in New Zealand when Freyberg was Governor-General – was in 29 Division at Gallipoli serving alongside the RND, and heard the story from those at other tables who were present in the *Grantully Castle*. Charles Lister was wounded in the June battles on Gallipoli and evacuated to Egypt. While there he was offered a job in 10 Downing Street, which was short-handed at the time, but without consulting anyone he turned it down to remain with the Hood. He was wounded twice more, on the last occasion fatally. He died of his wounds in the hospital ship *Gascon* on 28 August 1915.[19]

The battalion doctor was Staff Surgeon W. J. McCracken. He carved out a unique niche for himself in the Hood, through his bravery under fire, and through the countless lives he saved in the four years he was with the unit, including Freyberg's in November 1916 at the battle of the Ancre. McCracken's career with the RND began at Blandford, and he served from the first heavy fighting at Gallipoli in 1915 until he himself was severely wounded at Helles on 21 May and invalided home to England. Back later with the Hood in France, he served throughout 1916 and 1917, being recommended for the VC at the battle of Gavrelle in June 1917, for which he received a DSO; a bar was added after further heavy fighting later that year. Earlier he had gained the MC and bar. In August 1918 a stray bullet fractured his skull, and he was out of the war for good. Notwithstanding these wounds,

[46]

McCracken was one of the few original Hood officers who lived to see old age.

Probably 'the most brilliant of all the Balliol men killed in the war' (as he has been called) was Patrick Shaw-Stewart.[22] He had been a shy Eton scholar who succeeded in 1904 in winning the Reynolds scholarship, even against Ronald Knox with whom he continued to compete at Oxford, where they both won classical scholarships and prizes. In September 1914 Patrick was commissioned a Sub-Lieutenant in the RNVR. After a few weeks in France and Belgium as an interpreter he joined the RND and trained at Crystal Palace and Blandford. He survived the Gallipoli campaign, proving his qualities as a soldier, and cheering his companions with his wit and high spirits.

At the beginning of 1917 he returned home on leave from Salonika, where he was working at GHQ as a staff officer; he was far from well, but succeeded in his efforts to rejoin the Hood Battalion in France. He remained with it for the rest of the year, at the end being in temporary command. In the early morning of 30 December, as he was going round the line, the Germans put up a barrage. Patrick was hit in the head by a bullet. He carried on, and was finally killed by a shell which burst on the parapet.[22]

Patrick's letters from Gallipoli are full of his passion for the classics, and typify how he and his scholarly companions were to see the Gallipoli landings as a romantic adventure to classical territory – and how cruelly their excitement was rewarded. On 29 April, just after the landings started, he wrote to Ronald Knox: 'Thence we came straight to the very edge of the tyranny of Miltiades, in sight of the *notissima fama insula*, in sight of Samothrace, in imaginary sight of windy Illios itself . . .'[23]

And on 28 June he wrote to Raymond Asquith: 'It is delightful to me, to bathe every day in the Hellespont, looking straight over to Troy, to see the sun set over Samothrace, to be fighting for the command of the Aegospotami, and to restate Miltiades' problem of Bulair.'[23]

After Patrick was killed a poem of his was found scribbled in his copy of *A Shropshire Lad* by A. E. Housman. The last two verses are:

> Was it so hard, Achilles
>   So very hard to die?
> Thou knowest and I know not –
>   So much the happier I.

> I will go back this morning
>   from Imbros over the sea;
> Stand in the trench, Achilles,
> flame capped, and shout for me.[19]

Freyberg's close association with such cultured and lively individuals over a period of months had a profound and lasting effect on him. He was made aware for the first time of the intellectual world, and the curiosity of trained minds. Their understanding and appreciation of the arts, and of the beauty of poetry and the classics was a revelation to him. As Geoffrey Cox later explained in *The Road to Trieste*:

> It is not difficult to envisage the impact which these men had on the open, curious and vigorous mind of the young New Zealander . . .
> There was nothing in the educational system of New Zealand at that time which could have given him similar intellectual development, for he had grown up in the robust but Philistine atmosphere from which his contemporary Katherine Mansfield had fled to Bloomsbury. But he had the intelligence and interest enough to appreciate their gifts. In these later years, in his occasional periods of reminiscence, he would recall the Latin tags which they flung at each other under bombardments . . .[24]

During his time at Blandford Freyberg began to be introduced into the homes of these extrovert individuals, and to meet their parents, sisters and girlfriends. At the age of twenty-five he was tall, good-looking and presentable. Although Freyberg had always been able to communicate easily with people whatever their background, doors now began to open for him into English social life, which would not have happened without the RND key.

The Hood Battalion was at Blandford Camp for just over three months, from the middle of November 1914 until the end of February 1915. The camp consisted of newly constructed huts, but because of winter rains and the absence of proper tarmac roads and paths it was soon reduced to a sea of mud. The huts themselves were quite comfortable, and as far as the officers were concerned consisted of individual cubicles, some fifteen feet by eight feet, whose furnishings were largely left to their personal choice. At this period of 'A' Company Freyberg was Company Commander; his second-in-command was Oc Asquith; and the subalterns were Denis Browne, Johnny Dodge, Patrick Shaw-Stewart and Rupert Brooke.[21]

Christmas day at Blandford was described by Rupert Brooke in a letter to Violet Asquith:

> Never say we're not a hilarious nation. Christmas Day in the Naval Division is a revelation. The Battalion CPO, a very fat man, who has been drunk since dawn, is conducting the band in an Irish jig in the middle of the parade-ground. He can't beat time, but he dances very convincingly . . .
> Half my stokers are dancing half-naked in their huts. They spent the night

on cheap gin. The surrounding woods are full of lost and sleeping stokers. I expect most of them froze overnight.[20]

The New Year brought rumours of impending moves. Churchill arrived to inspect the Division in February and it poured with rain. Rupert Brooke describes Edward Marsh lunching with him and Freyberg afterwards in the Hood mess: 'he told us all the jokes from *The Times*, and all the atrocity stories: things we never hear. The wardroom was fascinated by him, and said in chorus, when he left, "What odd eyebrows." '[21]

Three days later Quilter addressed the officers and broke the news that the Division was shortly to leave for the Mediterranean and the Dardanelles. The effect on the battalion was electrifying. Rupert Brooke wrote ecstatically to Violet Asquith: 'Oh Violet, it's too wonderful for belief. I had not imagined Fate could be so benign. I almost suspect her.'[21]

On 25 February King George V came to review the Division. Mrs Churchill and Violet Asquith watched the parade, and afterwards lunched in the Hood wardroom. Violet describes the occasion: 'I sat next to Freyberg, Rupert's Company Commander... He loves fighting as a musician loves music – for its own sake. He said to me, "I'm different from Oc and Rupert. I've got to make my own fortune, as well as England's, out of the war." '[7] She also portrayed the chaos of the camp the afternoon before the Battalion left: '500 marvellous mules as big as hunters dragging helpless, baffled stokers in all directions while equally nonplussed NCOs bellowed directions at them'. But in spite of the attempts to be lighthearted her conclusion was melancholy: 'Every form of luxury – grapefruit, marrons glacés, foie gras and champagne had been procured by Patrick. It wasn't quite the fun it ought to have been. I felt a tightening of the heart throughout.'[7]

By the last morning, the day of departure, the atmosphere had become more frenzied:

The camp had disintegrated overnight. Great wagons packed with blankets lay across the road becalmed in a sea of mud. Mules still rioted, stokers tore about, officers whistled, formations of men stood here and there being counted and equipped... Saw Freyberg for a moment who said to me pathetically that as all the others had had their photographs taken he had done so too. 'I have got 6 Cabinet photogravures 12 × 8 and I don't know a single woman in England to give one to. (hastily) Would you like one?' Of course, I leapt at it and carried back a huge military portrait inscribed 'Kia Ora' [meaning 'Good health' in Maori].[7]

[49]

At 7.15 p.m. on Saturday, 27 February the Hood marched 10 miles from Blandford Camp to Shillingstone station where the battalion entrained for the Avonmouth Docks. There they boarded the *Grantully Castle*, a Union Castle liner of 7,500 tons, in the early hours of the next day. The ship sailed the same evening.

The *Grantully Castle* arrived at Malta on 8 March 1915, resumed her voyage the next day, and two days later dropped anchor in Mudros Bay, Lemnos, where there was a huge assembly of ships. After a week, on 18 March she sailed for Turkish waters in the vicinity of Gallipoli. Those on board half expected to be put on shore, but the operation was a feint, aimed at making the Turks disclose the strength and dispositions of their defences, which at the time were negligible. It coincided with the Navy's attempt to force the Straits, which ended in failure and the loss of four old battleships, blown up on minefields in the Dardanelles. Afterwards the *Grantully Castle* returned to Lemnos, and later left for Port Said, which she reached on 27 March. The object of this diversion was to allow the forces destined for the Gallipoli landings to reorganise for battle after their hasty and ill-prepared despatch from England. This month-long delay was one of the many reasons for the Gallipoli disaster, however, for it also gave the Turks time to prepare their defences – and warning that they needed to do so.

The Hood Battalion disembarked in Egypt for a fortnight and went into a temporary camp, where Freyberg shared a tent with Dodge, E. W. Nelson, who had been on Scott's last expedition, and Rupert Brooke. After a couple of nights the junior officers went off to visit Cairo and the pyramids. Soon afterwards many went down with dysentery and were away from the battalion for some days in consequence. Eventually all the Hood foregathered again on the *Grantully Castle*, and on 10 April sailed once more for Mudros, this time proceeding very slowly because they were towing barges to be used in the landings. They arrived at Lemnos on 16 April but the harbour was so congested that they were diverted to Trebuki Bay on the southern tip of Skyros, which they reached the next day.

Rupert Brooke had been one of those who caught dysentery in Egypt, and was still feeling weak when he embarked on the *Grantully Castle*. He did not regain his strength on the sea journey as the others did, and because of this his resistance to infection was low. When he was bitten on his lip by an insect, the bite became poisoned. He took part in an exercise on Skyros on 20 April; after it was over Freyberg, Lister and Brooke happened to be together on the beach when someone suggested swimming back to the ship, about a mile away. Brooke said he wished he could join them but he did not feel up to it. So the others plunged in, and he followed seated among their clothes in a fisherman's boat.[21]

Freyberg wrote an article in 1961 describing Rupert Brooke's illness, death and burial on the island of Skyros.[25] After pointing out that only three of the officers who dug Rupert's grave had survived the Great War, he said that two of them, Arthur Asquith and Johnny Dodge, had since died, leaving himself the sole survivor. He related:

> Rupert Brooke was in my Company as a platoon commander in the Hood Battalion of the Royal Naval Division. Though his personal interests were of a very different order, he was an excellent young officer and commander. When the Royal Naval Division moved to the Middle East in 1915 Rupert and I shared a cabin in the troopship *Grantully Castle* on the voyage from Alexandria to the Gallipoli landing.[25]

Freyberg later used to tell of how Rupert Brooke spoke very little on his last voyage, 'and kept to himself, apart though not aloof, as if he already knew the fate that awaited him'. Freyberg's account continues:

> Our ship was anchored off the island of Skyros. It was here that the poison from an insect bite on the lip which Rupert had contracted earlier spread to a general condition of acute blood poisoning.
>
> When he became seriously ill, he was transferred to a nearby hospital ship, as our ship was under orders to sail at short notice. He died in the hospital ship only a few hours later.
>
> Situated as we were, and expecting the order to move at any moment, we wanted to make the most of such few hours as we were likely to have to pay our last tribute to Rupert Brooke before we were moved on.
>
> The Colonel of our Hood Battalion, Arnold Quilter, and Rupert's brother officers of A Company went ashore and we chose the site for his grave – a lovely olive grove high above the bay, where we had been at anchor.
>
> Seven young officers who had shared Rupert's last months dug his grave, Denis Browne, Charles Lister, Cleg Kelly, Patrick Shaw-Stewart, Arthur Asquith, Johnny Dodge and myself.[25]

A more detailed account of this famous scene is given in Christopher Hassall's biography of Rupert Brooke.[21] Hassall describes how the site, which Brooke had himself found 'very pleasant', was chosen, and the grave marked beneath one of twelve olive trees. Rupert's coffin was on the French hospital ship, the *Duguay-Trouin*, and her men surrounded the coffin with small palm trees and covered it with a British flag. As there was no time to engrave a plate Asquith burnt Rupert

Brooke's name and the date into the wood of the coffin with a cauterising iron.

A party of twelve officers came with Quilter and collected the coffin from the *Duguay-Trouin* and then made for the shore with two other boats all with their lights on:

Twelve bearers, petty officers of the Hood, mostly Australians, and a guard of honour commanded by Shaw-Stewart, were drawn up on the quay. The moon was clouded, the way up the watercourse . . . was rough with loose rocks and stones, and men with lamps had to be posted every twenty yards of the way inland to the rendezvous. It took the bearers just under two hours to negotiate a distance of less than a mile. Shortly before eleven o'clock, Lister and Asquith saw a man with a lantern coming slowly up the gorge. Behind him walked Platoon-Sergeant Saunders of No. 4 Platoon, holding aloft a big, roughly put-together cross painted white, and along the cross-beam, painted in black, the name of the man they were burying; then came Shaw-Stewart with drawn sword, leading the firing party, then the bearers with the coffin, and General Paris walking behind it.

When Asquith saw the coffin, he asked for a spade and jumped into the grave and lengthened it a little, and he found it all lined with sprigs of olive and flowering sage. When all was ready and the men assembled, Quilter threw in a wreath of olive. The moon remained clouded, and a slight breeze got up, stirring the foliage, as the Chaplain read the burial service of the Church of England . . . Three volleys were fired into the air, Shaw-Stewart presented arms . . .

The parade broke up and they found their way down to the shore, while Freyberg, Kelly, Asquith, Lister and Browne stayed behind and gathered lumps of the pink and white marble from round about and heaped them into a cairn over the grave.[21]

All those present were struck by the beauty and aptness of Rupert's grave; as Kelly wrote in his journal, 'It was as though one were involved in the origin of some classical myth.'

But Rupert Brooke's death and burial were not good omens for what lay ahead. Four hours after the service was over the *Grantully Castle* weighed anchor at Trebuki Bay and headed for Gallipoli.

(Top left) Bernard Freyberg in 1894, aged 5; *(top right)* at Brisbane in 1905; *(below)* view of Wellington town and part of Lambton harbour, *c.* 1900, taken from Mount Victoria *(Alexander Turnbull Library)*

REG. HEALY
880 Yards

M. E. CHAMPION
220, 440 Yards and 1 Mile.

B. C. FREYBERG
100 Yards.

NEW ZEALAND CHAMPIONS, 1910.

Swimming and sailing played a big part in Freyberg's youth: *(top left)* Bernard at 16; *(top right)* a group of New Zealand champions, 1910; *(below)* the Te Aro Baths, Wellington, 1908, Freyberg at second left *(Evening Post)*

Y.M.C.A. SWIMMING SPORTS 1.2.08;
(START FOR THE 100YDS. HDCP.)
ZAK: PHOTO: WOTON N.Z. 546:

Four of the five Freyberg brothers *(clockwise from top left)* – Oscar, Paul, Bernard and Cuthbert. Neither Oscar nor Paul survived the First World War. Bernard, photographed in 1914, is wearing the Royal Naval Division uniform which gained him the nickname 'Khaki Jack'

(Left) The brothers' 33-foot keeler *Viking*

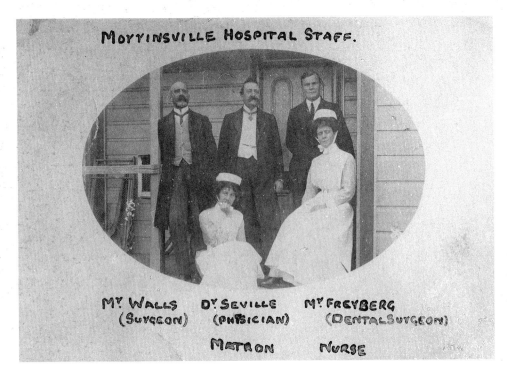

MOYYINSVILLE HOSPITAL STAFF.

M*. WALLS   Dʳ SEVILLE   Mʳ FREYBERG
(SURGEON)   (PHYSICIAN)   (DENTAL SURGEON)

MATRON   NURSE

Morrinsville, ninety miles south-east of Auckland, *c.* 1911. *(Above)* The hospital staff, including 'Mr Freyberg, Dental Surgeon'; *(below)* Thames Street *(Turnbull Library)*

THAMES STREET.   MORRINSVILLE.   No 615E.

(Above) A group of strikebreakers in the Wellington dock strike of 1913, Freyberg standing, in bow tie, centre; *(below left)* Freyberg at the wheel of RMS *Tahiti* en route to San Francisco, April 1914; *(right)* Freyberg with Queenie *(left)* and Lucinda Penboss in Tahiti

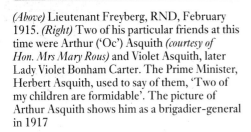

(Above) Lieutenant Freyberg, RND, February 1915. *(Right)* Two of his particular friends at this time were Arthur ('Oc') Asquith *(courtesy of Hon. Mrs Mary Rous)* and Violet Asquith, later Lady Violet Bonham Carter. The Prime Minister, Herbert Asquith, used to say of them, 'Two of my children are formidable'. The picture of Arthur Asquith shows him as a brigadier-general in 1917

BACK ROW
2nd LIEUT. ARTHUR ASQUITH. LIEUT. JACOB DE LILLE. LIEUT. WALLER. LIEUT. SHADBOLT. R.

MIDDLE ROW
LT. NELSON. FLT. R. BROOKE. FLT. EGERTON. FLT. JOHN DODGE. FLT. DENIS BROWNE. FLT. LESTER. FLT. MARTIN. FLT. GAMMAGE. FLT. CASSEY. LT. E.QM. NOBBS

FRONT ROW
PAY. GILLIARD. LT. FERGUSON. LT. COM. FREBERS. LT. COM. PARSONS. LT. COM. GRAHAM. ADJ. COL. QUILTER. LT. COM. BURNETT. LT. COM. DAGLISH. LT. HUGHES. MID. JACOB. LT. HENDERVICK.

(Above) The officers of the Hood Battalion, RND, at Blandford Camp, December 1914. *(Middle)* Rupert Brooke, 1913, and Surgeon W. J. McCracken; *(bottom)* Patrick Shaw-Stewart, and Johnny Dodge

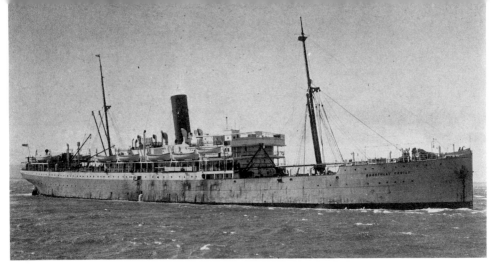

(Above) The troopship *Grantully Castle* which carried the Hood Battalion from England to the Dardanelles; (left) the raft which Freyberg towed on his famous swim in the Gulf of Saros on 25-26 April 1915; (below) Freyberg in the trenches at Gallipoli, June 1915

5

Gallipoli

The Royal Naval Division's role at the beginning of the Gallipoli campaign was to make an appearance in its ships at Bulair, and try to persuade the Turks that a landing there was imminent. The RND ships were still anchored off Skyros in the early morning of 24 April 1915, after Rupert Brooke's burial the night before; but at 5.30 a.m. the fleet of fourteen liners and their naval escorts left Trebuki Bay and the next day entered the Gulf of Saros.

Commodore Backhouse's diary describes what happened:

Sunday, 25 April.
Up at 4.30 a.m. and found ship close off Bulair village. Glorious morning, quite calm, lovely sunrise. Shore on both sides exquisitely beautiful, very lovely effect. Very sad to think of approaching desolation of war. Went into action at 5.30 and opened fire with *Lydite* at Fort Sultan at 5.15 firing about 20 rounds without producing any reply. No sign of life or movement of men or animals. Trenches plainly visible everywhere but all vacant of troops.[1]

Seaplane reconnaissance had shown that there were no troops moving on the roads of the peninsula. Later Backhouse went further into the bay and could see the maze of trenches and barbed wire with the naked eye, but still no sign of life. Another ship found the northern shore of the Gulf of Saros equally deserted. So Backhouse:

steamed to slopes of hills all the way from Yeniloi to Bulair. System of trenches quite marvellous in extent especially close to Fort Napoleon.

[53]

Turks evidently expected landing by Bulair. Fine view of Bulair village approaching from East'd at 3 p.m. – very much in ruins from previous bombardment. Further reconnaissance showed at 4 p.m. Bulair lines and forts and trenches quite deserted. The mystery quite inexplicable. Returned to rendezvous 5 miles WSW of [Island of] Saros by 5.30 p.m.

Some of the warships and transports then left to do a feint along the north shore of the Gulf of Saros, while to the south the liners *Franconia*, *Issunnetoulia*, *Alnwick Castle*, *Royal George* and *Grantully Castle* stopped some 6,000 yards out from the Bulair shore. At 6.50 that evening, eight ship's boats, each manned by twenty men, were hoisted out of each of the liners.

A plan had been devised to send a whole platoon from Freyberg's A Company to land by boat near to the Bulair lines, and to light flares at intervals along the coast. The object was to make the Turks believe that these flares were being lit to guide the ship's boats loaded with soldiers to the shore. That was why the boats had been allowed to be seen leaving the troopships just before last light, to give the impression that they were going to land during the night. Freyberg, however, disliked the thought of one of his platoons stumbling about in the dark on an unknown beach, risking becoming casualties or being taken prisoner unnecessarily. He felt it was possible to achieve the same object by using one or two swimmers instead. He therefore suggested to his Commanding Officer, Colonel Quilter, that he and one other be allowed to carry out the task. When the plan was accepted Freyberg then asked that Oc Asquith accompany him. This Quilter refused, saying that he was prepared to risk the life of one New Zealander, but was damned if he was going to be held responsible for drowning the son of the Prime Minister! So Freyberg did the swim on his own.[2]

Freyberg was covered in dark, heavy grease to protect him from the icy waters, and so as to make him as inconspicuous as possible. A wooden canvas raft was made by some of the engineers for him to tow, and in it were placed oil flares, calcium lights, a signalling light and a revolver. What happened next Freyberg himself described in his report the day after his return:

At 9 p.m. last night (25 April) . . . we were taken in tow by the steam pinnace of HMS *Dartmouth*, and towed to within three miles of the shore, when we slipped and rowed in another mile. It now became evident that to proceed further without being seen would be impossible.

26 April. At 12.40 this morning, therefore, I started swimming to cover the remaining distances, towing a waterproof canvas bag containing three oil flares and five calcium lights, a knife, signalling light, and a revolver.

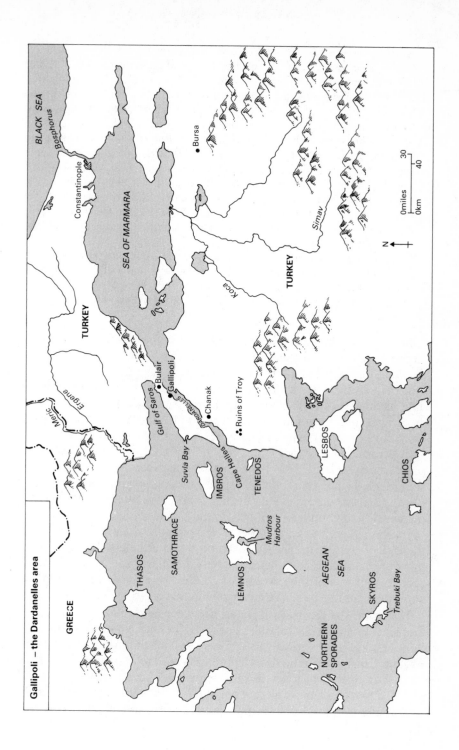

Gallipoli – the Dardanelles area

GREECE

BLACK SEA

Bosphorus

Constantinople

SEA OF MARMARA

TURKEY

TURKEY

Bursa

Simav

Koca

Meric

Ergene

Gulf of Saros

Bulair

Gallipoli

DARDANELLES

Chanak

Ruins of Troy

Suvla Bay

Cape Helles

IMBROS

TENEDOS

THASOS

SAMOTHRACE

LEMNOS

Mudros Harbour

LESBOS

CHIOS

AEGEAN SEA

NORTHERN SPORADES

SKYROS

Trebuki Bay

N

0 miles 30
0 km 40

After an hour and a quarter's hard swimming in bitterly cold water I reached the shore and lighted my first flare, and again took to the water and swam towards the east, and landed about 300 yards away, where I lighted my second flare and hid among some bushes to await developments. Nothing happening, I crawled up a slope to where some trenches were located the morning before. I discovered they were only dummies, consisting of a pile of earth about two feet high and 100 yards long, and looked to be quite newly made. I crawled in about 350 yards and listened for some time, but could discover nothing. I now went to the beach, where I lighted my last flare, and left on a bearing due north. After swimming for a considerable distance I was picked up by Lieut. Nelson in our cutter some time after 3 a.m. Our cutter, in company with the pinnace and the destroyer *Kennet*, searched the shore with 12-pdr and machine-gun fire, but could get no answer from the shore.

It is my opinion that the shore was not occupied, but from the appearance and lights on the tops of the hills during the early hours of the morning, I feel sure that numbers of the enemy were there, but owing to chance of being captured, and as I had cramp badly, I could not get further.[3]

Several points need to be made about Freyberg's swim. He was a strong swimmer, and from the length of time he was in the water the distance for each leg, there and back, must have been closer to two miles, as he himself stated, than the 600 yards originally expected.[1] The likelihood of re-establishing contact with the blacked-out cutter on a dark night with no moon was slight, and the operation was hazardous in the extreme. Finally, as he mentions, Freyberg began to suffer from cramp as a result of the intense cold. This was becoming acute when a large fish leapt out of the water and brushed his shoulders. 'I got such a fright,' Freyberg said on rejoining the *Grantully Castle*, 'that the cramp pains vanished, and I was able to swim without further difficulty until I eventually found the cutter.'

Joseph Murray was a member of the platoon which was relieved of the task of landing on the Turkish coast. Nevertheless the men spent most of that night in an open boat near the shore, and Murray's main recollection was of the extreme cold. He wrote in his diary, 'Only a superman could have survived so long in that icy-cold sea.'[4]

For a time the diversion at Bulair had a considerable effect upon the German Commander of the Turkish forces, General Liman von Sanders. He had been woken at 5 a.m. at his headquarters in the old French Consulate in the town of Gallipoli, and told that the Allies had landed at various beaches in the Helles and Anzac areas. But what alarmed him much more were reports that further landings appeared to be imminent in the Bulair region. Von Sanders immediately ordered troops from near Gallipoli itself to march north and he himself rode at once to Bulair, where, from the high ground above the Gulf of Saros, he had a broad view of the diversion being carried out by the ships carrying the Royal Naval Division and the warships:

> About twenty large enemy ships, some war vessels, some transports, could be counted in front of us [he wrote]. Some individual vessels were lying close in under the steep slopes of the coast. Others were farther out in the gulf or were still underway. From the broadsides of the warships came an uninterrupted stream of fire and smoke and the entire coast including our ridge was covered with shells and shrapnel. It was an unforgettable picture.[5]

While the RND was off Bulair rumours began to circulate that all was not well with the main landings at Cape Helles and Ari Burnu. Instead of the light resistance that had been expected, there were wireless reports of heavy fighting on the beaches at Cape Helles; and at Ari Burnu (later named Anzac Cove) there were alarming stories that the original shallow beachheads were in danger of being driven back into the sea. From all sides came reports of heavy casualties and, far from capturing the first day's objectives, the troops were only able to secure a few of the preliminary ones. After several days it became clear that the Turks had succeeded in bringing in substantial reinforcements. The small bridgeheads that had been gained were soon sealed off, and the war of attrition began.

Although the main body of the RND had been employed for the feint at Bulair, General Paris was also asked to provide some 300 ratings with sea experience to help with the disembarkation of 29 Division. One such detachment, commanded by Sub-Lieutenant Johnny Dodge, accompanied the Dublin Fusiliers on the *River Clyde* to 'V' Beach. But as the casualties began to mount, it was not long before the Naval Brigades were needed to participate in the land battle.[6]

The *Grantully Castle* and the *Royal George* arrived off Cape Helles at 5 p.m. on Friday, 30 April and Commodore Backhouse went ashore to receive orders from General Hunter-Weston, Commander of 29 Division and of the Helles front. The Howe Battalion landed that night, and the Hood Battalion, with Freyberg commanding A Company, was all ashore by 4 a.m. the following day, 1 May.[4]

When Freyberg landed at Cape Helles he knew that the justification for the British, French, Australian and New Zealand forces invading Turkey was that an attempt had to be made to break the stalemate already set in on the Western Front in France. The purpose of the

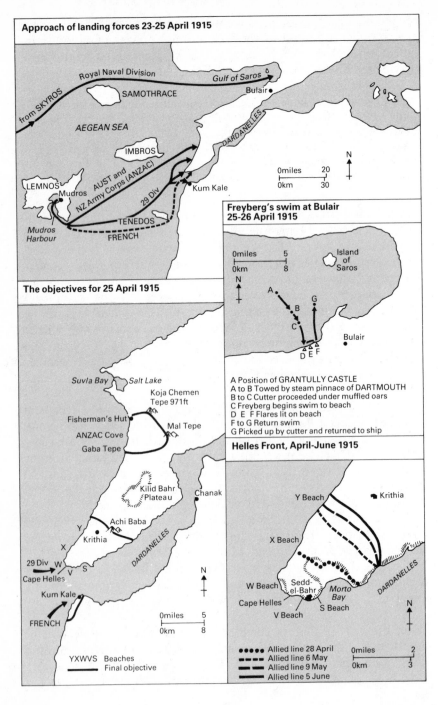

Approach of landing forces 23-25 April 1915

Royal Naval Division

Gulf of Saros

from SKYROS

SAMOTHRACE

Bulair

DARDANELLES

AEGEAN SEA

IMBROS

AUST and NZ Army Corps (ANZAC)

LEMNOS

Mudros

29 Div

Kum Kale

TENEDOS

Mudros Harbour

FRENCH

0miles 20
0km 30

N

Freyberg's swim at Bulair 25-26 April 1915

0miles 5
0km 8

N

Island of Saros

A

B

G

C

D E F

Bulair

A Position of GRANTULLY CASTLE
A to B Towed by steam pinnace of DARTMOUTH
B to C Cutter proceeded under muffled oars
C Freyberg begins swim to beach
D E F Flares lit on beach
F to G Return swim
G Picked up by cutter and returned to ship

The objectives for 25 April 1915

Suvla Bay

Salt Lake

Koja Chemen Tepe 971ft

Fisherman's Hut

Mal Tepe

ANZAC Cove

Gaba Tepe

Kilid Bahr Plateau

Chanak

Achi Baba

Y

Krithia

X

DARDANELLES

29 Div W

V S

Cape Helles

Kum Kale

N

FRENCH

0miles 5
0km 8

YXWVS Beaches
——— Final objective

Helles Front, April-June 1915

Y Beach

Krithia

X Beach

DARDANELLES

W Beach

Sedd-el-Bahr

Morto Bay

Cape Helles

S Beach

V Beach

N

••••• Allied line 28 April
– – – Allied line 6 May
——— Allied line 9 May
——— Allied line 5 June

0miles 2
0km 3

[58]

Gallipoli campaign was to open up to Allied shipping the narrow waterway that runs from the Aegean Sea to the Black Sea through the Dardanelles, the Sea of Marmara and the Bosphorus at Constantinople. This would provide a warm water route to Russia, who needed munitions and supplies of all kinds if she was to continue fighting on the Allied side in the war against Germany. Additionally the defeat of Turkey would probably have had the advantage of eliminating German influence in the Levant and the Middle East.

In December 1913 the Germans had secured the appointment of a Military Mission to Turkey, headed by General Liman von Sanders. A series of diplomatic incidents followed during the first seven months of 1914, culminating in the arrival of the German cruisers *Goeben* and *Breslau* at the entrance of the Dardanelles on 10 August 1914. These warships were reluctantly admitted into Turkish waters, in contravention of three international treaties governing the status of the waterways. The British Naval Mission to Turkey ceased to function in September 1914. On 27 October 1914 Admiral Souchon, with the *Goeben*, *Breslau* and ships of the Turkish Fleet, made an attack on Sevastopol, Odessa and other Russian Black Sea bases. Russia then declared war on the Ottoman Empire on 2 November, quickly followed by Britain and France on 5 November. It was this realignment that gave rise to the idea of an Allied expedition to take the Gallipoli peninsula and open the Dardanelles.[7]

The plan was an ambitious one, but two elements were of crucial importance. The first was to gain tactical surprise – strategic surprise was never again possible after the failure of the naval assault at the Narrows on 18 March 1915. The second was to land in an area that was favourable to the Allied forces.

In the original attempt to force the Narrows on 18 March, however, the French lost two old battleships, *Gaulois* and *Bouvet*, in Turkish minefields, while the British lost *Ocean* and *Irresistible*. This convinced the admirals that the Straits were too heavily mined for the Allied fleets to find a way through. The army command, and General Sir Ian Hamilton, the British commander, in particular did not realise until later, however, that the navy had already given up the intention to make further attempts to force the Narrows, so subsequent military operations were planned in the belief that there would be full naval support in any combined attack on the Gallipoli peninsula. In fact, when the army assumed responsibility for forcing the Dardanelles the military ceased to be 'in support' of the navy, and took over the primary role. The failure to appreciate that the whole nature of the Dardanelles operation had thus changed, and that in future the army plan should be based solely on military considerations, lay at the heart of the Gallipoli tragedy.*

Shortly after the naval attempt to force the Narrows on 18 March, Enver Pasha, the Turkish Minister for War, summoned Liman von Sanders to his office in Constantinople and invited him to take command of the Turkish Fifth Army at the Dardanelles. Von Sanders agreed to do so at once, and arrived at the town of Gallipoli on 26 March 1915 with only his Turkish Chief of Staff and two German officers.[5]

In theory there were three ways in which the Allied ground forces could attack the Gallipoli peninsula. They could assault the Asiatic mainland at Kum Kale and eventually occupy the eastern shores of the Narrows; they could land at Bulair, cut off the rest of the peninsula from its land communications with Europe and gradually 'roll it up' from north to south; or they could land on the south-western shores of the Gallipoli peninsula. In April 1915 General Sir Ian Hamilton had the resources to undertake only one of these options.

The first two can be dismissed quickly. A landing on the Asiatic mainland could have developed into an enormous military commitment, and Kitchener, Secretary of State, ruled it out from the beginning. A landing at Bulair had been closely studied by General Birdwood, one of the senior officers in the Middle East before Hamilton was appointed to command. Birdwood relates how his staff had urged this plan on him. He finally rejected their advice, his most important reason being that 'the great distance from our base at Mudros would impose an almost impossible task on the navy in keeping us supplied'.[9]

This reduced Hamilton's options for landing-places to the south-western shores of the peninsula, which, from south to north, can be divided into the Cape Helles sector, the Ari Burnu or Anzac Cove sector, and the Suvla Bay sector.

Soon after Hamilton arrived in the Mediterranean he took the fateful decision to land at the south-westernmost end of the peninsula. The main factor was his desire to keep in close touch with the navy; but in choosing Helles and Anzac he had to deploy his troops in very confined areas which gave almost no room for manoeuvre. There were

---

* In 1924 an American historian, Major Sherman Miles, commented in a report that was shown to Sir Ian Hamilton: 'Certainly General Hamilton did not suspect that naval co-operation would be so limited, and to a large extent his plans during the following month were based . . . on the assumption of a combined attack with the Fleet.'[8] In the margin of this statement Hamilton wrote 'correct'.

to be two main landings, the first on each side of Cape Helles at the entrance to the Dardanelles, to be carried out by the British regular 29 Division. Its principal objective was to capture the commanding height of Achi Baba which overlooks the southern approaches to the Narrows. The second landing further north was to be by the Australian and New Zealand Army Corps (Anzac). The objective was the high ground at Mal Tepe, inland from Gaba Tepe and Ari Burnu, and south of the Sari Bair range. When both objectives were in Allied hands the two forces were to link up.

There were also to be two 'feints'. These operations were intended to make the Turks unsure where the main weight of the attack was going to fall and to delay them in reinforcing their troops opposite to 29 Division and the Anzacs. In the first feint the French were to land at Kum Kale, on the shore opposite to the Dardanelles peninsula, in order to give the impression that they were the vanguard of Allied landings on the Asiatic mainland. The second feint was the demonstration by the Royal Naval Division at Bulair, in which Freyberg was involved.

The five beaches where the original landings took place at Cape Helles are situated at the tip of the Gallipoli peninsula, and follow each other from Morto Bay and Sedd el Bahr round to V Beach, Tekke Burnu Beach, Gully Beach and Y Beach near Krithia. This area of land is basically flat, but it is intersected by ravines (nullahs). Although some of it is now under cultivation or covered with trees and shrubs, it is not difficult to visualise from the open ground that still exists how bare it must have been in 1915.

What immediately strikes even the visitor of today is how small and confined is the space that was to be captured at such high price. The distance of the front line across the peninsula at its widest point is only three miles, while the deepest penetration into the Turkish positions in early June was no more than four miles from the tip of Cape Helles. Into this area, at various times during the period May to July 1915, were concentrated over six British and French divisions.

By contrast the area at Anzac Cove, 15 miles to the north of Cape Helles, is made up of very hilly country consisting almost entirely of high ridges and steep valleys criss-crossing the landscape in a pattern of bewildering complexity. A modern road has now been carved out of the coastal hillside between Gaba Tepe and Ari Burnu, but in 1915 the hills disappeared straight into the sea.

At the summit of the Sari Bair range (above Anzac Cove) are three high points. The first is Chunuk Bair, which was captured and held by New Zealand troops for a short time during the final offensive of

[61]

6–10 August, at heavy cost; hence the New Zealand memorial there. Further along is Hill 'Q', and finally Koja Chemen Tepe which, at 971 feet, is the highest in the range. From Koja Chemen Tepe on a sunny day the Aegean Sea can be seen gleaming to the west from Suvla Point to Cape Helles, while in the east the Dardanelles sparkles on its way to the Sea of Marmara or, in the opposite direction, dwindles to a pinpoint of light as it approaches the Narrows at Canakkale (Chanak).

Beyond Ari Burnu the modern coast road enters Suvla Plain. At the western end lies Suvla Bay and its Salt Lake. The bay consists of a half-circle of about five miles of beaches between Suvla and Nibrunessi Points, with about two miles of water between them in a direct line. Inland lies the large expanse of Suvla Plain, which stretches in a half moon from the high ground to the north and east, past the two Anafarta villages to the foothills of the Sari Bair range, down to Ari Burnu. Within this half-moon is a large expanse of flat country, interspersed by small hills, with very fertile soil and provided with ample springs and water.

A perfectly feasible alternative to landing at Cape Helles and Anzac Cove was thus available, that is, to concentrate the whole attack at Suvla Bay. What made this proposition even more attractive was that the Suvla Bay area was virtually undefended on 25 April, whereas there were two enemy divisions near to both Kum Kale and Bulair; while 9 and 19 Turkish Divisions were already in position at Cape Helles and Anzac respectively.

Hamilton had been in trouble with the Gallipoli operation long before the attack began. When he arrived at the naval base at Tenedos on 17 March with a hastily gathered staff he found that there was no proper command structure. No machinery existed for co-ordinating the actions of the navy and army in the field, and no one officer was in charge of the whole operation. The commander of each service was answerable to his professional head in London, but even there no staff existed to co-ordinate common policy. Co-operation between the admiral and general on the spot worked smoothly enough in defining what they both wanted to achieve, but the means with which to carry it out were sadly lacking. At the height of the planning for the Gallipoli landings the navy and army staffs were located at Tenedos and Alexandria respectively, separated by several hundred miles.[5] Other examples of lack of support for the expedition was the refusal of the UK authorities to provide any specialised landing craft, although these existed, or to produce any form of army air service, which was essential for reconnaissance and Intelligence.

Not the least of Hamilton's difficulties was the speed with which his forces had been dispatched from England, particularly 29 Division and the Naval Division. To quote from *Gallipoli* by Robert Rhodes James:

> His army was scattered around the Mediterranean in spectacular confusion; battalions were split up, wagons were separated from their horses, guns from their ammunition, shells from their fuses.
>
> An officer of the 29 Division reported that 'the arrangements for the embarkation had been made, and the ships taken up in such a hurry that it was impossible to tell in what ships the various stores and vehicles of the Division were situated' . . . Wemyss [the Commanding Admiral], struggling to transform Mudros into the expedition base, wrote more bluntly that 'the slipshod manner in which the troops have been sent out from England is something awful'.[5]

The only way of disentangling this muddle was to send the ships to Alexandria and Port Said to reorganise their equipment, and to reload them in the order in which troops and their supplies would be required on the Gallipoli beaches. Not only was this a time-consuming process when time was in short supply, but it also involved another hazard, that of security. The Turks soon became well aware of the size and purpose of the British forces in Egypt, and rapidly moved their troops from the Bulair front and the mainland of Asia, to Cape Helles and Ari Burnu.

During the first ten days of May an offensive took place which later became known as the second battle of Krithia (the first battle of Krithia had been an attempt to capture the village on 28 April). Krithia, now called Alcitepe, was two miles from Achi Baba, which had been the main objective of 29 Division on the first day. Not only was Achi Baba never captured, nor was the intermediate objective of Krithia itself. By early May the Turks had their 7 and 9 Divisions on the Cape Helles front, which was three miles across. These troops had excellent defensive positions in the foothills of Achi Baba, with open country in front of them overlooking the British positions; and because there was no room for manoeuvre Krithia soon became little more than a killing-ground for many thousands of British troops.

Some idea of the scale of the slaughter can be gathered from the casualties incurred by 2 Naval Brigade in the first week of May. On 1 May the Howe, Anson and Hood Battalions were up to full strength with approximately 30 officers and 800 men each. Six days later less than half were left, with the Hood Battalion down to 10 officers and 343 men.[4] In the attack on 6 May the Commanding Officer Arnold Quilter was killed instantly early in the advance. On the following day Freyberg suffered an abdominal wound which was sufficiently serious for him to be evacuated to a hospital in Egypt.

The journey from Gallipoli to Egypt was a nightmare which haunted Freyberg for the rest of his life. He recalled even in 1951:

> It fell to my lot to be wounded and evacuated twice from Gallipoli, once in May, and later in July 1915. I was evacuated each time in a troopship, the SS *Grantully Castle*. It was one of the lessons I never forgot. It taught me the importance from the morale point of view of the medical and nursing service. I am not saying that every General should have a similar experience, but it did teach me about the all-important question of a fighting force in the field. The first time I was wounded, the journey to Egypt by so-called hospital ship was an example of how not to do things. We had no nurses, and one overworked doctor and two medical orderlies to 800 serious cases. On my second journey arrangements had improved, and we had the staff of an Army Casualty Clearing Station, with eight nursing sisters. The less said of the first journey the better.[10]

Meanwhile in England, and to the great dismay of the Royal Naval Division, Winston Churchill had been forced to resign as First Lord of the Admiralty. Freyberg had a message sent from Egypt to Churchill via Hoe Farm, Hascombe, near Godalming (where Churchill was living after leaving Admiralty House), through Eddie Marsh, exhorting Eddie to 'tell him that we feel that he is our father, and we will look to him for help as we always have'.[11]

At this time Violet Asquith was visiting Egypt for a month to be with her brother Oc, who had also been wounded at Gallipoli. She describes the sense of disillusionment that was widespread in the RND at the beginning of June 1915, by which time it was obvious to the troops that they were trying to capture an impregnable position:

> I found him [Oc] and his companions in the RND bewildered and distraught by the news that Winston had left the Admiralty and been relegated to the Duchy of Lancaster – a Cabinet wastepaper basket. How had it happened? What could it mean?
> In the Hood Battalion this sense of loss was especially acute, for they had had three 'private wires' with the powers-that-be. They could reach Winston through Eddie Marsh, my father through Oc, and both Winston and my father through me. Now two of the three wires were cut. Arthur Balfour (the new First Lord) was a remote, impersonal figure of whom they

knew nothing. I did my best to reassure them. At least I could tell them with my hand on my heart that he was and always had been a firm believer in the Gallipoli operation and had supported it throughout. But I could not honestly pretend that he resembled Winston in any other respect whatever.[12]

Violet Asquith also explained why the RND men felt disillusioned with the way the fighting was being conducted:

Again and again when an advance was made at heavy cost there were no reserves behind to follow up the thrust and push it through. At best they were halted in their tracks, at worst driven back over dearly gained ground. This gave the Turks a breathing space to re-form and reinforce themselves and strengthen their positions. The Gallipoli campaign had already become a tragic example of giving too little and too late. As Winston wrote: 'We have always sent two-thirds of what was necessary a month too late'.[12]

Freyberg's wound was on the mend in a few weeks, and he took to bathing every day at Stanley Bay near Alexandria. Violet Asquith describes how large the waves were and how:

Freyberg takes me in – right in – and as they arch their necks and tower high and dark above us he lifts me right off my feet and we are borne over them together in a swirl of foaming surf. Water is his element and when unhampered by me he goes shooting and bounding through the centre of the waves like a porpoise. All this with an abdominal wound which has not yet healed![12]

It was while he was still in Egypt on 3 June that the *London Gazette* announced that Freyberg had been awarded the Distinguished Service Order for his swim at Bulair. A few days later, however, there came bad news, which Violet recorded:

On the eve of Freyberg's return to Gallipoli, we had a farewell dinner with him at the Savoy, which we were all determined to make a gay one. Halfway through it, Schlesinger (a doctor with the RND) came in, very excited and overwrought, bringing us terribly bad news of the RND. The Artillery had shelled a dummy trench and they were then told to advance and take it. They found it to be a dummy and went on to the next, which was quite intact. This they captured with great gallantry and terrible losses, taking six machine-guns. They were then shelled both by the Turkish artillery and our own, heavily counter-attacked and had to retire, leaving their guns, the officers being practically wiped out in the retreat. Howe, Hood and the new Collingwood battalions had all suffered cruelly. Denis Browne was wounded and missing and the COs who all (with the exception of Collins of the Hood) led their battalions in the charge, were killed or wounded to a man. Freyberg, whose brother [Oscar] had just joined the Collingwood, said he didn't want to ask or know anything more about it as this was his last evening and he wanted to enjoy it. I could see that he was very upset and feared that his brother was dead. We went on to a place called Le Jardin de Rosette, where we tried to lasso objects with rings and watched a rather bad performance from a box. But all our hearts were chilled with fear.[12]

The casualties sustained in the third battle of Krithia, 4–16 June, were horrifying, coming on top of the previous disasters. The battle cost the RND alone nearly 1,400 casualties, and the British and French armies over 4,500 and 2,000 respectively. The story of the Collingwood Battalion epitomises the fate of the other battalions. It had landed on the peninsula on 30 May, and took part in the third battle of Krithia on 4 June. At 12.15 p.m., as if on parade, the battalion moved forward in a long extended line. They marched across the bare ground into merciless Turkish fire. By that evening 16 officers were dead, 8 wounded and over 500 men were casualties. The Collingwood Battalion literally ceased to exist, and on 8 June the survivors were posted to other units in the RND.[6] Among the officers killed was Oscar Freyberg, exactly as Bernard had feared. He was last seen alive in a Turkish trench with a pistol in each hand but, like so many others, his body was never found. In the first seven weeks of the Gallipoli campaign British and Dominion troops suffered nearly 40,000 casualties, and French losses amounted to some 20,000 more.[13]

Freyberg returned to the Hood Battalion in the second week of June 1915, but it was a sombre occasion for him. He had been looking forward to meeting his brother again. Now Oscar was dead. So too were many of Bernard's fellow-officers in the battalion, including Denis Browne. Surgeon McCracken had been badly wounded and sent back to England. Few of the original members of the battalion were left, and those that were had had their morale and confidence shaken.

The results of the third battle of Krithia finally persuaded the British commanders that there was no future in making any further attempts at frontal attacks in the Cape Helles area. At last the high command began to look towards Suvla Bay, where, it was now realised, lay the only hope of opening the door into the Dardanelles, and which, on purely military grounds, ought to have been the choice for the original landings. The Turkish Army's presence in the peninsula had never been so strong, and any chance of reversing the long catalogue of failures depended on the timing, surprise and above all the leadership of the new initiative.

Freyberg was now the senior survivor of the battalion: Colonel Quilter had been killed on 6 May; his successor Crawford-Stewart was badly wounded soon afterwards; and six other Hood officers were killed in the 4 June battle. Lieutenant-Colonel Collins commanded for a short period in June, and then he and Myburgh, the only other officer senior to Freyberg, both went sick and had to be evacuated. Freyberg assumed command of the Hood on 25 June, but in the third week of July he sustained another wound. There is conflicting evidence about the exact date, as neither Commodore Backhouse's diary nor Charles Lister's letter to his father Lord Ribblesdale nor Freyberg's own memory, says quite the same thing. This confusion seems hardly surprising in the circumstances. At all events Freyberg was badly wounded in the stomach, around 19 or 20 July, and had to be evacuated on a stretcher.

There was a rule at Gallipoli that an officer who sustained wounds would be kept on the strength of his unit for twenty-eight days before being struck off, it being assumed that he was not returning in the foreseeable future; and another officer was then appointed to his command. Charles Lister, in a letter to his father dated 19 August 1915, wrote, 'Freyberg, after an absence of twenty-five days, has returned. This must be a record for anyone hit in the stomach. He was brilliantly operated on, and the gash is perfectly healed.'[14] This was one of the last letters Charles Lister wrote. On 26 August he wrote to his father from the hospital ship *Gascon* to say that he had been wounded for the third time, and died from his wounds two days later. Freyberg was greatly upset by his death.

While Freyberg was in hospital in Egypt, the new landings at Suvla Bay began on 6 August, and for the next three days the fate of Gallipoli hung in the balance. For a few hours the vital high ground at Chunuk Bair and elsewhere on the Sari Bair range was in New Zealand and Gurkha hands, and it looked as though the tide might have turned at last. But once again there were not enough supporting troops properly positioned to deal with the inevitable strong counter-attacks, or to exploit the gains that had been made, and the Turks managed to re-establish themselves firmly on the commanding heights. Freyberg commented later that this attack 'might have had the element of success, but failed because of faulty planning and hopeless leadership'.[15]

Freyberg's return to the Hood Battalion at Helles in mid-August 1915 coincided with the end of serious offensive action. The last major attack took place in the Suvla Bay sector on 21 August, when another 5,000 British casualties were incurred in a further futile and senseless action. After it was over even the ever-optimistic Hamilton, who had convinced himself that one more effort would bring victory, had to accept that there was no longer any prospect of overcoming the Turkish positions at Gallipoli.

Freyberg always recognised that, because of the restricted space, there was never any possibility of making progress at Helles, where he fought, nor at the Anzac bridgehead, which he visited. Suvla was different because there was more room for manoeuvre. The elderly British commanders of the Suvla Bay landings were General Stopford (aged sixty-one) commanding IX Corps, and Generals Mahon and Hammersley commanding 10 Division and 11 Division. These officers ought to have been up with their forward troops to arrange the flow and direction of reinforcing units to the vital high ground. Instead they remained on the Suvla beaches or stayed on board the landing ships. The decisive moment passed, never to return. As Freyberg wrote later, if only some of the excellent war-experienced Anzac leaders – such as Monash, Brudenell White, Russell or Blamey – had been in command at Suvla, 'the result would have been very different, and might even have ended in success'.[15]

It is interesting to note the sharp contrast between Hamilton's procrastination in replacing Stopford, and Liman von Sanders' decisive sacking of his Corps Commander on 8 August for allowing his troops to rest after marching non-stop from Bulair. As Freyberg remarked:

> Further factors which reduced our chances of success were the splendid fighting qualities in defence of the Turkish soldier and the excellent leadership of the 5th Turkish Army. Marshal Liman von Sanders won high distinction in Gallipoli, and he received great support in his critical period at the Suvla landing from Mustafa Kemal.[15]

The task that faced Freyberg and his Hood Battalion in the final four and a half months can be summed up in one word, 'survival'. The officers and men were exhausted, not only from the strain of battle and the casualties but by the heat, the flies and, increasingly, by disease. By this stage sickness had become even more of a scourge than the human enemy. In the heat of the Turkish summer millions of flies fed on the corpses of both sides in no-man's-land, which could not be buried because of snipers. This not only created the most nauseating stench but brought with it every manner of pestilence. The toll of death and sickness mounted alarmingly in the already depleted units, and to overcome the problem required a high degree of personal hygiene and self-discipline (for example, drinking only 'safe' liquid). This placed a heavy responsibility on the senior battalion officers to ensure that every possible precaution was taken. By the end of the campaign the health of the troops was once again under control, but between the middle of August and the end of November 63 officers and over 4,000 men from what was left of the Naval Division had to be evacuated because of fever and sickness. Similar figures occurred in other divisions, until the hospitals in Egypt, Malta and even England were filled to overflowing.[6]

In any other theatre of war, such as France, the RND would have been pulled out of the line for a prolonged rest and refit, but this was not possible in the peninsula. Originally the Naval Division had been organised into three brigades (one marine and two naval), each of four battalions. At the beginning of the campaign the RND strength totalled 16,500, but after the June disaster it had sunk to 7,000, and by early August it was down to just over 5,000. There was no alternative but to disband one of the brigades, and so 2 Naval Brigade had to disappear and Commodore Backhouse was returned to sea. This left a mixed marine–naval brigade, and 1 Naval Brigade comprising the Drake, Nelson, Hawke and Hood Battalions. On 15 August the much reduced RND took over 29 Division's old sector between Gully Ravine and the Krithia nullah. They remained there for three months in a defensive position. In addition to losing large numbers because of sickness, there was a constant trickle of killed and wounded caused by shellfire and snipers.[6]

The total British Empire casualties during the whole campaign (five months fighting and four months dug into positions and ravaged by disease) amounted to over 112,000, including 37,500 killed or died from wounds or disease. In addition 90,000 men were evacuated from the peninsula because of sickness. The French suffered 47,000 casualties and the Turks upwards of 250,000, giving a total of some half a million casualties during the nine months of the campaign on Gallipoli, of whom over 135,000 died.[13]

General Sir Ian Hamilton was recalled to London, and left his headquarters on 16 October 1915. He had lost the confidence of the government, his military superiors at home, and even his own staff, by his over-optimism and unrealistic assessments of the difficulties. The appointment required an absolutely ruthless commander, if the almost insuperable obstacles were to be overcome. Hamilton was too civilised and cultured a man to be able to deal with the problems. In his heart he realised this and many years later wrote of his own 'hero': 'Lord

Roberts had not succeeded in grafting on to me his gift for taking the bull by the horns.'[16]

Lord Kitchener's reputation also had fallen steadily throughout the campaign. He brought in General Sir Charles Monro to replace Hamilton, and then dithered over accepting his advice, which was for immediate evacuation. In the end, in mid-November, Kitchener went out to Gallipoli to see the situation on the ground for himself. Like all newcomers to Gallipoli he was depressed by the smallness of the Allied toeholds on the peninsula, and the strength of the Turkish positions. Unwillingly he recommended to the Cabinet on 22 November that Suvla and Anzac should be evacuated, and by implication that Helles should follow. Asquith replied that the War Cabinet was in favour of total evacuation.

Although only a few commanders and staff were told of the decision at the time, the troops, having observed the procession of high-ranking visitors, realised that there were only two possible alternatives, either massive reinforcement leading to new offensives, or evacuation. Since there was no indication of any new troops it was obvious that they must be about to leave the peninsula. It remained only to work out the details. Ironically, the withdrawal was the one operation of the entire campaign that was both efficiently planned and executed with faultless precision.

The tribulations of the troops were not yet over, however. On the night of 26–7 November there was a torrential gale, followed for the next three days by unprecedented frost and snowstorms. Two hundred men died of the cold and many thousands more were frostbitten and had to be taken off the peninsula as a result of the freak conditions. In compensation the freeze also killed off the flies, and this led to a notable improvement in health. When Suvla and Anzac were finally evacuated just before Christmas, on 19–20 December, the force at Cape Helles knew that their turn would come soon.

As the New Year arrived the troops started to thin out until only four divisions remained (facing twenty-one Turkish divisions). These four were 13 Division on the left, 29 Division and 52 Division in the centre, and the RND on the right, whose flank rested on the Dardanelles. The Hood and Drake Battalions of 1 Naval Brigade, and 1 Royal Marine and the Howe Battalions of the composite brigade were in the front line, with the remainder of the division in reserve. The date for the final evacuation was fixed for 8 January. By 7 January the RND was reduced to a total of 4,400 men. As evening fell on 8 January the line was held by 845 men drawn from the four battalions. Freyberg was with the Hood contingent as they made their way through the checkpoints to the evacuation beaches. The main bodies boarded their ships at 11.30

p.m., followed three hours later by the final covering parties. Freyberg left Gallipoli for the last time at 2.30 a.m. on 9 January 1916.[6]

Three-quarters of a century has elapsed since the tragedy of Gallipoli, but disagreements still persist about the causes of the disaster. Some historians maintain that the campaign was doomed before it started because of the failure in London to agree on the nature of the operation, or to provide sufficient military resources at the beginning to achieve the aim. Others have blamed the uncharacteristic loss of nerve on the part of the Royal Navy in failing to continue to force the Narrows, when success could have been within its grasp. It has also been argued that the fatal flaw was the fact that no one commander or service was in overall charge of the operation either at home or in the Eastern Mediterranean. Yet another view is that the country was ill-prepared after many years of peace to mount a major amphibious operation against a hostile shore so far from home.

Freyberg was quite clear in his own mind where the main blame lay. In 1956 he reviewed Alan Moorehead's book, *Gallipoli*:

> In examining the causes of failure of the British Army in Gallipoli certain important factors should be remembered. Lord Kitchener had never previously served in the War Office and did not understand the excellent machine over which he presided; he endeavoured to combine the position of Chief of the Imperial General Staff and Secretary of State, and thus destroyed the General Staff system so wisely and skilfully devised by Lord Haldane. He was in point of fact a military dictator.[15]

He also referred to an extraordinary decision:

> One of the most remarkable revelations is the story of the vital War Council meeting in London on 13 January 1915 when the plan to intervene in Turkey was considered: Lord Fisher, Admiral of the Fleet Sir Arthur Wilson, and Lord Kitchener were all present when the following decision was taken: 'That the Admiralty should prepare for a Naval Expedition in February to bombard and take the Gallipoli Peninsula, with Constantinople as its objective.' At this meeting there was not a dissenting voice. After the evacuation, the Dardanelles Commission, in its report in 1917, commented on the vagueness of the decision. 'How,' it was asked, 'can a fleet take a peninsula, or capture an objective such as Constantinople?'[15]

By the time Freyberg was writing this he had enjoyed high command and, as a Deputy Director in the Staff Duties Directorate of the War Office in 1933–4, had come to understand the War Office mechanism for controlling and co-ordinating the military machine. This gave him an insight into what had been lacking at Gallipoli which he did not have at the time. But he was also echoing the opinion of General Sir Ian Hamilton himself, who wrote a series of essays which were only published in 1957, ten years after his death. In one of them he described the scene in Whitehall early in 1915, and discussed Lord Esher's book, *The Tragedy of Lord Kitchener*:

> My headquarters was at the Horse Guards, just across the road from the vast apartment in which K shivered at the War Office. Every day almost, I used to run in and burst into a sweat from the two blazing fires and the antics of that poor untamed bull in the china shop.
>
> What Lord Esher, and, more so, many others have failed to realise is that K was utterly out of his depth . . . because for the first time in a high place, he found himself saddled with an organisation which he had to accept. He was so used to working with his own ad hoc headquarters organisation, had always been too disinterested [sic], too impatient, to study the detailed staff system of the War Office and Army that he was unable to use that vast organisation in Whitehall which was there solely to do his bidding.[16]

Thus the one organisation that should have been able to monitor the Turkish military build-up at Gallipoli, and warn Hamilton of the risks he was running in attacking the obvious landing places, was paralysed at the top, and unable to function properly.

In the 1920s and 1930s Freyberg used to have many discussions about the Gallipoli campaign with his old friend Brigadier-General C. F. Aspinall-Oglander, who had served on Hamilton's staff and later wrote the two volumes of the Official History which were published in 1929 and 1932.[3] Both he and Freyberg were too loyal to their old chief to criticise him in public, indeed in his *Sunday Times* article Freyberg commented as follows on Alan Moorehead's strictures on Sir Ian Hamilton:

> Moorehead is outspoken in his opinion of General Hamilton and his senior commanders. For myself I can only add that, although these commanders may not have been good, they were the best we had. When the Expeditionary Force went to France in August 1914, it took all the high-grade commanders and staff officers, and for that reason alone it was wrong to attempt any operation as difficult and as complicated as the Gallipoli campaign. I am sure that we are seldom taken in by excuses for defeat. I can

only say, after two long and difficult wars, that I have never known British troops failing to fight when properly led and commanded.[15]

On one occasion as a boy I can remember staying with my parents at the Aspinall-Oglanders' house at Nunwell Park on the Isle of Wight, and hearing the soldiers discuss what a great opportunity had been missed in disregarding the Suvla Bay option in April 1915. They believed, on purely military grounds, that it would have been the correct solution for attacking the Dardanelles and that if it had been adopted from the outset it would have led to the successful conclusion of the Gallipoli campaign at a fraction of the cost. That this point of view was widely held by officers at Gallipoli was confirmed to me in conversations in the early 1980s with Brigadier B. B. Rackham of the Hawke Battalion and other members of the RND. The attraction of the Suvla Bay alternative was also emphasised fifty years ago by Lieutenant-Colonel C. O. Head in his book, *A Glance at Gallipoli*.[17]

In April 1915 the only Turkish force within the Suvla Bay crescent was one battalion of mounted gendarmes. All the rest of the Turkish forces on the southern part of the peninsula were guarding the landing places near Cape Helles and Anzac Cove, or were in reserve behind. If it had been decided to go ashore at Suvla Bay in April instead of at Helles and Anzac, the landing would have been virtually unopposed. Nor were there any practical difficulties in landing at Suvla because the beaches are gently shelving, with flat, easily accessible exits behind them, and indeed this part of the operation was successfully carried out in August 1915. It was no more difficult from the administrative point of view to maintain a force at Suvla from Mudros than at Helles and Anzac – in fact from several points of view it was easier. The area was favourable for offensive operations, since the large open space in the Suvla Plain was suitable for concentrating a number of divisions without enemy interference. And because Suvla was a less obvious place for landing than Cape Helles and Anzac Cove, surprise would have been more likely.

The Allied force would have been operating as a single force under a headquarters established ashore (which it never was in 1915), with obvious advantages in command and control. The administrative problems would have been less difficult, and those of the Turks, with longer lines of communication from Canakkale, would have been that much greater. The Allies would not have suffered the shortage of water they had at Anzac, nor would they have been subjected to artillery fire from the Asiatic mainland, which caused so many casualties at Helles. Most importantly, the lie of the land would have been more favourable

[73]

than at Anzac and Helles, since the ground sloped progressively upwards to the high ground of the Sari Bair range over a frontage of five miles between Biyuk Anafarta and Ari Burnu. From Anzac Cove troops had to move across the grain of the country on a comparatively narrow front, while at Helles there was no room to manoeuvre at all. Above all there would have been much more space for assembling a large force at Suvla, which could have been deployed against the Turks in any one of several directions, or combination of directions. Not only was the high ground at Chunuk Bair more accessible from Suvla, but beyond the Anafarta villages were valleys that led straight to the waters of the Dardanelles near the Narrows, which by-passed the Sari Bair range altogether. These options were absent in the very confined spaces at Helles and Anzac.

It is pointless to speculate on the way in which a campaign based on Suvla might have developed. Hard fighting and many losses would doubtless have been incurred, but because the Turks would not have been able to command such strong defensive positions, the casualties would probably not have been on the same scale. Equally the size and timing of the reinforcements that the home authorities provided would have determined the outcome and the moment when it proved possible to capture the high ground overlooking the Narrows, and/or to turn the flank of any line of Turkish defences based on the commanding heights. Freyberg and Aspinall-Oglander argued that an Allied army based on Suvla Bay, given the necessary men, equipment and determination to succeed, would ultimately have been able to force the Straits, whereas one boxed up in Helles and at Anzac never had any such chance. As Freyberg wrote: 'The Gallipoli Campaign, because of the high hopes with which it started and the poignant ending as a dismal and costly failure, will always be one of the world's classic tragedies.'[15]

6

The Somme and the Battle of the Ancre, 1916

On the morning of 10 January 1916 Freyberg and the much depleted RND stepped ashore at Mudros Harbour. The Hood Battalion's first need was to restore the health and morale of its men and get them back to a more normal life and routine. After a few days of rest, regular meals and the unaccustomed absence of enemy shellfire and sniping, however, the majority of the officers and men quickly recovered. They were mostly young and resilient, and soon the uppermost thought in their minds was what was likely to happen to them next.

At this stage of the war the future of the Royal Naval Division was being actively reconsidered, both by the Admiralty in London and by Army Command in the Mediterranean. The RND had come into being, of course, because of the surplus of naval reservists in September 1914; but this surplus had significantly decreased after a few months by replacing normal wastage in the Fleet, and had disappeared completely in the casualties at Gallipoli. Could the continuation of a naval formation in an army role therefore be justified? Could it even be sustained? On more than one occasion orders were issued for the disbandment of the Division, only to be rescinded. For a time it seemed likely that the RND might be retained in the Mediterranean, and indeed one of the naval brigades was soon sent temporarily to join the Salonika Army.[1]

While the future of the RND hung in the balance, the survivors of the original Hood Battalion were sent on leave to England. On 27

February 1916 Freyberg, Oc Asquith, Cleg Kelly and a number of the other Gallipoli veterans sailed from Mudros in the SS *Olympia*, almost a year to the day after they had left the Avonmouth Docks in the *Grantully Castle*.[2]

The ship docked at Marseilles, and the party then travelled across France, arriving in England in the first week of March 1916. They were to stay in the UK for the next ten weeks. Although Freyberg's wounds had outwardly healed they were still causing him discomfort, and he spent some time in and out of hospital. He also made a point of visiting as many relatives as possible of all ranks killed at Gallipoli. He saw Rupert Brooke's mother on several occasions (and continued to do so after the war); called on Lord Ribblesdale, Charles Lister's father; and made a special visit to Suffolk to see Lady Quilter, the mother of his first CO, Arnold Quilter. Because of his admiration for her son, he confided to her, he hoped in due course to join his regiment, the Grenadier Guards.

Freyberg had in fact decided to make soldiering his career, and he used his leave in England to apply for a transfer to the British Army. He did so with the full support of his former Brigade Commander, Commodore Backhouse, whose character reference was a notable one:

Commander Bernard C. Freyberg, DSO, RNVR has served in the 2nd RN Brigade under my command during the operations at Antwerp and during the whole period of the Dardanelles operations, and has throughout performed his duties in the most praiseworthy and efficient manner. He showed conspicuous gallantry on more than one occasion, and in recognition of these services and of his high qualities of leadership and boldness he was promoted from the post of Company Commander when a vacancy occurred. He was also awarded the DSO and was mentioned in dispatches.

Commander Freyberg is gifted with the highest instincts of fearlessness, determination and leadership, and I cannot speak too highly of his admirable qualities. I am very pleased to record my high appreciation of him, with my strong recommendation for special employment in which these qualities are especially needed.[3]

General Paris, Freyberg's Divisional Commander, wrote in similar terms, and on 19 May 1916 he was gazetted a Captain in the Royal West Surrey Regiment. In the same gazette he was also shown as a temporary Lieutenant-Colonel commanding the Hood Battalion of the RND, a regularisation of his position that was necessary now that he was no longer a naval officer.[3]

During these weeks of leave Freyberg led an active social life. He took a flat in Jermyn Street[4] and from this base set forth on numerous journeys about the country including, on one occasion, travelling to Eastbourne to act as best man at the wedding of Lieutenant Molesworth, the naval surgeon who had taken over temporarily as the Hood doctor after McCracken was wounded.

Violet Asquith had announced her engagement to Maurice Bonham Carter soon after her return from Egypt in June 1915, and they were married that November. In March 1916, when her brother Oc arrived in England from Gallipoli, she gave a party at her new home, Dorset House in Marylebone, to welcome him back, and Bernard was one of the guests. So too was a twenty-eight-year-old friend of Violet's, Barbara McLaren. She saw Bernard across the room, he saw her, and according to their later accounts both stood motionless. 'There was a song in vogue at the time,' wrote Barbara many years later, 'with the refrain, "I took one look at you and then my heart stood still", and something of the sort happened when I looked across a crowded room and first saw Bernard.'[5] Bernard felt the same, and when he returned to the Hood Battalion in France he confided to Dr McCracken that he had met 'the most wonderful girl' while he was in England; but he added sadly that she was already married.[6]

Freyberg visited 10 Downing Street several times following Oc and Violet's introduction of him to their parents. H. H. Asquith had been Prime Minister for nearly eight years, and it is evident from contemporary letters from his wife Margot that Freyberg made a good impression on them both.[3] One such visit is recorded in the diary of Cynthia Asquith – she was married to Herbert Asquith, junior, nicknamed 'Beb', who at this time was serving with the Artillery in France – as having taken place on 29 April 1916 – the first of many references to Freyberg.[7] In this entry Cynthia mentions the death of Freyberg's 'brother', and makes Bernard appear indifferent to it; this was due, however, to a misunderstanding. The person concerned was Lieutenant-Commander Lancelot Freyberg, who was drowned when HMS *Russell*, while waiting to enter Malta Harbour on 27 April, was torpedoed and sunk by a German submarine. He was a cousin from Bernard's father James's first family, and Bernard had never met him.

At this time, and as Winston Churchill was out of office, it was generally believed in the RND that one of the main reasons why the Naval Division was not disbanded was the lobbying of the Prime Minister by Oc Asquith, supported by Freyberg. Certainly they had the opportunity of putting their case privately, and believed strongly that the *esprit de corps* that had been built up was too valuable an asset to be allowed to disappear because of organisational difficulties. Indeed it would have been out of character had they failed to take advantage of

[77]

their access to the Prime Minister's ear. Whatever the truth, however, it was decided early in May 1916 that the RND was to continue in being, and that it was to move to the main theatre of war in France.

On 16 May, therefore, the Hood and Nelson Battalions sailed from Mudros on the *Ivonian*, arriving at Marseilles five days later.[2] By 24 May the men had detrained a few miles from Abbeville, and later that day arrived in their new concentration area at the village of Citerne. At the same time most of those on leave left London to join them, including Bernard Freyberg, Oc Asquith, E. W. Nelson, Cleg Kelly, Vere Harmsworth, and Douglas Jerrold, later the historian of the RND. The party was seen off at Waterloo Station by Margot Asquith.[8]

For the RND, their arrival in France direct from the Eastern Mediterranean, and the transition to the conditions of the Western Front, marked a very sharp change. First, however, they had to be re-equipped and forced into the mould of the other divisions of the British Expeditionary Force; and the men needed to be trained in the use of such weapons as the Lewis gun, the rifle grenade and trench mortar, which had been unknown to the RND in Gallipoli. The energies of the lines of communication, remount and ordnance departments were concentrated upon the Naval Division and, since they had just finished similar missions with 29 Division and the Anzac divisions, which had arrived in France before the RND, they carried out the retraining with great speed and skill. Lorry after lorry arrived at Citerne with the new kit, departing with the old, and a detachment was sent to draw the battalion first line transport, which they accomplished in an hour. They marched back into their billets the same night with the field kitchens, water carts and ammunition limbers complete in every detail. In a week and a half all the mobilisation stores were drawn, and the units were then ready to receive the stream of instructors sent from the army schools. After a month's continuous hard work the RND was standardised with the rest of the British divisions in France.

While Freyberg was in the Abbeville area the Hood Battalion headquarters officers were billeted at the house of the mayor, who owned some fine horses. This enabled the officers to ride out together, but in doing so an accident occurred which added to Freyberg's number of injuries, and which also involved Dr McCracken, who wrote:

Unfortunately, the horse allotted to the CO had a vicious habit – which we did not know about – of rearing right up on his hind legs when mounted. Friz [Freyberg's nickname in the Hood] came out and said 'what about a ride' – we were quite keen. The groom held the brute and F mounted, and to my horror the horse rose straight and he fell backwards on the paved stable yard. F looked very shocked and pale and he complained of a pain in his elbow.

When it was uncovered, I found a fracture of the ulna, 3″ from point of elbow. I bandaged very firmly and we picked a quiet horse and we rode two or three miles to a small field hospital, and the MO admitted him and I said I would call to see him the next day.

During our slow journey there, he quizzed me about the best treatment for such an injury. I said, 'if you were in London, Arbuthnott Lane would wire it for you and it would heal quickly'. I was about to set out for the hospital next morning when I was shattered to see him coming into our billet. As far as I remember, I said, 'How did you escape?' 'Well,' he said, 'I told him your yarn about Arbuthnott Lane. He said I can have it done when I am next wounded and in London' – and I am almost certain he did just that!![9]

The progressive training and preparations of the RND were continued to the point when the Division was reckoned to be ready to take part in operations. But the whole policy of defence in France was quite different to what the RND had been accustomed to, owing to the artillery employed and the great amount of ammunition used. As a first step in its tactical re-education the Hood Battalion was attached by companies to battalions of 47 Division.

Notwithstanding their experiences at Gallipoli, the RND battalions were treated exactly as though they were unblooded novices fresh from England. This, not surprisingly, vexed some of the veterans but looking back after the war Freyberg considered that it had been the right policy to adopt.

This comment was made by Freyberg in a personal account of his activities from the time he arrived in France in May 1916 almost until the Armistice in 1918. 'A Linesman in Picardy' is a narrative of some 230 typewritten pages, which he was encouraged to write by J. M. Barrie whom he met later in 1916 (see Chapter 7). He began writing 'A Linesman in Picardy' in 1919 and finished it in 1921: it is not therefore a contemporary document, but was written within three years of the events described. Freyberg had a retentive memory and his account, which has never been published, appears to be factually accurate.

As soon as the RND was deemed fit for the next stage it was moved by train to IV Corps area, and on 19 July the Hood Battalion took over the Souchez Sector from 17 Battalion of the London Regiment. There they had their first taste of the procedures and routine of a battalion holding part of the front: the standing to at dawn and dusk, the system of sentries and patrols, digging and wiring parties, how and when meals were taken, and when it was possible to arrange for periods of rest and relief. 'The fact that seemed evident even to the novice,' Freyberg wrote, 'was that in war only an infinitesimal percentage of the work that was done had any close relationship with fighting.' It was a hard and unremitting life even in a quiet sector; but it came to an end in the late summer of 1916, and by September the RND was considered ready to take part in active operations on the Western Front.

The battle of the Somme had been launched on 1 July 1916. Its strategic purpose was, first, to divert German pressure away from the French who had suffered great setbacks and losses, especially in the vicinity of Verdun; and, second, to try and take some of the pressure off the Russian front. By and large these objectives were achieved, but at grievous cost. On the opening day of the British offensive there were 60,000 casualties, and three months later, by the end of September, the British armies had been fought to a standstill at the cost of 400,000 casualties. Nowhere had there been any tangible successes to show for the sacrifices made, and the territorial gains were modest.

Even so the British high command decided to launch one final offensive before the winter set in. This was the background to the battle of the Ancre. The attacks were to be carried out by the II, V and XIII Corps of the Fifth Army, commanded by General Sir Hubert Gough. The Royal Naval Division, now given the additional title of 63 Division, was assigned to V Corps on 4 October, and warned to prepare immediately for the forthcoming attack; but the battle, because of bad weather, had repeatedly to be postponed. The battle plan, as finally adopted, was for an attack on Serre, Beaumont Hamel, Beaucourt and St Pierre Division by 2 Division of XIII Corps; 3, 51 and Naval Divisions of V Corps, and 31 Division of II Corps. The Naval Division's sector, (1,200 yards in width) was immediately north of the Ancre river, at right angles to the river valley which ran almost due east to Beaucourt. The RND trenches and those of the enemy ran roughly north and south. The Division's objective was Beaucourt itself and the intervening positions opposite to their front.[1]

At a distance of from 180 to 250 yards from our assembly trenches, on higher ground, was the German front line system, consisting as usual of three lines of trenches [wrote the RND historian]. The last was known, for that purpose, as the Dotted Green Line. Behind the front line system, and separated from it by a valley, through which ran the road known as 'Station Road', was a second ridge, running from Beaumont Hamel to Beaucourt Station. On this ridge was a strongly fortified position, called the Green

The Somme and the Battle of the Ancre, 1916

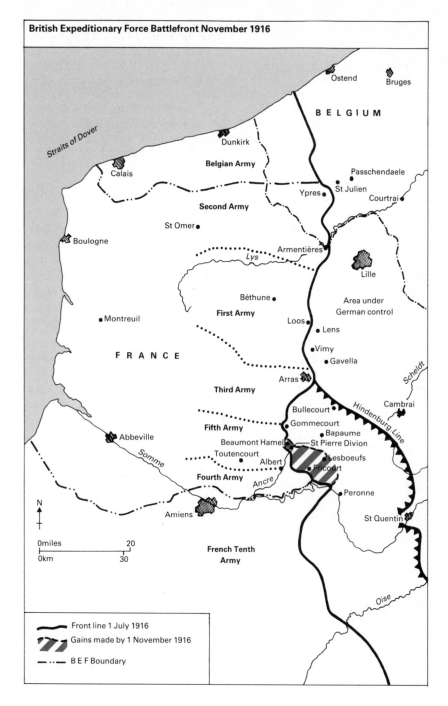

British Expeditionary Force Battlefront November 1916

Straits of Dover

Ostend

Bruges

BELGIUM

Dunkirk

Calais

Belgian Army

Passchendaele

St Julien

Ypres

Courtrai

Second Army

St Omer

Boulogne

Armentières

Lys

Lille

Béthune

Area under
German control

First Army

Loos

Lens

Montreuil

Vimy

Gavella

FRANCE

Scheldt

Arras

Third Army

Cambrai

Bullecourt

Gommecourt

Fifth Army

Bapaume

Beaumont Hamel

St Pierre Divion

Abbeville

Toutencourt

Lesboeufs

Somme

Albert

Fricourt

Fourth Army

Ancre

Peronne

N

Amiens

St Quentin

0miles   20
0km   30

French Tenth
Army

Oise

Front line 1 July 1916

Gains made by 1 November 1916

B E F Boundary

[81]

Line. This was the second defined objective. The country immediately behind this line was featureless, except the right front of the Divisional sector, where it slopes up to the hill immediately in front of Beaucourt, which commanded the enemy's communications with his forward systems on this part of the front. On the western face of this hill was a trench, which continued parallel to the front across the more level ground on the left. This trench was known as the Yellow Line, and formed the Division's third objective. The final objective, known as the Red Line, was a roughly-defined position to be taken up beyond Beaucourt, the capture of which would be, for the Naval Division, the real proof of success.[1]

In 'A Linesman in Picardy' Freyberg begins his account of the Ancre battle (13–15 November 1916) with a description of the 'strong natural position' of the Germans which the RND were ordered to attack, and which 'all the talent of modern military engineering had made into a line of fortresses, linked together laterally; in addition, all the high ground was in their hands'. On the right of the Ancre the Germans had the labyrinth of St Pierre Divion – and Thiepval Hill – flanked by the Schwaben Redoubt; on the left, they had the deep dug-out systems of the railway cutting, 'Y' ravine and Beaumont Hamel, flanked by the marshes of Serre.

Between 17 October and 1 November Freyberg's battalion moved back and forth between the line and the rest billets, constantly ready to stage the attack at two days' notice, 'which kept us all at constant fever heat of strain and excitement'. On 1 November they were told that, owing to the rain, the attack would be postponed indefinitely, and later that day that it would take place but no date had been fixed.

On 6 November the RND took over the Hamel sector of defence. They were then warned that they were definitely going to stage the attack because the French had just gone on the offensive at Verdun and recaptured Forts Vaux and Douaumont. But in order to ensure that the attack was a surprise its date was concealed from the troops taking part until the last moment. Freyberg wrote:

The plan was to assault the enemy positions, one after another, assembling in the dark and advancing at dawn as close to each trench or part of the defensive system as the bursting 18-pounder shells would allow; then to rush in and capture them when the guns lifted their fire on to the next position. When once the attack was launched, the wall of bursting shells ahead (or barrage) was the sole guide, and as no alteration in the plan during the attack was possible, great care had to be exercised to ensure that no part of the enemy position escaped from the bombardment, and also that the

[82]

barrage moved back slowly enough to give the overladen infantry soldier time to stagger forward across the mud.

The attack was at last staged for 13 November, and zero hour, the moment for the attack to be launched, was settled for 5.45 a.m., just before it was light.

It was accepted generally that heavy casualties were inevitable. This comes out again and again in 'A Linesman in Picardy'. During the planning for the Ancre battle an analysis was made of casualties in other divisions in similar circumstances, and it became chillingly evident that during the next month numbers in the RND would be thinned out by more than half. This forecast was never referred to, but it was uppermost in the minds of the more senior officers, with the result that, as Freyberg put it, 'we all became far kinder and more considerate to one another'.

At this stage the Hood Battalion was part of 189 Brigade. Freyberg's account of the battle itself begins as the battalion assembled on the left of the river Ancre on a frontage of 300 yards, within 200 yards of the enemy from V line. They formed up about one man to every two yards. Immediately behind were two other battalions, the Drake and the 1 HAC, assembled on the same plan; so that in all there were twelve waves assembled one behind the other on a piece of ground 300 yards

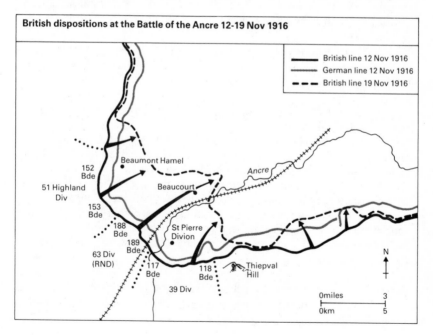

British dispositions at the Battle of the Ancre 12-19 Nov 1916

—————— British line 12 Nov 1916
—————— German line 12 Nov 1916
– – – British line 19 Nov 1916

Beaumont Hamel

152 Bde

51 Highland Div

Beaucourt

Ancre

153 Bde

188 Bde

St Pierre Divion

189 Bde

63 Div (RND)

117 Bde

118 Bde

Thiepval Hill

39 Div

N

0miles 3
0km 5

wide and not more than 100 yards deep. In front of each wave were four
subaltern officers, whose duty it was to direct all movement during the
battle and reorganise afterwards, whenever the opportunity allowed.
The whole Fifth Army attack was on a frontage of eight miles, and for
four miles on either side of the road to Beaucourt a similar number of
men were lying. Freyberg wrote:

> The Company and Battalion Commanders travelled with the second wave
> during the attack, while the Adjutant with the signallers and runners came
> on just in rear of the Battalion. The officers who commanded my first wave
> were Lieutenants Hart, Hall, Chapman and Cresswell, and it was their
> unenviable lot to rush out and get within a few yards of the wall of bursting
> shells, ready to rush in and dispute the possession of the trenches as soon as
> our guns lengthened their range. It was to these officers, and the men they
> led, that the Fifth Army owed their victory that day. The officers were all hit
> within a few minutes of the commencement, leading their men in the
> desperate attack on Railway Redoubt; some of the officers and men were
> wounded by our own shells which fell short of the main bombardment, but
> they boldly risked being shelled to make certain of getting the trenches and
> dug-outs before the enemy could recover from our barrage.
> We were the only battalion north of the river to get our objective that
> morning; all the other divisions had failed – in many cases in the same way
> as in July and September. Our lodgement enabled the Fifth Corps to exploit
> northwards, turn Whaleback Redoubt, and change what might have been a
> most costly failure into our greatest success on the Western front.

Freyberg's description of the actual attack tells of his personal feelings
of loss, the brutalities of the attack, and the individual deaths it gave rise
to. It also gives a clear picture of the sequence of battle tactics:

> At 5.30 a.m., with fifteen minutes to go, I went across quickly to see that
> everything was in order.
> The patrol in front was in trouble, some bombs were thrown, and it
> retaliated as it withdrew. On the extreme right I stopped to talk to Kelly,
> who commanded B Company. I wanted to take both his hands and wish him
> 'God speed', but somehow it seemed too theatrical; instead we talked rather
> awkwardly, and synchronised our watches. I walked back along our sector,
> speaking to the men I recognised. The old hands, whom I called by name,
> answered with a 'Yes, Sir, I'm here again', which recalled similar meetings
> on dark nights, and made me wonder which of them would answer the call
> at the next attack.

One 'old hand', who vividly remembered the tension that night, was
Joseph Murray, at the time an Ordinary Rating, who had also been at
Gallipoli. He wrote in *Call to Arms*:

[84]

It is extremely dark, I cannot see the hands of my watch but I can feel the dampness of the mist on my face and assume it is about midnight. I may be hopelessly in error but it doesn't really matter, for nothing matters any more. Each and every hour is the same. I fancy I can see a figure approaching on my left; maybe it's a ghost; I cannot hear any footsteps and there is no reason for anyone to be wandering about; we are all supposed to be sleeping. After what seems to be an eternity, I realise it is no ghost; it is my colonel, Colonel Freyberg, who is having a quiet chat with the chap in the next hole to me. I sit up with much difficulty. He apparently recognised an 'old hand' maybe because I had been the Prime Minister's son, Sub-Lieutenant Asquith's, runner while we were in England, on the *Grantully Castle* during our voyage east and when we landed on the Gallipoli peninsula. As such, I had on many, many occasions the honour of addressing him with the usual preface, 'With Mr Asquith's compliments, Sir' and deliver the message.

'You, too, are still with us. So pleased to see you. Make yourself as comfortable as you can and good luck. Do try to get some sleep.'

With these parting words he disappears in the darkness.[10]

Freyberg's own account continues:

At 5.40 a.m. all the assaulting troops fixed bayonets: they muffled the bayonet catch and ring, and the rifle muzzle. The shower of enemy lights and bursting shells in front and flashes of our guns behind, was minimised by the thickness of the atmosphere.

The officers stood counting the minutes to zero, looking at their luminous watches, and at 5.45 a.m. to the second the whole sky in rear was suddenly lit up by hundreds of flashes, and the guns had fired. The sound reached us some seconds later, and about 7 seconds after the sound thousands of shells passed a few feet over our heads and burst in an impenetrable wall 150 yards beyond. Our 12 waves were now running hard to get clear of the enemy counter-barrage which we knew was due to fall in our assembly trenches in 8 minutes.

Once the leading battalion had crossed no-man's-land it was well poised to capture the first three lines of enemy trenches. Meanwhile the two following battalions took what cover they could in the open until it was time for them to pass through the first battalion. The danger of this method of attack, as Freyberg pointed out, was that if the front battalion failed to capture its objective there was no means of stopping the second and third battalions getting prematurely involved, and usually suffering severe casualties in the open. This happened to the troops on the left of the Hood battalion that day, as it had happened many times before.

[85]

Our task in the battle resolved itself into capturing the front line system; it was composed of three lines, all more or less wired before our bombardment. First the outpost line, which was only occupied at night by small posts of two or three men, who sent up lights and fired field machine-guns to show that they were there. In the event of an attack these men did not attempt to hold the position but bolted back on to their second line, which was a resistance line, with deep dug-outs, which were joined together and laterally and from front to rear with those of the second line trenches. The dug-outs were most elaborate with electric light, and, in one case a lift nearly 100 feet underground. The trenches were hopelessly battered about, past all recognition, and had we relied on sight alone for guidance we should have been lost. Each Section Commander and Officer had a compass for direction, and a watch to check the distance (they knew that at 6.05 a.m. if they kept up with the barrage they would be assaulting the main line of resistance).

As we moved forward north-east by compass, we passed the burning entrances of dug-outs which showed that our phosphorus bombs were doing their work. Day broke as we neared our objective, and found us trying to collect the disorganised parts of our force. In a valley to the right I saw about 300 men, who I thought at first were some of our Companies reorganising, but on getting closer I found them to be from a large German dug-out, which two of our officers and a few men had taken. At 6.05 a.m. we had captured the first objective, and we reorganised and took stock of our losses.

My Adjutant and Signal Officer had been killed, also Kelly, commanding B Company, gallantly rushing a machine-gun, which he and some men scuppered, when hesitation and his failure would have endangered the whole operation.

Five other officers had also been killed and eight wounded, which left only five still able to fight. Similarly, out of 535 other ranks who had crossed no-man's-land twenty minutes earlier only 250 answered the roll-call on the captured objective. 'In return for these losses,' Freyberg wrote:

we could only point to a strip of pock-marked muddy ground, 300 yards wide and 800 deep. But those 2½ thousand square yards of ground were the most precious we possessed; they were the sole avenue of approach by which reinforcements could be hurried during darkness to our hard-pressed line. Had the enemy been able to close this hole between themselves and the river, the whole history of the battle of the Ancre would have had to be re-written.

After taking the main line we lay down to await the capture of the second objective (Beaucourt trench) by the Drake Battalion, who were due to pass through us at 6.05 to continue the advance behind the barrage. But the only troops of the Drake battalion to arrive were 3 officers and 70 men – Lieutenants Constable, Fox . . . and Beak . . .

In the mist and confusion after the initial assault the remainder of the Drake battalion had apparently followed the slope of the ground and strayed to the left of their sector in the direction of the hostile rifle fire. A great many of them were killed in front of Whaleback Redoubt.

With only three minutes before the barrage was due to move back, Freyberg relates how it was decided to attack the Drake Battalion's objective with all the troops at their disposal – a fraction of those who had been intended to take part in this action. Their right flank was secure on the river Ancre, but their left had lost touch with any of their troops, and as far as they could gather – or rather see – the attack to the north of them had failed:

> We advanced at the appointed time up the Beaucourt slopes, capturing Engine and Beaucourt trenches. The barrage was now playing on Beaucourt village, which was just on the far side of a small ridge that ran across our front, the summit of which was keenly fought for but remained neutral.
>
> Later in the morning a message came from the Divisional Commander to the effect that, owing to the failure of the troops on our left he was afraid of our pushing too far forward and becoming surrounded. He had, therefore, decided not to lift the barrage off Beaucourt which prevented us from capturing it. Very definite orders were sent as to the importance of holding our gains at any cost, and the message finished with a promise of help after dark.
>
> We were therefore forced to dig in, and as we were too thin on the ground to dig a trench, we consolidated a line of shell holes, throwing back our left flank.

Later on in the morning they were able to get in touch with a battalion of the Cambridgeshires on the river at Mill House, and at Handsar line, who sent runners and men with news of the rest of the Division; it was not encouraging. All the battalion commanders in their brigade were casualties, with two dead.

At the junction of the Beaucourt Road and Engine trench they discovered a large mail and ration dump belonging to a brigade of the German 3 Guards Division:

> We sent back the letters as quickly as possible to our Intelligence Department, while the food and tobacco were divided amongst the men who did very well out of this free issue. I got a message from one of the subalterns

[87]

demanding 25 large cigars for his wiring party, saying that the Company on his left were all fitted out with them.

However, Freyberg went on, they were not left in peace for long. Heavy and accurate sniping started, driving them to earth and making it impossible even to move from one shell hole to another:

Our own heavy howitzers started to fire short and all round our posts. Some men were wounded, and then one shell landed plumb in a large shell crater full of men; it seemed certain that everyone must have been killed, but as the smoke cleared away, we saw the men from the occupied shell hole running in all directions; after dark we discovered that only one man had been killed, and nobody else had been hurt. This short shooting continued all day and shook us considerably; we couldn't stop it, as it was impossible for us to get a runner back alive with a message. We could hear the reports of the 9.2-inch guns being fired, and we strained to hear the sound of the approaching shells; first we heard a whistle which quickly swelled into a roar, culminating with a tremendous concussion; the impact with the earth of the quarter-ton projectile driven at that rate through the air was frightening – quite the most vicious sound imaginable. The shell-bursts themselves were not as destructive as they might have been, owing to the great amount of mud on the ground, which stopped the fragments from flying about.

But even the midst of battle was not without its funny incidents:

About noon, my orderly room clerk discovered a jar of liquor, rather like rum in appearance and strength. After having drunk a good deal, he climbed out of the shell hole, and lay in full view of the enemy position, his commander thought, killed. He lay there all the afternoon until dusk, when they pulled him in by the legs, to find him untouched!

At dusk they were able to assess their position again, and an accumulation of messages arrived from the rear, announcing the failure of the troops on their left – 'This we already knew from the German firework display that was still going on in their old front lines' – while General Shute, the new commander of the RND in succession to General Paris, answered their request for reinforcements by sending part of 190 and 111 Brigades to their immediate aid. He told Freyberg to put them into position and be ready at 7.45 the next morning to attack Beaucourt village, and to consolidate on the far side.

After dusk fell they received rations and water and a batch of ten fresh officers to replace their battalion casualties: 13 Battalion of the KRRC 60 Rifles (111 Brigade) arrived just before midnight and were positioned as an extension of the force to the left; half an hour after they were settled in the HAC dug in just behind and to the left of Freyberg and his men. The Hawke, Hood, Drake and Nelson battalions were concentrated next to the river. The entire fighting force consisted of 300 men from the Hood Battalion and 200 men of the Drake Battalion with elements from both the Hawke and Nelson Battalions in addition to 13 Battalion of the KRRC, and 12 Battalion of the HAC (190 Brigade) – about 800 men in total.

The plan for the morning was for the HAC on the right and the 60 Rifles on the left to go forward and assault the village when the artillery opened fire on Beaucourt at 7.45 a.m. Elements of 189 Brigade were to support them and to keep their position secure in the event of the attack failing. But that plan was spoilt by the arrival of 4 Battalion Royal Fusiliers who, owing to a misunderstanding, marched up the 'bullet-swept slope' behind Freyberg and his men ten minutes before the attack was due to commence. This caused considerable confusion:

The enemy machine-guns from the near edge of Beaucourt were very active, and as we looked back we saw men drop all along the line. As the Royal Fusiliers came level the HAC got up from their trenches and the two battalions advanced mixed together. When they got up to our trench they were forced to take cover owing to casualties, and they came in with us.

We now had in our trench the three battalions – our own, the HAC and 4 Royal Fusiliers, all mixed up, and each with different orders, which they commenced to pass up and down the line until everybody was completely fogged as to what the instructions were. One battalion passed messages giving their men orders to attack, another orders not to attack, while the third passed messages to the effect that they were in reserve. In desperation several officers tried to reorganise, and to do this they got out of their trenches and were immediately sniped.

The barrage had now opened, but was ineffective. The 60 Rifles had started to work round the left of the village and our only chance was to push on with them. Several officers of our battalion got up calling to the men to follow them. I had not gone 10 yards when a bullet hit my tin helmet, breaking the chinstrap and knocking me on my back. We didn't expect to get far as the machine-gun fire was murderous, but we hoped to create a diversion and attract the enemy's attention from the 60 Rifles, who were working round behind the village.

To our surprise the enemy started to surrender, and in a minute were swarming all over Beaucourt. We moved through the ruins and picked out 800 prisoners from the deep dug-outs; there was very little fighting. While we were advancing through a barbed-wire entanglement an egg bomb landed at my feet, and in my hurry to get clear of its zone and influence, I became caught in the barbed wire, and held a prisoner. I threw myself on

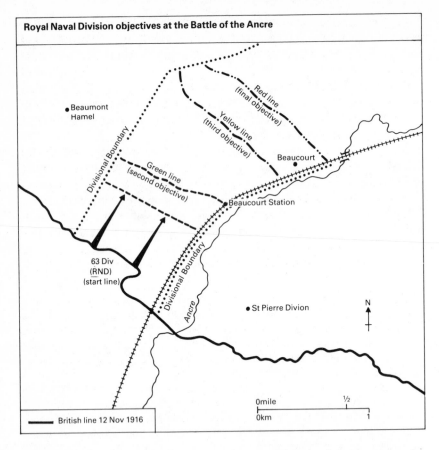

Royal Naval Division objectives at the Battle of the Ancre

the ground as the bomb exploded, but it did little damage except for splinters.

The sight of 800 prisoners marching back from Beaucourt aroused the curiosity, as Freyberg put it, 'of every soldier in sight, and drew them like a magnet to the place the prisoners had just left'. This was the last thing that was wanted, because senior officers knew very well that when the Germans discovered that Beaucourt had fallen, they would direct all their artillery on it, and, as the forward troops were in a salient, they would be shot at from both flanks as well as from the group of guns in front of them near Mirimont. Two of the main party hurried back to the principal crossroads to send everyone away from the village, 'the HAC to dig in on the right, the Royal Fusiliers in the centre, and the 60 Rifles on the left. All that remained of 189 Brigade were sent back to the trench that they had occupied the night before.'

The men were just clear of the village when the shelling started. They had to run for cover to a little drain at the side of the road where they became trapped – because the road which was their only line of escape was swept with shells. But if they stayed where they were they were equally likely to be hit. Freyberg and Captain 'Cardy' Montague, commanding D Company of the Hood, elected to stay in a scratch in the ground about one foot deep. There was an HAC man on Freyberg's left, Montague on his left and some Drake Battalion men beyond him. A ruined red wall stood about 10 yards behind them with bricks piled around it on the ground, and every time the bricks were hit a red cloud was thrown up which looked like gas and made them put their masks on.

The shelling was very heavy by now, bursting continually on the ground and on the wall:

> The ground shook with the concussions and the dust and cordite fumes were choking us; we had a good many close calls, and then there was a bang, a curious ringing note in my ear and I lost consciousness. When I came to, my head gave me a good deal of pain, and as I lay face downwards hot blood was dropping from my nose and chin. I thought at first my head had been smashed, but I located the wound in my neck with two dirty fingers. I looked at the man on my left; he was curled up. I moved his head, and found he was grey and dead. Montague was also hit by the same shell, but not badly. He came across to me at considerable risk and bound up my neck, saying, 'God how you bleed, I must get you back as quickly as possible, it's your only chance.'

Cardy Montague, in a letter to his mother a few days later, told the story from a slightly different viewpoint, and how it ended:

> One shell fell a bit closer than the others. I felt something hit me on the small of the back but it did not seem to hurt at all. Then I heard Freyberg say 'Goodbye Montague' and then 'Steady Hood', and I saw he was hit and going a very bad colour. He asked me if I had any morphia and I said 'no'. He then produced a tube and asked me to give him some. I gave him a quarter grain and labelled him to say that I had done so. I then dressed his wound with my field dressing (he had none) as best I could. There was a hole in his neck which was bleeding rather profusely. He lay there for about ten minutes and I thought he was going to die; I told him I would go and get two or three men to carry him down, but he told me on no account to move. It was just as well because the chances of getting men to carry him down during the heavy shelling were slight and he weighs about 16 stone. He kept giving me orders about informing the senior officer of the HAC and the troops on our flank. Suddenly he said, much to my surprise, 'do you think I

could walk to the dressing station?' I told him it was quite safe (which it was not, owing to the heavy shelling which still went on), but the going was very rough. He got up with less difficulty than I expected, and walked down leaning heavily on my arm . . .

I shall never forget that walk down; it was curious how instinctively one chooses the best going for oneself and I had to make an effort to find a patch for his feet round the shell holes. The heavy shelling still continued but the worst part was passing the badly wounded men who prayed me to help them. He faltered badly once, but I told him he had GOT to go on another 30 yards. The regimental aid post was down a very steep bank, and here I found most of the remnants of the Hood and Drake. There were naturally plenty of people to take over Freyberg and he immediately had a good dressing from our splendid regimental doctor [McCracken]. He handed over the battalion to me telling me to carry on and giving orders all the time.[11]

Freyberg's main worry as he lay injured on the ground had been that he had 'kept the reins in my hands so tightly that I was the only one who knew the scheme'. His account goes on:

It was now essential to get orders to the Commanding Officers of the various units, telling them the plan, that the present regime had ended, and that they must deal direct with the General [Shute], and shift for themselves. I sent these messages out by some runners, and then with my arm over Montague's shoulder we staggered drunkenly back along the road.

He describes the same 'heartbreaking' journey, viewing the many dead and being begged for help from the badly wounded, 'us, who could barely weather the storm ourselves'. At the dressing station they found a hundred or so wounded men who had been brought in for safety and were waiting for a lull in the bombardment before being evacuated. Freyberg describes his last waking moments:

After making some final arrangements I lay down, not to get up again for six weeks. With the loss of blood, and the immobility, all resistance broke down, and it was a much frightened man who was carried back along the shelled road. We stopped at Brigade headquarters and gave them the latest situation report, and I told the General that all of 189 Brigade were unfit to remain in the battle, and should be taken out of the line without loss of time.

Freyberg had an even closer encounter with death in the field dressing station than on the battlefield. It was the practice when there were mass casualties to divide the wounded into three categories: the walking and lightly wounded, the seriously wounded who were expected to live; and those expected to die. When Freyberg arrived at the dressing station with his four wounds, his head and eyes covered in blood-soaked bandages and all colour gone through loss of blood, the stretcher bearers took him at once to the tent of those who were not expected to live and were given no treatment except for painkilling drugs. Later he remembered hearing a quiet, gentle voice giving orders for him to be moved to another tent, where he received full medical attention and the chance to live, but at that time he never saw or knew the name of the doctor responsible.

The officer involved was Captain S. S. Greaves, who in the Second World War commanded the hospital ship *Atlantis*. One day early in 1941 the *Atlantis* arrived in Egypt, and Greaves went to Cairo to obtain medical supplies for his ship. He lunched at Shepheard's Hotel, and while he was talking with his companions in the hotel foyer beforehand he became aware of a senior army officer who was watching him intently. Presently he came over, and asked Greaves if he had been at a dressing station on the Ancre in November 1916. Freyberg had recognised the softly-spoken voice which, twenty-five years before, had given the instructions that were to save his life.[12]

'The success of the Hood and Drake battalions was both brilliant and astonishing, and it was decisive,' states the RND history.[1] The British lodgement in the German lines at Beaucourt soon spread to the flanks, enabling the neighbouring strongholds at St Pierre Divion and Beaumont Hamel to be captured as well. This gave the British High Command its first success for many months.

The repercussions of the fighting on the Ancre had consequences that went far beyond the battlefield, however. In her book *Somme*, Lyn Macdonald writes:

> The outcome of the gamble had been limited success and less than General Gough had hoped for. But the capture of St Pierre Divion, of Beaucourt and Beaumont Hamel were three trump cards. The previous evening Gough had had the gratification of placing them in the hand of his Commander-in-Chief and that morning Haig laid them on the table at the opening session of the Chantilly Conference where they had the desired effect of mollifying the French. He played them again next day at the Paris Conference of the Anglo-French Governments and they even trumped Lloyd George. He had come prepared, with all the powers of his formidable rhetoric, to plead the case for shifting the main arena of the battle away from the atrophy of the Western Front and, even after the Prime Minister had insisted on his deleting the most virulent and inflammatory passages of Lloyd George's prepared speech, it had promised to be a lively meeting.

Now all was changed. The Conference, which had set out to curb the powers of the Military, unanimously accepted the conclusions which the Military Commanders had reached at Chantilly and endorsed their plans for the continuance of the war in the spring.[13]

Freyberg's exploits at Beaucourt were by this time being recorded in the British press. *The Times* war correspondent wrote on 23 November:

The capture of Beaucourt, though accomplished at the last with unexpected ease, was a brilliant piece of work, and it gave England another hero, whose name will come to be famous as the commanding officer of one of the battalions of the Naval Division, who lies at present in hospital with four wounds in him. There is every prospect, however, of his recovering to learn what the country thinks of him.

Not that he was the only hero of that day, for again I say, what I have said many times, that heroism is the normal behaviour of our men in every action. Yet out of all and above all, this one man's action stands conspicuous, so that every man in the Division is proud of him, and already his fame is beginning to spread through the army.[14]

Freyberg meanwhile was being taken through the base hospitals in France on his way to England. He ended up in Mrs Guest's (Johnny Dodge's mother) nursing home at 26 Park Lane in Mayfair, where he was a patient until mid-January. Violet Bonham Carter visited him there as soon as he arrived and brought some astonishing news: 'I told him that Philip Sassoon [Private Secretary to Haig] had come to Downing Street that very day bearing the C-in-C's recommendation for the VC.'[15]

Freyberg was still confined to his bed in mid-December when the award of his Victoria Cross was announced in the *London Gazette*. The official citation is:

For most conspicuous bravery and brilliant leading as a Battalion Commander.

By his splendid personal gallantry he carried the initial attack straight through the enemy's front system of trenches. Owing to mist and heavy fire of all descriptions, Lieutenant-Colonel Freyberg's command was much disorganised after the capture of his first objective. He personally rallied and re-formed his men, including men from other units who had become intermixed.

He inspired all with his own contempt of danger. At the appointed time he led his men to the successful assault of the second objective, many prisoners being captured.

During this advance he was twice wounded. He again rallied and re-formed all who were with him, and although unsupported in a very advanced position, he held his ground for the remainder of the day, and throughout the night, under heavy artillery and machine-gun fire. When reinforced on the following morning, he organised the attack on a strongly fortified village and showed a fine example of dash in personally leading the assault, capturing the village and five hundred prisoners. In this operation he was again wounded.

Later in the afternoon, he was again wounded severely, but refused to leave the line till he had issued final instructions.

The personality, valour and utter contempt of danger on the part of this single officer enabled the lodgement in the most advanced objective of the Corps to be permanently held, and on this *point d'appui* the line was eventually formed.[16]

It was after the award of the Victoria Cross that Freyberg began to keep correspondence for the first time, instead of throwing papers away as before – press cuttings, telegrams and letters of congratulation. The Asquith family was particularly attentive and there are many letters from Oc, Margot and Violet. There were more from brother officers and from former commanders such as Generals Paris, Hunter-Weston and Shute. What gave him particular pleasure were those from old friends in New Zealand, which only arrived after their six-week journey by sea. The letter he had from his old headmaster, the redoubtable J. P. Firth, is typical of these:

> I wonder whether you can really understand how proud we all are of you, and how heartily we congratulate you and your mother?
>
> From all here kindest remembrances and warmest good wishes for complete recovery, and soon. We have read of your great deeds, with many a thrill. Good luck and God bless you![17]

In *The Story of the 29th Division* the achievement of Freyberg at Beaucourt is put in its simplest and clearest terms; it was originally contributed anonymously in 1925 by General Sir Beauvoir de Lisle, who was to command Freyberg later on in the war:

> At nightfall on the 13th after the most bloody casualties it was realised that the attack had again failed, but Lieutenant-Colonel Freyberg, though wounded, collected every man who had got through the left of the German defences. This party of about 350 he led during the night up the spur to attack Beaucourt redoubt. He took the redoubt and the remainder of the ridge, and next morning 5,000 Germans between this ridge and the Beaumont Hamel defences surrendered. By his initiative, fine leading and bravery Lieutenant-Colonel Freyberg won the battle of Ancre. Probably this was the most distinguished personal act in the war.[18]

[95]

But perhaps the most personal and human tribute that was paid to Freyberg was from Chief Petty Officer Tobin, who described how he had been close to Freyberg throughout the Ancre battle and helped Surgeon McCracken to get him down and away:

> ... a giant in stature, as strong as an ox, brave as a lion, yet gentle, kind and [he] understood the men's humour. He never talked down to them and didn't expect them to talk up to him ... They were proud of him and more than proud to call themselves 'Freyberg's men'.[3]

7

The Hindenburg Line and Passchendaele, 1917

Freyberg had been a keen admirer of Captain Robert Falcon Scott, and had followed closely the details of Scott's last expedition to the Antarctic. When Freyberg joined the Hood Battalion he found that one of its officers, E. W. Nelson, had been a member of that expedition. On his return to England at the end of the Gallipoli campaign Freyberg asked Nelson to introduce him to Lady Scott, and this had been arranged. After he was wounded in the Ancre battle Lady Scott visited him in Mrs Guest's nursing home where he was recovering. She thought it might interest Sir James Barrie, the playwright and author of *Peter Pan*, to meet Freyberg, and on a second visit brought Barrie with her. Freyberg's close friendship with Barrie began from that moment.

The disparity of the characters and backgrounds of Barrie and Freyberg made their relationship a puzzle to some who knew them both, but in truth there was no great mystery about it. Each found in the other something that had been missing in his own life. In 1916 Barrie was fifty-six, lonely and depressed, melancholy ever since his wife had left him after fifteen years of marriage, and with no children. Freyberg was twenty-seven; he had not had a happy or affectionate relationship with his own father, nor had much guidance from an older and more experienced man. For Barrie it was almost a repeat of the father-son relationship that he had had with Captain Scott. As he lay dying in the Antarctic Scott had written one of his last letters to Barrie, in which he said that he had never met a man whom he admired and loved so much,

[97]

but that he was unable to show how much his friendship meant to him, 'for you had so much to give and I nothing'. Freyberg felt much as Scott had done, as one of Barrie's biographers, Denis Mackail, describes. But Barrie also thought highly of Freyberg, initially because of his military exploits; then because he enjoyed his company. After stating that Freyberg was as kind as he was brave, Mackail goes on, echoing some of Barrie's own reactions:

> And as simple? Yes and no. Simple always in every sense connoting honesty and virtue, but the very last man to describe as all brawn and body and no brains. The body, scarred all over, remained tremendously impressive. But Bernard Freyberg adjusted himself, with something more than ordinary intelligence, to flattery and fame. In that Royal Naval Division, and afterwards, there were friends of a very different upbringing and stamp. They couldn't and didn't attempt to hide their admiration, yet as Freyberg passed more and more into this circle, how easily – if he hadn't been Freyberg – it might have softened him or turned him into a snob. It didn't. He remained entirely himself. The background altered, but nothing could touch his integrity. If that's being simple, then simple is one of the right words. And of course he was infinitely simpler than Barrie.[1]

There were two phases in Freyberg's relationship with Barrie. The first lasted from 1916 until 1922 and culminated in Barrie's famous address on 'Courage' at St Andrew's University, in which he referred to Freyberg's swim at Gallipoli. This was a period during which they saw each other a great deal and were on close terms, to the point where Barrie kept a room for Freyberg in his Adelphi Terrace flat; when Barrie encouraged Freyberg to write the account of his experiences in the First World War; and helped him over his war wounds – just as Freyberg looked after Barrie when he was seriously ill in 1921 and later. It came to an end with Freyberg's marriage in 1922, at which Barrie was best man.

The second phase, inevitably, was less intimate though more mellow. Freyberg, who was no longer living in officers' messes or London clubs and had a settled home, did not have the opportunity to descend on Barrie's flat with the same frequency. In spite of this, though, they did not drift apart. They kept in close touch on the telephone, and whenever either of them had a special lunch or dinner party, the other was usually one of the guests. Thus Barrie came to Freyberg's dinner for the Winston Churchills in 1934; and Freyberg was generally included in Barrie's celebrated lunches and dinners for his literary and political friends.

Freyberg remained in the nursing home in Park Lane until early

[98]

January 1917. Lady Cynthia Asquith mentions him frequently in her diaries, and her entry for 18 January shows that by then he was up and about again and that he gave a dinner at the Carlton Grill for her, Eddie Marsh and Irene Lawley, daughter of Lord and Lady Wenlock.[2] Afterwards they went to see a Harry Lauder show, probably the first of Freyberg's many visits to the old-style music-hall which was still in its prime, and which he always enjoyed. In later life he often used to repeat a Harry Lauder song that went:

> I was playing golf one day
> when the Germans landed,
> all our troops had run away,
> and all our ships were stranded.
> And when I thought of England's shame,
> it *almost* put me off my game.

Lady Cynthia's diaries also mention that he went before a medical board on 6 February 1917 and was passed fit.[2]

A further new element now appears – Bernard began to write to Barbara McLaren. Their first meeting had been in Violet Bonham Carter's house in March 1916; and they saw each other on several occasions during the winter of 1916–17 while Bernard was convalescing in London: 'In case I failed to convey how much I loved your parties, I do so now,' wrote Bernard after he returned to France. 'It was great fun for me, I enjoy things like a child. I suppose it's wrong and *un-English!*'

During the course of the next five years (until they were married in June 1922) he wrote several hundred letters to her. This was the first, written on his return to the Hood Battalion in France in the middle of February 1917:

Trenches, Same Battalion   25 February 1917
God how one misses Cleg [Kelly] – one remembers him more vividly each day – he was a rare and beloved creature – I hope he misses us a little. I went over the ground we had our show on, yesterday, and saw it all again – it was great fun – I went to the shell-hole where I was hit and found my steel helmet lying just as I had left it, all smashed about and with a bullet hole through it.

Life here I find very complete – lots of maps, guns and noise; even the mud and snow are amusing. I am back to my battalion again and find it in very low ebb as regards men and officers. We have had wastage in our last couple of shows. The battalion has again done most wonderfully well and has increased its reputation as a fighting unit. Oc's DSO has been a very popular decoration and nobody has earned one more – all the men are very bucked over it.

The most amusing fellow here is our surgeon [McCracken]. I spend most of my spare time with him and we walk, bathe and ride together whenever we get the chance. He is the only original officer I have left – he knew Rupert – Charles – Patrick etc. and is a topper. He is very much in love with somebody and when ratted about it blushes like a girl; we get a lot of fun out of him . . .

Please write me anything that concerns 1. Oc. 2. Patrick. 3. Any London mail news. I did enjoy my dinners and theatres in town. You were very kind to me. Bless you.

Bernard Freyberg.[3]

Many years later McCracken remembered accompanying Freyberg to the exact spot where he had been wounded for the fourth time. He recalled their finding Freyberg's battered helmet, and how they cleaned it up before sending it off to Sir James Barrie.[4]

The 'Patrick' in Freyberg's letter was of course Patrick Shaw-Stewart. At this time he was working reluctantly as a staff officer at GHQ Salonika, and trying to rejoin the Hood in France. He wrote to Freyberg at Christmas 1916, but the letter did not arrive until May 1917. In it Patrick congratulates him on his 'amazing exploits at Beaumont Hamel', but had not yet heard of Freyberg's VC:

. . . before hearing your name mentioned I heard all about it under the title of a 'a battalion commander of the RND' and I said to myself with complete certainty, 'that's him'.

. . . I wish I knew how bad your wounds are: one would be inclined to say they oughtn't to be really bad if you went on taking Beaumont Hamel with them all inside you, but as I know what you generally do with holes in your stomach and splinters in your penis and unsutured nerves in your arm, I am inclined to be suspicious.

. . . I can't tell you how sad I am about Cleg: I got very much attached to him at Helles, as I know you did. I admired enormously the way he militarised himself, quite against his nature, and the way he stuck to the Battalion. Do you remember how quaint we all thought him at first, and how absolutely we all came round to him? I can remember nothing funnier than him on Nelson and old Buck: one could always rely on Cleg to have a little feud on . . .[5]

Freyberg had gone back to France to what he described as 'the harshest weather conditions of the war' in February and March 1917 'with the exception of the Gallipoli blizzard in November 1915':

... during the heavy frosts, when the ground was too ironlike for any impression to be made upon it, even with a pick, men were forced to take cover in shell-holes, or any unsuitable depression. Burying our dead became an engineering feat, graves being blasted out with explosives. The petrol tins of drinking water froze hard, and had to be opened with a tin opener, pieces of ice chipped off with the bayonet and forced into the water bottle, where they remained in a solid state till mealtime. When a drink was required the ice had to be thawed by placing the water bottle inside the shirt. Washing and shaving were an impossibility.

The occupied shell-holes were usually half full of ice, upon which the men had to lie or kneel during the day; at night only was it possible to move about and stretch out the creases that had been frozen into their bodies during the cramped hours of daylight. Men were often frozen to death, as they lay facing the enemy, with their rifles still tightly gripped as if ready for use. Visiting rounds frequently arrested what they believed to be sleeping sentries, only to discover their melancholy error. Under these conditions of cold our wounded stood little or no chance; drowsiness followed any loss of blood, which in turn gave way to death.

The period that followed in April saw the preparations for the next stage of the war. By this time the Germans had retreated to the Hindenburg Line, the line of field fortifications taken up by the German armies in their retreat after the battle of the Somme and developed into a formidable defensive system by their military engineers. The British armies' next task was to try and break through these positions. An extract from a letter Freyberg wrote to Barbara McLaren on 16 April 1917 demonstrates how enthusiastic he felt about military life:

We are all very fit and keen; life can never be more interesting than it is at present – thank goodness one had a sense of proportion to enjoy it to its full: it really is electric. We are very busy, and there are plans for us to be *very much* busier. Your last letter was much more cheerful than the one before which made me unhappy to think that people at home might feel miserable over the ultimate result of the war. WE ARE going to win this war and perhaps within the year. Nothing can stand up to us, we are invincible. I hope I see the finish of it, but who can tell. Anyway, one feels that one has really lived for two years to some effect; I feel I mean quite a lot to my battalion. This is the last time I will write and depress you, but I felt I wanted to say it. You must know how hard it is to have to enjoy one's feelings alone.

Freyberg spent the first three weeks of April making preparations for the attack by the Hood Battalion on Gavrelle, but on 20 April, three days before the attack (the battle of Arras) was due, he was posted to

[101]

take command of 173 Brigade in 58 Division, 'and since it was possible my new command was on the verge of this same offensive, I was not allowed to stay for the battle,' he wrote. Oc Asquith was ordered to return from a staff appointment to take over the Hood at 24 hours notice and the attack on Gavrelle was successfully carried out. It was a disorganised battle and of the officers Asquith alone was unscathed.

Freyberg's hurried departure from the Hood Battalion had been a moment of real sadness for him because, as he wrote to Patrick Shaw-Stewart, he had tremendous sentiment for everything to do with 'The Steadies', as they were known. Later to Cynthia Asquith 'he spoke with tears in his eyes at his pain at leaving the Hood Battalion, and of how his men had cut off his buttons as souvenirs – said he meant to run his Brigade as intimately as he had his Battalion'.[2] The new appointment was an impressive one, and meant that he was the youngest general in the British Army. On arrival at the new head-quarters Freyberg reported to his divisional commander, General Hew Fanshawe, who was having tea with his brother General Edward Fanshawe, the commander of V Corps. When he was announced they looked hard at him and asked his age. They had been told he was twenty-three, and were relieved to hear he was all of twenty-eight.

Freyberg stayed with 173 Infantry Brigade for almost five months, from the end of April until 20 September 1917, but, as he discovered when he arrived, 58 Division was a second line territorial division which had been badly mishandled. The Division had been retained in England for home defence until the end of 1916 and had been the victim of newspaper attacks since the battle of the Somme had started – about when they were going to France. In addition they had been so harried and dragooned by inspecting officers that everyone had lost confidence in themselves. Nor had matters improved since the division had come to France. They had not yet seen any action, and most of the officers who had nursed them through their earlier difficulties had been sent home. Now they were about to be engaged in operations for which they had neither the training nor the leadership.

Freyberg was horrified by the amateurishness and the slipshod methods of the staff of 58 Division. As usual he got on well with his immediate subordinate commanders, and he admired the fighting spirit of the men of the Brigade. The trouble came when he was instructed to carry out operations that he considered unsound. This happened on several occasions and made him unpopular with his superiors, as he accurately predicted what would happen.

'Taking over a force which had been mishandled to such an extent,' Freyberg wrote, however, 'was a much easier task than taking over a formation which had a great fighting record; because although my new brigade was ignorant of battle conditions, the material was good.' His commanding officers included a clergyman and a professor of mathematics from London University; among his brigade staff were a city businessman and an actor, 'one of the ablest of men'. The troops came from London, 'very intelligent cockneys' quick to learn, but with so little experience of battle that they needed proper training and initiation. Freyberg started to work on this new command with his usual enthusiasm and determination. To Barbara he wrote:

> Such fun; I am bit by bit putting things in order and sorting things and people out. Some are going and others I am changing round. I am working at maps and am having a great time. About tactics, I am working up my scheme of infantry in the assault, and doing it the same way as I did with my battalion. My divisional general and all concerned think a great deal of it, and I am certain it is a sound way of fighting. I find being a general comes naturally and easily and is, to say the least, absorbing. Of course I miss my dear battalion – more than I can say, so you must be kind and write to me . . .

Shortly after this, he had to return to London for one day – probably to obtain the uniform and insignia of his new rank as Brigadier-General – and lunched with Cynthia Asquith. She noted his complete self-confidence. He reiterated that he planned to run his brigade of London Territorials in the same way as he had the Hood Battalion, and she got the impression that his firmest resolve was to quarrel with his superiors.[2] He also saw Barbara on this occasion and afterwards wrote to her: 'I am glad you enjoyed yourself on the 24th; it was fun for me – but I think the greatest fun is being a Brig. and arranging big things out here – nothing is too much trouble or worry.'

The effect that Freyberg had on the officers and men of his new command was electric:

> I clearly remember a fine sunny morning [wrote Charles Howard, forty-three years later] when we were in the line near Bullecourt, manning a machine-gun, when along came our 'Brig' quite alone, coming to see for himself and asking many questions, shrewdly assessing the situation in front of us. We got quite a thrill out of it and we were very proud of our commander, a VC and the youngest Brigadier in the British Army – a fine handsome man full of quiet confidence, and indeed giving us confidence

too. We needed every encouragement in the following weeks. During that terrible time at Bullecourt we lost two hundred men out of two hundred and sixty.[6]

The operations for which 58 Division was destined were also attempts to break the Hindenburg Line. This had been prepared and sited so that, should any part of it fall into Allied hands, the Germans could enfilade the trenches which the Allies would then be occupying.

On 3 May the Fifth and Third Armies launched their attack; but unfortunately zero hour, which was set for daylight, was timed too early. The Fifth Army's attack centred on Bullecourt. The offensive was a costly failure, except for the lodgement gained by the Australian Corps, 'after some of the most desperate hand-to-hand fighting of the war', which threatened the most vital part of the Hindenburg defensive position. The attention the Germans paid to the Australian gains over the next fortnight showed that they were fully aware of the threat, and from shelling alone the Australians were reduced to half their original numbers in a few days. To relieve them became urgent, and on 11 May 173 Infantry Brigade (in Third Army) was ordered to replace 15 Australian Brigade, in a position where an attack was known to be pending.

Freyberg was dismayed at the prospect of taking over this sector with inexperienced troops. He had hoped to take his untried brigade into the line by easy stages, starting with a period of simple garrison work in a quiet sector. Instead they were having to take over the most active part of the British front.

The reality proved even worse than he feared. The relief, carried out after dark on the night of 12 May (there were only five hours of darkness at this time of year) was, in Freyberg's words 'a nightmare'. It took place during heavy bombardment by the Germans, who feared another Australian attack. The officers and senior NCOs were warned of the difficulties honestly, also that the shelling would be heavy and the casualties severe but, they were told, the job was not impossible. General Gough, commanding the Fifth Army, decided to leave the Australian artillery and machine-gunners in the line until the infantry got used to the sector and had organised their defence scheme. The 2/4 Battalion of the London Regiment passed brigade headquarters at about 11 p.m. on the way to the front line 1,500 yards further on, and casualties started to arrive at the dressing station almost immediately. The 2/3 Battalion, which followed, also ran into a heavy bombardment that split them into two parts. By dawn, when the relief was nearly complete, it had already cost over 150 casualties.

Freyberg crawled to the front line an hour after dawn, when the shelling eased off, through trenches filled with Australian dead – often black and so swollen that their trousers and jackets had split – having to embrace dead bodies in order to get round heavily shelled corners; the ground was so churned up that corpses that had been buried lay on the surface.

But Freyberg particularly remembered the men of 15 Australian Infantry Brigade for their behaviour under fire, and the conduct of their stretcher-bearers:

> As we crawled into the line, we saw the Australian stretcher-bearers carrying back their wounded under fire. The foremost troops of the enemy would not allow anyone to come forward, so these stretcher-bearers had to crawl into the line as we had done, pulling their stretchers behind them on a rope. But once there, they were allowed to leave without being shot at by the enemy infantry. However they still had to run the gauntlet through the enemy artillery fire.
>
> These Australian stretcher-bearers were all but naked, wearing boots, socks and a thin pair of khaki shorts, with a water bottle slung across their sun-tanned naked shoulders. They looked magnificent primitive creatures as they stalked out through the shellfire, sweat running in little streams down their muscular backs and legs; some picked their way by unshelled routes, while others went straight, but neither lot looking back, nor had the appearance of hurrying. It was a wonderful sight, that got completely under one's guard and made us all very proud to be fighting alongside such men.

The military position was not the only problem. Water supplies were crucial to the men's survival, and they had gone to the front with just two days supply; more supplies were brought in on the night of 13 May, but out of 100 men bringing 100 tins of water only seventy survived. On the morning of 14 May the lines were heavily shelled, and all the telephone wires cut, not only forward to the battalion in the line, but also back to the Division and the artillery; a German prisoner was taken who revealed that an attack was to be launched at dawn the following day, and this was borne out by the increased shelling which continued all day without respite. Worse still, the signal office was destroyed by a direct hit from a large shell and the whole signal section killed. A message was sent back to the division headquarters at dusk, telling them that the two supporting battalions might have to be moved forward during the battle. An hour after dark Freyberg went forward with two runners to find out what was happening in the forward positions. The shelling was so heavy, especially round the Hindenburg Line, which was their objective for the night, that on the way the younger of the two orderlies broke down, and confessed that he was only seventeen and could not stand the strain. He was left behind with the reserve company while Freyberg and the other orderly pressed on to one of the tunnel dug-outs in the Hindenburg support line:

> After going 300 yards further and within a similar distance from the front line, the remaining runner was killed, and a few minutes later I was forced to take cover under a little bank not a hundred yards from my objective. It was now impossible to move either forward or back, and from eleven till two o'clock I waited, but without success, for a lull, to rush into the dugout.
>
> I was not the only inhabitant of this little depression, for an Australian machine-gun sergeant was already in residence. He had his machine-gun in the bottom, wrapped in a blanket to keep the mechanism free from the earth, which was flying about during the bombardment. He seemed to know I was an officer, although my jacket was buttoned to my throat like a private soldier's, and I was wearing a tin helmet. He evinced no interest, however, in what I was doing, taking me on trust, feeling no doubt that I must be there on duty and not from curiosity. I asked him where the rest of his gun team were? To which he replied, 'they are all beat to the wide and have turned in for the night'.
>
> He had decided to keep a lonely watch at the gun during the hours of darkness. I asked where they had gone to? To which he answered: 'I don't know, but they'll turn up all right when the time comes.' When the noise wasn't too great we talked as we lay close together. He told me what he thought about Sydney and the girls he used to meet on Circular Quay – recited many verses of 'Mademoiselle from Armentières' – and just before we parted company, he decided we were the two worst soldiers in the British Army.

Freyberg hurried back, knowing that the bombardment was now unlikely to decrease, and that his presence was necessary to launch the counter-attack of the 2/1 and 2/2 London battalions, should the Germans succeed in regaining the ground lost to the Australians. At 3.15 a.m., the bombardment reached its fiercest, and the SOS signal (a parachute rocket, red over green over yellow) was sent up all along the British front. The battle commenced immediately. The German infantry advanced and by 3.50 a.m. had effected a lodgement in the Australian line; but by 5.30 they had been repelled again by an Australian and an English company.

By the following morning the Hindenburg Line had been reduced to a string of shell-holes in which it was impossible to distinguish the original line at any point; 500 men were lost during the two days in the line, while the dug-outs were full of stretcher cases. In addition twelve Lewis guns had been destroyed and all the reserve ammunition and bombs had been blown up or buried. The two worn-out and depleted battalions were replaced, and the whole Brigade was eventually relieved on the night of 20 May. As Freyberg wrote, 'it was with *very* different feelings that the men now faced their tormentors and critics. They had been in action and had done well.'

While Freyberg was in the line at Bullecourt he got a summons from Buckingham Palace to attend an investiture in Hyde Park on 2 June 1917 to receive his VC from the King. In the circumstances he had to request that the award be conferred at a later date. However certain newspapers had noticed that his name had been the thirteenth on the list to be presented and had some fun suggesting he had requested the postponement out of superstition.

He replied to Patrick Shaw-Stewart's Salonika letter just after the battle at Bullecourt, which he described, listing the casualties and the decorations won. He also wrote, 'Most amusing. They treat me with great respect here. I like dealing with CRAs, Div and Corps Commanders in the same way that you love Duchesses.'

173 Brigade returned to the line on 29 May; they were, Freyberg reported, in excellent spirits in spite of the heavy casualties and the difficult times they had been through. The line now was directly to the north of Bullecourt, in the area of Mort Homme, but it was a quiet sector in comparison to their last one, and they managed to hold it without many casualties.

In the second week of June Freyberg received a visit from Winston Churchill, who, out of office, was on a private visit as a guest of the French government. After lunch he was shown a copy of orders for a raid in which the last paragraph stated that the object was 'to get a prisoner (only one is wanted)'. On reading this Churchill jumped to the erroneous conclusion that all the other prisoners were to be slaughtered. Freyberg continued: 'Churchill appeared greatly moved by this and, taking me on one side, said, with an almost ingenuous expression on his face, "My boy – you should pray for humility".'

On 12 June 173 Brigade received a warning order to attack and capture part of the Hindenburg Line in conjunction with a brigade of 21 Division on their left. This division, from a different corps, had already captured the front line of the objective, and asked that 173 Brigade should be invited to capture the enemy front line opposite to them, and then both brigades, starting off on even terms the following morning, should attack at 'Tunnel trench', the main Hindenburg Line. Freyberg and 173 Brigade wanted to accomplish the whole operation in one attack because, once they had captured the front line, they felt they would have 'advertised' their ultimate intention.

This brought Freyberg up against a problem which he was to

encounter on a number of occasions in both world wars, namely, what to do if he strongly disagreed with his superior officers over the conduct of future operations. On this occasion the divisional and the corps commanders concerned could not agree on the plan, so the method of attack was settled by General Allenby (then commanding the Third Army) who ruled in favour of two attacks being made. Freyberg had no confidence in the plan and after 'two miserable days and nights' went to his divisional commander, General Hew Fanshawe, prepared to refuse to do it. Fanshawe warned him that if he did refuse he would be sent home and someone else – who would be largely ignorant of the ground and the men – would be brought in at the last moment. He also told him that the attack was only one part of a big scheme and that his section had to co-operate as a counter-irritant, to prevent the enemy from moving troops to reinforce the armies opposite Messines, where the Allies were carrying out another series of attacks. Freyberg knew that the last part of this argument was true, and he also realised that if he refused to take part his men would learn why he had been sent home, which would unsettle them more and lessen their already doubtful chances of success. He felt himself 'in a cleft stick'.

The 2/3 and 2/4 Battalions were concentrated at St Leger, ready for the first part of the attack which was launched at 2.50 a.m. on 15 June. After stiff fighting they captured 1,100 yards of the Hindenburg front line, with 43 prisoners, who were mostly wounded. The remainder of the Brigade assembled there on the night of 15 June, but at midnight the enemy attacked and recaptured part of the recently occupied line. Freyberg's troops now had to recapture their assembly area without any artillery support, and then continue with the main attack at 3.10 a.m. The assembly area recapture was not completed till 3 a.m., leaving no time to reorganise for the bigger attack, and the men went forward in a disorganised state.

The enemy were expecting them at Tunnel trench, and 173 Brigade's casualties were substantial; the few men who reached the objective were immediately repulsed by the counter-attack of a German 'Sturmtruppen' battalion. By dusk the extent of their defeat was confirmed. Freyberg wrote, '174 Brigade relieved the remnants of our battalions, and a very unhappy and dispirited lot of men moved back to Ypres where we refitted'.

He summed up his feelings as follows:

The judgement of but few commanders is so implicitly trusted by their superiors that they can refuse to carry out an attack which involves even a simple straightout issue. Yet, when the issue concerns no other troops save those under your command, it is the duty of the commander to refuse to commit his men to a bad plan.

During the war it fell to the lot of most commanders to experience a disaster similar in cause and nature to our abortive attack, on 15–16 June, to capture the Hindenburg Line.

It falls to the lot of fewer commanders, however, to foresee such a disaster in the making, and when this happens, there is often a situation in which to the uninitiated, there seems to be a nicely struck balance between subordination and stupidity. But when such an issue involves large bodies of troops no junior commander, after having registered his opinion, has a right to prejudice the success of operations by using undue pressure.

The really difficult part of the whole business for me was that I had to tell my commanding officers I had confidence in the attack. I know that my last statement will shock a number of readers, and many have suggested that the course they would have adopted would have been to avoid expressing any opinion upon the plan. They quite naturally don't know that, during the period before any attack, each of the harassed unit commanders would ask, probably a dozen times, what you thought were the chances of success. In fact, they would come to ask you when you were in bed, and even when you were in your bath. There is no way of hoodwinking people over such a vital question.

This situation was not Freyberg's only reason to feel despondent. He was looking forward to seeing his brother Paul, who had recently arrived in France to join 1 New Zealand Division, which was fighting in the Messines area 10 miles south of Ypres, not all that far from where Bernard was, near Bullecourt. In the second week in June, during heavy fighting at Basseville, Paul was mortally wounded and on 18 June 1917, on his way to hospital in England, died at Boulogne and was buried in the military cemetery there. In later life Bernard often quoted the lines written on Paul's death by his friend Elsdon Best, the New Zealand poet:

> Today the lonely winds are loose
> And crying goes the rain.
> While here we walk the field they knew
> The dead who died in pain.
> The fields that wait the slow hours long
> For sounds that shall not come.
> In other fields, in other earth
> The laughing hearts are dumb.

The next month was mainly spent reorganising and absorbing new drafts. On 16 July 173 Brigade occupied the Beaucamp sector, but it was a quiet time and they were even able to enjoy the mass of wild strawberries that they found in the Havrincourt Woods. They were relieved by 27 Infantry Brigade on 29 July, and moved by rail to the Mannin Training area close to Arras.

The move was the prelude to their participation in the Third Battle of Ypres, later known as Passchendaele. At the end of August 58 Division was transferred from the Third Army to the Fifth Army and became part of General Sir Ivor Maxse's XVIII Corps. Maxse's first words to Freyberg after they met were, 'I hate you bloody gallant Brigadier-Generals – what the devil do *you* know about training men?' Maxse had a disagreeable technique for imposing his will, but militarily he was extremely able, and the well-trained New Zealand Division of the Second World War owed much of its excellence to the methods devised by General Maxse and taught to Freyberg in 1917. 173 Brigade spent the first three weeks of August in the training area under Maxse's direction, commencing early in the morning and carrying on until it was dark, often until the men almost dropped with fatigue.

Towards the end of August the Brigade moved to a camp near to the battlefield, and on 11 September took over the line in front of St Julien, where they first saw the appalling geographical difficulties that were to confront them. The name Passchendaele is synonymous with war fought in the mud. Freyberg describes it thus:

> The morasses of mud, which paralysed the British attacks, were caused by the breakdown of the drainage systems of Flanders, once the shelling by both sides had destroyed the culverts and small streams. Even the slopes of hills were reduced to the consistency of a bog, while the valleys of the Stroombeek, the Raveek and the Haanbeek became impenetrable marshes.

As a result, Freyberg went on:

> During some of the fighting, attacking companies waded knee-deep, and often up to their waists in mud before gaining their objective, while, in many cases, whole waves disappeared, or were held captives in the mud within speaking distance of the British line, until they either died from exposure or were blown to pieces by artillery fire. It was a most wicked battle and the night after any attack, men with ladders and ropes worked away in the most appalling danger, trying to save those who were bogged.
>
> There were no roads, just a few shellswept duckboard tracks, and wheeled transport could not reach the gun positions with ammunition. Packhorses carried forward eight rounds at a time, and the slaughter of these animals, to say nothing of their leaders, threatened to cause a horse shortage. Advancing the guns in this fluid country was a problem which had

[110]

to be solved; in some cases a light railway was laid on brushwood or any other available debris, and the guns were taken forward in pieces and reassembled.

In the autumn of 1917 Passchendaele and its ridge of high ground to the east of Ypres was the scene of some of the most costly and bitter fighting of the entire war. The German defences had been strengthened with numerous 'pill-boxes', or concrete redoubts, which bristled with machine-guns. These were difficult to reduce with artillery fire, and were fatal to attacking infantry.

Freyberg's final battle began badly when, on 14 September, he had to carry out another minor, but disastrous, operation. This time he was attacking in front of St Julien with a company, to capture Winnipeg crossroads and the cemetery:

Most of our men lost themselves in the dark, or became bogged, and several ' wandered about between our lines for days. On 16 September one of our low-flying aeroplanes reported that three men in khaki had signalled from a shell-hole in no-man's-land. An officer went out in broad daylight and brought these men in, who stated on oath that, the morning after the attack, they saw a party of our men, after being disarmed and made prisoner, bayoneted by the enemy. They said the men's screams were dreadful. They could do nothing because their rifles were jammed with mud and out of action.

The large attack the brigade was to take part in was to be launched by the Second and Fifth Armies on the morning of 20 September upon an eight mile front, and with tanks co-operating with them along the St Julien road. The 2/4 Battalion of the London Regiment was to deliver the attack and capture the valley between Schuler and Worst farms. It was to form up through 2/3 Battalion, which was then holding the line and suffering badly from the mud and cold.

In the afternoon of 19 September, a few hours before the troops were due to move to their assembly areas, Brigade headquarters received reports that 2/3 Battalion was in trouble, and that men were drifting back from their positions. Their Commanding Officer was condoning their conduct by being sympathetic rather than sending stragglers back to their posts. It was a difficult situation, because the enemy was aware of the impending attack and was putting the forward troops under heavy bombardment. Freyberg held a conference in a pill-box forward of St Julien at which the Commanding Officer concerned, Colonel Beresford, and all his company commanders were present. They were ordered to get matters in hand before the concentration began, and the pill-box was shelled as they talked. The officers ran from the pill-box in pairs; the company commanders to their outpost line and Freyberg and his runner back to their headquarters to arrange final details for the attack. They had gone 50 yards when they were bowled over by a 5.9-inch shell which burst in the mud at their feet. 'We were badly shaken,' Freyberg reported, 'but managed to crawl on all-fours a distance of three hundred yards through deep mud to a first-aid post, where they bound up the runner's head and chest and my chest and thigh which now rendered me immobile.'

Freyberg's account continues:

> A change of command at this stage of an attack (owing to the shortness of time to grasp all the details) meant either a change of policy, or leaving all arrangements in the hands of subordinate commanders: and as neither of the alternatives would enhance our chance of success, I decided to keep the fact that I had been wounded from the troops, to command the brigade from brigade battle headquarters by telephone, to send the brigade major round the troops in the assembly area and to hand over command to Colonel Dann when the objectives were captured some time during the following morning.
>
> The approach march and assembly were difficult. It was a pitch dark night, and as the men marched down the St Julien road they were heavily shelled. After passing St Julien, where the men left the road, they had to be roped together by platoons to prevent individuals from getting lost. The artillery of both sides were harassing the forward areas; we to prevent the enemy relief from taking place, and they to prevent us from assembling. And to add to our difficulties, it was raining as we waded in with mud over our knees. The men were just as frightened of being swallowed up in the mud as of being blown to bits by the enemy shells.
>
> At one o'clock in the morning we received the welcome message by telephone that the assembly was complete. This was a great relief to us, and at 5.40 a.m. (20 September) the barrage opened, and the Second and Fifth Armies had launched the attack which is known in history as 'the Battle of the Menin Road'.
>
> All our objectives were captured to plan, but not many prisoners were taken by our men. The incident of a few days before [the bayoneting] was too fresh in our minds.

Just before noon Colonel Dann was brought in to take over command, and Freyberg was moved back to the casualty clearing station (CCS). It was the eighth time he had been wounded and evacuated, but he found that, in spite of the large numbers of casualties at Remy Siding CCS, the scale and extent of the facilities were far greater than those he had experienced earlier in the war. The hospital, he wrote, seemed large enough to take a whole army:

It was a town of big Indian marquees that covered many acres. They had wooden floors and were comfortably furnished, whilst the nursing staff, equipment and doctors were sufficient even for the thousands that passed through in a single day during a battle.

The constant stream of patients at the casualty clearing station was registered at a central registry – there was no confusion – and hot food was always ready for those who could eat it. The badly wounded cases usually arrived wrapped in blankets, without a stitch of clothing and with no personal belongings except an identity disc, and, perhaps, a wrist watch.

When the wounded arrived, they were hung with labels which stated the treatment and drugs that had been given forward in the line, especially in event of preparations of opium having been administered and injections for anti-tetanus. These data were now transferred to the patient's chart, giving a continuous history of the case from the moment of becoming a casualty.

But it was the organisation of the operating theatre that amazed those who saw it. The excising of bits of shell or bullets when possible was done at once. Simple cases were X-rayed under a screen, and the body marked with pencil, before taking the patients to the operating theatre where they took their place in a long queue of cases.

Inside the tent eight teams of operators were working simultaneously. As soon as one patient was finished, he was carried away, still under the anaesthetic, to make room for another anaesthetised man who was put on the operating table. I waited in a queue for my turn for the anaesthetic, which was given to me by a woman doctor.

When I came to after my operation, I was in bed with sheets and hot water bottles; while the stertorous gasps of half-anaesthetised men were coming from most of the beds. At daylight all of us who could be moved were taken back to the base hospitals to make room for the next day's stream of wounded.

Freyberg had been admitted to the CCS on 20 September, and then evacuated to England on 25 September. He was taken to Bryanston Square Hospital in London, and the fact that he had been seriously wounded was in the newspapers on 2 October. Among his first visitors was Cynthia Asquith, who recorded the main facts of Freyberg's condition and convalescence over the next three months.[2]

Freyberg had indeed been seriously wounded. He had been hit in five places by the heavy shell that had burst at his feet, right through a lung in one place, and in his thigh was a hole the size of his fist. Lady Cynthia described him as 'riddled like St Sebastian' and very white and subdued when she first visited him. She went to see him every week for the two months he was in hospital, and during the first weeks there were fears that he might lose a leg – or even his life. On 15 October she recorded that his thigh wound had gone septic, and that he was looking and feeling very miserable and ill. But after the first month he began to improve, and by the middle of November he was starting to get up. By the end of the month he had left hospital.[7]

On 1 December 1917 Lady Cynthia went down to see him in Brighton and he met her at the station:

> He is staying at the Royal York, but we drove straight to the Metropole for luncheon. He was looking better and had a fine appetite. With his youthful face and the insignia of his anomalous rank (his medals and preposterous number of gold stripes*), he is very conspicuous and much stared at – obsequious deference from the waiters. I insisted on taking him to Professor Severn, the phrenologist, but he was hopelessly out about him, marking him low for self-esteem and concentration. Freyberg's contemptuous indignation was such that he threw his chart into the mud directly he got out of the house. Twice it was picked up and returned to him. We went to the Kitchener Hospital to have his wound dressed. We had tea at the dear Old Royal York, then I made him go and rest while I read in the lounge. We walked to dinner at the Metropole. His eyes shine and he becomes poeticised talking of military adventures, and I was touched to see his eyes fill with tears once when he was talking about his men. I find him very, very attractive.
>
> He drove me to the station to catch the 9.40. He made love to me all day – with simplicity and sweetness and I don't know what to do. Several times he said he thought he had better not see me any more, and I suppose I ought to take him at his word: it is the candle that should withdraw, the moth cannot, but it would require considerable unselfishness on my part. I should hate to give him up altogether – conscience tells me I should . . . He kept asking me if I would have married him had I been free. I enjoyed the day very much – injudicious as it was.[2]

Four days later Cynthia Asquith was again confiding to her diary about Freyberg:

> I went to stay one night at Seaford House – lunching with Margot and Lord Howard de Walden. Freyberg called for me there and we dined at the Trocadero, and sat till late listening to music. He interested me enormously. He has the stamp of a high calling which I have hardly ever recognised in anyone. I believe him to be a genius. He said he would 'do his damnedest' to forget me when he went out. I have never had the type of

---

* The gold stripes denoted the number of times he had been wounded.

admirer who hates the 'yoke' and I respect him for it, and yet he wants the friendship side of the relationship and complains of loneliness.[2]

One of Cynthia Asquith's characteristics was that she was exceedingly vain. Her diaries abound with examples of her vanity, recorded with such artless abandon as to indicate that they were kept mainly for her own amusement and were not intended for publication – or at any rate not in her lifetime. In fact they did not appear in print until 1968, eight years after her death, and even then there were difficulties, as the (unsigned) Introduction to them explains: 'She wrote with the be-wildering fullness of a still leisured age – and very, very frankly, so that even now many excisions have been made for reasons other than length, before it was possible to publish this selection covering the period of the First World War.' Almost certainly Freyberg knew nothing about the diary, either at the time or later. He had no knowledge therefore that his remarks had been recorded within a few hours of their being uttered. Some of his comments and observations would now seem melodramatic if they were torn out of the context of the extraordinary background and atmosphere of the 1914–18 war. But if the diary had not been kept very little would now be known about his life during those four months from September 1917 to January 1918.

Cynthia Asquith was obviously attracted to Freyberg and liked his gentle manner, which was combined with forthright views. She was aware of his growing reputation, and was flattered by his attention. There is a passage in which she mentioned their lunch together in April to Ambrose McEvoy, who was painting her portrait, and who also painted a portrait of Freyberg later in the war: 'he congratulated me on the feather in my cap of having shared Freyberg's one lunch with him – said it would arouse great jealousy' and she purred with pleasure when 'Freyberg told me Ian Hamilton had said I was "the most beautiful creature in the world"'.[2]

For his part Freyberg was greatly taken by her beauty, now at its zenith, and found her intelligent and sympathetic companionship stimulating. He was at last beginning to recover from his multiple wounds, and Cynthia helped to restore his zest for life. However, many references in her diaries for December 1917 and January 1918 reveal that he had come to realise that there was no long-term future in their relationship.

Shortly before Bernard was wounded at Passchendaele, in August 1917, Barbara McLaren's husband, Francis, had been killed in a flying accident in Scotland while serving with the Royal Flying Corps. Barbara did not keep a diary at this period, but subsequent references

BERNARD FREYBERG, VC

in Bernard's letters to her show that they met each other while he was convalescing.

On 2 January 1918 Freyberg went to Buckingham Palace to be presented with his Victoria Cross by King George V. The King noted in his diary: 'Held an Investiture at 12 when I gave decorations to over 300 officers including 8 VCs.'[8] Afterwards Freyberg went to stay at Stanway in Gloucestershire, the home of the Wemyss family. There is a story in Cynthia's diary of one of the children there: 'Gabriel, showing herself a real daughter of Eve, sat cosily in Freyberg's lap, toying with his VC, and stroking his hair.'[2]

1917 had been a year of mixed fortune for Freyberg. He had earned his Brigade and commanded it with distinction, but he had had to lead it into situations which he knew would end in failure and unnecessary casualties. He had also received the most severe wounds he ever had to endure. Secretly, perhaps, he was relieved when these wounds terminated his association with 173 Brigade; for although, in later life, he was a loyal member of the RND and 29 Divisional Associations, he rarely participated in anything to do with 58 Division. Also the death of his brother Paul had greatly upset Bernard, and he was much saddened too when Patrick Shaw-Stewart was killed six months later, on 30 December 1917. In addition Oc Asquith had been grievously injured on 20 December, only two days after assuming command of one of the Naval Brigades.

Freyberg left England again for France on 11 January 1918. Next day he arrived at Third Army Headquarters at Albert and was writing to Barbara McLaren: 'I had a long and tiresome journey here with many luggage difficulties . . . I wonder if you know how grateful I feel for your help and companionship during those last few days in town – I shall always remember our little party on the 10th.' A few days later he wrote again: 'Dearest – I got your letter dated the 11th, I am glad you wrote it and glad you felt sad I was going, rather a mean thing to be glad about anybody being sad.'

Freyberg visited Oc Asquith in hospital at Le Treport:

He was having a bloody time while they were trying to save his leg [he wrote to Barbara on 21 January]. Yesterday I heard from his surgeon to say they had operated and taken off his leg (they must have meant foot) for which I am delighted, because I felt sure they would never be able to do anything with it as it was, and all that suffering would be needless. I wrote to Violet advising her to come out. So I expect she will be at Le T now . . . My love to you dear,

Bernard.

Freyberg was staying at Third Army headquarters. It was the practice at this time to keep a few senior officers at each army headquarters to fill vacancies when they occurred – from promotion, sickness or casualties – and Freyberg waited for ten days for the next appointment to arise. On the night of 12 January he dined with General Julian Byng, the Army Commander, who impressed him with his intelligence, friendliness and simple mode of living. Byng was an exceptional officer, whose daring plan for the battle of Cambrai on 19 November 1917, with its then novel employment of tanks on the battlefield, made a lasting impression on tactics in the First World War.[9] When the meal was over Byng asked him how he wanted to spend his time while he was waiting. Freyberg asked if he could read the orders and instructions for the battle of Cambrai, and was given access to them including the General's secret files and his correspondence with Sir Douglas Haig.

Freyberg also spent some time accompanying the Army Commander on training, and one afternoon (18 January) he listened to a discussion between the Fifth Army Commander, General Gough, and one of his corps commanders, General Maxse, whom he already knew, as they talked about 'the sudden change of policy and the taking-over from the French of the front down to La Fère'. At the age of twenty-eight Freyberg was being given an insight into the higher direction of war, and for the first time seeing the workings of an army staff from within:

> The conversation between General Gough and General Maxse made a great impression on me. I had never before heard a plan of campaign discussed by two such senior commanders and I gathered from their conversation that:
>
> (a) The Fifth Army had been given an impossible task to do. That they had too few men either to hold the line in its present condition, or to put it in a satisfactory state of defence before the Germans launched their attack in the spring, and
>
> (b) That even if we had sufficient men to dig the necessary defences, we hadn't sufficient engineers' material (i.e. wire and pickets, etc.).
>
> I learned also that the British General Headquarters Reserves available in event of a crisis, after the Fifth Army moves were completed, would not be more than seven weak divisions.

In addition Gough and Maxse accurately predicted the course of the impending German onslaught in March 1918, just two months away.

88 Brigade: Bailleul, Last Ypres and Lessines

The Allies' war situation at the beginning of 1918 was precarious. The Russian Revolution had deprived them of their 'second front' in Europe, so that the Germans were able to transfer a large number of divisions from the east to their armies in the west. The French Army had been decimated, and the mutinies of 1917 had called into question the reliability of their forces in the field. The Germans were known to be massing for a final onslaught and almost certainly this would be launched before the main American armies (the US had declared war on Germany in April 1917) could be deployed in Europe. The resolution and steadiness of the British Army on the Western Front, therefore, was going to be of crucial importance in determining the outcome of the war.

On 21 January Freyberg was appointed to command 88 Infantry Brigade, then in the Ypres–Passchendaele area. This was a regular brigade in the renowned 29 Division, which he had served alongside during the Gallipoli campaign. He was pleased with the appointment, he told Barbara McLaren, and admired his new divisional commander, Major-General Sir Beauvoir de Lisle, as a soldier. Field Marshal Birdwood once referred to de Lisle as 'a real thruster. Everyone hates him as he is a brute, with no thoughts for others, rude to everyone.'[1] When the officers at Third Army headquarters heard that Freyberg was going to 29 Division they told him stories of officers who had lasted only a few days with de Lisle. He was prepared therefore for any kind of reception from his new divisional commander, and on his arrival de Lisle gave him an assessment of the characters of his battalion commanders and his brigade staff officers that was detailed and accurate. Freyberg noticed in his divisional mess that all the officers listened in silence to everything de Lisle said.

Freyberg took over command at Wieltje dug-outs at 7 p.m. on 22 January and spent all that night until after daylight next morning reading defence schemes, scanning maps and generally putting himself into the Ypres picture. On 26 January the Brigade took over the line again and concentrated its energies on wiring the outposts, which were in an insecure condition.

On 4 February it moved back to the Winnezeele area to train, and became part of the general reserve of seven divisions, ready to move by bus or rail to any part of the Allied front when required. While there Freyberg experienced de Lisle's intransigence:

> Part of our training task while back at Winnezeele was a brigade ceremonial parade, when the division commander inspected the turnout and smartness of the men, and presented medal ribbons to those who had won decorations in action. This parade required a large piece of flat ground to allow room for the brigade to march past. When I told General de Lisle we couldn't find a suitable field, his reply was characteristic: 'I'll find you one this afternoon.'
>
> He took me to a piece of ground that was half under water and said: 'What's wrong with this one?' 'It's under water, sir.' 'Drain it, my boy,' was his answer as he rode away; and drain it we had to. It took us three days but we had our ceremonial parade.
>
> I give this small instance to show the character of our general. Probably no other man would have achieved a brigade ceremonial parade under the adverse weather conditions. It was just the same in battle. Once he had decided upon his plan, which he did after considerable thought, he never altered it. He was a very difficult man to serve, but in the long run he was far more satisfactory to be under than the good-natured commander who listened too much to the difficulties from below and altered the plan so many times that eventually everybody was muddled and uncertain. With General de Lisle you knew where you were.

It was while he was waiting for 'the blow to fall', the German spring offensive, that two letters reached Freyberg from Barrie. The first was dated 25 January 1918:

> If you smell tobacco in this page you are to conceive it coming from your pipe. It was immensely good of you to give it to me, and here am I showing my gratitude . . . We have now got the chimney of my study under control, and a nation that can do that can assuredly win the war. We really succeeded

[119]

in accomplishing this by following the most orthodox methods at the front. We made a powerful attack before which the smoke fell back, and then we quickly brought up our reserves (which were available briefly) and pushed forward during the period while the enemy was broken. Thus, he could not counter-attack; all the time you were explaining this method to me you little knew that what I was thinking of was my chimney.

I saw Winston C yesterday and he seemed very pleased to be able to say that it was he who gave you your commission. I suppose you saw Asquith in France. Lady Bonham Carter told me they were waiting longingly to hear from you about him, and now I see that he has had to lose his foot. I think the lady ought to give him hers as a substitute, instead of, in the old phrase, giving him her hand.

I shall be very glad to hear from you at any time, and to adapt an old Scottish proverb 'Be careful of yourself, and if you can't be careful, be as careful as you can'. You are just at the beginning of your career if all goes well.[2]

The second letter from Barrie was written on 18 February 1918:

We have again reached that time o' the month when we raise our eyes skywards as we walk abroad. We need no sermons to tell us that the moon has once again got past the coast defences. Some six millions more or less see her the moment she steals into light. She is not the popular light she was once, even lovers have scarce a good word for her. She reminds me of the English tourists who climbed a Scotch mountain to see the sun rise. They didn't want to see the sun rise. They wanted to lie abed, but they were driven to the exploit as something everybody must attempt once. The mountain was arduous and the adventurers were stout and when they did reach the top they were grumpy. So when the sun did rise they didn't think much of it, and they *hissed*. That is how we feel about the moon . . .

There have been some good things in the papers about Shaw-Stewart, mostly by school and college friends . . . It is obvious that if ever a boy lay on the knees of the gods it was SS. A poem in the *Eton Chronicle* says of him:

> What was hid in that supple being?
> What was hid in that subtle mould?
> Poise of power and thought far-seeing,
> Kindled stubble and alchemed gold;
> Scorn that would mock at Faith and feeling
> Wit as keen as a Damask blade,
> Yet could you draw and bind hearts to you,
> Never to find their trust betrayed.

I hope your leg is able to cope with all that mud, which must be more with you than even shells. Such a thing is war, you pause in a letter to carry in your runner as I might pause to put another log on the fire. That fire, by the way, would like to see you back at it again.[2]

On 7 March Freyberg and 88 Brigade took over part of the line from 8 Division, who were to replace them again in three weeks' time, and then carried on their defensive work. They suffered considerable bombardment and some gas shelling. On 14 March they went back to Poperinghe for a week. At 11 a.m. on 21 March the long expected news came through by signal that the Germans had started their big offensive on the Somme. Freyberg pleaded with the corps commander's ADC to intercede with his general to cancel his inspection of 88 Brigade which was due that same day, as they were getting ready for whatever operational tasks they might be given in the coming crisis. But the answer received stated that the corps commander had read up the necessary handbooks upon inspection of soldiers and was determined to air his knowledge.

The corps commander was General Hunter-Weston, who had commanded 29 Division at Gallipoli, and who, on writing to Freyberg to congratulate him on his command of 88 Infantry Brigade, had advised him to: 'Take it easy and do not overdo yourself in this mud. I shall want all your energies whenever the ground dries up and makes fighting possible. Then will come the time for us to kill Boshes.'[3]

'Hunter Bunter', as he was universally known, had a handlebar moustache and could have walked on to the stage of any production of *The Pirates of Penzance* as the epitome of a 'modern Major-General'; and he certainly turned the inspection of 21 March 1918 into an almost operatic farce. Before the inspection he sent an officer to Brigade HQ to demand, among other things, that there should be 'a subaltern's bedroom tastefully arranged; a kitchen cleaned up, and a good show of bones in the stock-pot; a water-cart as complete as possible; a clean mincing machine.' During the inspection great attention was paid as to whether the same blades were being used for mincing meat and bread, the different dishes that could be prepared with its aid; and when the bread blade was only discovered after a long hunt, completely rusty and filthy, further inspection of the mess ceased while the officers and men 'listened breathlessly to a list of diseases which were directly attribut-able to dirty mincing machines'. So excited was 'Hunter Bunter' that he forgot to inspect the rest of the not-so-clean kitchen.

As the inspection proceeded, 'Hunter Bunter' explained how to date the bones in the stock-pot, ran out of the bedroom when confronted with a picture of a naked woman beneath a piece of mistletoe, walked faster than anyone else, and finally discovered no spare parts in the Newfoundland Regiment's water-cart, but only a mangy ham bone. At this point all the staff officers shrieked with laughter, and the inspection was terminated. As Freyberg summed it all up:

[121]

It will seem inconceivable to all those who have not experienced the ironies of war, that while this comedy was being acted, the gallant Fifth Army were living a drama in real life, as with odds of 18 to 1 against them they were fighting it out, in many cases to a finish, only a few miles away.

The Germans had concentrated altogether 129 divisions, many of them from the Russian front, against the British Army. On 21 March 1918 (Freyberg's twenty-ninth birthday) they launched their attack against the Third and Fifth Armies on a 60-mile front with 62 of those divisions. The German objective was to drive a wedge between the British and the French south of Amiens with a view to separating their common front and forcing the British armies back towards the Channel ports. This would then leave the French to face the numerically superior German forces on their own. The six German armies assigned to this part of the plan were deployed as shown in the map.

The main attack by the 17 and 18 German Armies was to fall on the British Fifth Army under General Gough. But this did not become apparent for some days. Meanwhile, as soon as the direction and thrust of the main enemy attacks became clearer, it was part of the British defensive plan to start to denude other parts of the line in order to form reserves to plug the gaps.

Freyberg's own experiences during the last great German attack of the war followed much the same pattern as that of the battle. When the offensive began 88 Brigade and 29 Division were holding a sector of the Passchendaele salient at Poperinghe, to the north of where the main fighting was to take place. It was a sea of mud many feet deep which was kept in a fluid state by constant churning from artillery fire. The corps' reserve division (8 Division) was sent south almost immediately, to be followed shortly afterwards by the second reserve (35 Division). This left the troops that remained holding well over twice the normal frontage in the Ypres–Passchendaele sector (roughly 4,000 yards – the length of front supposed to be held by a division) and 88 Brigade was deployed thus for over a fortnight without any form of relief. Eventually, last of all the brigades, its turn came to go south, and it was replaced by a mangled and tired 123 Brigade from the front.

They had almost been sent south two days after 8 Division – and if this had happened they would have been completely destroyed. In the end Freyberg and his men marched out from the salient at 5 a.m. on 10 April for a planned rest of a day and a night; but as they left he was handed a signal that ordered him to embus his brigade immediately and

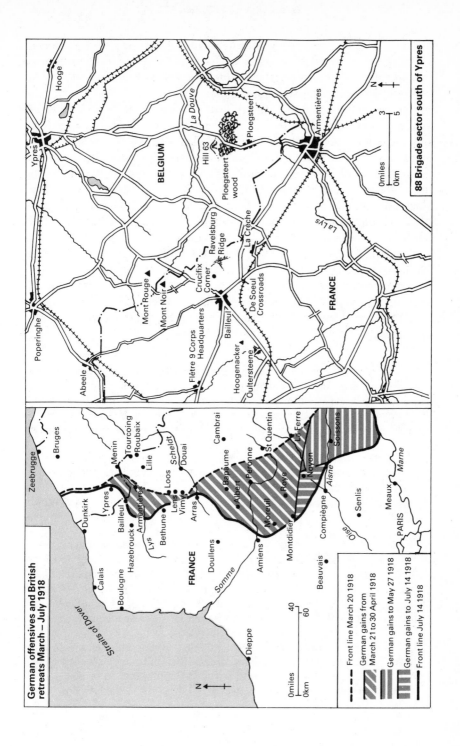

German offensives and British retreats March – July 1918

Zeebrugge
Bruges
Calais
Boulogne
Straits of Dover
Dieppe
Dunkirk
Ypres
Menin
Tourcoing
Roubaix
Lille
Bailleul
Armentières
Lens
Vimy
Arras
Douai
Scheldt
Cambrai
St Quentin
La Ferre
Soissons
Noyon
Aisne
Compiègne
Senlis
Meaux
Marne
PARIS
Beauvais
Oise
Montdidier
Roye
Moreuil
Albert
Bapaume
Peronne
Amiens
Somme
Doullens
FRANCE
Hazebrouck
Bethune
Lys

0 miles 40
0 km 60

N

- – – Front line March 20 1918
- German gains from March 21 to 30 April 1918
- German gains to May 27 1918
- German gains to July 14 1918
- —— Front line July 14 1918

88 Brigade sector south of Ypres

Poperinghe
Abeele
Hooge
Ypres
BELGIUM
La Douve
Ploegsteert
Hill 63
Ploegsteert wood
Armentières
La Crèche
Ravelsburg Ridge
Crucifix Corner
Mont Rouge
Mont Noir
Flêtre 9 Corps Headquarters
Bailleul
Hoogenacker
Oultersteene
De Soeul Crossroads
FRANCE
La Lys

N

0 miles 3
0 km 5

go to De Soeul crossroads where he would be met by a staff officer of IX Corps with orders. The signal ended 'you will be fighting on arrival this afternoon'. The originator was Headquarters Second Army, which by then had taken over some of the most threatened sectors previously the responsibility of the Fifth Army. De Soeul was in the area of Bailleul, which was defended by 25 Division and 34 Division, who were holding a long sector of the line and being strongly pressed by large enemy forces. For the battles which followed, 88 Brigade came under General Nicholson's 34 Division. At this stage Freyberg was lamenting: 'Here we were, wet through, caked with mud, weary from want of sleep and filthy from lack of baths – none of us having had our clothes off for twenty odd days, and immediately being thrown into another battle, which would keep us busy for a long time.'

While his Brigade was moving to its assembly area Freyberg went to IX Corps headquarters at Flêtre, where he found an emergency conference in progress. In addition to the corps commander, Lieutenant-General Hamilton Gordon, and several other generals, the Commander of the Second Army, General Sir Herbert Plumer, was also present. Freyberg's account continues:

> The situation now was as follows: there were no reserves in either the First or Second Army that had not been involved, except our Brigade Group, and there was a gap in the line of several miles. About this stage in the proceedings we arrived, and interrupted the gathering by knocking loudly and somewhat unceremoniously at the door. This drew an angry General:
>
> BRIGADIER GENERAL IX CORPS (angrily): 'What do you want?'
> GENERAL COMMANDING 88 INFANTRY BRIGADE: 'I command the 88th' (no time to say Brigade).
> BRIGADIER GENERAL IX CORPS (hurriedly and with show of welcome): 'Come in.'
>
> In an eager voice he announced me in a way that convinced me that my entry had interrupted a discussion as to our employment. The discussion now continued between the Corps and Army Commanders, at which I felt like a convicted prisoner, hearing a debate upon the method by which he was to be exterminated. The war map was put in front of General Plumer, while all the other generals leaned forward with their heads close together.
>
> COMMANDER IX CORPS TO GENERAL PLUMER: 'We might attack with him here,' indicating an enemy lodgment being driven back by a sweep of his hand across the map from north-west to south-east. 'Or else here,' indicating a gap which existed between 34 Division and the Division on its right.

General Plumer sat quite silent, and nodded his head to show that he heard, but gave no decision. Just then a wire came in saying: 'Enemy working north-west along the valley from Steenwerck in the direction of Bailleul.' They knew that should Bailleul go in the next two days, it threatened the whole retreat of the 34 and 25 Divisions. This situation was critical. More wires arrived, but only gave confirmation of earlier reports. A telephone conversation now took place between the GOC 34 Division and the Corps Commander, on the question of withdrawing to another line; this took General Plumer's attention for a moment from the map. When the conversation was finished he turned to me, and in a kind and considerate voice said: 'Where are your Brigade?' To which I answered, 'En route to Bailleul.' 'Will they arrive by 4 p.m. in Bailleul?' To which I said, 'No, about 4.30 as well as I can say.'

General Plumer then took a pencil out of his pocket and placing the point on the map at a place called La Crèche, on the right of the main Bailleul–Armentières road, said, 'Take your Brigade group to here; you must fight it out with the utmost resistance; there must be no withdrawal until the others have got out of that salient.' This was a very definite and feasible order, giving us a mission with a definite degree of resistance.

GENERAL 88 BRIGADE TO GENERAL PLUMER: 'We are in buses, sir, can we risk them under fire to get our men up there quickly?'
GENERAL PLUMER: 'My dear boy, the situation is critical, you cannot consider the loss of a few buses. Take them up as far as you can to gain time.'

Freyberg obtained maps with the latest information about the positions of British and German troops, and then went to the De Soeul crossroads to redirect his brigade, which had set off for battle in London omnibuses. Here the men debussed and began their advance on La Crèche. It was a dispiriting march as the road was jammed with civilian refugees, ammunition and supply wagons, field and heavy artillery, ambulances and fragments of broken units, 'the salvage of a beaten army, drifting back on Bailleul'. Rifle fire was turned on them as they neared La Crèche, and they reached their final battle position advancing in diamond battle formation through a brigade of field artillery who were endeavouring to keep back enemy artillery.

Brigade headquarters was established behind a mangel clump on the Bailleul Road, and the brigade then started to fight. Every hour they gathered more troops, as everyone who came down the main road lost or without orders was collected and reorganised into auxiliary companies. By the night of 10–11 April the troops under Freyberg's orders were:

3 Battalions of Infantry
2 Companies of Machine-Gunners
2 Companies of Royal Engineers
1 Battalion Pioneers
1 Section Cyclists
1 Light Trench Mortar Battery
6 Batteries of 18-pounders
2 Batteries of 4.5-Howitzers
1 Battery of 60-Pounders

... and in addition 600 stragglers from all units were organised into companies and were used as the tactical situation demanded.

88 Brigade hung on to their positions, while the infantry of 34 Division and 147 Brigade were withdrawn through them, in spite of the fact that they were nearly surrounded and were being very hard-pressed by the Germans who at times were only a few yards away. On 10 April units counter-attacked at dusk, and then managed to slip away that night in the resulting confusion. In the Neuve-Eglise sector on the left of the British position the enemy found and eventually occupied the weak position in the line. The divisional commander, General Nicholson, gave orders for 88 Brigade to withdraw when his own troops were clear of the salient, as by 11 April the position had become untenable.

The men were so worn out that they fell asleep if halted, even when standing up, so extra special care had to be taken not to leave anyone behind. In the late afternoon the German artillery started to shell with an 11-inch high-velocity gun, destroying the headquarters of one battalion and a stable beside Freyberg's brigade headquarters. Freyberg and the other commanders were in a cellar dictating orders for the defence of the new position at Ravelsburg Ridge. By dusk the divisional headquarters had been reconnected by telephone, and all arrangements for withdrawal were complete. At about 9.30 p.m. Field Marshal Haig's Special Order of the Day, issued on 11 April, was sent through to the commanders, who were ordered to read it to their men. The final paragraph stated:

There is no other course open to us but to fight it out. Every position must be held to the last man: there must be no retirement. With our backs to the wall and believing in the justice of our cause each one of us must fight on to the end. The safety of our homes and the freedom of mankind alike depend upon the conduct of each one of us at this critical moment.[4]

The withdrawal order from 34 Division was therefore cancelled, and 88 Brigade was instructed to fight it out where they stood. Freyberg knew that his men were in a desperate state, and that their line was badly smashed in one place. The Germans had already occupied all the high ground to their left rear, and come next morning would be shooting into their backs. Freyberg told his divisional commander that, if they stayed in their present positions, two hours of daylight would see the men of his brigade either killed or taken prisoner, which would leave a gap in their lines of many miles, whereas if they withdrew now in the dark, they could re-form a new continuous line based on the Ravelsburg Ridge. Nicholson referred the situation to the Army Commander, and eventually to General Headquarters, and Freyberg was told that the orders were to stay where they were, but that if the situation really was as he claimed he could take the responsibility for the withdrawal and justify his actions afterwards. And so the original plan for withdrawal was reinstated, and he started to move his brigade back at 11 p.m.

The withdrawal was supposed to be completed by 2 a.m., with three hours to move back 2 miles, leaving a further three hours to dig a new defensive position before first light. The Worcestershires withdrew on time at midnight, but there was no sign of the Monmouthshires for two and a half hours. 'I went up in rather a panic, and met Colonel Evans just coming away,' Freyberg continues. 'He reported "withdrawal complete", as he passed our brigade headquarters at 3 a.m.'

We closed our headquarters and started back to Ravelsburg Ridge. The enemy machine-guns seemed very close, and as there were no troops between us and the enemy we didn't waste any time. Just as we started to come away, one of the brigade signallers said: 'What are we to do with the two wounded men?' It then came out that when the barn had been knocked down by the enemy shelling, two men had been extricated, badly wounded. They had been dressed and fed, but so far no action had been taken to evacuate them. There was nothing left but to carry them on our backs. We couldn't leave them behind. It was that journey back that made me realise how done we were. My voice had completely gone and carrying this not very heavy man, which normally would have been nothing, made me move very slowly, and many times, when going up a small rise, my legs lost all power of movement.

When we got nearly back to our fresh position, we came up with some other stretcher-bearers, who took over our wounded. They had been wonderfully uncomplaining, and so grateful for not being left; even when we jolted their broken limbs, they encouraged us.

After the withdrawal, when they had reached their new position, Freyberg went to 2 Battalion, Hampshire Regiment with Colonel

Westmoreland, its CO, to see how they were digging. It was an hour before daylight.

> When we arrived, we found the whole battalion asleep, lying in every kind of position. They lay there with their arms limply by their sides, lying in heaps like great fish, in a trench not more than a foot deep . . . The men in some cases had fallen asleep as they dug; they worked till they dropped, all knowing that within an hour or two they would be under heavy fire again.
>
> Westmoreland, Brown [a South African lieutenant] and I went about shaking the men; but they were past rousing, so we let them sleep and trusted to Providence, and our hope that the enemy were as tired as we were. Anyhow, they didn't come on until too late, and when they did we were dug in and awake again. The two or three hours sleep revived the men, and tided them over until the arrival of 59 Division, who relieved us early on the morning of 15 April.

They went back to Croix de Poperinghe for a rest in billets in front of Mont Noir. That afternoon a staff officer of 34 Division, Major Tower, came with orders for the Brigade to go and assemble near Hooge-nacker, ready to counter-attack the Haegedorne line, as 59 Division had been heavily attacked near the Crucifix Corner line, and had been driven back suffering heavy casualties. Freyberg then sent for his battalion commanders:

> When they arrived I gave them a meal. They went to sleep between the two courses, while my Brigade Major lay asleep face downward on a stone floor. Major Tower and I walked the floor, drinking whisky to keep awake. I don't think any of us will forget that conference – we were all in; we had all lost our voices and our grip on things was slipping. I read the counter-attack scheme to a snoring audience, waking individuals when wanted by pulling their hair and saying: 'Here you! Wake up!' And then detailing off their part in the scheme, following up with each battalion commander in turn. When we had finished, we gave them hot coffee and turned them out into the night.
>
> Our great fear now was – would the Battalion Commanders be able to rouse their men, and move them to the position in time, or would they go back to their headquarters, and doze off to sleep as they had in mine?

After several minutes Freyberg and his groom set off on horses to visit each battalion, and discovered the same situation as at brigade head-quarters – colonels reading orders to snoring company commanders. Then something unexpected happened:

> About midnight several Germans walked into our lines and one, who was asleep, drove a cart through our outposts. This cheered our men consider-

ably: they said: 'The Germans are more done than we are.' We got the prisoners and told them that we had no use for them, and were sending them back, to which the sergeant said: 'Don't send us back; we will work very hard'... Of course we had no intention of sending them back, we only wanted to find out what state they were in.

The next day was uneventful, and about midday on 17 April horsemen in French grey uniform were seen at the fringe of the woods in front of Mont Noir – the French cavalry had arrived. They sent their horses back and dug a reserve line. Freyberg reported that 'everything alive and eatable immediately disappeared. They quite lived up to their reputation in this respect.' He added, 'They also gallantly came forward and helped our stretcher-bearers who were in difficulty carrying injured men on a shelled slope. On the evening of 19 April they were told that the big German offensive was to resume on them the following morning, 20 April':

At 3 next morning to the stroke, the whole crests of Mont Noir, Mont Rouge and Mont Vidaine in rear, were a sheet of flame; the air was filled with a noise like flocks of birds flying towards the German lines; and then came the welcome sound of hundreds of French 75s in action, followed by the flashing crash of thousands of high explosive shells, bursting in front of our lines. We knew then that the French infantry division had arrived, and the most desperate part of our rearguard battle was finished. The French counter-preparation swept and searched all the enemy approaches in front of our lines for two miles back, and continued to do so until after daylight, which prevented the enemy assembling to attack us.

All that remained for them now was to prepare to hand over the position to their relief, which would take place on the night of 20–21 April. The handing over was funny enough. The Assistant Staff Captain, an Australian, Captain Seabrook, did the handing over of such stores as there were; he couldn't speak French and the French Adjutant couldn't speak English, so they handed over in German, while sitting a little away, the old French Regimental Commander (who was about sixty-five) refused to discuss the position of our line, the enemy, the defence scheme, or anything to do with the tactical situation. All he wanted to do was to tell me about his mistress he had left in Amiens.

I can see him sitting on the ground kissing his hand, or rather the tips of his fingers, repeating in a fervent voice every few minutes: '*Elle est adorable*' – '*Elle est magnifique*'. The attitude of the French colonel amused us all very much at the time. Anyhow it made us all wonder if we didn't take things just a little too seriously.

The relief itself was simple. It was a moonlight night and the 401 Regiment of French Infantry (part of 133 Division) looked magnificent as they marched in, in step, with their large packs, with the extra pair of boots on top. They were in wonderful form, as well they might be. They were part of the French Groupe d'Armées de reserve and had been out of the line for months near Rheims. We handed over, and marched out to our camp near Abeele.

After the action the commander of 34 Division, General Nicholson, under whom 88 Brigade had been serving, wrote the following report:

88 Infantry Brigade
(Brigadier-General B. C. Freyberg, VC, DSO)

This Brigade came under my orders on the 10th April. Throughout the succeeding days it showed a gallantry and tenacity well worthy of its reputation.

Among the most notable of its exploits, were the covering of the retreat from Nieppe on the night of the 11th–12th April, when the Infantry of the 34 Division and 147 Brigade passed through it; the steadiness shown on the night of 13th–14th April when the retirement to the Mont de Lille–Crucifix Corner Line took place, and the efficient assistance rendered to the hard pressed left of the Division when on the Haegedorne Line.

General Freyberg exhibited to the full those qualities of personal gallantry, energy and driving power for which he is well known throughout the army and his handling of his Brigade was beyond all praise.[5]

For forty days from 21 March until the end of April 1918 the main strength of Germany had been devoted to the battery and destruction of the British Army and assaulted fifty-eight British divisions, at a cost to them of 14,803 officers and 228,066 men. The German casualties totalled 12,806 officers and 335,962 men.[6] But no vital British positions were lost, and their morale and cohesion remained intact, while the supreme German effort for victory was made in vain.

It was some time before Freyberg was able to write his own account of his 'backs to the wall' period to Barrie, and some further weeks before his letter reached Barrie in Scotland, so it was not until August that the following reply was received – in which Barrie refers to the offensives that had occurred meanwhile:

I am immensely interested in the account you sent me of those grim days and the really splendid report on it to GHQ. Owing to my being wandering in Scotland at present they reach me late. It makes me very happy that you should be written of in this way and also that you should give me the opportunity of knowing precisely what you are doing and what those in authority say about it. The fact is that even in these strange days your

[130]

position is a unique one – you have arrived at it by such short cuts that you must sometimes find yourself a bit lost, and I want you thoroughly to understand that I am as keen to know of your doings and have the same feelings of pride in them as if we had some family tie. You can always unburden yourself to me with perfect confidence in my taking it in the right light. . . .

What a month of it you had! How can I after this decide to ease myself by taking off my boots after walking a few miles! And that state of deadly tiredness and sleepiness! No need of the sleeping draught for you with which I frequently regale myself before seeking my couch. I hope you will never have such a grim time again as that with which you concluded the month. Fighting as hard I daresay, but with, one may hope, your back to the wall. Before you went out this time you were looking forward to defensive warfare, and you have had a good drink of it! Of course, we are all very excited over our new offensive, which has certainly come as a surprise to us. I presume it was a surprise to all of you. I was breakfasting with the PM no time ago and certainly he did not then expect that we should do anything in this way until next spring. How has it come about? Are we suddenly inspired or is Foch a man of genius or is the German morale giving way? Without making too much of it it is all very heartening.[2]

Throughout 1918, Freyberg wrote intermittently to Barbara McLaren and some twenty-four of these letters have survived. Most were written before the German offensive in March, and there is only one in the three months between the third week in March and the second week of July 1918. Quite apart from the situation on the battlefield, Barbara herself was on the move. After her husband was killed in August 1917 she had returned to her house in London with her two small sons, aged four and two. Understandably, she was unsettled and undecided about what to do next. Her mother and sister thought that she needed a complete change of scene, and it was arranged for her to go and stay with friends in America. Preparations for the journey had reached an advanced stage when the project was suddenly cancelled. At that period of the war there was a heavy rate of sinking of Allied ships in the Atlantic, and Barbara was not prepared to take the risk of her two boys being orphaned.

So, to get herself away from London, Barbara became a nurse in a convalescent hospital for officers at Escrick Park near York, the home of the Wenlock family, whose daughter Irene (Lawley) was one of her closest friends. Barbara installed herself and her children in a small cottage in the grounds during the early summer of 1918. Evidently she had discovered that Bernard had been wounded yet again, and as she had not heard from him for some time she became increasingly anxious, and asked Oc Asquith, who by then was working in the War Office, to find out about it. Oc responded with this note: 'The latest available news at WO about our Limited Liability Coy is "wounded remained at duty". Isn't that a comfort, but it's high time he got home for a bit. I hope you are happy and well.'[7]

It transpired that Freyberg had in fact written a letter to Barbara on 2 June 1918, the day before he was wounded, explaining why he had not written for nearly two months:

> We are at last out for a day or two but go in again almost at once. I miss your letters, they were the only mail I got – I have neither received nor have I written any letters for ages.
>
> We are in for a great deal of heavy fighting this summer and I long to see all of it – the chance of staying the distance is remote. On the whole I am satisfied with my battles since I last saw you. I have worked harder than ever and haven't had a minute to myself . . . Writing will be more difficult in a day or two. Forgive me and bless you.
>
> Bernard.

Freyberg was wounded for the ninth time on 3 June, as he related in a subsequent letter:

> I was wounded by a big shell during a minor operation. I was very shaken for a bit; it threw me several yards and wounded me in the leg and head. I had the bits out at the CCS and it is all healed now. It was rather an ordeal. I have had flu again. The man next to me had two legs and an arm off. It was sweet of you to send me chocolates. I wonder when I shall see you again. The chances seem very remote.
>
> Bless you from Bernard.

His injuries were in fact bad enough to be described as severe wounds.

After the failure of the German spring offensive, a period of regrouping had followed on both sides. The Allies expected the enemy to resume their attacks in a short while, and only gradually came to realise how exhausted in fact the Germans were. 29 Division had been used piecemeal to plug the gaps during the March crisis, and was still widely dispersed at the end of April. It did not come together again until 16 May, and for the next six weeks carried out a series of minor operations to hold their part of the line.[8] Early in August, 29 Division relieved 1 Australian Division and took over the Merris sector of the line between Hazebrouck and Bailleul, in the Second Army zone.[8] It was while the Division was here that General Sir Henry Rawlinson and his Fourth Army in the south of the British sector carried out the attack which Ludendorff later described as 'the Black Day of the German Army'.[9] The Official History calls 8 August 'the great turning-point in the War'. Freyberg wrote in his account:

> On 8 August our suspicions were confirmed, when it was announced that the Fourth Army/Australian Corps with other troops had attacked in front of Amiens, capturing all their objectives and thousands of prisoners.
> I think it was from this date that we realised the corner had been turned, and the dread of another huge German attack had no further awe for us. From now onwards, feelings of a purely defensive nature disappeared, and as we seized the initiative once more the human tide surged back again across the fields of Flanders and Picardy.

The fighting continued, of course, but now it was the Allied force which had the initiative. Gradually the five British armies pushed the enemy from the gains they had made in the March 1918 offensive, up to and beyond the various battlefields of the previous four years, back to where the war had begun in 1914. 29 Division was now part of General Plumer's Second Army, the most northerly of the British armies. For the next three months Freyberg and 88 Brigade were in almost continuous action.

From mid-August to mid-September 88 Brigade pushed the Germans back over ground which they had defended in previous battles – Hoegnacher Ridge, the village of Oultersteene, the town of Bailleul, and the De Soeul crossroads, where they came across some of their own unburied dead. After heavy fighting they cleared Ploegsteert Wood and captured Hill 63, and on 17 September Bernard wrote to Barbara, 'We pushed him back 8,000 yards over the ground we fought on in April, usual congratulations from C-in-C, Army and Corps Commanders – they wonder how we did it with so few men.'

On 17 September 29 Division was transferred to II Corps, which meant that it was to go to the Ypres sector for another battle. II Corps, commanded by Lieutenant-General Sir Claud Jacob, consisted of 9 and 36 Divisions. The operation in which they and 29 Division were about to take part was the battle of Gheluvelt and the last battle of Ypres, in which they joined with the Belgian Army.

On 23 September General Jacob went to 29 Division's headquarters to explain the plan of attack. 88 Brigade's task was to exploit any gains made by the other two brigades in the division; Jacob told Freyberg he was to push forward as far as possible. At this stage 88 Brigade consisted of 4 Battalion the Worcestershire Regiment; 2 Battalion the Hampshire Regiment; and 2 Battalion the Leinsters.

The attack by 29 Division was timed for daylight on 28 September, and the two leading brigades set off as planned. Rain had now set in, and the appalling state of the country for the next few miles was almost worse than the weak enemy reaction. Close to Hooge a series of huge mine craters was where the road should have been. Despite a certain amount of machine-gun fire, by 9.25 a.m. 86 and 87 Brigades had taken all their objectives and were holding the top of the ridge. At 9.30 a.m. 88 Brigade topped the summit and pushed down the Menin road in the duly appointed diamond battle formation. With no artillery support, the advance relied for success upon speed; and by 10.15 a.m. the 4 Worcestershire had captured Gheluvelt while the other two battalions had, as Freyberg wrote, 'got in among the German field guns, capturing many batteries. The German gunners made no effort to defend their position and surrendered freely without firing a shot.'

After the capture of Gheluvelt enemy resistance increased as reserves were rushed to the area. The 88 Brigade headquarters was bombed from the air by their own aircraft; attempts to outflank the German outpost line failed, and the weather conditions were miserable. The men were wet through, covered in mud and suffering from the cold.

The key to the next objective, Gheluwe, was the high ground at Kruiseik just beyond Gheluvelt. After several attempts the Worcestershires managed to get to the top of the ridge in the early morning of 30 September and reached the outskirts of Gheluwe, where they were relieved at dusk by the Hampshires. 88 Brigade itself was relieved on the night of 2–3 October and returned to camp, and then, on 5 October, to Ypres, to be ready for the next offensive.

During this period Bernard wrote to Barbara on 11 October: 'A line to say we are busy and fighting hard . . . I commanded my brigade from a horse (an ugly white German one) and advanced under a barrage on it until it was killed.'

The story of the horse was picked up by *The Times*, and on 12 October Barrie was writing:

> What times we are living in, even we at home, and we can measure by that what times you are having. I saw in *The Times* how a famous Brigadier who was also a VC, had ridden into a recaptured town on a horse lost by the enemy; and Lady Cynthia (I told you she was my secretary now, didn't I?) and I decided that it must be you tho' no name was given. We all warn each other against being too optimistic but find it difficult to learn the lesson ourselves. That was a fine feat of your brigade in Ploegsteert Wood.[2]

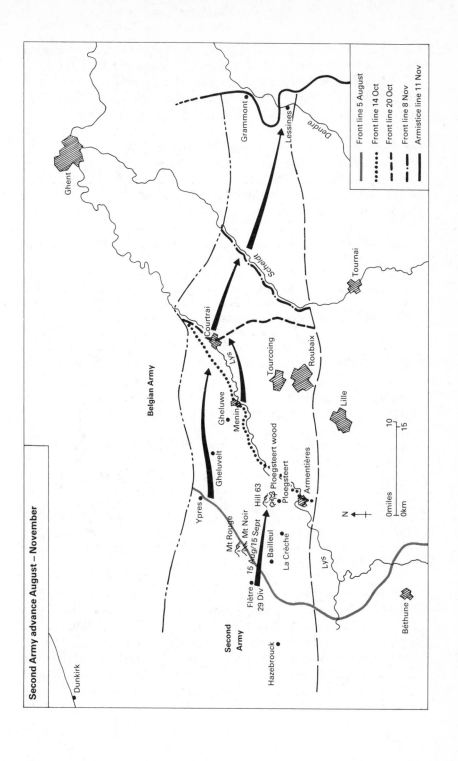

Second Army advance August – November

Dunkirk

Hazebrouck

Second Army

Flêtre
29 Div
15 Aug/15 Sept
Mt Rouge
Mt Noir
Hill 63
Bailleul
La Crèche
Ploegsteert wood
Ploegsteert
Armentières

Ypres

Gheluvelt

Gheluwe
Menin

Lille

Béthune

N

0 miles
0 km

10
15

Belgian Army

Courtrai

Lys

Lys

Tourcoing

Roubaix

Ghent

Scheldt

Grammont

Lessines

Dendre

Tournai

Front line 5 August
Front line 14 Oct
Front line 20 Oct
Front line 8 Nov
Armistice line 11 Nov

For his action at Gheluvelt Freyberg was awarded a bar to his DSO. Part of the citation reads: 'The success of the operations of his brigade near Gheluvelt on the 28 September and the following days was largely owing to his inspired example. Wherever the fighting was hardest he was always to be found encouraging and directing his troops.'[10]

On 9 October 88 Brigade relieved 86 Brigade in the Ledeghem area, and preparations were made for the next advance. All was ready by 14 October, and the attack planned for dawn (5.35 a.m.) with 88 Brigade on the right and 86 on the left, and 87 in reserve. One part of the preparation did not go as planned, however:

> The officer commanding Leinster Regiment, Lieutenant-Colonel Weldon, walked back to his headquarters about 600 yards in rear. There he discovered his brigadier a reeking mass of filthy black slime. General Freyberg had walked head first into a farmyard pond in the dark. The odour was so unpleasant that the interview was limited to the very briefest narrative of facts, and a hasty advance again on Colonel Weldon's part to the danger zone. 'Anything rather than a continuation of that dreadful stink!' he wrote. As General Freyberg remarked the next day, 'It was bad enough to fall into the mess, but worse to have everyone avoiding me.'[8]

Freyberg also noticed on 13 October when he went round the Assembly Area how the attitude of the men had changed:

> It was a fine starlight night when I went round the Assembly Area. The men were all sitting with their legs dangling into the newly dug trenches ready to disappear into them should the shelling become dangerous. I told the men all the latest news, and said that in my opinion the war would be over with another few attacks. I was very much struck by the nonchalance of the men, who seemed to have become automatons in the last few weeks; there was no life in them; their pulses were slower than usual. An attack had ceased long since to act as a stimulant; only the feeling that it had to be gone through with kept the men going.

II Corps attacked on 14 October on a front of three divisions with 29 Division in the centre. On the following day the corps had advanced 4 miles, and by the 16th they were in the vicinity of Courtrai, a big Belgian town of 30,000 inhabitants, where enemy troops were based. On 17 October 88 Brigade was ordered to take over from 9 Division on the banks of the Lys. Next day it was quiet, but when a patrol was sent to the far bank the Germans were found to be still in position. 88 Brigade was given orders to force the crossing of the Lys on the night of the

18–19 October, which they succeeded in doing, whereupon the enemy bolted the following morning. At this stage the British attacks were hampered by the enthusiasm of the Belgian civilian population:

> During the battles the civilians looked on with keen interest, shouting 'Vive les Anglais!' and in many cases rushing after our attacking lines of Infantry which were often under fire, giving the men a kind of hot coffee made from burnt beans. This giving of refreshments threatened to delay the whole attack and became a positive danger to us in the thickly populated parts.

At 8.30 a.m. they had captured Staceghem and pushed posts forward on to the Essher Road. At 3 p.m. 86 Brigade passed through and carried on with the attack. 88 Brigade went into reserve, and went back into billets at Staceghem:

> It had begun to rain hard and we were tired out. We rested in these billets until the 25th, always on the verge of another attack, but always having our arrangements cancelled at the last moment.

These are among the last passages in 'A Linesman in Picardy'. By this time the Germans had opened negotiations for an armistice. 29 Division spent the last week of October and the first week in November resting in the vicinity of Roubaix. The strain of the previous few weeks is evident in the letter Bernard wrote to Barbara soon afterwards on 23 October:

> A line to thank you for your letter and to say that I am here and doing battle very often. Today I feel old and rather tired – perhaps reaction after two heavy battles – we come out of the line for three days and I am getting a car to take me clear for a few hours and a meal at a decent restaurant. Do you remember meals in town we had in January – nearly ten months ago? What a volume of water has flown under the bridge since then . . .
> I have commanded a brigade now for nearly two years (not quite), and with a certain degree of success. When this period of fighting finishes I intend to come to London on business for a day or two. I have just read your letter dated 18 Oct. One of our Brigadiers named Cheape has asked me to be godfather to his small son. I am terribly pleased that anybody should want me to be godfather. Somehow I have never thought of myself as anything but a soldier – I wonder how Oc is and if he is happy. We are all rather tired physically and mentally, and the few days rest won't do us any harm. But of late I don't seem to care if I live except to see the finish of Germany. Somehow one couldn't have lived and lost.

But the fighting was not quite over yet. On 7 November the 29 Division took over the line again near Bossuyt on the left bank of the river Scheldt, in preparation for the crossing. The river, 60 yards wide and very deep, was a formidable obstacle, especially as the British bank was overlooked by commanding heights on the enemy's side.

The attack was planned for 10 November, but one day earlier the enemy retired, and 88 Brigade, who were holding the front, pursued. They improvised foot-bridges (they had used empty beer casks to cross the Lys a month earlier), and progressed as far as Celles that evening, but still made no contact. Bridges had to be repaired to enable guns and vehicles to cross, while pack animals with rations were ferried across the river.

Early in the morning of 11 November 1918 the news was received that an armistice would come into force at 11 a.m., when the opposing sides would remain on the ground on which they found themselves at that hour. At 9.30 a.m. Freyberg received orders to push on at once with his advance guard to try and seize the important bridges over the river Dendre at Lessines to prevent them from being destroyed – before the armistice came into force.

Freyberg immediately gave orders for the squadron of 7 Dragoon Guards under his command to saddle up, and he galloped the 10 miles of the hilly road to Lessines with them, although fired on by German outposts on the way, who put a bullet into his saddle. They arrived on the outskirts a few minutes before eleven o'clock, when the squadron immediately rushed into the town and captured the Dendre bridges which had been prepared for demolition, so preventing their destruction. They took 3 German officers and 100 men prisoner, and the whole transaction was completed by 10.59 a.m. It was a fitting climax to Freyberg's four years of war.

The action gained for Freyberg a second bar to his DSO[11] and the townsfolk named a street in Lessines 'Rue Général Freyberg' to commemorate this episode. It still bears his name.

Following the armistice the whole 29 Division began to concentrate in the Lessines area and shortly afterwards came the news that the 29 and 9 Divisions had been chosen to lead the advance of the British Army into Germany itself.

Freyberg commanded the Guard of Honour, drawn from all British infantry units, for the state entry into Brussels of the King and Queen of the Belgians on 22 November. He led the march past afterwards on a horse, wearing his nine gold wound stripes and his medals. The British

Army's reception from the Belgian crowds was tumultuous, and Freyberg was asked to grant an extra day's leave for the Guard, which he did without demur, observing, 'Some of them look as though they need a little rest before reporting back.'[12]

29 Division's line of march *en route* for Germany, which began on 18 November, took it not only across the field of Waterloo, but also past Ramillies, one of Marlborough's celebrated battlefields more than 200 years before. They crossed the Meuse at Huy, and then climbed and descended the steep hills and valleys of the Ardennes. All the time the division was marching through Belgium they received an ecstatic welcome from the inhabitants. But from the moment they passed the German frontier near Malmedy on 4 December they were greeted with sullen hostility. The outskirts of Cologne were reached on 9 December and on Friday, 13 December 1918, in pouring rain, 29 Division crossed the Rhine by the Hohenzollern Bridge, where General Plumer, now commanding the Army of Occupation, took the salute.[8] There the long drawn out saga of 29 Division came to an end, and with it Freyberg's participation in the Great War.

After four years of war, what were Freyberg's feelings? Inevitably they were mixed, but something of their nature, and of Freyberg's sheer fatigue after ten months in action, are shown by this letter which he wrote to Barbara on 18 November, before the march into Germany.

Barbara dear
A line to say we are going forward into Germany and in a day we pass Waterloo – it's thrilling to think of the British Army marching past with the French, a little over a hundred years afterwards.

How conditions have altered. Napoleon's headquarters at Belle Alliance were a mile from Wellington's at Mount St Jeanne.

Nowadays Foch and Ludendorff sit at tables separated by hundreds of miles. The morning of the battle Wellington was joy-riding in Brussels at a ball, while we sit all day and most nights for a long time before a battle of only moderate size.

We are marching most days. I shall stay here long enough to finish our march into Germany and for peace to be signed, then I shall come home for a rest. I am tired and rather worn out. I show it and have changed a little. What will eventually happen to me – I cannot say. I know an excellent solution will occur . . .

I can't define my feelings at peace – I don't know if I am glad or sorry to be left alive – I only know it wasn't my fault I am alive. Bless you.
Bernard.

9

Return to England

After 88 Brigade became part of the British Army of Occupation in Germany, Bernard Freyberg was able to return on leave to England several times.[1] Usually he stayed in London with Barrie at his Adelphi Terrace flat; and during these visits led an active social life. But his most immediate and pressing problem was to decide what he should do next.

He was thirty years old. After his wartime experiences in Europe he did not intend to return to his old life in New Zealand – and certainly not to dentistry. He had, of course, joined the British Army but initially at any rate he did not fancy the idea of peacetime soldiering in England, nor of reverting down in rank from Brigadier-General to Captain, which also meant a corresponding fall in pay. There were suggestions that he might accompany General Rawlinson on his mission to Archangel in the White Sea, or go to Mesopotamia or India in other capacities, but for different reasons none of these ideas came to fruition.[1]

Freyberg had joined the Royal Naval Division in August 1914 as a temporary Sub-Lieutenant RNVR; he was promoted to Lieutenant, owing to his territorial service in New Zealand, and then successively to Lieutenant-Commander and then Commander RNVR. In 1916 he transferred to the army as a junior 'hostilities only' officer, with the army equivalent temporary rank of Lieutenant-Colonel. For the last two years of the war he served as a temporary Brigadier-General, which in those days was rated as a General Officer. He was given the brevet rank of Major on 3 June 1917, and Brevet Lieutenant-Colonel on 1 January 1918. A brevet enables an officer to hold a higher rank temporarily than that for which he is paid, so that Freyberg was only able to date his substantive rank from the beginning of the war.

Freyberg's post-war restlessness was such that some of his friends, in particular Barrie and Oc Asquith, strongly urged him to calm down and accustom himself to a more normal kind of existence. He had had more than his full ration of action and adventure. They reminded him that the war had shown he had a natural gift for soldiering and leadership, and that it would be a waste to throw this experience away by starting again from scratch in another profession. They also pointed out that his record had been so remarkable that, in spite of having to accept immediate demotion, in time he would be bound to climb the ladder again to a high position in the army. As he recovered from his exhaustion and became more objective he realised that his friends were right, but another factor influenced him even more strongly. He was very much in love with Barbara McLaren. She was a widow, but he hoped she would soon become his wife.

After some weeks therefore he applied, as he had forecast to Arnold Quilter's mother, for a regular commission in the Grenadier Guards. His application was approved and the notification appeared in the *London Gazette* early in March 1919.

The final episode of this unsettled period was Freyberg's departure from the command of 88 Brigade in Germany. As with most armies of Occupation, once the novelty of being in the heart of enemy country had worn off the main problem was that of dealing with the boredom of troops isolated in a strange and hostile land. Even though Freyberg was there for only three months he was glad to leave. In the days before his departure he was entertained to a number of pleasant formal dinners by his battalions and units and, still dressed as a Brigadier-General, was given a rousing send-off from his headquarters on 15 March 1919 in a car towed by ropes manned by officers and men.

In his final confidential report about Freyberg the commander of 29 Division, General Douglas Cayley, wrote:

A Brigadier of marked personality and power of leadership, whose courage in the field is of the highest order. He is an indefatigable worker and most thorough in all his plans. He has the gift of inspiring all under him with his own keenness and determination. At present he lacks experience as a trainer. He is an efficient organiser and disciplinarian. Physically very strong, and nearly incapable of fatigue.[1]

On his return to England he reverted to his substantive rank of Captain.

[141]

Freyberg was nominated for a place on the first post-war course at the Staff College, Camberley, which began in April 1919. The officers were selected on the basis of their war records rather than the normal competitive examinations. The 1919 course was quite unlike any other, before or since, as many of the students had held high command in the war and were ex-generals, like Freyberg. Five were holders of the Victoria Cross, 95 had the Distinguished Service Order, and nearly all the remainder had the Military Cross and other decorations.[3] Their combined knowledge was formidable, and the directing staff had the unenviable task of instructing officers who had mostly had more experience of war than they had. But the atmosphere was informal and relaxed, and Freyberg enjoyed it. Perhaps the most important, lasting aspect of the course was that so many of the students were later to hold senior appointments. Three of them became Field Marshals (Gort, Alan Brooke, and Wilson), five would be full Generals (Williams, Giffard, Riddell-Webster, Platt and Marshall-Cornwall); eight were later Lieutenant-Generals (Barker, Bond, Carr, Lindsell, Massy, Miles, Osborne and Freyberg himself), and twenty became Major-Generals.[3]

During the summer of 1919, however, a crisis occurred in Freyberg's relationship with Barbara McLaren. After years of wartime seclusion, looking after small children, enduring the misery of widowhood and being nurse to convalescent officers, she was beginning to enjoy life again, and embarked on travels which took her out of England for weeks at a time. In March 1919 she went to Spain with Violet Bonham Carter and her father H. H. Asquith.[1] The Spanish government placed every facility at the disposal of the ex-Prime Minister and his party. Barbara next planned to stay with friends during September at the Villa Medici in Florence, and the following January to go to Mürren in Switzerland with Irene Lawley for winter sports. In the midst of all this she had less time to spend in Bernard's company than he would have liked.

Her behaviour and feelings in the immediate post-war years were understandable and normal. It was but two years since her husband was killed, and she was only now getting over the shock and trauma of his death. She was unwilling to commit herself to anyone else for the time being, and though she cared very much for Bernard, she felt that she had to be sure that any new arrangement would benefit her two young sons as well as herself. Barbara needed time to readjust and to see her way ahead clearly.

During this time Bernard remained in England, in his off-duty times often bored and lonely. He found the reversal of their roles trying and was ill-equipped to deal with a situation that required understanding, patience and tact. Some sort of explosion was bound to occur sooner or later, and it came in August 1919, almost certainly in Paris when Barbara passed through on her way to Italy, and where Bernard was studying French. Bernard had gone to Paris during the Staff College summer break to try to learn French so that he could sit the interpreter's exam. This would have given him a better chance of gaining interesting appointments abroad; but he had no natural gift for languages and became increasingly discouraged as time went by.

None of Bernard's letters to Barbara between August and December 1919 has survived. They were almost certainly later destroyed by Barbara because they showed him in an unfavourable light. Most probably Bernard complained that Barbara was selfish in not being prepared to marry him at once, and told her he resented her having fun without him. This was hardly the way to win her. Indeed such complaints would have been guaranteed to alienate Barbara, and brief references to him in letters to her mother show that she was not in a conciliatory mood in the summer of 1919.[1]

Bernard must soon have realised that he was well on the way to losing her. In many respects Barbara was as strong a character as he was, and he was having to accept that she was not going to be made to do anything except on her own terms and in her own time. His letters to her resume in early January 1920 and are written in a much gentler tone than some of the earlier ones.[1] The whole episode had clearly been a considerable shock to him.

At the end of 1919 Freyberg toyed with the idea of applying to go to Balliol, Patrick Shaw-Stewart's old college. Bernard went to see the Admissions tutor who told him that he would be offered a place, probably to read history, and confirmed it in writing.[1] But having joined the Grenadier Guards Freyberg clearly had to serve with the regiment before he could go elsewhere, and 1920 was already out of the question. A year later he was ill and had to go to New Zealand to recuperate, and so the possibility of going to Oxford receded and eventually disappeared.

The Staff College course finished just before Christmas 1919, and Freyberg was gazetted as 'psc' (Passed Staff College) in Army Orders dated 16 January 1920.[2] He went on leave for three weeks and was then posted to 1 Battalion Grenadier Guards, stationed in the Tower of London.[2] This was an unusual home for a battalion, and indeed its use as a station was later discontinued. One particular disadvantage was due to an historical reason: the 'Ceremony of the Keys' had taken place every night for hundreds of years, after which everybody was locked in or out of the Tower until six next morning. In 1920 this meant that if unmarried officers wanted to live in the mess (as was normally the case) they had to leave their outside pursuits in London early if they were to be back before the entrance door of the Tower was bolted. So most officers not on duty lived outside barracks. Freyberg had a room in the officers' mess but spent most evenings at one of his clubs. His was thus a somewhat nomadic existence, divided between the Tower in the morning, the Bath Club where he went for exercise and a swim in the afternoon, and, when he was not doing anything in particular, spending the evening with Barrie or at the Guards Club, where he usually slept.

Freyberg often went to the studio of the sculptor Sir William Reid Dick where he met Mary Motley as a child. In her reminiscences, *Morning Glory*, she recalled that 'Freyberg's fame had reached even into the nursery':

> Mama said that he was the bravest man that had ever lived, he had swum across the Dardanelles with a lighted candle in his mouth to guide the British troops to the Turkish shore. This version of what had happened was quite good enough for me. I hero-worshipped General Freyberg. One day, quite unexpectedly, he decided to take me to the Tower of London. He was wearing civilian clothes (this was a sore disappointment to me), but the word got round or someone recognised him, and the Beefeaters turned out and presented arms. My hero took me by the hand, and together we inspected the guard. I was in Seventh Heaven: 'the air was full of trumpets and gorgeously coloured fire'. I was overwhelmed by the importance of Generals; and my General was the most important one of all. It was intensely gratifying.[4]

By the time Freyberg joined the battalion at the beginning of 1920 the Brigade of Guards was in the process of returning to its pre-war, peacetime routine. The day usually began early with a drill parade and was followed by individual training such as musketry, map reading, PT or lectures, which lasted until lunchtime. Afterwards there were games, route marches or other physical activities. Individual training was a prelude to section, platoon and company training later in the summer, to be followed by battalion and formation exercises in the autumn. Until group training began Freyberg had few military calls in the afternoons. In the evenings he mostly dined out.

Outside his military duties Freyberg's main interests were writing his Great War story, which Barrie had so much encouraged him to do, and stocks and shares. Of the former Cynthia Asquith comments: 'I remember Barrie's amused pride when Freyberg showed how well he could wield a pen in place of the sword he had been compelled to sheathe. Barrie wrote:

Freyberg was in last night. The first I'd heard of him for a week. The fury of
writing, for which he has a great natural gift, is the cause. I have seldom seen
anyone so struck down by the malady. He already looks the pale student of
the midnight oil. He may talk vaguely of mundane affairs but all the time
words like 'no adjectives' or 'by style I mean' keep falling off his lips where
they gather unbeknown; and every hour of the day, so to speak, he is going
over the top, waving manuscripts and reading them to prisoners.[5]

As a keen follower of the stock market Freyberg watched share
prices lynx-like, devoured the city columns in newspapers, and (on
arriving at his club) went straight to the ticker-tape to pore over how
prices were moving. Having had little money in his youth he was keenly
aware of its importance, and became shrewd at investments. His letters
to Barbara at this time are full of reasons for backing certain companies,
and the level his shares had to reach to make him sell them. During the
war years he had had few expenses and managed to save most of his pay.
After sending a generous allowance to his mother in New Zealand he
invested the remainder very well. Later on it was said by some that he
married Barbara for financial security, but by 1921 he had stocks and
shares amounting to a considerable sum. In fact his disposable assets
were probably as much as hers, because, with no husband to support
her yet with two young children and a household to maintain, Barbara
was having difficulty in 'keeping her financial head above water'.

In the middle of August Freyberg's regiment left the Tower of
London for Pirbright Camp in Surrey, where they stayed until the
middle of October. During these two months the battalion put in a
great deal of field training and firing on the ranges. Freyberg preferred
these activities to the public duties in London, largely because the unit
was all together in one place and it was much easier to get to know
everybody.

Although it was an obvious 'come down' to command a company
after being a brigade commander, Freyberg made no complaint and
adapted well to the change. One of his subalterns was Allan Adair, who
commanded the Guards Armoured Division in the Second World
War. During the last exercise in 1920, Adair recalled, at the critical
moment of the final attack Freyberg led his company through a railway
tunnel under Chobham Ridges (which the directing staff had forgotten
to put out of bounds), and they suddenly appeared in the rear of the
opposing side, much to their discomfort and to the consternation of the
umpires. The exercise had to be abandoned, causing great hilarity in
the battalion, and providing a talking point for years to come.[6]

At the end of August 1920 Bernard was asked to stay with Lady

Edward Cecil (widow of Lord Edward Cecil who had many Grenadier links) at her Kent home, South Park, Penshurst. One afternoon she took her house party over to nearby Bateman's, Rudyard Kipling's home. Bernard and Kipling got on so well that Kipling asked him to come for the weekend in the middle of September. He enjoyed his visit enormously and said that they had talked a great deal about most subjects: 'Kipling is great fun and rather like a boy in his enthusiasms over life in general,' he wrote to Barbara. Bernard became an avid reader of Kipling's poems, many of which he knew by heart.

Barbara meanwhile spent the first of several summers holidaying at Menabilly, a house on the coast of south Cornwall which she, her sister Pamela McKenna, and Lady Gwendolyn Churchill took for their children.[1] It had a romantic atmosphere – later Daphne du Maurier wrote her novel *Rebecca* while living there. The entrance lodge, the long drive to the house through woods lined with rhododendrons and azaleas, and the path from Menabilly (Manderley in the book) to the little bay and the sea, were all as she described them in *Rebecca*.

On 11 November 1920, two years after the armistice, the funeral and burial of the Unknown Soldier took place. Freyberg commanded 'The VC Guard of Valour' composed of holders of the Victoria Cross from all three services, which was mounted outside Westminster Abbey. Sir Alan Lascelles, later Private Secretary to King George VI and Queen Elizabeth II, recorded the scene as he watched:

> The Unknown British Soldier passed down the Mall to his new grave in Westminster Abbey. Pipers marched before him, Admirals of the Fleet and Field Marshals of England on his right hand and on his left, and all London stood bare-headed as he went; while on his coffin lay the steel helmet which each one of us wore, and the long crusader's sword selected for him alone from the King's armoury. He has no name; of all symbols, he is the most nameless, the most symbolic; yet few that Man has ever devised can have given such a clear-cut image of reality; for every one of us who has his own dead could not fail to see that they too went with him; that, after two years of waiting, we could at last lay a wreath to the memory of that great company.[7]

Late autumn 1920 found the battalion back in London. Freyberg took part in – and usually won – swimming races organised by the Household Brigade Swimming Association at the Bath Club; and often dined with the King's Guard at St James's Palace, where officers on duty at Buckingham Palace lived during their tour. He was the Captain at Christmas, and Barrie wrote to Cynthia Asquith on 23 December: 'I am to dine with the Guards on Christmas Eve at St James's Palace, and expect it will be interesting or at least "massive and concrete".' Denis

Mackail, Barrie's biographer, wrote that it was 'a highly successful evening; even though the innocent warriors let out that all their other invitations had been refused'.[8]

All was not well, however, with Freyberg's health. Considering that he had been wounded on nine separate occasions in the Great War – once at Antwerp, twice at Gallipoli, four times in the battle of the Ancre, again at Passchendaele in 1917 (multiple wounds), and in June 1918 in the Forêt de Nieppe – this was perhaps hardly surprising. Nor does that include the breaking of his elbow when he was thrown from his horse in May 1916. Nature was rebelling. In June 1920 Barrie recorded how he had 'been busy with poor Freyberg most of the day'. He

> got him to 17 Park Lane [Sir Douglas Shields' nursing home, much used by Barrie and his friends] about 3 and have lately got back from a second visit. It was very necessary he should be there, as his leg has gone discoloured, and at best this will spread before he gets better. They have had many such cases with soldiers as the result of wounds, and the best that can be said at present is that though troublesome it is not considered dangerous.[9]

Freyberg was subject to recurring bouts of illness throughout the 1920s. During the course of these illnesses fragments of metal were expelled from his wounds, and more had to be extracted surgically. This happened intermittently for approximately fifteen years after the war ended. The wounds that gave the most trouble were those in his neck and leg. The big trench in his neck, acquired in the action when he won the VC, affected his hearing and required several major operations. These were painful and worrying too, because at one stage he was almost completely deaf, but eventually most of the damage was repaired. The wound in his leg was less serious but gave him continual trouble.

Winston Churchill was once, during the 1920s, staying at a country house where Freyberg was staying too. 'I asked him,' Churchill wrote in *The Grand Alliance*, 'to show me his wounds. He stripped himself, and I counted twenty-seven separate scars and gashes. To these he was to add in the Second World War another three. But of course, as he explained, "You nearly always get two wounds for every bullet or splinter, because mostly they have to go out as well as go in".'[10]

Barrie was a 'tower of strength' to Freyberg during the immediate post-war years. He was often far from well himself, and he and Freyberg took it in turns to nurse each other, as Cynthia Asquith records in her *Portrait of Barrie*:

Now and again, one of Freyberg's nine wounds would break out and send his temperature soaring, upon which Barrie, self-appointing himself 'next of kin', would firmly take charge, confer with the doctors, and – an office he specially loved to perform – keep off other would-be visitors. Freyberg too, when his turn came, was an excellent nurse, displaying skill, tact and sympathy and also – for it must be remembered that Barrie's illnesses were no light business for others – commendable patience. I remember how Freyberg once slept at the flat with a string tied round his wrist for the patient to pull. This was during the illness in which Barrie was given heroin, then a newly discovered drug prescribed to make the patient sleep. The doctor was disappointed. Barrie, blissfully exhilarated by his injection, defiantly sat straight up in bed all night. Sleep! What was sleep? This new sensation was far too good an experience to lose, by unconsciousness. 'I feel all silver,' he exclaimed ecstatically, 'entirely silver.'[5]

Freyberg was ill again early in 1921, when he and Barrie twice visited Brighton. After this the army doctors decided he needed a complete change of scene and air. He wanted to go to New Zealand in any case to see his mother and it was decided to combine the two needs. An obscure pre-war rule was unearthed which allowed him to be sent on sick leave at public expense, even as far as New Zealand. The rule was cancelled by an enraged Treasury immediately after it had been invoked, but not before it was honoured for the last time.

For the first nine months of 1921 Bernard saw very little of Barbara, though he wrote to her on average every other day.[1] At the end of December 1920 she had taken her two sons to stay with their paternal (Aberconway) grandparents at the Château de la Garoupe near Antibes. They were away for a month, and by the time she came back Bernard was already starting to make preparations for his journey to New Zealand. When he left Southampton on 5 May 1921 on the RMS *Arawa* Barbara did not come to see him off because she was again at Menabilly with her sons. In his last letter to her before he sailed Bernard wrote: 'I can't help thinking of the time twenty-nine years ago when as a very small bullet-headed boy I made the same journey – but round the Cape.'[1]

Arawa, a ship of some 5,000 tons belonging to the Shaw, Savill and Albion Company, was nineteen years old, coal-fired and very slow. The journey was uneventful but agreeable, and Bernard spent much of his time finishing off 'A Linesman in Picardy'. Two days before reaching the Panama Canal he saw the Southern Cross again: 'I remember seeing it disappear below the horizon eight-odd years ago, from the stern of the *Tahiti*. During the war I often wondered if I should ever see it again.'

(Above) The Ancre Valley – scene of the Hood Battalion's advance on 13 November 1916 and where Freyberg gained his VC *(Imperial War Museum); (below left)* Freyberg, 1916, in uniform of Royal West Surrey Regiment; *(right)* with staff officers of 173 Brigade, 1917

(*Above left*) James Barrie, in a photograph he sent to Freyberg as a Christmas card. (*Above right*) Lady Cynthia Asquith, née Charteris (*courtesy of Lord Neidpath*); (*below left*) Freyberg liked to take an early morning ride but was less at home on a horse than in the water; (*right*) Freyberg, 1918, with wound stripes

Lessines
Rue Général Freyberg et Pont de pierre.

(Above) Rue Général Freyberg in Lessines. Freyberg's dashing action, capturing the bridge over the River Dendre at 10.59am on 11 November 1918, earned him a bar to his DSO and a street which still bears his name. *(Below)* On Freyberg's relinquishing command of 88 Brigade in Germany on 5 March 1919, his car was towed by his staff as a gesture of farewell. *(Right)* Freyberg, March 1919

(Above) Bernard Freyberg and Barbara McLaren at the time of their marriage, in 1922. *(Below)* Barbara's sister Pamela and her husband Reginald McKenna, one-time First Lord of the Admiralty, Chancellor of the Exchequer and later Chairman of the Midland Bank

CARDIFF PARLIAMENTARY ELECTION.
SOUTH DIVISION.

Election News.

FREYBERG		FREYBERG
STANDS FOR		STANDS FOR
Economy		Social Reform
Free Trade		Cheap Food
League of Nations		Universal Peace
The Irish Treaty		Child Welfare
International Friendship		Co-operation between Employer & Employee

Lieut.-Colonel BERNARD FREYBERG, V.C., C.M.G., D.S.O., LL.D., the Independent Candidate.

Vote for **FREYBERG**
and **PROGRESSIVE PRINCIPLES.**

Vote for **FREYBERG**
and **MORE EMPLOYMENT.**

"THE COUNTRY MUST AT ALL TIMES
COME BEFORE PARTY."

Vote for **FREYBERG,** the Independent Candidate.

(Left) It was not necessary for Freyberg, when he stood for Parliament in 1922, to resign his commission unless he were elected. *(Below)* At St Andrews University on 3 May 1922 Barrie gave a lecture on 'Courage', mentioning Freyberg as an example. Barrie is seated on the left of Field Marshal Earl Haig, Chancellor of the University, and Freyberg is standing behind them. On Barrie's left is the actress Ellen Terry

COL. FREYBERG'S GLORIOUS FAILURE : THE CHANNEL WINS AGAIN.

1. WITHIN 500 YARDS OF THE ENGLISH WHITE CLIFFS : THE GALLANT SWIMMER BATTLING AGAINST THE VIOLENT COASTAL EBB.
2. EMPLOYING THE OLD ENGLISH SIDE STROKE, WHICH HE USED ALMOST EXCLUSIVELY : COLONEL FREYBERG WITHIN SIGHT OF DOVER HARBOUR.
3. AFTER HIS SIXTEEN AND THREE-QUARTER HOUR STRUGGLE : COLONEL FREYBERG, UTTERLY EXHAUSTED, BEING ASSISTED FROM THE WATER.

Lieutenant-Colonel Freyberg, V.C., D.S.O., made a most gallant attempt last week to swim the English Channel and was within five hundred yards of the shore at Dover when, exhausted by the violence of the coastal ebb, he was forced to give up. Colonel Freyberg won the V.C. in France for "most conspicuous bravery" and at Gallipoli, in 1915, he won the D.S.O. for swimming ashore alone and lighting flares within a few yards of the Turks to deceive them as to where the landing was to be made.

In 1925 (and again in 1926) Freyberg attempted to fulfil a boyhood ambition by swimming the English Channel. *The Illustrated Sporting and Dramatic News* carried the story of a 'glorious failure'

When Freyberg took command of 1 Bn, The Manchester Regiment, he found its morale low. He sought King George V's consent to becoming Colonel-in-Chief, signified by a special parade *(above)* at Buckingham Palace on 16 May 1930. *(Below)* Freyberg's aunt by marriage Gertrude Jekyll, even in extreme old age, was able to help on the design of the Commanding Officer's garden *(NPG)*

When Freyberg was invalided out of the army in the late 1930s, one of the tasks he turned his energies to was building. *(Above)* Gillham's Farm, near Haslemere, after considerable restoration under his direction. *(Right)* On the outbreak of war in September 1939 he was recalled for 'home only duties', but soon after was medically upgraded 'forward everywhere'

Bernard arrived in Wellington on 19 June 1921, and his first letter to Barbara, from the Wellington Club, is dated 20 June:

> A line to say I have just arrived and that I am not well. My leg swelled up again and I had a temperature to land with. I was met by my mother and Cuthbert and his wife, and Claud, my brother who is just older than me. They are all unchanged except my mother, bless her, who is quite white and who has lost all incisiveness and kick. She is very quiet and has a look in her face that wasn't there when I last saw her.

Because he was unwell Bernard asked that a civic reception planned in his honour should be cancelled. The only ceremonial event of his visit was the inspection of the cadets of his old school, Wellington College, when over 700 boys were on parade. Afterwards he addressed the whole college:

> In the seven years I was here I learned many things, not so much as I ought – I am sorry to say that a great deal of my time and energies were spent in avoiding what I thought was unnecessary work. I am not going to say (as I remember all visiting old boys said in my time) that the years I spent here were my happiest. They should have been had I worked. I don't expect anyone to profit from my advice . . .[11]

He was entertained to dinner one evening by his old swimming friends, and was very touched to be made a life member of the Returned Soldiers' Association. Otherwise his five weeks in New Zealand were spent entirely with his family. He never saw his mother again, for she died in 1936 and Bernard did not return to New Zealand until Christmas Day 1939. Bernard went back to England on the *Arawa*, this time sailing via Cape Horn. He walked into Barrie's Adelphi Terrace flat on 7 September 1921, having been met earlier that day at Southampton by Barbara.[9]

The immediate problem for Bernard on his return was his fitness for duty. The rest and the long sea journeys had certainly done him good, and he was passed fit by a medical board and told he could rejoin his unit. But it was not for long. At the end of 1921, after two years regimental duty, he was due for a change. His next appointment was GSO2 at HQ 44 (Home Counties) Division TA, stationed at Woolwich.

Barrie's health, however, was still far from good, and that autumn Freyberg again had to help look after him. It was another occasion when he slept in the room next to Barrie with a string round his wrist. This time there was a nurse as well – likewise with a string – of whom

[149]

Freyberg evidently disapproved, a sentiment that was reciprocated. When Barrie pulled his strings the two would arrive in his room simultaneously and glare at each other across his recumbent body.[9]

In a letter to Barbara on 3 October 1921 there is a significant phrase. After thanking her for the happy evening they had spent together, Bernard wrote: 'We recaptured the hour we lost two years before.' His letters at this time reveal a new tone, a change in the atmosphere of their relationship. From then on they spent a great deal of time together, and by December Barbara was taking her parents and sister into her confidence. Her mother, Lady Jekyll, wrote a letter to Barbara on 17 December:

> My darling precious Barbara
> I have been thinking of you all day and talking with Pamela of nothing else. You will have heard one version of a damp and dark walk and talk – and I think she felt after talking with him that you cared in a way that meant the ultimate decision had really been already made. If only *you* are at peace and happy, that is the only thing that *really* matters and if any feeling that you were going against those who cared for you so greatly had held you back and vexed your soul, that need not do so darling, for once your decision is taken, we shall all be on that side and he will win love as easily as he has won admiration for all the great qualities he has shown in the war years. If you feel too racked or indecisive at heart don't let yourself be rushed, but if you know deep down that you can live and be happy together, we shall all be joyful with you. I don't think money matters much, or profession, and he is sure to make a success of his life – affinity and sympathy and kindred likings matter a good deal – and in all the things which he may lack you can so greatly supplement and help – and what outside friends and the world say or think matters not a jot, only the sympathy of your nearest and dearest which you have in abundant measure. I will come or send the car if you want me, and I am your most devoted and I think really very understanding
> Mother.[1]

Christmas 1921 was spent at the Jekyll family home at Munstead House, near Godalming, and it was then that Bernard and Barbara got engaged; but only the immediate family knew. One of the first to be told, of course, was James Barrie, who wrote enthusiastically:

> It is grand news, and tho' I am of course not surprised by it I am quite excited. You know how much your happiness means to me, and I am sure that this is the happiest thing that could come to you. I have long guessed that your Barbara is a very delightful person, as she ought to be to be worthy of you, and I hope she is now to become a great friend of mine. I thereby take her to my heart.[1]

Barbara had planned some months earlier to take her sons Martin and Guy for a second visit to their grandparents in France, and they left England on 29 December. For this reason the formal announcement of the engagement was delayed until mid-February. It attracted so much unwanted publicity of a personal nature that they were determined to avoid any more for the wedding itself.

On 3 May 1922 Bernard went to St Andrews where he and others were to have honorary degrees conferred upon them by the Chancellor of the University, Earl Haig. This was the occasion of Barrie's installation as Rector when Freyberg was one of several people he recommended to receive degrees (others included Ellen Terry and Thomas Hardy), and the ceremony was marked by his famous address on 'Courage'. Barrie's theme was 'all goes if courage goes'. In this he was echoing Goethe's 'Possessions lost – something lost; honour lost, much lost; courage lost, everything lost.' Barrie gave two examples of courage. The first was Captain Scott and his death in the Antarctic. The second was that of Freyberg, which he put in these words:

> There is an officer who was the first of our Army to land at Gallipoli. He was dropped overboard to light decoys on the shore, so as to deceive the Turks as to where the landing was to be. He pushed a raft containing these in front of him. It was a frosty night, and he was naked and painted black. Firing from the ships was going on all round. It was a two-hour swim in pitch darkness. He did it, crawled through the scrub to listen to the talk of the enemy, who were so near that he could have shaken hands with them, lit his decoys and swam back. He seems to look on this as a gay affair. He is a VC now, and you would not think to look at him that he could ever have presented such a disreputable appearance. Would you? (indicating Colonel Freyberg).[12]

Just before the wedding Bernard sent his medals by post to his future wife. The marriage itself took place quietly on the morning of 14 June 1922 at the church of St Martha, three miles from Guildford near the village of Albury. The date was chosen because it was Barbara's birthday. The church had always been 'special' in the family, and is on a high hill on the Pilgrim's Way, inaccessible by car to this day, and with magnificent views over the surrounding countryside. The press did not find out about the time and place of the wedding, but in order to keep the event quiet no photographers were present, and consequently there were no wedding photographs. Barrie was best man. A short announcement of the event was put in the papers next day. The ceremony was followed by a wedding lunch at Munstead for relatives

[151]

and close friends. Afterwards Bernard and Barbara were driven to London to catch a train from Euston to Bodnant in North Wales for the first part of their honeymoon. The second half was spent some weeks later at the Palazzo Barbarigo in Venice, the home of Barbara's aunt Caroline Eden.

10

A New Family

Bernard and Barbara's marriage marked a new beginning for both of them. It ended five years of widowhood for Barbara, after a first marriage which in later years she herself described as having been very much 'a boy and girl affair'; and it gave Bernard the first settled home of his adult life.

Barbara had been born Barbara Jekyll in 1887, second of the three children of Sir Herbert and Lady Jekyll. The Jekylls were an old English family who came originally from Lincolnshire and East Anglia. Their most famous forebear was Sir Joseph Jekyll, Master of the Rolls in the reign of Queen Anne. Another Joseph Jekyll was a famous wit and a prominent member of the Prince Regent's circle.

Colonel Sir Herbert Jekyll was educated at 'The Shop' – Woolwich Academy – where he won the Sword of Honour and went on to serve with the Royal Engineers in the Ashanti War. As Private Secretary to Lord Carnarvon, and as Secretary to the Royal Commission for the Defence of British Possessions and Commerce Overseas, he travelled to Singapore and Ceylon to report on fortifications and to design new ones. His other posts included being Private Secretary for three years to Lord Crewe while he was Lord Lieutenant of Ireland (1892–5); British Commissioner of the 1900 Paris Exhibition, for which he appointed Edwin Lutyens to design the British Pavilion; and Secretary of the Board of Trade. In addition Herbert was a keen gardener, a gifted wood carver, an organist and a founder member of the Bach Choir. In 1881 he married Agnes, daughter of William Graham, Liberal MP for Glasgow, whose numerous projects included managing a maternity home in the East End, working as chairman of the visiting

[153]

committee for a girls' Borstal and chairman of a hospital supplies warehouse for St John of Jerusalem during the Great War. At the first dinner party of their married life the guests included Robert Browning, John Ruskin and Sir Edward Burne-Jones. She was the first person to supply recipes to *The Times*, which were later published in 1922 as *Kitchen Essays, with recipes and their occasions.*

Barbara's early years were spent at Munstead in a close-knit and happy family. As was the custom of the period, she and her younger sister Pamela were educated mostly at home, and only her brother Timmy was sent to boarding school. Timmy had a brilliant beginning, getting into College at Eton, where he won the classical Newcastle Scholarship in 1900 and then an Exhibition to Balliol College, Oxford; but unfortunately his early promise did not endure. Barbara and Pamela, a lively and intelligent pair of sisters remained close, however, all their lives. In 1908, at the age of eighteen, Pamela married Reginald McKenna, then First Lord of the Admiralty, who was twenty-four years older than she was. By the time Bernard first met him in 1916 he was Chancellor of the Exchequer. In 1922, when Bernard and Barbara married, he was Chairman of the Midland Bank, a position he retained until his death. 'Reggie' was one of the few people of whom Bernard was always much in awe and he frequently turned to him for advice. 'Reggie is undoubtedly the wisest man I know,' Bernard used to say.

Bernard also acquired a number of lively aunts by his marriage. The most remarkable as well as the most formidable was Gertrude Jekyll (1843–1932). Through her books she probably did more than anyone else to change the face of English gardening at the beginning of the century. Her talents were wide-ranging and diverse. She was a competent painter, and from her workshop came a steady stream of metalwork including salvers worked in silver. She was an expert at carving in wood, and also a photographer, who developed and printed her own films. For nearly forty years she and Sir Edwin Lutyens worked together – he as architect of the house, she designing the garden – culminating in the Viceroy's House in New Delhi. When Bernard knew her she had entered the last decade of her life.

In one respect Gertrude was fortunate, namely the age in which she lived. When she was born gardens were mostly elaborately formal, laid out in accordance with a rigid Italianate pattern. By the time she began to take an interest in gardening in the late 1870s the tradition was ripe for change. In conjunction with other kindred spirits, such as William Robinson, Gertrude began to experiment with more informal garden layouts. The first was at her new home at Munstead House, which was built the year after her father's death in 1876. Gradually, as her scope and experience increased, she started to write articles in the *Journal of the Royal Horticultural Society*, *Country Life* and other papers and magazines. By the turn of the century she was ready to consolidate her knowledge into a series of gardening books which became classics in her own lifetime. In her later years she became more and more of a recluse, cutting herself off from a world with which she felt increasingly out of sympathy. At heart she was a Victorian countrywoman who rejoiced in nature's order of things.

Bernard and Gertrude got on well together. When Bernard went to Moore Barracks at Shorncliffe in 1929 Gertrude made a design for the Commanding Officer's small garden there. It was among the last things she did. After Sir Herbert Jekyll's funeral on 3 October 1932, Sir Edwin Lutyens went to see Gertrude:

> Afterwards I saw Bumps [Sir Edwin's nickname for Gertrude], self-possessed and herself – very feeble she was in her bedroom with a delicious dark blue felt cap on her head. She was very happy with Bernard [Freyberg] who sees a good deal of her and asks her endless questions and waits for her deliberate answers in which she delights.[1]

Gertrude died two months later on 8 December 1932.

Caroline Eden (née Jekyll) was another gardening aunt of Barbara's. Born in 1837, she was the eldest sister of Herbert and Gertrude. In 1867 she married Frederick Eden and because he suffered from poor health they decided to make their home in Venice. Caroline lived there for the next fifty years. Their house, called the Palazzo Barbarigo, was at the entrance to the Grand Canal and they also had a large garden on the Guidecca, which inevitably became known to the considerable English community in Venice as the Garden of Eden.

Aunt Caroline's (or 'Cary's') house in Venice was very popular with her family in England. It gave them not only the excuse for visits but a comfortable residence once they got there, after the twenty-four hour journey on the Orient Express. Barbara stayed at the Palazzo Barbarigo several times before the First World War. After Frederick Eden died in 1916 Cary decided to remain until the war was over. She was still there in July 1922 when Bernard and Barbara stayed during the second part of their honeymoon. She died in London in 1928 aged ninety-one.

Barbara's mother Agnes had four sisters, of whom the closest to her was Frances. In 1883 Frances married Sir John Horner of Mells Manor near Frome in Somerset. Mells was that rarest and most desirable of all properties, a *small* Elizabethan manor house. It had come into the Horner family after the Dissolution of the Monasteries in

1537, and before then had belonged to the Abbey of Glastonbury. This was the origin of the nursery rhyme about Little Jack Horner pulling out a plum – Mells Manor. Lady Horner, an intellectual and a leading hostess in Edwardian times, was one of the 'Souls' – the group, including Arthur Balfour and Margot Asquith, who used to meet from time to time in each other's houses to discuss philosophy and the topics of the day. For nearly half a century, because of Frances and Agnes, there was a close link between Munstead and Mells. This continued into the next generation through Pamela and Barbara, for when the time came for the McKennas to find themselves a country house in the early 1920s they came to an arrangement with the Horners and commissioned Sir Edwin Lutyens to rebuild Mells Park, which had burnt down in 1917. Bernard and Barbara used frequently to visit Mells in the early years of their marriage.

Alice Hogg was another of Barbara's aunts. By the time Bernard came on the scene she was dead, but her son Douglas was much in their life at this period. In later years as Lord Hailsham he was appointed Lord Chancellor (1928–9 and 1935–8), an office held in 1970 and 1979 by his son, the irrepressible Quintin.

In the early years of his marriage Bernard also came into frequent contact with the first Lord and Lady Aberconway, the parents of Barbara's first husband Francis McLaren. They always took a close interest in their grandsons and lent their house, Bodnant, to Barbara and Bernard for their honeymoon.

The Freyberg 'family' consisted of Bernard, Barbara and Paul (born 1923); but also Barbara's two sons, Bernard's stepsons, Martin and Guy McLaren. One of the reasons why Barbara took so long to agree to marry Bernard had been because she wanted to be certain that her sons would accept him in place of their own father, whom they were too young to remember. She also wanted to be sure that Bernard would treat them as if they were his own children. On both counts she never had any cause for regret.

Martin and Guy were quite different from each other. Martin was serious-minded, scholarly, good at games, fond of music and with a keen sense of history and of beauty. Guy was an extrovert, interested in people rather than abstract theory. He was particularly good at making friends and enjoying life, and was more at home on the racecourse than in the library.

One other important member of our family circle was my mother's maid Muriel Tolley, or Milly as she was invariably called, who came from Breamore in Wiltshire. Although strictly speaking she was not one of the family, she was certainly one by adoption. She was the principal prop of the household and played a major part in my father's life for thirty years. Cooks, parlourmaids, housemaids and nannies came and went, but Milly was always there – even during the Second World War when my mother travelled to Egypt and Italy with 2 NZEF – and because of her continuity she acquired a remarkable influence and authority. All of us, my mother, my father and we three boys, were devoted to Milly, and I believe that the feeling was returned, although there were moments when this was far from obvious. Milly could be very much of a disciplinarian, and when I was little and had done something I should not have done I was far more concerned about what Milly, rather than my parents, might say. When roused she had a remarkable command of the English language, and could give a more effective 'rocket' than any I ever heard in twenty-five years in the Grenadier Guards. In the early days my brothers and I would say to each other, 'Watch out, Milly's on the warpath,' in tones of alarm tinged with no little apprehension. Even my father was not immune from Milly's strictures. Although she was devoted to him her first loyalty was always to my mother. Several generations of ADCs would testify that in small matters my father was often vague and absent-minded. But none of them would have dared to say to him what Milly did when he lost the special gloves my mother had given him, or forgot her birthday.

My parents' marriage was an extremely happy one. They were to go through many anxious times together, particularly during the Second World War, but it was made sustainable by the deep love and affection they had for each other. Bernard and Barbara were both strong characters, but because they were quick to adapt to each other's ways their personalities complemented one another and rarely clashed. Thus it was that in the early years Bernard made it his business to become a part of Barbara's family and to fit into English life. Later, in the Second World War and at Government House, when Bernard returned to his New Zealand background, it was Barbara who had to do the adapting. It says much for both of them that they were able to adjust to each other's environment with so little difficulty.

11

Only Five Hundred Yards Short

Although Barbara had a house in Little College Street, Westminster, which was designed for her by Sir Edwin Lutyens, it dated from her first marriage and she did not want to live there now. Instead she and Bernard found a house in a quiet street to the north of Hyde Park, connecting with Hyde Park Square. Barbara wrote:

> 7 Clarendon Place was to be our base for thirty years and, during a great part of the time, our home. It was a cheerful, pleasant house with half of the windows in Hyde Park Square and the front door and south windows in Clarendon Place, with a view to the Park.

She was again able to obtain the help and advice of 'Ned' Lutyens as a close family friend: 'Ned's usual abundance of ideas, including lining the dining-room with mirrors, soon helped us to transform it into an attractive house of charm.' The family was able to move into Clarendon Place a few days before their son Paul was born there on 27 May 1923.

Soon after Bernard returned from New Zealand in 1921, he had been given a staff appointment at the headquarters of 44 Division. The job of GSO2 of a territorial division in England in peacetime was not a demanding one and ideal therefore for someone at the start of his married life. It was full-time only in the summer months when camps and training were taking place. At other times it consisted of routine administration and the writing of defence and training schemes. The location of the headquarters of 44 Division at Woolwich was convenient enough for Bernard as it enabled him to establish his new home in London, and to commute daily to his office. It also gave him time to decide whether he was wise to stay in the army.

Over the years Bernard had become increasingly interested in politics. The ending of the war had increased rather than diminished political pressures in England. For over 200 years the two main parties, the Whigs and Tories, or, as they became, Liberals and Conservatives, had more or less taken it in turn to govern the country. However, under the strain of the early years of the war, the ruling Liberal party split into two factions headed respectively by Asquith and Lloyd George. Another factor in the immediate post-war period was the arrival on the parliamentary scene of numbers of Labour members. In 1922 the political situation was still fluid and no one foresaw that both the Asquith and Lloyd George sections of the Liberal Party would soon be reduced to impotent rumps.

Although Bernard seemed intent on making the army his career, it was not without some misgiving. Understandably a pacifist element was developing in England in the early 1920s which held that the cost of the Great War had been so terrible that it was inconceivable that another war could be allowed to happen. In 1922 this seemed a plausible proposition, and with the 'Geddes Axe' cutting down the size of the services, and the ten-year rule coming into operation – which laid down that post-war military plans must be based on the assumption that no war would break out for a minimum of ten years – the prospects of a worthwhile career in the army did not look particularly promising. Bernard was ambitious and it was natural he should explore other possibilities before deciding finally to settle down as a professional soldier.

Barbara's first husband Francis McLaren had been the Liberal Member of Parliament for the Holland with Boston constituency of Lincolnshire. As Barbara's family and friends were mostly Liberals of the Asquith persuasion, Bernard, newly arrived on the scene, naturally gravitated to the Liberal cause. Throughout his life he was a political moderate who detested the extremes, whether the Nazi regime in Germany, the Fascists in Italy, the Franco dictatorship of Spain or Communism in any of its guises; and later he was to find the moderate Labour leaders of the 1940s – Clement Attlee and his colleagues in Britain, and Peter Fraser and Walter Nash in New Zealand – easy and pleasant to work with. In the early 1920s the moderate party seemed to be the Asquith Liberals.

Lloyd George's coalition government had continued to be supported by the Conservative Party for some time after the war, but with increasing restlessness. At a meeting of Conservative MPs at the

Carlton Club on 18 October 1922 they voted to discontinue support, which led to the fall of Lloyd George's government and to a General Election. The powerful committee of Conservative backbenchers is still known as the 1922 Committee.

The election of 1922 was called in a great hurry, and Bernard only had a few days in which to find a constituency and get adopted. On 28 October he presented himself before a meeting of the Liberal Association for the constituency of Cardiff South, and within two days was adopted as their official candidate.[1] The General Election was held on 15 November. Freyberg's election literature places more emphasis on his status as an 'Independent Liberal' than in identifying himself with the policies of the warring Liberal factions. His main opponent was the sitting Conservative Member, Sir John Cory, who had had a majority of 3,150 at the previous election. Freyberg was defeated, but not without reducing this majority by nearly two-thirds to 933, gaining 6,996 votes to Cory's 7929. Labour came third.

Whether Freyberg would have made a good politician seems doubtful, but as it turned out this was the only election he ever fought, and in those days serving officers were not required to resign their commissions *unless* they were elected. It was, however, one of the deciding factors in making up his mind that he should turn all his energies to soldiering.

With his marriage and the election 1922 had been an important year for Freyberg. By way of contrast 1923 and 1924 were years of consolidation, of the completion of his new house and the birth of his son. He worked diligently as GSO2 44 Division at Woolwich, but this still left him plenty of time for outside pursuits including the resumption of swimming. In August Bernard was writing from Dover describing visits to the South Goodwin lightship, the state and direction of the tides and the temperature of the water.[1] What he was up to was preparing to swim the English Channel, which he had first dreamt of doing back on the Waihou river in 1911.

On 25 April 1925 Bernard was present at the unveiling, timed for the tenth anniversary of the landing at Gallipoli, of the memorial to the fallen of the Royal Naval Division, which then stood at the Admiralty corner of Horse Guards Parade. The memorial took the form of a fountain designed by Edwin Lutyens, on the west side of which were inscribed two of Rupert Brooke's poems: the one beginning 'If I should die think only this of me'; and the other containing the words 'These laid the world away, and poured out the red sweet wine of youth'. The ceremony was performed by General Sir Archibald Paris, who had commanded the Naval Division for the first years of its existence. The climax came with an address by Winston Churchill:

> Here, under the shadow of the Admiralty building, where, eleven years ago, the Royal Naval Division was called into martial life, this monument now records their fame and preserves their memory. Their memory is thus linked for ever with the Royal Navy, whose child they were, and whose long annals, rich with romantic and splendid feats of arms, contains no brighter page than theirs.[1]

Early in May Bernard made the first of two battlefield visits, to Valenciennes with a group studying the opening phases of military operations in 1914.[1] On the second occasion in the middle of September he returned to the Ancre Valley for an exercise that he had set his Territorials. In between these two visits he made his first attempt to swim the English Channel.

In an article for the *Household Brigade Mazagine*, entitled 'On training for the Channel swim',[2] Bernard described his preparations. He had visited the British Museum Library to read newspaper articles about previous Channel swims, and had studied a professional swimmer's account of the training he underwent. This consisted of an extremely arduous and spartan regime which, to Bernard's mind, insisted on making training conditions as uncomfortable and miserable as possible. Bernard was determined to avoid this, while at the same time making himself as fit as he could.

During his first two months of training he walked ten miles every two days, and on the third day swam for two hours at the Bath Club. During the next two months the length of his walks was increased to fifteen miles, and the swimming was transferred to the open sea. A major problem was how to get accustomed to the cold, since even in summer the temperature in the Channel rarely rose above 60° F. Previous swimmers had lost between 10 lb and 14 lb in weight in as many hours in the water, due to the body burning up tissue in its vain effort to maintain normal temperature. There seemed to be no very satisfactory answer to this problem: although one long training swim was recommended in order to experience some of the difficulties likely to be encountered, it was thought that repeated lengthy swims did more harm than good. Bernard's main endurance test immediately before the swim was a 35-mile walk unbroken over ten hours.

In preparation for the Channel swim my parents rented a house on the coast. This was Gun House, New Romney, not far from Folkestone and Dover. My brothers Martin and Guy and I went there too. The swim started at Cap Gris Nez at 8.16 p.m. on 4 August 1925. It attracted a huge amount of publicity – swimming the Channel was a relatively new kind of venture and no Englishman had yet succeeded in doing so. It had been accomplished from France to England by only two swimmers, Enrico Tiraboschi of Italy, and Charles Toth, an American, both in 1923.[3] Since then, of course, the number who have done so is so great that the feat no longer seems to merit mention in the newspapers. Another reason for the amount of publicity was that Freyberg was known to the press as a 'war hero', and there was genuine admiration that anyone who had been so often and so badly wounded should still take on such a gruelling physical challenge. Moreover the particular details of Freyberg's swim provided a dramatic story. The Special Correspondent of *The Times*, who was in the accompanying tug from start to finish, wrote:

> Lieutenant-Colonel Bernard Freyberg, VC, DSO, has today ended a swim here which lasted 16 hours 44 minutes and was only 500 yards short of a Channel swim. At 1 o'clock this afternoon he was taken out of the water close to the rocks below the Dover Patrol Memorial, exhausted but quite

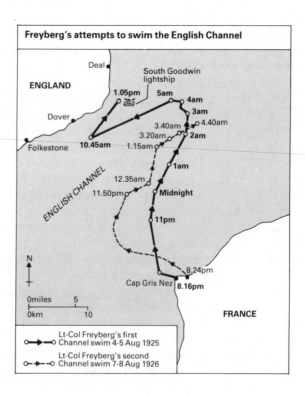

prepared to go on with the struggle if his pilot and trainer had thought him equal to a prolongation of his task by six hours.

That is what continuance of the swim would have meant, for he had arrived about two miles off Dover just an hour too late for the tide to allow him to get to the shore. At 11.15 this morning he was swimming strongly towards the shore, and was little more than a mile from the west entrance to the harbour. Twenty minutes later the tide had turned and he actually began to lose ground. Changing his objective, and gaining something from the northward sweep of the outflowing tide, he made towards the rocks, and passed gradually northwards until at last the hope of getting out of the tidal ebb failed and the only course remaining was to float for four hours until the next flow, or abandon the attempt. Though Colonel Freyberg was unsuccessful, his was a magnificent failure.

The next day, 6 August 1925, Barbara wrote a personal version of the attempt to her parents:

> Bernard was so wonderful through it all, and very philosophical about the end. Actually he was so completely exhausted that I think he realised very little of the last few minutes. The alternative to giving up at the point where he came out, was to drift out to sea for another 4 hours, and then be brought back on the tide after – a matter of at least another 6 hours in the water, and this was altogether out of the question. The last 3 hours after he began to get tired were very agonising, for I didn't want him to give up while there was a hope of his doing it, but this meant egging him on for an extra effort – it felt like beating a willing horse up an impossible hill and when the wrong tide caught us and the hard-won yards up to the Dover Harbour entrance were wiped out in a few minutes and we were swept back and back it was heartbreaking, but the struggle went on for 7 or 8 miles along the coast – always a chance that a few hundred yards of hard swimming would get him in beyond the strong tide, and enable him to land – he would have made nothing of it when he was fresh, but at the end he had all the will and the courage but absolutely no strength left.[1]

At the end of 1925 Bernard's four years as GSO2 of 44 Division came to an end. In his final report General Henry Hodgson wrote:

> I am sorry to be losing him – his work has been of great value . . . I consider him fully qualified for a 1st Grade Staff Appointment – and yet he is so interested in the Territorial Army that I am sure he would command a TA Infantry Brigade with great success – and I would like to have him in my Division.[4]

The Army Commander General Sir George Milne (later to become CIGS and a peer) added, 'I agree. A very able officer whose promotion should be accelerated in the interests of the Army.'[4]

· · · · ·

It was time for Bernard to return to regimental duty. In January 1926 he was posted back to 1 Battalion Grenadier Guards, then stationed at Victoria Barracks at Windsor. It was not necessary for him to move house since he could stay overnight in the officers' mess when occasion required, and otherwise he commuted to and from London. Apart from his military duties he was determined to have another try at swimming the Channel, and again he took his training seriously. The only difference this time, compared with 1925, was that he took his Grenadier Company with him.

Fifteen years later, after I had joined the regiment, there were still a few senior Warrant Officers in the training battalion who had been with my father at Windsor in 1926–7. When I used to close the sergeants' mess as Picquet Officer they would often give me a drink and reminisce about my father. 'He was a fine officer,' they would say; and then rather glazed looks would come over their faces as once again they force-marched behind him over the endless miles of Windsor Great Park and Salisbury Plain, 'but thank heaven I'm not in his Company any more!'

Bernard made his second attempt to swim the Channel on 7–8 August 1926. He entered the water from the little sandy beach to the north of Cap Gris Nez at 8.42 p.m., cheered by a fairly big crowd of onlookers. He started off at a brisk pace of nineteen strokes to the minute using overarm sidestroke, and during the first hours made good progress. *The Times* Special Correspondent reported that 'he began to travel towards England at a pace never approached by him last year'. At 1.15 a.m. the captain of the launch reported that he was only 7 miles from the South Goodwin lightship. But two hours later he was still 7 miles away. Freyberg's leg wound had caused him intense pain in his groin and deprived him of the power to kick his legs. He remained in the water for a further hour and a half, in the hope that his ability to swim might return. When it did not he gave up, at 4.40 a.m.[1] This was his last attempt to fulfil his principal swimming ambition.

Six months later Bernard and Barbara took a month's holiday, which began with a four-day sea journey to Gibraltar where they arrived on 8 February 1927. They set off from Gibraltar by car and rail for leisurely visits to Malaga, Granada and Ronda in southern Spain until 18 February, when they returned to Gibraltar via Algeciras. The *Iron Duke*, Jellicoe's flagship at Jutland, was in harbour and they went on board to have tea with the captain. On 19 February they crossed over to Tangier, and their visit to Morocco included Tetuan, Rabat, Meknes, Fez, Casablanca and Marrakesh.

Back at home the spring and summer of 1927 was the time when Freyberg acquired a greyhound called Jealous Branty[1] who proceeded to win a lot of races at the White City and make large sums of prize money for his delighted owner. But on 31 August Freyberg was warned by the War Office to stand by for a staff job in October. This turned out to be at Headquarters Eastern Command, at the Horse Guards.[1] Although it was another GSO2 appointment as a Brevet Lieutenant-Colonel he was now a *substantive* major, and the probability was that he would not do a full tour before command of a battalion came his way. In the meantime he and Barbara could continue to live at Clarendon Place without any upheaval.

This was just as well because 1928 began with another operation, this time on Freyberg's ear. Fortunately it was very successful and restored his hearing to something approaching normal. On 8 March he and Barbara went to the south of France to recuperate with Pamela and Reggie McKenna, who had been lent a yacht, the *Cutty Sark*, by the Duke of Westminster, the extraordinary 'Bendor'. A fellow guest was Admiral Jellicoe, full of stories of his happy five years as Governor-General of New Zealand immediately after the war.[1]

Freyberg's name came to the top of the Brevet List in the early autumn of 1928 at the same time as the Military Secretary was looking for a new commanding officer for 1 Battalion Manchester Regiment based at Moore Barracks, Shorncliffe near Folkestone. He was offered the appointment, which he accepted. On his leaving Eastern Command the Chief of Staff, Major-General H. J. Elles, made an important assessment of Freyberg's military prospects:

Freyberg has had a remarkable career and at the age of 39 will command a battalion. Owing to an early brevet he will on promotion to Full Colonel find himself at the top of the Colonels' List before the age of 45. Everything in his record up to date including a most distinguished war record makes me anticipate his promotion to Major-General at a very early age and his consequent eligibility for the highest ranks of the Army. His career therefore becomes public property and should be so devised that he may be able to give the Service the fullest return.

Of his capacity for command in the field I can have no doubt. He has had great experience and has exceptional personality. His staff experience has not been wide, that is a matter of time. As a staff officer he is a tremendous worker, exceptionally thorough and methodical and of astounding persistence. What he will require on completion of his command is not staff work of a detailed nature for which he is already well equipped by nature and habit, but employment at work which deals with problems in their broader aspects.

I would suggest training at the Imperial Defence College or in Military Operations at the War Office.

[165]

Given this, he has the qualities to take him very high.
I have had a delightful year with him.[4]

The C-in-C, General Sir R. Whigham, concurred:

I have formed the highest opinion of Lt.-Colonel Freyberg's capacity for
work, and I endorse all that Major-General Elles has written of his
personality. He will certainly go far in the Service and I recommend that
after a suitable term in command of a battalion he be employed at the War
Office. His capacity for command has been proved in the war. What he
needs is experience in the higher sphere of military administration.[4]

12

Unit Administration and Half-Pay

Freyberg took command of 1 Battalion Manchester Regiment in March 1929. Under the Cardwell system* still in operation, the Manchester Regiment had one battalion at home and one abroad. Priority for reinforcements and the best officers was given to the overseas battalion. As a result, the morale and general standing of the home battalion tended to suffer; indeed Freyberg discovered a considerable restlessness in the battalion when he arrived.

From the day of his arrival he identified himself completely with all aspects of the battalion's life; and after a period of stunned disbelief the men responded enthusiastically. The officers' mess cook, Sergeant Worsman, was both a good cook and a very observant NCO – indeed, when in 1939 Freyberg took command of the New Zealand Division he obtained the services of Worsman as head cook for his 'A' mess. Worsman declared that 'the General's interest in the welfare and safety of the private soldier was a revelation to his brother officers'. He wrote:

> When he came to Shorncliffe I was the first to meet him; all the officers got out of the way because, to be quite honest, they were scared stiff. The very next morning Freyberg went over to the cookhouse unattended, and from that time onwards my Regiment became the best fed in the Army. The men won everything that was possible, and they were proud of their Commanding Officer.[1]

*The Cardwell system of linked battalions was part of Lord Cardwell's army reforms of 1871–2. They included the abolition of the purchase of commissions.

This observation identifies two of the characteristics that marked Freyberg's attitude to peacetime soldiering: the men had to be properly looked after first, and only then could they be asked to give of their best on the ranges, at sport, on manoeuvres or whatever. If this sounds obvious, in the 1920s and 1930s it was rare for a commanding officer to concern himself so directly with his soldiers' welfare.

The commanding officer's house at Moore Barracks was situated at the far end of the main officers' mess block. The barracks were old and most of the battalion transport was still horse-drawn. The house was quite small and built of unappealing dark-red brick. Barbara wrote:

> I shall never forget my first sight of our new home. With my snob views on houses after the spoiling experience of my Lutyens home, I could hardly believe it was true when I saw the long, redbrick, slate-tiled building of the Officers' Mess, terminating in the bay windows of the Commanding Officer's quarters. To make matters worse, there had been a flood and, being winter and a cold one at that, the floor of the drawing-room was a sheet of ice.[2]

The family moved down from London soon after my father took over, and my mother quickly became immersed in welfare committees, wives' clubs and the Married Families' Club, which she started and which grew and grew. 'Our two years in that little house,' she wrote, 'were completely happy and full of interest, fun and enjoyment.'

The 1 Manchester was one of the battalions of 10 Infantry Brigade which, in turn, was part of 4 Division. This meant that Freyberg spent a busy time on training during the manoeuvre season in the autumn of 1929. His first Confidential Report as a battalion commander contained the usual compliments, so that it is almost a relief to read that his new brigade commander did not think much of his 'horsemanship'!

On 9 November 1929 Freyberg attended the Princes Chamber of the House of Lords for the largest ever gathering of holders of the Victoria Cross at a dinner given by the Prince of Wales. Some 320 VC holders were present, the oldest aged eighty-six, having won the decoration fifty years before against the Zulus at Rorke's Drift. Two days later all the VCs attended the British Legion's Festival of Remembrance at the Royal Albert Hall.

To try and raise the morale of the home battalion and to 'put them on the map' Freyberg made a request to the King, George V, that he become Colonel-in-Chief of the regiment. After some delicate negotiations with the Palace the proposal was eventually agreed, and a big parade was planned. Much of the early part of 1930 was spent on drill and smartening up the soldiers' appearance. Eventually the day came, 16 May 1930, when the battalion marched to Buckingham Palace and was inspected by the King in the garden. Speeches by Freyberg and the King followed, three cheers were given, and eventually the battalion marched back to Wellington Barracks. Contemporary accounts confirm that the officers and men were very pleased with the occasion, and that it did give the necessary boost to the battalion's morale.

While Freyberg was with the Manchester Regiment, he began to consider writing a book about the best way to look after and administer army units. Although *A Study of Unit Administration* was not published until 1933, most of the work that went into it was done at Shorncliffe and immediately afterwards at Salisbury in 1931–2 when his role brought him into greater contact with administrative details.[3] Incidentally it was the only book Freyberg published, and even then it came out anonymously.

Freyberg described his book as a short study 'written for the guidance of Regimental and Staff Officers serving with units on the Home Establishments'. He went on:

If, however, it should get into the hands of anyone unversed in Army methods, I should like to explain that the criticisms given are ones of detail and they must not be twisted into an attack on the whole system of unit administration. That units are able to feed their men, and feed them excellently, on a ration that costs less than 9d per man per day, is ample proof of the high standard and efficiency of the system . . . It is in the spirit of a search for further improvement under modern conditions that this book has been written.[3]

The year 1929 was of course that of the crash on Wall Street, which had severe repercussions throughout Britain. Individuals in almost all walks of life faced considerable difficulties with falling incomes, and in the armed services in particular pay was reduced by a quarter. This effect was made worse because the issue was handled with so little explanation and such insensitivity that, in the Royal Navy, there was a mutiny at Invergordon. Freyberg was keenly aware of the hardships caused to the ordinary soldier, and especially to those who were married but not 'on strength': for reasons of economy the Treasury had ruled that only a small proportion of soldiers in a battalion could receive marriage allowance or be housed in army quarters. The rest had no provision made for them, so that, officially, the existence of their families was ignored. As Freyberg wrote:

To give an idea of the extent of the fall, the following comparison is made between the conditions as they were when the scale of living was arranged in 1921, and the conditions in 1930.

[In an average infantry battalion]

	1921	1930
Pay per man per day	3/6	2/-
Value of rations per man per day	1/10	8d

. . . Moreover, because of the Depression the whole system of unit messing has been thrown out of gear by the uneven fluctuation of the wholesale and retail prices of foodstuffs.[3]

Obviously Freyberg could do nothing about the general economic situation; but where he felt he could contribute was in making sure that the administrative resources available to units were utilised to their best advantage. In this, as in his immediate attention to the men's food and welfare when he arrived at Shorncliffe, Freyberg was well ahead of his time. Most commanding officers of the period left the administration of their units to the quartermaster, and intervened only when something went wrong. Freyberg took the view that it was one of a CO's first duties to concern himself directly with all aspects of the administration of a battalion:

The planning of an administrative policy requires not only an intimate knowledge of regulations, but also of the reasons which led up to their being written. If regulations are unintelligently applied, they frequently defeat the very object for which they were framed. For this reason, Commanding Officers must review the whole ground to be covered, and then lay down a clear and complete unit administrative policy.[3]

He also felt the need for a proper budget forecast:

Even when the financial situation is made clear, it is difficult to get units to alter their scale of living. Any change is deprecated; teams continue to be sent to Bisley, boxing coaches are engaged, and commitments entered into upon the same scale as in 1920, when unit finances were in a flourishing condition. In this way a unit finds itself harnessed to an expenditure out of proportion to its income, and when the Canteen account is exhausted, the men themselves are put under stoppages of pay, to make good the gap. This is the start of a thoroughly vicious administrative system . . .[3]

[170]

Freyberg noticed that there was a direct relationship between petty crime and a badly fed unit, and that this followed a well-established pattern. Barbara recorded how he linked the two when he took over command:

He started by inspecting the kitchen refuse tubs and, as he had expected, found them full of loaves of bread and only half-consumed joints of meat, and it was soon apparent that the meals in the messrooms were unpalatable. Hence, early in the week the soldiers were hungry and spent their money in the NAAFI buying the food that ought to have been provided as part of their regular fare. When the money was spent and the hunger still unassuaged, other ways of raising funds had to be found and a campaign of theft began – hence the lengthy crime sheets.

It was only a matter of days before the regimental cooks were taken in hand, with fresh ideas for menus introduced and a general revival of interest with competition as to which mess could produce the most attractive and appetising meals and the chain began to unwind – less need for substitute NAAFI food, so less expenditure, and with more money still unspent the urge toward theft diminished.[2]

Whenever Freyberg inspected a unit – as in his next appointment as Assistant Quartermaster-General (AQMG), Southern Command – the first thing he always asked to see were the crime statistics. If they were above average he suspected something was wrong with the unit's administration. His next port of call would be the swill tubs in the cookhouse. In a badly administered unit these were usually full, indicating bad planning and unnecessary wastage – for example, loaves of bread thrown away indicated that the unit did not make its own sausages. Further investigation of how the unit spent its ration money usually confirmed that it was buying the wrong items and did not use its resources to purchase fresh fruit and vegetables, which could only be obtained locally with cash.

Before the Second World War the feeding arrangements of the British Army were based on three elements. There was a Royal Army Service Corps (RASC) ration, which was issued in kind by weight; second was a NAAFI portion consisting of various commodities, again supplied in kind; and third, a messing cash allowance for the purchase of local produce. These were all scaled according to the number of men in the unit, the ration strength. The art of a well-administered unit lay in knowing how to use the various components to the best advantage, when to overdraw some items and underdraw others and where to purchase in bulk from the cheapest sources. The system allowed for great flexibility and endless permutations, but only for those who knew their way around.

As Freyberg wrote, the meat ration per person was enough for one meat meal a day, plus sufficient to make rissoles or sausages for four breakfast meals a week. If a unit was buying sausages rather than making them it indicated the wrong use of resources, in that money was being spent on sausages from the cash allowance, which ought to have been used only for, say, fresh vegetables which could not be provided any other way. If units failed to provide the number of meat meals required it pointed to faulty planning, bad butchering or theft.

He also examined the different uses that could be made of the basic commodities:

> The problem, therefore, of getting the best value out of the goods issued at contract rates is an interesting one. There does not appear to be any difficulty in consuming any of the commodities, except bacon, cheese and perhaps a small proportion of the jam. As it is permissible to overdraw any other cheap commodities, it is suggested that the solution would appear to be to overdraw the sugar, flour and margarine, and start to bake cakes and make puddings, upon a scale at present not generally attempted. Several units which have lately sent their cooks to learn cake-making at Lyons, Cadby Hall, and other bakers, are now successfully producing slab cake, buns, sponge-cake and doughnuts, etc. at a cost of just over twopence per pound.[3]

In his book Freyberg went into detail about how to get the best value out of the resources available – from selling swill and dripping to the need for a separate unofficial clothing account – insisting that men should not be made to pay for necessities such as extra coal in severe weather; and he defined the exact responsibilities of the commanding officer, the messing officer, the quartermaster and the master cook to obtain the most satisfactory results. Although the figures he used are now out of date and the feeding standards required in the 1930s were less sophisticated than they are today, the principles he set out for unit administration are still valid. What was unusual was to find a commanding officer who knew more about the finer details of the system than most quartermasters and RASC officers, and was able to describe them with such clarity. *A Study of Unit Administration* had a steady sale through the 1930s, became an accepted army manual and rapidly sold out at the beginning of the Second World War.

Freyberg's knowledge and experience in this field proved to be invaluable when it came to devising a suitable framework for the administration of the New Zealand Expeditionary Force in the Second World War.

In 1930 Freyberg had a busy autumn with manoeuvres which lasted for the whole of August and until the third week of September. He commanded 10 Infantry Brigade on exercises and at the end of the year his commander-in-chief considered him well fitted to command a brigade.

The policy in the 1920s and 1930s was for commanding officers to be given short rather than long tours in command in order to ease the promotion blockage that then existed. Freyberg stayed with the 1 Manchesters for just two years and left early in 1931. He had been notified in the autumn that his next appointment was to be as AQMG Southern Command. At the same time his Brevet automatically made him a full colonel, which was back-dated so that his seniority as a colonel dated from 1 January 1922 and meant that he was already a long way up the list for his next promotion. The quick advancement that Barrie and Oc Asquith had predicted for him was coming about.

As AQMG Southern Command Freyberg was no longer involved with the military training side but with the administrative and 'Q', or 'Quartermaster', branches. As Barbara describes:

> His Shorncliffe experience stood him in good stead for it fell to him to sort out the problems of the large number of regiments under Southern Command and he soon found himself again making for the pig buckets, and finding the usual sequence of problems arising from poorly run messes and wasteful use of rations, which were perfectly adequate if used with intelligence. Southern Command covered a big area and his work took him far and wide, including the big concentration of camps at Bulford and Tidworth.[2]

In 1931 Headquarters Southern Command was situated in the middle of Salisbury, so the Freyberg family rented a house not far from the centre. It was a typical early twentieth-century dwelling of the 'stockbroker' type, known as Harnham Croft; but it had magnificent views of Salisbury Cathedral across the meadows and must have been close to the spot where Constable painted his picture of the cathedral a century before. The family would go for early morning rides on the downs, and Barbara in particular was able to enjoy the cathedral music under Sir Walter Alcock.

Martin and Guy at this time were at Eton, while Paul attended the Cathedral Choir school, a day school in the Cathedral Close. Barbara sang in the Three Choirs Festival, held that year in Gloucester

[173]

Cathedral. James Barrie came to stay in early May and in August Bernard and Barbara went on holiday for the first time in two years, taking Martin and Guy with them and visiting Normandy, Brittany and the Loire Valley. Christmas was spent at Munstead for a special reason. On 29 December Herbert and Agnes Jekyll celebrated their golden wedding, and the whole family turned out for the occasion. In fact it was the last such gathering and, for the family, marked the end of an era.

The first of them to die was Sir Herbert Jekyll, at the end of September 1932, followed ten weeks later by his sister Gertrude Jekyll on 8 December. Less than a month afterwards, on 4 January 1933, Lady Aberconway died in the south of France; and Lord Aberconway died there a year later. Lady Jekyll lingered on for four more years. But already the next generation including Bernard and Barbara had become the senior members of the family.

1932 started with a minor disaster when Harnham Croft was sold over the heads of the family, who were given very short notice to leave. Barbara wrote:

> A few rather desperate days followed, for the house was comfortable and suited us well, and houses in and around Salisbury were not easy to come by. However, a miracle happened to save us! There was a charming old lady known to her friends as 'Auntie Bar', who lived in Mompesson House, the dream house of all the exquisite houses in the Close. It looked on to the little playing field of the Choir School and beyond to the Cathedral – a gem of architectural perfection; stone pineapples on the gateposts of the beautiful ironwork gate, magnolias on the walls – to call it breathtaking is no exaggeration, and its beauty has long been recognised, for when it came on to the market at a later stage, it was acquired for the National Trust and is safely endowed as one of the star small houses of the county.
>
> So it was indeed an unbelievable stroke of luck when sweet old Auntie Bar (Miss Townsend), whom I had met and knew slightly, heard of our homeless plight and sent us word that she was about to go for her annual three months holiday to Bournemouth and would let the house to us while she was away. Our time at Mompesson House was sweet but short, but it gave us the flavour of the Salisbury Close as nothing else could have done.[2]

Afterwards the family moved to a tiny house just outside the southern gate of the Close, called De Vaux Place – a fortunate move for financial reasons, Barbara states in her diary, since 1932 was the year when 'every home was feeling the pinch'.

Martin and Guy lived at home after leaving school, while preparing to take the Oxford University entrance examination; and Bernard wrote to Paul nearly every day the following year, when he first went to boarding school. These letters were mostly about family and home doings, but they included other snippets of news – how Bernard went to inspect a School Corps in Birmingham, or watched Dorothy Round playing tennis at Wimbledon.

At the end of 1932 it was announced that Colonel Freyberg had been appointed GSO1 at the War Office with effect from the early summer of 1933. The last few months at Salisbury passed quickly and smoothly with increasing social life and activities. The last Confidential Report on Freyberg from Southern Command contains the first recommendation for his command of a division and promotion to Major-General. His C-in-C General Radcliffe ended the report as follows: 'In addition to the prestige of a most outstanding war record, Colonel Freyberg has a mental ability much above the average, originality, initiative and great force of character. He devotes these qualities untiringly to the interests of the service, in which he should go very far.'

In the summer and autumn of 1933 Bernard was in the process of taking over his new appointment in the Staff Duties Branch of the War Office, the department responsible for the organisation and co-ordination of army units and formations, both at home and abroad. At the same time he and Barbara re-established themselves at Clarendon Place. Martin, who had joined the Supplementary Reserve of the Grenadiers, went to New College, Oxford, and Guy disappeared to Switzerland to work for his Oxford exam. It was a busy time socially, but Barbara was again able to sing with the Bach Choir.

Bernard wrote later of this time:

> This opportunity had given me precise knowledge of the Army system, which though it may seem ponderous and slow, does finally achieve its objectives. I am a great admirer of the War Office, and in my opinion it is an excellent administrative and operational organisation. For anyone who has worked there, especially if they have entered on a low level and climbed the ladder, it is simple to find out the answer to any problem.[4]

On 23 January 1934 Bernard and Barbara went to Southampton to see off his old command, 1 Battalion Manchester Regiment, *en route* to India. In the middle of May Bernard received a letter from the Military Secretary stating he was to be promoted to the rank of Major-General on a date to be announced later. On 16 July the Military Secretary wrote again to inform him that the date would take effect from 'today' and would be published in the *London Gazette* of 'tomorrow'. In fact the news had already been given to the Military Correspondent of *The Times* who, in anticipation of the public announcement, had produced a long article about Freyberg, which began: 'It will certainly arouse special interest, as the one case in which a "New Army" officer has risen from a temporary wartime commission to a Major-General. He is only 45.'[5]

Letters of congratulations poured in. Bernard's promotion meant, of course, that he had to vacate his colonel's post at the War Office, and the handover to his successor took place in September. He was placed on the half-pay list with effect from 16 October. The system that operated in those days was that, if there was no immediate appointment available, officers were placed on half-pay until a vacancy occurred in their new rank.

One of those who wrote to congratulate Freyberg was Winston Churchill. At this time Churchill was beginning to warn the nation about the rise of the Nazi menace in Germany, and on 21 February 1934 Bernard and Barbara had gone to support him at a lecture he gave in London. Winston sent him a copy of Volume II of his *Marlborough: his Life and Times*, which was just published, and on the flyleaf he wrote in his own hand: 'To Bernard Freyberg from Winston S. Churchill Oct. 21 1934. With sincere congratulations on a significant promotion.' Bernard responded at once with an invitation to dinner. This was held on 15 November at Clarendon Place and was probably the most remarkable dinner my parents ever gave, for its consequences affected them both for the rest of their lives. That afternoon my father wrote to me from the Bath Club and sent me the 'placement' for the party – Winston sat between my mother and Lady Horner, and Mrs Churchill between my father and J. M. Barrie. The other men were Samuel Courtauld and Bruce Ottley; and the ladies were Enid Bagnold, the author, and Viscountess Gladstone.

The occasion went with a bang from the word go. After the ladies retired at the end of dinner, as was the custom, the men stayed on at the dinner-table discussing what was likely to happen in Europe with the rise of Hitler. They lost all sense of time. When eventually they broke up Winston went up to the drawing-room to apologise for their lateness, to find only my mother there. The rest of the ladies had gone home, including, to his consternation, his wife Clementine. It was four in the morning. My father had to go round the following day with large boxes of chocolates for Mrs Churchill and the other ladies as a peace offering.

Barrie wrote an apologetic letter to my mother:

You must have felt it shocking our sitting downstairs so long – and it was. But I want you to understand that, putting this aside as after all a mere social transgression, your dinner party was in my opinion (and I doubt not in the opinion of all the men present) the most successful dinner party I have attended for a long time. Winston was in his very best form and we all know how good it can be, but Bernard has never to my knowledge talked so delightfully in a company though he is sometimes thus to me when we are alone. I realised that we were shamefully outstaying our sitting and could have suggested an adjournment, and the one and only reason I didn't was that I was feeling mighty proud of him and determined that everyone of them should have this fine sample of him uncurtailed. He showed the intellect I have always known him to possess and his manner was equally gracious. I was as cocky about him as if I was presenting him to the public.[6]

At the time of this dinner Winston Churchill had known Bernard for over twenty years. They had met before and after the RND expedition to Antwerp. Bernard had sent messages of encouragement from Gallipoli after Winston's political career had seemed to have ended; and Winston had made a special visit to Beaucourt, had seen Freyberg in command of 173 Brigade in 1917, and had written glowingly about him in the Foreword of the RND History. Bernard had canvassed for Winston in the 1923 General Election, and they found themselves in each other's company on many other occasions in the 1920s and 1930s, while their wives had been personal friends for even longer. Now, in November 1934, Winston saw Bernard at the age of forty-five, a newly promoted major-general glowing with self-confidence and at the height of his powers both of intellect and, to outward appearances at least, of physical well-being. The impact he made was considerable, and from that moment Bernard was, in Winston's eyes, a 'marked man'.

Soon after Bernard had been placed on the half-pay list he was invited to attend a staff course at Versailles in December together with two other major-generals, Wavell and Marshall-Cornwall, who were also on the half-pay list. He spent much of that autumn attempting to brush up his French in anticipation of the visit. At this time he also had further trouble with his leg. He wrote to me in October, 'Here is my weekend letter to you, this time from bed where I have been since Friday midday. I am not very ill – just my old leg.'

On 27 October my parents went to New College, Oxford, where Martin was an undergraduate, to stay for the weekend with the Warden and his wife, H. A. L. and Mrs Fisher. Fisher was close to finishing his

[177]

magnum opus, *A History of Europe*. His brother William was then
Commander-in-Chief, Mediterranean Fleet and my parents were to
lunch with him at his headquarters in Malta the following summer. At
the end of the Oxford visit my father gave one of the other guests a lift
back to London. The journey took twice as long as usual because there
was dense fog. Many years later Diana Hopkinson described this drive
in *The Incense Tree*:

> That same weekend I drove home from the Warden's Lodgings with a
> military character, who had been a fellow guest, Bernard Freyberg, the New
> Zealand VC. I listened enthralled to his conversation on themes of which I
> knew nothing but feared much, such as the likelihood of the use of gas in the
> next war. He forecast that it would not be used, but hinted at more terrible
> weapons. As there was a dense fog and the journey took us four hours, we
> had a long, and to me, memorable conversation. I had never met an
> intellectual soldier before. He completely disarmed my grandmother at two
> in the morning by explaining politely that he had seldom had so enjoyable a
> journey back from Oxford. He had disarmed me by not having asked
> questions about what the Younger Generation thought.[7]

November 1934 was a particularly busy month with two or three
engagements each day. Thursday, 1 November, for example, began
with a French lesson for my father at 11 a.m., then Lesley Jowitt and
Enid Lawson came to lunch, and Oc and Betty Asquith to dine. The
final few days of November my parents spent preparing for their three
week visit to Paris for the staff course at Versailles. My father left
London by car on 29 November and arrived in Paris the following day,
in time to meet my mother and Irene Forbes-Adam (née Lawley) who
arrived by train at 6 p.m. The whole party, the Wavells, the Marshall-
Cornwalls, my parents and Irene, stayed at the Hotel Majestic in the
Avenue Kleber, near to the Place de L'Etoile. The military purpose of
the visit was later summed up by Marshall-Cornwall:

> The DMI (Director of Military Intelligence) explained to me that he was
> rather puzzled by the very eulogistic reports he had received from the last
> two Military Attachés in Paris, Gordon Heywood and Paddy Beaumont-
> Nesbit, about the high standard of training and efficiency of the French
> Army, and he would like information from another source. Usually one
> British officer was invited each year to attend this course, which had the
> cumbrous title of *Cycle d'information pour les généraux et colonels*, but this time
> he had got permission for three to attend. The other two were to be Archie
> Wavell and Bernard Freyberg. As he thought my knowledge of French was
> better than that of the other two, I was to make notes of all lectures and
> exercises and assist the others in drawing up the joint final report . . .

Each morning we drove out to Versailles in Bernard's car to attend the lectures and take part in the exercises in the open country, the students being in mixed syndicates. Every evening Archie, Bernard and I met in the hotel and recorded our impressions of the day's work. At the end of the course, which finished just before Christmas, we submitted to the War Office a unanimous report to the effect that the French, far from being leaders in military doctrine, had made no progress whatever since the end of the Great War. They had, for instance, no conception of exploiting the mobility of armoured divisions in tactical manoeuvre. Every attack was envisaged as a head-on frontal assault, with the infantry of one division supported by the artillery of three divisions. It was a complete reversion to the tactics of 1914–18. Needless to say, the War Office was considerably shaken by our evaluation, which differed so widely from that of their Military Attachés.[8]

On 1 December my father gave me an engagingly frank account of his first morning in a letter: 'I went to my military school this morning and started work. We had three lectures all given in French and I found they talked very fast, too fast for me to follow, but I managed to get more or less what they were talking about.'

Fortunately in Marshall-Cornwall they had an expert linguist, and my father was able to participate increasingly in discussions afterwards as the course wore on. His letters mainly describe his other activities. For example, on their first Sunday:

I had no work so we planned a day in the country. Gen. Wavell and wife and daughter aged 15 and mother, Rene Forbes-Adam and I. We bought some food for a picnic and we went off to Chartres to see the most lovely Cathedral that we have ever seen. We had lunch before we arrived and then spent several hours sightseeing. Afterwards we came back and we had dinner in a little restaurant in Paris.[4]

The finale of this pleasant interlude was a luncheon given in their honour at Les Invalides by the Military Governor of Paris, General Gouraud, on 16 December 1934. A few days later my parents returned home for Christmas at Clarendon Place in the best of spirits.

13

Change of Direction

When Freyberg joined the Staff Duties Directorate of the War Office in 1933 he had quickly established a routine for himself. He would leave Clarendon Place each morning after breakfast and walk the two miles to Whitehall across Hyde Park, Green Park and St James's Park, arriving by 9.30. After he finished the day's work he would go to the Bath Club in Dover Street for an hour's exercise before being collected in the car by my mother. His exercises usually consisted of a strenuous half an hour in the gymnasium, followed by a further half hour of energetic swimming up and down the club baths.

One day in the autumn of 1934 he was approached by a fellow member of the club who was a doctor and had been watching Freyberg's activities for some time. He warned him that if he continued to take such punishing exercise in his mid-forties, sooner or later he would strain his heart. That evening my father related to my mother what had been said to him, treating it as a bit of a joke; and took no further notice.

By the end of 1934 Freyberg was due for a new appointment; he had been on the half-pay list since 16 October, and as he had held regimental and staff appointments in England since 1919, this was likely to be an overseas posting. The first indication of where he might be sent came in a letter from an Indian clerk in Calcutta soliciting employment for a relative. Sure enough a few days later, early in January 1935, Freyberg received an official letter from the Military Secretary telling him that the Appointments Board had selected him to be the next GOC of the Presidency and Assam District. This District, together with those of Lucknow and Meerut, made up the Eastern

Command of India based on Calcutta, and had its headquarters nearby at Jalapahar.

In 1935 the Presidency and Assam District commanded two infantry brigades – 6 Lucknow and 9 Jhansi – and several independent battalions.[1] There were twelve regular infantry battalions in the District, made up in the usual proportion prevailing in India at the time of two to one, that is, eight Indian and Gurkha battalions and four British battalions (1 Devonshire, 1 East Yorkshire, 1 Bedfordshire and Hertfordshire, and 1 Black Watch). The Commander-in-Chief Eastern Command was General Sir Norman Macmullen, then the most senior Indian Army general, and his chief staff officer was Brigadier Philip Neame, VC. The senior staff officer of the Presidency and Assam District in 1935 was Lieutenant-Colonel William Gott.

'Arrangements were already far advanced,' Barbara wrote in her diary. 'Our date for departure had been decided and our passage booked – we had even chosen the pattern of the drawing-room curtains.' She went on:

Then Bernard was told that a medical examination of all officers going to India was required and, as he was very well at the time and had been in good health for years, we had no reason for concern. I remember vividly the shattering shock of his return from his interview.

The medical boards took place in London on two separate occasions, the first on 8 February 1935, and the second a week later, which confirmed the findings of the first. The diagnosis was 'a diastolic murmur of the aortic valve of the heart' and it cancelled any question of his being passed fit for India. The cause of it, as Freyberg stated in a subsequent submission to the Secretary of State for War, was precisely what he had been warned about by the doctor in the Bath Club: 'In my case, it has been established beyond doubt as being due to strain, caused by too violent exercise for one of my mature age, and not in any way attributable to disease.'[2]

Freyberg was advised to take to his bed immediately and to spend the next few weeks resting quietly, which he did. When in April 1935 I came home from boarding-school I found him in the unfamiliar posture of lying in bed and reading the papers. Even at the age of twelve I realised that his medical downgrading had been a traumatic experience for him, but I could not fully understand until later quite what a shock the whole incident was, and how it would affect his and our lives. My father tried to treat his misfortune lightly for the sake of my mother and me, and even made jokes about it. There was a popular song of the

moment which he first heard on BBC radio immediately after returning from the medical board, and he pointed out how very appropriate it
was to his condition: it was called 'Why does my heart go Boom?'.

What made the situation almost unendurable was that he felt he had
brought it on himself – he had had what amounted to an obsession
about physical fitness dating from his New Zealand swimming days. His
condition would have been far less distressing if it had been caused by
war wounds. As it was, once the cause of the disability was established
my father was unable to harness the goodwill that undoubtedly existed
for his many wounds in the First World War. The chief problem,
however, was that when first diagnosed the 'murmur' appeared to be
permanent.

Freyberg decided to consult a specialist and sought out Dr T. F.
Cotton, an eminent cardiologist. Cotton confirmed the army medical
board's original diagnosis of his case, and took a serious view of
Freyberg's condition. By this time the posting to India had been
cancelled, and what was now at stake was whether in fact he was fit
enough to stay in the army.

My father soon got bored with lying in bed with nothing to do, and
his first effort to find some way of employing his time was to get himself
appointed as one of the examiners and markers of the current staff
college entrance exam. At this period, therefore, whenever I went into
his room his bed was strewn with exam papers and marking sheets. I
remember in particular that there was an entrant from New Zealand, a
fact which pleased my father.

Dr Cotton was a great help to my father at this time, not only on the
medical side but also in steering him in the right direction to make the
equally important psychological readjustments in coming to terms with
his condition. Cotton's main theme was that my father must learn to
stop worrying about something he could not do anything about, and
having tried his hardest to influence events where that was in his power,
that he should stop thinking about the might-have-beens and *switch off*.
It was a philosophy that guided my father through much of his later life,
long after the troubles that had brought it about were past; and he often
used to repeat the advice to me.

During the summer of 1935 the family went on a month-long cruise
to the Mediterranean in the *Viceroy of India*. We were a large party, with
my father and mother, us three boys and my grandmother, plus several
friends including Field Marshal Lord Birdwood. We visited Malta,
Egypt, the Holy Land, Greece and some of the islands, Turkey, Sicily,
Algiers and Portugal. The highlight, undoubtedly, was steaming slowly
through the Dardanelles on our way to and from Istanbul, and having

the battlefields of Gallipoli pointed out as we passed, as well as hearing first-hand accounts of the battles of twenty years ago related by Birdwood and my father. The cruise relaxed my father very noticeably, and enabled him to put his worries about his military future into perspective. By the time we returned to Tilbury on 7 September he was glowing with health and vigour.

By the autumn of 1935 Dr Cotton noted the improvement in Freyberg's condition. He discarded his original diagnosis as the strained condition of the heart had subsided and all the symptoms of disability disappeared. 'I agree that you can play golf, tennis and swim,' he wrote. 'I see no reason why you should not apply for a Medical Board at an early date for I think you are fit for full military duty.'

Freyberg sent Dr Cotton's report to the army doctors, and applied for another medical board. He was very disappointed when it still refused to pass him fit.

I was then advised that my case would be greatly strengthened if I could get another eminent cardiologist to support Dr Cotton's report. So I consulted Sir Maurice Cassidy in October last, and after having examined me over a period of six months, he reported on April 15 [1936], that in his opinion, the damage was due to excessively violent exercise, and it was non-progressive and symptomless, and that he considered that I was fit to perform the duties of a Major-General in India or elsewhere . . .

This means that so long as I avoid such violent forms of exercise in future, the condition will remain stabilised, to use Sir Maurice's own words: 'at its present symptomless condition', which, in view of the blood pressure being 140–80, proves that in spite of the murmur, there is no loss of pressure due to valvular inefficiency.[2]

In one respect the cancellation of my father's appointment had been a relief, especially for my mother. In those days a posting to India usually meant a minimum of three years away from England. My grandmother had become increasingly frail and it was unlikely that she would survive that long. In the event she died in January 1937, leaving many family complications to be sorted out. Moreover Martin and Guy were about to finish at Oxford, while I was in my final year at preparatory school before going on to Eton, which would have involved another set of problems as there was no question of children going on long journeys by sea to join their parents even for the summer holidays.

The autumn, winter and spring of 1935–6 saw the beginning of a new pattern in my father's life. For the first time since 1914 he had no

[183]

form of army employment to occupy his working hours; in consequence he turned most of his attention to two challenges. One was the restoration of a house, Gillham's Farm, and the other was his attempt to re-establish his medical credentials in the eyes of the army doctors.

When Lord Aberconway died early in 1934 he had left my mother and his McLaren grandsons some property in the Haslemere area. At one time the Aberconways had themselves lived in the main house, which was called Hilders, but as it had not been lived in properly for many years, both Hilders and the nearby property known as Gillham's Farm had become very run down. When my parents thought they were being posted to India they had decided to hand over the management to local agents. Now my father was glad of the opportunity to manage them himself, and he formed a small property company, Trust Developments Ltd. My mother's diaries for the next few years until the outbreak of the Second World War record innumerable visits to Hilders, Gillham's and a third place soon to be christened Cherry Tree Avenue. The family was grateful that this new interest had come along at just the right time to absorb my father's formidable energies, once he had resigned himself to the possibility of being invalided out of the army.

Gillham's Farm, situated three miles south of Haslemere in Surrey, looks towards the South Downs across the rolling Sussex countryside. The farmhouse itself was of considerable antiquity, with timbered beams that had come originally from Elizabethan ships, and there was a magnificent tithe barn. But when my mother inherited it the house and its surroundings were dilapidated, with livestock running in and out of the house and huge piles of dirt and manure everywhere. As it stood it was worth very little, but it had such obvious potential that my parents thought it worthwhile to 'do it up' before putting it on the market. What started off as a temporary cleaning-up operation, however, quickly developed into a full-scale building project, for soon after returning from the summer cruise my father decided to employ direct labour rather than put the work out to contract. This entailed regular visits to Gillham's to supervise the work, besides ordering the materials needed, engaging specialists to put in electricity, plumbing and central heating, paying the workforce and generally acting as overseer of the whole project, which went well despite the usual delays.

My father's efforts to satisfy the army doctors were less successful, however. The label 'heart condition' was like a millstone tied round his neck, for although the condition had stabilised to the point where it posed no threat to his ability to tackle any activity he was likely to undertake in the military world, there was no disguising the fact that the 'murmur' existed and was unlikely to disappear. In the 1930s this situation was much less well understood medically than it is today, when it is accepted that a stabilised 'murmur' is not a dangerous condition in itself, and certainly not one meriting compulsory retirement. But although Freyberg's own cardiologists were satisfied that he could be safely re-employed, they were unable to persuade the army specialists. This situation continued until the middle of 1936, after further medical boards still refused to certify him fit for service.

Meanwhile family life continued much as before, with a large number of events, visits to and from friends, concerts, and plays. On 14 November 1935, the day of the last General Election to be held in Britain for ten years, the Conservatives were returned with a large majority. The All Blacks team of 1935–6 arrived and we went to several of their matches, including one very exciting international at Cardiff. One of their players was Jack Griffiths who, as a result of meeting Freyberg on this tour, later became his ADC. In January 1936 King George V died and my parents visited the lying-in-state on 24 January, the day my father was to have attended an investiture to receive his newly awarded CB. This was presented to him by King Edward VIII on 18 February.

On 14 May 1936 Freyberg went before yet another medical board in London. The result was the same as the previous ones; the heart murmur was audible, and the board again declined to pass him fit. Nearly eighteen months had elapsed since he was downgraded, and so later that month he decided to make a formal appeal to HM the King (which he was allowed to do under the provisions of King's Regulations) against the decisions of the Army Council, 'with regards to my physical fitness for general service'. His appeal contained a resumé of the medical facts of the case and ended: 'Under these circumstances I submit that it would be a great hardship if I am prevented from pursuing my career as an officer in HM Forces, for which I have spent so many years in endeavouring to fit myself.'[2] The appeal was to the King but of course he consulted and took advice from the Army Council, who considered the matter with care. No decision was arrived at for a considerable time.

While on holiday that August, at a shooting lodge in Argyllshire on the eastern shores of the Mull of Kintyre (where my father, characteristically, insisted we should all have a swim in the freezing cold sea, before breakfast), my father received a telegram to say that his mother Julia had died in Wellington on 13 August 1936. He had realised that he was unlikely to see her again, but he was always faithful in writing to her regularly, and helping her financially. Since Julia had come from

[185]

Argyllshire it somehow seemed fitting that we should learn about her death in her native county; and it was also one of the few occasions when my father talked about his early days in New Zealand, of what a wonderful person his mother had been, and how she had brought up five strapping sons with little help or money.

Five months later, on 28 January 1937, my other grandmother, Lady Jekyll, died in her sleep at Munstead House. She left Munstead to my mother, but its old-fashioned state and the fact that it had had little money spent on it for many years provided another challenge for my father. He not only modernised the house over the next year, but devised ways of making the flower and kitchen gardens more labour-saving and productive.

On Saturday, 12 June, when on a weekend visit to friends at Hayling Island, my father got a telephone message that Sir James Barrie had had to go into a nursing home and had specially asked to see him. He returned to London the next morning to find the following letter waiting for him at Clarendon Place. It was written by Barrie on the afternoon of 12 June: 'I have come to this nursing home for a bit. It strikes me as very good. This is just to say that any time you can come to see me, you will be welcome and far more than welcome. I do miss you.'[3] My father saw Barrie that Sunday and stayed with him for as long as he was allowed to. Barrie lingered on for another five days in and out of a coma, and died in the early hours of Saturday, 19 June. My father went to Scotland on 24 June for the funeral at Barrie's birthplace, Kirriemuir, and attended the memorial service in London on 30 June.

Meanwhile during the summer of 1936 the Army Council had been considering Freyberg's appeal. The army medical board had been justified in declining to pass Freyberg as fit when it originally examined him in early 1935, as his own cardiologists agreed. It was also the case, as the army doctors maintained, that having once acquired a 'diastolic murmur', such a condition would stay with him for the rest of his life, in one form or another. When the military doctors started to advise about the consequences of such a condition, however, they were venturing on less certain ground.

Dr Cotton and Sir Maurice Cassidy took the view that, after a prolonged period of quiet and rest, Freyberg's murmur had stabilised. There was no reason why he should not live a perfectly normal life in all respects, including a normal military life, which could even involve going to India if necessary. The army doctors disagreed. It was generally believed at that time that a heart murmur was permanent not only in itself, but also in its consequences, irrespective of whether the condition had stabilised or not.

The Army Council's deliberations continued: the case was obviously a difficult one, though Freyberg was not aware of the substance of the discussions. In the end he was asked if he wished to be considered for a sedentary or semi-sedentary appointment. He said at once that he did. His main object by this time, with the Second World War looming, was to 'keep his foot in the door'. But how was 'sedentary or semi-sedentary' to be defined in relation to a major-general's employment? In fact there were probably no more than two or three appointments that could be considered 'sedentary'; and by the time it was decided that Freyberg could be offered such a position he was approximately two-thirds of the way towards the maximum period of three years anyone was allowed to be kept on half-pay, and the possible appointments were either already filled during the timescale or had been promised elsewhere. A further year then elapsed, from the summer of 1936 until the summer of 1937, without any new developments on the medical or appointments fronts.

Was there any truth in the often repeated story that Freyberg challenged the army doctors to walk up Mount Snowdon with him, and to examine him medically when they reached the top? I have found no direct evidence about this, although he did write the following into his Appeal: 'On May 3 last (1936), I climbed a mountain of 1,200 feet in North Wales in an hour, without any effort and no after-effects. I should be quite prepared to carry out any physical test that might be thought necessary.'[2] Knowing my father, however, I believe it is more likely than not that he did issue an oral challenge along these lines to the doctors. If he did, however, they did not respond.

By the summer of 1937 little had changed. The army doctors still refused to pass him as fit and no 'sedentary' military job had become available. Shortly after returning from his summer holiday in Venice at the beginning of September my father received the following letter from General Deedes, the Military Secretary:

> I am directed to inform you that as you will have been three years unemployed on 16 October 1937, you are due to be placed on retired pay from that date inclusive, in accordance with the provisions of Article 568, Pay Warrant 1931. It is with great regret that I have to inform you that you were found Medically Unfit for General Service by the Medical Board that examined you lately.[2]

There was nothing more to be done. On 27 September Freyberg wrote his final letter to the Military Secretary: 'In view of the decision of the last Medical Board not to pass me fit for General Service, I beg now to be allowed to retire upon retired pay.'[2]

[187]

Freyberg would have been less than human, however, if he had never speculated on the different course his career might have taken had it not been for these medical problems. In the 1930s it was the usual practice for major-generals to be given two tours of duty in the rank, one in command, and the other on the staff. At the beginning of 1935 Freyberg had been appointed to the Presidency and Assam District in command of twelve regular battalions. This was an important military post, and a satisfactory tour of duty there would have further enhanced his position in the army. He would have spent three years in the appointment by the end of 1937, and the likelihood is that he would then have returned to England and been given a staff job, such as Chief of Staff of one of the commands, or in the War Office as Director of Military Operations or Staff Duties.

By the time the war broke out in September 1939 Freyberg would have nearly completed his second tour as a major-general and reached the top of the list of that rank, where he would be well placed to be considered for one of the higher positions in the army at the beginning of the war. As a major-general he was already senior to all but three of the officers who achieved prominence in the Second World War. Gort, Auchinleck, Alan Brooke, Alexander, O'Connor and Wilson were all junior to him at this time, while Montgomery, Slim, McCreery, Leese and Horrocks, to mention but a few of the others, were still only colonels. The three senior to him – Ironside, Dill and Wavell – for various different reasons took no further part in the central direction of the war after 1941. Furthermore Freyberg's own fighting record and his ability to get on with Churchill, unlike some of the others, would probably have ensured that he was considered for the top appointments.

Although it is now an academic exercise to think about such might-have-beens, they must have included being in the running for the command of one of the corps in the BEF in 1939–40 or one of the Middle East commands, such as Western Desert Force or GHQ Middle East. Later in the war, when he had seen what happened to those who had had the thankless task of commanding the British armies during the locust years, and when he realised that but for his medical problem he would not have linked up again with his New Zealand background, he had good cause for thankfulness.

Many years later my father wrote about the shock caused to him when his military career appeared to have ended:

At first I felt my interest in life had stopped, but this was only temporary. The War Office would not reconsider their opinion as to my fitness to remain on the active list and although they hesitated once, I was retired. I bowed to the inevitable and left.

At this stage my brother-in-law, Reginald McKenna, came to my assistance with advice and help. He said he had left politics and entered the City as a banker at the age of fifty-three – why should not I leave the Army and enter business with politics thrown in as a background? This I decided to do.[4]

It says much for my father's contentment and equanimity that he was able to take such a blow in his stride. In the five years between 1935 and 1939 I saw more of him than in any other period of our lives, because we were both at home during the school holidays and he often came to visit me in term-time. I never once remember his complaining about how he had been treated, still less indulging in any form of self-pity. At the end of the waiting period, when he realised that the break with the army was inevitable, he set the military world on one side, and started to make a new life for himself elsewhere.

By 1937 my parents had been married for fifteen years and had evolved a most agreeable way of life together, shared with many friends and relations. This made his departure from the military world infinitely less stark and upsetting than it might otherwise have been. Indeed our life in 1938 and 1939 hardly seemed any different from the years that had gone before. My mother was unconcerned by the loss of my father's army career in itself, her only worry was that he would be disheartened by the rather bleak manner of its ending. During the three years he was on half-pay, of course, he had had plenty of time to think about what he would do if he was forced to leave the army; indeed after three years of wrangling with the army doctors it came almost as a relief when he did finally depart. He had always been fascinated by politics and it was a more or less automatic decision that, if he could not continue soldiering, he would return to the political scene, even though his experience amounted to little more than a brief flirtation in 1922 when he had stood as an Independent Liberal at Cardiff.

My father's first priority on leaving the army, therefore, was to try and get into the House of Commons. Since his Cardiff candidature both sections of the Liberal Party had been reduced to relative impotence. The Labour Party, after achieving office at the end of the 1920s, had itself been almost decimated by the traumas of the financial crash of the early 1930s. The Conservative Party alone had survived virtually undamaged and now occupied the centre of the political stage. My father had little difficulty in identifying himself with the moderate politics of the Tory Party of those days, and put his name down at

Central Office to be considered as a candidate for a constituency. By this time the government under Stanley Baldwin, elected in 1935, was approaching the half-way mark of its five-year term of office.

At the beginning of 1938 Freyberg was shortlisted for the Ipswich constituency where a by-election had been caused by the elevation to the peerage of Lord Belstead, the sitting Tory member. At first all appeared to go well at his interview, until he was asked if he would be prepared to go and live in the constituency, which he was unable to undertake because of family commitments at Munstead and Clarendon Place. He was not surprised therefore when another candidate, Henry Willink, was chosen. In point of fact he had had a lucky escape. The Labour Party put up a strong candidate in R. R. Stokes, who later became a minister in the 1945 Labour government, and the Conservatives were beaten into second place by some 3,000 votes.

Shortly afterwards Freyberg was again shortlisted, this time for the Spelthorne Division of Middlesex where the sitting member, Sir Reginald Blaker, was not contesting the seat at the next General Election, due in 1940. This time no conditions were suggested, and the selection committee unanimously offered my father the impending vacancy, which he accepted with alacrity. Geographically the constituency was ideally situated for him, being adjacent to where Heathrow Airport was later to be built and therefore almost equidistant from both Munstead and Clarendon Place. In the 1930s it was a safe Conservative seat with a majority of over 16,000. He worked hard at constituency matters during the next eighteen months and attended a course at the Conservative Party country headquarters at Ashridge in Hertfordshire to learn some of the finer details of party policy.

My father needed paid work, however, to supplement his army pension which, because he had not recently been employed as a General Officer, was only at the rate for a full colonel. In 1938 he became a director of Birmingham Small Arms Company (BSA), the engineering group based in the Midlands. He hoped it would be the forerunner of a number of other directorships: but in the short time before war broke out it was the only directorship he was offered.

In the late 1930s BSA was a thriving company under the dynamic chairmanship of Sir Dudley Docker, manufacturing a wide range of products such as specialist steels at the Jessop works at Sheffield; and vans, motor bicycles, pedal bicycles and cars, especially Daimlers, which they supplied to the Royal Family. But its most important function was the making of small arms – rifles and bren guns in particular – as well as a variety of ancillary military equipment. This made the BSA works, notably the arms factories in the vicinity of Small

Heath outside Birmingham, prime potential targets for air attack by the Germans if war did come.

Freyberg's main task therefore was to devise and put into effect a system which would safeguard the large workforce from attacks by German bombers, and at the same time try to minimise loss of production. The requirement demanded cool judgment and the balancing of conflicting risks. Freyberg had to formulate a policy to cover the many factories, including the design, siting and construction of air raid shelters for the workforce when attacks were imminent, while ensuring that they occupied these shelters for no longer than was absolutely necessary. He spent a great deal of his time in 1938 and 1939 touring the BSA factories, and in school holidays I often went with him. The world of factory managers, trade union leaders and urban workers was very different to the barrack squares and military headquarters he had been used to, but he approached the many difficulties with the same practicality and attention to detail as he had military administration. I can remember him at dinner at our hotels discussing possible solutions to the problems he had encountered during the day, how much money they were likely to cost, and how he proposed to present them to the Board of Directors.

Meanwhile Gillham's Farm had been finished, put on the market and was eventually sold. It did not make as much profit as my parents had hoped, for one good reason: they had done the property up to the highest standards as if they were going to live in it themselves. After it was sold, Gillham's House was started in an adjoining field in 1938, and a large tree-planting programme was begun to screen the houses from each other, and to make future sites attractive for further houses. In all my father planned to build a further five or six medium-size houses on sites at Gillham's and in the Linchmere area. In the event none of the latter was built and Gillham's House was only just finished before war began.

Another project my father started was at Cherry Tree Avenue. This was on the edge of Haslemere itself and when work started the site consisted of a bare, steeply-sloping field of about fifteen acres. He planned to build about forty-five houses there, each to a slightly different design and with a third of an acre of garden. He began from scratch, and the first thing that had to be done was to put in a road and a main drainage system. During the planning stage the conversation at home was dominated for weeks by words like 'hardcore' and 'bitumen', and by the cost of the different kinds of gravel. Visitors to Munstead, particularly my mother's artistic friends, would be startled at finding themselves drawn into discussion of the merits of different kinds of sewers, and asked for their opinions. In all fifteen houses were built before the war, and were rapidly sold. It is a sobering reminder of the changing value of money that they cost less than £1,000 each. When Barrie died he left my father £500, and his reaction was that it would enable him to build another house!

At this period Reggie and Pammie McKenna were among the people my parents saw most frequently. Reggie, as Chairman of the Midland Bank, occupied the flat at the top of the Pall Mall branch. It was next door to St James's Palace and had fine views over the park and Marlborough House. The rooms were spacious, faced south and were ideal for entertaining, whether for Reggie's political and business colleagues or Pammie's artistic and musical friends. As the Second World War loomed Pammie took an increasing interest in the Order of St John of Jerusalem, and became in effect its Number Two. Its head, Edwina Mountbatten, was a frequent guest for lunch and one I found easy to talk to, no doubt because she had children of the same age as myself.

Another frequent visitor was Maynard Keynes and his Russian wife Lydia Lopokova, one of the star ballerinas of Diaghilev's company. Reggie McKenna and Maynard Keynes loved to linger after lunch, puffing huge cigars and setting the world to rights while my father and I listened; on one occasion they claimed that they were the only two people in Britain who really understood how to manage 'money' and that when they were gone no one else would have the necessary knowledge about which were the right financial levers to pull at the right time.

My parents' closest friends then were the two Asquith families, Violet and 'Bongie' Bonham Carter, and Oc and Betty Asquith. Oc had married the Hon. Betty Manners just before the end of the First World War, and my father was godfather to the eldest of their four daughters, April Mary. They lived at Clovelly Court in North Devon, at the top of Clovelly village, and we visited them several times in the 1930s.

Another old friend from my father's Naval Division days was A. P. Herbert. APH, as he was known, was a prolific and lively writer who represented Oxford University as a Member of Parliament from 1935 until 1950, when university representation in Parliament was abolished. Other friends he also saw frequently at this period were Lesley Jowitt and her husband William, who became a Liberal Member of Parliament for the Hartlepools in 1922 and caused a sensation a few years later when he crossed the floor of the House to join the Labour Party. He was Attorney-General in the Labour government of 1929–32 and Solicitor-General in the Second World War. In the Attlee government of 1945–51 he was Lord Chancellor, and became the first and last Earl Jowitt. Also lifelong friends were Fred and Enid Lawson; Fred Lawson became Director of Public Relations at the War Office in the Second World War, and afterwards Managing Director of the *Daily Telegraph*, having inherited the title of Lord Burnham in 1943.

One of the most curious dinner parties which my parents ever attended was that given by Sir Roderick and Lady Jones in 1936 to meet Ribbentrop, later the German Foreign Minister, the only time my father met any of the senior Nazis. My mother was an old school friend of Lady Jones, the author Enid Bagnold, who in 1936 had just published her best-known novel *National Velvet*. Sir Roderick, the head of Reuters, had a reputation for being pro-German, although his autobiography, *A Life in Reuters*,[5] shows that this extended only to the old regime, not to Hitler and his associates:

> I shall always remember particularly [he wrote] the third and last time that Joachim von Ribbentrop ('von' now having put in its appearance) came to our house. It was on the night of April 8, 1936. He had just completed the mission with which he was charged directly before he became Ambassador in London – the mission to negotiate the ill-starred Anglo–German Naval Treaty . . . He was to leave the following morning for Berlin, and I had invited him to a small dinner party at Hyde Park Gate. Herr von Hoesch [then German Ambassador] also was a guest; the others were the American Ambassador and Mrs Bingham, Lady Carlisle, Count Dürckheim, Lord and Lady Camrose, the Comte and Comtesse de Gaillard de la Valdène, General Sir Bernard and Lady Freyberg [sic] and Miss Jeanne Stourton [Lady Camoys].[5]

The placement (see overleaf) involved my mother sitting on the right of Herr von Hoesch, whom she found cultivated and civilised, while my father was next to Lady Camrose, who was sitting nearly opposite to Ribbentrop. According to the account that circulated in the family afterwards, towards the end of dinner Ribbentrop started to tell his end of the table about what was in Hitler's mind, and of the German intention to get her colonies back and expand to the east. After he had talked in this vein for a time, it became too much for my father and he told Ribbentrop that they would not be 'allowed to get away with it'. A furious argument then resulted, which Dowager Lady Camoys described to me in detail many years later. My mother told me subsequently that she had been acutely embarrassed that my father had had a row while he was a guest in a friend's house, but not about his side of the argument, with which she entirely agreed.

Mrs Freyberg

29 HYDE PARK GATE, S.W.7.

April 8, 1936.

WINDOW.

Lady Jones.

Herr von Ribbentrop.	The American Ambassador.
The Countess of Carlisle.	Lady Camrose.
Comte de Gaillard de la Valdène.	General Freyberg.
	Count Durkheim.
Miss Jeanne Stourton.	Mrs. Freyberg.
Lord Camrose.	The German Ambassador.
Comtesse de Gaillard de la Valdène.	The Hon. Mrs. Bingham.

Sir Roderick Jones.

ENTRANCE.   FIREPLACE.

There was, though, a chilling and sinister sequel to this dinner party. Sir Roderick Jones's account of the evening concludes:

Meanwhile, at my end of the table Herr von Hoesch was in good spirits, occasioned perhaps, by the prospect of Ribbentrop's early departure. Next morning at Croydon he saw Ribbentrop off to Germany. Twenty-four hours later he was dead – from (officially) a heart attack! There was

[194]

something tragic, to many something mysterious, in this event and its timing; not unnaturally, bearing in mind the Nazi record, it gave rise to suspicions, and to dark rumours which I cannot either confirm or refute.

A sinister story, which perfectly detailed the death scene and the ominously-hurried embalming (involving the emptying of the body of blood and of all traces of what it had contained), was told to my wife in a ship's corridor off Madeira – by an eyewitness! . . . it had curious, rather un-inventable details, particularly as to a telephone message sent before Hoesch's actual last moment.*

In August 1938 we had what was to be our last family holiday together before the war – motoring in the south-west of France. On our return to Clarendon Place at the beginning of September we were surprised to see trenches being dug in Hyde Park. This reflected the Sudetenland crisis in Czechoslovakia which ended in the Munich agreement of 29 September 1938. At the time this caused furious controversy between those in favour of 'appeasement' and those in favour of taking a strong line. My father never had the slightest doubt that war was coming, and frequently said so. For him it was a question not of 'if', but when and how. He agreed with Churchill and Duff Cooper in rejecting the Munich agreement.

For the rest of 1938 there was an uneasy lull. I went back to Eton, and my parents' diary records engagements in Spelthorne, at BSA, in Haslemere, and at various social events during the remainder of the year. They were invited to the launch of the *Queen Elizabeth* at John Brown's shipyard on the Clyde on 27 September. We spent a family Christmas together at Munstead; but already peacetime life was beginning to change. My mother had taken on one of the St John Ambulance divisions in the Paddington area, and attended St John meetings and first-aid classes. Also, since Godalming was in an evacuation zone where children from London were to be sent to escape from the expected bombing of the capital, it was arranged that Munstead House was to provide accommodation for the Cynthia Mosley Day Nursery, consisting of some fifty children aged from three to five and their staff, who were due to arrive from the East End of London on the outbreak of war.

Freyberg, thanks to the rider attached to the declaration that he was

---

* After Hoesch's death Ribbentrop became German Ambassador to Great Britain.

medically unfit for general service in 1937, which stated that in war he could be employed in a non-active service capacity in England, was offered a mobilisation appointment as GOC Salisbury Plain Area, to command all the troops in the Bulford–Tidworth district of the Plain, with its headquarters in Bulford itself, should war break out. He had no hesitation in accepting the offer. Although it was far from being the kind of employment he sought, at least it held out the prospect of getting back into the army on a full-time basis.

Against this background of ever-increasing tension Guy, who had joined the Coldstream Guards in 1938, was selected to take a draft of 100 men to join their 3 Battalion at Mustafa Barracks in Alexandria, and left from Southampton on 1 August on HM troopship *Nevasa*. Two weeks later Martin joined the Grenadiers at Tidworth for his fortnight's annual training with the Supplementary Reserve. He was not released from the Colours for over six years.

On 9 August my parents and I motored to Treglos Hotel at Constantine's Bay, St Merryn in north Cornwall, to begin a rather half-hearted holiday. It was a pleasant enough place but we spent more and more time reading the newspapers or glued to the radio. There was another, more personal cause for gloom. Arthur Asquith had become mortally ill and my father abandoned the holiday on 21 August to visit him at his home at Clovelly. Oc died on 25 August aged only fifty-six; he had never fully recovered from the wound to his leg in 1917. My father gave the Address at Oc's funeral in Clovelly Church a few days later. 'With his passing,' Freyberg said, 'goes one of the last war links with that brilliant gathering of young men that fell in the war with the RND . . . He was the best sharer in the world . . . I remember being enthralled and delighted by Asquith's constant flow of intimate letters from his devoted stepmother and brilliant sister Violet, all of which he shared with his friends, and I often think with gratitude of their help. They did us more good than all the medical comforts supplied by HM Government.'[4]

The two closest, warmest friendships in my father's life outside his marriage were with James Barrie and Oc Asquith, and they had died within two years of each other.

On 30 August a furniture van came to Clarendon Place to remove our favourite possessions to Munstead. The next day the evacuation of children from the main towns was ordered, and we spent a frantic twenty-four hours at Munstead clearing the furniture from the rooms earmarked for the day nursery, and putting it into store. On 1 September Germany invaded Poland, and at 12.30 p.m. the same day two red double-decker London buses arrived at the gates of Munstead

[196]

with the children. The buses were too tall to pass under the lower branches of the lime trees leading to the house, so everyone got out on the main road and walked the final stage with their luggage.

A few days before war was declared my father had come down to dinner one evening at Munstead in his blue patrols, to see whether they still fitted – which they did, although he had not worn uniform for five years. On Sunday, 3 September the Prime Minister, Neville Chamberlain, broadcast to the nation at 11 a.m. and announced that we were at war with Germany. 'In common with all others on the Reserve,' Freyberg wrote, 'I was told over the wireless to go at once to my mobilisation appointment, and took up my job as GOC Salisbury Plain Area':

> My work there was to mobilise a number of units of the British Expeditionary Force and despatch them to France. My area then was to form the large groups of Training Units of reinforcements of officers and other ranks for the Field Army. In the process we would expand from being a garrison in peacetime of 6,000 to one of probably ten times that size. We increased to about 20,000 in one leap. As a result of the strain thrown on our cookhouses, administrative services and dining-halls, comfortable meals were almost an impossibility. Knowing peacetime routine as a former AQMG at Southern Command, I realised that normal procedure would take years to deal with the shortages. The only way to cope with the problems that arose was to act first and get authority afterwards, taking the worse cases first.[4]

Salisbury Plain Area was a new District Headquarters and, to begin with, only had very makeshift arrangements. In one of his letters in mid-September 1939 my father wrote, 'I live in the mess of 162 Field Regt – not very good food, quite plain and I am teetotal while I am here.'[6] One of the many problems was that no staff car was available. After waiting for some time he eventually persuaded the RASC to take over the family Packard, which otherwise would have been laid up because of petrol rationing. In another letter he wrote, 'I am working hard here and I am getting a good hang of things. All my Training Regiments are now working away and in the next few weeks I shall be able to see how they are doing.'[6]

Freyberg's main preoccupation in the first month of the war was how to get himself medically upgraded. He was still in the lowly HO (Home Only) category to which he had been relegated by the 1937 board, and unless this could be changed he was condemned to employment in military backwaters in England for the rest of the war. There had, however, been an important development soon after Freyberg's arrival at Bulford. As one of the main holding and reinforcement districts for the BEF in France the Salisbury Plain Area would need to process drafts for the BEF in a hurry. This meant that, among other requirements, all medical documentation had to be up to date and accurate. It could be achieved only by mass examination of the many thousands of regulars and reservists in the area, and instructions for this to be done were issued by the Medical Branch of the War Office.

When the time came for his own headquarters to be examined Freyberg presented himself at the Medical Centre alongside his junior officers, clerks, cooks, signallers and drivers. It may be that the doctors were somewhat surprised to find in their queue of corporals and subalterns a large, burly and apparently fit General Officer. It is unlikely that they had the time to examine him at greater length than the others or that they questioned him about his medical history, and certainly he did not volunteer any information. The upshot was that the board graded him FE (Forward Everywhere) – the highest medical category. This examination took place on 11 October, and the head of the board, Dr Eric Shipper, signed the following certificate: 'Major-General Freyberg has today been examined by me and is found fit for general service.'[2] Just as Freyberg's medical crisis had come quite unexpectedly out of the blue, so had its correction.

Barbara's diary adds:

> When his examination loomed up, he had become not only familiar with the procedure but resourceful as to how to handle it. He talked all the time the doctor was listening through the stethoscope, with the results that the murmur, which had probably diminished in any case, was unnoticed.[7]

After all the heartache and disappointment of being invalided out of the service two years before, Freyberg could hardly have failed to relish the unexpected turn of events. With his tongue in his cheek he sent a copy of the precious certificate to the CIGS General Sir Edmund Ironside, with a covering letter dated 12 October:

> Please forgive me for writing to you direct in this way when I know you are so very busy. You will, I know, understand why I write and sympathise.
>
> By the attached medical report you will see that the Medical Specialist at Salisbury Plain at my Medical Board has certified that I am fit for General Service. This was no surprise as I have always been fit. Last summer I climbed the Gornergrat (10,000 ft) at Zermatt in the Alps.
>
> I am writing to you to see if I could be considered for a training and fighting job in France. You know my capabilities. I am only just 50, and I think Bertie Fisher, my C-in-C here, would recommend me.[4]

One suspects that the medical authorities at the War Office must have been far from amused by the new development, although Freyberg had done no more than comply with instructions they themselves had issued. However that may be, the War Office response was to call Freyberg before a full medical board which was held on Thursday, 2 November at Millbank.[2]

But times had changed. Not only was there a war on, but Freyberg could hardly be all that unfit if he had been passed 'FE' by the Bulford board. As lawyers say, 'the burden of proof had again shifted'. Freyberg was put through the medical hoops once more, and once again the heart murmur was noticed. But this time the outcome was different. It was ruled that he might be allowed to go on active service, provided that it was in 'temperate climates' only.[2]

This was Freyberg's medical charter for the rest of the Second World War. The general who had been invalided out of the army two years earlier on the grounds that he was unfit to serve in peacetime, was now to experience five of the most strenuous and continuous years of active service of any general in the war, and in 'temperate climates' which were to include the Western Desert in summer.

14

Commander of 2 New Zealand Expeditionary Force

When Freyberg returned to Bulford after his medical board he found a telegram inviting him to dinner with Peter Fraser at his suite at the Savoy Hotel.[1] Fraser, Deputy Prime Minister of New Zealand, had come to England in the last days of October 1939 charged among other things with investigating possible commanders for the Expeditionary Force which New Zealand was intending to put into the field. At that particular moment the country did not have an officer of the right age and experience for the appointment. Their only General Officer, Major-General (later Sir) John Duigan, Chief of the General Staff, was primarily a staff officer and at fifty-eight was considered too old to lead troops in the field. Later in the war there were at least half a dozen suitable New Zealand officers, any one of whom would have made an admirable commander of their forces, but in 1939 they were still too junior and inexperienced to be considered. The decision had already been taken in principle, therefore, to find a commander from outside New Zealand.[2]

A few days after the war began, Freyberg had offered his services to the New Zealand government. His suitability for the appointment rested on three foundations. The first, of course, was his unique fighting record in the First World War. The second was that, at fifty, he was exactly the right age and seniority to command a division. In addition he was staff-trained, and his varied experience between the wars had further equipped him with the administrative knowledge

[200]

necessary to lead an independent force in the field. Finally, although not native born, in most other respects he could be regarded as a New Zealander.

After his first meeting with Fraser, Freyberg wrote at his request 'a short appreciation of the situation as I saw it on the question of training and concentration of the NZEF overseas'. Fraser meanwhile went through the motions of consulting a number of other authorities. Lieutenant-Colonel (later General) W. G. Stevens, then a staff officer in Fraser's entourage, was present at the interview with the CIGS when the question of a suitable officer was discussed.[2] General Ironside said that the whole of the British Army List was at New Zealand's disposal, and suggested that Stevens look through it with a member of his staff. Fraser himself had taken soundings elsewhere about Freyberg's suit-ability, including opinions from General Gort, General Mackesy (who had recently visited New Zealand and made a report on the New Zealand military forces), and Sir Stephen Allen (Freyberg's first NZ Territorial Army commanding officer)[1], and had also communicated with Winston Churchill, then First Lord of the Admiralty, who urged 'the desirability of appointing Freyberg, whom he regarded as pre-eminently suitable'. Fraser records what then happened:

> Armed with these views and opinions, when I saw General Ironside I told him that we were considering him (Freyberg) for the post of General Officer Commanding the New Zealand Expeditionary Force. He at once made it plain that in his opinion we could not make a better choice. He also spoke in the highest terms of Freyberg, whom he had known for a very lengthy period, and he expressed the opinion that Freyberg invariably took care of his men even at the risk of his own safety. He referred also to the wide experience which Freyberg had, not only in fighting, but in the organisation of large bodies of men on a war basis. He regarded him as an admirable man to command a division.[1]

Fraser telegraphed his recommendation to New Zealand, and on 15 November 1939 the reply came that the government had decided 'to offer the appointment of General Officer Commanding the New Zealand Expeditionary Force to Major-General Freyberg'. The next day Fraser made the offer to Freyberg, who later wrote, 'I told Mr Fraser I would be glad to accept the New Zealand Division, and agreed not to accept a Corps if offered one.'[3]

The public announcement of his appointment was made on 22 November 1939, and Freyberg took command the same day.[1] Freyberg's appointment was well timed. Major decisions about future policy for the New Zealand Expeditionary Force had still to be made, and he was able to take a prominent part in deciding what they should be: how and where the force was to be deployed, and what its role was to be. How was it to be organised and equipped? What administrative backing was required to keep it in being? How much training was needed before it was fit to take the field?

At the outset of hostilities the New Zealand government had decided that the country would make a contribution to the British war effort in all three of the fighting services. At sea and in the air they provided substantial reinforcements for the Royal Navy and Royal Air Force in ships, planes and, above all, personnel. But it was in the land forces that they were to make their major contribution. This was to take the form of a complete division.

Freyberg now wore two hats. He commanded 2 New Zealand Division, which was the fighting element (1 New Zealand Division was the force that had fought in the First World War); and also 2 New Zealand Expeditionary Force (2 NZEF), which included those services needed to keep the Division in the field – the reinforcement depots, training schools and allied organisations, and the specialist units such as hospitals, workshops, stores and supply columns, to name but some of the backing required.

The New Zealand Division was originally expected to be deployed in France and become part of the British Expeditionary Force. However Egypt, being more or less half-way between New Zealand and France, was an obvious place for them to stage *en route* to the European theatre. It was arranged that successive echelons would leave New Zealand as and when the units could be recruited and the shipping to move them was available. They would then be assembled into brigades in Egypt where they would marry up with their equipment and carry out training. When this process was completed the whole force would depart to France as a fighting division. At the same time the main base of 2 NZEF would move to England. Soon after taking over, in discussions with the Adjutant-General and Quartermaster-General, who offered him any site he wanted (except Aldershot, already promised to the Canadians), Freyberg provisionally agreed that the New Zealand Expeditionary Force would be based in Colchester.[1]

From the beginning the New Zealand Division was to be organised on the same lines, and with the same basic establishment, as a British infantry division. It was to consist of three infantry brigades of three battalions each, with the normal supporting arms and services. There were to be three field regiments of 25-pounder guns, an armoured car regiment known as the Divisional Cavalry, anti-tank and anti-aircraft regiments, plus the usual engineers and signals regiments, together with transport companies, field ambulances and other services. The main component that the Division lacked in the early days was armour. Later in the war a tank brigade was added, after experience in the Western Desert showed how vital it was for the New Zealand Division to have its own organic armour under the permanent control of its divisional headquarters.

One of Freyberg's first tasks was to establish an agreed charter, to define his powers as commander of the New Zealand forces in relation to the New Zealand government and any British commanders-in-chief under whom he might serve. In the 1914–18 war difficulties had arisen for General Currie of the Canadians, General Monash of the Australians and General Godley of 1 New Zealand Division, all of whom had disagreements with the British high command over their respective responsibilities. The problem was that the British military perception of such relationships had not kept pace with the political reality. Although the Dominions had achieved independence and self-government well before 1914, it took a major effort by the commanders of Dominion troops in that war to disabuse British generals of the notion that they could treat Canadian, Australian and New Zealand divisions as if they were British divisions, and use their battalions to plug gaps in British brigades so that they were no longer fighting as a national force. Some of these misconceptions lingered on into the Second World War, as Freyberg was to discover.

Furthermore Freyberg was employed as a British army officer seconded to the New Zealand forces; so although he was the servant of the New Zealand government and paid by it, he continued to appear in the British Army List; unlike, for example, General Sir Thomas Blamey, the Australian commander, who had always been listed as an officer of the Australian military forces. As a result some senior British officers at GHQ Middle East in the early years of the war believed that, if there were any conflict of interest or loyalty, British officers would always side with their own hierarchy. In thinking this about Freyberg they could not have been more mistaken, but it took a series of monumental rows for him to establish his independence and the fact that he could not be compelled to accept British orders without his agreement or that of the New Zealand government.

Freyberg consulted the Director of Military Operations at the War Office, General R. H. Dewing, about the powers which the commander of an independent force would require, and the charter he should receive from his government. Dewing suggested that this agreement should be negotiated between the New Zealand Cabinet and the War Cabinet in London. This would in effect take future problems out of the hands of any British commander-in-chief or CIGS, and give Freyberg both the fullest authority to disagree with the commander-in-chief and the right to report any situation back to the New Zealand government, which would then negotiate directly with the British government.

The main points of this arrangement were:

1 The New Zealand government should at all times have direct access to Freyberg's views on matters relating to the employment and well-being of New Zealand forces.
2 The administration, discipline, promotion and pay of their officers and men came completely under the New Zealand government control.
3 The New Zealand Division should not be committed to active operations until they were adequately equipped and trained.
4 The Division should be employed as a complete formation, and not be split up or used piecemeal.

Freyberg telegraphed these proposals to New Zealand for consideration together with a request for certain financial powers he was advised to seek for use in emergencies. He also included matters such as choosing the base and training areas in Egypt, and the standardisation of the food ration. These were all questions he needed to discuss with his government, which he would do in person when he visited New Zealand.

Before he went there, however, Freyberg visited the British Expeditionary Force (BEF) in France to familiarise himself with the conditions the New Zealand Division would be expected to face. He left on 24 November 1939 by train because 'the state of the war prevented using an aeroplane, and enemy submarines made us cross by night instead of by day'.[3] In France Freyberg stayed with his old friend General Gort, the commander of the BEF. A full programme was arranged for his week's visit, including two days at Metz near the Maginot Line with General Condé, the commander of the French Third Army, which convinced him that the line, though strong, could easily be turned because it did not properly cover France's border with Belgium. He was given a detailed briefing at GHQ BEF by General Neame, Deputy Chief of Staff, on the operational plans in the event of the Germans invading Belgium, with Project I being the Allied advance to the position of the river Scheldt, and Project II a more ambitious plan to establish a forward line from Antwerp, Malines, Louvain and Namur to the existing French defences at Sedan. Freyberg considered this second plan unworkable.[3]

Freyberg's technical knowledge, garnered from his time at BSA, also came into play, for he found the work being done in the British zone badly planned and disorganised:

> My feelings at seeing the British Army trying to build an area of ferro-concrete pillboxes, involving the handling of many thousands of tons of material without light railways or power-driven concrete mixers, made me very unhappy. The men were trying to do with shovels and wheelbarrows what was plainly a job for machinery.[3]

On 30 November Freyberg arrived back at Victoria Station and was met by a special messenger who told him his plans had been changed. Originally the first convoy with the first echelon of 2 NZEF had been due to leave New Zealand on 20 January 1940. The Admiralty had now decided to combine the Australian and New Zealand convoys under one large naval escort. This required the departure of the New Zealand contingent on 6 January, which in turn advanced the date of Freyberg's leaving England by a fortnight to 4 December. This left him four days in which to complete his arrangements at the War Office, pack all his uniform, sort out his personal affairs and say goodbye to his family. He even found time to see me at school on Sunday, 3 December.

It was a wet and cold morning when Freyberg left Heston Aerodrome on Monday, 4 December 1939, but he was exhilarated by the change in his fortunes over the past month. After years of civilian life he was not only back in uniform but playing a prominent part in military and national life; and he was delighted in particular to be linking up again with his New Zealand past.

A flight to New Zealand in 1939 was still something of an adventure; it was the practice to fly mainly by day, starting at dawn and coming down two or three times to refuel, with night stops at hotels. The short range of the aircraft, and the need of the Flying Boats of Imperial Airways to land on water, tied the flights to a route passing mainly through the countries of the old British Empire and its protectorates. Freyberg's journey from Heston on that first day ended at Marseilles and he spent the night at the Splendide Hotel, where he had stayed in 1916 on his way back to England from Gallipoli with Oc Asquith and Cleg Kelly. Both were now dead, and to Freyberg the place appeared eerie and haunted.

On 5 December it was on to Malta for another night stop; and the third day was spent coasting along the shores of North Africa in time to

[205]

arrive in Cairo at 4 p.m. on 6 December.[3] Just before departure from
Heston Freyberg had been handed the following letter:

> To GOC Commanding New Zealand Forces Overseas   2 December 1939
> You are empowered to make all arrangements for the reception, accom-
> modation, drawing of equipment, training and comfort of the New Zealand
> Expeditionary Force when it arrives in Egypt.
> > Peter Fraser
> > Deputy Prime Minister of New Zealand[3]

Since Freyberg was in Egypt for only five days and had no staff with
him, this was a tall order. But in that time, after consultation with those
who knew Egypt well and careful reconnaissance of other alternatives,
he settled on Maadi for the New Zealand base camp:

> In those days, of course [he wrote], Egypt was only a sideshow. There were
> only a few British troops there and we were offered the whole country, so to
> speak, for a camping ground. This did not really ease matters as I had only
> three and a half days to see the site, select the camps and arrange for them to
> be built and ready for occupation in ten weeks time.[3]

None the less Maadi proved a fortunate and wise choice. It was near a
pleasant garden city on the Nile, adjacent to good desert training areas
and with a reputation for being healthy. It also had a frequent, fast train
service to Cairo, six miles away. For the next six years it was the main
New Zealand overseas base, and between 1940 and 1946 some 76,000
New Zealanders passed through it on their way to and from the Second
World War.

Freyberg's next step was to settle the terms of the tenure; and to
arrange to have the building of the hutments put out to contract, and
prepare other contracts for the provision of water, electricity, sewerage
and all the other services that an army camp requires. Freyberg then
cabled the New Zealand government to tell them what he had done,
and to warn them that owing to the lateness of the decisions the camps
would be only partially finished by the time the first troops arrived. As
the stationing of troops in Egypt was thought to be a temporary measure
the New Zealanders arranged to rent the camp from the British at the
rate of 4d per man per day rather than buy it outright; when 2 NZEF
departed for France Maadi was to be handed back to the British, who
had laid down the scale of the buildings to be erected and were
supervising the work.

After that Freyberg flew to Alexandria to await Peter Fraser, who arrived on the Imperial Airways Flying Boat *Canopus*, on his way to Sydney. The party consisted both of the New Zealand delegation and a large Australian one headed by Richard Casey, the Australian Minister of Supply. This was the first long-distance journey by air that Freyberg had undertaken:

> The journey was better than anything I could have imagined. There was one strange result of flying due east – we reduced the length of the days from 24 hours to 22 hours and daylight was correspondingly much shorter. Usually therefore we arrived at our destination in the dark. We left Alexandria harbour at dawn [11 December 1939] and we were flying over the confluence of the Euphrates and Tigris as light was fading. We circled above the lights of Basra as we lost height . . . Next day it was on to Karachi, and then to Calcutta, Rangoon and Bangkok, eventually reaching Singapore on 15 December.[3]

The scenery throughout was a constant joy to him. He was particularly struck by the great beauty of the evening approach to Basra with the whole sparkling panorama of city lights reflected on the river. But he also had to get through a lot of paperwork:

> I started in with my motor pen* at six in the morning and plied it hard until the end of the journey. In the four days and nights I completed my rough drafts, wrote my appreciation of the situation for Mr Fraser, prepared the plans for the base in England in outline, and set out all the arrangements made and to be made for the concentration of the New Zealand troops in Egypt. In addition to these I had worked out a complete précis of all the conditions that I was going to advise the New Zealand Government to consider and if possible decide upon in respect of the force that I was to command.
> I cabled OC Troops Singapore that I was arriving and asked if he would have some typewriting done for me. In anticipation I corrected my drafts all next day and when the plane arrived I handed my work to the Staff Officer who met the plane and asked him to let me have it back by 5 a.m. next day.[3]

Freyberg stayed that night in Government House, Singapore, and dined with his old command, 1 Battalion Manchester Regiment, where he spent 'a very moving evening'.[3] Then they continued the flight over the Dutch East Indies to Sourabaya, where they spent the day visiting the hill stations in the jungles just beneath volcanic mountains, and the next morning flew on to Darwin with Freyberg correcting his drafts yet again. After Darwin it was on to Townsville for their last overnight stop,

* A 'motor pen' was an expression for continuous writing, not a special kind of pen.

[207]

from where the final lap of the journey took the flying boat over lovely country down the east coast of Australia to Sydney Harbour, where the delegation was made guests of the Commonwealth government for the remainder of their stay.

The next days in Australia were hectic. Australia and New Zealand had long had close associations on defence matters, and now had common interests over their expeditionary forces. It was essential for their commanders to be in broad agreement over policy matters. One of the problems they discussed was whether to accept the British army ration for their overseas forces, which was smaller than the Australian and New Zealand ration, with almost half the amount of butter and meat per day. The New Zealand government was only willing to accept the proposed reduction if the Australians also agreed to it. Freyberg argued strongly that for practical reasons the British ration was adequate, the men would be doing the same job and they should accept the British scale. Gradually he won the Australians round, but on one point he was defeated: the British ration in the Middle East contained margarine instead of butter because unrefrigerated butter melts in the heat. But for the Australian government to accept margarine was regarded as 'political suicide', so a 'fudge' was agreed whereby 'butter if available' was left in as part of the ration.[3] Freyberg later calculated that in reducing the food ration he saved the New Zealand government approximately a shilling per man per day, which for 32,000 men for six years amounted to a saving of approximately £3.5 million! He maintained that the cuts also improved administrative efficiency and saved thousands of tons of valuable shipping space.

Freyberg had several useful conversations during this interlude, including a long talk with Robert Menzies, Prime Minister of Australia, and was impressed by the forceful outspokenness he encountered. He called on General Sir Brudenell White, who had been Chief of Staff to Field Marshal Birdwood in the Great War, and as something of an elder statesman was able to give advice about the difficulties Freyberg would encounter when he took the NZ Expeditionary Force overseas. Freyberg also had discussions with General Squires, Chief of Australian Staff, and with his opposite number in command of the Australian Imperial Force (AIF), General Blamey, whom he was to see continually during the next two years. He found Blamey able, outspoken and ruthless in argument, but on fundamentals they were in general agreement.[3]

At the end of the Australian visit, on 23 December, he sailed on to New Zealand in the TSS *Awatea*:

Christmas morning saw us up very early and we picked up the coast at daylight and steamed into Wellington harbour. Twenty-five years had not changed that stormswept coastline, which except for one brief visit in 1921 I had not seen since March 1914. As we turned towards the City round Point Halswell on this lovely Christmas morning of 1939 I looked and thought that it was a truly beautiful setting; but how could it appear otherwise to one who was coming home?[3]

The next twelve days were among the busiest and most demanding in Freyberg's life. He was trying to carry out three separate activities simultaneously: negotiating with Ministers the terms under which he was to lead the expeditionary force during the next critical years; inspecting the troops he was to take overseas; and agreeing the senior officer appointments in the Division. In addition he was asked to show himself in public and to meet as many of the people of New Zealand as he could. Finally all this had to be done within a timescale which could not be extended. The first echelon had to embark on their troopships on 5 January 1940.[1]

Freyberg began by having breakfast at the Waterloo Hotel with his brothers Cuthbert and Claud, whom he had not seen since 1921. After that he attended the Christmas day service, following which he met some of the senior regular officers who would accompany him overseas. He went over his programme of engagements with them to decide how best to divide up his time. The following morning at nine he met the Minister of Defence, the Hon. Frederick Jones, at Parliament Buildings, and gave him a full account of his work in London, France and Egypt, and told him what he hoped to achieve in New Zealand. He handed over the précis he had prepared of the special powers he considered the New Zealand government should vest in him, and the powers which he thought they should reserve to themselves. He also produced a diagram showing the suggested channel of communication for administrative and general staff matters.[3]

Their next subject was the base organisation. Freyberg explained his tentative arrangements to locate the administrative services at Colchester in the longer term, where he had been promised the facilities of a barracks complex where all the administrative troops could be concentrated in one area. After considering the matter in detail the Defence Minister approved these proposals.[3] In the afternoon the question of the concentration and training areas in Egypt was discussed. By New Zealand standards Egypt was an unhealthy country, and a very close watch would have to be taken to safeguard the well-being of the troops and provide the necessary medical precautions. Freyberg's choice of Maadi as their camp was also approved. The final matter for that day

BERNARD FREYBERG, VC

concerned the legal position of the special powers Freyberg sought, and how they were expected to be applied in emergency. It was agreed to refer these to the Attorney-General and his staff before they were submitted to the New Zealand Cabinet.

It was late when Freyberg looked at his engagements for the next day, and remembered that he had a civic reception in the Town Hall:

> I was glad that I had already given a certain amount of thought to what I was going to say: I felt that it was one of the big moments of my life. Some thousands of men and women of my home town had gathered to give me a homecoming welcome. It was not just the welcome that is given to the stranger within their gates, and I should have been wanting in imagination if I had not realised that it was something much deeper – something of a very personal nature. I could come before them with a clear conscience in one respect. I could face them and say with truth that in all my life abroad I had always remained at heart true to my country. New Zealand has always been my first and dearest love. It was a most moving meeting and I had the greatest difficulty in not showing my emotions.[3]

The occasion did not pass without incident, however. After beginning his speech with sincere personal remarks and sentiments he went on to discuss the war situation, and then, in his own words, 'I dropped a tremendous political brick.' The New Zealand government had pledged themselves not to bring in conscription, and thereby caused a heated controversy in the country, of which Freyberg was unaware. So as he warmed to his subject and spoke of his admiration for the way in which the British public had accepted the sacrifices needed for waging war he cited, as an example, that they had taken conscription in their stride. He was astonished when the audience rose to their feet as one, cheered him loudly and yelled abuse at the Defence Minister and Deputy Premier who were sitting on the platform at his side:

> I was embarrassed by the situation I had precipitated. Eventually I stopped them, and then by way of putting myself right with my Minister I said that the English people had also accepted 7/- in the £ income tax with cheers. This caused a certain amount of laughter and the meeting subsided. The lesson was not wasted on me.[3]

The following morning Freyberg, with Fraser and Jones, went to call on the Prime Minister, Michael Joseph Savage, who was mortally ill; but what was intended as a visit of ten minutes took up the best part of the morning. Freyberg records that he had rarely met anyone with a more striking personality.

[210]

That evening he boarded the overnight ferry boat to Lyttelton for a civic reception in Christchurch. He breakfasted with the Mayor, and afterwards addressed a crowd of several thousand from a balcony. Then it was out to Burnham Camp for a visit to troops of the first echelon. That night he returned by the ferry to Wellington for another day with the troops and a visit to Trentham Camp. He caught the train the following night for Hamilton, to visit Hopuhopu Camp and more of the first echelon; and then on to Papakura to see the Auckland Regiment and the Divisional Cavalry. He was then taken by car to the Town Hall in Auckland for a further civic reception with another large audience. By then he was so tired he was scarcely registering what was happening, for during this period he had also had to interview all the commanding officers and senior members of the Division to confirm their provisional appointments.

Although Freyberg had reservations about several of these officers he kept his thoughts to himself. His principal concern was that some of them were too old; and although they had gallant First World War records their military experience had been in the slow-moving conditions of the trenches.

The most difficult case for Freyberg was that of Brigadier James Hargest, born in 1891. He had an impressive record in the First World War, and was now the Member of Parliament for Awarua as well as being in the Territorial Army. He was in line for a senior military job by virtue of his seniority and length of service, but Freyberg was concerned that Hargest had undergone very little military training since the 1914–18 war and lacked modern knowledge, in addition to being middle-aged in military terms. He was reluctant therefore to confirm Hargest in such an important position as one of the three Brigade commanders. Political pressure was then brought to bear and, as Chief of Staff, Duigan wrote to Freyberg from Army Headquarters, Wellington: 'Regarding the 5th Brigade Commander: this was a Government decision, and they took all responsibility from myself and the DMS.'[4]

There was also the problem of 'the four colonels', as they were known. While they were still on the Territorial Army Reserve these officers had made a political attack in the press on the defence policy of the government. They were immediately placed on the retired list, but they were among the most experienced officers in the country and but for their misdemeanour would have been in the running for senior appointments. Freyberg asked for guidance as to their availability and was told that the main consideration was that he should have the best officers, and if he wanted any of them he was to have them. In the event he took three of 'the four colonels'.[3]

[211]

Another important appointment made was that of Freyberg's Personal Assistant. This was John White, who was introduced by an old friend of Freyberg's, Mr Justice Ostler. John White, who served Freyberg devotedly and with great discretion for over five years, was in charge of his private office and all his paper work, including his dealings with the New Zealand government. A lawyer by profession, and later a distinguished judge, John White had an impressive range of skills, which included shorthand. In the many battles to come he listened in on a second handset to all Freyberg's telephone conversations with other commanders, and was present at conferences. Immediately afterwards he would record what had been said, and the decisions taken. He was also a fine photographer; Freyberg gave him a Leica camera, and John became the unofficial photographer to the Division.

Friday, 5 January, Freyberg's final day, was a crucial one. In the morning he appeared before a meeting of the Cabinet to explain, paragraph by paragraph, the powers he sought from them and to answer questions. After a hasty lunch he spent the afternoon in front of the all-party Defence Committee where he was again closely questioned and cross-examined. He emerged satisfactorily from both ordeals; indeed he was given a vote of thanks at the latter for being prepared to discuss matters so fully. He got back to his hotel just as the first of thirty ministers and other guests began to arrive for a final dinner before his departure. Between the soup and the fish he had to slip out and broadcast a farewell message to the people of New Zealand. He later said he went to the microphone 'not knowing what I was going to say and not knowing what I had said when I had finished'. The same applied to the speech he had to make at the dinner itself, before those who were embarking left to join their ships at eleven o'clock that night.[3]

The convoy did not weigh anchor, however, until 6 a.m. on 6 January, when it steamed slowly out of Port Nicholson into the Cook Strait, escorted by the battleship *Ramillies* and cruisers of the Royal Navy and the Royal Australian and New Zealand navies. Freyberg watched the departure from the bridge of his troopship, the liner *Empress of Canada*. It was a moving moment for him. Two of his brothers had failed to return from the Great War, and now here he was himself departing for war in Europe entrusted with the lives of the next generation. The men of the first echelon were all on the decks of their ships or hanging from the riggings. The civilian population in their thousands lined the hills near the harbour entrance. In Freyberg's words, 'it was an inspiring send-off and one that will be remembered as long as memory lasts'; but his final thought as the ships moved out of sight of land was that 'my responsibilities did not bear thinking about'.[3]

The next thirty-six hours Freyberg spent in bed recovering from exhaustion and an inoculation that had given him a temperature. By the time he felt fit to get up again the convoy was approaching Sydney. That afternoon he received a message from Captain Baillie-Grohmann, commanding *Ramillies*, that he was going to pass through the convoy. This was done with the ship's decks fully manned, its band playing, and the crew giving 'three cheers' as they passed the *Empress of Canada*, while she signalled 'God bless you and your gallant men from all who sail in HMS *Ramillies*'. The spectacle reminded Freyberg of the occasion, twenty-five years earlier at Mudros, just before Gallipoli.

Next day the *Empress of Canada* left the convoy with HMAS *Canberra*, and put in to Sydney, where Freyberg and his chief doctor, Brigadier MacCormick, were taken off by launch.[1] They were intending to fly on ahead to Egypt, but had to wait three days before the next flying boat left. Freyberg went and 'shot the surf at Little Coogee', which he had last visited thirty-four years before. MacCormick and he talked to the Australian military medical authorities, who gave them a thought-provoking report about the Abyssinian campaign, written by the Italian medical chief, Aldo Castillagri. This attributed the Italian troops' freedom from disease to the great care that had been taken over the treatment of water supplies, and the fact that they were allowed to drink only bottled water shipped all the way from Italy. Freyberg and MacCormick spent the next three days looking at mineral water factories and making calculations about the millions of bottles they would need; fortunately when they got to Egypt they found that the water supply was hygienic!

They left Sydney on 13 January, reached Singapore on 16 January, and landed at Alexandria on 22 January 1940. In the six weeks since leaving Heston Freyberg had travelled 27,000 miles.[3]

Back in Cairo Freyberg stayed at the Continental Hotel, because work on the Maadi camp had been delayed by shortages of materials. Indeed Freyberg only managed to take up residence there on 8 February, four days before the first echelon arrived at Suez.[3]

The combined Australian and New Zealand convoys were met by a high-powered delegation which included Anthony Eden, then Dominions Secretary, Sir Miles Lampson the British ambassador and General Sir Archibald Wavell, C-in-C Middle East, as well as Generals Blamey and Freyberg. The arrival received massive news coverage; the British papers proclaimed it an historic occasion,

[213]

comparable to the arrival of the Anzacs prior to the Gallipoli campaign; and there were descriptions of the ships carrying the Australians and New Zealanders as one of the biggest troop convoys in history – 'a wonderfully inspiring sight' – with the panorama of liners and naval escorts stretching as far as the eye could see.[5]

The New Zealand troops went by rail to Maadi, which was still in the hands of the contractors. Peacetime conditions continued to prevail in Egypt, which meant that the troops could train without interruption. Egypt had no dispute with Germany or Italy, and the presence of Allied forces there was largely due to the British interest and presence in Egypt since the previous century. This had been finalised in the Anglo-Egyptian Treaty of 1936, which provided for the gradual withdrawal of British forces over a period of twenty years, except from the Canal Zone.

The assembly of the New Zealand Division had been planned around the first three echelons, each of which comprised approximately a Brigade Group, plus a proportion of divisional troops, and numbering about 7,000 men each. The rate of arrival was governed by their recruitment and initial training in New Zealand, followed by their despatch overseas in fast troopships. The second echelon was due three months later, towards the end of May 1940, and the third actually arrived at the end of September. Had things gone as originally planned the concentration of the Division would have been complete by the beginning of October 1940.

One of Freyberg's concerns as its commander was how to maintain a high standard of health care:

I made up my mind, when I took over the 2 NZEF that I would not leave the medical side of our force to chance . . . We set our doctors off on research in a big way. They investigated conditions not only with regard to water-borne disease, but food-borne disease, fly-borne diseases, venereal disease; and on the surgical side, the question of mobile surgical units, blood transfusion units, saline baths, and the like. As I say, nothing was neglected.

They made the fly, which included, of course, the mosquito, enemy No. 1, and had a campaign to stop them from breeding in our base area. Latrines were fly-proofed; casual water was oiled [to prevent insects breeding]; water for human consumption was specially treated – it was filtered, boiled or chlorinated; food was carefully protected at all stages; all utensils that came in contact with food or drink, including plates, cups, knives, forks and spoons, were sterilised – they were boiled, and kept under fly-proof covers until the men wanted to use them. To guard against hand contamination, men were made to dip their hands in 2 per cent solution of creosote before entering the dining-halls. I cannot pass an opinion on the efficiency of this system, but as a drill it had its effect. It showed the men that great thought was being given to the protection of their health, and this made everyone health-conscious.

Then we had to consider the list of infected foods and drinks that could be bought by the troops in the bazaars in Cairo or on leave in other parts of the Middle East. They were all highly dangerous, but the worst of them were fresh fruit, particularly melons, salads, and ice-cream, while native drink in all the bazaars was a serious source of trouble.[6]

The establishment of clubs in Cairo – and later in Italy and England too, in fact wherever New Zealand troops were based – was another innovation. Freyberg had observed in 1914–18 how the British Army appeared to wash its hands of responsibility for its soldiers' activities once they were off duty. This seemed to him wrong, especially considering some of the inhospitable places in which they were required to serve. He was determined to establish centres to which his soldiers could go when not on duty, where they could get a decent meal cheaply, read the New Zealand papers, write letters, post parcels home and get advice about where to go and what to see locally. Freyberg added:

> We made fresh fruit drinks under hygienic conditions. We started a bakery with the most modern cake-making machinery brought out from England. All the natives who were employed were medically examined, and had to bath and change into clean clothes before starting work.[6]

By the end of 1940 the organisation of the New Zealand clubs was well established, with a considerable staff from the New Zealand Women's War Services Auxiliary (WWSA) to help run them, and a large financial turnover. Beer bars were also established in the clubs, although these came in for a good deal of criticism in New Zealand, so much so that the subject became politically sensitive.

The trouble with the bars was that the soldiers would return on leave, after many weeks of danger and discomfort in forward areas, determined to enjoy themselves and with large sums of money in their pockets. Inevitably some men drank more than they should, and it was not long before lurid and exaggerated stories started to appear in the New Zealand press. This caused distress and concern among relatives, and the military authorities overseas were blamed for encouraging drunkenness by allowing the sale of beer in the clubs. Equally inevitably, there were calls for them to be closed.

Freyberg would have none of it. He resisted pressures to close the bars, which recurred from time to time throughout the war. He knew perfectly well that, if that had happened, the soldiers would go to some

[215]

alternative civilian establishment in Cairo where no supervision was possible. There they would buy arak, a form of native brandy, and other strong intoxicants; they might be robbed when drunk and even get a knife in the back if they tried to resist. There were a number of instances of this happening to British troops who did not have clubs to go to.

Military training started almost immediately the first echelon arrived in Egypt:

> Although there were delays in the training and equipping of our force [Freyberg wrote], the men put a high quality of energy and thought into all they did, and it was a delight to be associated with them. As I was to find out, they were by nature obedient and most practical. They required only to be told what to do – and rarely how to do it. We tightened up the administration and tested out their physical fitness, and could see their improvement week by week.[3]

By 22 April Freyberg considered that the individual training for the first echelon had been completed. He then divided the force into two and took them south into the desert for their first full-scale exercise. This, as he described it:

> was an uncontrolled battle, heavily umpired, although we did not use live ammunition. It was great fun and the honours were even. The men enjoyed it, and were so much above themselves that they burned the Camp Cinema that night on their return to Maadi to show how tough they were.[3]

But Freyberg the commander, and his compatriots the officers and men of 2 NZEF, needed some time before they began to settle down together. Initially both parties were wary of each other; nor did Freyberg, in spite of his strong character, determination and reputation, find his feet immediately in his relationships with his subordinates. In their turn, these officers did not quite know what to make of Freyberg. In outward appearance he looked formidable and every bit the general in command who expected to be obeyed; and they felt in some awe because of his reputation and his VC. He was tall, well-built, with an expression on his face that at times could be grim, even though he might merely be preoccupied with the problem of the moment. Those who came into early contact with him were misled about his nature by their first impressions, and sensed some distance in his approach because he had been subject to British influences for the last twenty-five years.

Yet as General Stevens explains:

Nothing could have been further from the truth than those first beliefs. We found a man who was kind, considerate, gentle, compassionate, always ready to listen, always approachable. I never heard him raise his voice in anger, or say a harsh or unkind word . . . He was never peremptory, never curt, never dictatorial, never criticised anyone in front of anyone else, and if he did criticise one's work, was so gentle about it that it was hard to realise that criticism was intended. There may be differences of opinion about Freyberg's conduct of operations; but there are none at all about these personal characteristics.

He was dignified under provocation or under rudeness, or when someone took advantage of his forbearance, for he was understanding and tolerant of human weaknesses. In a word he was simpleness and gentleness personified.[2]

Stevens also suggests that Freyberg's attitude altered as a result of the misfortunes of the Greek and Crete campaigns of 1941, which made him 'as one' with the Division. This was only partly true. His analysis of the main elements of Freyberg's personality was accurate, but there was no sudden change in Freyberg's behaviour. What altered was the New Zealanders' perception of him. If there was one adjective that Stevens identified as summing up Freyberg's everyday approach, it was that he was a *gentle* man.

It took time for this view of Freyberg to percolate through to the Division. His staff and immediate subordinates were the first to 'warm' to him, but stories about his attitudes soon began to circulate: his acute awareness that he was dealing with civilians who had only recently donned uniform; his concern about their health and well-being; his determination to render their off-duty moments as pleasant as possible by establishing the clubs. As Stevens says, the New Zealanders' attitude towards Freyberg changed from puzzlement into understanding and then respect; and ultimately affection.

His approach to discipline was very different from that of a great many generals. Freyberg had authority to adopt whatever kind of discipline he thought most suitable, but in his opinion discipline was a means to an end, and not an end in itself.[3] In the New Zealand forces the officers, NCOs and men all came from the same source – the same towns and villages. They usually knew each other well, and in many cases were close friends or even relatives, and for this reason Freyberg felt that the British system of discipline would not work with them. It would fail because it depended on a factor that did not exist in the new countries – the existence of three distinct army classes: the Officer, the NCO and the Other Rank. The British system, which worked also with the Germans and to a lesser extent with the Americans, depended on keeping the classes separate when off duty.

Freyberg was interested in discipline only to the extent that it helped in the winning of battles or affected the well-being of the men or the good name of New Zealand. Right from the beginning, therefore, he decided to adopt an elastic style of discipline. He did away with minor crimes because they created bad feeling rather than comradeship, and concentrated upon guards and picquets, ceremonial parades, close order drill and march discipline, relying on the common sense of New Zealanders to respond to example and reason. As a Division they held more brigade ceremonials than any other formation, and at every opportunity guests were invited, and a function made of it.

No doubt the New Zealanders did fall below the high standard of smartness achieved by the regular British units in Cairo. Freyberg, however, was aiming at a wartime goal which depended on other factors, the main one being the speed with which his forces could be fitted for battle. The justification of any system in wartime could thus be tested. Did the formation take and hold its objectives? Did the trained military force hold together in a crisis? Was there much real crime? Freyberg challenged anyone to fault the New Zealand Division in these vital matters. That it excelled in battle was due to the superb material available, to good leadership from top to bottom, and to the common sense of the New Zealand soldier. That there was practically no desertion in the face of the enemy, and very little crime, was a reflection on the efficiency of the military set-up and the way discipline was applied.

The first echelon had been in Egypt for three months when, on 10 May 1940, the Germans attacked the Western Front in France. Freyberg heard of the unfolding events with anguish but without surprise. His visit to the BEF and French armies six months before had revealed to him how easily the Maginot Line could be turned, and the Allied armies were quickly beaten in the open country by the superior German armour, supported by their formidable air force. The only consolation that Freyberg could see as a result of the crisis was that his old friend Winston Churchill became Prime Minister.

At the same time the second New Zealand echelon was *en route* for Egypt and, by the middle of May, had reached the Indian Ocean. However, in view of the likelihood of Italy entering the war, the Admiralty decided that it was no longer prudent to risk exposing such a target to enemy air action from bases in Abyssinia as it entered the Red

Sea. The second echelon was diverted to Cape Town therefore, and then proceeded direct to England.

By early June the BEF had largely been evacuated from France, and on 10 June Italy declared war on France and Britain, bringing fighting to Egypt's very doorstep because of the Italian armies in Libya. Thus, within a month Freyberg's situation had changed completely. His New Zealand force had been intended to concentrate in Egypt as the staging post before the Division moved on to join the BEF in France. Now that the BEF had virtually evacuated the Continent and the future of a front in France was in doubt, Egypt itself was likely soon to become a battlefield; but because the second echelon convoy had been diverted in the Indian Ocean, Freyberg's command was split almost equally between Egypt and England.

This put Freyberg in a quandary. Should he stay in Egypt in view of the possibility of an Italian attack from Cyrenaica, or should he return to England to oversee the training of the second echelon? His instincts told him that the Italian threat in the Western Desert was not likely to be a serious one to begin with, especially during the coming hot summer months. On the other hand he felt that his presence in England was certain to be needed, in view of the inexperience of the officers of the second echelon. At this time, moreover, there was no suggestion that France would cease to fight.

From 25 May to 17 June a series of signals was exchanged between Maadi and Wellington about whether or not Freyberg ought to go to the UK.[7] Initially the New Zealand government believed that a major Italian attack was impending in the Western Desert, and Peter Fraser, now Prime Minister after the death of Savage on 26 March 1940, felt that Freyberg should stay in Egypt. Freyberg, however, was able to persuade his government that no Italian attack was likely before the cooler weather in September; and he explained further: 'What I want my Ministers to realise is that none of my senior officers with the second echelon bound for England is fit to start training without being trained himself.'[7]

Even so Freyberg waited until the situation cleared. On 10 June, when Italy finally came into the war, the Italians in Cairo were rounded up. After allowing a few more days for affairs to settle – with the battle in France growing more ominous, and the air routes through the Mediterranean closing – Freyberg decided to set off for London.

15

'If you are not careful you will lose Egypt'

Freyberg left Cairo on Monday, 17 June 1940 in a Lockheed 14. In addition to two other military passengers there was mail for the War Office, Admiralty and Air Ministry from the Middle East, and a large accumulation of Foreign Office mail from the Balkans, Turkey and Syria. The Italian entry into the war had made it impossible to use the usual air routes through the Mediterranean, so the only alternative, given the limited range of aircraft, was to hop across Central Africa. As they arrived in Khartoum on the evening of 18 June,

> the radio started to boom its doleful news. The situation appeared much worse and later in the evening we got two cipher messages, one from the Air Ministry at Bristol telling us to go back to Cairo, and another from the Foreign Office, signed by Lord Halifax [the Foreign Secretary], telling us to come on with all haste to England. The reason for all this interest in such high places was not any concern for the safety of the passengers, but purely because of the vital diplomatic mail.[1]

During the night further cipher messages arrived directing the aircraft back to Cairo. However just as the party was about to board the aircraft another cable was received from Lord Halifax directing the pilot to proceed with all speed across the Sahara and on to England. Before starting they heard the news that France had asked for an armistice. This was shattering enough in itself, but it also raised doubts about the

[220]

availability of French airfields in West and North Africa. However the Foreign Office had known about this when it ordered the flight to continue; so the aircraft duly set off. The journey in an overladen plane without proper maps or wireless beacons was a hazardous one.

There were a number of incidents during the first part of the journey from Khartoum, including a smashed back wheel. They proceeded with difficulty to Gao, a French town on the banks of the river Niger, where a message arrived from London diverting the aircraft away from Dakar, and instructing it to continue via Oran. The military passengers were also ordered to change into civilian clothes. The most difficult and dangerous part of the journey was now before them:

We set off before it was light for Aoullton, a distance of 750 miles with nothing to guide us except a compass bearing and a featureless map. The landing ground we were making for was just a clear stretch of desert with a small petrol hut. When we did try to land we found that it would be pure luck to find so small a mark. We had been flying for several hours and as we were overdue the pilot started to search round in a large circle. After a long period of indecision, to our great relief the pilot picked up a landmark which he recognised on the map and after another hour's flying we came down with not very much petrol left.

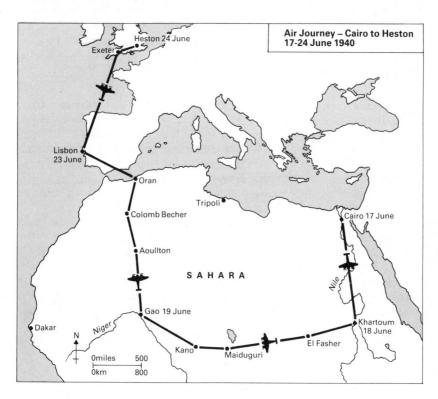

Air Journey – Cairo to Heston
17-24 June 1940

Aoullton, to my mind, was the most desolate spot I have ever seen. The temperature when we landed was over 130 degrees in the shade; the only shade, incidentally, was under the aeroplane wings. The air hit us like a blow in the face after the cool of the cabin. The place itself had only one inhabitant, a Frenchman who stayed there alone for three months on end. The last inhabitant had gone mad and committed suicide. The present inhabitant did not seem very sane.[1]

When the aircraft eventually reached Oran, they found the French in a state of shock, unable to understand the catastrophe that had overtaken their country. Then, as Freyberg put it: 'On 23 June, dressed as civilians, complete with Bombay bowlers and looking like music-hall Empire builders, we left for Lisbon, a hop of 650 miles.' They stayed there for one night, and next day flew the final leg to Exeter, and then on to Heston. Freyberg concluded his account of this 'strange journey':

I was filled with admiration for the skill of the pilot and the aeroplane's personnel . . . Of course Captain Pelly was a famous airman, and it was he who was chosen to take Mr Chamberlain to Munich. That we finished our journey safely was surprising, and indicated a large amount of luck.[2]

Freyberg arrived at Clarendon Place at 6.30 p.m. on 24 June. The following morning he went straight to the War Office to get an appreciation of the strategic position after Dunkirk, the fall of France and the loss of so much equipment; and then he began to discuss the NZ requirements with the Staff Duties Branch:

It was only when I dug into the question of equipment that I realised what a ghastly mess we had got ourselves into . . . we had not only lost the full equipment of the Field Army, but also the War Reserves which had been built up on the Lines of Communication in France. Nothing remained. When I talked about the chance of getting any guns I was told there were none in the country. With the exception of the Canadian Division, which was completely equipped, there was extremely little of anything, arms or equipment, in the United Kingdom.

When I discussed the role of the New Zealand troops in England I told them that they had done section training, but not platoon, company or battalion training. I asked their opinion as to what would be the best way for us to help. They did not pass any opinion other than to say that it would probably be better for us to go away to some back area and complete our training. When I asked about equipment they said that troops which had an operational role would have priority and that they would not be able to give us any equipment.

I considered the position very carefully. It was a little bit tricky because, before I left Egypt, I had cabled my Government and said that I could not recommend the New Zealand Forces for an operational role unless we were adequately trained and equipped for the operation to which we were committed. Troops with two months training to a standard of section-commanding armed with a rifle and bayonet did not appear to fall into the required category; and yet it seemed inconceivable that New Zealand troops in uniform should be in England and stand aside and let others defend the home country.[1]

Freyberg cabled to this effect to the New Zealand government and urged them to give him authority to take an operational role. The New Zealand second echelon had arrived in England in mid-June, some ten days before Freyberg, and had gone into camp in and around Mytchett near Aldershot. It consisted of a full Brigade Group plus a large slice of divisional troops including two further battalions. The New Zealand government accepted Freyberg's recommendations and, as he wrote:

we were released to be used as and when we were required. So I went hat in hand to the CIGS [now General Sir John Dill] and said, 'Give us what equipment you can spare and give us an active operational role.' We thus became part of GHQ Reserve which was at this stage composed of the 1st Canadian Division, 1st Armoured Division and the NZEF (United Kingdom).[2]

Freyberg set up a small headquarters and officers mess at Mytchett Place, and as soon as his negotiations at the War Office were success-fully concluded he got down to training. 'The Staff Duties Branch gave us twenty-five per cent of our arms and equipment, sufficient ammunition for our first and second echelons and two London bus companies to make us entirely mobile.'

He was faced with having to cram many months of training into seven days because he was assured that the Germans could start their invasion any time after 1 July:

However I was facing an easy problem in one way because we had few if any arms other than rifles and bayonets, bren guns and anti-tank guns. We worked night and day until everybody had developed certain proficiency. I organised the force into three groups; a so-called Armoured Group consisting of the Divisional Cavalry Squadron of light tanks, carriers and a battalion of gunners masquerading as infantry; the Fifth Infantry Brigade Group complete; the 7th Infantry Brigade consisting of a reinforcement battalion and the Maoris.[2]

Training started during the last days of June and continued through-out July. The New Zealand brigades travelled in their buses all over southern England, across the Sussex Weald and Kent, camping in Petworth Park and in the shadow of Arundel Castle, and were deployed on the Sussex Downs to repel imaginary German landings at Seaford, Brighton and Littlehampton. 'No part of Kent, Sussex or Hampshire,' Freyberg wrote, 'was without car and bus loads of men with the broad-brimmed New Zealand felt hat.' He added, 'We were inspired by, and I think in turn we also inspired the civil population. There was a deep feeling of mutual esteem between our men and the population of the towns we moved through.'

To begin with the officers and troops 'made every mistake possible'. For example, Freyberg's units and the Royal Army Service Corps (RASC) had no knowledge or experience of drawing supplies in the field. 'The first night at the ration meeting-point, unit guides waited for their rations to arrive until daylight without results. The next night it was better, everybody got something and by the fourth night they started to get the hang of the job.' So it was in every other department: 'I learnt a good deal about my force during that period; that they had soft feet, bad boots and socks, and that they could not march.' So Freyberg organised long route marches to get the men fit after many weeks at sea, and they spent a considerable time firing their small arms weapons on the ranges.

When the New Zealand government agreed on 29 June to the second echelon accepting an operational role, Freyberg had been delighted:

> The scheme of action was that we were to move to any part of the south coast of Great Britain where a German landing had taken place. It was a satisfactory role because we were able to remain concentrated to train and at the same time were certain to take part in the main battle wherever it might be.[1]

King George VI visited Mytchett Camp on 6 July, and after inspect-ing New Zealand troops on parade stayed to lunch in the officers' mess. The District Commander, Major-General D. G. Johnson, VC, was present, as was the High Commissioner for New Zealand, William Jordan, who amused the King on his arrival by saying, 'Allow me to introduce your Majesty to two VCs and one BF.'

The Prime Minister heard that Freyberg was back in England, and invited him and Barbara to dine on 17 July at 10 Downing Street. Mr and Mrs Duncan Sandys (Churchill's son-in-law and daughter), and Professor Lindemann, Churchill's scientific adviser (later Lord Cher-

[224]

well), were also present as they sat down to a late meal. Freyberg
describes the occasion:

The Prime Minister was in the best of spirits with a bright seraphic smile,
and a most engaging welcome. His opening remark to the gathering was: 'I
am tired; you're tired; we're all tired! Let's have some bubbly.' He talked
buoyantly throughout the meal, with no hint of the critical and very
precarious state of our position.

He was full of interest and enquiries. 'Were our men fit?' He would not
ask about equipment, but he impressed upon me that 'there was no need to
worry. The equipment would soon be here and then you will have guns
galore.' He said that guns were arriving at all ports from the United States.
Then the conversation switched.

'This is the most interesting government I have ever been in – far the
most interesting.' He added that he had made himself Chairman of the
Committee of Defence, and had purposely refrained from defining his
duties, as he intended to do exactly what he considered necessary.

Towards the end of the dinner the Prime Minister took another line.
'This' (meaning England), he said, 'is the decisive theatre. If we are
defeated here, the war is lost.' He repeated this remark many times during
the evening. We all agreed on the need to defeat or prevent an invasion.

Mr Churchill also said to me that he was going to insist that convoys
should come through the Mediterranean. It was evident that the dangers
and difficulties of the situation were only acting as a spur to him. I had never
seen him in better form, and he told me he was glad to have me in England
with my men. I tried to turn the conversation to the Middle East, without
much effect, and after one or two attempts I gave up the unequal struggle.

As we were saying goodbye, Mr Churchill said to me, 'I'm going to bring
all your Anzacs home through the Mediterranean.' To this impossible
proposal I replied, 'You're not!' This was the first time I had been able to
make any impression, but he was quite unmoved, and enquired: 'You don't
think they will attempt invasion?' to which I replied: 'I don't think they will
succeed, but if you are not careful, you will lose Egypt.' He swept my
remarks aside, and I felt that my counter-attack had not had any effect.
Before leaving he said to me again, '*You* don't think they will attempt an
invasion. Neither do I – but you must not say so.'[2]

The sequel to this dinner was to come ten days later, on the afternoon
of 27 July. While Freyberg was watching the last of his men leave
Aldershot for a full-scale exercise, Anthony Eden's Private Secretary
rang from the War Office. The Secretary of State for War wanted to
see Freyberg at once, either at 6 p.m. or 10 p.m. that night. If he came at
the later time Eden would have longer to spare. Freyberg, having seen
his columns leave camp, went up late to the War Office in battledress,

all ready to go straight back into bivouac at Coleman's Hatch near Crowborough in Sussex. He described what occurred:

> When I went to the War Office I had no idea what was afoot with the Secretary of State. But when you are in a subordinate position in one of the Services, especially during a war, it is always a thrill to be sent for by the head of your service. When in doubt there is a phrase in Field Service Regulations which in life I find a great guide: 'Time spent on reconnaissance is seldom wasted.' So I planned to arrive at the rendezvous ten minutes early and see the Secretary of State's private secretary to get a line on what particular aspect of the war I was being consulted upon. When I said that I did not know what I was wanted for the Private Secretary passed over a sheet of foolscap with the following words typed on it:
>
> Secretary of State for War
> Freyberg is home. Get him to write an appreciation of the situation in the Middle East.
> 27 July 1940   WSC [in red ink].[2]

Freyberg realised at once that, unless he was careful, he was in danger of finding himself in a difficult position *vis-à-vis* his commander-in-chief in the Middle East; so he went along the corridor to General Dill, the CIGS, explained what was afoot and asked Dill to come and hear what was said.

> In we went, and Mr Eden then asked me if I would do an Appreciation of the Middle East for the Prime Minister. The situation was not an easy one for me. I was as busy as could be training my troops, working the clock round, and I said so, and told him that I was on my way out on an exercise at the moment. Further I told him that it was a big subject and one that I was not competent to review because I only knew a small part of the picture. Further I did not know either the naval or air situations and without knowing either no appreciation could be attempted, and I said so. He had anticipated this answer and said I could have access to all the reports and information in the Air Ministry and Admiralty. I said there was nothing that I would have liked to do more, but that it would take me a month's hard reading before I could cover all the ground. I also said that I had to train and possibly fight in a matter of days. He suggested that I could get somebody else to do the job. This of course was not a possible solution. However, as something would have to be done for the Prime Minister I agreed to put on paper my views on the defence of Egypt and the Suez Canal. I had a shrewd suspicion that nobody wanted my opinion except Mr Churchill.[2]

It was finally agreed that Freyberg should prepare his paper for the consideration of the Middle East Committee which had just been set up, composed of Lord Lloyd, Leo Amery and Eden. Afterwards he said, 'I do not know if they ever read what I wrote, but I know that Mr Churchill did, although it ran contrary to his considered opinions, as he said himself.'[2]

Freyberg wrote his report in two days and signed it, 'In Bivouac, Coleman's Hatch, Sussex, 29 July 1940.' Its main theme was to the effect that, at the time, there were two schools of thought about defence, which he described as 'Defence of London versus Defence of the Empire'. The first advocated a policy of concentrating all military resources to safeguard the British Isles until the danger of invasion was over; the second considered that such a priority must include as well the problems of the defence of the Suez Canal and Singapore.

In considering the options open to their German and Italian enemies, Freyberg pointed out that one of the most important factors was the weather. If the Germans were unable to launch an attack across the Channel by 20 September they would then run the risk of encountering the equinoctial gales; while in Egypt the position was the other way round – the best time for operations in the desert was from October onwards. He argued therefore that, as the Germans had less than two months in which to mount an invasion of England, it was unlikely that they would try, and those who argued that nothing should be sent from England before the autumn were over-insuring at the expense of the Middle East. He went on:

> In my opinion, the Italian forces alone do not constitute a menace, because the Italians in the past have lacked incisiveness to attempt such an operation and the offensive spirit necessary to carry through to a successful conclusion a project of this nature. If, however, Italy is helped by Germany with up-to-date methods and equipment, then the whole position of the defence of Egypt is altered.[2]

Freyberg also pointed out that the garrison in Egypt was totally inadequate in numbers of men and in equipment. It was a mixture of units hastily thrown together, with old, out-of-date tanks and armoured cars, obsolete artillery and inadequate war reserves. He said that there was not a single properly constituted division in Egypt. The only armoured division was very poorly equipped. The 4 Indian Division had only two brigades. The Australian and New Zealand forces were incomplete both in numbers and equipment. He recommended that, as a first step, the decision should immediately be taken to send reinforcements in men and equipment round the Cape without waiting for the autumn. He later summed up the paper and its contents as follows:

It was a closely argued paper emphasising the peril that threatened Egypt and strongly urging that equipment, reinforcements for the Army and the Air Force should be sent there without any further delay.

A week later General Wavell arrived home and from that date on there was a complete change in Government policy and convoys of ships started to leave for the East in quick succession taking equipment and men. I hope that my attack may have helped this state of affairs to come about. If it did then my labour at 'Coleman's Hatch' during the last week of July will not have been wasted.

However it is seldom in everyday life that one is able to lecture one's seniors, and in this case, betters. To be able to do so in a world crisis is probably one chance in a lifetime. I had the opportunity to say exactly what I thought about a subject I understood without any feeling of restraint. Seldom have I enjoyed doing anything so much. What was even more kind, Mr Churchill sent me six copies of the report and said that I was to send one to my own New Zealand government.[2]

The paper had been hastily prepared, but it was one of the most important Freyberg ever wrote. The argument may have gone counter to the Prime Minister's own opinion at the time, but Churchill not only had it printed but circulated it to the War Cabinet and Chiefs of Staff.

Shortly afterwards Freyberg got a telephone message asking him to dine and stay the night at Chequers, which he did on 2–3 August:

The party for the weekend was a small one [Freyberg wrote] – Mr and Mrs Churchill, their kinsman Lord Ivor Spencer Churchill, General Ismay, the Military Secretary to the Prime Minister, and myself. I wondered what was in the wind, and sure enough after dinner the Prime Minister developed his theory upon the defence of Egypt. It was an ingenious one. Later he asked me to give an opinion upon the possibility – not the advisability – of a certain minor operation against the Italians should they advance from Libya. By this time I was placed in an even more difficult position than before, because the official advisers knew as well as I did that the only operation that we could contemplate in the defence of Egypt for many months was to hang on by every means possible and hope that the Germans in their madness would attempt an invasion of Great Britain. What we really dreaded was that she would switch all her air power to the Middle East to help the Italians turn us out of the Western Desert and consequently the Suez Canal and the Mediterranean.[2]

They sat late over their meal, talking and not getting to bed till after 2 a.m. The Prime Minister was deep in his plan for defeating the Italians in Libya. Freyberg's account continues:

Roughly his plan was to allow them to advance along the coast road in the direction of Mersa Matruh and then, when they had stretched their communications to the utmost, to land in force behind them from the sea and stop the flow forward of food, petrol and water to the fighting troops. He said that what he was after was 'Strangulatory Hernia'.

He was now a little more approachable on the question of the Middle East. I found out afterwards that the C-in-C, General Wavell, had cabled to the Cabinet that the way they were heading would end in the loss of Egypt and the Suez Canal and I made the most of what opportunities offered and kept at him about the great disadvantage we were working under, and the fact that to reinforce Egypt now took forty days by fastest surface ships while the slowest took as long as 120 days. The Axis could carry out their reinforcements by air in a week. He listened and brooded, muttered to himself, and then sought shelter behind the formula, 'This is the decisive theatre' – a general statement with which I did not agree. I kept on whenever I got the chance on the lines which did not appear to be congenial to the Prime Minister. I did not believe in the possibility of a German invasion of England; that it was the Middle East which was in peril; that we should send by the quickest route, through the Mediterranean if possible, all the aeroplanes, equipment and munitions possible – but above all aircraft.

I needed to get back to say farewell to some of my troops who were going out to the Middle East. I had to start before luncheon as they were to leave Aldershot at 4 p.m. I did not see the Prime Minister until 1 p.m. on 3 August, but when he came downstairs he walked up and down telling me how he visualised committing 'Strangulatory Hernia' upon the Italians in Libya. He was very pleased with the phrase. Just before I left he said that I must stay for lunch as General de Gaulle was coming. I wish I could have stayed on but one cannot be in two places at once. His parting shot dealt with the air situation in the Middle East. He said, 'We cannot increase the number of squadrons in Egypt but we can see that the pilots have good polo ponies.'

He liked that statement too because when I took leave, he added, 'Yes, we can mount them well, with the best polo ponies.'[2]

While Freyberg was at Chequers he wrote a letter on 2 August to the New Zealand Prime Minister:

I am writing to you from the Long Library here after a long talk to the Prime Minister. He asked me to send you his greetings and to say how much he felt cheered to have the New Zealanders here in England. He also sent special messages of his confidence of ultimate victory.

I am here today to talk over an appreciation of the Egyptian situation which I prepared for him at his special request. I am sending out to you a copy of it for your information.[2]

[229]

Throughout August training for all the battalions went on at considerable pressure. At the end of a month there were two high-ranking visitors. The first was the C-in-C Home Forces, General Sir Alan Brooke, who made a thorough inspection on 31 August and, at the end of it, 28 (Maori) and 29 Battalions – looking superb, physically fit and bronzed – marched past at a swinging pace.[2] The second visitor was Mr Churchill himself, who had promised to visit and did so on 5 September. His method of 'inspection', as Freyberg wrote, was quite different from General Brooke's:

> 'I don't want to see any training,' he said, 'I just want to walk along the lines of men and look them in the eye.' It was arranged therefore that they should be drawn up in lines, and he went along line after line of men always looking them in the face, and he stopped at every few men and ran his fingers over the point of their bayonets. This was a source of great amusement to everybody.
>
> One of the men in the rear rank 'lost his name for talking during inspection' and was duly crimed. 'What remark did he make?' said the Prime Minister, intensely interested in all the proceedings, none of which were lost on him. He was told that he had made a highly improper remark, which was, 'He's a pugnacious looking b. . .' This pleased the Prime Minister enormously and he chuckled away as he added, 'I hope that justice will be tempered with mercy in this case.'[2]

Meanwhile orders had arrived from the War Office that the New Zealand second echelon was to leave England for Egypt in a convoy departing on 25 September. Instructions were issued for the soldiers to be sent on embarkation leave, and everything appeared to be settled. However during the first week of September General Paget, Chief of Staff GHQ Home Forces, telephoned Freyberg to ask if the New Zealand force would accept an urgent operational role. He was informed that they were already under orders to move overseas. Freyberg was then asked to go to GHQ. On arrival it was explained to him that there had just been a heavy bombardment of Dover from Cap Gris Nez, and an invasion was expected at any moment. Churchill had ordered that, if Dover was captured, it must be retaken at once and at all costs, and a special force was to be positioned immediately for this purpose. Would the New Zealanders take it on? In such an emergency Freyberg felt he could not refuse to act, but he made it abundantly clear that he accepted the commitment on the understanding that it was to last only for a few days, and that immediately the invasion scare was over his force would be released.

After the instructions for the move overseas were suspended, the

New Zealand force left the Aldershot area and was placed under the operational control of XII Corps Headquarters at Tunbridge Wells: 5 NZ Brigade Group was positioned to the east of Maidstone; 7 NZ Brigade deployed north of the Maidstone–Charing Road, and the Armoured Group went to the area of Charing itself. All three were alerted to carry out immediate counter-attacks on Dover and/or Folkestone. The invasion was expected on 10 September. In the meantime large formations of German bombers came overhead protected by hundreds of fighters, and the climax of the Battle of Britain was fought out in the sky above.

When 10 September came and went without invasion it was agreed that the New Zealand force should leave Kent on 12 September, complete its mobilisation for overseas by 17 September, and join the convoy to the Middle East on 25 September. Churchill then put back the date of the sailing of the convoy by a week, and kept the New Zealand force in Kent until 19 September, when he changed his mind again and deleted the NZ second echelon and the Armoured Division from sailing in the convoy at all. To Freyberg this cancellation was a great disappointment. It postponed the concentration of the New Zealand Division in Egypt by some four months, and this had a number of undesirable consequences.

At the same time as the invasion scare in England the Italians suddenly advanced from Cyrenaica into Egypt on 10 September and quickly reached Sidi Barrani. Freyberg was faced with another dilemma. Should he remain in England to help deal with an invasion which he believed to be less and less likely with every day that passed, or should he fly back to Egypt to be with the main part of the New Zealand Division? He decided that his place was in Egypt, and on 20 September it was agreed at the War Office that he should fly there by Wellington bomber two days later. This was subject to Churchill's agreement, which was only given very reluctantly at the last moment.

Freyberg and his chief of staff, Colonel Keith Stewart, drove by car to Stradishall in Norfolk and I accompanied them to see them off. On leaving Eton I had joined 23 Infantry Battalion in 5 NZ Brigade at the beginning of August and was posted as a private soldier to 'C' Company. There were air battles going on overhead, and at Epping Forest we were diverted down a side-road by police, who mistook the divisional pennant on my father's car for that of a bomb disposal squad. When eventually we arrived at the airfield we were warmly received and given dinner. An hour before take-off Freyberg rang GHQ Home Forces and spoke to General Paget; the forecast for that night was: 'No wind in the Channel, sea calm, invasion imminent – all precautions to be put into effect – full alert. He asked whether similar warnings to this one had been issued before? The answer came back – "No". On that note the conversation ended.'[1]

Freyberg was deeply troubled about whether he had made the right decision – but it was too late now to turn back. He was provided with 'a thick woollen teddy bear suit, with a pair of white silk gloves under leather gauntlets and a leather helmet'. We walked over to the Wellington bomber sitting on the tarmac nearby and said goodbye. At 2230 hours on 22 September 1940 the aircraft roared down the runway, took off, and disappeared into the night.

Freyberg's seat in the bomber was on top of a pile of oil filters which were being flown out to Egypt for the tanks of the Armoured Division. The plane flew high over enemy-occupied France, and took ten hours to reach Malta. The pilot was unused to the clear visibility of the Mediterranean, and instead of landing the aircraft on the beginning of the runway he touched down in the middle. The result was that it overshot and crashed into a stone wall at the end. The plane had to be written off altogether, and all the filters were destroyed, but Freyberg and Stewart emerged unscathed, though shaken. They resumed their flight next day in another aircraft, and arrived in Egypt at 1700 hours on 24 September after a journey of 39 hours.[2]

The troubles of Freyberg's flight were but a prelude to those he was to encounter on his return to Egypt. During his absence he had been made aware by his second-in-command, Brigadier Edward Puttick, that unacceptabe changes had been proposed by GHQ Middle East for breaking up and dispersing the New Zealand forces. When Puttick had signalled to England the details of these proposals, Freyberg went straight to the CIGS and reminded General Dill that arrangements for the New Zealand troops could only be implemented with the consent of their GOC and of his government. Dill had told him, 'Archie [Wavell] cannot do this – leave it to me.'[1] Freyberg thought the matter had been resolved, but when he returned to Cairo he found that this was far from the case.

It had always been the intention of the New Zealand government to hand over a complete division to be employed *as a single entity* wherever it could be most effectively used. Before this stage could be reached however, the force had to be adequately equipped, and even more important, it had to be properly trained. But they could only be trained as a division if they were kept together as a division. Freyberg regarded their proper training as one of his most important tasks, and had been dismayed when the second echelon was diverted to England. He was

[232]

even more dismayed when the Prime Minister deleted the second echelon from sailing from the UK on 25 September. But for that decision the Division could have been concentrated together in Egypt during the first half of November, as by then the third echelon had arrived from New Zealand. Although the Division would not have been ready in time to participate in Wavell's initial assault against the Italians in early December, it would probably have been available to take part in the follow-through early in 1941 – a role that was ultimately under-taken by 6 Australian Division.

The problem was that GHQ Middle East considered there was no reason why, in the meantime, the New Zealand Division should not be broken up to undertake non-operational tasks, thereby releasing Brit-ish troops to take part in the forthcoming offensive against the Italians. They regarded the military resources in the Middle East as a pool, available to be drawn on irrespective of nationality. Wavell told Freyberg that, as commander-in-chief, he had the right and duty to make whatever dispositions he thought were necessary in the overall interests of the theatre. In other words, he had reverted to the First World War policy that Dominion troops were part of the British Army, that they must conform to an overall plan, and that the New Zealand government's instructions to keep the Division together were, in effect, to be disregarded.

The process started even before Freyberg had departed for England, when the Western Desert Force Headquarters first came into being. Headquarters British Troops Egypt (HQ BTE) telephoned Freyberg and asked him if he would lend his Divisional Signals to the newly formed headquarters for three weeks, pending the arrival of signallers from England. At the time it seemed a reasonable request, and he had agreed. It was a gesture he came to regret afterwards, because it was the first of many similar requests. In the event the loan stretched to five months – and even then the signallers were only returned when he made an issue of the matter. He subsequently discovered that the Australian commander, Blamey, had also been asked to lend units, but had refused point-blank. Blamey told Freyberg he had been a fool to lend anything, and that it had been the cause of the major rows in the First World War between Monash and Haig. When Freyberg returned he found that, far from the compact body of New Zealand troops at Maadi he had been led to expect, they had been dispersed into six separate detachments stationed throughout the Middle East. All he had left under his direct control was his own headquarters. In other words the original plan of dispersal, which he thought the CIGS had countermanded, had been enacted under another guise.

Freyberg was incensed, and on 29 September wrote to HQ BTE pointing out that in the past he had met nearly every request for detachments in an effort to help. In future, he declared, he was no longer prepared to comply with such requests, and must now require the return of all these detachments to his own control. Matters came to a head early in October in an interview with Generals Wavell and Maitland Wilson (commanding BTE) when, he said, 'I was treated as though I were a fifth columnist.'

In spite of the fact that their two families had been friends for many years, Freyberg had an ambivalent relationship with Wavell. Wavell was a scholar and an intellectual soldier in a way in which Freyberg was not; on the other hand Freyberg was articulate and a good communicator when Wavell was often tongue-tied. These factors played an important part in their relations with the Prime Minister Winston Churchill. Freyberg was not in awe of Churchill and was quite prepared to tell him to his face when he thought he was wrong, as when he warned that Cabinet Policy was in danger of losing Egypt.

The Prime Minister was mystified by Wavell's reluctance to engage in argument with him, and was unimpressed by his Caledonian silences. The contrast in Wavell and Freyberg's relationships with Churchill during the fateful days of 1940 and 1941 undoubtedly added to their strained feelings over the deployment of the New Zealand forces, and caused Wavell to become even more uncommunicative than usual. This was particularly unfortunate because, had Wavell been prepared to discuss his difficulties with Freyberg that autumn and ask for his help, the latter would unquestionably have responded. Basically Freyberg wanted to co-operate with the British Command, as had already been shown by his action in Egypt in the first half of 1940. But when Freyberg sought to protect the interests of his New Zealand force, Wavell reacted with a lack of understanding, and even hostility.

Wavell asked Freyberg for his reactions to using New Zealand troops piecemeal in an offensive. He said it was out of the question for Freyberg to ask permission of the New Zealand government for the troops to be so used, since it would give away the fact that an offensive was being planned in the Western Desert. As New Zealand troops in Egypt were still without some of their equipment, and nearly all training had ceased for some months because of the way in which the force had been broken up, Freyberg refused to agree that they could be used offensively. In any case it was outside the terms of the charter from his government to commit the troops in such circumstances without its concurrence. Freyberg wrote:

By 19 October, everyone could see that we were building up for an offensive against the Italians. I had a very difficult problem to decide. I had my duty to the New Zealand Government to concentrate the New Zealand Forces. The New Zealand Government would have insisted, as did the Australian Government, that their Forces were to be so concentrated, and I had only to give my Government the word, and Generals Wavell and Wilson would have been told to return the New Zealand troops forthwith. On the other hand, if I had followed this course, the offensive which had been planned would have had to be called off.[2]

After agonising over the problem, he decided against taking any extreme action. Instead he wrote to General Wilson at HQ, BTE:

The New Zealand Forces are not an integral part of the British Army – they are a distinct New Zealand Force, proud of their own identity. They cannot be split up and used piecemeal except with the consent of the New Zealand Government. The past, I know, has been unfortunate, and for that I must take my share of the blame. We came over here in February keen and willing to help everybody, and have never refused a request of any sort. It has been a mistake, and the efficiency of the Division has suffered grievously. Now, because we are insisting on concentrating as a force, we are most unpopular. I feel I let our force in for this by not saying 'No' right at the beginning, as I believe did the AIF.

For your information, I send you a copy of the special powers vested in me by the New Zealand Government. They were granted to me when I accepted the command of the NZEF.

The NZEF will, I hope, be assembling fast in the next few months, and when equipment is available here, I am empowered by my Government to raise an Armoured Brigade.

The position is quite clear; in an emergency we will all work under anybody's command, and do any job for which we are trained and equipped. The Division meanwhile cannot be used piecemeal. When the equipment has been completed up to an operational scale and has been in its possession for at least a month, the NZEF will be handed over by the New Zealand Government and placed under command of the AIF or BTE, or it may even take part in some theatre of war not yet decided upon.[2]

This letter cleared the air but did not improve personal relationships, and the attitude at GHQ was that Freyberg could no longer be trusted to co-operate. For his part Freyberg felt that the British High Command had not been straight with him. When it appeared that Egypt was about to be invaded by the Italians he had agreed to certain dispersals of the New Zealand forces in order to help counter this threat. Now the British were seeking to perpetuate this redeployment for quite different reasons – to release British troops to take part in offensive

[235]

operations. In addition they were using security to prevent him from explaining to his government what was happening.

This was not the only pressure to which Freyberg was subjected, because on 22 October he met Anthony Eden at Baggush aerodrome:

> Mr Eden asked why I would not let 4 New Zealand Brigade Group take part in the offensive, and I gave the ordinary commonsense reply that my job was to concentrate the New Zealanders for use as a Division. In a crisis, I would allow New Zealand Forces to be used piecemeal, but not otherwise. When I added that the New Zealand Government would not agree to breaking up the Division, I was given the astonishing reply – 'What, those dear old men, they would agree to anything.'
>
> Although this comment may have been flattering to the Cabinet as individuals [sic], it was a very imperfect appreciation of the characters of those shrewd, careful, and intensely loyal people. For six years I worked with them in close harmony, and learnt how careful and wise they were, and what strict control was exercised from New Zealand.[2]

On 6–7 December 1940 British and Indian troops carried out their attack in the Western Desert under General Richard O'Connor, and won a notable victory over the Italians in Egypt and Cyrenaica. It was a considerable feat of arms in the face of a numerically superior enemy, and their achievement was acclaimed. However this success was made possible only through the New Zealanders continuing to undertake commitments which allowed the force taking part to be released for the attack. Despite this and the victory, there was no improvement in the relationship between the British generals and the New Zealand commanders. As Freyberg expressed it: 'My relationship with the higher command was not good, and I had a difficult and unpleasant meeting with the Commander-in-Chief on 27 December which ended in a clash, when things were said that cannot be too quickly forgotten.'[2]

The British generals in the Middle East at this time seemed to be determined to avoid sharing military decision-making with anyone else, even when the majority of the troops involved did not come from the United Kingdom. Next year, when the moment came to send an expeditionary force to Greece, General Maitland Wilson was appointed to command it, even though most of the fighting troops came from Australia and New Zealand. General Blamey, who later had even more bitter quarrels with General Auchinleck than Freyberg had with Wavell, put the problem to the Australian Prime Minister, saying that experience had taught him 'to look with misgivings on a situation where British leaders have control of considerable bodies of first-class

Dominion troops while Dominion commanders are excluded from all responsibility in control, planning and policy.'[3]

Also, in a letter dated 8 September 1941 to Sir Percy Spender, Minister of the Australian Army, Blamey wrote:

> I am meeting considerable difficulties in my effort to assemble the AIF as a single body. It seems quite impossible for the ordinary English Officer to appreciate the position from our point of view, and once any Australian unit gets into the command of the UK formation, it's like prising open the jaws of an alligator to get them back again.[3]

This attempt to run the army in the Middle East as an exclusively British preserve was a concept the days of which were numbered; but it took a series of disasters and the dismissal of two commanders-in-chief before the fact of Dominion forces' independence was finally accepted. Only when Generals Alexander and Montgomery arrived on the Middle East scene in the summer of 1942 were the realities of the situation acknowledged, the Dominion troops treated separately from the British Army, and everyone's time and energies at last released to concentrate on defeating the enemy.

As it was, as 1940 came to an end, Freyberg recorded:

> From October 1940 to the end of that year, we went through a very unhappy period. It was not a pleasant situation to be treated as a 'black sheep' by one's old friends in the British Army, with whom I had spent so many happy years. But the British generals greatly misunderstood my character if they thought that I and the New Zealanders would allow ourselves to be bulldozed. We could all see that the war was going to be long and difficult, but nothing was going to deflect me from the trust that had been handed to me of producing the New Zealand Division fit to take the field in as rapid a time as possible.[2]

Looking back it seems tragic, as Freyberg himself records, that friction of this nature should have entered into the relations of the British, the Australian and the New Zealand commanders in the Middle East.

16

The Campaign in Greece

On 17 February 1941 Freyberg was sent for by General Wavell, who told him that the New Zealand Division was under orders to move to Greece. It was to be the advance guard of a force including two Australian divisions and a British armoured brigade, which would be commanded by General Sir Henry Maitland Wilson. 'We were to disembark at either Piraeus or Volos, thence moving by road or rail to take up a line which I understood had been dug already along the mountains in Macedonia,' wrote Freyberg several years later. He went on:

> The Australians were to take over this line and the NZ Division were then to go into Force Reserve ready to operate northwards should there be any threat from Monastir.* There was always a possibility that after concentration we should move forward to support the Greek Army who were holding the high ground north and east of Salonika.[1]

Freyberg asked whether this was being done with the knowledge and agreement of the New Zealand government. Wavell assured him that it had been consulted by the British government and had given approval for the Division to participate in the expedition. In fact the situation was far more complicated, with both Freyberg and the New Zealand government believing the other to be better informed about the situation than was the case.

The security constraints were so tight that the only person with

---

* The 'Monastir Gap' (Monastir is the old Turkish name for Bitolj) is the key route from Southern Yugoslavia into Greece.

[238]

whom Freyberg could discuss the operation was General Blamey, his Australian opposite number, who had been given a similar warning to move to Greece. The two met on 18 February, and both expressed disquiet. On 24 February Freyberg informed his brigadiers singly of the plan – Puttick in charge of 4 Brigade, Barrowclough of 6 Brigade, and Miles, the CRA, but Hargest and 5 Brigade were still on the high seas and he did not arrive until 3 March – and they too were forbidden to discuss it with each other.

The New Zealand Division was still widely dispersed in February 1941, with 4 NZ Brigade in a support role in the Western Desert (although under orders to move to Helwan near Cairo), and 6 NZ Brigade at the Base Camp at Maadi, where it had been training since early October 1940 when it arrived in Egypt. The 5 NZ Brigade had left England in mid-January 1941 and was expected to reach Suez at the beginning of March.[2]

Freyberg was expected to get his force ready to leave Egypt in less than three weeks from the warning order. The Division had never yet been together in one place, let alone trained as a whole, and much reorganisation of units and individuals was required before it could take to the field. Moreover new equipment and vehicles still outstanding were in the process of being delivered, many of them coming direct from England with 5 NZ Brigade.

Freyberg was given scant information about the background of the despatch of the British force to Greece, and knew very little about the diplomatic and political developments unfolding there. He also had so little information about the military situation in Greece that he would have found it impossible to give the New Zealand government an 'Appreciation of the Situation'. The bulk of the Greek Army was still engaged against Italian troops in Albania, from where, on 28 October 1940, Mussolini had ordered an attack on Greece. The Greeks were resisting valiantly and, although outnumbered, had driven the Italians back into Albania. Greece was not at war with Germany but she had pledged herself on the Allied side and asked for help from the Allies in the event of a German attack.

General Wavell and Air Marshal Longmore, Air Officer Commanding Middle East, had paid a secret visit to Athens early in January 1941, when they had had a series of meetings with General Metaxas, the Greek Prime Minister. The latter appreciated that the British were not in a position to send a large expeditionary force to Greece, but considered that if the British government could not send ten divisions they should not come at all. Reinforced with ten British divisions the Greek Army could hold a front in the face of a German attack on

[239]

Greece from Bulgaria; but a smaller force would probably achieve the worst of both worlds by provoking an attack and yet not being sufficiently strong to stop it. In this situation Metaxas felt that Wavell's best contribution would be to eject the Italians from North Africa.

In his book, *Foreign Body in the Eye*, one of the best-informed accounts of the British involvement in Greece, Sir Charles Mott-Radclyffe sums up the position in mid-January 1941: 'A very limited British offer of assistance had been made and declined by Metaxas with both courtesy and understanding. The Chiefs of Staff in London and the Joint Planning Staff at GHQ, Middle East, simultaneously heaved sighs of relief.'[3] On 29 January, however, General Metaxas suddenly died, and this created a completely different situation:

> Metaxas had been an unabashed dictator by ability, by ruthlessness, by force of character and by circumstances. He had organised the Greek Army and galvanised the Greek people to a high pitch of morale which had enabled them first to hold, and subsequently to defeat the Italians in the Albanian mountains. Had they been able to capture the port of Valona and to interrupt the Italian seaborne supplies from Bari, there is little doubt that the Italian Army would have been completely routed, but at the crucial moment they lacked the essential supplies and, above all, air support which we were unable to give them.[3]

Meanwhile in the Western Desert at the beginning of February General Richard O'Connor, commanding XIII Corps, captured Benghazi; and on 5–6 February rounded up the remaining elements of the Italian Tenth Army at Beda Fomm. For a brief moment the door to Tripolitania was open with no organised Italian defences between the British Army in Cyrenaica, and Tripoli; a situation that might have led to the elimination of the Italian military presence in Libya. On 7 February in fact armoured cars of 11 Hussars were 40 miles to the west of El Agheila, and O'Connor was later to write:

> But on that afternoon [7 February], when the battle of Beda Fomm was over, a brigade of 6 Australian Division, lorryborne, with supplies of petrol, was drawn up on the Benghazi and Sirte road, facing south, all ready to advance on Sirte and Tripoli. I have never really forgiven myself for not using them.[4]

O'Connor's plan for the next stage was to advance on Tripoli and, had he been successful, as Brigadier Barclay wrote in *Against Great Odds*, he 'would in all probability have saved us the tribulation of more than two years of fluctuating and desperate fighting in North Africa'.[5]

But it was not to be. The eyes of the Cabinet in London and of General Wavell in Cairo were focused in a northerly direction in the belief that the desert flank was secure. On 12 February the Prime Minister sent Wavell a long directive, paragraph 3 of which reads:

> 3. We should have been content with making a safe flank for Egypt at Tobruk, and we told you that thereafter Greece and/or Turkey must have priority, but that if you could get Benghazi easily and without prejudice to European calls so much the better. We are delighted that you have got this prize three weeks ahead of expectation, but this does not alter, indeed it rather confirms, our previous directive, namely, that your major effort must now be to aid Greece and/or Turkey. This rules out any serious effort against Tripoli, although minor demonstrations thitherwards would be a useful feint. You should therefore make yourself secure in Benghazi and concentrate all available forces in the Delta in preparation for movement to Europe.[6a]

On the very day that Churchill sent this signal General Erwin Rommel and the first units of the German Afrika Korps arrived in Tripoli. This was not known in Cairo for some days.

Metaxas was succeeded as Prime Minister of Greece by Korizis, a banker with little experience of public life. He soon threw out feelers as to the possibility of British forces being despatched to Greece, and reaffirmed the pledge given by Metaxas that Greece would resist any German attack at all costs. The question now was whether a British force should be sent, which, alongside the Greek forces, would be sufficient to hold off a German attack and encourage Yugoslavia and Turkey to drop their neutrality and become belligerents on the Allied side. Eden, the Foreign Secretary, and Dill, the CIGS, decided to discuss these problems on the spot. They arrived with Wavell in Athens on 22 February, after being delayed in transit from London for a week by bad weather, and having broken their journey from Cairo at El Adem in the Western Desert to tell General Wilson that, if a force was sent to Greece, he would be given the command.

An important aspect of the defence of Greece was the situation in Yugoslavia. If Yugoslavia succeeded in remaining neutral, and was not overrun by the German Army, then the flanks of the Greek Army, both in Albania and on the front opposite to Bulgaria, would be secure, while the second flanks would rest on the Adriatic and Aegean respectively. But if Germany attacked Yugoslavia any hope of defending Greece would have to be based on a line much further to the south, because of the vulnerability of defensive positions in northern Greece to German attacks through the Monastir Gap.

A series of conferences took place in Tatoi Palace, outside Athens, on 22–3 February. Assuming that the Greeks would accept British assistance on a limited scale, what line could be held? The Nestos and Struma positions were rejected as too far north and easily turned by the Germans. The latter, it is true, covered Salonika, essential to the Yugoslavs, but the Yugoslav attitude to the whole operation was unknown. The alternative, the Aliakmon Line (named after the river which formed part of it), which ran from the Gulf of Salonika to the Yugoslav border, was finally decided upon. General Papagos, the Greek commander-in-chief, thought, and Wavell agreed, that there was a good chance of holding the Aliakmon Line provided the Greek troops manning the Metaxas Line in Western Thrace and Macedonia (three divisions) were immediately withdrawn behind it, plus another division from Albania, and provided too that the British force began to move there at once from Egypt. The total force was to consist of seven and a half divisions, four Greek and three Dominion, plus one British armoured brigade.

When Wavell, Eden and Dill left the conference they were under the firm impression that this arrangement was to be implemented immediately; but Papagos maintained at the time, and after the war, that the choice of a defence line was dependent on the attitude of the Yugoslavs, and that the port of Salonika should not be abandoned until this was known, in case the Yugoslavs came into the war on the Allied side.

On 20 February, two days before Eden and Dill arrived in Athens, Colonel Guy Salisbury-Jones, second in command to General Heywood, Head of the Military Mission to Greece, stated in a telegram to Cairo that Papagos had warned him personally that, if a German attack was mounted before the Albanian situation was cleared up, disaster was bound to follow, for the Greek troops in Albania would be cut off. The Greeks were anxious therefore that nothing should precipitate a German attack until they had made one more attempt to reach Valona, because that would, if successful, release a considerable number of Greek divisions for the Macedonian front. Salisbury-Jones also pointed out that, while the strategic advantages of the Aliakmon Line were obvious, it was questionable whether Greek national morale would withstand losing so much territory. Moreover the Greek Army was not prepared for a war against Germany. At the same time Air Marshal D'Albiac, the RAF Liaison Officer with the Greeks, made it clear that the small RAF contingent already in Greece could give only very limited assistance to a military campaign.[3]

When Eden and Dill paid their second visit to Athens on 2 March (the same day the German forces crossed the Danube and Bulgaria joined the Axis powers) they discovered that the withdrawal of Greek troops from Thrace and Macedonia, which they thought had been agreed and expected to find in progress, had not even begun. A new situation arose, little short of a nightmare. Was it too late to call off the whole operation? If so, how would it be interpreted by the rest of the world and, in particular, by America? To allow the Germans to overrun Greece would not only put paid to any chance of the Turks or the Yugoslavs joining the Allies, it would damage Britain's reputation almost as greatly as a military defeat. On the other hand, if the British landing were to go ahead, would the Germans attack Greece before the Aliakmon Line was properly occupied and fortified?

In London the Prime Minister and the chiefs of staff began to have serious doubts. Eden and Dill had gone to Turkey seeking help but left (on 1 March) empty-handed, and there was still no reply from Yugoslavia to appeals from Britain and Greece for assistance. The tone of the telegrams from London began to change. No longer was it a matter of honouring 'our obligation to the Greeks'. The Prime Minister telegraphed to the Foreign Secretary:

> We must liberate the Greeks from feeling bound to reject a German ultimatum. If on their own they resolve to fight, we must to some extent share their ordeal. But rapid German advance will probably prevent any appreciable British Imperial forces from being engaged. . . Loss of Greece and Balkans by no means a major catastrophe for us, provided Turkey remains honest neutral.[6b]

The final decision to send the British force to Greece was taken at the conference held on 4 March, at which Eden and Dill were again present, and for which Wavell flew out from Cairo. Colonel Jasper Blunt, the British Military Attaché in Greece, wrote in his diary:

> Our representatives sat in the drawing-room of the Legation; the secretaries came and went with telegrams; Sir Michael Palairet [the British Minister] played host, the harassed King, the serious face of General Papagos, the deathly pallor of the Greek Premier, the suspense as the King and his advisers conferred behind the closed doors of the Minister's study. The minutes passed and I watched the scenes as a completely unconsulted onlooker. I was a spectator with a seat in the front row of the stalls at a drama

[243]

as intense as any played on the classical Greek stage with the added interest that I knew the plot, the authors and the players.[3]

Mott-Radclyffe continues the story:

> When it was over, Blunt drove down with Palairet to the seaplane base and watched the [British] party leave. The die was cast and as the plane took off he remarked to Palairet that our troops destined for Greece would be lost before they ever set sail from Egypt. The British Minister was greatly upset by this forecast, as pessimistic as it was accurate.[3]

Admiral Sir Andrew Cunningham, Commander-in-Chief Mediterranean, recorded how the decision to send troops to Greece was uneasily confirmed:

> At the final meeting in Cairo with Wavell, Eden and Dill, I gave it as my opinion that though politically we were correct, I had grave uncertainty of its military expedience. Dill himself had doubts, and said to me after the meeting: 'Well, we've taken the decision. I'm not at all sure it's the right one.'[7]

There can be little doubt that the decision to break off pursuit of the beaten Italian Army in Tripolitania in favour of the Greek expedition was one of the biggest British military blunders of the Second World War. It diverted two well-found divisions, an armoured brigade, a number of RAF squadrons and a large administrative component from pursuing a limited and attainable objective in Africa in favour of an unlimited and unattainable one in Europe. And in the event, when equipment was in such short supply as it was in early 1941, the loss in Greece of the guns for seven field regiments, two medium regiments, three anti-tank regiments, and numerous heavy and light anti-aircraft batteries, to say nothing of 100 tanks and over 8,000 vehicles of all kinds, amounted to a major setback in itself.[8]

These disasters affected the future of the British and Dominion forces in the Middle East not only for the rest of 1941 but also during the subsequent struggle in the Western Desert. Freyberg and the New Zealand Division were to pay a high price for these misjudgments. As he wrote subsequently: 'So we muddled into the Greek Campaign. It was a campaign entered into for political reasons, and came near to losing us the Middle East.'[9]

On 3 March Freyberg went to Suez to meet 5 NZ Brigade on its arrival from England. He talked to Brigadier Hargest and all the senior officers and warned them of the difficult times that lay ahead. On 5 March he left Helwan Camp by road for Alexandria *en route* for Greece. At 11 a.m. he called at GHQ Cairo to say goodbye to General Wavell, who was just back from Athens. The C-in-C gave him an outline of the plan, but at that stage Freyberg had not seen the British Order of Battle. He gathered that only a small contingent of the RAF would be available and that the British would be heavily outnumbered in the air. When he said goodbye Freyberg told Wavell that he had no illusions about how tough the Greek campaign was going to be.

The following morning Freyberg embarked in the British cruiser HMS *York* with the first echelon of the New Zealand Division. While waiting on board to depart they watched a constant stream of guns and vehicles moving to nearby ships, to be loaded and carried to Greece. At midday in company with HMS *Bonaventure* and HMS *Gloucester* they sailed from Alexandria. The crossing took less than twenty-four hours, the sea was calm, and on the morning of 7 March the squadron steamed into Piraeus harbour. 'Operation Lustre', had begun.[1]

Although the New Zealand Division had already started to move to Greece, negotiations over their terms of employment were still under-way between London and Wellington. The NZ government was worried about the operation, and on 9 March in reply to a signal from London the Prime Minister sent a long signal on behalf of the members of his government, which began: 'Their first reaction is that the operation, which they had always regarded as highly dangerous and speculative, is now obviously much more hazardous than that pre-viously contemplated.'[10] Nevertheless the NZ government gave its reluctant agreement to participate in the operation, subject to certain conditions, some of which were not carried out. These included the stipulation that plans of evacuation should immediately be drawn up.

While this exchange was going on General Blamey was making his views on the campaign known to his government. Blamey and Freyberg were the two most experienced commanders in the Middle East, yet neither was asked for his views on the Greek operation. Blamey was in a better position to protest than Freyberg. He was a Lieutenant-General (an important factor in the rank-conscious Headquarters Middle East) and in command of a force of three divisions. Moreover, unlike Freyberg, as a corps commander he was not weighed down with organisational and administration problems. And since the Australian formations were not due to start for Greece for two to three weeks he had more time in which to set out his opinions on paper.

Blamey drew attention to the large size of the fully-equipped German forces available for operations in the Balkans, especially their air force, and the comparatively small force at the disposal of the Allies. He commented on 10 March: 'Military operation extremely hazardous in view of the disparity between opposing forces in numbers and training.'[9] Blamey's appreciation was cabled from London back to Cairo where it caused considerable offence to Wavell and Dill (who was still in Egypt). When they protested to Blamey about the late expression of his views he replied that he had said nothing when originally told of the proposals on 18 February because he had not been consulted before the decision to go to Greece had been made; and when he was told, he was given instructions and not asked for his opinion. Freyberg, having been treated in the same way, was in a similar position to Blamey.

The arrival in Piraeus of British and New Zealand troops came as a surprise to the inhabitants of Athens. The disembarkation was completed quickly and without interruption, the troops moving from the docks in motor transport to wooded bivouac areas on the outskirts of the capital, with snow-capped hills beyond. These surroundings reminded the New Zealanders of their own country, and they were touched too by the welcome the Greek people gave them, and continued to give them, throughout the Greek campaign.

If Freyberg was still unaware of the British Order of Battle, the German Military Attaché in Athens was somewhat better informed, as Mott-Radclyffe relates:

Advance parties began to land at Piraeus on 7 March under security arrangements that were merely a farce. The Greeks were not yet at war with the Germans, and the German Military Attaché, who spoke excellent English and dressed like an Englishman, spent a good deal of his time wandering about on the quayside at Piraeus greeting various units as they landed. 'Fancy seeing the well-known cap badge of the Northumberland Hussars!' he exclaimed gleefully to an officer who had just disembarked on the quay and who had no reason to suppose that the tweedy individual in a homburg hat was any other than an English resident in Athens. 'Many a good day's hunting I have had in the past with the Percy hounds,' the conversation continued. 'What have you done with your horses?' 'Oh,' said the officer, 'we had to leave them behind. We now have anti-tank guns instead, but they are quite useless, and in any case we have no ammunition with us because the ships were wrongly loaded in Alexandria.' A few more conversations of this kind no doubt enabled the German Military Attaché to compile without much difficulty the complete order of battle.[3]

[246]

General Maitland Wilson, commander of 'W' Force (the name given to the expedition), had gone north on reconnaissance in civilian clothes and under the pseudonym of Mr Watt. Freyberg had known 'Jumbo' Wilson since 1919 when they were at the staff college at Camberley together. Their paths were to cross on a number of occasions in the Middle East in the Second World War, first in 1940 when Wilson was in command of BTE, then during the Greek campaign of 1941, and later in 1942 when he was commanding the Ninth Army in the Levant. They had a perfectly harmonious relationship, but Freyberg had little respect for Wilson's military judgment, and even less for the way in which he looked after 'number one'. He regarded Jumbo as an amiable 'yes man' who would always bend in the wind and side with those in authority. Another contemporary, General Richard O'Connor, was to write later, 'I don't really know why he ever became a Field Marshal.'[4] Freyberg was less mystified by Jumbo Wilson's subsequent elevation, which he attributed to his sympathetic treatment of Churchill's imprudent intervention in Cos and Leros later in the war.

Freyberg spent his first day in Greece gathering as much information as he could from the British community in Athens. He then decided to go north to assess the conditions under which his Division would be operating, and the next day, 8 March, flew from Athens to Larissa accompanied by his chief of staff, Colonel Stewart, plus a Greek liaison officer and an interpreter.[1]

From Larissa (which had suffered an earthquake only days before) Freyberg went by road to Kozani, Veroia and then back via Katerini. He called on the Greek commander of the Central Macedonian Army, General Kotulas, and on the GOCs of 12 and 19 Greek Divisions, who disconcerted him by declaring that it was impossible to fight in mountainous country without mule transport or pack artillery. Indeed the Greek first-line transport consisted entirely of ox wagons which moved at a slower pace than marching troops. Freyberg returned to Athens from Larissa by air on 9 March and, with a growing sense of unease, issued orders for the move of the division northwards.[1]

The move of the NZ Division from Egypt to Greece had been organised by GHQ Movement Staff in Cairo. They had planned this without consulting Freyberg or his staff, with the result that the components arrived in the wrong order. Divisional headquarters, which should have been one of the first units on the ground, was kept back to the end, so that Freyberg's own headquarters and signals did not reach the forward area until 25 March, nearly three weeks after he did. Other essential elements, such as the anti-tank regiment, only arrived just before the German attack, emphasising the folly of depriving commanders of the management and movement of their own divisions in the field.[1]

Over the next three weeks from 10 March, the New Zealand Division was dribbled northwards by road and rail from the Athens area as and when they were ferried across from Egypt. Units of 4 NZ Brigade were the first to arrive. After long discussions with the local Greek generals it was decided that the brigade should take up a position near the Aliakmon river, to the left of the Greek 19 Motorised Division on the coast and 12 Greek Division further inland. Freyberg later wrote:

> By 1 April the great moment for which I had been praying had arrived. The Second New Zealand Division had concentrated at last, after fifteen months. I had fought long for this moment, and in the process had not endeared myself to the Higher Command, who all said they quite understood my desire to get our forces together, and then imposed a series of obstacles to prevent its accomplishment. It is a severe criticism of Middle East Staff and Commanders that this was the first occasion when we had the opportunity to run-in the Division with its complete Staff, Signals and Artillery. Our first full-scale divisional exercise was, therefore, not a training exercise or a battle rehearsal, but a bitter battle.[9]

At the beginning of March 1941, when 5 NZ Brigade arrived at Suez, I had seen my father briefly in Egypt. We now met in northern Greece in early April at a rather run-down café/bar in Katerini. I was serving with 23 Battalion. No sooner did our food arrive than so did some twenty to thirty members of the NZ Divisional Cavalry, who had already imbibed well of the local ouzo. The moment they spotted my father they crowded round our table demanding to know when he was going to let them fight the Germans. We only managed to eat a few mouthfuls before we had to beat a retreat to his staff car, which was waiting round the corner.

On 2 April divisional headquarters moved to Gannokhura near the Aegean coast. That evening Freyberg received a mysterious signal telling him to be at Katerini Station at 4.30 next morning to meet 'certain important people'. These turned out to be Eden, Dill and Wilson *en route* to Florina for a conference with the Yugoslav General Staff. Freyberg travelled with them as far as Aiginion, the next station up the line. They were in high spirits in the belief that Yugoslavia was soon coming into the war, and were discussing new plans including a possible advance by British forces to the Rupel Pass, north of Salonika. Freyberg was horrified by what he considered their unwarranted optimism and did his best to discourage it. On returning to his headquarters he wrote in his diary: 'The situation is a grave one; we shall be fighting against heavy odds in a plan that has been ill-conceived and one that violates every principle of military strategy.'[1]

The odds against success lengthened when, the same day as Freyberg's meeting at Katerini, Rommel captured Benghazi; and a few days later the three senior British commanders in the Western Desert, Generals O'Connor, Neame and Gambier-Parry, were taken prisoner together with much of the only British armoured division left in Cyrenaica. In Churchill's words, 'Rommel has torn the new-won laurels from Wavell's brow and thrown them in the sand.'[6c]

The caving in of the desert flank, which had been thought inviolable, meant that, from then onwards, all military resources in Egypt had to be rushed to Tobruk and the Western Desert, because the defence of Cyrenaica was vital to the safety of Egypt and the whole British position in the Middle East; by comparison events in Greece were only a sideshow. The move to Greece of 7 Australian Division and the Polish Brigade, both part of the original planned force, was immediately cancelled.

The short-sightedness of undertaking the expedition to Greece could not have been demonstrated more quickly and clearly than it was in the course of that first week in April 1941. The strong warnings that Blamey had uttered less than a month before, and with which Freyberg completely agreed, were totally vindicated. Ironically it was to be left mainly to these two officers to extricate the Expeditionary Force from Greece as best they could.

On 5 April the New Zealand Division was placed under command of I Australian Corps, whose headquarters had opened at Gerania, 10 miles north of Elasson. General Blamey became responsible for the line from the Aegean coast to the Veroia Pass, 30 miles inland. The NZ Division was now complete, but 6 Australian Division under General Mackay was still in the process of moving to Greece and by the start of the German attack only two brigades had arrived there.

On the next day the Germans invaded Yugoslavia and Greece. The German Twelfth Army under Feldmarschall von List began its attack on Greece from Bulgaria. The Twelfth Army consisted of two Panzer divisions, one motorised division, one mountain division and six infantry divisions – a force of ten divisions in all. They had assembled in Rumania, and then moved quickly into Bulgaria. In the attack on Greece some of these divisions were directed at Salonika, and others moved through southern Yugoslavia in the direction first of the Monastir Gap and then the Florina area.

On 7 April Generals Blamey and Mackay came to the headquarters of the NZ Division, and Freyberg took them to see 4 and 6 NZ Brigades on the Aliakmon river. The NZ Division was holding a front of 28,500 yards – or about 16 miles – which, in Freyberg's view, was an impossible task for a division. Later that day they were joined by General Wilson who agreed that the position was too spread out to withstand a co-ordinated German attack. They decided to withdraw to the area of the Mount Olympus passes, where the troops would have better defensive positions, even though this meant abandoning a line on which much work had been done and which contained a large proportion of the division's wire and mines; it also involved giving up the railhead at Katerini. Meanwhile the swift collapse of resistance in southern Yugoslavia soon gave the Germans access to northern Greece. A composite force, including elements of the British 1 Armoured Brigade and 16 Australian Brigade, was sent to try and plug the gaps south of Florina and in the direction of the Veroia Pass.[9]

On the afternoon of 8 April, in heavy snowstorms, 4 NZ Brigade moved out of its position on the left sector of the Aliakmon Line and across to the Servia Pass area, to take up new defensive positions where they could act as a pivot for the subsequent withdrawal of 12 Greek Division and 16 Australian Infantry Brigade. The 6 NZ Brigade withdrew in stages to the Katerini area and then to reserve at Dolikhe, west of Mount Olympus, leaving 5 NZ Brigade guarding the Olympus passes. This redeployment was completed by the night of 10–11 April without loss, but in the face of considerable German air activity.

The resulting Allied situation was still precarious, because the direction of the enemy advance southwards from Florina was beginning to outflank the Olympus passes.[1] Indeed Freyberg later wrote: 'If we had been forced to stay and fight on the Aliakmon Line, we should all have been rounded up in the first phase of the campaign.'[9] John White, Freyberg's Personal Assistant, remembers the first impact of the German Air Force in Greece at this time, how Salonika could be seen burning, and the ever-present air recce, with yellow-bellied Stukas and strafing fighters. The latter became so prevalent that daytime movement on the roads had to be abandoned.

On 12 April it was announced that I Australian Corps was to be renamed the Australian and New Zealand Army Corps (ANZAC). It is difficult for those without associations in Australasia to understand fully the magic those initials have for Australians and New Zealanders. They symbolise the coming of age of their two nations epitomised by the sacrifices and sufferings at Gallipoli. Most such military trade marks disappear once the original situation which called them into

[250]

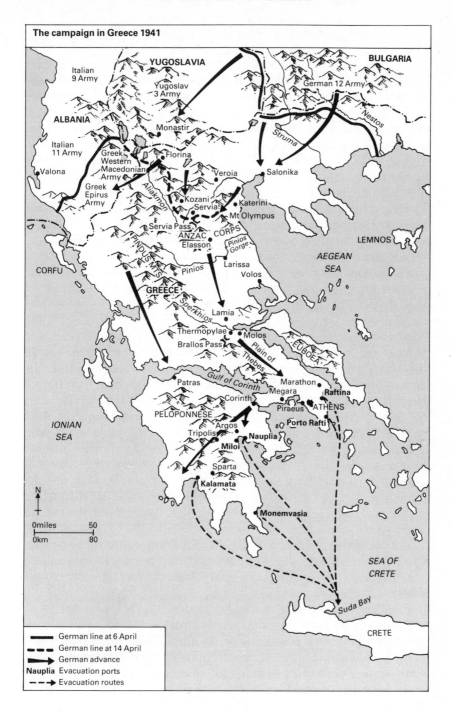

The campaign in Greece 1941

ALBANIA

Italian
9 Army

YUGOSLAVIA

Yugoslav
3 Army

BULGARIA

German 12 Army

Nestos

Italian
11 Army

Monastir

Struma

Valona

Greek
Western
Macedonian
Army

Florina

Veroia

Salonika

Greek
Epirus
Army

Aliakmon

Kozani
Servia

Katerini

Mt Olympus

LEMNOS

Servia Pass

ANZAC CORPS

PINDUS MTS

Elasson

Pinios
Gorge

AEGEAN
SEA

CORFU

Pinios

Larissa

Volos

GREECE

Sperkhios

Lamia

Thermopylae

Molos

Brallos Pass

Plain of
Thebes

EUBOEA

Patras

Gulf of Corinth

Marathon

Megara

Raftina

IONIAN
SEA

Corinth

Piraeus

ATHENS

PELOPONNESE

Argos

Porto Rafti

Tripolis

Nauplia

Miloi

Sparta

Kalamata

N

Monemvasia

0 miles   50
0 km   80

SEA OF
CRETE

Suda Bay

CRETE

——— German line at 6 April
- - - German line at 14 April
——▶ German advance
Nauplia Evacuation ports
- -▶ Evacuation routes

[251]

being fades away, but ANZAC remains part of the language. Later in 1941 an attempt was made to keep ANZAC in being, with Freyberg spoken of as a possible commander, but the idea came to nothing for organisational reasons, and after the battle of Alamein in 1942 the Australians were withdrawn from the Middle East. But for a brief time in April 1941 ANZAC lived again, to the pride of all ranks of the 6 Australian and 2 New Zealand Divisions, and to the satisfaction of their peoples back home.

Also on 12 April the Greek Western Macedonian and Epirus armies began their withdrawal from Albania; but as Salisbury-Jones had predicted the large German attack developing from the Monastir and Florina areas quickly threatened the flank and rear of the retreating Greeks. During the next few days this withdrawal developed into a shambles. After their heroic fight against the Italians in Albania the Greek Army no longer had the military or transport resources to disengage and move the considerable distance to new battlefields in the north-eastern sector of Greece; and the Greek troops themselves were too exhausted to take on the Germans.

While the Allied forces were beginning their withdrawal from the Aliakmon Line, Feldmarschall List ordered the German XL Corps to move south from Florina and make for Kozani, to outflank the rear of the Australasian forces attempting to establish the defensive line in the area of the Servia and Olympus passes. By 13 April both 4 and 5 NZ Brigades were heavily involved in fending off German attacks; while the Luftwaffe had established air supremacy and its planes were constantly bombing and strafing everything that moved by day behind Allied lines. Freyberg's diary records on 13 April: 'I travelled 500 miles by car to visit all my detachments, and throughout the day was frequently shot up from the air.' German air power had become the dominating feature of the campaign, and never again, apart from the fighting in Crete, did the British Army have to contend with it on such a scale.

When Freyberg visited ANZAC headquarters on 14 April he found that the German outflanking threat was already causing Blamey and his staff to plan a new line right back at Thermopylae, 100 miles to the south.

Freyberg commanded the withdrawal of the NZ Division in an efficient manner, and at no time was control lost in spite of the chaotic conditions. Fighting continued on 15 April, both 4 and 5 Brigades being heavily engaged, while reports of considerable forces deploying were coming in from 21 Battalion. Preparations were undoubtedly in train for a heavy attack on the whole front. The action was being dictated by the Germans, yet sometimes this had surprising results, as Freyberg describes:

> At Servia, enemy infantry launched an attack at 6 a.m. supported by air or artillery against a company of 19 Battalion. The result was interesting. Fifty-three of the enemy were killed including three officers, and 150 prisoners were taken. Our casualties were two killed and five wounded. There were several dive-bombing attacks during the day and artillery action. At the tunnel in Pinios Gorge, there was shelling by both sides during the 15th, the enemy fire increasing towards six o'clock when an infantry attack was launched. This was repulsed and an attempt by enemy tanks was also driven back. Reports from 5 Brigade indicated that fighting had extended to both flanks. This line was being held with confidence however and heavy casualties had been inflicted on the enemy, the artillery fire of the 5 Field Regiment being particularly accurate against concentrations of enemy motor transport and tanks.[1]

Freyberg's account reveals how hard the fighting was at this stage – and how tough the prospects were:

> 16 April was a most anxious day. As time for the withdrawal to Thermopylae approached, it became a question as to whether 4 and 5 NZ Brigades, who were being heavily attacked, would be able to disengage at dusk, and withdraw.
>
> Meanwhile, at the Servia Pass the enemy launched a heavy infantry attack, supported by dive bombers, during the afternoon. Here they had a complete setback, and were repulsed with heavy losses. Our 4 Brigade, who were greatly outnumbered, fought with courage and steadiness.
>
> On the Katerini front, 5 Brigade were in trouble, and a very difficult situation was developing. The enemy was infiltrating, and trying to outflank the 23 Battalion and Maoris. At midnight on the 16th I had a telephone message from Brigadier Hargest that both these Battalions were surrounded and could not be withdrawn. However, eventually they did fight their way out, and after anxious delays and a very hard night, they reached the top of the Mount Olympus Pass. We also had a signal from the 21 Battalion at the Tunnel position [Pinios Gorge], to the effect that a company was being overrun, which, alas, was only too true.[9]

In 23 Battalion we had to beat off attacks on our defensive positions near the Mount Olympus Pass road, as well as try to deal with the enemy attempts to outflank our line. It was bitterly cold (so much so that many men suffered from frost-bite), and eventually we were ordered to try and withdraw to the top of the pass at about midnight. It was a difficult operation in the dark, made all the more so because the

Germans had infiltrated the tracks we were using and had to be dislodged. We reached a village at the summit of the pass as dawn was breaking.

> At daylight on 17 April [Freyberg wrote] our situation all round was as bad as it could be. An unofficial rumour had reached us that the Greek Army had asked the German Commander-in-Chief for an armistice. We had also heard that our only maintenance port, Piraeus, had been made unusable by the first German air raids to penetrate so far south, and that the ship with all our gun ammunition on board had been blown up. Finally, all our aircraft had been destroyed on the ground at the Larissa aerodrome, so that we would have no air cover during our long and difficult withdrawal, which was likely to be heavily interfered with by hostile air attack, without the possibility of counter-measures.[9]

By the morning of 17 April the situation on the scattered front held by the New Zealand Division was as follows: 5 Brigade Group was still in position at the top of the Olympus Pass; 4 Brigade was preparing to withdraw from the Servia Pass; 21 Battalion was withdrawing through the Pinios Gorge near the Aegean coast; and 6 Brigade was preparing defensive positions south of Elasson. The Divisional Cavalry, which had been detached, was due to revert to HQ NZ divisional control that day to take over a rearguard role.[9] With the force so widely dispersed, and wireless communications difficult in the mountains, Freyberg found it hard to keep in touch with his Division. He spent much of his time on the road, visiting his detachments and co-ordinating their next moves. The Luftwaffe made this a hazardous occupation. Whenever air strafing commenced, part of the drill was to abandon the vehicles and shelter in nearby ditches. Several of Freyberg's staff cars were destroyed or rendered unserviceable.

Between 17 and 19 April there was a general withdrawal southwards from the Olympian passes and 4 and 5 NZ Brigades managed to extricate themselves, but not without difficulties and considerable casualties. 19 Australian Brigade moved to the Domokas Pass as a rearguard, while 16 Australian Brigade covered the Kalabaka to Larissa road, to enable 1 British Armoured Brigade to withdraw behind them. The whole Expeditionary Force had difficulty in negotiating a way through the Larissa Plain since the main road had become completely congested with traffic, even though by now all movement was at night. On one occasion at the Larissa crossroads Freyberg got out of his vehicle and directed traffic himself to get rid of a bottleneck. 'Put on your lights and drive like hell,' he told the drivers. The bulk of the New Zealand Division found a more satisfactory alternative route

[254]

via the coast road through Volos, Almireo and Lamia and then to Molos, covered by the NZ Divisional Cavalry.[1]

By 19 April the whole of the NZ Division, except for a few stragglers, had withdrawn to the Molos area, or in rear of it, and were preparing a strong defensive position at Thermopylae in the narrow pass between the sea and the mountains – where Leonidas and his 300 Spartans had made their stand in the fifth century BC. Freyberg and his New Zealanders were on the coast, with 5 and 6 Brigades forward; while on their left were 19 and 17 Australian Brigades, with 4 NZ and 16 Australian Brigades behind in reserve.

During the last fortnight Freyberg had been far too preoccupied with the military situation, and with his efforts to keep his Division intact, to concern himself with political developments; but the penultimate part of the Greek tragedy was even then being enacted in Athens. News reached Athens on 20 April that the Greek commanders in Albania were about to surrender to the Germans. General Wilson was immediately informed by Colonel Blunt, who had had a secret meeting with General Pangalos (a former C-in-C of the Greek Army), and when Blunt had finished his account Wilson stood silent for a moment and then simply said, 'I thought so.'[3]

A couple of days earlier, on 18 April, the Greek government had been confronted with this very crisis: and then thrown into turmoil, as Mott-Radclyffe relates:

> The sands of time were running out and Korizis [the Prime Minister] was torn in the nightmare of two conflicting loyalties. The King and the bulk of the Greek people were steadfast in their determination to help British troops to the last minute and to go down with colours flying. The Greek High Command realised that with the German Army attacking Greece in the rear across the Albanian front, the Greek Army had shot its bolt. Was the Government to leave Athens or not? Was Korizis to give orders for the necessary shipping to facilitate the evacuation of the British forces? The Prime Minister rose from the Meeting of Ministers and walking towards the ante-room promised that he would give his reply in a few minutes, and the reply was a revolver shot.[3]

By nightfall on 20 April no hint had yet reached ANZAC in the field that any change was in the wind. The two divisional commanders, Mackay and Freyberg, had been impressing on their subordinates that there would be no more withdrawals. Brigadier Vasey, commanding the force astride the Brallos Pass, had given the order: 'Here we bloody well are, and here we bloody well stay.' His brigade major translated this instruction into rather more diplomatic language: 'The 19th Brigade will hold its present defensive position come what may.'[11]

Shortly afterwards, however, Wavell arrived at Blamey's head-quarters. It was about 2 a.m. on 21 April, and Wavell informed him that the Greeks had surrendered, and that the British force would have to be evacuated.[3] The news reached Freyberg at 0600 hours on 22 April – twenty-eight hours later – when a liaison officer brought a warning order stating that the evacuation of Greece was to begin.[1] He immediately called a conference of brigadiers to discuss the orders, which were explicit:

> Everything was to be destroyed except rifles, automatic weapons, brens, optical stores, and some SAA. Each man was to carry rifle, equipment and one blanket while rations would be provided on the beaches and ships. Fires or explosions which would indicate a withdrawal were prohibited and to ensure surprise there was to be no movement to the rear by day. There was also a tentative programme of embarkation, very little of which was destined to be carried out unaltered. Force and Corps Operation Orders which arrived later in the day conflicted but, as was to be expected, neither in the end covered the rapid changes of the situation.[1]

The situation should have been anticipated and prepared for:

> Although the immediate consideration of evacuation plans was one of the conditions laid down by the New Zealand Government when they consented to their Division going to Greece [Freyberg later wrote], this condition was lamentably and totally unfulfilled, in spite of Mr Churchill's cable to the New Zealand Prime Minister before the Greek Campaign, when he stated that: 'To make good the request and assumption at the end of your message shall be our faithful, unremitting endeavour.'[6d] No evacuation plan had been made, or apparently, even considered, until we were almost back on the beaches.[1]

And yet the Joint Planning Staff in the UK had accurately forecast the result of the hurried intervention in Greece: 'To intervene in the Balkans was to invite a second and even more disastrous Dunkirk.'[12]

Freyberg continued: 'Here in Greece we had all the conditions which had existed at Dunkirk a year before, but with two further problems – a much longer carry back by ship, and an enemy with complete air supremacy and air bases in the Dodecanese Islands close to our withdrawal routes.'[9]

When General Wavell gave instructions on 21 April for the evacuation of the British and dominion forces from Greece, he gave specific orders, confirmed in writing, that Blamey and Freyberg were to be consulted about the arrangements, and that Australian and New Zealand representatives were to be included on the staff that worked out the details. However Wilson and 'W' Force Headquarters never consulted Blamey or Freyberg, and their hastily devised evacuation plan nearly ended in complete disaster:

> I had had considerable experience of evacuations and retreats [Freyberg wrote] and knew something of what can be achieved, and how many men can be got away from seemingly impossible positions.
>
> A retreat should never be hurried, and as far as possible, it should be deliberate. There is, however, one principle that must always be borne in mind, namely that a retreating force must never stop fighting and must hit hard all the time. The only weapons that are of use are guns, and they must be fought fiercely to the muzzles.
>
> In the evacuation plan from Greece, the Force Commander, however, ordered us to destroy our guns on the night of 24 April. 4 NZ Brigade owe their survival to the fact that Brigadier Puttick disobeyed this order and used his guns on the beaches to within a few minutes of embarkation in the face of a German armoured force of 100 vehicles.[9]

Freyberg was highly critical of the plans which *were* finally made for evacuation.

> I fully believe that a proper withdrawal plan could have been made ... However, the Staff who prepared the plan were inadequate, and in my opinion their scheme was a thoroughly bad one. Even at that late hour, they could have evacuated the whole of our Force from the Peloponnese. I have no doubt that the New Zealand Division could have held our sector of the Thermopylae Line for some days longer, and 6 Australian Division were even better placed.[9]

Freyberg considered that the obvious route for the withdrawal was via the Peloponnese, because, being almost an island, it was easily defensible once ANZAC had retired into it with their 200 field and medium guns, plus their numerous tanks. Moreover the distance between the Peloponnese's southern anchorages of Kalamata and Monemvasia and Suda Bay in Crete was only some 120–50 nautical miles. The crossing between the two took approximately five to six hours by fast cruiser and destroyer, so that the navy could have evacuated the whole force in an orderly manner under cover of darkness, over as many nights as were needed. However, instead of an orderly withdrawal through the Peloponnese, the evacuation was done in a great hurry, mainly using the embarkation beaches east of Athens and at Megara.

On the morning of 23 April Freyberg and Brigadier Puttick went to

Corps headquarters for further orders. 4 Brigade was to take up a covering position south of Kriekouki that night. It was a very strong defensive position on a ridge overlooking the plain of Thebes, with two battalions forward, the third in reserve and with 2/3 Australian Field Regiment in support. 5 Brigade also withdrew that night to Agar Constantia, prior to moving the next night to the Marathon beaches at Porto Rafti – due east of Athens – for embarkation on HMS *Calcutta*, HMAS *Perth*, and one of the Glen ships (*Glengyle*) which sailed for Crete at 3.40 a.m. on 25 April, Anzac day. The ships were bombed after daylight but arrived safely at Suda Bay at 4 p.m.; about 4,000 men of 5 Brigade were lifted.[9]

Freyberg's attention on 24 April was focused on the 6 Brigade front at Thermopylae. The bridge over the Sperkhios river was kept under fire by 6 Brigade, but German tanks got across further inland and during the day the enemy deployed in strength. In the afternoon German infantry and tanks attacked and there were numerous bomber and fighter raids. NZ/British artillery accounted for at least 13 German tanks and no enemy progress was made along the coast. The Germans also advanced along the high ground but this movement was countered and at nightfall there was no break in the line.

In the afternoon both Mackay and Freyberg received an order from Wilson's headquarters that they and their staffs were to embark that night. In consequence the officers and men of Mackay's headquarters set off for the fishing port of Miloi in the Peloponnese late that afternoon. Mackay and his aide-de-camp embarked in a flying boat and were flown to Crete early next morning. The remainder of his staff sailed in a cruiser during the night.

Freyberg, on the other hand, disregarded the order to embark. When it arrived his forward troops were in the midst of a hard fight against German tanks at the Thermopylae Pass. He wrote:

> I cabled back to GHQ Athens, and told them I was being attacked by tanks, fighting a battle on a two-brigade front, and asked who was to command the New Zealand troops if I left. I was given the answer of 'Movement Control'. I naturally went on with the battle. After that I never received an order as to my disposal.[1]

Freyberg tried to get in touch with headquarters ANZAC at Mandra on the morning of 25 April but found that it had closed down without notifying the New Zealand Division, and that 'W' Force Headquarters had taken over the final stages of the evacuation. General Blamey and his staff had already returned to Egypt on orders from General Wilson issued before breakfast on 24 April. When Freyberg discovered that both Blamey and Mackay had obeyed their orders to leave Greece while their troops were still in the field, he was astonished. He found a telephone and learned that General Wilson wished to see him urgently; so he set off at once for the Acropole Hotel in Athens:

> It was with rather an uneasy feeling that I went into Athens, wondering what attitude the Greeks would adopt towards the British troops and whether German Fifth Column would have an effect upon them. As a matter of fact, the attitude of the Greek population, both military and civil, was perfect. They were most courteous and eager to help us in any way, and they appeared heartbroken that our efforts to help them had brought disaster upon our forces.
>
> I arrived with the C-in-C just in time for a combined Naval, Military and Air Force Conference which was going into the ways and means of evacuating our troops from Greece. Until that moment I had not realised the great difficulties under which the Navy had been working. Many ships had been sunk in heavy bombing attacks. It must have been obvious to the C-in-C that only a proportion of the men still in Greece could be evacuated with the shipping available. The alternative methods of evacuating the NZ brigades were discussed. Originally it had been intended to send us to the beaches east of Athens but these beaches were now in close range of the dive-bombers and fighters. It was eventually decided that only one more embarkation would take place from Marathon and that the balance of the troops should move to the Peloponnese. Units which had been grouped under Brigadier Miles [the NZ Commander Royal Artillery] dribbled through Athens during daylight preparatory to embarkation. In the afternoon I gave orders that the Divisional Cavalry (less two squadrons) should assist the 1 Armoured Bde in covering the Marathon embarkation.[9]

The 6 Brigade disengaged from Thermopylae on the night of 24–5 April, passing through the 4 Brigade covering-position south of Thebes before dawn. 19 Australian Brigade had preceded them, leaving Colonel Clifton's rearguard at Thermopylae to follow after firing a series of delaying demolitions along the road. The plan was for 6 Brigade and Divisional Headquarters to cross over the Corinth Canal on the night of 25–6 April and continue to Miloi in the Peloponnese; and for 4 Brigade to pass over the canal on the following night. The first part of the plan worked smoothly and 6 Brigade passed through Corinth itself, which had been set on fire, and went into concealed positions in olive groves south of Miloi; while the NZ Division set up its headquarters alongside those of General Wilson nearby.

Saturday, 26 April was a critical day in the evacuation. In the early hours of the morning a heavy air attack was mounted against the area of the Corinth Canal and its bridge. An hour or so later 1,200 German parachute troops were dropped, and quickly overwhelmed the small British force in the immediate vicinity, thereby severing all communications between the Peloponnese and the rest of Greece. This placed 4 Brigade in a critical position, as it was situated to the east of the canal which it had been going to cross that night. Frantic efforts were made all day to get in touch with Brigadier Puttick and warn him of the danger, without avail. Meanwhile the Germans had crossed over into the Peloponnese higher up the Gulf of Corinth in the vicinity of Patras and were beginning to make their way south. To Freyberg:

> It appeared more than likely that two of our three Brigade Groups would, with Div HQ, be surrounded and captured. At this stage, although our position in the Peloponnese was insecure enough, the position of 4 Brigade was infinitely worse and one of grave peril.[9]

In a private letter which Freyberg sent to Fraser about this crisis after he had reached Crete, he wrote:

> I know how very anxious we have made you in New Zealand. I only trust you did not know the full truth at the time. On 26 April I thought that we were all caught except 5 Brigade who had embarked. I spent three very anxious days at the end. I am sad that we have a certain number of missing. In my opinion the men at base in Athens should have been evacuated. They were not under me and I am furious that nobody grasped the fact that to leave them to the last was only increasing our difficulty.[9]

The last sentences referred to 2,000 New Zealand reinforcements. Along with about 16,000 other reinforcements held in back areas, they were sent to Kalamata at the southern end of the Peloponnese. The navy managed to evacuate half of them, but 8,000 were left to become POWs, including the NZ reinforcements. Not until he reached Crete did Freyberg know that they had gone to Kalamata and had not been embarked.[2] As it was, out of some 62,000 (in round figures) British and Commonwealth troops originally landed in Greece, some 46,000 were successfully evacuated. Just under 1,000 were killed, just over 1,000 wounded, and a total of 14,000 became prisoners of war.[8] After a day of acute anxiety a message in clear was eventually got through to Puttick via the HQ of the British Armoured Brigade, which had not yet embarked, telling him to cancel the move of 4 Brigade to the Peloponnese and to go to the Marathon beaches instead. This they did, but the Germans were closing in on them and were held off only with difficulty. Almost miraculously the navy came in that night and embarked the whole of the brigade, and they arrived safely at Suda Bay in the late afternoon of 27 April.[1]

On the night of 26 April the C-in-C General Wilson left by flying boat, taking with him his Force Headquarters. He bade Freyberg farewell at 4 p.m., saying, 'Bernard, I hand over Greece to you.' A few days later there was to be a repeat performance as he departed from Suda Bay: 'Bernard, I hand over Crete to you.'

While 4 Brigade was embarking from the Marathon beaches, 6 Brigade began to move to the southern part of the Peloponnese and, during the night of 26–7 April on to the high ground of a small village just south-east of Tripolis. Freyberg's account continues:

> I was in close and constant touch with the men, and I learned a great deal about New Zealand character and also something of their superstitious sense. On 27 April we were outside a large stone Greek Orthodox Church where we were preparing breakfast. I told the officers that the situation reminded me of an occasion 26 years ago before the landing in Gallipoli, when I found myself in front of a Greek Church in Mudros. By a coincidence we were also at that time planning the landing at Gallipoli and were worried about the weather and the arrival of the Royal Navy to guide our convoy to the right beach. Patrick Shaw-Stewart had said that he was going to the local church to light the biggest candle he could find to Aeos Nicholas, the Saint of the Sea. We had all lit our candles as well. Now in 1941, I said I would try the same plan, but in the stress of the moment I forgot to light my candle, and only remembered just as we were moving off. I stopped my car, and went back into the Church to look for the shrine of my patron saint. I then discovered that the shrine was already blazing with hundreds of lights, for my story had gone the rounds and all and sundry had rushed in and had lighted their candles. I put mine with the rest, and as I was carrying a very large sum of Greek money, I put the equivalent of a fortune into the box.[9]

The 6 NZ Brigade moved through Sparta, and before first light on 28 April was concealed in olive groves fifteen miles from Monemvasia. No movement was allowed during the day, and rations, petrol and explosives were in short supply. Freyberg had gone on ahead, hoping to make contact with the embarkation staff, but none could be found. NZ Division HQ had no communication with the navy, and had nothing definite to go on except a promise from General Wilson before he left that he would try and arrange for ships to go into Monemvasia on the night of 28–9 April. 'This uncertainty which surrounded the last hours in Greece, was the most unnerving part of the whole evacuation,' Freyberg commented later.[1]

At midday on 28 April Admiral Baillie-Grohmann arrived at

Monemvasia in a small launch from a village along the coast. He was uncertain as to whether the ships would come that night, but had sent off his signal and was hoping for the best. That afternoon the New Zealanders had found a dozen or so rowing-boats and two Greek caiques in the harbour and got crews for them.

As soon as it was dark the troops of 6 Brigade moved down to the beach ready to embark, and the vehicles that conveyed them there were broken up and made unserviceable. There were some 4,000 men to be taken off, and the ships were not due to arrive until 11 p.m. It was estimated that they would have to leave by 3 a.m. next day if they were to be out of range of German dive-bombers by daylight, and anyone not embarked by then would have to be left behind. At 11.30 p.m. no ships were in sight and, as Freyberg said, 'we were in a state of desperation'. Then, at midnight, a signal was seen from the sea and the destroyer HMS *Havock*, the first of five warships, slipped in near the shore:

> When, lo, out of the darkness, there was light.
> There in the sea were England and her ships.[13]

Embarkation started at once, and by one o'clock it was in full swing. The dozen rowing-boats and two caiques took off 800 men between them. There was difficulty in getting some of the stretcher cases on board, but by 3.15 a.m. everyone was clear of the beaches. Admiral Baillie-Grohmann, Colonel Keith Stewart and Freyberg, with his PA and ADC, were the last to leave, and clambered up the nets on to the deck of the cruiser HMS *Ajax*. The squadron immediately headed for the open sea at full speed.

Freyberg's account of 'The New Zealand Division in Greece' ends: 'Shortly after daylight the snowcapped mountains of Crete could be seen and by breakfast time on a lovely morning we were at anchor in Suda Bay. The ill-fated Greek adventure was over. The grim battle for Crete was about to begin.'[1]

17

Crete – The Prelude

When Italy declared war on Britain and France on 10 June 1940 the British Mediterranean Fleet was no longer based at Malta, as it had been for more than a century, because the island was vulnerable to bombing from Sicily, some 50 miles away. The Fleet's new harbour at Alexandria, however, was too far from the Italian Navy's main fields of operation: after allowing for the journey in both directions British warships had insufficient fuel to stay in the central Mediterranean for very long.

As early as 6 June 1940 Admiral Cunningham had strongly recommended to the Admiralty the occupation of Crete and establishing there a refuelling staging post.[1a] This could not be carried out at the time because Greece was neutral; but four months later, at the end of October 1940 when the Italians attacked Greece and the Greeks appealed for help, the Royal Navy was able to send its tankers into Suda Bay.[1b] The importance of Crete in the early stages of the war was thus almost entirely a naval one.

The navy quickly realised that Suda Bay could be turned into more than just a refuelling stop, and had the potential for becoming an advanced base for the Fleet. The Mobile Naval Base Defence Organisation (MNBDO) began to take shape therefore during the winter of 1940–1. Its main components, sent out from England, were assembled at Haifa, prior to beginning its move to Crete early in May 1941. The concept of establishing the MNBDO in Crete was based on the assumption that there would be a friendly regime on the mainland of Greece.

The MNBDO was a supply organisation for replenishing the Fleet, and a defence force to protect it. The defence element consisted of several heavy and light anti-aircraft regiments, a coastal defence regiment, a harbour protection force, searchlights and other ancillary units. The whole organisation, some 5,300 strong, was commanded by a major-general of the Royal Marines.

At the same time as the navy moved in to Suda Bay the RAF and Fleet Air Arm established a small presence at Heraklion and Maleme airfields in Crete, mainly to work with the Fleet, but occasionally to attack Italian targets in Albania. The first army unit to land on Crete – 2 Battalion York and Lancaster Regiment – arrived at Suda Bay on 30 October 1940.

The first British Army commander in Crete was Brigadier Tidbury, whose task was to defend the naval refuelling base and to co-operate with local Greek forces.[2] These originally included a Cretan Division which, however, was sent to Albania in the middle of November and was not replaced. Later the British garrison was increased to two battalions and two commandos, with some heavy and light anti-aircraft batteries, under Headquarters 14 British Infantry Brigade. During the six months from November 1940 to April 1941 there were five different commanders of this army garrison. Brigadier Tidbury was succeeded by Major-General Gambier-Parry, who was followed by Brigadier Galloway. In March the latter was replaced by Brigadier Chappell, who in turn handed over to Major-General Weston (Royal Marines). These officers each received different instructions, and no overall policy on long-term defence arrangements was laid down. 'From the outset there was ambiguity as to the role of the Garrison. The appointment of five commanders in six months could hardly produce the best results,' was the later comment of an inter-services report on Crete.[2]

No formal study was ever carried out by the Joint Planning Staffs in London or Cairo about the implications of defending Crete. This was in spite of the Prime Minister's 'repeated injunctions to have Suda Bay fortified', as he wrote:

> I had even used the expression 'a second Scapa' ... The Middle East Command should have made a more careful study of the conditions under which Crete might have to be defended from air or sea attack. The need of providing if not a harbour at least landing facilities at the southern side of the island at Sphakia or Timbaki and the making of a road therefrom to Suda Bay and the airfields by which Western Crete could have been reinforced from Egypt was not foreseen.[3a]

The first directive in which Crete was even mentioned as a possible battlefield was dated 18 April 1941, just before the order was given to evacuate Greece. It was addressed by the Chiefs of Staff to the Commanders-in-Chief, Middle East:

Following Directive has been issued by the PM and Minister of Defence:

1   It is not possible to lay down precise sequence and priority between interests none of which can be wholly ignored, but the following may be a guide. The extrication of New Zealand, Australian, and British troops from Greece affects the whole Empire.
2   It ought to be possible to arrange shipping in and out of Tobruk either before or after the evacuation crisis, observing that Tobruk has two months' supplies.
3   You must divide between protecting evacuation and sustaining battle in Libya. But if these clash, which may be avoidable, emphasis must be given to victory in Libya.
4   Don't worry about Iraq for the present. It looks like going smoothly.
5   Crete will at first only be a receptacle of whatever can get there from Greece. Its fuller defence must be organised later. In the meanwhile all forces there must protect themselves from air bombing by dispersion and use their bayonets against parachutists or airborne intruders if any.
6   Subject to the above general remarks, victory in Libya counts first, evacuation of troops from Greece second. Tobruk shipping, unless indispensable to victory, must be fitted in as convenient. Iraq can be ignored and Crete be worked up later.[3b]

Such, very briefly, was the background of the British presence in Crete; and it was only one month after the Minister of Defence's directive that thousands of German parachutists descended upon the island.

HMS *Ajax* and her squadron arrived in Suda Bay from Greece at 9 a.m. on 29 April 1941, carrying 6 NZ Brigade and NZ Divisional HQ from Monemvasia in the Peloponnese. Freyberg himself was very tired:

During the last six weeks we had all been through a hard time of great anxiety. Our clothes were looking the worse for wear . . . and most of us showed the strain under which we had been living. I had no thoughts of plans to defend Crete. It was clear to me, however, that the force which had been evacuated from Greece was a very mixed one and not in good shape. Further, there were no facilities for re-equipping it on the island.

It had been arranged that the New Zealand Divisional Headquarters and 6 New Zealand Brigade were to go in their ships to Alexandria as soon as it was dark, and I was to see 4 and 5 New Zealand Brigades that afternoon and

fly on to Egypt before daylight on 30 April. There was no mention at that
time of Crete being attacked.[4]

Meanwhile in England there had been a series of meetings and
discussions as to what should be done next, culminating in a signal from
the War Office at 0115 hours on 30 April: 'Personal for General Wavell
from CIGS: Would suggest Freyberg to succeed Weston in Crete. It
need only be temporary command and Freyberg could collect later his
scattered flock.'[5]

When Freyberg woke at about 7 a.m. on the 30th he found a
telegram from Middle East HQ telling him to go with his Chief Staff
Officer to a conference at 11 a.m. When he arrived he found General
Wavell, who 'had just arrived by air from Cairo, looked drawn and
haggard, and even more tired than any of us'. Others made the same
observation, including General Ismay: 'All of us at the centre, including Wavell's particular friends and advisers, got the impression that he
had been tremendously affected by the breach of his desert flank . . . I
seem to remember Eden saying that Wavell had "aged ten years in the
night".'[3d]

The conference met under an awning on the flat roof of a small villa
between Maleme and Canea, under arrangements made by 1 Battalion
Welsh Regiment. Those who attended were:

General Sir Archibald Wavell	GHQ Middle East
Lieutenant-General Sir H. M. Wilson }	W Force
Brigadier Galloway }	(HQ Greece)
Major-General Freyberg }	NZ Div
Colonel Stewart }	
Major-General Weston	Comd Crete
Air Commodore D'Albiac }	RAF
Group Captain Beamish }	
Captain Fern	RN
Sir Michael Palairet	Ambassador to Greece
Major-General Heywood	Mission to Greece

Freyberg's account goes on:

Prior to sitting down at the conference table, General Wavell and General
Wilson got together in the corner. They appeared to be having a heart to
heart talk, and it was only later I realised what they were discussing. I had
been nominated by Whitehall by name to take over command of Crete.

After a few minutes, the Commander-in-Chief called me over. Our
relationship had been strained for several months, but there was a background of friendship going back to the First War, and he was a man for

whom I had affection. General Wavell had always been a man of very few
words, and I could see that something was afoot. He started by saying what I
knew to be true – how well the New Zealand Division had carried out their
difficult role in Greece. His next remark came as a complete surprise. He
said: 'You are to take command of all the troops in Crete,' and went on to
say that he considered Crete would be attacked in the next few days.

I immediately said that I could not agree to that. I was the servant of the
New Zealand Government, and my job was to get the New Zealand Forces
together again and get them retrained and re-equipped, and that the New
Zealand Government would not agree to their being split between Crete
and Egypt.

General Wavell then said that he considered it was my duty to remain and
take command, and that I could be a Lieutenant-General. In the circumstances I felt I could do nothing other than accept, but I insisted upon
remaining a Major-General as I did not require any inducement to do my
duty.[4]

After this exchange the conference sat down. Wavell was at the head of
the table, and Freyberg at the other end opposite the C-in-C.
Freyberg's account of the proceedings includes the following:

1   Crete was to be held.
2   General Wavell considered that the island would be attacked in the next
    few days.
3   The objectives of the air attack were considered to be the aerodromes at
    Heraklion and Maleme.
4   No additional air support would be forthcoming.
5   General Freyberg to command. Brigadier [previously Colonel] Stewart
    as Brigadier General Staff (BGS), Brigadier Brunskill as Deputy
    Adjutant and Quartermaster General (DA and QMG). General Wes-
    ton to command British troops in Suda Bay area.
6   General Weston, Royal Marines, pointed out that a seaborne landing
    was very probable, and that as far as he could see, the Royal Navy would
    not be able to do much about it.
        The Commander-in-Chief said he would talk it over with Admiral
    Cunningham.
7   Air Commodore D'Albiac said the RAF had nothing to offer us.
8   The object of the defence was defined as: 'To deny to the enemy the use
    of Crete as an air base.'[4]

Freyberg then asked the Commander-in-Chief the expected date
when the enemy would be ready to launch his assault, and the scale of
attack envisaged. Wavell said that the attack could be delivered in the
next few days, and that the scale was likely to be 5,000 to 6,000 airborne
troops in the first sortie, plus a possible sea-force landing with tanks.

Upon receiving these replies, and in view of the unsatisfactory air position, I got up from the conference table and asked the Commander-in-Chief to come away where we could talk in private. I then told him that from my knowledge, I could see that the Garrison was unprepared and unequipped, and that in my opinion the decision to hold Crete should be reviewed. General Wavell said that we could not evacuate Crete as we did not have the necessary ships. There was, then, nothing further to be said, and I accepted my task without more comment.[4]

After the conference was over, Wavell took Freyberg into the garden of the villa for a further talk in private. What then took place is crucial to an understanding of what happened in Crete in the next four weeks. Wavell told Freyberg that he was to be given the ULTRA intelligence; but as Freyberg had never heard of ULTRA Wavell had to tell him what it was, where it came from, and how it would be brought to him. He explained that ULTRA was a very special source of intelligence obtained by the British possessing the Enigma machine, which could decode or decrypt German wireless transmissions.

Having briefed him about ULTRA, Wavell then gave Freyberg two specific orders. First he was not to mention the existence of ULTRA to anyone else on Crete. Second, he was never to take any action as a result of what he learnt from ULTRA *alone*. Wavell emphasised that this was a fundamental rule which must be strictly obeyed and could not be varied without his personal authorisation. If the rule was not adhered to, there was a danger that the enemy might realise that his codes had been broken.

In some later accounts of Freyberg's induction into the ULTRA secret, and particularly in Anthony Cave Brown's biography of Sir Stewart Menzies, head of MI5, it has been stated that Freyberg was not given the full background information about ULTRA and was only told the 'cover story'.[6] The cover story was that the intelligence came from a highly placed agent in Athens, and those officers who had to be given the ULTRA intelligence at Headquarters CREFORCE were so informed about the source. However my father told me definitely that Wavell explained to him at his garden briefing that ULTRA involved the decrypting of German wireless transmissions, adding that it soon became obvious from the contents and the timing of the ULTRA signals (which started to flow to Crete towards the end of the first week of May 1941) that the information could not have been obtained by any other means in the time available. An example my father gave was advance warnings of enemy bombing attacks, which were carried out within a few hours of their being notified.[7]

Originally the breaking of the German code had been called 'Boniface', after St Boniface, the English missionary monk and martyr of 675–754, known in the Church as the 'Apostle of Germany', but it became known as ULTRA later. One of the earlier practitioners at Bletchley Park in Buckinghamshire – the nerve-centre of British cipher intelligence – was Wing Commander (later Group Captain) Humphreys, who was in charge of the Air Section of Hut 3, where the Middle East wireless traffic was handled. In an important paper, now in the Public Record Office at Kew. Humphreys has described how ULTRA was first made available to the Middle East Command in February 1941.[8] The Middle East Intelligence Bureau at Heliopolis had first been called into being to handle 'Y' information (the interception and dissemination of German low-level wireless traffic in the field), but subsequently 'U' (ULTRA) traffic was added. German wireless intercepts in the Middle East ended up at Hut 3 where they were deciphered, and the more important information went to JIC (Joint Intelligence Committee) and to Broadway, where 'C' (the 'Chief') and his staff were responsible for keeping the Prime Minister informed. An ULTRA link had been provided in Greece on General Wilson's staff, and just before Freyberg was appointed C-in-C Crete another had been established in Crete.

The ULTRA liaison officer in Crete was Group Captain Beamish, Air Officer Commanding, who had a wireless set powerful enough to communicate directly with Bletchley Park. Under the system that operated in May 1941 enemy operation orders were transmitted by wireless from XI Fliegerkorps Headquarters in Athens to German Army and Air Force Formation Headquarters on Greek airfields and islands targeted on Crete; these transmissions were recorded at British listening posts at Sarafand, Heliopolis, Malta and elsewhere, and then signalled to Bletchley Park, where they were decoded and read. The more interesting information was sent to Broadway and the Joint Intelligence Committee, and then, where appropriate, encoded on 'one-time pads' (that is, codes which were used only once) and sent to the Middle East Bureau at Heliopolis. The really urgent intelligence went direct from Bletchley Park to Group Captain Beamish in Canea, and reached Freyberg within a matter of hours.

After leaving General Wavell, Freyberg went immediately to Force Headquarters at Telegraph Hill on the outskirts of Canea. He found that General Weston's headquarters of the MNBDO had moved out and had swept the place clean, leaving nothing. CREFORCE headquarters, as his command was styled, did not exist:

There were no Staff, Signals or Clerks, and only a little stationery, ink, pencils and office equipment of any kind. General Weston very kindly left me a few of his Naval Signallers to see me through until I was able to get others, but this was all. I inherited a car, an RASC driver, and a cook. I turned over the organisation of Headquarters to Brigadier Stewart, who co-opted suitable men from the New Zealand Brigade Groups. In the next few hours we assembled a staff of sorts, and they worked well, but we could not consider them as an adequate Force staff.

When I arrived in Crete I had with me my Divisional Staff and Headquarters, including Signals, with as much equipment as we had been able to carry up the rope ladders over the ships' sides. In the convoy were the complete 6 New Zealand Infantry Brigade Group under their able and resolute commander, Brigadier Barrowclough. They remained on their ships.

The naval convoy, with our well organised units, lay all day on 29 April in Suda Bay, and at dusk left, taking my Divisional Headquarters and the fine Infantry Brigade. By the time I took over command of Crete on 30 April, this valuable part of the New Zealand Division had already arrived in Alexandria. For all these mistakes – for which Whitehall, the Commanders-in-Chief Middle East and 'W' Force and their staffs were responsible – we were to pay a high price.[9]

Freyberg's appointment as C-in-C in Crete required someone else to command the New Zealand Division. Brigadier Puttick, commanding 4 NZ Brigade, was the next most senior officer, and he was promoted Major-General and became Divisional Commander. Brigadier Inglis replaced him at 4 NZ Brigade.

After Freyberg had taken over command in Crete he was presented with three documents. The first was a local appreciation of the situation jointly prepared by General Maitland Wilson and the former GOC Crete, General Weston. This included the following statement about the seaborne threat:

> The enemy's sea approach to the island is comparatively easy and he can provide air protection for a seaborne landing. It is difficult for our Navy in the face of air superiority to interfere with a seaborne expedition. It is therefore not improbable that he will attempt a seaborne expedition of limited strength, in conjunction with an airborne attack in the near future. A Note by General Weston is attached as Appendix 'C'.[10]

Appendix 'C' was headed 'The Possibility of Seaborne Attack', in which the Royal Marine General Weston stressed the short distance of sea passage between Greece and Crete, the speed with which light forces could cover the distance, the difficulty for the Royal Navy in intercepting such forces without air cover, and the unlimited forces which the enemy possessed to build up his landing.

The second document Freyberg received was a précis of the scale of attack expected on Crete.[11] The German Order of Battle in southern Greece at the beginning of May was already known to consist of the XI Air Corps under General Kurt Student, with the 7 Airlanding Division, possibly 22 Airborne Division, and both the 5 and 6 Mountain Divisions, all earmarked and available for the attack on Crete.

The third document – which arrived next day, 1 May – was the War Cabinet JIC Appreciation.[12] This envisaged an initial parachute or airlanding drop of up to 3,000 troops, or possibly 4,000 if gliders were used; and it was estimated that this would need two or possibly three sorties per day. But the JIC Appreciation also reckoned, since ample German troops and shipping were available, that the enemy was likely to make a *combined* airborne and seaborne assault in approximately equal numbers.

Freyberg's reactions to these appreciations were immediate:

I could scarcely believe my eyes. I realised how great were our difficulties if the appreciations proved correct and I felt that the sooner I introduced a little reality into the calculations for the defence of Crete the better. I therefore sent off the following telegrams to Middle East Headquarters and the New Zealand Government:

To Headquarters Middle East
Forces at my disposal are totally inadequate to meet attack envisaged. Unless fighter aircraft are greatly increased and naval forces made available to deal with seaborne attack I cannot hope to hold out with land forces alone which as result of campaign in Greece are now devoid of any artillery, have insufficient tools for digging, very little transport and inadequate war reserves of equipment and ammunition. Force here can and will fight but without full support from Navy and Air Force cannot hope to repel invasion. If for other reasons these cannot be made available at once urge that question of holding Crete should be reconsidered. I feel that under terms of my charter it is my duty to inform NZ Government of situation in which greater part of my Division is now placed.
2155 hrs 1 May 41.[4]

To the Prime Minister of New Zealand
Feel it my duty to report military situation in Crete. Decision taken in London that Crete must be held at all costs. Have received appreciation scale of attack (sent separately). In my opinion Crete can only be held with full support from Navy and Air Force. There is no evidence of naval forces capable of guaranteeing us against seaborne invasion and air force in island consists of 6 Hurricanes and 17 obsolete aircraft . . . Would strongly

[271]

represent to your Government grave situation in which bulk of NZ Division is placed and recommend you bring pressure to bear on highest plane in London to either supply us with sufficient means to defend island or to review decision Crete must be held. I have of course made my official representation on this matter to C-in-C Middle East.[4]

Afterwards Freyberg spelt out the reasons why he had sent such an uncompromising signal to his government in Wellington:

I was outspoken with him [Wavell] because arrangements had been so bad in Greece that we could not afford to have any further misunderstandings. I wanted him to know clearly how bad the situation in Crete was. We now know that he failed to make Whitehall understand the fully gravity of the position. On the other hand, I had foreseen this possibility, and my telegram to the New Zealand Government was quite clear and precise on this vital point.[4]

As a result of Freyberg's signal to New Zealand, Mr Fraser decided to fly at once to Egypt, in order to be on hand when decisions were being taken concerning the fate of the New Zealand Division.

One of the major difficulties in defending Crete was the geography of the island, which adversely affected the navy's ability to deal with any seaborne threat from the north. Crete is 160 miles long from east to west, with a width varying between about 35 and 8 miles north to south. A backbone of high mountains runs nearly its whole length, which can be crossed in only a few places, and which, on the southern side, slopes abruptly down to the sea. Admiral Cunningham describes the main problems in greater detail:

All the bays and harbours are on the northern coast, an unfortunate fact for us as they could only be reached through the Kaso Straits at the east end of the island, and the Antikithera and Kithera Channels to the west, all of which were in easy range of enemy aerodromes. No port or real anchorage exists on the south coast, while the only country suitable for airfields is on the northern side. We had two airfields, one at Maleme, about 10 miles west of Suda Bay, and the other near Heraklion, a small port about 65 miles to the eastward. There was also a small landing strip at Retimo, about 20 miles east of Suda. From the point of view of defence it would have suited us much better if the island could have been turned upside-down.[1c]

If a proper study been carried out during the six months of British occupation it would have identified two interrelated difficulties. The first was the vulnerability of the northern airfields and ports to air attack from an enemy established in Greece. Second, any British administrative arrangements that depended on these would be in the front line from the moment an attack started. In addition there was only one road along the north coast that connected the towns, ports and airfields of the island. A modern tarmacadam road was still under construction in 1941; many of the bridges were weak; and because of the road's primitive condition vehicles could move along it only very slowly. The military implications were that each of the three sectors of Maleme/ Suda Bay, Retimo and Heraklion had to be self-contained for defence purposes, because it was very difficult to reinforce one from another.

Freyberg was soon made aware of other problems:

> After taking over Command, the first message I received was from Admiral Cunningham who drew my attention to the fact that he could not use the northern ports of Suda Bay and Heraklion to maintain Creforce and asked whether I could develop the south coast ports of Sphakia and Timbaki. Given a clear month and the necessary mechanical equipment, this could have been done.[9]

Freyberg's conclusion was inescapable: 'Had a careful study been made of the conditions under which Crete might have been held against air and sea attacks, many of the administrative difficulties could have been avoided.'

From air and car reconnaissance Freyberg discovered that the island was for the most part tankproof and very rocky. He also found, like Admiral Cunningham, that 'from a defence point of view, Crete faced the wrong way. After having made a rough survey of the island, the grave doubts that I had at the beginning were not allayed.' He was worried also about some of the troops:

> I knew that after a hurried evacuation from Greece over open beaches under heavy enemy pressure, all units would be disorganised and short of equipment. I did not realise the true position, however, until I had visited the men in their camp areas. It was not unusual to find that men had no arms or equipment, and no plates, knives, forks or spoons and that they ate and drank from bully beef or cigarette tins. There was no Unit transport, and most Units had no tools. The morale of the men from the unequipped and non-fighting Units was low.[4]

In an attempt to boost morale, and to stem rumour-mongering, Freyberg instituted a troops' newspaper. Second-Lieutenant Geoffrey Cox, a journalist in civilian life, was given on 5 May the task of

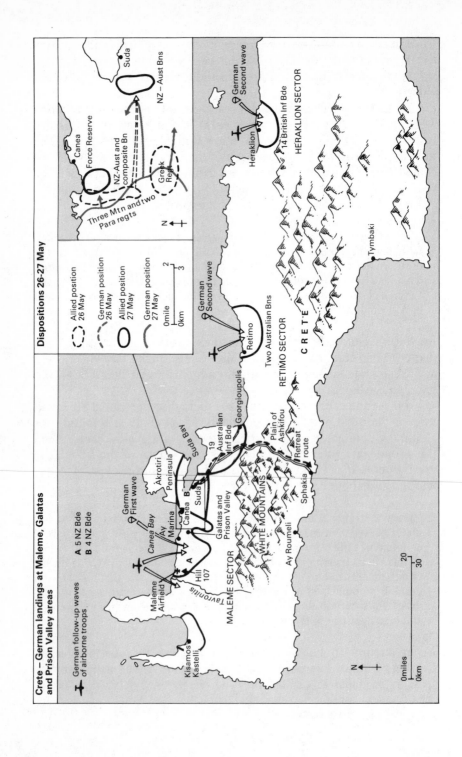

Crete – German landings at Maleme, Galatas and Prison Valley areas

German follow-up waves of airborne troops

A 5 NZ Bde
B 4 NZ Bde

German First wave

Kisamos
Kastelli

Canea Bay

Maleme
Airfield

Hill 107

Tavronitis

Ay Marina

Ákrotiri Peninsula

Canea

A

B

Suda

Suda Bay

Galatas and Prison Valley

MALEME SECTOR

WHITE MOUNTAINS

Ay Roumeli

Sphakia

Retreat route

Plain of Ashkifou

Georgioupolis

19 Australian Inf Bde

German Second wave

Retimo

Two Australian Bns

RETIMO SECTOR

C R E T E

German Second wave

Heraklion

14 British Inf Bde

HERAKLION SECTOR

Tymbaki

0 miles 20
0 km 30

N

Dispositions 26-27 May

Allied position 26 May
German position 26 May
Allied position 27 May
German position 27 May

0 mile 2
0 km 3

Canea
Force Reserve

Suda

NZ-Aust and composite Bn

NZ – Aust Bns

Three Mtn and two Para regts

Greek Regt

N

producing the newspaper. This he did, and *Crete News* appeared on 14 and 19 May before the battle and on 22 and 24 May during it!

Freyberg now had to face the problem of reorganising his force:

> The men had to be told the urgency of the situation in a way that would prepare them for the battle which was now about to burst upon them. At the same time, it was important to say nothing which would reveal to them my grave doubts as to our ability to hold Crete. Only five people at that time on Crete knew the seriousness of our position. In addition to myself they were General Weston, my Chief of Staff (Brigadier Stewart), my Personal Assistant (Captain John White) who typed my cables, and the Cypher Officer, who coded and decoded all high-grade cypher messages. These men were secure, and kept their doubts to themselves. I hope that my attitude was soldierly, and that outwardly I managed to look the part of a man with complete confidence in the situation.[4]

Robin Bell, one of Freyberg's Intelligence Officers, describes how Freyberg used to travel all round Crete to supervise preparations. On one occasion he accompanied Freyberg to Retimo:

> . . . with air photographs taken from a crashed German aircraft, to show the Australians there what could be seen by attacking aircraft, so that they could take precautions accordingly. Another time I went with Freyberg to Brigadier Vasey at Georgioupolis and other places. On these occasions he seemed to relax a little and from his conversation I gained the impression he had been reluctant to take command of all troops on Crete.[4]

To his troops and to the world generally Freyberg had to radiate optimism about the impending battle; only to his immediate superiors could he unburden himself and weigh the odds objectively. Inevitably he was to find later that several of his pre-battle statements were quoted against him as examples of over-confidence.

At the beginning of May the defence of Crete was laid out against, as the JIC Appreciation had foreseen, a seaborne attack of the same scale as the parachute and airborne assault. In the crucial Maleme–Canea–Suda Bay area, for example, the New Zealand Division and other troops were strung out along the shores of Canea Bay, with only one infantry company on Maleme airfield itself. The distance from the most westerly point of 5 NZ Brigade on the Tavronitis river, to the most easterly point of 4 NZ Brigade on the outskirts of Canea town, was 10 miles. An ad hoc 10 NZ Brigade was interposed between 4 and 5 Brigades. Nearly all the units in these brigades were responsible for looking after a stretch of the coast. Similar arrangements were made to

[275]

tackle the combined sea and airborne threats to Heraklion and Retimo, which were the responsibility of 14 British Brigade and an ad hoc Australian force respectively. At this stage the information provided by ULTRA began to come through to Crete.

The man largely responsible for Freyberg's appointment as C-in-C Crete was Winston Churchill. 'I had suggested to the CIGS,' Churchill wrote in *The Second World War*, 'that General Freyberg should be placed in command of Crete, and he proposed this to Wavell who had immediately agreed.'[3f] Churchill was determined therefore to give Freyberg the maximum amount of information available. As the way in which ULTRA information was handled was to play a crucial and decisive part in the fate of Crete, it is important to understand the mechanics of how it worked. Wing Commander Humphreys explains:

> As much as possible, consistent with the security, was made of this intelligence in preparing the defence of the Island, but the danger of giving complete information to GOC Crete, in his exposed position, presented a grave problem. On the Prime Minister's decision, the Bletchley Park (BP) 'U' Air Intelligence Section produced a paper purporting to be a compendium of German documents obtained through Secret Service channels from General Headquarters at Athens, the summary being couched in terms consistent with such an 'alibi'. This was then signalled to GOC Crete over a special link, using 'One-Time-Pad' cypher procedure.[8]

That 'compendium of documents' was known as OL (or Orange Leonard) 302. It was the cover story for ULTRA, which successfully concealed the real source from the intelligence staff at Headquarters CREFORCE. The general belief among the officers who handled it was that the information came from Admiral Canaris.*

It is not certain exactly when OL 302 reached Freyberg. It may have arrived as early as 6 May, but although the information was available in London late that evening it probably did not reach Crete until some time on 7 May. The signal was repeated to Heliopolis 'for information' on 13 May and added that Freyberg had already been informed direct.

OL 302 was nothing less than a summary of the German plan for the attack on Crete. The operational picture that emerged was of massive air attacks by fighters and bombers, a force of some 600 transport aircraft and gliders available to move 7 Air Division, 'some 12,000 will be parachute-landing contingent', together with 'Airlanding of Eleven Air Corps, including the Corps Headquarters and elements of the

---

*Admiral Canaris was head of the German Military Intelligence, the Abwehr. He had many contacts with Allied countries and was thought to be a double agent. He was executed by Hitler in 1945 for his part in the July 1944 assassination attempt.[13]

Army placed under its command, probably including the 22 Division', and a seaborne force of 10,000 men. The breakdown of this force was therefore approximately as follows:

parachute troops	12,000
airlanding	8,000–13,000
seaborne	10,000
	30,000–35,000

Freyberg was taken aback. The information was factual and, coming from where it did, obviously authentic. It showed a far heavier weight of parachute and airlanding troops than had been mentioned at his take-over conference, or in the JIC Appreciation, and it increased the threat from the air compared with that from the sea by a ratio of well over two to one. But, worst of all, the intelligence showed for the first time that the deployment along the beaches was wrongly placed to counter an airborne invasion of such dimensions and directed against the airfields, particularly at Maleme. This was the overriding problem that concerned Freyberg for the rest of the pre-attack phase in Crete.

A glance at the dispositions on the map (page 274) indicates what was wrong. Because, when the original deployment was decided, the seaborne threat was thought to be a serious one, the New Zealand Division was strung out over a distance of 10 miles along the shores of Canea Bay. The critical sector occupied by 5 NZ Brigade stretched from the Tavronitis river in the west to the village of Ay Marina to the east, a distance of 7 miles. The 28 Maori Battalion – one of the strongest – and the Brigade Headquarters were 5 miles from the aerodrome. All units of 5 NZ Brigade were responsible for looking after stretches of beach within this sector.

The country to the west of the Tavronitis river was flat and unoccupied by any defending troops. What was particularly dangerous was that this open flank went right up to the perimeter of the airfield, so that the most westerly defending troops were in the area of the runway itself. German airborne troops, should they land to the west of the Tavronitis river, would meet no opposition on the ground, and have an undisputed approach right up to Maleme airfield. There were insufficient troops available to look after both the beaches and the area to the west of the airfield.

Once Freyberg knew from ULTRA the increased scale of attack on Maleme, he told me, what he wanted to do was to close up the four-battalion 5 NZ Brigade so that they occupied the ground on both sides of the airfield. Leaving 22 NZ Battalion astride the airfield, he planned to deploy one New Zealand battalion to the west of the Tavronitis river together with a Greek battalion nearby in support. A counter-attack force of two battalions was to be positioned immediately to the east of the aerodrome. The troops from 4 NZ Brigade near Canea would have had to extend westwards to take over some of the area vacated by 5 Brigade. There was still sufficient time in which to carry out such a redeployment before the date of the German attack indicated by ULTRA. At that stage the target date for the start of operations was given as 17 May. In the event there were to be two postponements, first to 19 May, followed by a further day's delay to 20 May.

In several of Freyberg's papers about Crete, written after the war, there are references to his regret that a New Zealand battalion had not been placed to the west of Maleme airfield, and the difference that this might have made to the outcome of the battle. In later years indeed he often used to repeat a sentence from Field Service Regulations: 'It is rarely possible to recover in battle from a faulty deployment.'

Freyberg was unable to send any messages to Wavell by word of mouth since he was forbidden to mention the existence of ULTRA to anyone else in Crete, so the discussion between them had to be conducted by sealed letters taken by trusted officers. As in the second week of May there were considerable comings and goings between HQ CREFORCE in Canea and GHQ Cairo, there was no shortage of secure messengers.

No documentary evidence survives of the operational messages that passed between Wavell and Freyberg concerning the ULTRA information because they were all burnt immediately after being read, in conformity with security instructions. Major-General Sir Digby Raeburn, who was an ULTRA reader at GHQ Cairo in 1941, confirms this: 'When I was privy to ULTRA, it was certainly the practice to destroy all messages after they had been communicated to those entitled to know – a small band. In my day none of the material was ever filed.'[14]

There is evidence, however, to support what my father told me, namely that he planned to send his Chief of Staff back to Cairo, to explain the tactical situation in Crete to Wavell, and to emphasise why it was so important to change the dispositions in the Maleme–Canea area. In a signal file in the Public Record Office there is a letter from the Chief Signal Officer Crete to his Signal Officer-in-Chief Cairo, dated 11 May: 'Your letter dated 8th May arrived this afternoon, and I am hurrying to get an answer off by the BGS who leaves tomorrow morning.'[15] But the BGS, Keith Stewart, did not fly to Cairo on 12

May. Instead a high-powered emissary from Cairo had arrived at Maleme airfield on the afternoon of 11 May.

In his history, *The Second World War*, Winston Churchill explains the setting in which the preparations for the Crete battle were made:

> We had known for a long time the efforts Goering had made to create and develop a powerful airborne force, capable of a large-scale descent from the air. This had appealed to the ardent and devoted Nazi youth of Germany. The German Parachute Division was a *corps d'élite*, which had played its part in our thoughts about home defence against invasion. All such plans however require at least the temporary command of the daylight air. This the Germans had failed to gain in Britain. Crete was a different tale.[3c]

This account was published in 1950, almost a quarter of a century before ULTRA was declassified. Our subsequent knowledge makes it easy to read between the lines of Churchill's next few sentences:

> At no moment in the war was our Intelligence so truly and precisely informed. In the exultant confusion of their seizure of Athens the German staffs preserved less than their usual secrecy, and our agents in Greece were active and daring. In the last week in April we obtained from trustworthy sources good information about the next German stroke. The movements and excitement of the German 11th Air Corps, and also the frantic collection of small craft in Greek harbours, could not be concealed from attentive eyes and ears. All pointed to an impending attack on Crete, both by air and sea. In no operation did I take more personal pains to study and weigh the evidence or to make sure that the magnitude of the impending onslaught was impressed upon the Commanders-in-Chief and imparted to the general on the actual scene.[3e]

By the time *Finest Hour* by Martin Gilbert was published in 1983 no security restriction remained, and the Prime Minister's wishes could be spelt out in full. Gilbert writes:

> On May 10 Churchill contemplated a desperate course, to save Crete. The Enigma decrypts were providing a complete picture of exactly where the Germans intended to land in Crete. One feature of these plans was the seizure of airfields by glider and airborne landings.
> Studying these decrypts, Churchill thought of a plan, to send the 'actual text of all the messages' to Freyberg, 'by special officer, by air', so that

Freyberg could be shown 'personally' all the German messages relating to the seizure of airfields. 'These messages could then be destroyed by fire.' The officer taking them out, Churchill continued, 'would be answerable for their destruction in the event of engine failure *en route*. No one should be informed but the General who would give his orders to his subordinates without explaining his full reasons.'[16]

A minute from the office of the Minister of Defence on 12 May 1941 and signed L. C. Hollis reads as follows:

MOST SECRET

Prime Minister
With reference to your Minute, the Chiefs of Staff had considered the problem of how best to help the Commanders-in-Chief, Middle East, and in consequence sent a telegram making a suggestion on the same lines as that contained in your minute.

The Commander-in-Chief has accepted these suggestions and has sent a special Officer to see General Freyberg. The actual text of the special messages have been sent to the Commanders-in-Chief, Middle East.[17]

In the Prime Minister's own handwriting is written '*put by WSC*'.

It is clear that the Prime Minister wanted Freyberg to be given a free hand to defeat the impending German assault on Crete. There was, however, one major difficulty in allowing him to take the military measures required. It would also have been necessary to suspend, temporarily, the fundamental rule that commanders were forbidden to take action on information that was derived *solely* from ULTRA.

How this rule was applied in practice can be illustrated by an event a few weeks before the battle of Crete. On 27 March Admiral Cunningham learnt from ULTRA that the Italian Fleet was at sea off Cape Matapan. According to the rules he was not allowed to take any offensive naval action on this information alone. But there was nothing in the standing orders to prevent air reconnaissance, so he despatched a flying boat to the spot and confirmed that the Italian ships were indeed there.[18] He was then free to launch the British Fleet and attack the Italians. Again, in the Humphreys Report is the statement: 'Security restrictions on the use to which the Intelligence obtained was put operationally were rigid, so that, unless there was corroboration from other sources, no specific operational ACTION was taken on any specific piece of 'U' intelligence.'[8]

Professor Sir Harry Hinsley, the historian of British Intelligence and author of *British Intelligence in the Second World War*, has confirmed how these rules were applied in 1941:

[280]

The rules were being constantly kept under review and they were always aimed at avoiding any action by commanders on the basis of information derived solely from ULTRA. My feeling is that the rules were if anything even more rigorous in the spring and summer of 1941, when ULTRA on any scale was a very recent acquisition, than they became later, when more resources were available in the way of air reconnaissance and prisoners of war which could provide cover for the ULTRA evidence.[19]

We have no means of knowing about the discussions and heart-searchings that took place in London between Churchill and Sir Stewart Menzies, who controlled ULTRA intelligence, before the fateful decision was taken over the use to which the ULTRA information could be put in Crete. Menzies had originally agreed that ULTRA could go to the British C-in-C Greece (General Wilson), because Wilson commanded an army headquarters, but Menzies made it a cardinal rule that the intelligence should not go to any lower formation such as a corps, division or brigade headquarters, on the grounds that these were liable to be overrun by the enemy. When it came to giving the full ULTRA information to the GOC Crete, Menzies balked and his biographer states that he was prepared to resign if it was insisted on by the Prime Minister.[6] According to the biography, however, a compromise was agreed whereby an officer was to be sent to Freyberg's headquarters to show him the full texts of the latest intercepts, without revealing their source. What Menzies clearly did not realise was that Wavell had already fully briefed Freyberg about ULTRA on 30 April. What Churchill, for his part, may not have realised, or had forgotten, was that ULTRA had the built-in safeguard that information derived solely from that source could not be used by commanders in the field *unless* this was specifically authorised. Martin Gilbert hints that no such authorisation was given, when he comments in *Finest Hour*: 'This bold plan was presumably judged far too dangerous: had the Germans learnt that Britain was decrypting the Enigma messages, the single most important British advantage of the war would have been irretrievably lost.'[16]

Nevertheless the relevant instructions from London to send an officer from Cairo to Crete with the updated ULTRA information arrived at GHQ Middle East early on 11 May. It was immediately decided to send the acting Director of Operations, Brigadier Eric Dorman-Smith, to Crete that same day. Dorman-Smith flew to Maleme airfield on the afternoon of 11 May in a Blenheim of 30 Squadron[20] and stayed the night of 11–12 May with Freyberg at Headquarters CREFORCE. Dorman-Smith attended a conference at 0900 hours on 12 May which Freyberg had with his heads of services, and flew back to Cairo that afternoon, leaving from Maleme at 1400 hours. This visit is recorded in Freyberg's engagement diary,[21] and in the Dorman-Smith papers.[22] Dorman-Smith (who was privy to ULTRA) brought with him three important items of information – a personal letter from Wavell to Freyberg, an updating of the latest ULTRA intelligence, and word-of-mouth orders from the Commander-in-Chief.

General Headquarters Middle East, Cairo

Personal and Confidential

8.5.41

My dear Bernard

Dorman-Smith who brings this can explain all about equipment and other plans. What I would like from you if you have time is a note on personalities, which I can't very well discuss with him verbally. How are you getting on with

Heywood
Weston
Brunskill
Chappell
Salisbury-Jones

are they all pulling their weight and do you want any changes?

We are sending you all we can and hope it will reach you safely and in time.

The air problem is the difficult one and I don't quite know the answer. Dorman-Smith will discuss it with you.

This Iraq business is giving me a lot of trouble and I don't like it.

No sign of Barbara yet, have you any word of her? Is Paul in Crete or in Egypt?

Good luck to you, you inspire great confidence.

Yours
Archie Wavell.

Be very careful of SECURITY, Crete is certain to have many enemy agents. Especially keep all knowledge of OL to yourself.[23]

OL, of course, stood for Orange Leonard – the codeword used in the Middle East in 1941 to identify ULTRA.

The updated ULTRA intelligence that Dorman-Smith brought was incorporated into an Appreciation that was issued next day by the BGS, to all commanders down to battalion level. As will be seen, the document was ordered to be burnt as soon as it had been read. As far as is known, Freyberg's personal copy is the only one to have survived:

MOST SECRET   ZF/GSI/16

Appreciation – German plan for attack on Crete

1   The following appreciation of possible German plan for attack on
    CRETE, is based on previous German air attacks, and on Intelligence
    reports of German resources in the BALKANS.
2   The first objective will almost certainly be the three aerodromes,
    HERAKLION, RETIMO and MALEME, the possession of which is
    an essential preliminary for the landing of troop carrying aircraft.
3   The second objective will be the seizure of SUDA BAY and HERAK-
    LION ports to enable ships to land further troops and heavy equipment
    required for the complete occupation of the Island.
4   The following is the probable sequence of events:

    a) *D – 2 and D – 1.* Heavy air attacks on RAF and troops, especially
        AA guns.
    b) *D 1 day.* Fighters and medium bombers low flying attacks on
        aerodrome perimeters to neutralise defences, to be followed
        almost immediately by parachutists.
    c) The first sortie of parachutists at each aerodrome will number
        about 500 in five coys, of 100 each, dropped from 30–40 JU 52.
        Height of jump will be about 300 ft. Parachutists will be landed all
        round the perimeter of the aerodromes and up to 1,500 yards from
        the perimeter. Coys will be formed up ready for action within
        12–15 minutes of jumping. They will have LMGs, MMGs, and
        mortars, and will probably make extensive use of smoke.
    d) Within half an hour of the dropping of parachutists, the first batch
        of airborne inf. will arrive. They will have heavier weapons. It is
        expected that this operation will be carried out irrespective of the
        success or failure of the parachutists. An estimate of 5,000 troops
        from 350 aircraft may be landed in the first sortie.
    e) The next step will be the landing of dive-bombers, fighter and
        recce aircraft closely followed by aerodrome staffs, fuel and AA
        weapons.
    f) the JU 52s used to drop parachutists will probably return with
        another 1,500 men which will be dropped at various key points
        to prepare the way for the capture of HERAKLION and SUDA
        BAY ports, and to cause disorganisation and confusion.
    g) *D 2.* Having seized and provisioned aerodromes, this day will be
        devoted to securing with the help of further air bomb troops, the
        ports of HERAKLION and SUDA BAY. Dive-bombers will
        operate in close support of ground troops.
        D 3 and subsequently
    h) Ships will commence to arrive on this day, and the complete
        occupation of the Island will follow as quickly as possible.

[283]

5   From the above appreciation it will be noted that the entire plan is based on the capture of the aerodromes. If the aerodromes hold out, as they will, the whole plan will fail.

6   It is to be stressed to all troops defending aerodromes that the only danger is from the preliminary low flying air attack. Provided men are properly dug-in, and where possible concealed, they have nothing to fear. It is important, however, that not only the men, but also their weapons must be protected during the preliminary air attack.

7   It is to be further noted, that up to the present, the aerodromes have NOT been bombed, nor have the ports been mined. The obvious deduction is that the Germans hope to use both themselves in the near future.

8   Although this appreciation has not mentioned sea landings on beaches, the possibility of these attacks must not be overlooked; but they will be of secondary importance to those from the air.

9   WHEN READ, THIS PAPER WILL BE DESTROYED BY FIRE.

GS1   K. L. STEWART
Force HQ   Brigadier
12 May 1941   General Staff[24]

Paragraph 5, it will be noted, recognised that the whole German plan was dependent on the capture of the aerodromes by their airborne forces, and according to sub-paragraph 4(h) seaborne troops were not due to start arriving until three days after the air landings had taken place. This information was in Freyberg's possession nine days before the attack began on 20 May.

The postscript to Wavell's letter confirms that Freyberg had been briefed by the C-in-C about ULTRA and it also shows that Freyberg was allowed to tell no one else in Crete of its existence. Dorman-Smith had brought with him one other item of crucial importance, namely an oral order from Wavell that in spite of the latest ULTRA information there could be no relaxation of the rule that action could not be taken on intelligence derived solely from ULTRA. In consequence Wavell told Freyberg that there was no question of allowing any redeployment at Maleme to deal with the assault that was about to be launched solely from the air.

In his paper, Group Captain Humphreys made it clear that ULTRA was rigidly controlled from London in the early days of its use in the Mediterranean. After Russia and America came into the war, and ULTRA was no longer quite so vital as it had been when Britain stood alone, the rules governing its employment were occasionally relaxed slightly. Thus in 1942 Commanders-in-Chief in the Middle East were permitted to attack Rommel's supply convoys to North Africa, even though the only information concerning their whereabouts came from ULTRA. However, on every occasion the authority to do so came from Broadway in London. In 1941 no such latitude was given.

When the Prime Minister decided on 10 May 1941 that Freyberg was to be given the German plans for the attack on Crete, as we have seen, he specified that '. . . no one should be informed but the General who would give his orders to his subordinates without explaining his full reasons'.[16] This obviously meant that Freyberg was to be given a free hand in making the best plan he could for the defence of the island. There was no point in making such special arrangements unless the Commander in Crete was allowed to act on this information.

But before Wavell, as the overall Commander-in-Chief, could authorise Freyberg to take the necessary measures, he had to be given specific orders from the ULTRA authorities in London that the standing instructions governing its use were to be temporarily suspended. In other words, that Freyberg could be given permission to alter his dispositions in the Maleme area, even though his only reason for doing so was the information provided by the ULTRA intelligence.

No orders were sent by the ULTRA authorities in London to the Commander-in-Chief in Cairo that the ULTRA Standing Instructions could be relaxed in Crete. In the absence of any such permission therefore, Wavell had no option but to continue to enforce these rules. That Churchill was unaware of this can be seen from his minute to the Chiefs of Staff on 14 June 1941 complaining about Wavell's and Freyberg's 'slowness in acting upon the precise intelligence with which they were furnished'.[25] The Prime Minister remained permanently under a misapprehension about Wavell's conduct: in the Diaries of Hugh Dalton there is the following entry for 3 August 1944 'The PM . . . speaks ill of Wavell. "He was a bad General. He let us down atrociously at Crete."'[26]

My father told me in 1962 that he instructed Dorman-Smith to warn Wavell that if this rule continued to be enforced it would lead to the loss of Crete, since the latest ULTRA information indicated that his forces were in the wrong positions from which to counter the greatly increased German airborne assault against the airfields. He had, of course, already warned his subordinates in his Appreciation what to expect, but to enable them to react more effectively he would have needed to cross that security-hazardous – indeed security-forbidden – line between warning and redeployment. It was an agonising dilemma.

In view of the date of the German attack, then expected on 17 May, Wavell sent Freyberg by special messenger a written reply next day, 13 May (burnt after being read), explaining that the rule could not be relaxed because, in my father's words to me, Wavell had written, 'the authorities in England would prefer to lose Crete rather than risk jeopardising ULTRA'. My father also told me that as soon as he had read Wavell's letter he knew for certain that Crete would be lost.

It was undoubtedly true that Menzies and the ULTRA authorities in England would have preferred to lose Crete rather than take any risks over the security of ULTRA. Had they thought otherwise they would have authorised Wavell on this occasion to disregard the 'no action' rule. They did not do so.

Freyberg remained under one misapprehension for the rest of his life. He had thought (as he told me) that, when Wavell referred to 'the authorities in England' preferring to lose Crete 'rather than risk jeopardising ULTRA' he was alluding to the Prime Minister himself. Wavell was unlikely to have known of the Churchill–Menzies clash, or that the Prime Minister intended that Freyberg should be given a free hand. Had Freyberg been aware of the disagreement in London he would certainly have drawn Churchill's attention to the facts of the situation in Crete, which he could easily have done over the direct ULTRA Crete–UK link. Even if such a signal had made no difference to the continued application of the ULTRA rule, it would at least have prevented the misunderstanding over Crete between Freyberg and Churchill that persisted after the battle was over, and for their lifetimes.

Although there is no direct evidence to show that the ULTRA prohibition on redeployment in Crete was applied right up to the moment of the German attack on 20 May, there are three separate indicators which suffice to establish it as fact. The first is that between early May and 20 May there was no change of any significance in the beach deployment of the battalions and brigades of the New Zealand Division in the Maleme–Canea sector. This was in spite of the fact that Freyberg knew, since 11 May, that there were to be no initial attacks from the sea, and that the entire German assault was to be concentrated on airborne landings directed at capturing the Cretan airfields.

Freyberg always took a great deal of notice of what his intelligence told him, as several of his intelligence officers have confirmed to me. For him to disregard the specific and detailed information that was especially presented to him nine days before the German attacks, can only be due to other reasons.

The second indicator was a sudden cancellation of the planned move of 1 Greek Regiment on 13 May. It had been decided to move 1 Greek Regiment from Kisamos Kastelli to the area next to Maleme airfield on the western side of the Tavronitis river, in order to try and reduce the vulnerability of this open flank. All the main authorities on the battle of

Crete refer with incomprehension to the fact that this move was suddenly cancelled without explanation. For example, the Salisbury-Jones Court of Inquiry later stated: 'The Commander of 5 NZ Brigade was very anxious about the area west of Maleme aerodrome and it was unfortunate that his intention to place a Greek battalion there had not been put into effect before the attack came.'[2]

The official NZ history, *Crete* by Dan Davin, refers to this incident in these words:

> There was one other weakness in the defensive system that gave Puttick great concern at this time. This was the ground west of Maleme Airfield. The troops of 5 Brigade were not numerous enough to extend far enough west to cover this ground effectively, and yet it was clear that it might prove a dangerous assembly area. The obvious force to use for holding it was 1 Greek Regiment; for where it was already placed, at Kisamos Kastelli, it was too isolated to be effective, while Kastelli itself might be assumed too remote from the main objectives to be important.[27]

I. McD. G. Stewart also mentions this in his book, *The Struggle for Crete*:

> At Kisamos Kastelli, fifteen miles further west, was stationed the 1st Greek Regiment, over a thousand strong . . . Freyberg had suggested that these Greeks should be moved into the area west of the Tavronitis . . .
> The move was cancelled . . . Certainly it is difficult to understand how objections could have been judged adequate to justify the neglect of a tactical area from which there might develop a deadly threat to the defence of the runway.[13]

The cancellation of this move was made the day after Brigadier Dorman-Smith left Headquarters CREFORCE, that is, when Freyberg had been told that he could not make any operational use of the information disclosed by the ULTRA intelligence. One theory put forward after the war to explain the cancellation of the move of 1 Greek Regiment was that there were insufficient picks and shovels available to enable the unit to dig in when it got to its new position. This suggestion did not gain any credence from the Crete historians, even before there was any knowledge of ULTRA involvement.

The third indicator that the ULTRA rules had been enforced in Crete is to be found in the statements Freyberg made to the Salisbury-Jones Court of Inquiry.[2] What came out very clearly from the inquiry was that there had been an alternative plan for deployment at Maleme to the one that had been in force at the start of the German invasion. This alternative had been designed to counter a purely airborne assault on Maleme airfield, but it was never implemented. This fact was not known to any of the historians who wrote accounts and histories of the battle of Crete between 1941 and 1972, for reasons that are explained in Chapter 19.

When I was investigating this aspect of the Crete evidence in 1982–3 I discussed it in detail with the late Major-General Sir Guy Salisbury-Jones, and we also had considerable correspondence about the Second Court of Inquiry on Crete. He wrote the following account about the conclusions of the First Inquiry:

> Immediately on my arrival in Egypt I was made Chairman of a Committee set up to report on the operations in Crete and to deduce the lessons therefrom. This was an Inter Services Committee formed by General Wavell and the other Cs-in-C. We sat for the whole of June 1941 examining evidence from many different sources, and we produced our Report in Cairo on the 2nd July '41. I then left Egypt to become Head of our Military Mission in South Africa.
>
> I discussed our proposed Report with General Freyberg on several occasions. None of our Committee knew about ULTRA, and of course Freyberg never mentioned its existence. However, during this period I was aware that he was unhappy that he had not been able to carry out the measures he had considered necessary to defend Crete properly, although he never said exactly why.
>
> We devised the form of words that was included in the Report under Summary of Lessons, after discussing it with Freyberg. This indicated that there had been two alternative forms of deployment. But by not spelling out the problems connected with adopting the second alternative, we avoided controversy and possible security objections. In the final paragraph we went so far as to hint that the result of the battle might have been different had the second alternative been adopted rather than the first.
>
> These are the exact facts as I remember them.[28]

There is one other significant fact about the pre-attack phase in Crete. On 16 May 2 Battalion Leicestershire Regiment was landed by the Royal Navy at Heraklion. Three days later 1 Battalion Argyll and Sutherland Highlanders was likewise put ashore at Timbaki on the south-east coast.[27] The arrival of these two battalions brought the strength of 14 British Infantry Brigade in the eastern sector of Crete up to six major units. The presence of these reinforcements was enough to prevent the Germans from capturing either the port of Heraklion or its airfield, which was the largest on the island and the only one with concrete runways. Although the German parachutists managed to establish themselves in the undefended approaches and outskirts of

Heraklion, they failed to capture, unlike at Maleme, any of their main objectives which would have enabled them to airland significant reinforcements during the all-important first few days.

A paradoxical situation thus existed. In the western half of the island Freyberg's freedom of manoeuvre to conduct the defence according to the tactical requirements was severely curtailed on instructions issued in Cairo, in compliance with the rules that governed the use to which information derived solely from ULTRA could be put; and this was not countermanded from London. But in the eastern half these constraints did not seem to apply. The reason for this was that the order for the reinforcement of Heraklion had been given at the beginning of May, when it was already apparent that the size of its garrisons was too small to be capable of withstanding even the limited scale of attack then envisaged, and before ULTRA had disclosed the increased size of the German airborne assault. The time taken to prepare and transport the two battalions from Egypt to Crete overlapped with the subsequent ULTRA information, but because the orders to move had already been issued they went ahead as planned.

But did it really make much sense to allow the substantial and unconcealable external reinforcement at Heraklion to go ahead, while forbidding the much less noticeable, but far more important internal redeployments that were required to rectify the tactical situation in the western sector? It is difficult to avoid the conclusion that such an arbitrary and contradictory distinction in the application of the ULTRA rules achieved the worst of both worlds. It hamstrung Freyberg, preventing him from putting into force the tactical measures that were needed to strengthen the defences around Maleme, while at the same time the last-minute reinforcement of Crete by two battalions might have led the Germans to suspect that this had been the result of the British deciphering their plan of attack.

One final point about these reinforcements. The eastern sector of Crete was not as important for the British defence of the island as the western sector. It would have been possible for a time to have lived with a situation in which the Germans held Heraklion and the eastern part of Crete, provided the main bases at Retimo, Suda Bay, Canea and Maleme remained in British hands. Whether that would have been a tolerable long-term posture in the face of continuing German air supremacy is another matter, but at least it would not have precipitated the immediate crisis that followed from the loss of Maleme airfield. The ultimate paradox lay in reinforcing the less important eastern sector while still leaving wide open the undefended vital ground to the west of the Tavronitis river.

18

Crete – The Battle

A number of special factors and constraints directly affected the battle in Crete in May 1941. The first was the composition of the garrison, made up of the original 14 British Infantry Brigade, units of the MNBDO, and the troops who had been evacuated from Greece. The 14 Infantry Brigade was composed of three Regular battalions – 2 Black Watch, 2 York and Lancaster Regiment, and 1 Welsh Regiment – and they were the only infantry troops on the island with the normal complement of equipment, weapons and vehicles.

By the time of the battle 1 Welsh Regiment had been detached to Force Reserve at Canea, while the remainder of the brigade was at Heraklion, where they were reinforced by 2/4 Australian Battalion and 7 Medium Regiment in an infantry role. They were joined at the last moment by 2 Leicestershire Regiment, and 1 Argyll and Sutherland Highlanders. The MNBDO, composed mainly of static anti-aircraft and coastal defence regiments in the process of arriving at Suda Bay from Haifa, was only half complete when the battle started.

The largest part of the Crete force consisted of the 30,000 troops evacuated from Greece. Altogether some 42,000 troops were taken off Greece by the navy, of which some 12,000, mostly fighting troops, had been sent direct to Egypt, including the whole of 6 NZ Brigade. Many of those who were landed on Crete while it was being used as a staging post were Lines of Communication troops of several different nationalities, whose units had in many cases disintegrated during the evacuation, leaving demoralised soldiers without officers, arms or equipment. There were several thousand of them, described by

Churchill as *bouches inutiles*, for they still had to be fed on the dwindling rations, and could not be evacuated to Egypt because of lack of shipping. In addition there were 15,000 Italian prisoners of war, mostly captured by the Greeks in Albania, who had to be guarded as well as fed.

The fighting troops from Greece comprised 4 and 5 New Zealand Brigades, numbering some 7,700 men, who were concentrated in the Maleme–Canea area, and 19 Australian Infantry Brigade, deployed in the Suda Bay–Georgioupolis sector.[1] There were also two strong Australian infantry battalions stationed east of Retimo and the battalion at Heraklion, bringing the total number of Australian troops to 6,500.[1] The New Zealand and Australian troops had managed to bring their bren guns, rifles and other small arms from Greece, but not much else. They had no heavy weapons, and hardly any signals equipment or transport. Their field guns, tanks and vehicles had all been destroyed before leaving Greece. Counting in also 5000–6000 British troops Freyberg had, therefore, had some 20,000 fighting troops on Crete organised into eighteen battalions, plus several improvised field batteries and static anti-aircraft and coastal defence units, who were dispersed between the four sectors of the island – Maleme–Canea, Suda Bay–Georgioupolis, Retimo, and Heraklion – a distance of over 100 miles from one end to the other. There were also scattered throughout the island some 13,000 poorly armed Greek troops and Cretan gendarmerie.[1]

There was no proper organisation in Crete to cope with the administrative needs of a force which had suddenly increased from one brigade of a few thousand strong to a ration strength of about 35,000.[1] The only practicable way was to pool the scarce resources of equipment and transport that were already on Crete, and during the days before the battle this took up most of the time of the harassed administrative staff. Before the enemy bombing campaign began in earnest they had made a start in replenishing equipment and stores, but there was little modern British equipment left in Egypt. For example, the artillery that was despatched consisted mainly of captured Italian guns, often without proper sights, fuses or even ammunition. The few tanks which reached Crete were likewise nearly all found to be mechanically defective. The number of vehicles on the island consisted of 150 15-cwt trucks and 117 other load carriers; and seven ambulances.

The lack of medical resources was indeed a serious problem. There was only one RAMC hospital and one properly equipped field ambulance on Crete. When Freyberg visited the tented 7 General Hospital at Suda Point he was horrified to find it already full[2a], with 500–600 wounded from Greece being looked after by British and New Zealand nursing sisters. He cabled for them to be evacuated at once:

> The hospital ship *Aba* came and lay off Canea, and loaded up 561 casualties and the entire female nursing staff. The nurses were furious at being sent away when they knew that a battle was pending, but I could not agree to women being mixed up in the shambles that was about to commence. I visited the ship on 15 May, and she started back at daylight. She was bombed and machine-gunned twice during her return journey, and had nine casualties, one killed.[3]

After this the Commander-in-Chief Mediterranean Fleet considered it too dangerous to allow any hospital ship to proceed to Crete. He and Freyberg arranged to send as many walking wounded as possible on the returning cruisers and destroyers, but these ships could not cope with the hundreds of stretcher cases.

The supply position too was becoming more and more critical, as were shipping losses. Three ships were hit in the Suda Bay harbour on 16 May and were wrecked or crippled, and an ammunition ship blew up on 17 May. By 19 May there were thirteen damaged ships in the harbour. In addition three big ships, the *Rawnsley*, *Dalesman* and *Logician*, were each a total loss at sea. As Freyberg wrote to the New Zealand Minister of Defence:

> It was a period of acute anxiety and frustration. We saw our ships were being destroyed, and realised that although large quantities of war stores and guns were being shipped from Alexandria, only a small proportion was getting through to Crete for distribution and use. It was an agonising experience to see these vital ships getting so close to land, and then being sunk.[3]

Freyberg and his staff carried on grimly, seeing ship after ship being sunk or set on fire, and eventually reached the stage where they could only handle ships which could be got in by dark and leave again before daylight. As Freyberg describes it:

> This required very fast vessels, ships of thirty knots, which meant nothing but destroyers and cruisers. These would arrive at Suda pier at 11.30 p.m. and had to move away again on the stroke of 3 a.m. With this plan, even if two ships arrived each night, which was an optimistic forecast, we could unload only approximately 100 tons per night. This arrangement continued sometimes for successive nights, and then for days on end no ships at all would arrive. Meanwhile, we were making serious inroads into our small reserves of food and consumable stores.[3]

Freyberg's relationship with the Greeks and Cretans was harmonious in spite of the horrendous problems they were experiencing. The considerable number of Greek soldiers in Crete were all placed under his command. He had a high opinion of them both as individuals and as soldiers, but unfortunately they were of only limited military value. Had there been time, and had modern arms been available, the material was there to form an excellent Greek division, which could have made a substantial contribution to the defence of the island. As it was, the Germans struck before the Greeks could be properly organised.

When Freyberg took over no one had mentioned to him that present in Canea were the King of Greece, several royal princesses and the Greek Prime Minister and his complete Cabinet, as well as their families. Their safety was to take up a disproportionate amount of his time. He was able to persuade them that they should all be evacuated to Egypt forthwith and the princesses and some families duly departed, but when the King was about to follow a signal arrived from the Foreign Office. This said that it would create a bad impression abroad if the King was seen to leave the last of unoccupied Greek soil. A long and at times acrimonious exchange of signals followed, in which Freyberg pointed out the dangers facing the King and his entourage. The Foreign Office believed the risks were being exaggerated. Even after the German invasion had begun Freyberg received a signal saying 'Do not consider present situation necessitates evacuation either of Royal Party or Ambassador's Party'. He replied tersely on 21 May:

> *This place is not fit abode for important people.* The King and Prime Minister were yesterday nearly taken prisoner when fifty parachute troops landed within 500 yards of their house in the hills. I learned of their escape only from a faint signal picked up last night. With their New Zealand escort, which I can ill afford to be without, the party will be on the south coast as per my [earlier] telegram. They are now out of touch with us even by wireless.
>
> The Minister left at 3 o'clock this morning to join the Royal Party if possible. They had been bombed all day, and the consul had actually to be dug out.[4]

Eventually the royal party and the ambassador's were escorted over the mountains to the village of Ag Rummelli on the south coast, where they were picked up by HMS *Decoy* and HMS *Hero* at 0400 hours on 23 May. On 25 May Sir Michael Palairet sent a message reporting their safe arrival in Egypt.[4]

Another special factor in the Crete campaign was the weakness of the Royal Air Force. What happened in Crete in 1941 might have happened in England in 1940, but for the Battle of Britain and the skill and gallantry of the pilots of Fighter Command. In the Middle East there were neither the planes nor the pilots available to protect the skies over the battlefields and the Mediterranean, and it was to take a further year before the RAF could be built up to achieve parity with the enemy air forces, and even longer to gain air superiority. In short the supremacy of the German Luftwaffe was the root cause of the Crete disaster.

There had been a small RAF and Fleet Air Arm contingent in Crete during the winter of 1940–1 – so small that its senior officer was a Flight Lieutenant. Wing Commander Beamish was appointed Air Officer Commanding on 17 April 1941, when RAF activities increased because of the Greek campaign. The RAF presence then included: 30 Squadron, with eight Blenheim Is (bombers); 33 and 80 Squadrons with six Hurricanes between them; 112 Squadron with six Gladiators, and 203 Squadron with nine Blenheim IVs. These, together with some fighters of the Fleet Air Arm, were operating from Heraklion and Maleme in support of the navy during the evacuation of British troops from Greece.[4]

Freyberg tells how from an air point of view they were not left in peace for very long to contemplate their many problems. 'Enemy aircraft made a thorough reconnaissance of our airfields, which they photographed, and then set about bombing and shooting up our aircraft both in the air and on the ground.' He went on:

> Even as early as 16 May all mention of air support in the actual battle for Crete had ceased. During this preliminary period our small fighter force had fought against great odds, and had shot down 23 enemy fighters and damaged many others. The enemy's great numerical superiority, however, resulted in the gradual elimination of our aircraft despite the arrival of ten new Hurricanes. By 19 May our Air Force was reduced to four Hurricanes and three Gladiators, the Blenheims having been sent away earlier as they were of no value against fighters.[3]

Everybody on Crete felt concern for the hopeless plight in which the remainder of the RAF was now placed. Freyberg told his Air Officer Commanding that it would be too painful to see the last aircraft and their gallant young pilots shot down on the first morning of the battle:

> On my recommendation the remaining four Hurricanes and three Gladiators were sent to one of the airfields in Egypt on 19 May. Situated as we were, no one could have wished to weaken the defences even by so slight an amount. I was criticised later for sending these few aircraft away, but I am certain that the decision was the right one.[3]

The Mediterranean Fleet, however, had shown itself to be more than a match for the Italian Navy and Regia Aeronautica (Italian Air Force) during the first nine months of war, and after the very successful offensive actions at Taranto in November 1940 and at Cape Matapan at the end of March 1941, the Italians avoided further encounters with His Majesty's ships. But the arrival in strength in the Mediterranean of the Luftwaffe started to tip the balance of power towards the Axis. Ever since the decision was taken to go to Greece at the beginning of March the Royal Navy had been under intense pressure. The task of transporting the 62,000 troops to Greece, and then evacuating them, had led to the loss of several ships including the 8-inch gun cruiser *York*, mined in Suda Bay, and the destroyers *Diamond* and *Wryneck*, sunk on 27 April by dive-bombers while attempting to rescue 500 soldiers (nearly all of whom perished) from the troopship *Slamat*, which had likewise been sunk after embarking these troops from the beaches at Nauplia in the Peloponnese.

There was considerable discussion over what role the Fleet should play in helping to defend Crete. Freyberg himself had grave doubts about the ability of the navy to survive dive-bombing, and had told Wavell so at the conference in Canea on 30 April:

> My lack of confidence was only in the power of the Royal Navy to withstand the air attack, and was not due to any lack of trust in their determination to see the battle of Crete through at any cost . . . In the battle for Crete, the Fleet would be required to defend the Island against seaborne invasion from Greece, for which fighter cover would be essential during daylight, especially whenever the Fleet or part of it was north of the Island. Instead of having this vital air protection, the British Fleet found itself pitted against an unopposed German air force of great strength, and forced to meet a concentrated offensive from aerial bombing such as no surface navy had ever been called upon to endure.[3]

As Freyberg feared, the Royal Navy was to pay a grievous price for operating in Cretan waters. On 21 May the destroyer *Juno* was sunk, and on the following day the cruisers *Gloucester* and *Fiji* and the destroyer *Greyhound*. On 23 May the destroyers *Kelly* and *Kashmir* sank after being dive-bombed. Five days later the destroyers *Imperial* and *Hereward* were sunk, and on 1 June the cruiser *Calcutta*. In addition no fewer than 21 other warships were damaged, some seriously, including the battleships *Warspite*, *Valiant* and *Barham*, the aircraft carrier *Formidable* and the cruisers *Ajax*, *Orion*, *Dido* and *Perth*, as well as many destroyers.

On 23 May Admiral Cunningham sent his appreciation of the situation to the Chiefs of Staff in London:

> ... the scale of air attack now made it no longer possible for the Navy to operate in the Aegean or in the vicinity of Crete by day. We could not guarantee to prevent seaborne landings without suffering losses which, added to those already sustained, would seriously prejudice the command of the Eastern Mediterranean.[5]

Something of the strain endured by the navy during the battle of Crete is conveyed by Admiral Cunningham describing events on 21–2 May:

> Meanwhile at Alexandria, as the afternoon gave way to evening, and evening to night, our hearts were heavy as the news of our casualties kept coming in. In my office ashore close to the war room where the positions of all our ships were plotted hour by hour on the large scale chart, I came to dread every ring on the telephone, every knock on the door, and the arrival of each fresh signal. In something less than twelve hours of fighting against the unhampered Luftwaffe we had lost so much, two cruisers and a destroyer sunk, with two battleships and two cruisers damaged.[5]

Cunningham called the battle of Crete 'a disastrous period in our naval history – a period of great tension and anxiety such as I have never experienced before or since'.[5] Freyberg was later to write:

> My admiration for the courage and efficiency of the Royal Navy, and its support during the campaigns in Greece and Crete knows no bounds. Of the three Services, the Navy made fewest mistakes either in the initial stages or in the battles themselves ... There were weak links in our chain of defence of Crete, but the Navy was not one of them.[4]

The story of the battle for Crete has often been told. For the first time in history an attack was launched entirely from the air from bases hundreds of miles away to seize enemy territory by force of arms. As such, it presented a spectacle that aroused the fascination of the world at the time, and has gripped the imagination of historians and writers ever since.

The account that follows focuses on what happened to Freyberg himself during those twelve momentous days 20–31 May, and highlights his personal experiences and reactions largely through his own narratives of the battle and his dispatches.

On 20 May everyone was up before daylight. The Luftwaffe arrived in strength at 8 a.m. as expected, and began bombing and machine-gunning with great intensity the Canea and Maleme sectors, particularly the latter with its important airfield. From his HQ above Canea Freyberg could see the battlefields with the naked eye; and he knew that the first object of the assault was to silence the AA batteries and prevent any use of the roads between Suda Bay, Canea and Maleme:

> The bombing attacks continued with great intensity and then, without any appreciable lull, the glider and parachute landings commenced three-quarters of an hour later. The big-scale 'Blitz' was an awe-inspiring spectacle. It had been heralded by the Canea air raid warnings sounding for the last time. There was no need for it afterwards as for the rest of the Battle for Crete the sky was full of enemy aircraft from daylight to dark.
>
> I stood out on the hill with other members of my staff enthralled by the magnitude of the operation. While we were still watching the bombers, we suddenly became aware of a strange sensation, a pulsation, a kind of throbbing in the air – it was pronounced in the moments of comparative quiet when the bombing eased. Looking out to sea with my field glasses, I picked out hundreds of enemy transport planes, tier upon tier coming towards us. Here were the troop carriers with the loads we were expecting. They came in quickly and with precision. We watched them circle counterclockwise over Maleme Aerodrome and then, when they were only two hundred feet above the ground, white specks suddenly appeared beneath them mixed with other colours as clouds of parachutists floated slowly to earth. The white parachutes carried men and the coloured arms and equipment. At approximately the same time, fifty gliders were landing west of the Maleme Aerodrome in the river bed.[3]

The main German attacks on Crete on 20 May 1941 were carried out in two phases. In the early morning some 6,000 parachute and glider troops were dropped in the western sector of the island. About half descended on Maleme airfield and the area to the west of the Tavronitis river, while a whole parachute regiment landed south of Galatas, in Prison Valley, and detachments were scattered elsewhere west of Canea and on the Akrotiri peninsula.

The troop carriers returned in mid-afternoon and deposited a further 3,500 parachutists on the central and eastern sectors, divided between Heraklion and Retimo. After spasmodic air activity during the morning, 200 troop carriers appeared at Heraklion at 1600 hours, arriving in two waves from the north and north-west. Four battalions of

[297]

parachutists were dropped west and south of the town and around the aerodrome. All the parachutists who landed within the battalion-defended perimeters were quickly disposed of, but some who dropped outside managed to get into the outskirts of the town and fighting continued through the night.

At Retimo, which was also assaulted from the air at 1600 hours, the landings were made all around the airstrip and especially on the high ground to the south-east. Most of the parachutists were mopped up next day, except for a strong position held on the high ground east of Retimo itself.

Freyberg was critical of the German plan of attack:

General Student, Commanding the Enemy Forces . . . had contempt for British troops and based his plan on the assumption that they would not fight and would, in fact, 'bolt'. This wrong assumption led the Germans to drop their Parachute Force on top of our garrisons – the only possible way to ensure that the bulk of them would be killed at the outset. (In point of fact, most of them were shot through the head.)

General Student could have captured Crete in the first days with very little loss had he appreciated the situation properly. He could have landed his airborne force well to the west of Maleme Airfield, instead of on top of our garrisons, they could have built up a strong attacking front without much interference on 20 May. Such artillery as we had was not mobile, and there were, therefore, no guns which could give close support to our Infantry attacks. The enemy also could have landed his tanks (which were brought in on 27 May at Kisamos Kastelli) at any time during daylight from 23 May onwards without interference from our fleet, because the British Naval forces could not face, by daylight, the overwhelming strength of the German Air Force.[4]

Soon after the start of the battle Freyberg's demeanour, as described by one eye-witness, was one of 'extraordinary calm and composure':

In particular I can see him at his Headquarters near Canea, quite unmoved, although all that he could see in front of him was an endless stream of enemy aircraft landing on Maleme aerodrome with reinforcements. All that he could see behind him was a continuous stream of smoke ascending from our ships which had been bombed in Suda Bay.[6]

Freyberg fought the first part of the battle from the CREFORCE headquarters, which was situated above Canea at the base of the Akrotiri Peninsula. Robin Bell recalls that it 'was in part of an old quarry, and we lived in little stone huts which reminded me of the Mappin Terraces of the zoo'.[4]

[298]

The enemy scored initial successes in the Maleme–Canea sector by occupying the undefended hospital, 6 Field Ambulance and an anti-aircraft battery, but these were recaptured by counter-attack later in the day. Fierce fighting took place wherever the parachutists landed in areas occupied by New Zealand troops. The first task of the defenders after the parachute landings was to clear up the unit areas; but communications between Force HQ and formations were very bad as a result of the bombing, and the cutting of telephone lines by the parachutists. As a result the 'fog of war' descended over the battlefield, but towards evening a more accurate picture emerged. On Maleme Aerodrome 22 Battalion had suffered heavy casualties in a particularly bitter battle. Some 1,800 parachutists – one regiment, together with stores and equipment – were actually landed on top of them. In addition two battalions landed by glider to the west. This was a very dangerous development because it meant, already on the first day, that the Germans had found the Achilles heel of the defence – the flat open ground to the west of the Tavronitis river, which was undefended because Freyberg had not been allowed to change his deployment.

At midnight on 20 May Freyberg cabled to Wavell:

> Today has been a hard one. We have been hard pressed. So far I think we hold Maleme, Heraklion and Retimo Aerodromes and the two harbours. Margin by which we hold them is a bare one and it would be wrong of me to paint optimistic picture. Fighting has been very heavy and we have killed large numbers of Germans. Communications are most difficult. Scale of air attacks upon troops has been severe. Everybody here realises vital issue and we will fight it out.[3]

But unbeknown to Freyberg a fateful decision had already been taken.

Colonel L. W. Andrew, VC, commander of 22 NZ Battalion, had had a particularly difficult time at Maleme. He was still holding Hill 107, which overlooked the airfield, but his troops had been heavily dive-bombed all day, and on the ground his battalion was being attacked from three sides. Communications with his companies had been cut, and he knew nothing of what was happening to them. As Andrew (whose VC was won in the First World War) himself expressed it: 'The Somme, Messines and Passchendaele were mere picnics compared to the bombardment on this morning.' Furthermore there had been no response to his appeals for help from HQ 5 NZ Brigade.

A later account of the battle not only describes the conditions but the inevitable consequences: 'Visibility was obliterated by the clouds of dust and smoke that resulted, and under cover of this effective screen a number of gliders, estimated at between 50 and 100, achieved a measure of surprise.' The area chosen for the glider landings was bombed until the last moment. Then the barrage shifted for a sufficient distance to give a clearing for the gliders, but at the same time leaving the impression that the area was still being bombed. Heads were thus effectively kept down and by the time the parachutists came down glider-troops were organised and able to give covering fire. The glider attack in fact enabled the enemy to build up a firm base in the river bed, from which they could launch their attacks:

> Meanwhile, wave after wave of troop carriers flew over the area disgorging their contents with clock-like precision . . . The main areas selected for descent were the river bed to the west of the aerodrome, east of Maleme village, in the valley between Galatas and the prison, and near the hospital. Some troop-carriers also crash-landed on the beach.
>
> In all cases where parachute troops landed in the vicinity of troops they were immediately dealt with. Indeed, the defenders have little to fear in such cases, but the few who survived caused confusion. Even the odd sniper made intercommunication difficult, for, when the telephone lines had been cut, orders could only be sent by runner, and in some cases it became necessary to use officers in carriers. The enemy was quick to exploit his footing in the river bed and throughout the day exerted heavy pressure against the western portion of the sector held by 22 Battalion. The difficulties of the Battalion were increased by the infiltration southwards of troops who had crash-landed on the beach near Maleme village. In spite of gallant counter-attacks assisted by 'I' tanks*, the situation became grave, and at nightfall the Commanding Officer considered his Battalion in danger of being cut off.[7]

Andrew took a decision on that evening, therefore, which proved to be the turning-point in the battle for Crete. At 10 p.m. he gave the order for his remaining troops to retreat to the east, to withdraw to the line occuped by 23 and 21 Battalions, and to abandon Maleme aerodrome. 22 Battalion were off Maleme aerodrome by nightfall on 20 May and the following morning had re-formed about half a mile away. Because of the bad communications in the forward area Freyberg and his headquarters did not receive news of this development until the morning of 21 May when it was too late – and too light – to move troops to the crucial area of the aerodrome. By that time the Maleme sector, the gun positions, and the forward troops in particular, were being subjected to a heavy dive-bombing attack, which had started before nine o'clock. With this and further parachute landings the enemy was

---

* British Infantry Support Tank, known as 'Matilda' or 'I' tank.

clearly determined to wrest control of the aerodrome from the New Zealanders. Worse still, Freyberg reported:

> We had made a miscalculation. It had not been considered feasible for aircraft to land in the river-bed west of the Maleme aerodrome. But during the morning, troop carriers began to crash-land there, and also on the beaches west of the aerodrome. These landings continued under constant shell fire from nine field guns and despite this observed artillery fire, which destroyed numbers of the enemy planes, it went on regardless of loss of machines or life. The enemy were prepared to lose any number of planes, for those which were wrecked in landing or from fire were simply dragged off the landing ground to make room for more to land where these had been destroyed. It was unfortunate that the artillery we had at Maleme were captured Italian guns, and not our own 25-pounder field guns, which would have been much more efficient for the task. From time to time our artillery had to stop firing because of the pounding it received from the air during the daylight.[3]

A very different situation existed in the eastern sector of Crete. The area being defended, which included the town of Heraklion, its harbour and the airfield, was smaller and more compact than the western sector. This made the task easier, as did the size of the force available for the defence.

The strongly reinforced British and Australian garrison at Heraklion, together with three battalions of Greeks, totalled over 8,000 troops. These units were well dug in, mutually supporting and adequately equipped, with a number of Bofors anti-aircraft guns, and eight medium and light tanks, although most of the latter were not mechanically reliable.

The enemy dropped 2,000 parachutists from the German 1 Parachute Regiment, in the vicinity of Heraklion during the afternoon of 20 May. The 2 Battalion landed near the airfield close to the Black Watch and the Australians, with, as Stewart's *The Struggle for Crete* records, 'most of them falling into a murderous fire from all arms'. Within an hour 12 officers and 300 men had been killed, and another 8 and 100 respectively wounded.[2b]

Other German units faced similar experiences and casualties:

> In two ways the scene had been unlike that at Maleme. The parachutists had nowhere fallen abruptly in large numbers, and few had been unopposed. There was no group to correspond with those 1,000 men who had arrived unseen among the sand dunes west of the Tavronitis.
>
> By nightfall the main defences had been cleared. Small parties of the

[301]

enemy still lurked near the docks and in the town, but the airfield was secure and no attempt to crash-land had been made by the troop-carriers. Already a thousand enemy dead had been counted within the perimeter.[2b]

By the evening of 22 May 1,450 of the 2,000 parachutists who had been dropped near Heraklion were dead, at a cost of only 50 British and Australian casualties. The 600 Germans that remained were scattered throughout the area, disorganised, demoralised, without supplies and for the time being posing little threat to the well-established garrison.[2c]

The situation at Retimo was different again. Here Colonel Campbell commanded an ad hoc force of two Australian battalions and two Greek battalions, whose main purpose was the defence of the landing strip to the east of Retimo. At about 4 p.m. on 20 May the Germans' parachute attack began, and by nightfall they had almost succeeded in capturing the high ground overlooking the airstrip. But a spirited counter-attack next day wrested the initiative from the Germans.

> The two Australian battalions, aided by the Greeks, completed the destruction of the enemy along that part of the coastal strip that faced the defence positions, together with the parachutists who had collected in the south. Those that remained were now split into two groups. A mile and a half east of the airfield a few score fugitives had succeeded in making their escape from Hill A to find shelter in the olive oil factory at Stavromenos, and in the west a somewhat larger collection was held confined between the 2/11 [Battalion] and the Cretan Police, who had ejected them from the outskirts of Retimo.[2d]

The commander of the German 1 Parachute Regiment, Colonel Sturm, had been taken prisoner along with the whole of his staff; and he was still carrying his written orders, which revealed to Campbell that 1,500 men had taken part in the attack. Stewart's account goes on:

> By nightfall his [Campbell's] Australians were back in their original lines, most of them equipped with enemy weapons. Several hundreds of the Germans were dead, and hundreds more taken prisoner or wounded. No reinforcement had reached them, and it was plain that the Luftwaffe was having great difficulty in identifying its own men on the ground. Some captured Australians had been rescued, and the two tanks salvaged. That evening Campbell sent a message to Freyberg saying that the situation was well in hand.[2d]

As early as the second day of the battle, however, the consequences of the original maldeployment, as Freyberg had warned Wavell, were becoming apparent. The absence of any New Zealand or Greek troops west of the Tavronitis river had given the Germans a secure and inviolable assembly area from which to launch attacks on Maleme airfield. Now they started to bring reinforcements in through the airfield by a continuous shuttle service of transport aircraft. Another consequence of the maldeployment was that there was no counter-attack force positioned close to Maleme airfield which could be launched at immediate notice to regain control.

By the afternoon of 21 May, when Freyberg realised the position was critical, he held a conference of his commanders to consider how to regain control of the landing grounds on and around Maleme airfield. A dawn attack on 22 May was planned to be carried out by 20 and 28 NZ Battalions. At the same time he decided to bring forward one Australian battalion from Georgioupolis as reinforcement.

As the CREFORCE commander, however, Freyberg had to be tactful with the senior officers of the New Zealand Division. His relations at this time with Brigadier Puttick, in command of the NZ Division, and Brigadier Hargest were delicate. Among the senior New Zealand officers there had been some disappointment that none of their number had been chosen to command 2 NZEF – a natural reaction, but it meant that Freyberg had to take special care to let them make their own decisions. An added complication was that he was unable to explain to them the nature of the ULTRA intelligence or its reliability. However neither Puttick nor Hargest reacted with the speed and determination that the situation required. As it was, Freyberg wrote:

> Our counter-attack to recapture the airfield with only two battalions of Infantry went in too late, and was badly planned. The weak Artillery support did not help, and the Air Force never turned up.* The men did get a footing on the airfield, but after dawn on 22 May, the Luftwaffe came over and our forward troops were again heavily bombed, and were driven back. No movement in the forward area was possible by daylight, and by the night of 22/23 the Germans had reinforced Maleme from Greece, and it was too late.[4]

Not only had the counter-attacks been badly planned and executed, but they were mounted very slowly when time was of the essence, and nobody at brigade or divisional level appeared to have the necessary 'grip' on the situation. By contrast Campbell, at Retimo, showed what

---

*RAF bombers were supposed to come from Egypt.

could be achieved by a really resourceful and determined commander when he was confronted with a situation just as daunting as the one at Maleme.

Freyberg never sought to blame any of his subordinate commanders for the early capture of Maleme airfield by the Germans. Despite the initial deployment, which he had not been allowed to change, Freyberg always accepted full responsibility for the loss of the aerodrome. However a number of New Zealanders felt afterwards that the battle of Crete was one of the very few occasions in the war when Freyberg did not receive as much support from some of those under him as he should have done. It was not that Puttick or Hargest or Andrew lacked gallantry: both Puttick and Hargest had bars to their DSOs while Andrew had a DSO in addition to his VC. Nevertheless it was thought that Andrew should not have withdrawn 22 Battalion from Maleme without orders or without giving warning of what he intended to do. If he had stayed put on the airfield during the night of 20–1 May it would have delayed the start of the enemy landing and take-off flights next day for a number of vital hours, and that might have made the difference between failure and success.

Freyberg wrote later that, on reflection, he felt he ought to have gone up and led the counter-attack in person on the second night:

> Being wise after the event, I feel that the only possible chance and a small one at that, would have been to take every available unit and counter-attack on the night of 21 May. It might have succeeded in recapturing the aerodrome, but I feel that without artillery or heavy equipment we could not have broken the enemy defences. The enemy were in depth at Maleme. Besides, most of our troops were already heavily engaged in their existing positions with the enemy. However, thanks to communications, which were bad, we did not know the full story at Maleme until many hours later.[4]

Freyberg blamed himself for many of the things that went wrong. The concern he had felt when he visited New Zealand in 1939–40, that some of the senior officers were too old, was borne out on the battlefield:

> I should also have realised that some of my Commanders, men from World War I, were too old for the hand-to-hand fighting, and were not likely to stand up to the strain of an all-out battle of the nature that eventually developed round the Maleme Airfield and its eastern approaches. I should have replaced the old age group with younger men who, as a rule, although less experienced as fighting soldiers, stood up much better to the physical and mental strain of a long and bitter series of battles.[4]

In the later stages of the war the average age of the brigade, battalion and company commanders of the New Zealand Division was ten to fifteen years younger than those who held these appointments in 1940–1; and many of the military errors that were made in Crete did not occur later when officers at all levels were more experienced.

Freyberg was particularly anxious that the men of 22 Battalion should not be blamed for the loss of Maleme. He wrote afterwards:

> I saw the battle and have a great deal of fighting experience. I should not criticise them. I feel they were given an impossible task. They were blown out of their defences by heavy bombs. Without air defence, without AA defence, no troops could withstand such concentrated and incessant low level bombing and machine gunning.[4]

On the night of 21–2 May there was another distraction. An enemy convoy of ships and caiques was intercepted by the Royal Navy 18 miles north of Canea, and the whole seaborne force was sunk or dispersed. The flashes and sounds of this operation could be clearly seen and heard by Freyberg and his staff from their headquarters, to their relief and satisfaction.

In the four days from 20 to 23 May the Germans brought some 17,530 parachute and airlanding troops into Crete. The breakdown is instructive:

May	Maleme Galatas Suda Bay	Retimo	Heraklion	Total
20	6,030	1,500	2,000	9,530
21	1,880	Nil	120	2,000
22	1,950	Nil	Nil	1,950
23	3,650	Nil	400	4,050
	13,510	1,500	2,520	17,530[4]

Nearly all the troops who arrived on 20 May were parachutists, with a further 500 parachuting the next day to the west of the Tavronitis river, and 120 into Heraklion. This accounted for over 10,000 of the 12,000 German parachute troops available. Owing to disorganisation on the Greek airfields some 600 parachutists, who had been earmarked to fly to Heraklion, were left behind to follow on the sea lift, some of which was sunk *en route*.[2e] This meant that there were then only a small number of parachutists in reserve, and that the German commander, Student, had few forces left under his hand to influence future operations. Also, because of the nature of parachute and glider troops landing inside defended battalion perimeters, a high proportion of them were killed at once, often before they reached the ground. Of more than 7,000 Germans killed on Crete, about half were parachutists, of which the majority were killed on the first day. In addition an unquantifiable number were wounded. Such a rate of casualties could not have been sustained in a conventional battle.

Hardly any German reinforcements reached Retimo or Heraklion on Days 2, 3 and 4; and because the parachutists failed to capture the airfields there, none of the airlanding troops of their two Mountain Divisons could be flown in. Nearly all the troops brought into Maleme after the first two days were from 5 Mountain Division. On 22 May the total number of soldiers airlanded was nearly 2,000, while on 23 May it was 3,650. Thereafter the floodgates were opened, as the rest of the division arrived by non-stop shuttle. The enemy was thus able to bring fresh troops to the scene of battle more quickly and in greater numbers than the defence could do. Moreover, as the New Zealand troops were subjected to almost non-stop dive-bombing, movement during daylight became almost impossible, a restriction that did not apply to the Germans. After several days of such treatment the defending troops, not unnaturally, became increasingly exhausted and dispirited.

What might have happened if Freyberg had been allowed to do what he wanted, namely to put a New Zealand battalion on the other side of Maleme airfield, to position 1 Greek Regiment west of the Tavronitis river and move two battalions of 5 NZ Brigade close to the eastern perimeter of the aerodrome in a counter-attack role? It seems unlikely, in those circumstances, that the Germans would have been able to capture Maleme airfield on the night of 20–1 May, and it is debatable whether they would have been able to do so for some time, or even at all. This was always Freyberg's view. Although 6,000 parachute troops were dropped in the western sector of Crete on the first day, the size of the Assault Regiment (or Ramcke's Group as it was called) which landed around Maleme aerodrome did not exceed 3,000 men. Since many of them became casualties, and many more would have if New Zealand and Greek troops had been in position west of the Tavronitis river, it was probably not beyond the capability of 5 NZ Brigade to deal with them.

What the Germans would have done, had they failed to capture Maleme airfield by 22 May, especially with the sinking of their seaborne force, is anybody's guess. The enemy had large forces in reserve in Greece, complete command of the air, and increasing control of the sea between Greece and Crete. So long as the Germans were determined to persevere whatever their temporary setbacks, they had it within their power to capture Crete whatever the defence did, as Freyberg well knew. But had the defensive arrangement been laid out differently, the original German airborne assault might not have succeeded.

After the failure of the counter-attack on Maleme on the night of 21–2 May, another was planned for the following night; but before it could be mounted the Germans, attacking from the direction of Prison Valley towards the village of Galatas, threatened to drive a wedge between 4 and 5 NZ Brigades on the coast. From that moment on the Germans had the initiative, and the New Zealand and British troops were increasingly on the defensive. It is clear from CREFORCE headquarters signals after 23 May that the situation was recognised as being out of control. That day a message was received from the Prime Minister: 'The whole world watches your splendid battle on which great things turn.' Freyberg's later comment on this was: 'However splendid the battle might appear in the eyes of the world, I knew the situation was deteriorating fast in the Maleme sector.'[4]

Not only was the tactical situation critical, but so was the supply position. The replenishment of vital food and ammuniton by fast warships to Suda Bay had ceased at the beginning of the German invasion, and only meagre stocks were left in the depots. In particular food was beginning to run out, so that the ration had to be reduced. On 24 and 25 May the Germans brought in further fresh troops, and started to attack from the Maleme area towards Canea and Suda Bay. By this time the New Zealand and British troops had suffered nearly 2,000 killed and wounded.

On 24 May Freyberg had to move his headquarters from above Canea to a new location near Suda Bay. As he wrote his report to Wavell on the night of Sunday, 25 May, after watching a savage air attack on the forward troops by dive-bombers, heavy bombers and twin-engined fighters with machine-guns and cannon guns, Freyberg knew that the last hopes of retrieving the situation were disappearing:

Today has been one of great anxiety to me here. The enemy carried out one small attack last night and this afternoon he attacked with little success. This evening at 1700 hours bombers and ground strafers came over and bombed our forward troops and then his ground troops launched an attack. It is still in progress and I am awaiting news.

[307]

Later. I have heard from Puttick that the line has gone and we are trying to stabilise. I don't know if they will be able to. I am apprehensive. I will send messages as I can later.[3]

Freyberg had another caller that night. One of the British officers attached to the Greek Army came to report that the Greeks were about to break. The following morning, 26 May, at about 9 a.m. 'I called a conference with the Naval Officer in Charge and the AOC. As a result I sent the following cable to Middle East':

I regret to have to report that in my opinion the limit of endurance has been reached by troops under my command here at Suda Bay. No matter what decision is taken by the Commanders-in-Chief, from a military point of view our position here is hopeless. A small, ill-equipped and immobile force such as ours cannot stand up against the concentrated bombing that we have been faced with during the last seven days. I feel I should tell you that from an administrative point of view the difficulties of extricating this force in full are now insuperable. Provided a decision is reached at once a certain proportion of the force might be embarked. Once this sector has been reduced the reduction of Retimo and Heraklion by the same methods will only be a matter of time. The troops we have, with the exception of the Welsh Regiment and the Commandos, are past any offensive action.

If you decide in view of whole Middle East position that hours help we will carry on. I would have to consider how this would be best achieved. Suda Bay may be under fire within twenty-four hours. Further casualties have been heavy, and we have lost the majority of our immobile guns.[3]

Freyberg later wrote:

The question of deciding when the campaign was lost was taken out of our hands by the enemy on the battlefield. When the Suda Bay front collapsed, the end had come. The decision to evacuate should have been taken on 26 May, because at midnight on 25 there were four fresh and vital factors at work against us.

1. The Royal Navy, who had already on 22 May told the Commanders in Chief and Chiefs of Staff that they could no longer protect Crete against a seaborne landing, now told them that they could not use the northern ports for maintenance or for reinforcement of Crete. As the road from Sphakia [on the south coast] was impassable to any traffic except lightly equipped men, there was no method of maintenance for the Island or its Garrison.

2. The German forces were pressing irresistibly towards our meagre food and ammunition dumps. We clearly would lose these supplies of food and ammunition in a matter of hours. We would then be foodless.

Freyberg, appointed commander of 2NZ Expeditionary Force in November 1939, flew to New Zealand to consult with the government and *(above)* senior army officers: from left to right, Lt-Col. S. H. Crump; Lt-Col. T. J. King; Lt-Col. K. L. Stewart; Major-General B. C. Freyberg; Major-General J. E. Duigan; Colonel E. Puttick; Colonel R. Miles; Lt-Col. W. G. Stevens. *(Below)* The arrival at Suez, on 12 February 1940, of 1st Echelon, 2NZEF. Anthony Eden, Dominions Secretary, is making a speech of welcome listened to by Sir Miles Lampson *(right)*, British Ambassador to Egypt, and General Sir Archibald Wavell, C-in-C, Middle East *(left*, next to Freyberg)

The New Zealand base camp
at Maadi, six miles from Cairo,
during a parade for King
Abdullah in 1940. *(Right)* The
2nd New Zealand Echelon was
diverted to England where they
were visited by King George VI
at Mytchett, near Aldershot, on
6 July 1940. Introducing
Freyberg to the King is Major-
General D. G. Johnson, VC

Greece, 1941. *(Above)* Freyberg and Colonel Keith Stewart reconnoitre the Aliakmon Line. *(Below)* General Sir Henry Maitland Wilson, C-in-C, with Freyberg and the Australian Forces commander, Lieutenant-General Sir Thomas Blamey *(left)*

Crete, 1941. Freyberg was
appointed C-in-C,
CREFORCE at the instigation
of Winston Churchill. *(Above)* A
famous embattled picture of
Freyberg at the start of the
fighting; *(left and below)* the
evacuation from Crete had to be
made from the southern coast,
near Sphakia, where Freyberg's
temporary headquarters were in
a cave

(Above left) Freyberg, back in Egypt, grim and determined; *(above right)* in 1941-2 the C-in-C, Middle East was General Sir Claude Auchinleck, with whose tactics Freyberg disagreed. *(Below)* Photograph of Freyberg outside his tent in the Western Desert, November 1941, on which Peter McIntyre, New Zealand official war artist, based a later painting

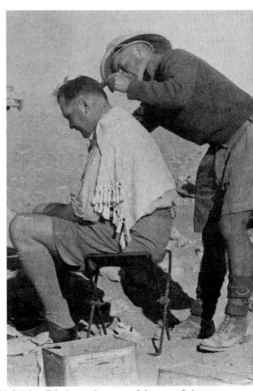

(Above left) Freyberg's ADC Jack Griffiths *(left)* and *(right)*, his PA through most of the war, John White, who kept the New Zealand Division Diary. *(Above right)* A quick haircut by a sheep-shearer; *(below)* Freyberg at Baggush with his son Paul, serving with the Long Range Desert Group, October 1941

(Above) Freyberg out on reconnaissance and (below) conducting an 'O' (or Orders) Group. His method of conducting these, which differed somewhat from English style, is described on page 411

(Above) Freyberg wounded at
the desperate, rearguard battle
at Minqar Qaim, June 1942.
(Right) Two months later he
is with Churchill, who was in
Egypt at the time of changes in
the Middle East Command

3. The gallant Greek forces had no ammunition left, and had informed me that they would be forced to lay down their arms.

4. The British front at Canea was reported to have collapsed.[1]

Although Freyberg sent his report stating that the position in Crete was hopeless at 9.30 a.m. on 26 May, he did not receive orders to evacuate the island until the afternoon of 27 May. Evidently Wavell had great difficulty in persuading London to accept that the end of the battle was imminent.

When the instructions to evacuate eventually arrived, Freyberg's first action was to try and get an order through to the troops at Retimo to withdraw to the south coast. Owing to a series of mishaps, including the shooting down of a message-carrying plane before it could deliver instructions, the garrison at Retimo never received the order to withdraw, and Colonel Campbell and his gallant Australians were eventually all taken prisoner, after a magnificent defence. The force at Heraklion was evacuated by the navy from the port, but in the process of being taken off by sea the troops suffered heavier losses than had been inflicted on them during the land battles.

Since the navy could no longer operate in the waters to the north of Crete, the only possible way to evacuate the force from the western sector was to use the anchorages on the south coast of the island. The only one that was accessible from the Canea and Suda Bay areas was at the small village of Sphakia, which was linked to the north by a rough track 'which required a 40-mile march' over the White Mountains. Even then the navy would only be able to embark troops under cover of darkness for two or three hours in the middle of the night, since its ships had to be out of range of German dive-bombers both before last light and after dawn the following morning.

Freyberg's account of his own journey across Crete (see map page 274) gives some idea of the 'nightmare' conditions when Force HQ left for Sphakia on the evening of 27 May:

The road from Suda Bay to Sphakia traversed steep mountains, and went through mountain passes to one of the most inhospitable coastlines imaginable. There were some units still sticking together and marching in order with their weapons, but in the main non-fighting troops in full flight – a disorganised rabble making its way doggedly and painfully to the south. There were thousands of unarmed troops including Cypriots and Palestinians. Without leadership, without any sort of discipline, it was impossible to expect anything else of troops who had not been trained as fighting soldiers. Someone said the words – 'withdrawal' and 'Sphakia' and all detached men in the Suda Bay area took a flying start in any transport they could steal.

[309]

This transport was later abandoned at the end of the road above Sphakia, where it remained thus revealing to the enemy our line of evacuation.

My driver chose this night to drop my car over the side of a bank just before we left, so Brigadier Stewart and I had to travel in a commandeered car which was already disintegrating owing to a bomb-torn radiator which would hold little or no water. After driving a few miles in the darkness the car would grind to a standstill, but it stayed the distance, being helped up hills by being pushed by the truck behind us.

Never shall I forget the disorganisation and almost complete lack of control of the masses on the move as we made our way slowly through that endless stream of trudging men. By first light we had reached a treeless plain where there were carriers in an anti-parachute role. At dawn we were still short of the Plain of Askifou with the coast not in sight. As I knew that the RAF had a wireless set at Sphakia which ought to be in touch with Middle East, I decided to go straight through to the coast. In ordinary times the scene as we came down to the Plain of Askifou, with its little villages and cultivated farms surrounded by high hills, would have excited our admiration. We pushed on to the end of the road at the top of what can only be described as a precipice. We climbed down to a rocky valley where Colonel Frowen, my Chief Gunner, RA, had already set up headquarters in a cave.[3]

Meanwhile the medical situation in the Maleme–Suda Bay area was becoming critical. Colonel Selwyn Kenrick, Assistant Director of Medical Services (ADMS), later described how all medical units including hospitals had been right in the battle area at one time or another, and what the problems were in moving the wounded to Sphakia for evacuation; for 4 and 5 (NZ) Field Ambulances had been called upon to treat 2,274 wounded during the campaign:

When evacuation was ordered, it was apparent that the Navy would be unable to embark stretcher cases even if these could have been transferred to the south coast. Approximately 700 stretcher cases had to be left in the Maleme–Suda Bay Sectors alone. In every case, Medical Officers and medical personnel remained voluntarily with parties of wounded, and in no case was it necessary for the ADMS to detail men for this duty. That over 1,500 walking wounded were able to embark was due to: The amazing fortitude displayed by the wounded men themselves, the courage and devotion to duty displayed by All Ranks of the Medical Services, and the co-operation of the Navy.[8]

Freyberg later commented:

Some of the country was too rough and mountainous for the movement of men to be possible by night, and the route was being heavily bombed by day. It was indeed an amazing achievement for this column of slow-moving

[310]

wounded men, led by a series of medical orderlies and doctors, many of the men with serious wounds, with improvised and unclean dressings, and many of them even having lost arms, to have made the journey to the ships of the Royal Navy and safety.[4]

During the night of 27–8 May 5 New Zealand Infantry Brigade and 19 Australian Brigade withdrew to the vicinity of Stilos, while the two newly arrived commandos under Brigadier Laycock were left as a rearguard occupying a defensive position near the cemetery east of Suda. The 5 NZ Brigade in its position at Stilos was attacked during the day by the enemy force which had been seen moving across country from Malaxa. This attack was from a new direction, due to the collapse of the Greek Army. A series of rearguard actions on the Suda Bay to Sphakia road by New Zealand, Australian and British forces bought time to evacuate many thousands of troops from Sphakia, which the Royal Navy did at night between 28 and 31 May.

Freyberg spent his final three days in the cave at Sphakia in touch with Egypt by wireless, trying to arrange for the maximum numbers to be evacuated. His main concern was to ensure that the combatant troops who had been foremost in the fighting should have top priority in the evacuation, but inevitably in the prevailing chaos there were some noteworthy units and individuals who were left behind.

Freyberg sent his personal staff with all his secret papers back to Egypt by the naval lift on the night of 28–9 May. Before they left Freyberg dictated a note to John White for him to give to Wavell on arrival. It sums up the situation as well as anything written later:

We have had a pretty tough time. The troops were not beaten by ordinary conditions, but by the great aerial concentration against us. The 'I' tank was suggested as a counter but they would not last more than a few minutes in the open being dive-bombed. The bombing is what has beaten us, the strafing having turned us out of position after position. Bombs of a heavy calibre from heights of about 200 feet simply blew our people out of the ground.

The actual parachute troops we annihilated and ordinary troops we knocked out in successful counter-attacks, only to be bombed out of our positions in the course of a few hours. We were bombed off Maleme aerodrome; we counter-attacked and retook it but the strafing of dive-bombers and extremely accurate heavy bombing and machine gunning drove us from it. Troops are retiring to Sphakia through a covering position. It is extremely doubtful whether that will hold if the enemy concentrates his full air attack against it. That is why I have asked that the embarkation should be accelerated. The troops are frightfully battered and if we get away with 25 per cent of our original strength we shall be very lucky . . .

We may have enemy troops, based on Suda, here at Sphakia in the next 24 hours. We were handicapped by lack of transport, communications and lack of staff. Everybody tried hard in most difficult circumstances. I am sorry Crete could not be held. It was certainly not the fault of the troops.[4]

Freyberg's assessment that they would be lucky to extricate 25 per cent of the original garrison fortunately proved over-pessimistic. In the event some 17,500 British and dominion troops were evacuated from Crete to Egypt, of which 13,000 (including the 1,500 walking wounded) left from Sphakia; and the total represented just over half the troops on Crete at the beginning of the battle. Some 1,751 men had been killed, and 12,254 were made prisoners of war, of whom 700 were stretcher cases.[4]

In view of what had happened in Greece when Freyberg remained with his troops to the very end, the faithful John White told Wavell that a direct order for Freyberg to leave would be essential if he was to be evacuated. Accordingly on 29 May Wavell signalled a Personal Order to him: 'You will return to Egypt first opportunity.' Freyberg did not comply with the instruction that night because there was some doubt about the size of the lift, and therefore of the numbers and priority of those who could be got away. In the event he waited until the night of 30–31 May before leaving. The last page of his report reads:

That night the Sunderlands [flying boats] arrived and also two destroyers, and 1,400 men were taken off.

General Weston took over from me to command for the last twenty-four hours.* My feelings can be imagined better than described. I was handing over a difficult situation with the enemy through in one place almost to the beaches from which we were to make our last attempt to get away the remnants of the fighting force that still held out, tired, hungry and thirsty on the heights above.

At about 3.30 on the morning of Saturday, 31 May – Day 12 in the Battle for Crete – I arrived back in Alexandria.[3]

*Weston was evacuated by the final flying boat to reach Crete on the night of 31 May–1 June.

19

Crete – The Inquiry and the Aftermath

The repercussions of the disasters in Greece and Crete were bound to be traumatic and their aftermath remained with Freyberg for the rest of his life. From the beginning he had realised that the expedition to Greece had all the makings of a disaster, but given its background and setting there was nothing he could have done to change the outcome of the venture. This feeling became even more pronounced when he assumed command in Crete, but there was no way he could have avoided the poisoned chalice because over half of the New Zealand Division was on the island. Nor could it be evacuated before the German attack.

Freyberg never doubted that he would be severely criticised for the loss of the island. He knew that he would be a sitting target for disappointed politicians and armchair critics for all that had gone wrong in Crete; and so it turned out from the moment on the morning of 31 May 1941 when he went from Alexandria straight to Cairo and reported to General Wavell:

> It was a difficult meeting, and we were both overwrought. I presented a dishevelled appearance as I had not had my clothes off for several days, and had no clothes except what I stood up in. I spent the night in the Commander-in-Chief's house. While there I learned from Lady Wavell how distraught the C-in-C had been. She said that in earlier battles he could always sleep, but that during the last few nights of the Crete campaign he had walked the floor and was unable to rest.[1]

[313]

Churchill insisted that a Court of Inquiry be held at once. Accordingly instructions were issued at the beginning of June to set up an Inter-Services Committee consisting of members of the three services under the chairmanship of Brigadier A. G. Salisbury-Jones; the naval member was Commander C. Wauchope, the air member Wing Commander E. C. Hudleston (in 1964 C-in-C Allied Air Forces Central Europe), and the army member Lieutenant-Colonel Bernard Fergusson (later Lord Ballantrae). The latter attended the first meeting only and was not replaced. This committee spent the whole of June examining a large number of witnesses, and held several interviews with Freyberg himself, who commented:

> After the Balkan adventure, the CIGS and General Wavell came in for adverse criticism. The Air Officer Commanding-in-Chief was changed, while, on a much lower plane, I, who had borne the brunt of the fighting in Greece and Crete, was having a Court of Inquiry assembled to investigate my conduct. I faced up to this criticism with spirit.[1]

The committee issued its Report at the beginning of July 1941.[2] It was a remarkable document, and its clarity and incisiveness owed much to the character of Salisbury-Jones himself.

Guy Salisbury-Jones was a Coldstreamer usually known by his nickname 'Guido'. As a very young officer he had fought in the First World War, been twice wounded and awarded two Military Crosses. Between the wars he had attended the Ecole Spéciale Militaire, St Cyr, and, as he was bilingual in French, a number of appropriate staff appointments followed, including that of liaison officer to General Weygand in Syria at the beginning of the Second World War. He commanded his regiment's 3 Battalion in Palestine in 1938–9, and was in Greece and Crete with the Greek forces in 1940–1. Later, in 1944–5, he was at HQ Supreme Allied Forces in France, and immediately after the war was appointed Head of the Military Mission to France as a major-general. After Salisbury-Jones retired he became Marshal of the Diplomatic Corps, and started a vineyard at his home at Hambledon in Hampshire. He also wrote a biography of Marshal de Lattre de Tassigny, *So Full a Glory*.

As might be expected from such a career, Guido Salisbury-Jones had a mind of his own, and was not afraid to speak it. Nor was he in the least overawed by officers of higher military rank. His integrity forbade compromises, whether to spare the feelings of those he judged had failed the national interest, or whether his own future might be affected by criticism of those senior to himself. The other members of his committee were of a similar calibre.

The Inter-Services Committee Report consisted of seventy pages of closely written typescript with detailed descriptions of every aspect of the Crete story. It was divided into four main sections, together with opening and closing remarks, and a number of appendixes. Throughout the committee was highly critical of the roles played by GHQ Middle East, and by HQ RAF Middle East, especially their failure to think about future requirements. By April 1941, when it became obvious that Greece was about to be overrun, the shortcomings of the defences in Crete were already past remedying. The committee's view on this was summed up in its 'Concluding Remarks':

(a) The major lesson of this campaign was that to defend with a relatively small force an island as large as Crete, lying under permanent domination of enemy fighter aircraft and out of range of our own, was impossible.

(b) Up to the last neither the Chiefs of Staff nor the C-in-C, ME, gave due weight to the vulnerability of the Navy and Merchant Ships.

(c) The Royal Air Force cannot claim to have shown greater foresight or energy than the Army.

(d) The planning of operations such as the defence of Crete demands exceptional foresight and the most intimate co-operation between the Services if due weight is to be given to the many factors involved. The Committee are of the opinion that until the eleventh hour no Service gave due weight to the preponderating factor affecting this problem, which was the overwhelming superiority of the German Air Force.[2]

In contrast the committee treated with sympathy and understanding the difficulties which faced Freyberg and the fighting troops, who, they considered, had done all that could be expected of them in an impossible situation. They had put up creditable resistance in the face of overwhelming odds, and had inflicted heavy losses on the Germans. The committee exonerated them from any blame for the disaster.

Because of the urgency with which the report was required in London, it was despatched, unread, by Wavell as soon as it was finished on 2 July 1941. It was given to Brigadier Laycock, who happened to be flying back to England. Laycock had been in charge of the Commandos in Crete, and was later Chief of Combined Operations. He subsequently told the story of his return to England in a letter to Salisbury-Jones, of which the first part reads as follows:

You may remember when you had finished writing your report it was decided that I should take it back to the War Office as I was to fly back in any case.

One usually had to wait days or even weeks for an air passage at that time but, most unexpectedly, I was suddenly told to leave a day earlier than anticipated.

Your report had only just come off the press and, when I went to collect it, Wavell hadn't had time to read it. He initialled a copy (which I was told to hand personally to the CIGS, Dill) with a covering note to say that he would comment on it as soon as he had studied it.

I asked Arthur Smith [Chief of Staff, Headquarters Middle East] if I could take a second copy back with me for my own boss, Roger Keyes (then Commodore, Combined Operations) since the Commandos had been involved and was told that there was no objection to this.

This second copy I read myself on the way home. As soon as I had finished it two things struck me: first that it was in every way an excellent report, but, secondly, that it was dynamite. You had given the ME HQ such a drubbing that they were bound to react violently – which they did.[3]

At the end of the first week of July 1941 Wavell left Cairo for India, where he had been appointed C-in-C, accompanied by Bernard Fergusson as his staff officer. Fergusson was present at the General's first reading of the Salisbury-Jones Report: 'Wavell did not see the finished product until we were in the aircraft flying from Cairo to Delhi after his supersession in July 1941, and he went through the roof. I had to send on his behalf from Baghdad a furious signal demanding its withdrawal.'[4]

Meanwhile Laycock, having been held up in Lagos, landed at Shannon instead of Poole Harbour and so reached England several days behind schedule:

When, at last, I arrived in London I dropped the second copy of the report on Roger Keyes at Richmond Terrace and went straight on to the War Office where I asked if I could see the CIGS. His Military Assistant (MA) told me that my chances of getting an interview with the CIGS were negligible. I said that I had a document for him and was immediately told to hand it over but this I refused to do on the grounds that I had been ordered by Wavell to hand it personally to Dill. The MA went in to see Dill who immediately sent for me and greeted me with, 'Come in – I have been waiting for you and want to see what you have brought me.' He explained that, during my time in transit, the wires between GHQ, ME, and the War Office had been practically white hot on account of the fervour with which the former demanded that the latter should completely disregard the report on Crete which Colonel Laycock was about to deliver.

I heard later from Roger Keyes that an officer was sent round to COHQ to demand his copy. It was the last he saw of it.

I myself went down that weekend to stay with Winston at Chequers and, upon being questioned, told him about your report and gave him the gist of it. He was extremely interested and said that he would send for it.[3]

The Salisbury-Jones Report caused consternation among the higher ranks of the staff in Cairo for two reasons: first the presumption by comparatively junior officers in criticising their superiors in an Official Report; second, a breach in the security of ULTRA which the committee had unknowingly committed. The report was as factually accurate as it was possible to be, because it was based on figures and information supplied by all the Middle East Departments concerned, but it was unacceptable to the military hierarchy because of the comments by the Court of Inquiry officers. The officers concerned were all 'high flyers' who, it was thought, should have 'known better' than to write as they did. What was even more unforgivable was that the committee had identified many of the Cairo staff's errors of judgment that had contributed to the Crete disaster, and had spelt them out unmercifully. There was therefore only one way to deal with the Salisbury-Jones Report, and that was to suppress it.

Fortunately for the military hierarchy there was an unanswerable reason for suppressing the report. One of its statements that had set alarm bells ringing in Baghdad, Cairo and London was in paragraph 6 of Part IV, which reads:

It is interesting to speculate as to whether the adoption of the second solution might have been more profitable. Maleme aerodrome might have remained intact, and the rapid reinforcement by airborne troops greatly delayed. It is even possible that the enemy might have been discouraged from continuing his attempts.[2]

This refers to the alternative deployment of concentrating entirely on the defence of Maleme airfield, and disregarding the beaches. Freyberg had told the Salisbury-Jones committee about this second plan, but he did not disclose why it had not been adopted for security reasons, as the committee members were not privy to ULTRA. Had the report been circulated in its original form, however, sooner rather than later questions would have been asked as to why the alternative deployment had not been implemented. Such a line of inquiry would have pointed straight at ULTRA; and to the fact that Freyberg had been given full details of the German plan of attack and was then prevented from acting on the information. It is hardly surprising, when they came to this part of the report, that Wavell should have 'gone through the roof' and that General Arthur Smith's signals to London caused the 'wires to become white hot'.

The GHQ Cairo file copy of the Salisbury-Jones Report was eventually lodged at the Public Record Office at Kew.[2] On the inside of its cover is annotated: 'Submitted by Brigadier Salisbury-Jones and later suppressed by GOC-in-C, MEF'; and it is further marked 'Closed until 1972'. Also in the Public Record Office is a file belonging to the Military Training Directorate of 1947 which reads: 'This report must have been *by the Second Inter-Services Committee presided over by Brigadier Erskine* [their underlining]. The Report by the first Committee was suppressed but we hold a copy.'[5]

Not much is known about the Second Court of Inquiry on Crete presided over by Brigadier Erskine, because it was held under conditions of strictest secrecy. Unlike the first inquiry, there does not appear to have been any written 'Terms of Reference', and neither Salisbury-Jones nor Freyberg knew of its existence at the time. Its sole purpose seems to have been to go through the original report, and to remove all those parts which might have compromised ULTRA, or were critical of the Middle East staffs. The second inquiry removed 29 paragraphs from the original report, including the all-important paragraphs 2–11 of Part IV (Summary of Lessons). What was then left was considered anodyne enough to be circulated as 'Lessons learnt from the Battle of Crete'.

There is a revealing indication of the attitude then prevailing in London in a comment the Director of Military Operations made to the CIGS in a minute forwarding Wavell's observations on Salisbury-Jones's Report, dated 26 September 1941, which reads:

> You will wish to see General Wavell's comments on the Inter-Services Committee Report on Operations in Crete. Copies of the Report have been given to Chief of Naval Staff and Chief of Air Staff only, and your copy has been only circulated within the Military Operations Directorate. This restricted circulation, you will remember, was necessary owing to the many injudicious and controversial remarks it contained.[6]

The Salisbury-Jones Report was eventually released to the Public Record Office in 1972 under the thirty-year rule. This fact is important, because the report's suppression removed from public knowledge for three decades the most detailed and authoritative official account of what happened in Crete – a factual record compiled within a month of the event from statements and cross-examination of dozens of eye-

[318]

witnesses who had participated in the battle. Also the main histories and articles about the battle of Crete were nearly all written several years after the war, by which time, inevitably, much of the detail of what had happened had become blurred. The authors of these accounts had mostly never heard of Salisbury-Jones, still less had they had any access to his report.

While Salisbury-Jones and his colleagues were conducting their Court of Inquiry in Cairo, in England at the beginning of June General Sir John Dill, the CIGS, asked Wavell to send a senior officer with experience of the fighting in Crete to the UK, to lecture to army audiences about how to counter German airborne troops. Freyberg was invited to nominate this officer, and he chose Brigadier L. M. Inglis, who had commanded 4 NZ Brigade near Canea. Inglis arrived in London at the beginning of the second week in June. As his evidence to Mr Churchill was later to cause a major row between Freyberg and Wavell it is important to establish just how his meeting with the Prime Minister came about. In the files of the Chiefs of Staff Secretariat there is a note from Colonel Ian Jacob to the Prime Minister's Private Secretary informing him of Inglis' arrival, and inquiring whether Mr Churchill wished to see him.[7]

Inglis was a member of the New Zealand Territorial Army, and in civilian life he was a lawyer. I. McD. G. Stewart, in *The Struggle for Crete*, comments on him as follows:

> As a soldier, there still clung to him something of the attitudes that he had learnt in his civilian profession as a lawyer. Highly intelligent, quick thinking and volatile in argument, he was also pugnacious and opinionated, adept at proving to his own satisfaction that any failure with which he might be associated could not relate to any inadequacy of his own. It is a skill that colleagues seldom find endearing.[8]

Brigadier Inglis duly went to 10 Downing Street for a talk with the Prime Minister on the evening of 13 June 1941. Next morning Churchill dictated a long minute to General Ismay, Chief Military Officer to the Minister of Defence, for transmission to the Chiefs of Staff. The opening paragraph, in full, says:

> Brigadier Inglis, with whom I had a long talk last night, gave a shocking account of the state of the troops in Crete before the battle. He stated that there were not above 10,000 men in the fighting units. None of the New Zealand battalions had been made up to strength or re-equipped after the Greek evacuation, except to a limited extent. Such transport and light tanks

as were available had to be fished up out of a sunken ship. There were no Mills grenades. The RASC, RAOC, and other troops, were quite un-armed, thoroughly disorganised, and represented *bouches inutiles*. Even the artillery and gunners had no personal arms. The only field guns available were Italian. The only well-equipped troops which reached the island were some British troops and Royal Marines, none of which took part in the battle until the retreat began.[9]

The minute continues by stating that Inglis' statements must be 'searchingly tested'. It went on to point out that they were in marked contrast with statements made before the battle by both Freyberg and Wavell, and that he, Churchill, did not feel 'that there was any real grip shown by Middle East HQ upon this operation of the defence of Crete'. Churchill further stated that the failure to remove the *bouches inutiles* from Crete was a great fault, and that the commanders' 'slowness in acting upon the precise intelligence with which they were furnished, and the general evidence of lack of drive and precision, filled me with disquiet about this Middle East Staff'. The minute goes on:

> I am far from reassured about the tactical conduct of the defence by General Freyberg, although full allowance must be made for the many deficiencies noted above. There appears to have been no counter-attack of any kind in the Western sector until more than 36 hours after the airborne descents had begun. There was no attempt to form a mobile reserve of the best troops, be it only a couple of battalions. There was no attempt to obstruct the Maleme Aerodrome, although General Freyberg knew he would have no air in the battle. The whole seems to have been of static defence of positions, instead of the rapid extirpation at all costs of the airborne landing parties.[9]

The Prime Minister ended by saying that there would have to be a detailed inquiry into the defence of Crete and all the facts would have to be established.

It is clear from this minute that the Prime Minister did not realise that Freyberg had been prevented from taking any remedial action to counter the German plan for the invasion. Also it is unlikely that Churchill appreciated that, before Wavell could have given Freyberg permission to change his dispositions at Maleme, he would have required special authorisation to suspend the ULTRA rule about not acting on information derived solely from ULTRA. Such a dispensation was never given.

The Chiefs of Staff replied to the Prime Minister through General Ismay on 17 June.[9] They agreed it was essential for the facts to be established not only for their own information, but also in justice to those officers 'whose arrangements of, and conduct of, the defence of the island have been the subject of criticism'. They noted that General Wavell had initiated a local enquiry in Egypt, and therefore recommended (in Paragraph 2) that a further inquiry 'should be entrusted to a Special Commission sent out to the Middle East from this country, under a Chairman who should not be a member of the fighting Services'. This produced an immediate response from the Prime Minister to General Ismay, for the COS Committee:

1   I do not approve of the proposal in Paragraph 2 of your minutes of June 17.
2   What is needed is a questionnaire which should be drawn up in the Office of the Minister of Defence, embodying the questions set forth in my minute with others that would readily occur. Let me see a draft of this as soon as possible.
    18.6.41   WSC.[9]

The questionnaire submitted to the Prime Minister consisted of nine extremely detailed questions about everything to do with the defence of Crete including the strength, equipment and location of all the main infantry, artillery and engineer units; particulars of the number of tanks and guns of all kinds; the strength of the non-fighting units and *bouches inutiles*; the number of Italian prisoners; and the position regarding supplies of food and medical stores. The final question was: 'What orders were issued by the GOC in Crete for the Tactical Conduct of the Battle?' This questionnaire was despatched to Headquarters Middle East on 19 June 1941.[9]

During the period immediately after the battle for Crete I was at the OCTU in Kasr el Nil Barracks in the centre of Cairo, while my father was living at Maadi Camp some six miles away. I saw him frequently. Not surprisingly he was in a sombre mood; and he was particularly upset that he had had no word from Winston Churchill. As a result he seemed to prefer my company to that of others, so we used to dine together once or twice a week, usually at the New Zealand Club or at Shepheard's Hotel.

Our routine was that he would call for me in his staff car at the OCTU and drop me there again on his way back to Maadi, after we had had dinner. On the evening of 19 June he called for me as usual but said that, just as he was leaving camp, he had had word that Wavell wished to see him as a matter of urgency. We would therefore have to call in at GHQ on our way. When we got there he asked me to wait in the car, saying that he would only be gone for a few minutes. He was away for well over an hour and when he reappeared he was as white as a sheet and trembling with rage. I had never seen my father in such a state before, nor was I ever to see him like it again. He told me nothing at the time, but after the war he confirmed that this had been the occasion when he had had a major row with the C-in-C, after the latter had said he no longer trusted him. Gradually the facts emerged.

The questionnaire signal, which had arrived that day at GHQ Middle East, could only have been compiled as a result of discussions with someone who had an inside knowledge of what happened in Crete. This made Wavell suspect that Freyberg had gone behind his back and briefed Inglis to go and see the Prime Minister and tell him what had gone wrong in Crete, including the fact that he had not been allowed to deploy his forces as he had wanted. Accused of doing the unforgivable, Freyberg reacted with great indignation. Neither Wavell nor Freyberg knew that Inglis had been thoroughly indiscreet and disloyal about both of them to Churchill, as the record of the interview shows.[9]

Wavell soon realised that his suspicions were unfounded, and he apologised to and made his peace with Freyberg. But he was right to have been upset by the signal. Two days later he received another one from London, announcing his dismissal. Martin Gilbert, in *Finest Hour*, tells the story in detail, including Churchill's interview with Brigadier Inglis, the Prime Minister's Minute to the Chiefs of Staff, and a visit to Chartwell on 19 June:

> Then when the others returned to London, Churchill left the train with Morton and Colville [his private Secretaries] to go once more to Chartwell, to which he sometimes went at times of crisis. 'There will be no weakening here,' Churchill had telegraphed to Roosevelt, earlier that day, with Operation 'Battleaxe' [Operation in the Western Desert] at a halt, with Brigadier Inglis' account of the Crete disaster very much on his mind.

A paragraph later is the sentence: 'Churchill had come to a decision of considerable moment: that Wavell must be replaced.'[10]

In the period immediately after the fall of Crete Freyberg's most pressing problem was his relationship with some of the senior officers of the Division, and with the New Zealand Prime Minister, Peter Fraser. The majority of officers who had served in Greece and Crete realised that the scale of the German attack had been such that no defence would have been capable of withstanding it for long, and the view of most of them appeared to have been that Freyberg had succeeded in leading the Division as well as could have been expected, considering all the adverse circumstances. But others, such as Inglis, felt otherwise. Another was Hargest, who had commanded 5 NZ Brigade at Maleme.

Hargest was very vocal in his criticism of Freyberg after he had returned to Egypt. Just after he arrived in Egypt from Crete, he had a meeting with Fraser which was witnessed by Sir Carl Berendsen, Fraser's chef de Cabinet, who 'said it was absolutely extraordinary the account Hargest gave of the campaign. He hadn't slept for days and nights and yet his case was completely lucid and utterly convincing.'[11]

Another account written much later relates:

> There was considerable discontent among certain elements of 2 NZEF on the Division's return from Crete. Brigadier Hargest was highly critical of the divisional input into his brigade's withdrawal from Olympus to Thermopylae – 'he [Freyberg] does not keep control over the conduct of operations which is essential for full supervision and co-ordination'. Furthermore, Hargest believed that Freyberg did not take his senior officers sufficiently into his confidence; they were sometimes left in doubt as to his intention. Hargest had already, so it appears, written to Fraser in 1940 urging him to come to England and see for himself the difficulties with Freyberg. In Cairo on 2 June 1941, Hargest poured out his complaints to the Prime Minister.[12]

His three main complaints about the handling of New Zealand forces in the Greece and Crete campaigns were:

1 The disaster at Kalamata, Greece, of the loss of the NZ Reinforcement Battalion.
2 The alleged loss of Divisional Headquarters' control during the withdrawal from Mount Olympus to the Thermopylae positions.
3 The maldeployment at Maleme, and the ineffectiveness of the counter-attacks on the airfield.

At Fraser's request these questions were referred to the Inter-Services Committee of Inquiry, and their findings on the first two were included as Appendix II to McClymont's official NZ history, *To Greece*, published in 1959.[13]

The NZ Reinforcement Battalion, under command of Headquarters 'W' Force (British Command Headquarters in Greece), was ordered to Kalamata by Movement Control. Freyberg and 2 NZ Division HQ were not responsible for the battalion, which should have been evacuated at an early stage of the withdrawal under the control of Forces Headquarters. Only when the NZ Divisional HQ arrived in Crete was it discovered that the battalion had been left behind in

Greece because the navy had been unable to evacuate the men in time.

The Inter-Services Committee did not find that Hargest's second point, the alleged loss of control on the retreat to Thermopylae, was proven:

> The Committee heard evidence from General Freyberg, Brigadiers Puttick and Hargest, and Colonel Keith Stewart. It was found that, 'on the whole, divisional control appears to have worked satisfactorily.' There was one period, however, when control became difficult. This was during the withdrawal from the Olympus positions to Thermopylae. As 6 Brigade was still in action at Elasson and Allen Force* at Pinios, General Freyberg decided to remain forward together with his GSO 1, Colonel Stewart, delegating to Brigadier Puttick the task of sorting out the units of the Division as they arrived at Thermopylae. The BGS Anzac Corps was to meet Puttick and was to allot positions.
>
> The Committee discussed the 'usual criticism' levelled against a divisional commander, that he is too often away from his headquarters, or that he does not leave it enough. It was 'strongly of the opinion that provided he does not tire himself unduly, the fault of going forward too often is the better of the two'. In this particular case there was 'ample evidence to prove . . . that General Freyberg, by his presence in the forward area at difficult moments was personally responsible for putting new heart into commanders and for stemming what might have developed into a rout'. A divisional commander must, the Committee added, ensure that when he does go forward his GSO 1 remains behind with a clear knowledge of his general intentions.[2]

When it came to dealing with the criticisms about the maldeployment of New Zealand troops at Maleme, Freyberg was in a cleft stick. He felt that these complaints were justified, but he was not able to explain, then or later, how this situation came about, because he was forbidden to mention anything to do with ULTRA.

Thus it was that the two operational New Zealand Brigade Commanders in Crete, Hargest and Inglis, thought that Freyberg had made a serious tactical mistake in the layout of the defensive positions in Crete. His own Chief of Staff, Keith Stewart, thought the same but was too loyal to say so at the time. However in 1958 Stewart wrote a letter to Brigadier Fairbrother (the successor as chief NZ military historian to General Kippenberger) about an interview with the NZ Premier in Wellington in November 1941:

---

*Brigadier A. S. Allen was given command of a joint Australian/New Zealand brigade group in the Pinios Gorge.

Fraser had me for a good half hour questioning me on Freyberg. It was most embarrassing but it was in accord with his usual practice. I had no option but to sing the praises of my boss. In point of fact my own private views at that time were completely different. Greece was all right, but I considered then and still do that General Freyberg made a balls of Crete.[12]

This was the view of a number of senior New Zealand officers. Many of them died before ULTRA was declassified, but even after the facts about ULTRA were made known some of the survivors still felt that, had Freyberg really wanted to change his dispositions, he could and should have found some way of doing so, whatever his orders to the contrary may have been.

The most important person Freyberg had to satisfy after the Greece and Crete disasters was, of course, Peter Fraser. Freyberg himself wrote:

Mr Fraser was a remarkable man, a good observer, and a Highlander like General Wavell, of whom he had a high opinion. I admired the open way in which Mr Fraser acted. He so obviously wanted to get at the truth of the situation. He also wanted to find out how I had measured up to the problems during the battle, and to know if I had the confidence of the men of the Division. I welcomed the inquiry, and would willingly have extended its scope.

Although Mr Fraser was not qualified to unravel the facts that led up to the mishandling of the whole expedition, his inquiries into questions of detail, such as the medical arrangements on Crete, had a salutary effect. Further, he was a good judge of form, and was not easily 'taken in' by the various reports. He met every ship that came back from Crete and questioned the New Zealanders, including those in hospital. He asked them point blank what they thought of the way in which the campaign had been laid on, and was quite willing to listen to the opinions of the men who had fought, on major strategy as well as on the tactical handling of their units. I do not take any exception to this procedure. I knew and trusted the sane qualities of the officers and the men. The New Zealanders had been trained by me for more than eighteen months, and after two campaigns they knew me well, and I was willing to abide by the opinions that they had formed.[1]

The most difficult problem Freyberg had to face in his relationship with Fraser and the New Zealand government was the fact that he had not warned them in advance of his doubts about the viability of the expedition to Greece. This was due partly to a misunderstanding by civilian ministers of military phraseology; but Freyberg had also not told them beforehand of his misgivings on military grounds, as he subsequently admitted readily. The debriefing meeting with Fraser took place at the British Embassy in Cairo during the first week of June. Freyberg wrote:

> I tackled Mr Fraser on the question of whether, on purely military grounds, the Greek Campaign should ever have been attempted. I was against it, and maintained that I had not been consulted about it. Mr Fraser said that I had agreed with the decision to go to Greece, basing his statement on an answer I gave the New Zealand Government in February 1941 to their question, 'Are you fit to go to Greece?' My reply had been 'Yes'. I explained that this merely meant in military language that we were fully trained and equipped, or in other words, that we were 'fit for war' – a term freely used and readily understood by Service people. I told him that I had never agreed with the plan to go to the aid of Greece, and that, in point of fact, secrecy restrictions were such that it would have been impossible to know the scope of the expedition before leaving Alexandria.
>
> Mr Fraser maintained that I had never put in a protest against going to Greece. My reply to this was that it was hard for a Divisional Commander to disagree with an Army Group Commander on major strategy. I had asked General Wavell if the New Zealand Government agreed to their Division being used, and I had been told that they had agreed.
>
> Mr Fraser then laid down a firm policy, that, no matter who was my Commander, I must always keep the New Zealand Government in the picture, and that if I disagreed with any major plan, I should report it to him immediately.
>
> I then made my main point. I said that the Prime Minister had a perfect right to consult whom he liked, and I hoped that he would do so, but that if he were to deal over my head with Commanders in Chief and did not ask for my opinion, the matter would be taken out of my hands and it would be very difficult for me to accept the full responsibility which I had assumed under the charter which the New Zealand War Cabinet had given me. There was agreement on this point.[1]

When he reported back to the New Zealand government Fraser discussed the repercussions of the decision to go to Greece:

> The campaign in Greece was carefully considered by us with a full knowledge of all the implications and dangers involved. It is, however, most regrettable that the possibility that the Germans would obtain such complete air superiority that they could operate quite unmolested, was apparently not foreseen by those, both here and in London, technically qualified to do so. I still think that the decision was right, although I find here a tendency to differ, and am surprised to learn now from Freyberg that he never considered the operation a feasible one, though I pointed out to him his telegrams to us conveyed a contrary impression.[14]

Fraser also signalled to his colleagues in Wellington about the involvement of New Zealand troops in Crete:

The operations in Crete seemed to me to have been largely the result of chance . . . as you know, we had no previous knowledge that it was intended to retain our troops on the island, or that it was intended to defend it, and it seems clear to me now that with the means at Freyberg's disposal, the island was in fact indefensible against the scale of attack which actually developed.

It seems to me also that it should have been as clear before the decision to defend Crete as it is now, that troops without adequate air protection (which it was known could not be provided) would be in a hopeless position, though obviously the scale of German air attack was larger and more intense than was foreseen.

As far as the New Zealand troops are concerned, the net result has been that all our care before committing them to battle, to ensure that they should fight only on reasonably even terms as far as equipment and supplies are concerned, and that they should have a fair opportunity to defend themselves, has been rendered nugatory by the turn of events.[14]

Fraser left Egypt on 8 June, but a delay in Lagos prevented him reaching England until 20 June.[15] He stayed there for almost exactly two months, during which time he brooded about Freyberg's alleged mishandling of the defence of Crete, and the criticism of him by some of his officers. Shortly before he was due to return to New Zealand Fraser asked the Director of Military Operations, Major-General Sir John Kennedy, to go and see him. Kennedy, in his book, *The Business of War*, left an account of the interview which took place on 18 August:

Some of his people had been criticising Freyberg, and [Fraser] was very exercised whether he should ask another man to command the New Zealand Division. He had had a talk with Wavell on the subject, and now, he said, he felt more or less satisfied to leave Freyberg in charge. I told him that, if he still had doubts, he should ask Auchinleck and Dill to advise him; that I had known Freyberg as a fine battalion and brigade commander, but did not know him well enough to be able to advise on his capacity for his present job.[16]

Fraser took Kennedy's advice and he called on the CIGS at the War Office. As a result the following signal was sent to General Wavell in India, and to General Sir Claude Auchinleck, Wavell's successor in Cairo:

New Zealand Prime Minister has had information from various sources which leads him to doubt if Freyberg is right man to command New

Zealand Division. While Mr Fraser likes Freyberg and is keeping an open mind this is causing him grave anxiety. It is clear that New Zealand's only division of such splendid men must have a really good commander. Could you let me have your opinions which I would communicate to Mr Fraser and if General Auchinleck is not satisfied I will ask him to initiate a confidential report.[17]

Wavell replied immediately:

Freyberg produced one of best trained disciplined and fittest divisions I have ever seen and he must be given fullest credit for their exploits in Greece and Crete. I am aware relations between him and his staff and Subordinate Commanders were not always happy due to Freyberg's passion for detail and desire to do everything personally instead of letting his staff work. I think he wore himself out in Crete through this tendency. If Freyberg is replaced in New Zealand division should be very pleased to have him in India. I have no Lt. General's appointment in sight but could give him Command of one of the new divisions being raised.[18]

A week later Wavell telegraphed again:

Has any decision been taken about Freyberg as it may affect appointments here. I think Fraser will be most ill-advised to displace him as no man could have done more for division. On reflection think I was wrong in what I said about relations with his Brigadiers I only meant that he is not always easy man to serve owing to his keenness. I propose to recommend him for KBE for his work in Greece and Crete and repeat I should like him in India if New Zealand does not want him though I think they will be wrong to lose him.[19]

At the beginning of September Auchinleck expressed similar views:

After careful inquiry consider it would be great mistake to move Freyberg from Command New Zealand Division to whose training and efficiency he has wholeheartedly devoted himself with excellent results. In action he is a first-class commander. In peaceful periods he is apt perhaps to centralise and pay too much attention to detail which possibly irritates his subordinate Commanders somewhat. This tendency probably due to his intense zeal for efficiency. On balance strongly recommend his retention.[20]

This exchange of signals brought to an end the only serious questioning of Freyberg's position during his command of the NZEF. He was to remain commander of the New Zealand Division for the rest of the war, until he finally relinquished the appointment on 22 November 1945, six years to the day of his assumption of it. It was to be the longest period of continuous and unbroken service by a senior officer in an operational command in any of the three services of the British and Commonwealth forces during the Second World War.

The Germans made a deliberate effort to play down the losses they had suffered in Crete. At the time they admitted to 6,000 casualties, of which 1,350 were killed. This figure for those killed was only one-third of the British estimate of enemy losses.

After the war was over Freyberg asked the Director of Military Intelligence to request that General Scobie (then British GOC in Greece) invite the War Graves Registration Unit in Crete to count the number of German graves on the island. This search produced very different figures:

> Germans killed in Crete during 1941 Campaign for certain 4,000 as counted from graves. In addition approximately 400 washed up after battle either crashed in sea from gliders, or sunk by Navy. In addition, 450 wounded flown to mainland [Greece] died and buried in Lonkinia cemetery. These figures still incomplete, and also inaccurate. Many graves still scattered round island, and not included. Big graves impossible to estimate true figure buried. Consider fair overall figure 5,000. Will forward further information as it becomes available.[21]

By the time that I. McD. G. Stewart came to publish *The Struggle for Crete* in 1966 the figures for German casualties had again been revised upwards. 'General Kippenberger had counted 4,400 German graves at Maleme and Galatas alone.' In addition there were '2,000 known dead in Retimo and Heraklion', plus the mortally wounded flown back to Greece and buried in Lonkinia cemetery, and those drowned in the attempted sea invasion. Altogether, the total of Germans killed was in excess of 7,000.[8]

None of the Crete histories gives firm figures for the total number of German wounded, and in view of the high proportion of Germans killed it is probable that the number of wounded was smaller than the usual ratio of two or three wounded to every one killed. Since the enemy was left in possession of the battlefield there were few German prisoners; also all the Italian prisoners of war on Crete were freed.

The most detailed breakdown of British and Dominion casualties in Crete was given in the Australian Official History as follows:

[329]

	Killed	Wounded	Prisoners	Total
British Army	612	224	5,315	6,151
Royal Marines (MNBDO)	114	30	1,035	1,179
Royal Air Force	71	9	226	306
Australian Army	274	507	3,102	3,883
New Zealand Army	671	1,455	1,692	3,818
	1,742	2,225	11,370	15,337
Royal Navy at Sea	2,000			2,000
	3,742			17,337[22]

At the end of the war a unit known as the Enemy Documents Section (EDS) with Historical Branch of the Cabinet offices in London, was set up to process the mass of material that became available after the German surrender. In a note to 'Developments in the Balkans', information was produced about German and Italian operations in Albania, Greece and Crete, taken from the German OKW (Operations Branch) War Diary kept from 18 March 1939 to 17 March 1943. This disclosed that on 28 October 1940 a 'Situation Conference' was held at the German OKW Headquarters to discuss Mussolini's letter about the forthcoming Italian attack on Greece. At this conference the Naval Staff made representations concerning the strategic importance of Crete, which had caused General Jodl, Chief-of-Staff, to look into the question thoroughly. Jodl produced a long memorandum on the military significance of Crete, and discussions followed on its strategic importance with General Halder, General von Paulus and other members of the German General Staff. In outline they regarded the occupation of Crete as an essential preliminary to their domination of the Eastern Mediterranean, for the subjugation of Malta, and ultimately to driving the British out of Egypt and the Suez Canal. For the next six months, until the parachutists descended on the island, these and later documents show that Crete was never far from the thoughts of the German High Command as, unfortunately, it was from British military minds.

The German objective in attacking Crete was twofold: first to deny Crete to the British, and in particular to prevent its use as an air base; second, to provide a jumping-off ground for further German operations. In this latter connection, the EDS Report is revealing:

22. It has been suggested that the severe losses suffered by the Germans in Crete deterred them from undertaking further airborne and parachute operations. [General] Student, when interrogated on 20 September 1945, stated that: 'the airborne assault on Crete was the first phase of an airborne offensive against the Suez Canal', but that Hitler, influenced by the losses, discouraged the undertaking of any further large-scale operation. If Student's proposals had been adopted, the next stepping stone would have been Cyprus. When the possibility of attacking this island was discussed by Keitel and Cavallero [German and Italian chiefs of staff] at the Brenner Pass on 2 June 1941, the Germans proposed that the Italians should carry out the operation from the Dodecanese, since German losses in Crete were too heavy to allow them to undertake the task with the necessary speed. The Italians, it is true, had not been informed of the Barbarossa plan [the invasion of Russia] at that time and this reason may have been given to conceal the German intentions of eliminating Russia before destroying England. It should also be borne in mind that the decision concerning Cyprus was in accordance with the fundamental German policy of making Italy primarily responsible for the occupation and protection of the Mediterranean.

23. The conquest of Crete did, however, prove to the Germans that a successful attack on a strongly defended island required naval and air superiority. At the time of Operation Merkur [the invasion of Crete] the Germans had air superiority, but even with the Italian Fleet they never achieved naval superiority in the Mediterranean. Student's suggestions for further airborne assaults in the Mediterranean were not supported, nor did any large-scale airborne operations take place after that date.[23]

In an Appendix to the main EDS Balkan Paper, there are details of General Student's further interrogation in September 1945:

Student, when interrogated, said that he pressed hard for a further strengthening of German airborne forces, but he could not secure acceptance of his idea that the presence in Germany of large forces of airborne troops would force the Allies to keep similarly large formations continuously available in the rear areas. No further extension or development was allowed in Germany after Crete.

While Crete was a German success it entailed the greatest losses for any single engagement up to that time and Hitler, influenced by these losses, discouraged the undertaking of any further large-scale operations. This proved a great disappointment to Student, 'Father' of the airborne idea and its champion throughout the war, but in spite of adverse decisions he continued to advocate the employment of airborne forces every time an opportunity presented itself. While many plans for the use of these forces were drafted, in Student's words 'Crete was the grave of German parachutists'.[23]

One of these plans was for a combined German–Italian attack on Malta in the late summer of 1942. General Student told how the Malta plan had reached an advanced stage with himself in command, and the Italian Airborne Division *La Spezia* of 10,000 men added to the reformed German XI Fliegerkorps of about 20,000, plus an Italian seaborne force to sail from Sicily. The British interrogator then asked:

BRITISH OFFICER: Do you think it would have succeeded?

GENERAL STUDENT: Yes, I'm certain of it. Of course difficulties would have cropped up, but it would have succeeded, and I think more easily than Crete. I was absolutely convinced of a victory there, of the fact that we could take it.

BRITISH OFFICER: Malta was a very great prize. Why was the operation turned down?

GENERAL STUDENT: I flew to the Führer for a final conference. That was in July. I went in and he simply turned it down flat, without giving me any reason, but said: 'The affair will go wrong and will cost too many losses', etc.

BRITISH OFFICER: Did he actually not give any other reasons for it?

GENERAL STUDENT: I had the impression that Hitler didn't trust the Italians at all, as he believed the German paratroops would be alone there, and he was unable at that time to place any further German troops at my disposal.

He told me afterwards, at breakfast the following day, 'Look here, as soon as you carry out this operation the English fleet will immediately put to sea from Alexandria and Malta, and as soon as the Italians hear that, the troop transport ships sailing for Malta will immediately turn back to Sicily again.' He thought the German airborne troops were too weak for the operation.[23]

One of the reasons why the battle of Crete has a continuous fascination is because it came at the lowest point in British fortunes in the Second World War. Less than a month after it was over the Germans invaded Russia; and within six months Japan bombed Pearl Harbor and Germany declared war on the United States of America. From then on the ultimate result of the conflict was never in doubt, however long and painful the road to victory might be. But the campaigns in Greece and Crete took place at a time when Britain and the Dominions still stood alone, and at the time they appeared to be unmitigated disasters.

The decision to try and hold Crete was, of course, the direct consequence of the evacuation from Greece, and Winston Churchill again moved to the centre of the stage. At first the Prime Minister, at a meeting of the Cabinet on 28 April, expressed himself as 'somewhat doubtful of our ability to hold Crete against a prolonged attack'.[24] But once ULTRA started to divulge the German plan of attack in such detail, he persuaded himself that there was a real chance of defeating the invasion. Clearly Churchill had little idea of conditions on the island, let alone the chaos, confusion and disorganisation of the army and RAF that resulted from the hurried evacuation from Greece; so that when the German assault was not defeated his disillusion found this expression: 'When the House meets we shall have to meet a good deal of criticism on Crete, most of it quite unjustified as regards action taken from here. Crete was a perfectly justifiable operation as there was a very good prospect of holding it.'[25]

In the emergency debate on Crete in the House of Commons on 10 June 1941 the Prime Minister defended the decision to stay and fight it out in Crete:

The question then arose as to whether we should try to defend Crete or yield it without a fight. No one who bears any responsibility for the decision to defend Crete was ignorant of the fact that conditions permitted of only the most meagre British air support to be provided for our troops in the island or for our Fleet operating round the island. It was not a fact that dawned upon the military and other authorities after the decision had been taken; it was the foundation of a difficult and harsh choice, as I shall show. The choice was: Should Crete be defended without effective air support or should the Germans be permitted to occupy it without opposition?

Suppose we had never gone to Greece and had never attempted to defend Crete? Where would the Germans be now? Suppose we had simply resigned territory and strategic islands to them without a fight? Might they not, at this early stage of the campaign in 1941, already be masters of Syria and Iraq and preparing themselves for an advance into Persia?

The Germans in this war have gained many victories. They have easily overrun great countries and beaten down strong Powers with little resistance offered to them. It is not only a question of the time that is gained by fighting strongly, even if at a disadvantage, for important points. There is also this vitally important principle of stubborn resistance to the will of the enemy . . . Again and again, it has been proved that fierce and stubborn resistance, even against heavy odds and under exceptional conditions of local disadvantage, is an essential element in victory. At any rate, the decision was taken to hold Crete. The decision to fight for Crete was taken with the full knowledge that air support would be at a minimum, as anyone can see – apart from the question of whether you have adequate supplies or not – who measures the distances from our airfields in Egypt and compares them with the distances from enemy airfields in Greece and who acquaints himself with the radius of action of dive-bombers and aircraft.[26]

But if Churchill had not insisted on Crete being defended, and if the defending troops had not inflicted heavy casualties on the German parachutists, then Student's airborne forces would have been able to move on to Cyprus, where they would have met little resistance, since at the time it was garrisoned only by a single weak brigade. Cyprus was within easy range of Port Said and was later used as the British base for their own airborne attack on Egypt during the Suez crisis in 1956. The Germans therefore would have been in a position, from 1941 onwards, to threaten Egypt from an additional direction to that of Rommel in the Western Desert. Moreover without the deterrent of the Crete casualties Malta would almost certainly have had to face an airborne invasion, possibly with fatal results, at a time when it had already been weakened by the long blockade. If either Cyprus, Malta or both had been lost in 1941–2, the British hold on the Eastern Mediterranean would have been even more gravely threatened than it already was.

Although Churchill largely blamed Wavell for the Crete disaster, Freyberg was also consigned to the Prime Ministerial doghouse, and for twelve months there was no communication between them. The silence was only broken a year later, when Freyberg was wounded at Minqar Qaim at the end of June 1942, following which he received an affectionate telegram from Winston – a prelude to a lasting reconciliation. Freyberg had been hurt and puzzled by Churchill's silence; and he was particularly upset when reports began to percolate back from England that the home authorities thought one of the reasons why Crete had been lost was because the troops there had not fought. This Freyberg knew to be untrue, but the German casualty figures were not then available, and the belief was only completely quashed when the true figures came out after the war.

Despite the fact that the disaster in Crete was his own lowest point in the Second World War, his subsequent talk with Peter Fraser proved very helpful from Freyberg's point of view. Their exchange of views in Cairo in June 1941 was 'a frank discussion which cleared the air and laid the foundations of a most harmonious and satisfactory association,' Freyberg wrote. The New Zealand Cabinet made it plain that they were not 'going blind' into any more operations. For his part, and for the rest of the war, Freyberg added, 'I was consulted on all aspects of our employment. I believe that this decision was to the advantage of both the British and the New Zealand forces. During the last four years of the war, the New Zealand government accepted all my recommendations without question.'[1]

After the end of the war Freyberg gave a dinner party in London on 27 January 1946 for Peter Fraser who was then in England. Except for Field Marshal Wavell, who was still in India, the party had a decidedly Cretan background. Freyberg wrote:

> When we resumed our seats after the ladies had withdrawn, I sat at the head of the table with Mr Fraser on my right, and the First Sea Lord, Lord Cunningham, on my left, with the Marshal of the Royal Air Force, Lord Tedder [C-in-C RAF Middle East] further down the table. Admiral Cunningham glared at me and said fiercely, 'Freyberg, I was glad when you lost Crete.' 'So was I,' said Tedder. I tried in vain to catch Mr Fraser's eye.[1]

The rest of the evening was spent in discussing, from the naval and administrative situations, what an impossible position would have resulted had Crete been successfully held.

When in 1949 Churchill did his research for *The Grand Alliance* – the third volume of his history of the Second World War – he sent the drafts of his two Crete chapters to Freyberg in New Zealand for comment. ULTRA was then still highly classified, and there is no mention in Freyberg's correspondence with Churchill of the intelligence aspect. However Freyberg took the opportunity to enlighten his old friend over many facts about the battle that Churchill had not previously known, and these he included in his book. In retrospect, Churchill displayed a more understanding attitude about what had happened in Crete in 1941 than the unsympathetic line he had taken at the time, and he summed up the episode:

> The battle of Crete is an example of the decisive results that may emerge from hard and well-sustained fighting apart from manoeuvring for strategic positions. We did not know how many parachute divisions the Germans had . . . But in fact the 7th Airborne Division was the only one which Goering had. This division was destroyed in the Battle of Crete. Upwards of five thousand of his bravest men were killed, and the whole structure of this organisation was irretrievably broken. It never appeared again in any effective form. The New Zealanders and other British, Imperial, and Greek troops who fought in the confused, disheartening, and vain struggle for Crete may feel that they played a definite part in an event which brought us far-reaching relief at a hinging moment.[27]

20

The Relief of Tobruk

While Freyberg and the New Zealand Division had been fighting in Greece and Crete, in the Western Desert Rommel had attacked at Agheila at the beginning of April 1941 and soon overwhelmed the small unprepared British force in Cyrenaica. Both General Neame and General O'Connor were captured, and the Desert Command was thrown into disarray. Before the month was out the Germans had surrounded the British garrison in Tobruk and pressed on as far as Capuzzo and Sollum on the Egyptian frontier.

On 15 May a force consisting of 7 Armoured Brigade and 22 Guards Brigade advanced along the top of the frontier escarpment and recaptured Capuzzo and Sollum; but the Germans quickly counter-attacked and regained them both later that day. Soon only Halfaya Pass remained in British hands. Freyberg's stepson Guy McLaren was a subaltern in 3 Battalion Coldstream Guards, which was part of 22 Guards Brigade. Guy was commanding an infantry company at Halfaya Pass on 26–7 May when the German 5 Light Division (shortly to be renamed 21 Panzer Division) launched a strong attack with 60 tanks. Some of these tanks overran Guy's company headquarters and during heavy fighting he was severely wounded. In the course of this action the Coldstream battalion lost eight officers and 165 men and it was not known for many weeks whether Guy was alive or dead.[1]

Freyberg, after returning from Crete on 31 May and his traumatic interview with the Commander-in-Chief, had to be told that Guy, of whom he was very fond, had been wounded and was missing, possibly dead. Peter Coates, Wavell's Military Assistant, recorded the occasion in his autobiography: 'As I write, General Freyberg is in my office,

[336]

sitting opposite me. A crushed Goliath, and almost in tears. His stepson, Guy McLaren, has been reported killed in the desert. What a homecoming the poor man has had.'[2]

During this time Bernard's wife Barbara was on her way to Egypt, travelling round the Cape. At the time of the Crete battle Barbara noted in her diary: 'Week of great suspense and anxiety. B. having terrible time – very little news but fighting must be ghastly.' Her ordeal was made all the harder by the Germans putting out in wireless broadcasts that Freyberg had been taken prisoner, and later that he had been killed.

Her ship, the *Strathaird*, was due to arrive at Suez on 14 June, and my father and I drove along the desert road from Cairo to meet her. We were both in a sombre mood, dreading the moment when she would have to be told the news about Guy. Her diary records how it happened:

Saturday June 14
Our 19th wedding day. Deck morning approaching Suez – Arrive wharf 3. Ashore in launch at 4.30. Major Dormewell, NZEF came to meet us. As we reached quay, *saw* Bernard *and* Paul (in OCTU uniform) walking across quay. Joy at seeing B. looking well, and great relief over Paul who had been in Greece. Bitter grief when B. had to tell me that Guy was wounded at Halfaya Pass. He is reported missing but there seems faint hope he may be prisoner.

There was no news of Guy for two months, but at the end of July 1941 we heard that he was in an Italian hospital near Naples with a shattered leg. Later he was moved to another hospital in northern Italy where he linked up with a Coldstream friend, John Fox-Strangways. They were both eventually repatriated in 1943 under a Red Cross exchange scheme for badly wounded prisoners of war.

Freyberg had wanted Barbara to come to Egypt for two specific reasons. First, to help organise the New Zealand Club. Suitable premises had been found in the centre of Cairo in Sharia Malika Farida, and Freyberg asked his government to recruit and send over initially thirty New Zealand girls to help run it. (Barbara christened them the 'Tuis' – a New Zealand bird – and the name stuck.) The numbers were later increased considerably. Cairo was the first and largest of the clubs, but others were established in the next few years in Bari, Rome, Florence, Venice and London. They became very popular and, under the initial guidance of Harvey Turner, an experienced businessman from Auckland who started them off on a sound basis, they flourished financially, enabling the large profits that were made to be ploughed back to provide extra amenities that would not otherwise have been available, such as the making of ice-cream in large quantities!

The second reason Freyberg needed Barbara's help was for entertaining. It was his intention to entertain privately as many of the officers of the Division as possible, particularly the junior ones, preferably for a meal, but at least for drinks. As there were many hundreds this was no light undertaking. He entertained other ranks in special categories, such as those who had had wounds or were escaped POWs. Barbara found a flat on two floors at 18 Sharia Dar el Shifa in Garden City, near the British Embassy, with spacious rooms and a large garden. All through the summer of 1941 on at least two evenings a week and at weekends some form of entertaining took place. It was a way for Freyberg to meet a large cross-section of the Division informally, and to be able to talk to them away from the parade ground and the officers' mess.

Later in the year, when casualties started to arrive as the result of the November battles, Barbara organised a system of hospital visits whereby a representative went to all the hospitals at least once a week to make sure that any special needs of the New Zealand wounded were attended to. It was comparatively straightforward to cover the New Zealand hospitals, but there were many British hospitals in the Nile Delta, and New Zealand soldiers would often be sent to them, for transport reasons or because they specialised in treating particular types of wound. Careful arrangements were necessary to make sure that no one slipped through the net.

After the German capture of Halfaya Pass the front stabilised for a few weeks on the Libyan–Egyptian border. The next operation was to be the British action codenamed 'Battleaxe', the objective of which was to defeat the enemy in the frontier area, push him back, and ultimately relieve Tobruk. The battle began on 15 June quite satisfactorily, but the Germans quickly reinforced their troops in the Capuzzo and Sidi Omar areas, and the British force of 25,000 soon encountered superior numbers which included 200 tanks. After a three-day battle which cost over 1,000 British casualties, Wavell was compelled to call off the action.[1] It was his final battle in the Middle East, and early in July he left to become C-in-C India. General Sir Claude Auchinleck was appointed in his place.

On 22 June 1941 the Germans attacked Russia, and this resulted in a much needed breathing-space in the Middle East. The British hold on Syria, Iraq and the Persian Gulf was consolidated, and in Abyssinia and East Africa the last vestiges of Italian occupation were removed. Only in the Western Desert did the German threat remain, but after the Battleaxe operation, and even though Auchinleck (who assumed command on 2 July) was pressed by Churchill to renew the offensive straightaway, there was a prolonged lull.

The Official New Zealand History describes how 'in the five convalescent months June to October the Division recovered its strength and grew stronger than ever'. Of the 16,700 New Zealanders who had gone to Greece and Crete, 5,816 did not return. The losses in units had been uneven. The 6 NZ Brigade, which had been evacuated from Greece to Egypt, was still largely intact. The main casualties had occurred in 4 and 5 NZ Brigades in Crete, where only 3,900 (out of 7,700) had been able to make their way over the mountains to Sphakia and eventually to Egypt.[3]

Meanwhile 4 and 5 Reinforcements (drafts from New Zealand) had arrived in Egypt and largely replaced these losses. The next drafts, 6 and 7 Reinforcements, were due to reach Egypt several months before the battles being planned for November. Also after nearly two years of war, arms and vehicles were rolling off the production lines in England in increasing quantities and being shipped to the Middle East. The re-equipment of the Division proceeded throughout the summer with gathering speed.

This enabled Freyberg to reorganise his troops at his own pace. The 6 NZ Brigade commanded by Brigadier Harold Barrowclough was concentrated in the Canal Zone in an anti-parachute invasion role; while 4 and 5 Brigades, commanded by Brigadiers Inglis and Hargest, started their re-grouping in the Helwan–Maadi areas of the Nile Delta, absorbing reinforcements and drawing new weapons, equipment and vehicles from the rapidly-filling depots. The records for June, July and August list Freyberg's many visits to, and inspections of, all units in the force as this process got under way.

Once the New Zealand Division was up to full strength again with 854 officers and 17,164 other ranks (not to mention reserves in the depots of over 10,000),[3] and issued with new weapons, equipment and vehicles, the next task to be tackled was its training. There are two reasons in particular why the New Zealand Division acquired its high reputation in the Second World War as a fighting force. The first was the high quality of its officers and men. The second because they were trained in the field to a more exacting standard than other divisions and indeed often to a better military standard than that reached by units of the British Regular Army. Freyberg's insistence on long and careful training, which he was fortunate in being able to carry out during the waiting period, was one of his most important contributions to the battleworthiness of his force. His strong views on the subject dated back to 1917 and his own thorough grounding by General de Lisle.

From June to November 1941, and especially during formation exercises in the last ten weeks, New Zealand troops were constantly out training in the desert. After the Division moved to Baggush, two dummy forts known as 'Sidi Clif' and 'Bir Stella' were established in the hinterland, and were mined and wired. Units in vehicles were required to carry out an approach march by night over 20 to 30 miles, ending with an assault on the forts at first light, often under a barrage of live 25-pounder shells and 3-inch mortar shells, while simultaneously establishing a path through the wire and minefields.

Freyberg was a great believer in night movement – he knew from experience that it kept down casualties. The brigades were constantly practised in long night marches by vehicle and on foot, and were taught how to navigate in the desert, a skill comparable to guiding a ship at sea. What gave this technique added point was that, certainly in the early days, the Germans disliked moving in the desert by night and avoided doing so whenever possible. Night movement also helped to avoid attack from the Luftwaffe – still powerful in 1941 – and greatly improved the chances of obtaining surprise.

Freyberg also made strenuous efforts to remedy any misunderstandings there may have been in the relationship with his senior officers and their methods of doing business. So much so that Hargest was soon writing to Peter Fraser:

> I have often worried over the anxiety I caused you when I unloaded my cares on you in Cairo. I have no doubt now of the justification for doing so, but the effect justified it all. The General met us in several conferences and we cleaned up a great deal of important details. I was forthright in my remarks and he was splendid about it all – but the results have been good beyond my strongest hopes. Now we meet in *conference* and the whole details are placed before us – we on the other hand are free to express ourselves – and we must accept a share of the responsibilities.[3]

Freyberg's continuing concern over the men's welfare is also evident in a letter he wrote to Fraser from Baggush on 29 September 1941:

> You know from my cables what the general position is here. The men after you left were tired, and in the hot and trying weather tended to lose a little weight. We watched them very carefully and those who looked the worse for wear were sent for a week's complete rest to the sea. It had a wonderful result and they came back like new men. Our holiday camp was staffed by our own cooks and was a great success. We had 500 men there through July, August and September. Our move to the coast here has been most popular.

Egypt and Cyrenaica

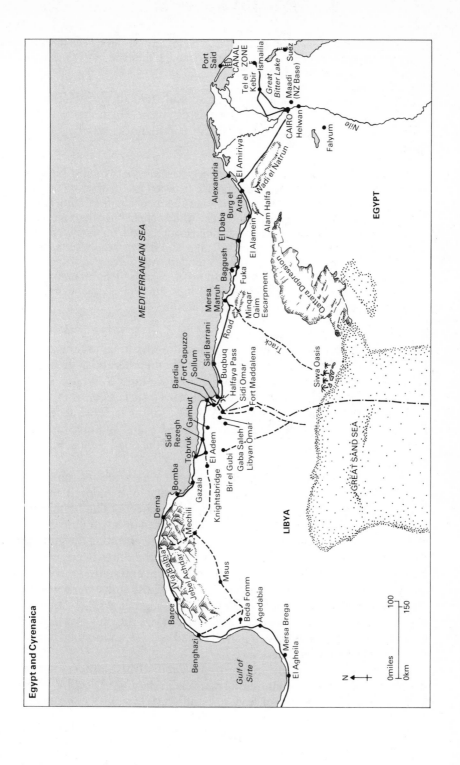

The cooler air and sea bathing has done wonders. I have never seen the men in better spirits. I hope with a little more training they will be as fit as they were when they went to Greece.[4]

But although he was able to organise and train the New Zealand Division in his own way, an important difference of military views between Freyberg and the other British commanders was becoming apparent:

> During this period of training and reorganisation [he wrote] it became obvious that there was a wide divergence between two distinct schools of thought – one represented by General Alan Cunningham [the Eighth Army Commander] and General Auchinleck, who thought that the Germans could be beaten by manoeuvre of small formations, and, on the other side, the school represented by General Blamey and myself, who were against the Brigade Group battle. It really was a fundamental difference of opinion, because it affected the whole question of organisation, training and fighting. We always moved by Brigade Groups, but concentrated to fight as a Division with our guns under Division control.[4]

The brigade group tactical concept was based on the brigade being the main fighting formation, and disregarded the divisional organisation. In the Western Desert it had originated in the theories and activities of General 'Strafer' Gott, and Brigadier Jock Campbell, whose small 'Jock columns' and 'defensive boxes' had proved successful when used against the Italians in the winter of 1940–1. But the lack of success of British tactics against the Germans in the spring and summer of 1941 ought to have alerted the British command to the need for a complete reappraisal.

These 'Jock columns' had usually consisted of a couple of companies of infantry in vehicles, supported by a squadron of armoured cars, a battery of 25-pounder guns and a troop of engineers. The 'defensive boxes' were sometimes larger, and might be based on a battalion group and its equivalent supporting arms, but never concentrating the guns of a division. The Germans' tactical doctrine, on the other hand, was to fight in divisions with their tanks and guns concentrated. To try and counter them with isolated brigade groups whose guns were widely dispersed could only result in defeat. Although it was obvious to Freyberg that a return to fighting as a division was the only way to deal with the Germans, the British generals had not yet understood that a different approach was needed.

This was in part because none of the senior British officers in the desert in 1941 had commanded formations in the First World War or had any other experience of how to handle artillery on a large scale.

[342]

Auchinleck, the C-in-C, had served mainly in the Indian Army, but never on the Western Front, and only once, briefly, against the Germans at Narvik in Norway in 1940. The Eighth Army commanders, first Alan Cunningham and later Ritchie, and the Corps commanders Norrie and Godwin-Austen, had served in France, but as junior regimental officers. By contrast Freyberg had been accustomed during his three years in France to the large fire plans needed in the Great War to counter the German Army.

On 14 September Rommel launched Operation 'Sommernachtstraum', 'Summer Night's Dream' – a deep raid by 21 Panzer Division into Egypt to find out the British state of preparedness in their forward area. The operation came near to a humiliating fiasco for him. The forward screen of British armoured cars fell back in good order, and the Germans found none of the forward dumps they had expected. When German tanks had penetrated some 50 miles beyond the frontier they ran short of petrol, and only regained their own lines with difficulty. Rommel came to the conclusion that British preparations for an attack from Egypt were much less advanced than in fact they were, and that he had plenty of time in which to make his long-planned assault on Tobruk. The effect of 'Summer Night's Dream' on the British Command, on the other hand, was to speed up the deployment of their forces into the desert, in case the German reconnaissance was the prelude to a major offensive.

The main New Zealand Divisional Headquarters left Helwan on 12 September, and Freyberg followed two days later. Their concentration area was at Baggush, some 30 miles east of Mersa Matruh. The arrival of Divisional Headquarters at Baggush saw the start of the 'GOC's Diary'. This daily summary was normally written by Captain John White, Freyberg's Personal Assistant. It recorded Freyberg's doings each day, and during battles went into great detail. The diary was kept with hardly any breaks (except when Freyberg was on convalescent leave or in the heat of battle when it would be written up later) for the next four years. It served as a record at the time, and later became an invaluable aide-memoire to the official historians.*

In the summer and autumn of 1941† the Germans held a frontier

---

*GOC's Diary will be drawn on extensively for the rest of the war, describing Freyberg's activities and those of the NZ Division.

†During this period I finished my OCTU course at Kasr el Nil Barracks, Cairo and was gazetted as a Second Lieutenant in the New Zealand Forces. I was posted to the Long Range Desert Group (LRDG) at the old Citadel in Cairo, and reported for duty at the beginning of October 1941. My first patrol left for the advanced LRDG base at Siwa shortly afterwards. I called in on my father at Baggush on the way on 23 October.

area of Sollum, Halfaya, Capuzzo and Bardia in some strength behind extensive minefields and wire, while immediately to their west was the Savona Division strung out as far as Libyan Omar. Four Italian divisions surrounded the British garrison in Tobruk, and in between the frontier area and Tobruk were the German Afrika Division (soon to be renamed 90 Light Division), 15 and 21 Panzer Divisions, and the Italian Ariete Armoured Division.

On 18 November Rommel was just getting into position to launch his attack on Tobruk, scheduled for 23 November, when the Eighth Army struck first. Two corps were involved, XIII Corps under Godwin-Austen on the right, consisting of 4 Indian, the New Zealand Division and 1 Army Tank Brigade; and XXX Corps under Norrie on the left, with 7 Armoured Division, two brigades of the South African Division, and 22 Guards Brigade. The 70 British Infantry Division and 32 Army Tank Brigade were holding Tobruk.

The broad plan was for the British armour to cross the Libyan frontier near Fort Maddalena in the south and destroy the enemy armoured formations near Tobruk; and subsequently for XXX Corps to relieve the fortress itself in conjunction with a sortie by its garrison. Meanwhile XIII Corps' task was to pin the enemy troops in the Sollum–Halfaya area from the front, while at the same time enveloping them round their western flank. Having done that, the corps would then clear the enemy from the whole area between the frontier and Tobruk. The operation was codenamed 'Crusader'.[3]

Freyberg's relationship with the Eighth Army Commander, General Alan Cunningham, was never close. A few days before the beginning of the 'Crusader' battle Freyberg sought an interview with Cunningham and subsequently wrote:

I could not see how XXX Corps, with only the 7th Armoured Division and two South African brigades plus the 22nd Guards Brigade, could fight their way through the whole Afrika Korps and Italian Army to relieve Tobruk. I expressed the opinion that if he, Cunningham, attacked Tobruk, which was surrounded by four Italian divisions and one German division, with two South African brigades he would fail, and it seemed to me that the New Zealand Division would then be ordered to march on Tobruk. I told him I had made all my plans to make this move and that all my officers had been studying the problem. I begged him, however, if the occasion should arise, to send us as a three-brigade division, and I pointed out the weakness in my opinion of a binary division in such an operation. I doubt if I made any impression on General Cunningham. He thought I was over-anxious and I thought him over-confident.[3]

[344]

Freyberg found Auchinleck equally difficult to work with. He wrote later that the high command was intolerant of any criticism of their plans from below, and that no British general who told the C-in-C the truth survived for long. But Freyberg himself had responsibilities to the New Zealand government, who had made it plain after Greece and Crete that they were 'not going blind into any more operations. They wanted to know about the plan and the Senior Commanders.' Before the 1941 'Crusader' battle the NZ government asked Freyberg his opinion of his corps and army commanders. Freyberg wrote:

> I applied to General Auchinleck, who gave me the answer to cable to the Prime Minister. This did not ease the tension between me and General Auchinleck, especially as he had to go back upon his opinion in the next few days and relieve the Army Commander [Cunningham]. Some time later the Corps Commander [Godwin-Austen], asked to be relieved of his command on the grounds that he could not carry on in view of the C-in-C's constant interference with his operations.[4]

The approach march of the New Zealand Division from their training area at Baggush to their assembly positions just inside Libya took eight days. It began on Armistice day, 11 November and was completed on 18 November 1941, the dates overlapping with the twenty-fifth anniversary of the battle of the Ancre. Freyberg took with him in his car the same bag he had had with him in 1916 for the attack on Beaucourt.

The move involved some 3,000 vehicles travelling dispersed in desert formation over a distance of 170 miles. After ten weeks of thorough training the troops were superbly fit, morale was sky high, and in the opinion of many who served throughout the war it was one of the peak moments in the six-year history of the Division, never before experienced, never again surpassed.

Its dramatic character can be sensed in two accounts – the first from *Infantry Brigadier* by Howard Kippenberger, who was then commanding 20 NZ Battalion:

> In the morning of 12 November we took our place in the column, moved through Matruh and down the Siwa road, and in the evening formed up at the head of 4 Brigade for the great approach march . . . The whole Eighth Army, Seventh Armoured Division, First South African Division, and the Second New Zealand and Fourth Indian Divisions moved westwards in an enormous column, the armour leading. The Army moved south of Sidi Barrani, past the desolate Italian camps of the previous year, along the

plateau south of the great escarpment, through the frontier wire into Libya, south of the enemy garrisons in the Sidi Omars, and wheeled north . . .

We did a short move, some 14 miles, and then two long day moves of 50 to 70 miles. These were easy, there was little dust and we rolled along, trucks 150 yards apart stretching far out of sight, a monotonous, never-changing procession like a convoy at sea. Then we started on the night moves. The trucks closed in until we were in 9 columns, not more than 20 yards apart and trucks almost head to tail. This was done just before last light each evening and meantime the provost sections went ahead planting posts with lanterns at ½ mile intervals along the intended bearing. All the brigades had different desert formations. In 4 Brigade at this time 20 Battalion led in 9 columns with companies abreast, 18 Battalion and 19 Battalion followed, each in 3 columns behind the flanks, and Brigade Headquarters and the attached troops, field, anti-tank, and anti-aircraft gunners, sappers, Field Ambulance, and supply vehicles followed the centre 3 columns. Fully closed up there was a mass of over 800 vehicles on a front of some 200 yards and a depth of 1,500 or so. When dispersed in the daytime the front was about 1 mile and the depth anything up to 10.[5]

At this time Sir Geoffrey Cox was one of the Intelligence officers of the NZ Division and he describes one of the day moves in his book, *A Tale of Two Battles*:

The entire Division moved forward in daylight a further forty-five miles westward, one of the rare occasions in the desert war on which it travelled as one single formation. We moved in lines of vehicles seven abreast, each vehicle two hundred yards from its neighbour, forming a vast column which stretched for nearly twenty-five miles. It was a clear, windless day, and the route lay for the most part over firm ground, so that there was little dust. On all sides trucks, Bren carriers, field guns, anti-tank guns, and staff cars lurched and bumped in one great moving fleet. It was an impressive spectacle. Early in the afternoon, above the sound of vehicles, we heard the sound of distant cheering, gradually growing louder. Up the centre of the column was moving a staff car, a Humber in desert camouflage colours. I recognised the General in it, with Jack Griffiths at his side.

The men in the trucks had recognised the General too and had begun to cheer. This was taken up in the vehicles around, and suddenly the whole column was cheering, with men waving from the backs of their three tonners, out of the cabs of trucks, from the carriers and the gun squads. As the General's car sped forward, the cheering sped with it. It was an emotive moment as, deep in the desert, with no one else to watch, these troops moving forward into battle cheered as if at a football match. It demonstrated not so much the popularity of the General – though that was one element – as of the men's confidence in him and in themselves for what lay ahead.[6]

[346]

The 'Crusader' operation began with the three Armoured Brigades (4, 7 and 22) and the support group of 7 Armoured Division all setting off on the morning of 18 November, and to begin with meeting little resistance. By the next day 7 Armoured Brigade was in the vicinity of Sidi Rezegh, where it was shortly to be joined by 7 Armoured Support Group. When 22 Armoured Brigade had reached Bir Gubi, held by the Italian Ariete Armoured Division, 4 Armoured Brigade had reached Gabr Saleh, in order to protect the western flank of XIII Corps. 7 Armoured Division was by then widely dispersed; 7 Armoured Brigade was some 25 miles to the north of 4 Armoured Brigade, which in turn was 20 miles from 22 Armoured Brigade.

Meanwhile 4 Indian Division had closed up to the German and Italian frontier groups, and 7 Indian Brigade was starting to work its way round the flanks of the Omars. The New Zealand Division crossed the frontier wire during the night of 18–19 November, and between 19 and 20 November moved slowly northwards to a position south-west of

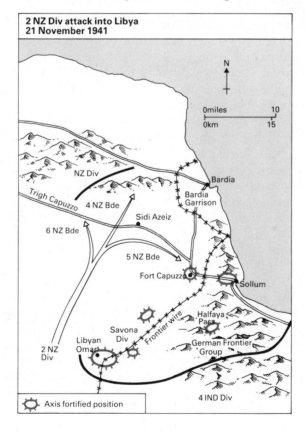

2 NZ Div attack into Libya
21 November 1941

Libyan Omar. Orders were received late on 20 November for a move forward of 10 to 11 miles next day.

The first phase of the NZ Division's offensive was very successful, as later reported in Freyberg's own account:

> 5th Brigade Group moved on by night and 22nd Battalion occupied Sidi Azeiz while 23rd Battalion moved against Capuzzo. It was a brilliant move and an excellent piece of desert navigation. The attack on Capuzzo was also an excellent piece of planning carried out at dawn with 'I' Tanks. The small force there was taken completely by surprise. It was like a dress rehearsal for the battle of 'Sidi Clif'. Two hundred prisoners (60 Germans and 140 Italians) were captured without casualties to ourselves and the Bardia water main to Halfaya was cut. So complete was the surprise that the Germans in Halfaya sent out an unarmed field company of 60 to mend the break and all of them were taken prisoner. The capture of Capuzzo played a most important part in disorganising the enemy because the Army Signal Exchange was situated there. In the afternoon 21st Battalion occupied Hafid Ridge.[7]

Freyberg sent a report to Godwin-Austen, XIII Corps Commander, at lunchtime on 22 November. In addition to the success of 5 Brigade, 4 Brigade had passed through 5 Brigade to the top of the escarpment west of Bardia, where they caught a number of Germans in a tented camp. Mopping-up operations continued and strong patrols were sent out to locate the positions of the enemy.

So far everything seemed to have gone according to plan. First reports about the armoured battle indicated that both 7 Armoured Brigade at Sidi Rezegh and 22 Armoured Brigade at Bir Gubi had fought successful actions and inflicted considerable casualties on the enemy. These reports were misleading, however, for the situation had become unsatisfactory even before 15 and 21 Panzer Divisions counter-attacked on 22 November. According to the New Zealand Official History, in the first four days of 'Crusader' the Eighth Army lost 530 tanks and the enemy about 100. 7 Armoured Division was down to fewer than 90 tanks, while the Germans still had 170 and the Italians 80. 7 Armoured Brigade had no tanks left, 22 Armoured Brigade was down to 30, and although 4 Armoured Brigade had between 50 and 60 Honey tanks, for the time being they were incapable of offensive action because their headquarters had been overrun.[3]

The first inkling of this disaster to reach the New Zealand Division was when a liaison officer arrived from XXX Corps on the afternoon of 22 November, followed shortly afterwards by another from General Gott to say that his support group was surrounded at Sidi Rezegh and that he needed help. Geoffrey Cox relates what happened next:

[348]

When the opening armoured battles ended in disaster for XXX Corps, and General Cunningham at Eighth Army considered cancelling the whole offensive, Freyberg's was a powerful voice against withdrawal. When he heard talk of this, he told General Godwin-Austen, 'You can't withdraw. You haven't even begun to fight.' This robust attitude was an invaluable buttress to Godwin-Austen's own instinct, which was to go forward rather than back. When the order came on 23 November for General Freyberg to establish a link with the Tobruk garrison he was able to move westward swiftly because he had trained his troops for night movement across the desert. Indeed the only formation in the Eighth Army in 'Crusader' which made use of the cover of darkness both to move and to attack was the 2nd New Zealand Division – and that was because Freyberg had seen far enough ahead to train his troops in these tactics.[6]

In fact Freyberg did not wait until 23 November before acting. On the afternoon of 22 November he despatched Brigadier Barrowclough and his 6 NZ Brigade Group, complete with its squadron of Valentine tanks, to Sidi Rezegh. After the war Godwin-Austen related how the attempt to call off the 'Crusader' operation had been prevented:

When we (XIII Corps HQ) were near Sidi Azeiz, I was called to a conference with Sandy Galloway (Chief of Staff, 8th Army), Lysaght Griffin (Chief Administrative Officer, XXX Corps), and Willoughby Norrie (XXX Corps Commander).

The last named could not come, but Major Carver* attended in his place with a R/T set netted to him . . . Galloway told me that orders were being considered for 'calling off' the whole offensive, and I was horrified. I spoke to Norrie who told me that XXX Corps was as good as 'finished'.

Galloway asked me if XIII Corps could relieve Tobruk. I said, 'NO, but Freyberg will.'

This conference ended by my telling Galloway that at all cost the offensive must continue, and the latter returned to HQ Eighth Army a very much happier man.[8]

When Galloway reached Eighth Army headquarters he put through a call to Cairo to make sure that Auchinleck was coming up, because General Cunningham had clearly lost his nerve. After assessing the situation on the spot the Commander-in-Chief returned to GHQ and decided on 25 November to relieve Cunningham of his command. Auchinleck appointed Lieutenant-General Neil Ritchie in Cunningham's place, and at the same time confirmed that the British offensive would continue.[3]

* Later Field Marshal Lord Carver.

[349]

On Sunday, 23 November Freyberg decided to make some changes to the plan for the advance on Tobruk. He detailed Hargest and 5 Brigade to contain Bardia and to deal with Musaid and Sollum, and asked XIII Corps to relieve them with 4 Indian Division as soon as possible. He also confirmed that the rest of the Division would be making for Tobruk. 6 Brigade was already on its way along the Trigh Capuzzo *en route* for Sidi Rezegh, and 4 Brigade was being directed on to Gambut as its immediate objective.

That same afternoon five miles south of the Trigh Capuzzo one of the heaviest tank attacks of the campaign was taking place: some 110 tanks of 8 Panzer Regiment overran and destroyed the 5 South African Brigade Group. Appropriately, in the Lutheran calendar Sunday, 23 November 1941 bore the name 'Totensonntag' – literally, 'Sunday of the Dead'.*

The week that followed saw some of the most confused and the fiercest fighting in the Desert War. It was confused because there were no established front lines, which meant that British and German mobile forces, both of armour and supply columns, were constantly intermingling in different parts of a battlefield that stretched for hundreds of square miles between Tobruk and the Egyptian frontier. And as far as the New Zealanders were concerned, in the end it became a straight fight between their Division and the Afrika Korps, with very heavy casualties on both sides.

There were two phases. The first lasted from 24 to 28 November when Freyberg and his Division marched westwards from their concentration area near Bardia, and linked up with a sortie by the Tobruk garrison at Ed Duda. The second phase lasted from 29 November to 1 December when Rommel returned to the Tobruk area with his Afrika Korps and attacked the New Zealand Division.

The sequence of events leading to the establishment of the Tobruk corridor may be clearly seen in date order:

24 November
Rommel started his dash to the frontier wire from south of Sidi Rezegh, with 15 Panzer Division directed at Bardia and 21 Panzer Division south of Libyan Omar.
4 and 6 NZ Brigades joined forces – 6 Brigade opposite Sidi Rezegh, 4 Brigade opposite Belhamed.

---

* Sometimes translated as 'Remembrance Sunday' or 'Day of the Fallen'.

25 November

NZ Brigades opposed by German Afrika Division in the Sidi Rezegh–Belhamed front. Reconnaissances and plans being made for attacks by both brigades.

Attack by 24 and 26 Battalions starts on escarpment south of Sidi Rezegh.

26 November

Night attack on Belhamed by 18 and 20 Battalions – final objective captured 0110 hours with 160 prisoners.

1600 hours TOBFORCE break out Tobruk perimeter near Ed Duda.

19 Battalion less two companies attack Zaafran to widen corridor.

6 NZ Brigade reach Sidi Rezegh.

27 November

Two companies of 19 Battalion attack Ed Duda taking 550 POWs.

5 NZ Brigade HQ outside Bardia is overrun by enemy tanks at 0700 hours, and Brigadier Hargest is taken prisoner.

Tobruk Garrison and NZ Division link up.

Frantic calls intercepted from General Westphal, Rommel's Chief of Staff, urging Rommel to return with Panzer Divisions to deal with New Zealand Division.

28 November

Further attacks by 18 and 20 Battalions south of Belhamed produced 600 more POWs.

Rommel's sudden dash to the frontier area with his Panzer Divisions on 24 November was meant to deliver a knock-out blow to the Eighth Army. Instead it was his undoing. Had the Germans kept 15 and 21 Panzer Divisions in the area of Sidi Rezegh, it is very unlikely that Freyberg and the New Zealand Division could have established their 'corridor' and reached Tobruk. As it was, they had an extremely tough fight to brush the German Afrika Division on one side and link up with the Tobruk garrison at Ed Duda. They could not have achieved this if the rest of the Afrika Korps had been there as well. Rommel's 'dash to the wire' certainly severely disrupted the British supply organisation, and caused the flight to Egypt of several thousand administrative vehicles, which became known as the 'Matruh Stakes'. But it did comparatively little operational damage – although one of its few adverse effects was to prevent the relief of 5 NZ Brigade in the frontier area so that it could not reinforce the rest of the NZ Division at Tobruk.

Tuesday, 25 November dawned a 'lovely day', night operations

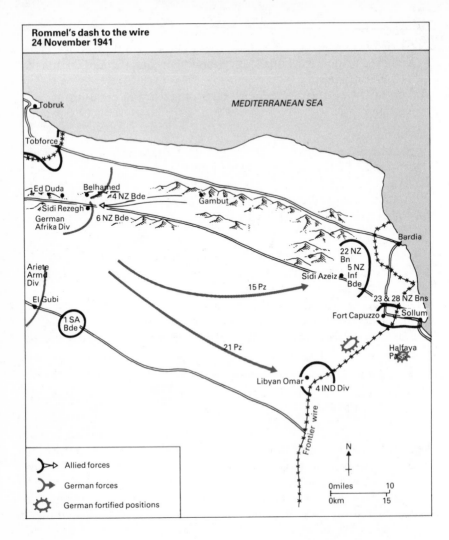

Rommel's dash to the wire
24 November 1941

having been completed according to plan, but Freyberg discovered that
the enemy were still ahead in strength when his two brigades collected
prisoners (4 Brigade took 300), which proved a considerable incon-
venience. Freyberg ordered new positions for 6 Brigade, went up to 4
Brigade, where he stopped 20 Battalion from carrying out a daylight
attack, and then went forward to have a look at the front line (of 18 and
19 Battalions) where he found splendid observation and targets but a
shortage of ammunition: 'Told them to dig in as they were already

being shelled – long range stuff which was skidding about.' The Diary for 25 November states:

> There is no doubt the enemy left these parts in a hurry. All the way along the edge of the escarpment [south of Trigh Capuzzo between Sidi Muftah, Point 175, and Sidi Rezegh] are tents full of personal gear, food and so on. A fair amount of 'ratting' has been done for shirts, underclothing, braces, badges, etc. We had stew for lunch containing olives, beans, carrots, turnip, meat (probably horse) – pretty oily and strongly seasoned but a good M and V [meat and veg]. An extraordinary war – while we eat his rations the Boche is sitting pretty in the south at present on one of our FSDs [Forward Supply Depots]. Freyberg then called in Inglis (4 NZ Brigade) and Barrowclough (6 NZ Brigade) for a conference at 1700 hours:
>
> The idea was to go in under cover of darkness some time before midnight or as early as possible. Message sent that Zero is 2200 tonight, meaning under the codes that Tobruk is expected to come out at the same time. One problem to decide is where to leave the great mass of MT [motor transport].[4]

It was decided that 6 Brigade should move on to Rezegh that night and 4 Brigade proceed to Belhamed at dawn, to coincide with the Tobruk sortie. 4 Brigade (18 and 20 Battalions) reached Belhamed in a dawn attack and 6 Brigade reached Rezegh on 26 November. But as the Diary states, 'fighting has been extremely tough and our successes have cost us casualties'. Kippenberger was wounded in both his legs and Colonel Peart, CO of 18 Battalion, was also wounded. The battalions had to advance across open ground on foot and capture enemy points with their bayonets. 6 Brigade found that Rezegh was strongly held, and once they were finally established there decided that it would be unsound to go forward to Ed Duda. Moreover the Tobruk garrison failed to come out as had been planned, 'because of the condition, no doubt, that we must first be on Ed Duda'.

Next day, 27 November, saw the planned link-up at Ed Duda. The Diary reports that as night approached the situation grew quieter. 'For the first time for some days we had a more or less uneventful evening and things were quiet on the front, the active role being temporarily handed over to Tobruk,' reported Freyberg, who added cheerfully: 'During the night Tobruk reported they had come out eight miles – felt inclined to send a reply that NZ Division had come out 308 miles!'

The next four days were the critical ones of the operation. Rommel had left his Chief of Staff, General Siegfried Westphal, at his main headquarters at El Adem, while he was in the frontier area with the Panzer divisions. Frantic messages from Westphal were intercepted on

27 November urging Rommel to return at once to deal with the New Zealand Division, now that it had linked up with Tobruk.[3] Rommel started back next day, initially with 21 Panzer Division on the Trigh Capuzzo and 15 Panzer further south, plus the Ariete Division. They were in fact following the route previously taken by the New Zealand Division, which, ultimately, would lead them to its rear.

The New Zealand troops were in good spirits on the morning of 28 November, in spite of the cold and overcast weather. The Diary records:

> As the day progressed, it certainly became one of extreme ups and downs. Just before lunch, 21 tanks were despatched to the east to dispose of enemy motorised transport reported separated from its tanks. No sooner had our reserve gone out than reports of an enemy column of tanks and motorised transport on the escarpment to the south came in and a little later the Ariete Division was reported on the Trigh Capuzzo! At about this stage, Corps moved to alongside and dug in – the Corps Command called and brought a bottle of whisky. During the afternoon there was pretty constant gunfire from the east and south, but that on the south went off that way and the reports were that the enemy in the east showed no inclination to advance.[4]

Later in the afternoon 4 Brigade attacked the Ariete Division in co-operation with the forces from Tobruk, and between them captured many prisoners. At the same time there was a German attack on Rezegh and Belhamed, the latter attack being caught before it reached Belhamed. The attack on 6 Brigade at Rezegh was a heavy one and supported by tanks. The NZ divisional reserve of 'I' tanks, of which there were nine, was sent out to assist 6 Brigade. At this stage the Diary, with other secret documents, was sent into Tobruk with most of the Division's HQ, and was brought up to date later at Baggush.

Freyberg meanwhile went up to see how 6 Brigade were getting on and had to take to slit trenches during heavy shelling. When he returned to Divisional HQ he found it under attack from a machine-gun force on the escarpment which had just released 1,200 German prisoners from a POW cage near the Medical Dressing Station (MDS). The Diary continues:

> Alarms and excursions continued as darkness came on. Tanks and Divisional Cavalry reported all quiet at the MDS and the enemy gone south. Verey lights all round showed the enemy rallying parties as usual. The loss of the prisoners will hardly bring the Boche an asset as they have no rations or water and 50 per cent are reported to have dysentery. Corps moved off to Tobruk at nightfall, followed by our Rear HQ and services. All

that was left, Advance HQ, moved up to near 4 Brigade so that the defence scheme could be closed in. Formed mobile column for guarding the rear. Hall produced a meal before start. Slept in office – very cold night.[4]

Rommel was now about to turn his full force on the New Zealand Division. It was Geoffrey Cox who recorded how the information reached Freyberg, because the Intelligence officers at XIII Corps had been listening in to the German wireless messages:

Though much enemy wireless traffic was in code, in the urgency of battle it was usually in clear providing a valuable and immediate source of information. I was on duty in our side of the 'G' [Operations] truck early on the morning of Friday, 28 November, when an urgent message from XIII Corps reached us. It was an intercept of an order sent by Rommel to the two German armoured divisions. It read; '15th and 21st Panzer Divisions are to rendezvous at Point 123456 (the exact map reference is not in my papers), destroy the New Zealand Division and advance on Tobruk.' I took it across to where the General's bivouac tent was pitched. He was washing in a green canvas basin. I read the message out to him. He finished drying his face, and then said, 'Where is Point 123456?'

I tried to sound in good heart. 'By my reckoning, sir, it is about the second tussock from where we are standing.'

'Read the message again.'

I did so. 'Destroy the New Zealand Division,' he said thoughtfully. Then a note of cheerful defiance came into his voice, and he said, 'We won't let 'em, Cox. We won't let 'em.'[6]

Every effort was now made to clear the decks. The NZ Administrative Group was sent into Tobruk that night, together with HQ XIII Corps, and Freyberg moved his own tactical headquarters right into the area which units of 4 and 6 Brigades were occupying. During the afternoon of 28 November there was a brush between 15 Panzer and 22 Armoured Brigade in which the latter lost 21 out of its remaining 45 tanks.

Saturday, 29 November was a dramatic day for the New Zealanders. In the early morning Brigadier George Clifton, a New Zealander at that time Chief Engineer to XXX Corps, arrived at a critical moment with 200 trucks containing water, rations, ammunition and an armoured escort of 15 American tanks and some armoured cars. Later that morning there was another excitement – the first German general to be taken prisoner in the Second World War was brought in. Soon after first light an outpost of 21 Battalion at Point 175 had opened fire at close range on an enemy car, and three Germans jumped out, one of them the general, who was sent on to NZ Divisional HQ. Geoffrey Cox described the incident:

> I found myself facing a man of middle age and middle height, with neat, sharp features, receding hair, a firm mouth and a quiet, self-composed manner. He had an Iron Cross around his neck, and another decoration which I did not recognise (it was the World War Pour Le Mérite, which despite its name, was a high German decoration equivalent almost to a British VC). He had given his name, when questioned at 6 Brigade, as Mueller. I had checked carefully through the lists of German officers supplied to us by Eighth Army but there was no General Mueller among them. It seemed highly unlikely that a new officer of such high rank could have arrived in Africa and been given a top command in the middle of a battle, but under my questioning he held adamantly to his story. It seemed all the more improbable because Mueller – the equivalent of our Miller – is a common German name, just the one at which one would grasp when seeking an alias.
>
> Bell told me to escort the prisoner to General Freyberg. In his red-banded cap, with four rows of medal ribbons on the tunic of his battledress, Freyberg looked a formidable figure as he stood alongside his staff car. Our prisoner halted before him, clicked his heels together with well-drilled formality, bowed, and, as was the German custom on being introduced to someone, gave his name. 'Ravenstein,' he said.

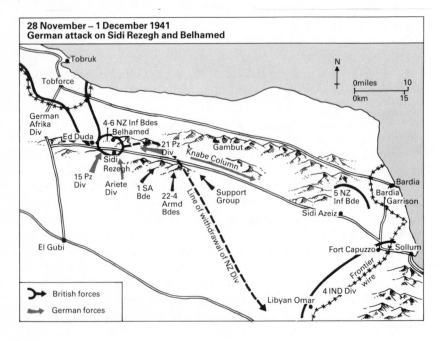

28 November – 1 December 1941
German attack on Sidi Rezegh and Belhamed

[356]

'But you said your name was Mueller?' I queried.

'So it is,' he insisted.

'Why then did you say Ravenstein?'

He shook his head. 'You have misheard me,' he said.

But I had heard enough. I knew, from my Baggush studies, that the commander of the 21 Panzer was Major-General von Ravenstein. I told General Freyberg that I was sure that our prisoner was the commander of 21 Panzer.[6]

Ravenstein's plans showed that there was to be a full-scale attack that day by 21 Panzer, directed on Belhamed and against the rear of the New Zealand Division, while the Ariete Division remained on the escarpment in reserve. 'Tanks are apparently to go round via Gambut to attack Belhamed,' the Diary recorded cautiously. 'The plan is ambitious – today will see how far it gets.' Enemy shelling of the New Zealand positions continued throughout the day, and in the afternoon John White's truck and 'I' Office were ordered to 4 Brigade HQ to ensure the safety of secret documents. Von Ravenstein was also sent to 4 Brigade HQ.

In the late afternoon, according to plan, the Ariete Division appeared at the New Zealanders' rear, 'at first being mistaken for South Africans!' The Ariete tanks advanced and overran 21 Battalion on Point 175. The whole of the available artillery was then turned on them and the Ariete departed east in haste leaving a considerable amount of knocked-out motorised transport behind. The Diary states that Inglis recommended Divisional HQ to follow XIII Corps into Tobruk; but Freyberg was unwilling as, in his mind, the only chance of holding Sidi Rezegh and Belhamed depended on co-ordination of plans with the South African Brigade Group – which could not be effected from within Tobruk.

The New Zealand Division at Sidi Rezegh and at Belhamed was now being attacked from all directions by the whole of the German Afrika Korps and the Italian Ariete Armoured Division. The only nearby possibility of help was the 1 South African Brigade Group under General Pienaar and the combined 4/22 British Armoured Brigade under Brigadier Gatehouse, both of which were to the south of the ridge near Point 175. But although they were repeatedly ordered to go to the assistance of the New Zealanders by retaking Point 175, they made no serious attempt to do so.

As John White wrote, Sunday, 30 November was a bad day for keeping a Diary as 'GOC's conferences were conducted in slit trenches'. The day also saw the climax of the New Zealand Division's action for the relief of Tobruk. First light showed the Ariete Division once again congregated on the edge of the escarpment, but they were seen off by a concentration of the artillery and made for the great open spaces 'a disorganised rabble'.

In the evening as the sun went down a heavy enemy attack supported by tanks was launched on Sidi Rezegh by 15 Panzer Division. Freyberg describes how 24 and 26 Battalions of 6 Brigade were overrun: 'The Ammunition of 6 Field Regiment ran out at the moment when tanks were grouping for attack and the infantry had no chance. Sent message to Corps at 1945: 'Infantry Brigade has been overwhelmed and enemy has Sidi Rezegh.'[4]

Freyberg was in communication by wireless with 1 South African Brigade, and urged them to 'push on, push with the bayonet' and retake Point 175 overlooking Sidi Rezegh. He sent two cavalry officers, Bonifant and Wilder, to contact the South Africans and explain the precarious situation due to the capture of Sidi Rezegh; they got through the enemy lines and 'returned with message next morning'. 'The South Africans' arrival alone on the flank of 6 Brigade could save the situation,' wrote Freyberg in the Diary. But in spite of prearranged plans and instructions, General Pienaar refused to attack, no doubt mindful of how 5 South African Brigade had been overrun and destroyed the week before and only a short distance away. Similar considerations affected 4/22 Armoured Brigade whose complement of tanks had now been increased to 120, but which was only too conscious of the fate of attacking British tanks earlier in the 'Crusader' engagement. During the evening of 30 November, when 15 Panzer Division overran most of 6 Brigade on Sidi Rezegh, there was no intervention from the South African or the British armour. The New Zealand battalions, however, continued to fight hard to the end, even though they had suffered severe casualties in the course of their long battle.

1 December was the final day of the battle, when the New Zealand Division was virtually surrounded and faced a daunting situation:

Was up at first light and made everyone dig again – very cold morning. Precautions were justified as enemy attack came from Sidi Rezegh direction and guns a few hundred yards from our HQ were attacked by tanks which brought up machine-guns, and the gunners were shot down by machine-gun fire. Battle HQ came under machine-gun and rifle fire and we escaped with nothing to spare. The Office Truck with a side down was abandoned. Brigadier Miles was wounded and later captured, Colonel Gentry's driver was killed and his car shot up, and there were other casualties. I went over to the 'I' tanks on Belhamed which were preparing to make a local counter-attack and there, too, the pressure was severe. Standing beside my car I was grazed by a splinter in the leg.[4]

The 18 and 20 Battalions of 4 Brigade were overrun at Belhamed by 15 Panzer early in the morning; what could be got away from both Sidi Rezegh and Belhamed either went into Tobruk or to Zaafran further to the east and the remnants from 6 Brigade streamed back in their vehicles into Zaafran, where NZ Division HQ was now located. Later that morning in Zaafran, Freyberg and Barrowclough met. The Diary records: 'I saw Barrowclough – it was a bitter blow, for the men could not have done more and now they had lost all the ground they had won.'

The situation on all fronts was critical. Nevertheless the decision to hang on at Zaafran was taken, and 4 Brigade, with the remainder of the 'I' tanks, repulsed sporadic German attacks during the day. They were also helped by four Valentines which Norrie sent out and which saw off fifteen or so Ariete tanks on the southern flank, while their own artillery and 'I' tanks held the attack from the west. 'It was an anxious day of waiting at Zaafran,' the Diary understated.

Freyberg decided against taking what remained of the Division into Tobruk, and instead moved south-east back towards the Egyptian frontier. Accordingly some 700 vehicles formed up at Zaafran in sight of the enemy, and at 6.45 p.m. set off due east accompanied by the remaining tanks and guns. After 3 miles they turned south-east and continued until they reached XXX Corps territory, passing through an area that was patrolled by troops of 4 Indian Division. Norrie was waiting near Bir el Chleta to meet Freyberg, who 'in spite of his adversities, was cool, calm, collected and in remarkable spirits'.[3] The move south in the moonlight had been done with uncanny ease, and the column pushed on until it reached Bir Gibni at about midnight, where it halted for a rest until dawn.

A considerable New Zealand presence on the battlefield still remained after Freyberg's withdrawal from the Tobruk corridor. One and a half battalions were helping the Tobruk garrison to keep open a modified form of corridor to XXX Corps; another 3,500 troops, mostly administrative personnel, were within the fortress itself, and about the same number again were with 5 NZ Brigade outside Bardia.

But the German and Italian armies were not in a position to continue the battle for Tobruk for much longer. The Afrika Korps had less than half the tanks and two-thirds of the guns with which it had started the campaign. Thanks to the activities of the Royal Navy, and the RAF operating from Malta, the enemy logistic situation was critical. After some half-hearted attempts to restore the situation between Tobruk and the Egyptian frontier in the first week of December, and as a result of prodding by mobile columns from 7 Armoured Division in the south, Rommel gave the order to start withdrawing from the Tobruk area on 7 December. By 12 December he was back at Gazala, where for a time 5 NZ Brigade followed up along the coast road. By 19 December 4 Indian Division had reached Derna, and entered Benghazi on 24 December. The whole of Cyrenaica was cleared of enemy troops by 6 January 1942. Bardia was captured on 2 January, and the remaining enemy positions in the frontier area surrendered a few days later.

Meanwhile Freyberg had re-established his headquarters in Baggush and nearly all his units had returned there by the New Year. New Zealand casualties during 'Crusader' came to 4,620 or a quarter of the Division's strength. The number killed or died of wounds came to 879, by far the highest proportion on the British side.[3]

The 1941 campaign to relieve Tobruk has been described as 'The Forgotten Battle'.[6] There are three reasons. First, it was such a complicated affair that historians have tended to ignore it in favour of the more straightforward and easily explained battles such as Alam Halfa and Alamein. Second, although the battle ended in defeat for the Germans and the occupation of the whole of Cyrenaica by the British, this phase did not last for long. Irrepressible as ever, Rommel soon hit back, and on 21 January 1942, only a fortnight after he had retreated to the El Agheila position, he again surprised and overwhelmed his opponents in Western Cyrenaica. By mid-February 1942 Rommel was back at Gazala, only two months after he had left it.

The third and the most important reason was because it coincided with the outbreak of war in the Far East. The Japanese attack on Pearl Harbor, their invasion of the Philippines, the sinking of the *Prince of Wales* and the *Repulse*, the attack on Malaya, the fall of Singapore, the threat to Australasia – these were the events and developments that dominated the headlines during the last month of 1941 and the early part of 1942. In comparison the campaigns in the Western Desert attracted little attention.

But one has only to reflect what would have happened had the November 1941 battles not been fought to realise how important they were. Had Rommel not been forcibly ejected from Eastern Cyrenaica in December 1941, he would have been able to start his 1942 offensive from the Egyptian frontier instead of from Gazala, 120 miles further west. Further, had he remained in possession of the East Cyrenaican battlefield, he would have been in a position to start his offensive into Egypt considerably earlier than when he attacked Gazala at the end of

May 1942. This would have happened before the arrival in Egypt from America in the summer of 1942 of the Sherman tanks and other equipment which did so much to turn the tide.

Seen in retrospect 1941 was a crucial year for the New Zealand Division under Freyberg's leadership. In the spring, in conjunction with the other defenders of Crete, they had helped to inflict such heavy losses on General Student's Fliegerkorps that his airborne forces were not able to proceed with their planned invasion of Cyprus or, ultimately, the Suez Canal. Furthermore, as a consequence of these losses, Hitler refused to allow them to be used against Malta in 1942. Then, that autumn in the Western Desert, the Division had marched on Tobruk at the critical moment in the battle, and had given Rommel and his Afrika Korps such a hammering that ultimately they were forced by the rest of the Eighth Army to withdraw from Cyrenaica altogether. This achievement, coming at a time when Allied fortunes in the Middle East were at a low ebb, helped to buy the time needed to reinforce the theatre with fresh forces and modern equipment, and laid the foundation on which future military victories were built.

In the 1942 New Year Honours List Freyberg was awarded the KBE. Murphy's Official New Zealand History volume *The Relief of Tobruk* assumes that this was in recognition of the part he played in the relief of Tobruk; but the system has rarely worked as fast as that even in wartime. The knighthood was given on Wavell's recommendation for Freyberg's services in Greece and Crete, and as recognition for the Division itself which, despite its heavy losses, had shown itself a fighting instrument of unique spirit.

The Lebanon and Minqar Qaim

The three months that followed the withdrawal of the New Zealand Division from the Tobruk corridor were increasingly taken up with disagreements about policy between Freyberg and GHQ Middle East. In essence, his disputes with Auchinleck were the same as those that had caused his differences with Wavell. Freyberg's priorities were to keep his Division together and to carry out his tasks in accordance with policy defined by the New Zealand government. Auchinleck, on the other hand, was as determined as Wavell that GHQ Middle East should decide policy, and that the NZ Division would conform in the same manner as a British formation. A clash was inevitable, and it came sooner than might have been expected. The new ingredient was that Freyberg had witnessed the tactical mistakes being made by the British Command in the desert and was more reluctant than ever to allow his men to suffer under what he considered foolish and damaging policies.

The first explosion was caused by orders Freyberg issued to Brigadier Wilder, the new commander of 5 NZ Brigade (Hargest having been taken prisoner in November 1941). When the rest of the Division returned to Baggush in December 1941, 5 Brigade had been left behind in Cyrenaica to help drive Rommel back to Tripolitania. Freyberg disliked detaching the Brigade from the rest of the Division, but recognised the importance of keeping up pressure on the Germans. He therefore agreed to 5 Brigade staying, on condition that it did not get involved in any more heavy fighting. The orders Freyberg gave to Brigadier Wilder were specific, for, having just incurred nearly 5,000 New Zealand casualties at Tobruk, he was not prepared to risk further substantial losses in subsidiary operations. Furthermore the outbreak of war in the Pacific in December 1941 made it likely that no further reinforcements from New Zealand would be forthcoming for some time.

When Wilder reported to XIII Corps Commander Godwin-Austen, who had taken over responsibility for the next phase of operations in Western Cyrenaica, he mentioned the restriction that had been placed on him. Godwin-Austen made no comment but reported it to Ritchie, the Eighth Army Commander, who in his turn informed Auchinleck. The latter was incensed, and on 11 December 1941 sent for Freyberg. Without giving him an opportunity to explain the C-in-C launched into a personal attack on Freyberg for 'interfering' with active operations, adding that this would not be tolerated. Freyberg was equally furious, and did not trust himself to reply at the time. He said that he would send Auchinleck a considered answer in writing, which took the form of a letter dated 12 December, the first three paragraphs of which state:

> C-in-C,
> I have now had time to go into the facts as I promised on the 11th and in doing so I have tried as far as I can, to see if the criticism levelled against me was merited. I have tried to find points of agreement with your charge rather than concentrate on points of obvious disagreement which I shall not refer to.
> The only controversial point that arises is the question of the employment of the 5 NZ Bde Gp. I know that you think I placed restrictions on the use of the 5 Bde Gp without reference to higher authority. If that had been the case I agree that I would have been entirely in the wrong. I am fully aware, however, of the normal channels of command and have always adhered to them.
> I did not attempt to answer the charge brought against me at our interview because you passed judgement upon me without asking me for my side of the case. I felt that it would be better to reply in writing.[1]

Freyberg then reminded the C-in-C more specifically that, after leaving the battlefield on 3 December, he had reported to Advanced Eighth Army Headquarters, where he had had a teatime discussion with the Army Commander Ritchie, and Auchinleck himself. At that meeting it was agreed that 5 NZ Brigade would not be used in further set-piece offensive operations, and Freyberg's instructions to his Brigade Commander were in accordance with these arrangements.

Auchinleck realised he had made a completely unjustifiable accusation. He told Freyberg in a letter three days later that he accepted his explanation unreservedly. After a half-hearted attempt to rationalise

[363]

his earlier attitude, he ended: 'I would like to thank you for your very straightforward and soldierly letter.'[1]

Although the matter was now closed, the episode left Freyberg with a nasty taste in his mouth. After all that his Division had done to relieve Tobruk at great cost to themselves, only a short time before, it seemed unreasonable that he should have been aggressively castigated for something that did not require explanation. There is no doubt that, had Freyberg chosen to report this incident, the New Zealand government would have been outraged. At that moment some 4,620 casualty notifications were dropping through letterboxes throughout New Zealand and no city or district was unaffected. The fact that he decided not to do so showed Freyberg's growing confidence in his ability to deal with his military superiors at GHQ. Indeed an alternative plan was already forming in his mind for future employment of the Division.

Freyberg had other reasons for dissatisfaction, of which two examples underscore the basic problem. When the Division ceased to have an immediate operational role it possessed more motor transport than it required, and Freyberg was prepared for this surplus to be sent where it was needed. In his view a quick staff study should have been made to identify the Division's continuing transport requirement for local administration and training; to decide what was in excess of these needs; and to suggest the best way of releasing the surplus. Instead Auchinleck and his Chief of Staff, General Arthur Smith, decreed which units in the NZ Division should provide the transport and even the type of vehicles to be supplied, often in ignorance of why their choice was unsuitable. Long and acrimonious arguments ensued; and Freyberg was unfavourably impressed that the C-in-C should allow himself to get personally involved in details that ought to have been settled at junior staff level. It was, incidentally, General Smith who was responsible for the origin of the oft-repeated story about Freyberg and the failure of New Zealand troops to salute. Arthur Smith was a stickler for orthodox military behaviour by other ranks towards officers. One day he complained to Freyberg about his men's lack of saluting. 'Try waving to them,' Freyberg replied. 'You'll find they'll always wave back.'

The second example caused Freyberg even more irritation and 'reinforced his doubts of the Middle East Command's wisdom and skill'.[2a] After the fight for Tobruk was over Freyberg decided to produce a detailed report describing what had happened. The exercise was designed solely for the benefit of the officers of the New Zealand Division, to help them with future training; and Freyberg's aim was twofold – to preserve a record of the battle, and to bring out the lessons that had been learned. Auchlinleck heard that this document was being prepared and, to Freyberg's considerable indignation, demanded to see and vet it before it was issued: 'as he feels that it is most important that nothing should go into it that is not in accordance with the policy he wishes adopted in tactical operations'.[2a] Freyberg foresaw correctly that this was an attempt to interfere with his ideas about fighting as a division, in favour of Auchinleck's brigade groups theory. The NZ Official History relates the outcome:

> The report was returned with the note: 'The only item I disagree with is the comment on battle-groups. Also it shows how badly we handle our "I" tanks.' Auchinleck ordered the deletion of a remark that 'the dangerous mistake of committing our small force piecemeal was gradually being corrected', and also references to the ineffectiveness of the binary, or two-brigade, division and the brigade-group organisation.[2a]

Freyberg was not the only commander of Dominion troops to suffer this sort of interference. The same thing happened both to the South African and to the Australian forces. The South African experience was not an exact parallel because Field Marshal Smuts was often in Cairo and kept direct control of the political and military aspects of the Union's forces. But General Blamey, the Australian commander, encountered problems similar to Freyberg's under both Wavell and Auchinleck.

One of Blamey's many disagreements with Auchinleck epitomises the attitude of the British/Indian Army commanders and staff in the Middle East towards the Dominion generals in the early years of the war. The 9 Australian Division had been locked up inside Tobruk since it was first invested by Rommel at the beginning of April 1941. By the summer the units were growing tired, and many of the men were in poor physical shape. Blamey asked for their relief, and this was eventually agreed, or so he thought. A Polish Brigade relieved 18 Australian Brigade at the end of August, but when it came to making arrangements to relieve the other two brigades, Auchinleck refused. At two stormy meetings at GHQ Cairo the following conversations were recorded:

AUCHINLECK: I want 9 Division to stay in Tobruk. You must support me, as my deputy.

BLAMEY: I am your deputy, but I'm also GOC AIF. I want them relieved.

AUCHINLECK: Talking of reliefs, if you take that tone I shall be compelled to ask for your relief.

BLAMEY: Go ahead and do it.[3]

And at the second meeting:

> The conference had begun badly. Auchinleck said that he had considered all the factors, and he decided that Tobruk could not be relieved. Then Blamey said: 'Gentlemen, I think you don't understand the position. If I were a French or an American commander making this demand, what would you say about it?'
>
> 'But you're not!' said Auchinleck.
>
> 'That's where you are wrong,' said Blamey. 'Australia is an independent nation. She came into this war under certain definite agreements. Now, gentlemen, in the name of my Government, I demand the relief of these troops.'[3]

Eventually Auchinleck had to give way, and the Australians were relieved in Tobruk without any major problems. But it was not until General Alexander arrived in Cairo in August 1942 that the Australian and New Zealand generals were left to run their commands without interference.

The New Year of 1942 brought the possibility of a further operational role for the New Zealand Division. GHQ, Middle East had had under consideration for some time a combined sea and land assault into Tripolitania known as operation 'Graduate' (sometimes referred to as 'Acrobat'). The object was to launch an early assault on Rommel from the sea in the Agheila area, using 5 NZ Brigade, and to follow this up on land with a link-up by the rest of the Division. The operation had certain superficial attractions, but the more Freyberg studied the details the less he liked the look of it. He told Middle East HQ that they did not know what reserves the Germans had behind Agheila, and that the danger was that Rommel could turn on the landing force before it was properly established, and destroy it.

During the first three weeks of January 1942 there were many discussions and arguments about the operation. Freyberg was in difficulty over the right attitude to adopt over a project he disagreed with – a problem he was to encounter again in the future. He had the power to refuse to undertake the operation, in which case he knew he would be supported by the New Zealand government. But he also knew that, if he did so, a British division would be employed in their stead, and it might then seem that the New Zealanders would undertake only easy operations and refuse the difficult ones. This he felt would be both morally wrong and understandably resented by the rest of the army. So he decided to accept the operation, and then argue against the project on its lack of merits. At the final conference, attended by about thirty officers from all three services:

Freyberg was so forthright in his comments and so argumentative that at length Admiral Cunningham, Commander-in-Chief, Eastern Mediterranean Fleet, beckoned him out of the room. Cunningham advised him not to worry. He said he had told Middle East Headquarters that the Navy would not go into the Gulf of Sirte unless air cover for twenty-four hours was guaranteed. As the aircraft were not available 'the show was off' so far as the Navy was concerned.[2b]

But unknown to the planners a more decisive factor was to bring the project to an end. On 21 January the Axis forces began to advance into Cyrenaica. As the New Zealand Official History comments, neither the New Zealanders nor any other British troops except captives were to see Agheila until nearly a year later.[2b]

Auchinleck interfered with British troops too. In late January 1942 his reversal of Godwin-Austen's orders for the defence of Western Cyrenaica resulted in the fiasco that led to the British retreat to the Gazala line. To Auchinleck's astonishment Godwin-Austen felt that he had no option but to resign, and asked to be relieved of his command of XIII Corps. He was succeeded by General Gott.[4]

Godwin-Austen came to dine with Freyberg in Cairo on 12 February 1942.* After dinner they had a long heart-to-heart talk. The move of the New Zealand Division to the Lebanon shortly afterwards suggests that Godwin-Austen's account of the mismanagement of the Eighth Army in Cyrenaica in late January 1942 confirmed Freyberg in his reasons for removing the Division from the Western Desert. At all events, after consultation between Freyberg, Auchinleck, and the New Zealand and British governments, it was agreed that the NZ Division should move to the Lebanon as soon as the necessary arrangements could be made.[5]

At the time it was announced that the New Zealand Division was being withdrawn to enable it to refit and recuperate after the battles to relieve Tobruk. However, in an interview at Government House in New Zealand on 3 May 1948, Freyberg told the historian J. L. Scoullar:

> I had seen what had happened in Greece and Crete and in the desert at Sidi Barrani and in Battleaxe. I had seen the Desert Command under Auchinleck. I knew their ideas and how faulty they were. I became firmly convinced that the only way to safeguard the interests of New Zealand and of the Division was to get the Division away from the Desert Command.[2a]

*I had been wounded with the LRDG in Cyrenaica in December 1941, and was staying in the family flat in Cairo on convalescent leave. I was present when Godwin-Austen came to dinner.

If the New Zealand Division was to leave the Western Desert, the obvious place for them to be employed was the Lebanon, which was still within range of the main NZ base in Egypt. Moreover some of the Australian troops were being withdrawn from the Lebanon to defend their homeland from the Japanese, and required relief.

The Division began its move at the end of February 1942 and Divisional Headquarters opened at Wavell Barracks, Baalbek on 27 February. At the beginning of March 4 NZ Brigade arrived followed immediately by 6 NZ Brigade; 5 NZ Brigade was still temporarily detached occupying a 'box' in the Gazala Line near Tobruk, but it left the Western Desert at the end of March and rejoined the rest of the Division at the beginning of April.[2c]

The NZ Division now became part of General Maitland Wilson's Ninth Army, the headquarters of which was at Beirut. The immediate responsibility of the command was to consolidate the British position in the Levant, which involved the security of Syria, the Lebanon, Palestine and Transjordan. The longer-term requirement was to go to the assistance of Turkey, should that country be attacked by Germany. At that time, early 1942, the German Army was still capable of mounting a two-pronged attack on Egypt, from the Western Desert and from the north through Turkey and the Lebanon.

Freyberg arrived in his new headquarters on 9 March. The Diary describes how 'The Mess is situated in a fine house on the outskirts of the township of the ancient Roman City of Baalbek – all stone, high ceilings – full of echoes.' The amenities included plenty of fresh food and good local wine; indeed the whole ambience could hardly have been in greater contrast to the bleakness of the Western Desert. Early spring in the Levant was very attractive, the temperature was pleasantly warm by day and cool at night, and the change of atmosphere was just what was needed to restore the Division's health and morale. Soon Freyberg was signalling to his Prime Minister how much the troops were revelling in the new conditions.

By the time the Division arrived in the Lebanon, none of the original brigade commanders was left. Brigadier Puttick had departed after the Crete campaign to become Chief of the General Staff in New Zealand. Brigadier Hargest and Brigadier Miles, Commander Royal Artillery (CRA), had both been taken prisoner during the November battles;* while Brigadier Barrowclough had been promoted Major-General and appointed to command the new 3 New Zealand Division being formed

---

*Hargest escaped and, after a series of adventures, reached England, but he was later killed observing action in France in August 1944.

to operate in the Pacific. Freyberg himself had been promoted to temporary Lieutenant-General in March 1942. The brigade commanders now were Brigadiers Inglis, Kippenberger and Clifton, with Brigadier C. E. Weir as the new CRA.[2n]

No one at this stage of the war knew how much of a threat the Japanese might prove to be to Australasia. Prudence suggested, however, that it should be taken seriously, particularly by the Australians. On the other hand there was a grave shortage of shipping to move the large Australian and New Zealand forces back to their home countries. In order to save shipping, President Roosevelt had undertaken to send three American Divisions to protect Australia and New Zealand, on the understanding that one Australian Division and the New Zealand Division should be left in the Middle East. For the time being, then, the future of 2 NZEF seemed settled; but there were many other factors to be considered.

The sailing of 8 Reinforcement from New Zealand to Egypt early in 1942 had been cancelled, so that manpower was now in much shorter supply. What was more of a worry for Freyberg was that he was required to send back to New Zealand a considerable number of 'middle-piece' officers to take senior appointments in 3 NZ Division. These were the officers he had been counting on to replace the many casualties amongst COs and company commanders suffered in the Tobruk battles.

Freyberg returned to Cairo twice for consultations with GHQ during his months in Lebanon, but apart from these short visits all communication between his wife and himself was by letter. These letters reveal what a large part of his time was taken up with training the new commanders. In addition he had agreed to help train the Greek Brigade which had been formed in the Middle East. There are several references to visits by Prince Peter, and on one occasion the King of Greece stayed for a weekend.

In a letter to Barbara dated 14 March 1942, when he had just returned from a tour of the Turkish frontier area, Freyberg spoke about how lovely the countryside was with the tops of the nearby mountains of the Lebanon and Anti-Lebanon still covered in snow: 'Yesterday we covered 450 miles over to the Euphrates, and then back via Palmyra, which has an extensive Roman town. I send you some small grape hyacinths picked from the banks of the Euphrates. Tomorrow, Sunday, I go off to Aleppo for three days.' These reconnaissances were all to do with the contingency plans to assist the Turks.[2d]

But his principal task was to improve the defences of Djedeide. This was a position of strategic importance in the Bekaa Valley, astride one of the two main roads from north to south through which any German attack must pass if the route to Egypt was to be opened up. The New Zealand Division, plus another brigade, was given the task of defending this line, while 9 Australian Division took up a similar defensive position near Tripoli, 50 miles north of Beirut, guarding the coastal road.

Freyberg's letters tell of a busy but pleasant life during the three months from early March to early June 1942. His mess had been lent some horses, and he was able to resume his First World War habit of a ride before breakfast in the cool of the morning. His Diary lists a constant stream of visitors, including the Duke of Gloucester, General Archibald Nye, the Vice-CIGS, and others, as well as the King of Greece, and Sir Thomas Russell Pasha, Chief of the Egyptian Police. But the news from the Far East was growing progressively worse, and everyone was also watching the Russian front: what happened there was even more likely to affect the Division's immediate future.

During the summer of 1942 the Germans resumed their attacks in southern Russia, with one group of armies moving eastwards towards Stalingrad, and a second towards the Caucasus. These developments meant that the Germans were unlikely to have sufficient troops for a simultaneous attack on Turkey, so that by the end of May 1942 pressure on the Ninth Army in the Levant had begun to ease. But as it did so the threat to Iran and Iraq increased. Nor was it fanciful to be apprehensive about what this might portend. Field Marshal von Manstein's memoirs make it clear that in 1942 Hitler at least had it in mind to drive through the Caucasus to the Near East and India.[6]

At the beginning of June 1942 therefore Freyberg was invited to carry out a reconnaissance into Iraq and Iran, in case this threat required the presence there of the New Zealand Division. The area was the responsibility of the Tenth Army under General Sir Edward Quinan, whose headquarters was in Baghdad. Tenth Army's resources, hitherto found mainly from India, consisted of a considerable infrastructure of headquarters and facilities stretching across Iraq and Iran, but contained very few fighting troops.

Having sent the rest of the reconnaissance party and vehicles ahead Freyberg left his headquarters at Baalbek with Colonel Gentry, his G1, on Friday, 5 June. They travelled from Damascus to Baghdad by Nairn Transport, that remarkable company which operated a direct coach service across the desert, and which usually travelled by night. They spent the morning of 6 June in conference with General Quinan and his staff. After he had lunched with his nephew David McKenna, who was serving in the Royal Engineers and was based in Baghdad,

Freyberg and his party caught the train for Khanikin, which they reached at 3.30 a.m. the next day, and linked up with their vehicles. On 7 June they crossed the Iranian frontier *en route* for Kermanshah, where they were met by General Mayne, commanding XXI Corps (staying the night at the big oil refinery there). Monday, 8 June was taken up in discussions with General Thompson (GOC 6 Indian Division) and Brigadier Furney (CO 26 Indian Brigade) and the following two days in reconnoitring places of tactical importance in the areas of Aquiz, the Sinnah Pass and Hamadan. The party started back the way it had come on 11 June, arriving in Baghdad in the late afternoon of Friday, 12 June.

On 27 May 1942, over a week before Freyberg left on his reconnaissance, Rommel had attacked at Gazala. The early reports of the battle suggested that the Eighth Army was more than holding its own, so Freyberg departed for Iran in a reasonably easy state of mind. However on 10 June, when he heard on the wireless that Bir Hacheim had fallen, he knew at once that the New Zealand Division would shortly be needed in Egypt. As soon as he reached Baghdad on 12 June, therefore, and before he received any orders, Freyberg made his arrangements. He despatched the reconnaissance party back to Baalbek by the fastest land route, with orders to pack up the Division immediately, prior to its moving by road to Egypt as soon as possible; and prepared to go on ahead by himself by air. At 0430 hours on 13 June Freyberg took off from Baghdad airfield in a RAF plane and arrived in Cairo that afternoon.

Freyberg immediately reported to GHQ, where he was greeted by Auchinleck with the words, 'I want to talk to you.'[2e] He was then given a warning order to move the New Zealand Division at once to the Western Desert. Bir Hacheim had been the first of the defensive positions of the Gazala Line to fall, and was an ominous pointer to the fact that the Eighth Army was losing its battle with Rommel. After a discussion about the precarious situation in the Tobruk area, Freyberg decided that this was the kind of emergency in which he was justified in giving the order to move the Division back to Egypt without awaiting the prior consent of the New Zealand government.

The distance of the move now to the area of Mersa Matruh varied between 900 and 1,000 miles, depending where the units of the Division were positioned. Main Divisional Headquarters left Baalbek early on the morning of 16 June and reopened a few miles west of Mersa Matruh at 9 p.m. on 20 June. They were followed on 17 June by 4 NZ Brigade, which arrived in the same area after a five-day journey. 5 NZ Brigade had been on an exercise east of Aleppo when the order to

move was received, and its main body reached 'Smuggler's Cove' at
Matruh on 22 June, after little more than four days on the road. 6 NZ
Brigade, which had been even more dispersed, took time to hand over
various commitments to the Australians and concentrate. One battalion travelled by rail and arrived at Mersa Matruh on 22 June. There
was insufficient motor transport to make this brigade as fully mobile as
the other two and so, for the time being, it was grounded at El Amiriya,
west of Alexandria.

Meanwhile Freyberg was recovering from a fortnight of non-stop
travelling. For the few days before his headquarters arrived from the
Lebanon he lived at the family flat in Cairo. He was thus able to be with
Barbara for her birthday on 14 June, which was also their twentieth
wedding anniversary. Soon afterwards he was laid low for forty-eight
hours. It was very hot, and the entry in Barbara's diary for 16 June
reads: 'I sat with B and rubbed his back till long after midnight.
He seemed a bit cooler and I don't think it is anything much, but, oh
dear, I so dread that hellish desert for him, and the news seems
pretty bad.'

The next three or four days were spent finding out precisely what
was happening in Libya, and making final preparations for setting out
into the desert. Whereas previously they had lived and worked in tents
when in the desert, divisional commanders were now being issued with
new office-cum-bunk-bed 3-ton vehicles equipped with telephones/
wirelesses, in which to work and sleep. Freyberg's caravan, having
arrived at Maadi, was being prepared for its first use in battle. Before
Freyberg left Cairo on Sunday, 21 June he called at GHQ, where he
heard that Tobruk had fallen and that the situation 'was obscure'. At
that time he understood that the plan was for the New Zealand Division
to concentrate on the coast 10 miles west of Mersa Matruh and then
move to the Libyan frontier. Barbara's diary records the moment of his
departure:

> I have had some anxious and unhappy partings but I think this was one of
> the worst, and the prospects for the moment are miserable. I am anxious too
> about B's health and know that he is feeling his heart. After he went, I went
> off to church, and was glad of the quiet to regain my control.

Although Freyberg was upset that all the hard fighting and losses
sustained in the November 1941 battles seemed to have been in vain,
he was so out of sympathy with the way the British Command was
conducting the war in the desert that he was not in the least surprised
that much of the Eighth Army was again being reduced to a shambles.

As the NZ Division advanced westwards the consequences of Auchinleck's misguided policies became apparent:

> As soon as the Division reached the desert road out of Alexandria, it
> encountered the Eighth Army in retreat ... The Divisional Cavalry
> Regiment, which had a particularly arduous journey from Syria and was the
> last unit to arrive, ran into Eighth Army convoys seemingly devoid of order
> and discipline. Hundreds of vehicles were parked along each mile of the
> road and a constant stream of traffic moving in the opposite direction,
> estimated at 750 vehicles each hour for the whole day, impeded progress.
>
> The congestion became worse as units and groups neared Mersa
> Matruh. Some senior officers bitterly described Eighth Army as a rabble.
> They were then meeting the flotsam and jetsam of an army in headlong
> retreat.[2e]

When Freyberg reached his headquarters near Mersa Matruh late
that afternoon he was told on the telephone that plans had been altered
and that the Division was to occupy the Matruh 'Box'. The Eighth
Army Commander Ritchie had decided to abandon the frontier area, in
the belief that this would buy sufficient time to build up an armoured
force behind the Matruh Box while a covering force from XIII Corps
imposed the maximum delay on the enemy between the frontier and
the Matruh defences.

But, although Freyberg had initially agreed to put the Division into
the Mersa Matruh fortress as ordered, he had no intention of fighting
the forthcoming battle in that box, or in any other box. He regarded box
defences as traps in which isolated defenders could be overrun by the
enemy at his convenience. More specifically he thought it completely
wrong to confine the highly mobile New Zealand Division inside a fixed
perimeter. Not only was the Division up to strength in men and
equipment, with a firepower that was equal to that of any two other
divisions of the Eighth Army, it had just been issued with the new
6-pounder anti-tank gun.

Freyberg put his views to General Norrie of XXX Corps, and again
to General Holmes of X Corps when the latter took command on 23
June. So strongly did he feel about it that he accompanied Holmes to
Ritchie's headquarters that afternoon, prepared to bring the issue to a
head. He was ready to say that the New Zealand Division would be
thrown away if it were kept in the Matruh Box and that, if necessary, he
would refer the matter to the New Zealand government. He told
Holmes he realised this might precipitate a crisis, but that the risk
would have to be taken for the sake of the Division and the people of

[373]

New Zealand. Holmes first saw Ritchie alone. When Freyberg was called in he was told that the Division would be relieved in Matruh by 10 Indian Division. The New Zealand Division would be allotted a mobile role in the open desert, with the task of attacking the open southern flank of the advancing enemy.[2e]

From 24 to 26 June the Mersa Matruh Box was evacuated and a defensive position taken up on the Minqar Qaim feature. This position left a lot to be desired, because, although the escarpment was tank-proof, instead of facing the approaching Germans at right angles, north to south – as ideally it should have done – it faced parallel to their line of advance, in other words from west to east. The problem, as General Kippenberger has written, was that 'the escarpment was a definite tank obstacle over a hundred feet high but [as] it ran east and west, the enemy were just as likely to come along the top as along the plain to the north'. Also there was no suitable feature to the south of Mersa Matruh, and the desert in the area was dead flat.[7] Moreover the New Zealand Division was tied to this general location if it was to keep in line with the defensive boxes of the Matruh position. In deploying in such a position on the Minqar Qaim feature Freyberg knew that he was risking being cut off from the rest of the Eighth Army, unless he could depend on 1 Armoured Division to keep his eastern flank open. For the Matruh battle, 1 Armoured Divison had 159 tanks of which 60 were Grants, so this risk seemed to be acceptable. By midnight on 26–7 June the New Zealand Division was disposed on the Minqar Qaim escarpment with 5 NZ Brigade Group on the western flank, Divisional Reserve Group next to it west of the Khalda track, and 4 NZ Brigade at Bir Abu Batta.[2f]

But on the evening of 25 June, while the NZ Division was taking up its position at Minqar Qaim, General Auchinleck decided to dismiss General Ritchie, whose conduct of operations had resulted in the retreat of the Eighth Army from Gazala, the fall of Tobruk, and the British withdrawal from Cyrenaica; and decided to take over command himself, with a change of policy.[2g] Auchinleck reversed the decision that the next battle should be fought on the Matruh position, and as he later wrote in his despatch, 'I therefore cancelled the orders to stand at Matruh and gave instructions for the Eighth Army to withdraw on El Alamein, delaying the enemy as much as possible in its retirement.'[2g]

A period of intense confusion followed. Eighth Army Operation Instruction No. 82 had been issued at midnight on 24–5 June stating clearly the intention to hold the Matruh position. Operation Instruction No. 83, issued at 0415 hours on 26 June, was to the effect that the Eighth Army was to retire to Alamein. The first instruction was received at NZ HQ, but as the Official NZ History states: 'There is no record that the New Zealand Division received Instruction No. 83.'[2g] Thus, while the Division was digging in at Minqar Qaim, Freyberg was under the impression that the Indian Division was still defending Matruh, and the Armoured Division was protecting his right flank.

The period that followed, from the end of June and through the first ten days of July 1942, were among the most disastrous of the Desert War. Freyberg was badly wounded on 27 June and so was out of action for the whole period. However, in view of the Court of Enquiry, Western Desert 1942 that followed the débâcle, and the close involvement of New Zealand troops, Freyberg later recorded his views:

> I would like to make a comment in general terms upon the cause of the disaster. General Auchinleck was well-known as a bad judge of a man, and he assembled round him a bad staff. I was apprehensive during the whole of this period, because most of us could see it approaching. The 'Jock Column' and 'Brigade Group', successful with the Italians, were doomed to end in disaster against the Germans, and these were the cause of our failures. It has been argued that our defeats were due to the lack of a good tank. I do not agree. It could have been offset, and it was in 1943 when the Sherman tank plus the use of Artillery saw off the 'Tiger' and the 'Panther'.
>
> The new set up of the Eighth Army would not work. You could not combine the duties of C-in-C Middle East with command of an army in the desert. The C-in-C should have put in a new Commander, who had not lost his nerve.
>
> Looking back, seeing the whole picture, many things are now obvious.
>
> 1 No success could be achieved if an Army Commander is allowed to re-organise on the lines of his scheme 27 June. This was quite fantastic, and would ruin any Army.
> 2 Auchinleck was completely out of the picture. Eighth Army Operation Instruction No. 83 of 26 June showed a lack of understanding of what had happened. The Army had for the moment disintegrated. The system of command had broken down. Neither Holmes nor Gott made any effort to keep their front intact. The 21 Panzer Division found a hole and went right through between 10 and 13 Corps. When this happened, instead of attacking to close the hole, the Commander-in-Chief issued the order to withdraw.
> 3 A study of the frequent change of plan shows that Auchinleck was badly served on the 'G' side. General Corbett [Chief of Staff to C-in-C Middle East] and Dorman-Smith [Deputy CGS Middle East] were bad choices. Ritchie also was badly served. Brigadier Walsh, BGS 10 Corps, was good. In his notes he said that on one day, I think about 23 or 24 June, his Corps got three separate sets of orders, all of them altering

the policy of defence. What was wanted at Mersa Matruh was for 10 Corps to start to get out early on 26 June and, if necessary, we should have fought an Army battle with the massed artillery of the two Corps side by side and in physical touch, with the Army Commander well forward.[1]

On 25 and 26 June Rommel closed up to the Matruh position round Charing Cross and Sidi Hamza with 90 Light and parts of 15 Panzer Divisions. At the same time 21 Panzer Division, under the command of Major-General von Bismarck (a cousin of the Iron Chancellor), was approaching the Siwa track, which it crossed at 7.30 in the morning of 27 June, in the vicinity of Bir el Gibb. Although the Germans knew that the New Zealand Division was back in the Western Desert, they had no idea that it had moved from Mersa Matruh to Minqar Qaim. In the meantime 21 Panzer continued eastwards along the low ground below the escarpment, in effect cutting off the New Zealanders from the coast road.

During the course of 27 June heavy artillery fire began to be directed against the New Zealand positions and a number of casualties resulted. Late in the afternoon German infantry attacks developed against the Minqar Qaim escarpment from the north, but these were beaten off with comparative ease. What alarmed Freyberg early in the afternoon of that day, however, was the news that 1 Armoured Division had received orders to withdraw to Bir Khalda, 15 miles to the south of Minqar Qaim, before moving further east, and was no longer support-ing the New Zealand Division. This was the first Freyberg knew of the change of plan and the withdrawal to the Alamein position. Freyberg quickly concluded that if the Division was to avoid being cut off it would have to break clear. Moreover it would have to rely on its own resources for the operation. Accordingly at 4.40 p.m. he issued detailed orders for what was to follow during the night of 27–8 June.[2i]

Freyberg then left his headquarters and motored up to see how the defence was coping with the latest German attacks. At five o'clock while watching this development from a forward position, he was hit in the neck by a shell splinter. His ADC Jack Griffiths assisted him to his car, and he was driven back to his headquarters where he received medical attention from the ADMS.

Freyberg later wrote from his hospital bed in Helwan, giving the following account of his wounding and what then happened:

We had been attacked four times without any success and a fifth attack was developing when we got orders to withdraw to the Alamein position. I was anxious to see if 5 NZ Brigade were pinned to the ground so I motored right up into the line and ran into a heavy shelling with nearly fatal results. A piece of shell the size of an egg entered below my left ear and passed through my neck. I had a hole that they passed a piece of gauze through the size of a handkerchief. I believe a photograph appeared in the *Mirror* of me after being hit. I believe I look rather sick in it. Well, I felt it!

After they had beaten off the last attack they began their 90-mile journey back, across very bad going:

The journey was eventful because we were surrounded and had to fight our way out, and then about midnight the Division, in desert formation 2,800 vehicles strong motored into the laager of 21 Panzer Division. Everybody shot in all directions and AT and AA guns fired tracer and we let off all our hand guns and threw bombs everywhere. I believe this charge did more to break the German morale than anything else. We had 250 casualties, mostly missing.[8]

That paragraph refers to one of the most famous actions of the New Zealand Division in the Second World War – the Minqar Qaim breakout. By this time Freyberg was no longer in command – indeed he had been given morphia by the ADMS – but he was conscious of all that was going on, and was reported to have said from his caravan bed at the height of the battle, 'By God, another Balaclava!'

The whole operation was organised by Brigadier Inglis with skill and efficiency. Three battalions of 4 NZ Brigade advanced in line on foot with their bayonets ready to punch a hole in the German positions; and they tore into the enemy with unprecedented ferocity. The attack was completely successful, and when all was over most of the transport of the Division passed through the hole made in the German line.[2k]

John White recounted in the Diary what happened to Freyberg during the action:

Jack [Griffiths] was in the caravan – turned into an ambulance with a Red Cross over it. It was in moving away from the infantry that the transport ran into the tank laager and the resulting burst of firing from that quarter. We turned away barring some vehicles on fire with 'tracer' sweeping across us – fortunately mostly high. A spandau [German machine-gun] hit the windows of the general's truck from behind, beside the driver's right ear!

Dawn on 28 June found the Division widely dispersed over the approaches to the Alamein position, but everyone knew that the rendezvous was at Deir el Harra and as the day continued more and more units reported to the check points until, to everyone's amazement, by last light virtually the whole of the New Zealand Division was once again reunited as a fighting force. Meanwhile Freyberg had been taken to an airfield on the coast, from where he was flown by air ambulance to Cairo.

Some interesting references to the Minqar Qaim breakout came from the German side in *The Rommel Papers*. Rommel himself described the action:

> The New Zealand Division under General Freyberg, an old acquaintance of mine from previous campaigns, did in fact concentrate in the night and break out in the south. A wild mêlée ensued, in which my Kampfstaffel Kiehl and units of the Littorio joined in the fighting. The firing between my forces and the New Zealanders grew to an extraordinary pitch of violence and my headquarters was soon ringed by burning vehicles, making it the target for continuous enemy fire. I soon had enough of this and ordered the headquarters and the staff to withdraw to the south-east. One can scarcely conceive the confusion which reigned that night. It was pitch-dark and impossible to see one's hand before one's eyes. The RAF bombed their own troops, and, with tracer flying in all directions, German units fired on each other.
>
> In the early hours of the morning, several hundred more New Zealand vehicles broke out through great gaps on the south-east side of our front. It is in fact extremely difficult in desert warfare to improvise a long front capable of withstanding the attack of a force which has retained its cohesion and is able, thanks to motorisation, to focus its strength suddenly.[9]

Rommel also wrote:

> Our men had once again fought with extraordinary courage. Unfortunately, the New Zealanders under Freyberg had escaped. This division, with which we had already become acquainted back in 1941–42, was among the élite of the British Army, and I should have been very much happier if it had been safely tucked away in our prison camps instead of still facing us.[9]

On 2 July 1942 the Prime Minister was replying to a challenge in the House of Commons on the government direction of the war. Churchill referred briefly to some of the steps being taken to rectify the situation in Egypt. He then said:

> Although I am not mentioning reinforcements there is one reinforcement which has come, which has been in close contact with the enemy and which he knows all about. I mean the New Zealand Division. (Cheers.) The Government of New Zealand, themselves under potential menace of

invasion, authorised the fullest use of their troops whom they had not withdrawn or weakened in any way. They have sent them into battle where, under the command of the heroic Freyberg, again wounded, they have acquitted themselves in a manner equal to all their former record. (Cheers.) They are fighting hard at this moment.[10]

Brigadier W. B. ('Bill') Stevens, then Chief Administrative Officer of 2 NZEF, has described how Freyberg on arrival in hospital was insistent on seeing the CGS Middle East, to tell him the position in the desert, and on sending a report to New Zealand:

Despite attempts to put him off by Lady Freyberg, various doctors and myself he persisted in this and was obviously upsetting himself so much that we had to fall in with his wishes. The CGS was hurriedly sent for from Cairo; and I took down at the General's dictation a message for the New Zealand Government. Only then would he agree to have his wound examined and re-dressed.[11]

Freyberg went into the New Zealand No. 2 General Hospital at Helwan on 28 June. On the day following admission, his neck was operated on and cleaned up. Basically he was extremely fortunate that, in spite of the size of the bit of shrapnel and the extremely sensitive area of its passage, no vital organ had been hit. However he was suffering from shock and exhaustion, and for the first few days was kept under sedation. After about ten days his condition began to improve and he was able to have visitors again. There were plenty of problems connected with the NZEF as a whole for him to be involved with. The officers in charge of administration and the New Zealand base were often at his bedside, and his personal staff were also in attendance.

When Freyberg was beginning to feel better and started to get up for an hour each day, the question came up of his going somewhere for convalescence. Field Marshal Smuts offered to send his personal Lodestar aircraft to Cairo to bring him and Barbara to South Africa, and to look after them until he was well enough to return. Barbara was keen to accept, but Freyberg felt that the trip would take him right away from the scene of action at a moment when crucial decisions might have to be made. Barbara's letter of thanks and regret to Smuts was so heartfelt that he sent her a charming reply in his own handwriting.

However Freyberg realised he was still too weak to think of returning to active operations without proper convalescence, and that the heat of Cairo in July was no place to recoup his strength. He began to think that the best compromise, offering a change of scenery without venturing too far away, was to go back to the Lebanon. Moreover the No. 3 New

Zealand General Hospital was still situated just outside Beirut, so that there was suitable back-up in case he should have a relapse.

On 20 July therefore the Freybergs flew in a small de Havilland aircraft from Almaza aerodrome near Cairo to the Lebanon. It was a lovely morning, and they refuelled at Port Said and Lydda, otherwise following the historic coast of the Holy Land. They lunched at the Normandie Hotel, Beirut, called in at the NZ General Hospital to have Freyberg's wound dressed, and then went on to the nearby Sofar Hotel, 2,000 feet up in the hills and much cooler than the plains. This was to be their base for the next fortnight. These two weeks were among the very few of relative peace and relaxation that Freyberg spent in the six years of the Second World War, and certainly the only ones in which Barbara participated as well. Many of those who came to dinner or entertained them there were personal friends, such as Sir Edward and Lady Spears,* or relations like Quintin Hogg. Other friends took them on motor expeditions to local beauty spots or for walks near the hotel through vineyards where wild flowers and columbines were a special feature.

But ominous rumours reached them about further battles in the Western Desert, and of more heavy casualties in the Division. The news from the Far East and from Russia seemed to be equally black, and then, just when Freyberg seemed to be nearly recovered, he suffered a setback which required further treatment. On several occasions his temperature rose alarmingly, and for two or three days he spent most of the time in bed. However this phase did not last for long, and by the end of the month he was feeling that he must return to Cairo, in spite of Barbara's plea for them to stay longer.

As they left on 1 August Barbara summed up this rare interlude:

From the personal point of view, I have much to be thankful for – B's wonderful recovery from what was so nearly a dangerous wound, and our perfect holiday together – such an oasis of happy, normal life at its loveliest in the midst of all the suspense and anxiety and, for so many, the sorrow. Personally I don't think I have ever had such a complete rest and am feeling all the better for it and for whatever may be ahead.

As soon as Freyberg arrived in Cairo, in spite of the fact that his wound had barely healed and he was still far from completely re-

*Major-General Sir Edward (Louis) Spears, MP 1922–4 and 1931–45 had a working military relationship with the French dating back to the First World War. He was Head of the Spears Mission, Syria and the Lebanon, July 1941 and First Minister to the Republics of Syria and the Lebanon 1942–4. He was also the author of *Liaison 1914: A Narrative of the Great Retreat* (1930; Second Edition, 1968).

covered, he found himself involved in the developing crisis. His original instinct not to go too far afield was proved right. During his absence in July the New Zealand Division had been involved in two major battles on Ruweisat Ridge and El Mreir which had gone badly wrong; partly because the same old problems with British Command had recurred. There had continued to be a disastrous lack of 'grip' in the leadership of Eighth Army and Corps HQ, with no proper co-ordination between infantry and supporting armour. Once again this had resulted in New Zealand infantry capturing their objectives, and then being overrun by enemy tanks in the absence of British armour to defend them.

Freyberg was appalled to find that New Zealand casualties in July had totalled over 4,000, including two battalions which had been decimated. He spent many hours with senior officers discussing how this could have happened, and found that troops had again been dribbled away in penny packets, supporting tanks ordered to leave infantry just when they were most needed, and the latter then left to face German armour without adequate means to defend themselves.[2m]

Freyberg was not the only person who was worried. Winston Churchill and the War Cabinet in London had supported Auchinleck until the July battles, but finally they too began to lose confidence, even though the 'front' had been stabilised at El Alamein, partly because Rommel's lines of communications were now so long. The CIGS, now General Sir Alan Brooke, arrived in Cairo at the beginning of August, followed shortly afterwards by the Prime Minister. Freyberg was asked to go and see Brooke at GHQ Middle East during the afternoon of 6 August. There is no record in Freyberg's papers about what they discussed, but if his views had been asked, which they almost certainly were, there is no doubt what he would have said.

The same Thursday, 6 August saw a personal reconciliation with Mr Churchill. There had been no communication between Freyberg and Churchill for over a year since the Crete disaster. The Prime Minister now knew much more about what had happened in Crete than he did in June 1941, and he had already paved the way by sending Freyberg a telegram on 4 July: 'Deeply moved to hear of your new wound and new glory. Trust that your injury is not serious and that you will soon be back commanding your splendid division. All good wishes to you and to them.'[12]

Freyberg lunched that day at the British Embassy and attended the conference with the Prime Minister, Smuts, Brooke, Wilson, Wavell and Auchinleck. Among other things Churchill discussed on that occasion were his War Aims, and the shape of the post world-war situation as he visualised it. But the shape of the Middle East Command was also under review.

Freyberg spent his final three days in Cairo getting ready for his return to the desert. He was still far from well, and in particular was suffering from a rash caused by the heavy dosages of the drugs he had been given against infection. Barbara's diary for 7 August concludes: 'He is getting stronger but his rash is still very heavy. He bears it with heroic patience and never complains.'

The Diary now resumed. It records that Freyberg's party left the New Zealand Club for the Western Desert at 1100 hours on 10 August 1942. They reached the desert road out of Alexandria without incident, but had some difficulty in finding 'C' Track due to a heavy sandstorm. Eventually they arrived at New Zealand Divisional Headquarters at 1800 hours that evening.

22

The Battles of Alam Halfa
and Alamein

When Freyberg returned to the desert and resumed command of the New Zealand Division he knew he was not properly fit; but big changes were impending. He was aware too that Inglis, his acting GOC, was suffering from the combined effects of jaundice, dysentery, an eye infection and insomnia. In fact when Inglis heard that Freyberg was about to return he anticipated the change in command by going to Cairo for medical treatment. The hand over of the Division took place at dinner in Freyberg's Cairo flat on the evening of 8 August, and more formally at Maadi Camp next morning.[1a]

Inglis had had an extremely difficult time in command of the Division. His physical discomforts had been bad enough, but much worse had been the continuing mismanagement of the Eighth Army; so much so that after the battles at Ruweisat and El Mreir Inglis had bluntly told the Corps Commander that he would refuse to take any further part if future arrangements followed the same pattern.[1b]

The military situation in the desert in the second week of August 1942 can be described in a few sentences. Rommel's attempts, from late May onwards, to force his way through to the Nile Delta had narrowly failed. There was then a pause, during which the Allies regrouped and, in particular, were able to bring forward the new tanks and other weapons that were arriving in quantity from England and America; but such a breathing space was likely to be of short duration.

Meanwhile General Sir Harold Alexander had been appointed

Commander-in-Chief Middle East in place of Auchinleck; and when Freyberg arrived back at his headquarters he was faced with another change. General Gott, selected to command the Eighth Army, had been killed on his way to Cairo to take up the position on 7 August, when his plane was shot down. General Renton, commanding 7 Armoured Division, took over temporary command of XIII Corps until Freyberg arrived in the desert on 10 August, when he replaced Renton. After Gott's death Lieutenant-General Sir Bernard Montgomery was appointed Commander of the Eighth Army.[2a]

On 13 August there occurred the first meeting between Freyberg and Montgomery. Freyberg was the only lieutenant-general left who had survived as a senior commander for much of the Desert War: two Cs-in-C, Wavell and Auchinleck, had been dismissed, as well as two army commanders, Cunningham and Ritchie; and the corps commanders who fell by the wayside for one reason or another included O'Connor, Neame, Beresford-Peirse, Godwin-Austen, Norrie, Holmes, Ramsden and, most recently, Gott.

Freyberg had been a strong critic of the previous regime's military policies and was therefore a 'survivor' from, rather than a supporter of, the old order. When he met Montgomery he was unhappy about the general situation in the desert and, according to Alan Moorehead's account in *Montgomery*, began the meeting by saying: 'I feel terribly sorry for you. This [Africa] is the grave of lieutenant-generals. None of them stay here more than a few months.'[3] Freyberg wrote:

> Our meeting took place at 1500 hours on 13 August 1942, as recorded at the time, and dealt entirely with Divisional organisation and control in battle.
>   I said to him, 'I want to talk about the control of the New Zealand Forces. I only come under your command for operations, not for discipline or training, and only for operations when the New Zealand Government have given their consent.' I also said to him, 'I have had great anxiety in the past with higher commanders who have a mania for breaking up military organisation.'[4]

Freyberg went on to complain about previous generals who had put their trust in jock columns, defensive boxes and brigade groups, and declared that he would refuse to take part in further battles unless he could fight as a division. To his surprise he found the new Army Commander agreed with him. Montgomery not only stated his intention to fight in divisions, but said he would centralise the control of artillery at divisional or even at corps headquarters level. Furthermore he would be giving orders that no more withdrawals were to take place,

[384]

and that troops would stay put and fight where they stood. He was also going to give instructions that the elaborate contingency plans to go back to the Nile Delta and beyond were to be torn up. According to Nigel Hamilton's account of the interview in *Monty: The Making of a General* Freyberg was 'delighted'. He was more than that – he was amazed. He realised that if Montgomery meant what he said, a new era really had begun.[2a]

Freyberg never forgot the debt of gratitude that was owed to Montgomery for his rehabilitation of the Eighth Army in the summer of 1942 after many months of mismanagement, and for the steps he took to restore its morale. He admired Montgomery's professionalism and his thorough grasp of military business. He agreed with his tactical concepts, both his determination to fight in divisions, and the full use he always made of artillery. He was in broad agreement too with his handling of the armoured commanders, and with his firmness in requiring them to comply with his orders. Moreover Montgomery and Freyberg shared an abhorrence of the senseless slaughter of the First World War that was epitomised by the battle of Passchendaele. In this connection Harold Macmillan noted in *Winds of Change 1914–1939* that the generals of the First World War were very different from their successors in the Second. Except on the rarest of occasions, the First World War generals hardly ever appeared in the line:

> Had they done so they could not have authorized the continuous and useless operations at Passchendaele, where 400,000 casualties were incurred to little purpose. The Second War was fought by great generals from their caravans. The First was conducted by men of lesser quality from their châteaux . . . many of the leading generals of the Second World War had served as regimental officers in the First War and had not forgotten their experiences. They also appeared constantly in the front line, and were well known to the troops. In this respect, the armies of the Second War were luckier.[5]

After the arrival of Alexander and Montgomery, Freyberg was no longer treated simply as part of the British Army and was left to make his New Zealand arrangements without interference. On a personal level Montgomery and Freyberg got on well together, and there were few of the disagreements that had marred the latter's relationship with earlier commanders-in-chief and army commanders. Later on, admittedly, Freyberg began to grow doubtful about certain aspects of Montgomery's behaviour – his growing personal vanity, his arrogance and intolerance towards those who disagreed with him, and his open contempt for the Americans; and after the war Freyberg was saddened by Montgomery's lack of loyalty to some of his old colleagues, particularly his treatment of his former Chief of Staff, General Sir Frederick de Guingand. But for the duration of the Desert War, Montgomery and Freyberg worked together harmoniously.

If the battles of Alam Halfa and Alamein were to mark the turning point, not just of the war in the Middle East but of the Second World War itself, the turning-point for Freyberg began on 13 August 1942. Before that date his references to the war in Egypt were gloomy; after it there was a new note of hope and growing confidence. On 14 August, for example, the Diary reports: 'Awoke to no sound of gunfire which was a relief – rash much better – felt a good deal better for both. Went to conference at NZ Div immediately after breakfast. Told them situation and policy of "New Brooms".'

At 0800 hours on 16 August Freyberg handed over XIII Corps to Lieutenant-General Brian Horrocks, and an hour later he gave a long talk to all the commanding officers of the NZ Division, for which he prepared the following notes:

> Big changes in command in Middle East. General Auchinleck has gone and General Alexander has taken over from midday yesterday. General Corbett has gone and also General Dorman-Smith. It has been a clean sweep. Always feel terribly sorry for a man like General Auchinleck who has had to face difficulties that few of us know about. C-in-C Middle East is a job that would do in anybody. However there is no doubt it is a good thing to get a completely new outlook on the situation here and I think we can all of us take that to heart. We have got into a desert warfare complex of moving backwards and forwards. I think it is a very good thing to get a completely new brain on to the thing . . .
>
> At the Army Commanders' conference yesterday he [Montgomery] gave his intention – while holding the present front against any attack – to prepare the Eighth Army for offensive operations to destroy the enemy in Egypt and Libya. We are to be on the defensive as short a time as possible and we shall be training on a long-term policy to resume the offensive as soon as it is possible.[4]

Four days later Freyberg was writing to Barbara: 'The position is much better and we can now look with a certain amount of confidence to the future, although the longer the Germans wait the better we shall be able to cope with them.' And again on 26 August, 'Here all goes well and on proper lines, now we have got down to it.'

On 20 August Winston Churchill spent a day with the Eighth Army on his return from visiting Moscow:

Everybody said what a change there was since Montgomery had taken
command. I could feel the truth of this with joy and comfort. We were to
lunch with Bernard Freyberg. My mind went back to a similar visit I had
paid him in Flanders, at his battle-post in the valley of the Scarpe, a quarter
of a century before, when he already commanded a brigade. Then he had
blithely offered to take me for a walk along his outposts. But knowing him
and knowing the line as I did I declined. Now it was the other way round. I
certainly hoped to see at least a forward observation post of these splendid
New Zealanders, who were in contact about five miles away. Alexander's
attitude showed he would not forbid but rather accompany the excursion.
But Bernard Freyberg flatly refused to take the responsibility, and this was
not a matter about which orders are usually given, even by the highest
authority.[6]

Referring to the visit Freyberg wrote to his wife: 'You will see the
admirable little speech Winston made to the representatives of the
Division. He was in very good form and I had a good deal of talk to him
at luncheon.' What the Prime Minister had said included:

In England not long before I left I heard someone say the New Zealanders
were 'a ball of fire'. It was said by someone quite impartial who had a great
opportunity of assessing your worth. You have played a magnificent part, a
notable and even decisive part, in stemming a great retreat which might
have been most detrimental to the whole cause of the British Empire and
the United Nations.
   I know that on the other side of the world in your homes in New Zealand
all eyes are fixed on you. But even more eyes in England watch you fighting
here with equal solicitude. I wish you good luck in the great days that lie
ahead – perhaps not so far ahead – of you.[4]

Two problems in particular occupied Freyberg during the late summer
of 1942. The first concerned manpower: no reinforcements had been
sent to Egypt since Japan entered the war; the relief of Tobruk had cost
nearly 4,700 casualties, and over 4,300 more had resulted from the July
1942 fighting; and in addition there was normal wastage, accentuated
by Middle East diseases, particularly jaundice, sandfly fever and
malaria. Instead of possessing a satisfactory reserve of reinforcements
in the base camps, as was the case in the first two years of the war, the
bottom of the manpower barrel was now being scraped to keep units up
to the minimum strength that was acceptable operationally.
   The second problem, which had been under discussion for some
time, concerned the raising of an armoured brigade. The July battles

had emphasised again how vital it was for the New Zealand Division to have its own organic armour permanently under the control of its headquarters. One of the most important lessons from the battles at Ruweisat and El Mreir, and indeed from Minqar Qaim and the relief of Tobruk before that, was that infantry/armoured co-operation had been most unsatisfactory. This was partly because tanks and infantry had rarely trained together before battle, and there was no common doctrine on how the two arms should co-operate in the field. Above all, New Zealand battalions had several times suffered from the fact that, when the infantry most needed protection from enemy armoured forces, their supporting tanks had been ordered to leave for another part of the battlefield. The only way to avoid such difficulties in future was by having a tank brigade under Freyberg's direct control.

By the early autumn of 1942 a compromise on both problems had been worked out. After the US victory in the battle of Midway on 4 June 1942 the Japanese threat to New Zealand had receded. A limited number of reinforcements could be allowed to 'top up' the Division in the Middle East. Also it was agreed that a New Zealand Armoured Brigade should be formed in Egypt. This required the conversion of one infantry brigade to armour. The choice fell on 4 NZ Brigade under Brigadier Inglis, which began its armoured training at Maadi Camp that autumn; but it took more than a year before new tanks and equipment were forthcoming and officers and men were trained in their use. This meant that for the rest of the war in North Africa the New Zealand Division consisted of only two infantry brigades.

In June and July the German and British armies had fought themselves to a standstill some 50 miles to the west of Alexandria. The Germans then regrouped and concentrated all their resources for a final attempt to reach the Nile Delta. Meanwhile the British Army had begun to change its strategy from a rearward defence in depth to a forward one in strength. That is, Montgomery had abandoned the concept of withdrawing under pressure in the hope of defeating Rommel by manoeuvre, and instead held the key forward ground strongly, with no thought of withdrawal. This policy required major adjustments in attitude and, above all, time to work out the new arrangements.

When Montgomery first outlined to Freyberg on 13 August the changes he proposed to make in the defensive posture, it was feared that the Germans might begin their attack in a week or ten days time. In fact some two and a half weeks passed before the next battle started. The most likely period for the attack coincided with the full moon on 26 August; but in the event Rommel began his offensive on 30

August. This delay gave the British just enough time to implement Montgomery's new arrangements for the impending defensive battle.

The dispositions of the Eighth Army were: XXX Corps – consisting of 9 Australian, 1 South African and 5 Indian Divisions – was holding the northern area between Ruweisat Ridge and the Mediterranean; further inland, to the south of Ruweisat Ridge, XIII Corps was deployed, consisting of the New Zealand Division, 7 and 10 Armoured Divisions, and 44 Infantry Division. This latter formation had been specially brought up from the Nile Delta by Montgomery to occupy the Alam Halfa Ridge, the high ground which dominated the rear area of the Eighth Army's position.

There were two courses open to the Germans. The first was to attack in the coastal area in the north; the second to make a wide outflanking movement to the south and then move in a north-easterly direction to seize the high ground at Alam Halfa, thus by-passing the defensive positions north and south of the Ruweisat Ridge at El Alamein. The XXX Corps defences north of Ruweisat, which were strongly held and well dug in behind wide belts of minefields and wire, would have required a prolonged battle to overcome. The southern flank was more open and vulnerable, and therefore the more likely area for German assault.

By the end of August it was the enemy who was up against the clock. His lines of communications stretched back for hundreds of miles to Tobruk, Benghazi and ultimately as far as Tripoli. Increasingly too the Germans were becoming short of petrol and ammunition, due to the sinking of their supply ships by the Royal Navy and the bombing of their transport system by the RAF, the tactics of both of which were guided by ULTRA decrypts. The British forces, on the other hand, were close to their main depots in Egypt, which were rapidly filling up with the requirements of a modern army. New American Sherman tanks, now beginning to arrive, would provide the first really effective equivalent to the German Mark III and IV tanks.

The knowledge that his own supply situation was critical – while that of his opponents was the opposite – made Rommel realise it was a case of now or never. But he could hardly have grasped the significance of the recent changes in the British high command. Rommel was expecting the British Army to continue to behave in the same way as they had done in the past, and laid his plans accordingly.

As there were insufficient British troops to occupy a continuous defensive position from the Mediterranean as far as the impassable Qattara Depression, some 40 miles to the south, the southern part of the front was heavily mined and patrolled by the armoured cars and

tanks of 7 Armoured Division. The New Zealand Division held Bare
Ridge, the most southerly of the main defensive positions below the
Ruweisat Ridge, and was hinged to face both to the west and to the
south. In theory there was nothing to stop Rommel from advancing
eastwards as far as he liked in the gap between the NZ Division and the
Qattara Depression; but the further east he travelled the longer his
flank became, and the more exposed his lines of communication to
attack from the north. In practice therefore his freedom of action to
move in the direction of the Nile Delta was strictly limited, and did not
extend eastwards beyond the area to the south of the Alam Halfa Ridge.

During the ten days before the German attack the British strengthened their defensive positions. The 44 British Division was brought up
to occupy the Alam Halfa position itself; the New Zealand Division was
on Bare Ridge; and both were dug in on the vital ground, protected by
minefields and wire. They were closely supported by large concentrations of field and medium artillery, plus 6-pounder anti-tank guns
and hull-down tanks, dug in so that only the turrets were exposed to an
advancing enemy.

The attack began on the night of 30–1 August with the advance into
the southern gap of three German and three Italian armoured and
motorised divisions. Rommel's intention was to move forward with his
usual speed and take the British by surprise. By first light on 31 August
he aimed to be within striking distance of Alam Halfa Ridge, and to
deal with what he expected would be the usual slow British reaction and
counter-attacks. But it worked out differently.

First the southern British minefields were much more extensive and
thick than the Germans had expected. Instead of getting clear of them
well before dawn, the Afrika Korps was still trying to find a way through
at first light and making so much noise about it that surprise was lost.
Heavy fire from the whole of the corps artillery, and incessant RAF
pattern-bombing on a massive scale were brought down on the advancing enemy during the morning, causing many casualties; General
Nehring, Commander Afrika Korps, was wounded, and General von
Bismarck, commanding 21 Panzer Division, was killed by a New
Zealand patrol from 25 Battalion.[1c]

Eventually by the afternoon of 31 August 90 Light Division, and 21
and 15 Panzer Divisions had reached positions between the New
Zealand Division and 44 Division.

At 1700 hours that afternoon the Germans launched a heavy
armoured attack on Point 102 on the western edge of the Alam Halfa
feature. It was met by 22 Armoured Brigade on ground of its own
choosing, and driven off with heavy casualties inflicted on the enemy.[2b]

This action was the turning-point of the battle, and a vindication of Montgomery's theories on defence. To Rommel it appeared unbeliev-able that, after what had happened in earlier desert battles, the New Zealand Division on Bare Ridge and 44 Division on Alam Halfa Ridge should have anticipated and countered the German attack. Neverthe-less by taking up strong positions on these ridges, with the infantry out of sight on reverse slopes, anti-tank guns defiladed on the flanks, tanks in hull-down positions and gunners with observation posts on the crest overlooking the surrounding desert, they had brought the assault to an abrupt halt.

As early as forty-eight hours after the start of the Alam Halfa battle Rommel already knew he was beaten and that he had no prospect of getting through to the Nile Delta. Partly this was brought about by his lack of logistic resources, but far more was due to his being faced by an opponent who refused to be stampeded into precipitative action. In previous battles troops had occupied brigade 'boxes' which were too isolated to support one another and whose artillery was dispersed in penny packets over a wide area. At Alam Halfa the infantry was deployed with brigades closely supporting each other and covered by

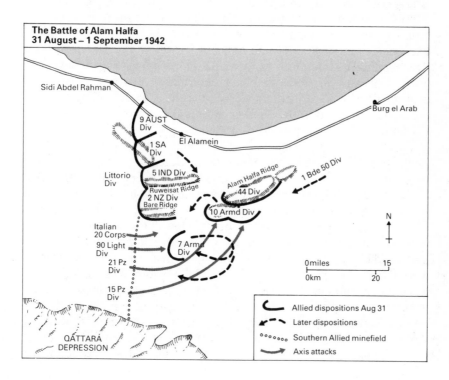

The Battle of Alam Halfa
31 August – 1 September 1942

regiments of artillery massed together under divisional and corps control. In this way, and by simply sitting tight on the vital ground, Montgomery had reversed the defence tactics that had proved fatal for his predecessors.

This was a remarkable achievement which had already transformed the desert fighting. For such a momentous battle the cost so far had been extremely light with under 700 British casualties. Unfortunately an operation known as 'Beresford' was then mounted which proved as costly as it was unproductive for the British side.

In moving towards the Alam Halfa feature Rommel had exposed the Afrika Korps' lines of communication to a possible counter-stroke from the north. On the map it looked an inviting prospect for the British to move south and cut off his retreat. The obvious place from which to start such an attack was Bare Ridge. General Horrocks, Corps Commander, who had been in the desert for just two weeks and lacked Freyberg's experience of the conduct of desert warfare against Rommel, decided to launch the operation and spent the first days of September trying to persuade Freyberg to mount it with New Zealand troops. But it was one thing to take on Rommel and his Panzer divisions from behind carefully prepared defensive positions, and quite another to go out into the open desert and meet them head-on without proper tank support. Less than two months previously the New Zealanders had been overrun by German tanks at Ruweisat and El Mreir, and Freyberg had no intention of exposing his Division to a repeat performance. Nor was he alone in being determined to resist Horrocks's orders: 'Freyberg's brigadiers were, from the start, unwilling to leave the defensive position they had so strenuously fortified,' wrote Nigel Hamilton in his biography of Montgomery.[2c]

When Horrocks realised that he could not persuade the New Zealanders to undertake the operation he decided to bring in another brigade to do the attack, and nominated 132 British Infantry Brigade.

For reasons of geography the 'Beresford' attack had had to be mounted from the positions held by the New Zealand Division on the Bare Ridge, and when the British brigade began to get into difficulties New Zealand commanders and troops tried to help them. The Germans had been presented by 132 Brigade with a soft target in the open desert, and by the time the Alam Halfa battle had ended on 7 September, another thousand British casualties were added, with no gains to show for them.[1d] Among many others, three outstanding NZ officers became casualties: Brigadier Clifton was taken prisoner, and Colonel Russell and Colonel Peart were killed. When Freyberg saw that the operation was degenerating into a shambles he called it off without consulting Horrocks.[2d] Later in the war Freyberg's coldness towards Horrocks was noticed on a number of occasions by different people. It was not just that he had forecast the 'Beresford' operation would end in disaster that caused Freyberg to mistrust Horrocks's military judgment;[4] he resented the unnecessary casualties which his insistence on the action had caused.

Apart from the excessive risks inherent in operation Beresford, there was an additional reason why Freyberg was strongly opposed to it: the New Zealand Division had been warned for relief at the beginning of September, and the usual hand-over/take-over procedures with the 44 Division had already been started when the German offensive began. The NZ Division had been in the desert since mid-June and had suffered over 4,500 casualties during those ten weeks. On his return from convalescence Freyberg had seen the strained look of troops who had been asked to carry on for too long. They could not, of course, be relieved until Rommel's final offensive had been repulsed, but as soon as that threat was over Freyberg lost no time in taking the Division out of the line.

The last casualty of the period was Freyberg himself. He had only recently recovered from his neck wound at Minqar Qaim and from the drugs prescribed to prevent infection. As he was driving from the forward area on 10 September his staff car collided at speed with a 3-ton ammunition lorry going in the other direction. His driver and ADC escaped unhurt, but Freyberg and his PA John White were thrown heavily and badly shaken. At first it was thought he had sustained a cracked rib, but a visit next day to the X-ray department of No. 8 General Hospital near Alexandria showed no fractured bones, only extensive bruising. His ribs however continued to hurt for the remainder of the month.

Meanwhile the Division was settling into a new rest area on the coast between El Hamman and Burg el Arab, some 25 to 30 miles to the east of El Alamein. Most of their vehicles and equipment had been sent to an out-of-the-way area some 15 miles inland, so that the troops had only themselves to look after. The weather was warm but not too hot, the sea bathing was superb, and the troops quickly recovered their health and morale. Soon leave parties were visiting Alexandria and Cairo, and Freyberg found he had a different set of problems on his hands. Most of the troops on leave behaved impeccably, but inevitably a small minority did not, and seemed to enjoy making trouble. Freyberg realised that if he waited the inevitable chiding letters would arrive from HQ, British Troops Egypt and the Military Police, so he decided to get in first and visit them personally. This had the hoped-for mollifying effect. The only mistake he made at this time was to visit the Beer Bar at the New Zealand Club to see conditions for himself. After a visit of seconds rather than minutes he was forced by the boisterousness of the celebrating soldiery to make an extremely rapid exit . . . 'it was the only time in the war,' recorded Brigadier W. G. Stevens, 'that I ever saw my chief turn tail'.[7]

When the ten days rest period came to an end the troops left their coastal bivouacs and, on 19 September, the Division joined up again with their vehicles and equipment in the open desert west of Wadi Natrum, some 40 miles inland. Training for the battle of Alamein was about to begin.

After the Alam Halfa operation, there was a six-week pause. Both sides used this to regroup but the Germans no longer had the resources for offensive action, and the initiative had passed to the British.

Montgomery's plan for the battle of Alamein was to attack the north of the German–Italian positions with four infantry divisions and to punch two holes in the enemy lines through which British armoured divisions would drive until they reached open country beyond. The original plan, called 'Lightfoot', envisaged that after a successful 'break-in' of the German–Italian lines, a 'corps de chasse' of two armoured divisions would then exploit the breakthrough and cut off the retreat of the Axis Army. The New Zealand Division was intended to participate in the 'break-in' operation under XXX Corps, and then switch to X Corps, the 'corps de chasse', for the break out.

The XXX Corps was commanded by General Oliver Leese, an old friend of Freyberg's. Montgomery originally intended X Corps to be commanded by Horrocks, but the latter asked to be excused on the somewhat unusual grounds that he might not be acceptable to cavalry regiments; and in the event the corps came under General Herbert Lumsden.[2e] The XIII Corps under Horrocks was given a less important deception role, being responsible for the southern sector.

Another development, which Freyberg welcomed, was that he was given as his third formation, replacing 4 NZ Brigade, the British 9 Armoured Brigade. This consisted of one Regular regiment, 3 Hussars; and two Yeomanry regiments, the Warwickshire and the Royal Wiltshire; plus their own battalion of infantry, 14 Foresters. They were equipped mainly with the new Sherman tanks. Moreover there was no nonsense about the brigade being 'in support', which would have meant they could have been ordered elsewhere at short notice. The 9 Armoured Brigade was firmly 'under command' of the New Zealand Division for the duration of the battle.

These arrangements filled Freyberg with confidence. For the first time since the war began in the Middle East he was under commanders whose tactical doctrines he approved, and he had been given the proper equipment for the forthcoming battle. On 3 October 1942, three weeks before the battle of Alamein, Freyberg sent a long signal to his government expressing that confidence:

> Complete change in Middle East management has cleared air. One good result they now insist Divisions must be kept intact. Result of this simple decision will be manifest in our future battles. It makes position here much easier . . . They have gone further and adopted German model of permanent Desert Corps kept intact to train and fight as such. New Zealand Division has been selected as infantry division for Desert Corps otherwise comprising armoured divisions.[8]

Freyberg added that he hoped the days were now past when New Zealand infantry could be overrun by enemy armour, as they had been on 1 December 1941, and on 15 and 22 July 1942. He ended:

> Weather now cooler and flies are fewer. As you know Division has been through difficult period but men are very fit and in excellent heart. Better equipped than ever before, your Division after present training period will be ready as part of Desert Corps for any future operations in Battle of Egypt.[8]

Training started as soon as the Division reassembled on 19 September after its short spell of leave. By this time 9 Armoured Brigade had arrived, so that for the first time all the important components of the force could be put through their paces together. The first major exercise began on 24 September. Known enemy defences that were to be attacked a month later were reproduced on a stretch of desert as near as possible to the original, and the exact drill was followed as if for real.

After the first exercise was over a number of post-mortems followed to analyse mistakes and correct the various drills. This in turn was followed by several smaller exercises designed to practise particular aspects of the operation. On 28 September Freyberg gave a dinner in Alexandria for selected officers of the Division and the Armoured Brigade to enable them to get to know each other and encourage co-operation. And on 30 September Montgomery inspected parades of the Division, and presented awards won in recent battles, including that of the VC to Sergeant Keith Elliott of 22 Battalion.[1e]

But one major problem had not been solved before the battle started, and no satisfactory answer was ever found. Indeed it was to recur later in the war in Normandy and elsewhere. The new brooms from England were slow to recognise it as a problem at all, although the 'old hands' had long known that it lay at the heart of the desert war. The Germans were past masters in using anti-tank guns to counter British armour. Even more damaging than the German Mark III and Mark IV tanks, was the effect of their 50mm anti-tank guns and the dreaded 88mm in 'brewing up' British tanks. The enemy had developed to a fine art the business of luring British armour on to well-concealed anti-tank gun screens, and then firing on the approaching tanks, with devastating results. A troop of 4 guns could destroy a couple of squadrons of 30 tanks in as many minutes, and had done so on a number of occasions – notably in 'Battleaxe' in June 1941; during the relief of Tobruk in November 1941; at Knightsbridge and Gazala in May 1942; and more recently at the first battle of Alamein in July 1942.

Armchair tacticians then and since have often criticised the timidity of British armoured regiments in the desert, but few of them can have had the experience of clearing up the aftermath of an encounter between British tanks and German anti-tank guns. The physical injuries inflicted on tank crews were often appalling, as the author saw both on the battlefield and as a patient in Tobruk General Hospital. The wounds caused by enemy armour-piercing ammunition were bad enough, but on occasions British tank ammunition also exploded after a direct hit; and worst of all the tanks' petrol tanks caught fire. In many cases soldiers killed outright were more fortunate than those left still alive.

It was experiences such as these that caused the armoured commanders to develop an attitude of extreme caution. This was particularly evident in the early stages of set-piece battles, when the infantry had punched a narrow hole in the enemy line and the intention was for the armour to push through the gap and then fan out beyond. On too many previous occasions the Germans had quickly thrown up improvised anti-tank gun screens beyond the gap, with fatal consequences for British tanks.

Freyberg was reasonably confident that the New Zealand Division would be able to capture its objectives, and with the help of 9 Armoured brigade and their Sherman tanks hold them against enemy armoured counter-attacks. But the other three attacking divisions had only Valentine tanks in support, and if any of these failed it might endanger the whole operation. The army plan insured against this by having the two armoured divisions of X Corps advance through the infantry along separate corridors. But after Freyberg had talked to Lumsden, commanding X Corps, and A. H. Gatehouse, now commanding 10 Armoured Division, he had considerable doubts about how their units would carry out the operation. Would the armoured formations be more likely to act with caution rather than determination?[1f]

When General Leese arrived in the desert in August 1942, according to Nigel Hamilton's account in *Monty*, he was 'horrified at the state of ill-feeling that existed between infantry and armour. Neither had confidence in the other. All mutual trust seemed to have been drained out in the previous battles.'[2h] Leese described how at his first corps conference before the battle he outlined the army plan to his infantry divisional commanders. They listened to him politely, and then expressed grave doubts whether the armoured divisions had the resolution to exploit the gaps in the enemy lines made by the infantry.

Montgomery himself later described the same conference in *Alamein and the Desert War*:

> Therefore, having considered the problem from every angle with my staff, we decided to drive two corridors through the enemy defensive area; both were well to the north of the centre of the Axis position. Infantry divisions were to clear the mines and open up the corridors; they were to be followed closely by the armoured divisions, and I ordered that if the infantry divisions were unable to clear the corridors completely the armoured divisions would fight their own way out into the open. This order was not popular with commanders of armoured formations and units, and when the Corps commander, General Leese gave it out at the conference with his subordinate commanders to tell them of the army plan, General Freyberg of the New Zealand Division remarked in a loud voice, 'They won't', and was quickly followed by General Morshead of 9 Australian Division with the same comment. General Leese had been in the desert only a few days and he was somewhat startled by such statements by two very experienced generals, so he said, 'Perhaps you don't know the Army Commander very well; what I have said is his order.'
>
> Both generals repeated 'They won't!' General Leese then wisely suggested they should all have a break for coffee, and during the break he discussed the difficulty with his Chief of Staff, an experienced officer, who was well aware of the discord between infantry and armour. When the conference reassembled General Leese laid it down that all would assume that planning would proceed in full accordance with the army plan – and this was done. It will appear later how nearly right the two divisional commanders were when both said 'They won't'.[9]

[397]

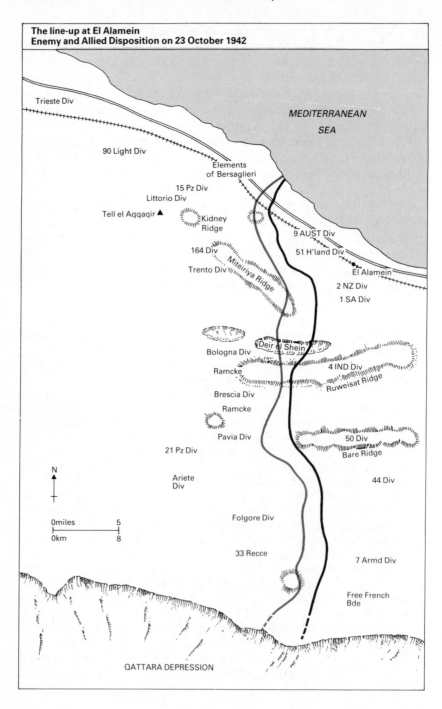

The line-up at El Alamein
Enemy and Allied Disposition on 23 October 1942

Trieste Div

MEDITERRANEAN
SEA

90 Light Div

Elements
of Bersaglieri

15 Pz Div
Littorio Div

Tell el Aqqaqir ▲

Kidney
Ridge

9 AUST Div

164 Div

51 H'land Div

Trento Div

Miteiriya Ridge

El Alamein

2 NZ Div
1 SA Div

Bologna Div

Deir el Shein

Ramcke

4 IND Div

Ruweisat Ridge

Brescia Div
Ramcke

Pavia Div

50 Div
Bare Ridge

21 Pz Div

N

Ariete
Div

44 Div

0miles   5
0km   8

Folgore Div

33 Recce

7 Armd Div

Free French
Bde

QATTARA DEPRESSION

Montgomery's intention had been to make the British armoured formations operate in the open beyond the minefields. As events proved, they were unwilling to do so and the Army Commander was forced to modify his plan during the battle. Freyberg's outspokenness was an important factor in making Montgomery change his mind when the first major crisis resulted in an impasse.

On 21 October Freyberg wrote to his wife from the Western Desert, 'We move into the line this evening.' And two days later:

> By the time you get this the cat will be loose and the result I hope will be satisfactory. We have had a hard task given to us. I wish we had our full number of men. My last few notes to you have been stultified affairs. It seems difficult to write when there is a censorship being imposed, somehow it paralyses thought.[4]

By the evening of 23 October four divisions – 9 Australian, 51 Highland, 2 New Zealand and 1 South African – forming XXX Corps were ready for the assault, which aimed to seize a bridgehead in time to pass the armour through by first light.

> After dusk all tracks [Freyberg's account stated], lit with their distinctive signs – Sun, Moon, Star, Bottle, Boat, and Hat – began to fill up with transport in orderly sequence from the rear areas, the heavy tanks of the armoured divisions rumbling in the rear. It was an impressive display of armoured strength. It was a brilliant and calm moonlight night. There was a tense atmosphere as everyone waited.[4]

At the Armoured Command Vehicle (ACV) at 5 Brigade Headquarters Brigadier Kippenberger recounted the moment when:

> the bombardment opened, the memorable opening bombardment of Alamein. Delivered by 800 guns it was the greatest there had ever been in Africa . . . The General was at the ACV, and we stood for a few minutes fascinated and awed and with our hearts praying for the gallant battalions going forward into the storm. 'If ever there was a just cause,' he said to himself, touched my shoulder, and departed.[10]

Freyberg's account continued:

> At 2140 hours all guns, field and medium, opened fire on suspected enemy batteries; it was a twenty-to-one concentration, twenty troops of artillery battering each enemy troop. Assembly forward, which had been proceeding feverishly but silently since dusk, went on even more actively. Noise no longer mattered. The bombardment continued for fifteen minutes,

El Alamein – The Break-in, 23-24 October 1942

.... Start line, 30 Corps

– – – – Infantry Objectives

← Armoured Division corridors

directed against enemy located batteries, and at 2200 hours switched on to the enemy forward defended localities (FDLs).

Meanwhile our infantry, who had assembled on a start line 1,700 yards from the enemy position, went forward to the attack in time to get right up to the bombardment before it started to lift back. Retaliation against our guns was negligible, confirming that we had gained tactical surprise, and demonstrating the efficiency of our counter-battery work.[4]

Both the New Zealand infantry brigades made a good start, with 5 Brigade on the right and 6 Brigade on the left. The capture of the corps' first objectives was confirmed by both brigades at 0300 hours on 24 October, after which Freyberg went forward with his Tactical

Headquarters to Miteiriya Ridge. At this time gaps in the first mine-field had been made, and leading elements of the New Zealand Divisional Cavalry and 9 Armoured Brigade were moving forward through them.[4]

The assault on the final objective – Miteiriya Ridge – met strong opposition from the German 164 Infantry Division and the Italian Trento Division. 5 Brigade on the right reached its objective shortly after 0400 hours, but 6 Brigade was held up, and Miteiriya Ridge was not finally taken until 0700 hours. 'But the appearance of the Sherman tanks of 9 Armoured Brigade with their 75mm guns was a great encouragement to the infantry,' wrote Freyberg. 'It gave their morale a great boost to have the tanks with them in the forward areas.'[4]

During the next three days the New Zealand Division straightened out its line on the corps' final objective, and consolidated its position. But all was far from well in other parts of the battlefield. Although the infantry had secured nearly all its main objectives, nowhere had the armour pushed through them into the country beyond. The pessimistic views of the infantry commanders about lack of determination on the part of armoured division commanders had unfortunately proved only too true.

The first crisis in the battle came on the evening of 24 October when Freyberg alerted Leese to the fact that he was not at all confident that 10 Armoured Division was being properly set up for its attack. It had been part of the 'Lightfoot' plan that when the corps' infantry objectives had been seized, 1 and 10 Armoured Divisions should pass through their special corridors, while the Australian and New Zealand Divisions continued their advances with 'crumbling' (continuous minor) operations.[2j]

But although the NZ Divisional Cavalry had led the way across the Miteiriya Ridge followed by their supporting armoured brigade, 10 Armoured Division held back. The Chief of Staff of the Eighth Army, General de Guingand, who had been closely monitoring the situation, decided that, notwithstanding the Army Commander's edict about not being woken in the night, this was a crisis only Montgomery could resolve. A meeting between him, Leese and Lumsden was assembled at 3.30 a.m. on 25 October 'to galvanise the whole show into action'. But the full facts were not known at that time and it was only the next morning that Montgomery discovered that 1 Armoured Division in the north was nowhere near reaching its objective, while in the south Horrocks had ordered 7 Armoured Division to cease any further attacks.

At 1130 hours on 25 October Montgomery went forward to the

tactical headquarters of the New Zealand Division on Miteiriya Ridge. There he discovered to his consternation that nowhere across the front had the British armoured divisions penetrated the enemy lines beyond the infantry positions. In the north 1 Armoured Division had only reached Kidney Ridge, held by 51 Highland Division; and in the centre Gatehouse's 10 Armoured Division had none of its armoured regiments beyond the Miteiriya Ridge, which was held by the New Zealand Division and 133 Lorried Infantry Brigade. Montgomery's plan for launching the armour into the open country beyond the original enemy lines had failed.[2m]

Montgomery's noonday conference at New Zealand Divisional headquarters on 25 October marked the first turning point of the battle.[2n] The Army Commander and Leese and Lumsden, the Corps Commanders, decided that Miteiriya Ridge should continue to be strongly held, but that the crumbling operation to the south-west should be discontinued. Instead XXX Corps would undertake crumbling operations northwards towards the coast, using 9 Australian Division reinforced by 10 Armoured Division. On the following day Montgomery decided to pull the New Zealand Division back into reserve, and to relieve them by sidestepping the South Africans and 4 Indian Division northwards. This move was to be completed by dawn on 28 October. As Corps Commander Leese explained:

> The Australians on the right were already in the midst of desperate fighting with the Panzer Divisions. Their job was by offensive action to contain the Panzer Corps on their front. Montgomery told me to reorganise the remainder of the line – to pull out the New Zealand Division and to form a new striking force under General Freyberg . . . He was making use of the magnetic leadership and personality of General Freyberg, with his most efficient headquarters, to drive the final wedge into the enemy front.[2p]

Montgomery had already made up his mind about his commanders: 'It was clear to me by now,' he wrote in his diary at noon, 28 October 1942, 'that my best Corps Commander was Oliver Leese; Lumsden was very poor. Easily my best fighting Divisional Commander is Freyberg, and then Morshead.'[2r] Montgomery's original intention had been to use the NZ Division to drive along the coast towards Sidi Rahman through the Australian bridgehead, but as the New Zealand infantry had suffered heavy casualties he reinforced the Division with two extra brigades, 151 and 152 from the Highland Division. On 29 October after prolonged discussions in which Alexander and his Chief of Staff General Richard McCreery were also involved, it was decided to change the direction of the next attack further to the south. It was to be mounted by the New Zealand Division between the north of the Miteiriya Ridge and the south of the Australian sector.[2s] Freyberg was delighted, and told Leese that the new plan, operation 'Supercharge', was what he had wanted to do earlier.[2t] This decision was the second turning point in the battle of Alamein.

On the eve of operation 'Supercharge' the position was that for ten days the Eighth Army had been attacking the German and Italian defensive positions at Alamein. Although the British and Commonwealth Infantry Divisions severely dented these defences, they had not succeeded in breaking the enemy line anywhere, nor had the British armoured divisions penetrated to the open country beyond. Nevertheless Rommel had used up the last of his reserves in countering the Australian thrust in the north when he committed the 90 Light Division opposite to 9 Australian Division. What was now required on the British side, therefore, was a final effort to tear a hole in the enemy's defences so large that he could not repair it.

In order to enable Freyberg to smash the German and Italian line, the following troops were placed under the command of the New Zealand Division for operation 'Supercharge':

(a)   5 and 6 NZ Infantry Brigades, consisting of seven battalions
(b)   151 and 152 Highland Brigades of six battalions
(c)   9 and 23 Armoured Brigades of six armoured regiments
(d)   Ten field and two medium artillery regiments.[4]

The New Zealand Division's attack had originally been timed to go in on the night of 31 October–1 November. However the situation on the ground was so confused that the GSO1 New Zealand Division and the G1 Plans of the Eighth Army were both told to identify all units not involved in 'Supercharge' and order them to leave the area immediately. For this and other reasons Freyberg had to ask for the attack to be postponed twenty-four hours and, as so much depended on Freyberg's leadership, Montgomery had no alternative but to agree.

Under the new timing of operation 'Supercharge' the infantry of 151 and 152 Brigades were to leave the start line at 0055 hours on 2 November. Zero was fixed at 0105 hours, which was when the artillery would open on the enemy FDLs. The objective was to be taken at 0345 hours. A creeping barrage was to begin at 0545 hours for one hour, during which 9 Armoured Brigade would advance a further 2,000 yards to the next objective. At 0645 hours 1 Armoured Division was due to pass through the 9 Armoured Brigade objectives.

Freyberg's account of the operation, however, describes the mixed success of the opening attack:

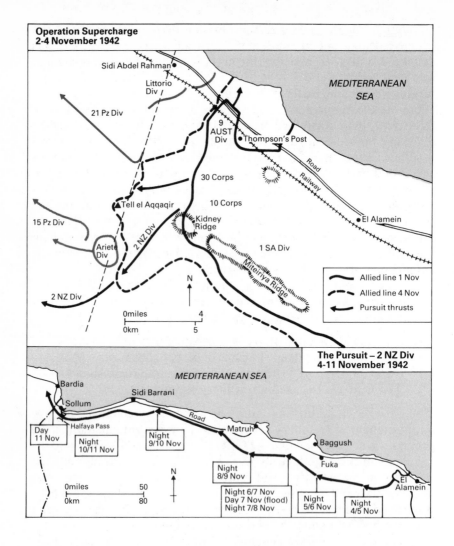

At 0105 hours on the morning of 2 November every gun on the Corps front which could reach, opened fire. 150,000 rounds were to be fired on the 4,000 yards front during the next 4 hours.

The attack provided an interesting comparison, as on the left everything went like clockwork while on the right resistance was stronger and the situation remained obscure for hours. On the left 152 Brigade Headquarters were in contact throughout with forward battalions, and encouraging progress reports were received at Divisional Headquarters from this Brigade as follows:

[404]

0148 hours: We are in touch with both battalions and everything appears to be going smoothly.

0218 hours: There is light shelling and moderate machine-gun fire on our front. We have taken some prisoners, a mixture of Italians and Germans. Everything appears to be going according to plan.[4]

During the later stages of the attack 152 Brigade encountered obstacles and enemy tanks, but at 0417 hours Brigade Headquarters announced that both the forward battalions had reached their objectives. Just over an hour later they reported again that the battalions were reorganising and linking up on the final objective, and that casualties would not exceed 40 per battalion. Freyberg commented: 'The attack has gone like a drill, objectives being taken according to schedule. It was a very fine performance.' On the right, however, there was greater resistance, and 151 Brigade Headquarters was out of touch with the attacking battalions. Freyberg's account continues:

Due to a misunderstanding they reported that the sappers (one of our own engineer companies) had not come up to make gaps in the minefield. It was not until 0400 hours that it was confirmed that the gaps had been made exactly as arranged, and that tanks and supporting arms were passing through satisfactorily. Not until 0525 hours could we inform Corps that 151 Brigade had definitely reached their first objective, although other sources had indicated that the Tynesiders [Durham Light Infantry of 151 Brigade] were getting forward despite stiff opposition. An hour earlier Corps was told that it was probable that the attack was successful on the whole front.

28 (Maori) Battalion had captured the area west of Point 29 and had linked up with the Australians on their right and handed over to them their prisoners. The operation was a typical assault by the Maori Battalion carried out efficiently against a strongly-held position.[4]

The situation on the right was cleared up just before 0600 hours when 151 Brigade reported that they were on their final objective. The northern corridor was completed but, as Freyberg commented, 'Even when the objectives were taken we did not paint too rosy a picture, for reorganisation had to be carried out and supporting arms dug in. Daylight would provide the answer, as we well knew.'

Meanwhile, and during the night, the armour had been moving forward slowly but steadily along the lane swept by the engineers, and marked by the provost, but:

The advance of the armour was too slow, and at 0500 hours I gave orders to press on with the Divisional Cavalry carriers in front, and not to wait for the

[405]

ground to be swept for mines. The barrage to cover the advance of 9 Armoured Brigade to their final objective had to be postponed for half an hour, i.e. to 0615 hours. This was a great pity. Had we had another hour's darkness 9 Armoured Brigade might have got through before first light.[4]

Other, more serious things were also going wrong:

3 Hussars had heavy casualties from shellfire during the advance, and when they reached the infantry objective they had no anti-tank guns. The regiment reached the Rahman track just before first light. The Royal Wilts in the centre also reached the Rahman track. The Warwickshire Yeomanry went too far south, mistaking high ground south-east of Tel el Aqqaqir for that feature. The three tank regiments were out of touch with one another and at first light all were hotly engaged by dug-in tanks and anti-tank guns at close range. In most cases the squadron leaders' tanks were blown up; wireless control was lost and tanks fought individually. 3 Hussars were reduced to three Crusaders and nine Shermans or Grants, but they knocked out fifteen anti-tank guns and two 88mm guns. The tanks of the Royal Wilts were nearly all knocked out, but they accounted for fourteen anti-tank guns. The Warwicks were engaged on three sides. They accounted for all anti-tank guns firing on them, but had only seven runners left at the end of the battle. It was a grim and gallant battle right in the enemy gun line.

Although 9 Brigade did not reach its objective and had heavy casualties, the action was a success in Freyberg's opinion as the enemy gun line was smashed. It may be argued, he went on, that it was a costly and incorrect method of using armour; but if one is to believe General von Thoma (commanding Afrika Korps) it may well prove to have been the deciding factor in breaking the German line, though advantage was not taken of the breach until later.[4]

Although 1 Armoured Division was not in a position to get forward by first light to take advantage of the gap, Corps HQ had warned that 15 and 21 Panzer Divisions were preparing to attack the large bulge that had been created in the British front line. The salient was not an easy place to hold if the enemy were to mount a strong counter-attack. The ground, 'as flat as a billiard table', was being so heavily shelled that the armour could not remain out in front. Casualties were mounting in 151 Brigade and in the Maori Battalion.

Freyberg's account continues:

The enemy armour counter-attacked in the early afternoon of 2 November. At one stage they broke across the salient and back again, but the Sherman, the Grant with its new ammunition, and the 6-pounder Crusader, when

[406]

mechanically efficient, proving more than a match for the German Mark III and IV Specials. 2nd Armoured Brigade claimed 25 enemy tanks knocked out after the first encounter, 18 of which were left burning.

The evening attack by 152nd Brigade under 51st Division was a complete success. They did a very fast advance of 1,500 yards in just over twenty minutes supported by the Army tanks of 50th Royal Tank Regiment. They had no casualties and took about 100 Italian prisoners.

On 2 November, in the battle for the bulge, the total number of prisoners taken was something approaching 2,000, including 200 who surrendered after a raid by Royal Air Force Bostons. By the end of the day it was clear that the enemy was cracking. I warned Brigadiers and CRA (Commander, Royal Artillery) to consider getting their transport ready for exploitation, as I was certain that the enemy must withdraw. I felt certain that the war on our front was over.[4]

The night of 2–3 November was spent in regrouping, and continuing to probe and make further gains into the enemy positions. There was no moon and the situation on the ground was confused. On the morning of 3 November Freyberg saw the Army Commander, who was visiting Corps HQ, and asked him to make up 9 Armoured Brigade in tanks. He agreed to do so but it was found to be impossible, and the remaining tanks were handed over to one regiment while the personnel of the others were withdrawn to refit. Various operations to get further elbow-room for the armour were carried out during the day. 2 and 8 Armoured Brigades made progress and there was considerable shelling by both sides.

Freyberg now saw as he went round the front that a great change was taking place:

Everything seemed to point to a general enemy withdrawal. Divisional Cavalry found the enemy were moving back from the north of the salient. The amount of fighting that had taken place was evident. The artillery barrage had certainly covered the area. Many dug-in tanks had been destroyed and there was a considerable amount of equipment and many German dead in No-Man's-Land.[4]

In the early afternoon of 3 November he saw the Army and Corps Commanders and reported that the battle was over, that the enemy was broken, and that there would be no more fighting. So certain was he that he drafted a cable to the New Zealand government giving them early news of the battles. In the final paragraph he wrote:

Present situation here is shaping well. I feel it is rash to make forecast regarding fighting here in Western Desert, which has been productive of so

[407]

many disappointments. For information of Government perhaps it would help if I gave my opinion for what it is worth. I feel future here is bright. I believe German resistance was finally broken by last attack and cumulative effect artillery fire during last ten days. I feel present German position is precarious, that we shall push him back in near future to frontier, and later under certain conditions I am led to hope we may eventually clear Africa.[8]

Operation 'Supercharge' was one of the most important battles Freyberg ever fought, for it ensured the decisive victory of El Alamein. After the battle Freyberg produced his usual account of the action for distribution to all units of the New Zealand Division: 'Narrative and Lessons – Operations "Lightfoot" and "Supercharge"'. Montgomery was asked to write the Foreword, the full text of which read:

> The Battle of Egypt was won by the good fighting qualities of the soldiers of the Empire. Of all these soldiers none were finer than the fighting men from New Zealand.
> This pamphlet tells the story of the part played by the 2nd New Zealand Division in that historic battle, and it contains many lessons that will influence the training of our Army.
> What this pamphlet does not bring out is the magnificent leadership of Lt-General Sir Bernard Freyberg, the Commander of the New Zealand Forces in the Middle East. His splendid example, untiring energy and infectious optimism were an inspiration to the whole Army; wherever the battle was most intense, there was General Freyberg to be found. Such outstanding leadership can rarely have been seen in the history of the British Army.
> I am proud to have the 2nd New Zealand Division in my Army.[4]

Freyberg suppressed the reference to himself and so when Montgomery's foreword was printed and distributed to the division it appeared without the third paragraph. On 20 November 1942 the New Zealand Prime Minister announced a special award of the KCB to Freyberg as a result of the battle of Alamein 'in recognition of the supreme gallantry and excellent achievements of the New Zealand troops and their commander in recent operations'. It was the second knighthood conferred on Freyberg in 1942.

23

The Salamander
of the British Empire

With the set-piece battle of Alamein over, the fighting in the desert now reverted to one of movement, at which Freyberg and the New Zealand Division excelled. During the next six months, as the Germans and Italians were pursued from Egypt through Libya all the way to Tunisia, Freyberg was to be given many opportunities to display his skill and leadership in mobile warfare, and to show the offensive spirit which played such an important part in the success of the New Zealand Division.

It must be admitted however that he was becoming more cautious about taking risks, and in consequence was criticised on occasions for being too slow. Opportunities, it was alleged, were missed to cut off the Germans immediately after the breakthrough at Alamein, at Fuka, and again during the Tebaga Gap battle in Tunisia. But there were reasons for his caution. The New Zealanders had learned from bitter experience of the ability of German armour to materialise unexpectedly from nowhere to savage the infantry. There was also a psychological reason that became more pronounced as the war continued. Freyberg felt that New Zealand, with its small population in 1939 of about 1,600,000 people*, had already incurred disproportionate losses in the early years of the war (in round figures 17,500 casualties) when the survival of the British position in the Middle East was at stake. Now that the outcome

* The population figure registered in 1986 was 3,307,084.

[409]

was no longer in doubt he was more anxious than ever to keep New Zealand casualties to the minimum.

But how had Freyberg exercised command of the New Zealand Division in action? What were his methods and systems? No one is better qualified to describe these than Lieutenant-General Sir Leonard Thornton, the Chief of the NZ Defence Staff from 1965 to 1971. He was GSO 2, Operations, at 2 NZ Division Headquarters at the battle of Alamein, and later GSO 1, Operations, in Italy:

> General Freyberg's approach to the task of command was entirely his own. It relied on his personal philosophy, his unequalled battle experience and his outstanding reputation. His dealings with higher commanders at Corps and Army levels were helped by personal acquaintance with most of the British officers concerned, almost all of whom were below him in seniority. As a result he enjoyed greater liberty and exercised greater influence than his compeers. He was able to affect the planning of operations to a greater extent than most commanders at his level, and to control more closely the destiny of his division. He enjoyed the advantage of having a measure of independence as the commander of a national force, limited only by the fact that he and his men were part of and dependent upon a British command and supply system.
>
> Freyberg's technique of command within the New Zealand Division was characterised by a degree of 'democracy' or informality not achieved in most allied armies – and therefore a source of mystification to casual observers. In the beginning, the General must have been conscious that his background separated him somewhat from his senior NZ officers, and there were no doubt reservations on both sides. However his sincerity, his fame as a fighting soldier, and the homogeneity and stable composition of his command all helped to improve the relationship, as did his own recognition of the quality of his subordinate commanders and senior staff. In spite of the adverse experiences in Greece and Crete there soon began to emerge the mutual trust and admiration which makes for success in command.[1]

Thornton goes on to describe how sound and efficient command arrangements, using British staff procedures, were evolved from the middle of 1941 onwards and remained virtually unchanged for the rest of the war. The system had been put to the test in the highly mobile phases of desert fighting during the 'Crusader' operations in November 1941, and now, again, during the 'Pursuit' in 1942–3 after Alamein, when wide distances, fluid situations and the need for quick decisions were the controlling factors:

[410]

General Freyberg did not hold regular 'orders groups' or 'O' groups – gatherings of commanders for the issuance of his orders – but called together the people concerned whenever necessary. In a rapidly changing scene there would be a conference at least every day, and before a set-piece battle there might be several conferences on successive days. The procedure varied little. After stating the general purpose of the conference, Freyberg would call on the senior Intelligence officer to outline the latest information on the enemy, either using a map enlargement or, when possible, a topographical model. After questions, Freyberg would indicate what task the Division was to perform, and would explain (usually after some sort of prior discussion with his senior operations staff) how he thought the job might be handled. He would then call for comments and suggestions from the brigade commanders affected and the commanders of supporting arms such as artillery and engineers. This would often produce vigorous discussion as various contingencies were explored, until Freyberg would note any consensus reached, and announce his decision on what was to be done, and by whom. That was invariably the end of the debate, and the General would then call on the senior administrative officer to explain what arrangements would obtain for supplies, ammunition, fuel, medical and other services, and a score of other matters.

After discussion of these arrangements, Freyberg would withdraw and there would be some deliberation about timings and general coordination between formations before the conference members dispersed. The operations staff, who would have been careful not to intervene earlier unless asked for a view, would now get to work to prepare and distribute a written order confirming the word-of-mouth instructions given, and to explain the detail further. The administrative staff might prepare a separate order covering their particular concerns; both types of orders would be used by formation staffs in preparing their own orders for the action that would follow. Freyberg always left that sort of detail to the staff, but would be consistently available to commanders during preparation and during operations.[1]

The period immediately following the battle of Alamein was both exhilarating and frustrating. It was exhilarating to know that Rommel and his Afrika Korps had been soundly defeated, and that church bells were being rung throughout Britain to celebrate the victory. A few days later came news of operation 'Torch', the Allied landings in Morocco and Algeria. Thus within the space of three weeks the military situation in North Africa was transformed, and the outlook at last was brighter than at any time since the beginning of the war.

What proved frustrating, however, was that on 6 and 7 November the heavens opened and in a few hours the rain turned the desert into a quagmire. More effectively than any action of the enemy, the elements brought the New Zealand Division to a complete standstill. Vehicles could not move in the mud, nor could supplies of petrol be brought forward. The deluge enabled a sizeable proportion of what was left of the enemy to slip away on the metalled coast road, even though it also grounded much German and Italian equipment which fell into Eighth Army hands.

After the breakout on 4 November Freyberg and his Division had moved about 50 miles to the west across country, and halted for the night of 5–6 November to the south of the Fuka escarpment. On the way they had encountered and knocked out eight German Mark III and IV tanks and captured a number of enemy personnel including the GOC and second-in-command of the Italian Trento Division. By this time 4 Light Armoured Brigade had been placed under command of the New Zealand Division for the advance, and it was they who captured General von Thoma, Commander of the Afrika Korps, while he was out on reconnaissance.

Because of the storm the Division was only able to get under way again on 8 November when it moved a further 30 miles to familiar country south of Mersa Matruh. Here 9 Armoured Brigade left the New Zealand Division for a much needed rest and refit. It had performed magnificently in the main battle, and Freyberg sent a heartfelt message of appreciation and good wishes. 6 NZ Brigade also had to be left behind at Matruh, for supply reasons.

On 9 November Freyberg pushed on 63 miles with 4 Light Armoured Brigade and 5 NZ Brigade to Sidi Barrani. By now the force had joined the coast road, while 7 Armoured Division moved westwards along an axis to the south of the frontier escarpment. On 10 November the NZ Division advanced a further 50 miles towards Sollum. Here they found that the pass by the sea had been blocked by the enemy, while Halfaya Pass was held in strength by Italian troops of the 'Pistoia' Division, whose motto was 'Valiant unto death'. Freyberg loved to tell the story of the company of 110 infantrymen of 21 Battalion who attacked before dawn on 11 November and, at a cost of 1 killed and 1 wounded, killed 60 and took 600 prisoners. It was the last encounter of the war to take place on Egyptian soil.[2a]

Later that day the New Zealand Division crossed into Libya and moved to a staging area at Sidi Azeiz to the west of Bardia. They were to remain there for the next three weeks as, by this time, the Eighth Army was in danger of outrunning its logistics – the supply depots being several hundred miles away to the east. To ease the position a New Zealand battalion was detailed to unload ships at Sollum.

On 13 November Freyberg was now able to write to his wife without having to worry about security:

I got your letter together with some much needed food. We are now down to rations – bully and biscuits. I am writing this note from my truck outside Bardia. The battle here is over and the Hun has had a very bad blow to his prestige as well as to his army here. The first ten days was hard slogging in which both he as well as ourselves had very heavy fighting and losses. The pursuit was less costly to us in casualties.[3]

The following day he wrote again describing the action at Halfaya Pass, where:

We bumped into the Pistoia Division bolstered up by a sprinkling of Germans. 100 men of the 21st Battalion attacked this very strong position and took 612 prisoners. They are a miserable lot. Yesterday I went to Sollum Bay to see what our working party was doing. While there I saw the C-in-C, Dick Casey and Lord Moyne and had a talk with them.[3]

The NZ Division spent the first fortnight outside Bardia 'catching up' after the strenuous battle and pursuit. Sufficient supplies were being ferried forward to allow 6 NZ Brigade to rejoin the Division on 22 November, and gradually other units arrived, such as a field bakery which produced the first bread the troops had seen for some time.

Freyberg took the opportunity of the break to return briefly to Cairo to discuss policy matters. The Australians were in the process of withdrawing all their troops from the Middle East because of the danger at home from the Japanese, and for a time it seemed possible that New Zealand might do the same. In the end it was decided to leave the NZ Division until the finish of the North African campaign at any rate.[2b]

While the New Zealand Division was resting near Bardia, the pursuit of the enemy continued. Rommel was not expected to make a stand until Agheila, nor did he do so. The 7 Armoured Division and 4 Light Amoured Brigade followed up along the coast road. Tobruk was entered on 13 November, and Benghazi was occupied for the third and last time on 20 November. This was an important gain because of the airfields it gave the RAF, from which to provide air cover for the supply convoys being sent to lift the siege of Malta.[2c]

The Germans finally retired to the El Agheila position on 24 November.

It soon became obvious from information filtered from ULTRA, however, that this time there would be no German counter-attack from

[413]

Agheila as there had been in 1941 and 1942, because the enemy was very short of supplies. The immediate tactical problem was how to eject the German and Italian forces from the Agheila defences in order to resume the westward march.

The Agheila position was a strong one. The coastal road followed a comparatively narrow neck of land with firm going, and was surrounded by marshland. The Germans had fortified the approaches with thick belts of minefields, and it was clear that frontal attacks against determined opposition would result in heavy casualties. The obvious alternative was a wide outflanking movement which would 'turn' the Agheila defences. But this involved covering long distances, required a big administrative effort in the provision of fuel, and above all meant going over country that was largely unreconnoitred, where sand drifts might be difficult to cross.

Planning for the turning of the Agheila position began in the last week of November. As XXX Corps had taken over responsibility for the operation, Freyberg and Leese were working together once again. The general scheme was to attack the main enemy position near the coast from Marsa Brega to Sidi Tabet with 7 Armoured and 51 Highland Divisions, and to send 2 NZ Division with 4 Light Armoured Brigade on a wide outflanking movement to the south, with Marble Arch, the airfield west of Agheila near the coast road, as the ultimate objective. Freyberg briefed his order group on 3 December, and 6 NZ Brigade left its rest area at Sidi Azeiz on 4 December, followed by 5 NZ Brigade the next day. The tanks and tracked vehicles were carried by transporters to the assembly area at El Haseiat, where they were due to concentrate by 10 December.

On 6 December Freyberg wrote to his wife 'on the move': 'I am writing this in my truck after an all day journey. Our routine for the last three days has been up at 5 a.m., breakfast at 5.30, away at 6.30, and finish at 4 p.m. It has been cold at night but quite pleasant in the middle of the day.'[3]

The 250- to 350-mile move across the desert to El Haseiat was uneventful, and each group arrived on time. The Division – less its tracked vehicles – was complete by the evening of 9 December. The armoured fighting vehicles went on transporters by the main road, and arrived at El Haseiat before dark on 10 December.[2d] Freyberg wrote to his wife before the operation started, on 12 December: 'We are just off and will be out of touch for a little while. I hope that luck is with us. I pray so.'[3]

Freyberg felt the need to keep well forward during this mobile phase, so that he could personally assess the developing situation and issue immediate orders to the leading units. The main New Zealand Division headquarters consisted of over 200 vehicles, and was too cumbersome and vulnerable to take into the forward areas. Freyberg therefore followed the method he had used before, and created a small tactical headquarters consisting of himself and one operations staff officer plus a signaller, travelling in a specially adapted light Honey tank protected by three light tanks from the Divisional Cavalry regiment. His ADC, artillery commander and a few administrative personnel followed in standard vehicles and enabled this small command group to be independent of main headquarters and stay out at night. Thus the chief staff officers controlled the move of the 2,500 vehicles of the Division from main headquarters, while Freyberg was free to direct the battle at the 'sharp end': in such a situation he was in his element.

An independent description of the beginning of the Agheila 'left hook' is given by Lord Rocksavage, who was serving at the time in the Royals (1 Royal Dragoons). The title of his book, *A Day's March Nearer Home*, was taken from Winston Churchill's speech to the Eighth Army in Tripoli on 3 February 1943: 'in the words of the old hymn, you have "nightly pitched your moving tents a day's march nearer home"':

> A Jeep patrol of the King's Dragoon Guards had done a long recce over this bit of ground, which had always been reported as being impassable for wheeled vehicles. But as they had managed to cross this stretch of the desert all right, a bold plan was decided upon. The New Zealand Division with the Greys in their Shermans, the Royals and the King's Dragoon Guards as the Armoured Car Regiments, and the rest of the 4th Light Armoured Brigade, would all march through the night in a vast left hook, and then come up and cut the coast road west of Agheila near the aerodrome of Marble Arch . . . Having traced out the route on our maps and worked out the mileage, which was considerable, we set off to join the main axis of the New Zealand Division. This was marked by tin signs on stakes, and it looked a pretty formidable sight to see this vast armada of vehicles moving relentlessly forward across the desert. On either side of the tins the might of the Division spread over about half a mile and was so long that we could not see either end of it.[4]

What happened next is described by Freyberg:

> This manoeuvre was complete surprise to enemy who had to turn and fight to get out of forward position or be surrounded. Our Force was too small to cover all lines of retreat and Panzer Army escaped but enemy were severely mauled by our armour artillery and infantry as they withdrew, losing tanks and considerable number anti-tank guns.[3]

[415]

At dawn on 17 December the armour and 5 NZ Brigade moved a further 30 miles to outflank enemy covering position west of Nofilia. The enemy rearguard was surprised by the speed of the New Zealand thrust and 250 prisoners were taken. The success of the operation, Freyberg felt, was largely due to the skill and efficiency of the drivers and mobile workshops that kept the vehicles in serviceable condition:

I have just visited our wounded. In isolated spot in Tripolitanian Desert they received best surgical treatment in what amounts to fully equipped field hospital being carried back by ambulances as soon as road was clear. Most serious cases were evacuated by air ambulances over many hundreds of miles of desert to our hospital in Egypt.

Our casualties I am thankful to say were comparatively light. 3 and 11 killed, 8 and 83 wounded, 3 and 9 missing.[3]

There was disappointment that the Division had not succeeded in trapping more units of the Afrika Korps and capturing a larger haul of prisoners. Freyberg told Corps HQ that if he had had twenty tanks on arrival at Nofilia the whole of the enemy garrison would have been 'in the bag'. But the disappointment did not last for long when it was realised that the operation had succeeded in forcing Rommel to abandon two extremely strong defensive positions and at very small cost. The Diary recorded on 18 December: 'General returned in time for dinner from Corps. Great difficulty in getting him to eat. He was in a very good humour. Corps apparently very pleased with the operations. Also Army Comd. "Thought they had set us a task we could not carry out."'[3]

Christmas 1942 was spent in the vicinity of Nofilia. The 'Q' (Supply) Services and NAAFI had made a great effort to deliver the full range of Christmas fare over the many hundreds of miles which now separated the Eighth Army from Egypt. Coupled with the already high state of morale this meant that the festive season was celebrated in as cheerful a frame of mind as could be expected of a force far from home and families. Freyberg's letter to his wife, dated 27 December 'In the West', indicates the general sentiment:

We have had a very good Christmas. We had until then been living on tinned bully and biscuit and the change even for two days has given us all a fresh start. Our last move has been in the papers so there is no secret that I am breaking. We had a series of very long and rather fast moves across the desert and came in and ragged the Afrika Korps. They were not liking our presence behind their lines and they were not happy. The men are in great form and everything goes very well. I have received a lot of telegrams [on the

[416]

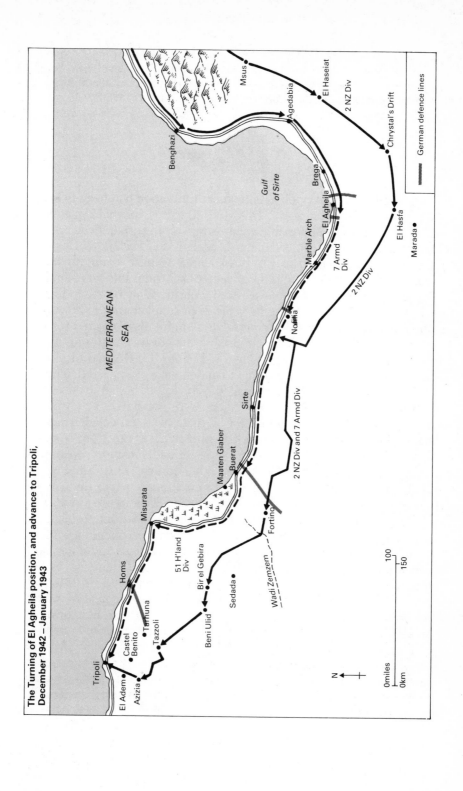

The Turning of El Agheila position, and advance to Tripoli,
December 1942 – January 1943

MEDITERRANEAN SEA

Gulf of Sirte

Tripoli
El Adem ●
Azizia ●
Castel Benito ●
Tarhuna ●
Tazzoli ●
Beni Ulid ●
Homs
Misurata
Sedada ●
Bir el Gebira ●
Wadi Zemzem
51 H'land Div
Maaten Giaber
Buerat
Sirte
Fortino
2 NZ Div and 7 Armd Div
Noffia
Marble Arch
El Agheila
Brega
7 Armd Div
2 NZ Div
Benghazi
Agedabia
El Haseiat
2 NZ Div
Msus
Chrystal's Drift
El Hasfa ●
Marada ●

German defence lines

N

0 miles   100
0 km   150

part played by the Division in the victory at Alamein and on Freyberg's
KCB] from England and New Zealand all of which have to be answered.
We are now a long way on the road to Tripoli. I think that its capture will
have a great morale effect upon the cause, and I am sure that the Allies have
turned the corner.[3]

For the advance to Tripoli Montgomery's intention had been to bring
up X Corps and for both XXX and X Corps to attack together.
However it proved impossible administratively to sustain two corps so
far from their bases – indeed it was difficult to keep even XXX Corps in
the field in the eastern part of Tripolitania because, owing to storm
damage, the port of Benghazi was temporarily unusable and supplies
had to come by road all the way from Tobruk. Only by grounding X
Corps completely and using its vehicles to supplement the lift was it
possible to bring forward the petrol and ammunition needed for the
next phase of operations. In continuing the advance with only three
divisions Montgomery was taking a risk, but ULTRA had disclosed
that Rommel was not in a position to undertake a prolonged defence.

The plan to capture Tripoli, called 'Fire-eater', hoped to cover the
200 miles to Tripoli in a week. There were two defensive positions
between Sirte and Tripoli where the Germans were expected to make a
stand. The stronger of the two, the Buerat Line, ran from Maaten
Giaber on the coast and followed a series of wadis inland.[2e] Nearer to
Tripoli was the line from Homs through Tarhuna to Garian. The 51
Highland Division followed the main coast road, while the axis of
advance for the 7 Armoured and New Zealand Divisions was a joint one.

On 3 January the New Zealand Division moved from Nofilia to a
position 10 miles to the south. After a week spent in planning conferences, exercises, and stocking up with ten days' rations and water, and
petrol for 350 miles, the move forward began on 9 January. In the
meantime 7 Armoured Division and 4 Light Armoured Brigade had
been closing up towards the Buerat position, so for the next four days
the NZ Division moved up slowly by day and rested at night in bivouac
areas. On 14 January they moved up to the start line opposite Fortino.[2f]

The advance proper began on 15 January. On the coast 51 Division
made contact with the enemy defensive line and prepared to attack it
that night. On the southern axis of advance 7 Armoured Division on the
right and the New Zealanders on its left also bumped into the enemy in
some strength in the area of Wadi Umm er Raml.

On the next day, 16 January, the Divisional Cavalry was operating in the area of Wadi Zemzem, south of Beni Ulid, and Freyberg was on advance reconnaissance in his light tank. As *The Times* reported, under a headline 'Three tanks captured by General Freyberg':

> Suddenly, in a shallow wadi, he came across a group of Italian M13s. His own tank was an easy mark for his opponents, but he moved smartly towards them as if to give battle. Up went the white flag from each enemy tank, and out popped the crews with their arms, to surrender.[5]

The tanks were from the Centauro Battle Group, and as the official historian commented, 'The crews who surrendered to the GOC himself said they were anti-German and glad to be out of the war.'[2g]

The advance now began to speed up. On 17 January 51 Highland Division on the main coast road reached Gioda, while 7 Armoured and 2 NZ Divisions occupied Sedada and pressed on to Bir el Gebira. The German 90 Light and 164 Divisions started to fall back towards the Homs–Tarhuna line, closely pursued by the Eighth Army. Soon the Highlanders were beyond Misurata and by 18 January the New Zealanders had reached Beni Ulid – a real oasis with lovely clear water. The next day 51 Division reached Homs and the Armoured Division was approaching Tarhuna. By this time ULTRA reports had made it clear that the enemy was not going to make a stand in front of Tripoli, because they were short of supplies.[2h]

When Freyberg went forward on 20 January expecting to join in an attack on Tarhuna, he found that 7 Armoured Division had already occupied the town. So he swung the axis of the advance to the left towards Tazzoli. It was bad going rather than the enemy that delayed the Division during 21 January, but by early the following morning the Divisional Cavalry had reached the plain of Tripoli, followed by 5 NZ Brigade. For a time it looked as if the enemy might make a stand at Azizia and Castel Benito, but by the end of that day the whole Division had debouched out of the hills and on to the plain. Tripoli was occupied on 23 January by the Highland Division, while the NZ Division confirmed that Azizia was clear of the enemy at first light. Freyberg instructed Brigadier Kippenberger, commanding 5 NZ Brigade, to push on to Tripoli itself, and the latter met General Wimberley, Commanding 51 Division, in the main square later that day.

The capture of Tripoli brought to an end a remarkable three months in which the New Zealand Division had fought the major action at Alamein, and several lesser ones along the way. During that time they had moved 1,500 miles across some of the most inhospitable country in the world. They had suffered heavy casualties in the initial battle, but by comparison the losses during the left hook at Agheila and on the advance to Tripoli had been light.

The New Zealand Division was now to be stationed in and around Tripoli from the last week in January until the beginning of March. During that period the most memorable occasion was the visit of 'Mr Bullfinch', which took place on the afternoon of 4 February 1943. New Zealanders do not normally relish ceremonial parades but the Tripoli parade was probably the most remarkable military review in New Zealand's history and, given the setting and personalities involved it is likely to remain a unique occasion. Over 10,000 troops took part, and it was the only time in the Second World War that the New Zealand Division as a whole 'paraded in review order'.

'Mr Bullfinch', or Winston Churchill, was dressed in the uniform of an Air Commodore. He arrived in an open car with General Montgomery, followed by the CIGS General Sir Alan Brooke, and the C-in-C General Sir Harold Alexander. As the escort of armoured cars swept into line beside the saluting base General Freyberg ordered a general salute. John White, on parade nearby, heard Churchill say with tears on his face as they met, 'Bernard, thank God you are here'. Freyberg got into the Prime Minister's car and, with Winston Churchill standing, they drove along the lines of the massed troops. After returning to the saluting base, Churchill addressed the New Zealand Division:

When I last saw your General, Bernard Freyberg, my friend of so many years of war and peace, the Salamander, as he may be called, of the British Empire, it was on those bare and rocky slopes to the south of Alamein where you were then preparing to receive what was expected to be a most dangerous and deadly thrust by the hitherto victorious Rommel . . .

But what a change has taken place since then! By the immortal victory of the battle of Egypt, the Axis Powers, who had fondly hoped and loudly boasted they would take Egypt and the Nile Valley, found their army broken – shattered; and ever since then, by a march unexampled in history for the speed and force of its advance, you have been driving the remnants of the enemy before you until now the would-be conqueror of Egypt is endeavouring to pass himself off as the 'Deliverer of Tunisia'. These events will long live in the annals of war, and will be studied minutely by other generations than our own. These feats of arms entitle the Army of the Desert to feel a deep-founded sense of comfort and pride based on valiant duty faithfully done.

Far away in New Zealand homes at the other side of the globe all hearts are swelling with pride at your deeds. It is the same throughout our small island of Britain, which stood alone for a year championed only by its children from overseas, and against dire odds. All are filled with admiration for the Desert Army. All are full of gratitude to the people of New Zealand who have sent this splendid division to win fame and honour across the oceans.[1]

At the end of the speech Freyberg called for three cheers for the Prime Minister, which were wholeheartedly given. Then, by groups, the Division marched past the saluting base to the music of the massed pipe bands of 51 Highland Division, with the troops nine abreast, an unorthodox formation but most suitable and impressive. The armoured and artillery units marched to their nearby vehicle parks, where they mounted their tanks, carriers and guns, and in columns of six vehicles abreast were again reviewed. So for half an hour an almost unbroken line of men, tanks, guns and vehicles passed in salute to the great war leader. For Freyberg it was 'the most impressive and moving parade of my career'.

Churchill's reference to Freyberg as the 'Salamander of the British Empire' had puzzled many people. The salamander is a lizard-like creature to which the superstition was once attached that it could live in fire. From this characteristic the parallel of Freyberg's career, involving battle after battle and wound after wound was an appropriate one. In the course of time, the arms of Baron Freyberg were to include as supporters 'on either side a Salamander Proper'.

[421]

The Last of the Desert

The rest of February 1943 passed quickly. It was a welcome change to stay in one place for a time, and the whole Division was concentrated in the area of Suani Ben Adem and Castel Benito amidst grass, groves of olives and fruit trees in blossom. The weather was sunny and warm but not too hot. There was plenty to do, the most important task being opening up the port of Tripoli. Although its facilities had been damaged by the retreating Germans the Royal Navy had repaired them, so that before long supplies at the rate of 2,000 tons a day were being unloaded. Labour was needed to move these stores, and New Zealand battalions were employed in this work for the rest of the month.[1a]

From 15 to 17 February the Eighth Army held a study period at the Waddan Hotel and Theatre in Tripoli. Freyberg and his staff were invited to run a discussion entitled 'The approach march of a motorised Division in open country in desert formation and first contact with the enemy'. There was a large gathering of senior officers, both from the Eighth Army and from the British and American armies in Algeria, including the American General George Patton.[2a]

The day after the conference ended Freyberg flew back to Cairo. The flight took seven and a half hours, with a refuelling stop at El Adem, and he was met at Almaza aerodrome by Barbara. He had returned principally to participate in two important parades. The first was that of 4 NZ (Armoured) Brigade, now close to completing its re-training, at Maadi on the morning of 19 February. Barbara's diary records: 'The Brigade looked grand. After the inspection B decorated 21 heroes and then came the march past in big blocks, which looked

[422]

much finer than the usual spidery columns.' Next day was the turn of 8 NZ Reinforcement, 3,000 of whom had just reached Egypt.

'You can't say I have given you a dull life,' remarked Freyberg to Barbara as they were called at 6 a.m. on 22 February. They were collected by John White and driven to Heliopolis airfield. Freyberg and White boarded a twin-engine Lockheed, which took off at 8.45 a.m. The weather was bad and, after refuelling at El Adem, they were forced to land at Benina near Benghazi. They continued the journey to Tripoli next morning, arriving at midday.

While the New Zealand Division had been resting in the Tripoli area other formations of the Eighth Army had continued their advance westwards. The Medenine area, with its four important airfields, was reached on 17 February, and 7 Armoured and 51 Highland Divisions then began probing towards the Mareth Line – a defence line, built by the French, running from Monts des Ksour (Matmata Hills) to the sea. Between 14 and 22 February Rommel had attacked the US II Corps at Kasserine, and inflicted heavy losses on them.[2b]

Towards the end of February it became evident from ULTRA that Rommel's attention was returning to Tripolitania, with an attack on the Eighth Army front impending. At the time there were comparatively few British troops in the forward area and it was essential therefore to reinforce the Medenine front. Late on 28 February Freyberg was warned to move the NZ Division there as quickly as possible.

Divisional Headquarters was first away at 9.30 p.m. on 1 March, followed an hour later by 5 NZ Brigade, with 6 NZ Brigade moving next morning. Two days later the whole Division had travelled the 200 miles by road and was taking up defensive positions west of Medenine itself. 5 NZ Brigade was at the southern end of a line formed by 51 Highland Division in the north, with 7 Armoured and the Guards Brigade in the middle and 6 NZ Brigade in reserve. The main German attack came on 6 March, two days after the New Zealanders were in position, and fell mainly on the 51 and 7 Armoured Divisions; although soon after first light 5 NZ Brigade came under attack from 10 Panzer Division. The British troops were in strength, well deployed and expecting the German attack, with the result that the Afrika Korps suffered one of its worst ever defeats, losing over 50 tanks during the course of the day – a third of its remaining strength – and nowhere making any penetration into the British positions. Rommel called off the attack that evening, and it proved to be his swan song. Three days later he left Sfax aerodrome for Austria, never to return to Africa.[2c]

As soon as the Medenine battle was over preparations were resumed for the assault on the Mareth Line. Advance planning for this had started immediately after Christmas and, in broad outline, it was to involve a major assault on the right across the Wadi Zigzaou near the sea opposite Zarat; while on the left there was to be an outflanking movement through the Matmata Hills to Gabes, which would penetrate behind the Mareth Line itself.

Montgomery had given Freyberg plenty of warning that he wanted the New Zealand Division to carry out this 'left hook', thus repeating the Agheila operation over an even greater distance and in more difficult country. The critical element was the 'going'. Before the war the French garrison of the Mareth Line had always believed the area of the Matmata Hills to be impassable for vehicles. For this reason Freyberg had kept in close touch with the New Zealand patrols of the Long Range Desert Group (LRDG) for many weeks before the Mareth operations took place. The Intelligence staff and engineers had constructed a plaster relief model of the area, and a route through had been plotted from air photographs and reports from LRDG patrols. There were two particular bottlenecks: 'Wilder's Gap' near the first assembly area, and the 'Tebaga Gap' which led to El Hamma, and ultimately to Gabes.

The troops under Freyberg's command, in addition to the NZ Division, included 8 Armoured Brigade (consisting of 3 Royal Tank Regiment, the Nottinghamshire Yeomanry, the Staffordshire Yeomanry and 1 Buffs) with 151 tanks; the King's Dragoon Guards (armoured cars), a medium, an anti-tank, and anti-aircraft regiments; and a Free French Force of 3,500 men under General Leclerc, who had made an epic march from Chad in French Equatorial Africa.[2d] This whole force was called the NZ Corps for the operation.

The move from Medenine to the staging area started at 8 a.m. on 11 March and involved travelling 60 miles in daylight. The assembly area (beyond Wilder's Gap) was 70 miles further on and, in order to conceal what was impending from the enemy, that move was carried out at night. The force was divided into seven major groupings, the first of which was 6 NZ Brigade Group, and the last 8 Armoured Brigade. The last arrived in the staging area on 14 March and was in position in the assembly area before dawn on 16 March.

On 18 March Freyberg was writing to his wife:

This is in a hurry. I am on my way by air to Army Headquarters. I now have an aeroplane of my own, a small recce plane called a Stinson which lands and takes off in twenty-five yards. This gives me greater freedom of movement and prevents those long car journeys.

How glad I shall be when it is all over and we can get back to normal life

[424]

again. Meanwhile we are pushing along and everybody is in very good spirits. It will be a great day when we push the German and Italian Armies out of Africa. There is every indication that he intends to hold on here and fight now, instead of running away. I am not in any doubt as to the difficulties facing us here. It will be tough and costly. My plane is waiting outside my Office truck. I have a small private aerodrome in the centre of the camp.[3]

Although he had to maintain an attitude of military enthusiasm and keenness to the outside world, this letter reveals privately that he was becoming weary of the war and longed for it to be over. It was a refrain he was to repeat to his wife and son with increasing frequency during the next two years.

The force of 27,000 men and 6,000 vehicles was self-contained, with eleven days' food, water and ammunition, and petrol for 350 miles. The plan for operation 'Pugilist', as it was code-named, was for the advance forward to the assembly area to be in three stages: stage 1 was a march of 20 to 30 miles on the night of 19–20 March to the area of Wadi bel Krecheb; stage 2 a move of 40 miles the next night to an area 10 miles short of the Tebaga Gap, which was to coincide with the main assault on the Mareth Line by XXX Corps; and stage 3 a night move on 20–1 March. But when Freyberg learnt that the enemy was aware of their approach he decided not to wait for darkness, nor waste any more time on deception, but rely on speed. In daylight on 20 March in desert formation he closed on 'Plum', the code-name for the entrance to the Tebaga Gap. This was the mountainous country that formed the north-western flank of the Mareth Line.

The 6 NZ Brigade reached enemy defences three hours before dark, which gave the artillery time to register. Then at 10 p.m., in full moonlight, 25 and 26 Battalions put in a major assault accompanied by a Field Company of Royal Engineers to clear gaps in the minefields, and allow through a squadron of Sherman tanks from 3 RTR. The attack succeeded brilliantly and the key position of Point 201 was captured along with 1,500 Italian prisoners. 21 Panzer Division, *en route* to take over from the Italians, arrived twelve hours too late.

However, although the NZ Corps had won a footing in the centre, the enemy still held the high ground on either side of the Tebaga Pass, and during the days that followed the troops were heavily shelled by large concentrations of enemy guns.

Also on 23 March XXX Corps' lodgement on the coast across the Wadi Zigzaou was lost. Lieutenant-Colonel Charles Richardson, who

[425]

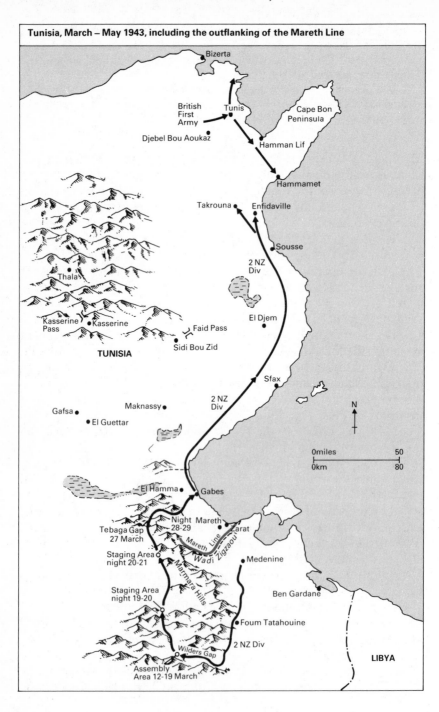

Tunisia, March – May 1943, including the outflanking of the Mareth Line

was then G1 Ops, has related in *Send for Freddie* how this news reached Eighth Army Headquarters:

Very early in the morning of 23 March, I was awakened at Main HQ by the telephone beside me. George Walsh, the BGS 30 Corps, told me that the assault had failed, and the remnants of 50th Division had been withdrawn across the wadi. I went to Freddie's [de Guingand] caravan and wakened him with the disastrous news. Further sleep was impossible. This was the first failure since the days of Auchinleck, and it was a great shock. Having driven the enemy 1,500 miles from Alamein, were we now to get bogged down so close to Tunis where the final curtain must fall?

At 2 a.m. Montgomery was wakened, and shortly afterwards Leese arrived in person at Tac HQ to confirm the failure of his attack. After a brief discussion, he was told to return in the morning for a conference at 9 a.m.

Montgomery immediately told his personal staff, 'Send for Freddie'. On arrival at Montgomery's map lorry, Freddie found that the Army Commander's usual composure had been badly shaken. For more than an hour the disaster was discussed between them; Freddie was then told to return to Main Headquarters to examine what could be done to strengthen Freyberg's 'left hook' and Montgomery retired to bed.[4]

Montgomery decided to switch his main thrust. He would reinforce the success of the New Zealand Corps' left hook by strengthening it with 1 Armoured Division and X Corps Headquarters. The main reason for sending X Corps HQ and its commander, Horrocks, to join Freyberg's left hook was to provide the administrative staff necessary to maintain a force of over 40,000 men, which NZ Corps HQ lacked. But the move also threw up a problem of command: Horrocks, as Corps Commander, would normally have been in charge. But because of the friction between Freyberg and Horrocks, and because Freyberg, as commander of an independent force, could not be superseded, Montgomery decided to set up a dual command – which was unusual, to say the least. In his letter to Freyberg of 24 March 1943 Montgomery said:

My dear Bernard

You will by now have got my message about X Corps and 1 Armoured Division . . .

I want to speed up your thrust as much as possible and I think we can do a very great deal to help you by heavy air bombing all night and day. To take full advantage of this you would have to do an afternoon attack, *with the sun behind you.*

The plan would be as follows:

(a) Continuous bombing by Wellingtons and Light Bombers on night
     D–1/D.
(b) Day bombing by Bostons & Mitchells from 0800 to 1400 hrs on
     D–Day.
(c) Kitty Bomber sorties in between each Boston sortie.
(d) Intensive artillery shelling for say 1 hour before zero. Smoke, etc. on
     high ground on flanks and/or to cover mine lifting.
(e) Air cover *and* attacks by fighters on any movement to and from battle
     area.

I do not believe that any enemy could stand up to such treatment and you
would, after it, burst through the defile quite easily and get to EL HAMMA
and GABES.

I believe it would be another 'Supercharge' which would do the trick like
we did it with 'Supercharge' at Alamein. The Army and Air staffs are
working it out and we can lay it on, if you agree and will accept it.

Date. The earlier the better . . .

Show this to Horrocks when he reaches you.

Good luck to you. I am delighted with what has been done on your flank.

Yours ever

B. L. Montgomery.[3]

While 1 Armoured Division was in transit during its three-day
approach march to join Freyberg, plans were made for the attack to
start as soon as the Division arrived. Opposite to the NZ Division was
21 Panzer Division which had been joined by the German 164
Division, and on the day of attack 15 Panzer Division was also switched
from the Mareth Line to the New Zealand front. The New Zealand
Corps' attack was due to start on the afternoon of 26 March.

Freyberg sent his own account of the action in a signal:

At 3 o'clock on 26 March as I drove up the valley in my tank all was quiet
except for occasional shell fire. There was no unusual movement or sign of
the coming attack. Exactly half an hour later first squadrons of RAF roared
overhead and relays of Spitfires, Kitty-bombers and tank-busters swept
over enemy positions giving greatest measure of air support ever seen by our
army. At 4 o'clock 200 Field and Medium guns opened their bombardment
on front of 5,000 yards. An instant attack developed and 150 tanks and
three battalions of infantry appeared as from nowhere advancing in natural
smoke screen provided by dust storm. It was the most awe-inspiring
spectacle of modern warfare. Roar of bombers and fighters ahead of our
advance merged with our barrage of bursting shells. Following close behind
this intense barrage as it advanced came waves of Sherman tank carriers
and infantry and sappers on foot preceded three squadrons of Crusader
tanks. Behind New Zealand Corps, coming down forward slopes just in

[428]

rear of our front line were 150 tanks of 1st Armoured Division followed by their Motor Brigade in lorries advancing in nine columns.

Hitherto all our big attacks had been by moonlight and, although the enemy was expecting us to attack, we again achieved surprise by attacking in daylight.

Without check our armour swept through to the final objective, a depth of 6,000 yards. Enemy tanks were destroyed or driven back. Anti-tank guns and artillery were overrun or captured. Meanwhile our infantry battalions, moving behind the armour attacked the remaining enemy strong points and fierce hand-to-hand fighting took place to clear objectives and secure high ground on both flanks. By dusk all enemy resistance had been overcome except for high ground at Point 209 and strong points outside left flank where German garrisons still held out. During the night 24th (Auckland) Battalion attacked and cleared left flank, taking a large number of prisoners.[5a]

The success of these attacks removed any remaining hopes the enemy may have had of being able to hold a front based on the Mareth Line. From 27 March the Germans began to fall back towards the next defensive position on the Wadi Akarit. Meanwhile the New Zealand Corps and 1 Armoured Division spent the final days of March closing in on El Hamma and Gabes, and rounding up large numbers of prisoners as far as the Mediterranean coast.

Freyberg had not been happy from the beginning about the dual command arrangements during the final phase of the Mareth left hook. He was well aware of how unprecedented it was to send two lieutenant-generals to command a force whose basic components consisted of two divisions: and when it came to sharing the operational direction of the battle he had not been prepared to co-operate. The Official New Zealand History alludes to the situation in these words:

There is some evidence that Montgomery knew that there might be difficulties, and certainly both Horrocks and de Guingand were aware of the prickly nature of the situation. Between them all they did their best to make things easier. Horrocks and de Guingand agreed that all messages sent from Army Headquarters should go to both commanders, and Montgomery was careful in the wording of his various telegrams and letters. But it is small wonder that Horrocks sensed a frigid atmosphere when he arrived. One must have sympathy with him, for he was innocent of any offence. Freyberg was determined to make sure that no newcomer should intrude in the handling of 2 NZ Division and was grim, firm and not at all forthcoming.[1b]

[429]

In Freyberg's eyes, however, Horrocks *had* committed an offence, the 'Beresford' débâcle, since when Freyberg had distrusted Horrocks's military judgment. Later in the war Churchill told Freyberg that as soon as he heard about the new command arrangements he had signalled to General Alexander to send him details of the commanders and troops involved in the left hook; and on 30 March he went specially to the House of Commons to make this announcement:

'Since I informed the House last week of the check sustained on the Mareth front, the situation has turned very much in our favour. General Montgomery's decision to throw his weight on to the turning movement instead of persisting in the frontal attack has been crowned with success.

'Another severe defeat has been inflicted by the Desert Army on the Axis forces they have so long pursued.

'According to my latest information, we occupied El Hamma last night. Our vanguards passed through Gabes this morning.' (loud cheers)

Mr Churchill then revealed that General Freyberg, VC was in command of the unit which turned the Mareth Line.

'The decisive break-through made by General Freyberg's turning force,' Mr Churchill went on, 'was aided to an extraordinary degree by novel forms of intense air attacks in which many hundreds of British aircraft were simultaneously employed.

'The enemy's losses in men and material have, of course, been very serious to him, and the Panzer divisions, in particular, are remarkably mauled and enfeebled.

'It is, however, too soon to say what proportion of the Italian 20th and 21st Army Corps has been left behind.' (laughter)

Answering a question, Mr Churchill said that 'New Zealand troops are those who have actually passed through Gabes this morning. That I am entitled to say as they are actually in contact with the enemy.' (cheers)[6]

After the drama of the turning of the Mareth Line it was inevitable that the final six weeks of the war in North Africa would be something of an anti-climax for Freyberg and his men. The Division was in reserve during the forcing of the Wadi Akarit Line, and its help was not needed. The 4 Indian, and the 50 and 51 Divisions from XXX Corps took part in the initial assault, and after twenty-four hours the enemy cracked and began to withdraw. There was no other defensive position for them south of Enfidaville nearly 200 miles to the north, which formed the bottom end of the defences of Tunis.

During the first fortnight of April the New Zealanders followed up the retreating enemy without any serious encounters. The weather and temperature were agreeable, the countryside contained a mass of wild flowers and there was an abundance of clear pure water – a welcome contrast to the brackish Libyan variety. Indeed the sand and the desert were soon but a memory. The coastal Tunisian plain, with its lush pastures and groves of olive and fruit trees, was a different world.[1c]

The Division was in almost a holiday mood as it wended its way past Sfax, past the ruins of the great Roman amphitheatre of El Djem, and into the town of Sousse where, as the first troops to arrive, they were given a big welcome by the inhabitants. Outside Sousse the New Zealanders had encountered, for the first time, British vehicles with unfamiliar camouflage and markings of the mailed fist. They belonged to 6 Armoured Division, which had come from Algeria, and was part of the First Army. The ring around the German and Italian armies was beginning to close. On 13 April the New Zealand Division started to enter the foothills of the Djebal Zaghoum, the range of high ground that extended to Tunis itself.

At the same time as the New Zealand Division was advancing northwards through Tunisia, Freyberg's future employment was under discussion. The New Zealand Minister of Defence, Fred Jones, was in London at the beginning of April, and was instructed by his Prime Minister Peter Fraser to discuss Freyberg's position with Churchill and Sir James Grigg, Secretary of State for War. The New Zealand Premier signalled by telegram:

> While it would, of course, have been preferable to have ascertained Freyberg's own feelings on the matter you could, I think, in the present circumstances raise the question somewhat in these terms: Freyberg has more than fulfilled all our expectations and we are deeply appreciative of his outstanding services to New Zealand. As Commander of the New Zealand Division in five campaigns, in which he has acquitted himself with the greatest distinction, we feel that he is due for some further recognition. You should make it clear that while nothing is further from our desires than to lose him, it would be a source of the greatest regret to us if his association with the New Zealand Forces should react detrimentally to his own prospects for a senior command.[5b]

This led to the following exchange between Churchill, Grigg and General Brooke, the CIGS:

Prime Minister to Secretary of
State for War and CIGS   17 Apr. 43

I am not satisfied about the position of General Freyberg. The services and experience of this officer are so outstanding that he should be promoted to the command of a corps. I cannot agree with the judgments which say, 'He is the finest Divisional Commander in the world, but that is the measure of his ability.' A man who wins such a position for himself has a right to be tried in the higher command, and the country has a right that a trial should be made of his services.

2. I shall be glad to know what happened when the Xth Corps was added to the New Zealand groups in the flanking movement to El Hamma. Did it pass under Freyberg's command, or did the Xth Corps Commander supersede him? In any case, Freyberg, as Commander of the New Zealand Corps, wrote a despatch to the New Zealand Government in which he mentioned a large number of other units which were under his command. It therefore looks as if he were in effective command of the whole of this turning movement. If so, he has proved his quality in a sphere much larger than that of a division. I could not help wondering why it was, considering the vital importance of the turning movement, it was left for me to mention his name in the account I gave to the House of Commons.

3. You will have also in your mind the representations made by the New Zealand Government and by Mr Jones, the Minister of Defence. Apart from Freyberg's position, to keep him at the head of the New Zealanders when normally he should have received promotion is to bar promotion in that division. Considering the work they have done, there must be brigadiers fit to take command. I should like to be able to tell Mr Fraser that if the New Zealand Division remains with us we hope that Freyberg will command the XXXth Corps.[7]

Shortly afterwards Churchill was told that it had been decided that Freyberg was to be given command of a corps in the British Army.

Prime Minister to CIGS   24 April 1943

Appointment of General Freyberg to the next vacant corps. I am very glad, and think it only an act of justice.[7]

The upshot of all this was that on 30 April Freyberg was instructed by Montgomery to take over command of X Corps from General Horrocks, who had left to command IX Corps in the First Army. Having talked it over with Jones, who was visiting the NZ Division after leaving London, Freyberg accepted the appointment, on a temporary basis only, until the end of the North African campaign. That it was far from being what he wanted can be seen from the letter he wrote to his wife next day:

I have now had a pistol placed at my head and been selected to command the X Corps. You know my feelings too well for me to have to put them down on paper. My feelings are the same, but I shall have to make a decision soon. I am taking over the Corps temporarily and will carry on until the end of this campaign. I shall also remain GOC 2 NZEF for the moment. Kippenberger will command the Division. The NZ Government have asked that I should have the NZ Div in my Corps. I wish I could see you to talk it over. Decisions like these are difficult.[3]

Freyberg's feelings on the matter were made explicit in a signal he sent to Fraser on 4 May:

While discussing this appointment with Mr Jones, he told me of a message he had handed to Mr Churchill from you concerning my possible war employment. I was very much touched and gratified that, at a time when you are so preoccupied with vital issues, you should have found time to think of this matter. That you did is, I feel, an expression of confidence in me for which I shall always be most grateful. For my part I am wholly contented. I feel that your Division, owing to its fighting qualities and efficiency, has been of incalculable value here in the Middle East, and has played a far greater part than that of any normal division. I feel, therefore, that as GOC 2 NZEF I have been of more use to the war effort than I should have been commanding an Army Corps.

I deeply appreciate your kind thought, but my personal wish is to return to the Division and the 2 NZEF. From a personal point of view I have no military ambitions save one – to be at the head of the New Zealand Expeditionary Force and bring it back at the end of the war, which, please God, will be soon. If for reasons of the higher conduct of the war I am required elsewhere, then I must review the situation, but the final decision will rest ultimately with the New Zealand War Cabinet, without whose knowledge I shall not of course act.[5b]

This signal summed up Freyberg's attitude to higher command. Any military ambition he may have had in the British Army between the wars had disappeared when he was compulsorily invalided out in 1937. He was only too conscious of the unfailing support he had always received from the New Zealand government in spite of the Greek and Crete disasters. This was in marked contrast to his difficult relationships with the British commanders in the Middle East, and although Wavell and Auchinleck had been replaced by the more understanding Alexander and Montgomery, Freyberg had no desire to return to a British Army command, especially as, at that time, May 1943, the war was expected to end some time in 1944.

The Eighth Army made little progress beyond Enfidaville, until the position was turned from the north nearly a month later. The New

Zealand Division's main contribution to these operations was the capture of Takrouna in an attack that began on 19 April. Freyberg describes Takrouna as 'a rocky crag surmounted by a village, which from the plain below, looked like some medieval castle. Fighting here was as hard as any experienced in the whole campaign.' Although the position was eventually taken, other strong defensive positions lay behind it and there was no prospect of a breakthrough without excessive cost. By the end of April the situation on the X Corps front had reached stalemate.

Freyberg took over X Corps at 4 p.m. on 30 April. Besides the New Zealand Division under Kippenberger the Corps consisted of 51 and 56 Infantry Divisions, 4 Light Armoured and 8 Armoured Brigades, plus a number of Free French troops who were detached from the neighbouring French XIX Corps in the Pont du Fahs area next door.[1d] Most of the operations that took place during his brief period of command were in providing artillery support to help the French to get forward. There was no major operation on the rest of the X Corps front during the first twelve days of May, only patrols and routine activities to ascertain what the enemy was up to.

Freyberg spent most of this time visiting his formations and in conference with his staff about future activities. The main military interest concerned the progress of Horrocks's IX Corps' offensive. The two 4 Divisions (4 Indian and 4 British) attacked from the area of Djebe Bou Aoukaz some 20 miles west of Tunis at first light on 6 May, and by midday 6 and 7 Armoured Divisions passed through them. By nightfall they were within 10 miles of Tunis. Next day the armoured divisions continued their offensive, and by early afternoon they entered the town. Opposition had been very light, and 7 Armoured Division lost only one tank.

Next day 7 Armoured Division fanned out northwards towards Bizerta, while 6 Armoured Division turned south towards Hammamet. They were delayed for two days at Hamman Lif at a defile where steep cliffs fall into the sea, for the position had been heavily mined and defended. By nightfall on 10 May 6 Armoured Division had reached Hammamet, and armoured cars were patrolling the Cap Bon peninsula, where many of the senior German and Italian commanders had their headquarters. The Royal Navy was out in force to prevent any escape by sea, and by then nearly all the enemy airfields had been overrun. Prisoners were coming in by tens of thousands – the total number of POWs in Tunisia came to just over a quarter of a million, of which some two-thirds were German.[1e]

Freyberg had been ordered to advance northwards from Enfidaville, but the situation was changing so rapidly that the move was soon overtaken by events and proved to be unnecessary. By 11 May the end was in sight, and on 12 May the terms of unconditional surrender were conveyed to the Italian Marshall Messe, who had succeeded Rommel in overall command. At midday on 13 May 1943 Messe and Major-General von Liebenstein, the German Commander of 164 Light Division, came to the headquarters of X Corps to surrender to General Freyberg. John White, who was present, recalls that it was a considerable satisfaction for Freyberg to accept the surrender of the Italian and German commanders after all that had happened, and to inform them that the terms were 'unconditional surrender'. There was no shaking of hands.

The day before, north of Enfidaville, at 8 a.m. Freyberg had accepted the surrender of General Graf von Sponeck, the Commander of the German 90 Light Division. This was witnessed by the war correspondent Alan Moorehead, who used the story 'of the two most famous infantry divisions of both armies' in his book, *The End in Africa*, to symbolise the climax and ending of the North African campaign:

> Von Sponeck's name stood almost as high in the Afrika Korps as Freyberg's stood in the Eighth Army. Their soldiers were the élite of the British and German armies. For two years they had mauled one another back and forth across the desert. We had killed two of the Ninetieth Light commanders. The 90 Light had almost killed Freyberg. They had charged up to the gates of Egypt in the previous summer, and it was the New Zealanders who broke the German division's heart outside Mersa Matruh. There is hardly a major battlefield in the desert where you will not find the graves of the New Zealanders and men of the Ninetieth Light.
>
> Now at last it was all over. This war within a war, this private vendetta between the two great divisions was finished. Von Sponeck saw that he could do no more.
>
> He put on his formal greatcoat, his insignia and his cap, and drove down the coast road. His only companions were a driver and an interpreter. Freyberg was waiting for him on the road, HIS road, the road that wound for nearly two thousand miles back to Egypt, the road he had done so much to conquer. The old lion looked a little shabby in his desert shirt, his shorts, his battered cap. He stood a little ahead of his officers on the road as von Sponeck got down stiffly from his car and drew himself to a full salute. Freyberg saluted slowly in reply. The two generals looked at one another for the first time. Suddenly there was nothing to say. It had all been too long, and too bitter. There were too many dead.
>
> Von Sponeck got back into his car and drove away to gather his men for the surrender. Freyberg turned round and walked down the road.[8]

25

Europe or the Pacific?

Once the fighting in Africa was over three things happened in quick succession. First Freyberg handed back the command of X Corps to General Horrocks. He told me himself, when I visited him shortly after the German capitulation, that it was an appointment he had neither sought nor wanted. Second, he returned to NZ Divisional Head-quarters immediately afterwards and resumed command. Third, the Division headed back to Maadi in the second half of May, like homing pigeons. It had taken them over six months to cover the distance in the face of the enemy; now, in the reverse direction and without opposition, it took just under three weeks. Unit convoys travelled in stages of 100 to 150 miles a day for the 2,000 miles back to Egypt, picking up petrol and supplies at the ports along the coasts. The first groups began to arrive at Maadi early in June 1943 and by the middle of the month the whole Division had returned.

Freyberg flew from El Djem airfield on 16 May and arrived in Cairo that evening. The main question, of course, was what was the future of the New Zealand forces overseas? The manpower situation in New Zealand made it impossible to maintain two divisions in the field at full strength, one in Europe and the other in the Pacific, as well as undertaking other commitments to the Royal Navy, RAF, Home Defence and food production. A simple choice had to be made, therefore, whether the future military contribution ought to be in Europe or in the Pacific. In the Mediterranean the Allies' next moves were aimed at knocking Italy out of the war. The immediate objective was to capture Sicily, as a prelude to invading southern Italy and bringing down Mussolini and his Fascist government.

[436]

The defence problems of Australia and New Zealand differed considerably at this time. Air attacks on mainland Darwin from Japanese bases in the Dutch East Indies had brought the war to Australia's doorstep. As her dependent territories of New Guinea and the Solomon Islands were also under sea, land and air attack, the Australian government wanted to withdraw all their forces from the Middle East. New Zealand, on the other hand, was some 2,000 miles further south-east of the Japanese war zone; but New Zealand had made an initial contribution to the defence of the Pacific in the garrisoning of New Caledonia by her newly raised 3 Division.

When the United States forces were ready to assume the offensive against the Japanese, the direct route from their main base in the Hawaiian Islands to the Philippines lay through the Japanese held island chains of the Marshalls, the Carolinas and the Marianas. The South Pacific archipelagos of the Solomon Islands and other neighbouring groups would soon be bypassed, and were therefore of little further strategic importance in the Pacific War. It made little military sense therefore for the main New Zealand contribution to be transferred there.

This was one of the reasons why the Combined Chiefs of Staff in Washington favoured the retention in the Middle East of 9 Australian and 2 New Zealand Divisions. The Australian government decided to disregard this request and to bring home its remaining Middle East Division after the battle of Alamein; but, after discussion between London, Washington and Wellington, the NZ House of Representatives decided in secret session early in December 1942 to leave their Division in the Middle East for the time being, without prejudice to the matter being raised again later. The Official NZ History sums up the situation in these words: 'There, except for expressions of gratitude by Churchill and Roosevelt, the matter rested for four months. None but the enemy would contend that the Division could have made better use of the time thus won than it did on the road from Bardia to Tunisia.'[1a]

It was a temporising decision, but Peter Fraser, the NZ Prime Minister, gave a pledge that the Division would not be employed elsewhere without the approval of the House, and promised that its future would be reviewed at the end of the North African campaign. A month before the German surrender, however, planning and training had begun for the invasion of Sicily, and the NZ Division was asked to participate. In view of Fraser's undertaking this request had to be refused, but Freyberg was not sorry. The Division had been in almost continuous action since Minqar Qaim nearly a year before, and

[437]

whatever its future role might be it was due for a considerable period of rest and reorganisation.

The House of Representatives met again behind closed doors on 20 and 21 May, while the Division was making its way back to Maadi. Since the previous debate there had been several new developments. The Minister of Defence, Mr Jones, had visited the Division and had long discussions with Freyberg and some of his officers. A scheme known as 'Ruapehu' had been evolved by which some 6,000 officers and men, who had formed part of the original Division and had been overseas without a break for three years, were to be sent back to New Zealand on three months leave (plus the travelling time). If such a scheme was implemented the members of the Division were likely to accept that the force should remain in the Mediterranean for the rest of the war.

At the same time as the House was in session, Roosevelt and Churchill were in conference in Washington, where they reaffirmed the principle that priority was to be given to ending the war in Europe. The American President's wish that the New Zealand Division remain in the Mediterranean impressed the New Zealand MPs. So too did a Special Report by Freyberg in which he outlined the trials and triumphs of the Division during the past year, the high repute in which it stood, and the confidence with which it would face the future of a European campaign if called on to do so. The Official History records: 'Between the lines of this message the least acute member of Parliament could not fail to read the pride of a general in his veterans and the desire that they should end together what they had begun and pursued through bad times and good.'[1b]

Finally there came a special message from Churchill to the NZ House of Representatives in which he strongly urged the retention of the New Zealand Division in Europe: 'in the magic of his style . . . to a House the more impressionable from its unfamiliarity with eloquence, he addressed sentences resonant with the cadences of Gibbon and ornamented by a reminiscence of Tennyson'. Thus the New Zealand War Cabinet now recommended unanimously that 2 New Zealand Expeditionary Force should remain in the Middle East and be made available for operations in Europe. After debate the House accepted these proposals without a vote.[1b]

The decision opened the way for fresh arrangements for the future of the Division. A few days earlier Fraser had asked Freyberg whether he would be prepared to fly to New Zealand to discuss such measures with the War Cabinet. Freyberg replied on 18 May that he would be delighted to make such a visit but, before he could leave Cairo, and because of the Ruapehu leave scheme he had to carry out a thorough review of every unit in the Division, and evaluate how fit for war they would be once the veterans had been replaced by new drafts. He needed to prepare a 'shopping list' of the minimum number of experienced personnel that were needed in each category to enable the Division to continue to operate efficiently in the field.

At midnight on Sunday, 6 June Freyberg left with John White in a converted Liberator bomber from Cairo West for Gibraltar, where they were greeted by Brigadier Reggie Parminter who had been Freyberg's second-in-command at Shorncliffe fourteen years earlier.[2] They continued the journey in daylight to Lyneham in England where they were amazed by the green countryside – a wonderful contrast to the desert environment they had just left. That night Freyberg slept in his own bed in London for the first time since 1940.

Next day, 8 June, was particularly busy, first at New Zealand House, where Freyberg conferred with Frederick Jones, the NZ Minister of Defence, and later at the War Office where he had meetings with the Secretary of State for War, the CIGS and the DMO, and discussed possible theatres and future roles for the NZ Division. Dinner followed at Clarendon Place, where Freyberg opened a bottle of champagne, noting that in the palmy days of peace it had cost 4s 3d a bottle, and was now worth £5. After that it was away to Euston Station with John White to catch the night train to Scotland. They left Prestwick in another converted Liberator early on 10 June, and flew via Newfoundland to New York where they were met by Geoffrey Cox, temporarily seconded to take charge of the NZ Legation, and an American general. John remembered that he and Freyberg dined that night in the King of the Sea Restaurant, with signs on the wall which proclaimed 'The fish you eat today slept last night in Chesapeake Bay'.[2]

The next stop was San Francisco before a thirteen-hour flight to Hawaii, then on to Christmas Island, Tutüila and finally New Caledonia, where Freyberg received a telegram asking him to address a reception in Auckland in two days time. On Sunday, 20 June Freyberg left New Caledonia in General Harman's Liberator 'Ever lovin' Heart'. The aircraft landed at Whenuapia, and the Diary records: 'as the plane taxied up to the hangar the gold chains of the Mayor and the black coats of the PM and members of the War Cabinet could be seen advancing towards us'. (Comment of the GOC: 'Well, John, we are for it.')[2]

The next three weeks were among the most moving in Freyberg's life. Almost uniquely as a divisional commander he was to come into close and countrywide contact with the parents and families of the men he

[439]

had led in two years of tough fighting. He had had no idea of the programme that had been prepared for him, but found that, in addition to extensive consultation with the New Zealand War Cabinet and Army Command, he was asked by the Prime Minister to do a tour of the main centres of population of both the North and South Islands. It was an extraordinary experience, not least because of the level of public acclaim he was accorded: but it also confirmed the extent to which Freyberg had won the trust of the NZ government and people.

John White kept the Diary for this visit, and his entry for the first day, Monday 21 June, in Auckland is typical of many that followed:

> The civic reception was held in the Town Hall during lunch hour. The general drove to the hall with the Prime Minister and Mr Nash [Deputy PM]. There were large numbers of people in the streets who gave the General a great welcome. He was almost mobbed at the entrance to the Hall and on going into the Chamber . . . the whole audience rose to their feet clapping and cheering as the General and the Mayor, followed by the rest of the official party, walked up from the back to the platform. It was several minutes before the clapping died down and the proceedings were able to begin . . . when the General rose to speak, the whole audience again stood and sang 'For he's a jolly good fellow', and again gave him a tremendous reception . . .
>
> His opening was extremely deliberate but none the less dramatic and from the beginning to the end of his speech, the whole audience followed his every word with the keenest attention. The address was often interrupted by great applause, not only clapping, but cheering. I personally have never seen anything like it.[2]

That night Freyberg left by the Limited Express for Wellington. He worked in the train on his speech for the civic reception next day, which followed the pattern established in Auckland and was broadcast over the national radio. He stayed at Government House for the next four days, and prepared for his meeting with the Cabinet on 23 June, which lasted for most of that day. On 24 June the Prime Minister gave a state luncheon for him attended by leaders of the community.

On 25 June Freyberg was required to deliver an address to both Houses of Parliament, which the Diary says 'was received with great enthusiasm'. Afterwards he was invited to call on the Anglican and Roman Catholic archbishops. He also took the opportunity of his visit to New Zealand to meet some of the families of men serving in the Division, and the relatives of those who had been killed, including Mrs McShane, the mother of one of his drivers who had died at Alamein.[2]

On Monday, 28 June Freyberg flew to Christchurch for five days in the South Island, which included visits to Invercargill, Dunedin and Timaru, where he was given a meal of Stewart Island oysters. He travelled by special train through Southland and Otago, stopping at many of the stations, with the crowds singing old Scottish songs. He made speeches at Edenvale, Mataura, Gore, Clinton, Balclutha and Milton. At Dunedin the party was piped into the town hall, which was packed to the doors. The weather was bitterly cold, with the ground covered in snow and ice.

On return to Wellington he spent three days in conferences with the War Cabinet, redrafting proposals for the future employment of the Division. No theatre of operations other than Italy seems to have been seriously considered during these discussions; yet Italy, with its mountains and narrow peninsula, was not ideal country for the employment of a fully mobile force, which would now have its own armoured brigade. Greater scope might have been found for the Division's style of fighting in the plains of northern Europe – much better country for mobile warfare. But there were other considerations, one of which counted heavily in Freyberg's mind: the likelihood of heavy casualties in the invasion of Europe. After the sacrifices New Zealand had already made in the war he was extremely reluctant to recommend this alternative. A further factor was that if the Division were to leave the Mediterranean its large overseas base would have had to move from Egypt to England. This in itself would have been a major operation and expensive in terms of shipping and finance, and as it was generally expected that the war would be over in 1944 the time and effort did not seem worthwhile. In sum, the disadvantages of transferring the future theatre of operations to France appeared to be so overwhelming that they were not considered any further.

On 4 July Freyberg flew to New Plymouth and the next day he addressed a civic reception there:

> I think I can tell you one reason for the success of the NZ Division, and that is the type of man that this country produces. NZers are tough and fit and intelligent. They have no preconceived military ideas, and they are therefore easy to train, and with the NZer you never have a dull moment. Your division has evolved during the last three and a half years into a very highly trained veteran division of the specialist kind. In the early days it started with three infantry brigades, but it was soon found in the desert that men could not fight on their feet simply with bayonets. We became one of the first mobile divisions, and we have gradually evolved into what is known as the new type division, comprised of two infantry brigades and an armoured brigade armed with heavy and light tanks. The NZer with his high standard

[441]

of intelligence and love of adventure is admirably suited to form a part of this type of division which often has to operate miles away from the main force.[3]

Leaving New Plymouth by railcar, and stopping at various places *en route*, Freyberg then motored to Massey College, which had been turned into a military Staff College. He gave a lecture there – his fifteenth speech of the day.[2] The warmth of Freyberg's reception was due to a number of factors. The people of New Zealand were proud of their Division and of the high reputation it had earned. Veterans of the First World War felt that those of the Second had fully upheld the standards they had set in Gallipoli and France, and that between them they had established a name for New Zealand in the world as a force to be reckoned with. The public realised how great had been the odds the Division had faced in the early days of Greece, Crete and the Western Desert, but they rejoiced that the persistence of their troops had contributed so much to the final victory in North Africa.

This visit to New Zealand affected Freyberg deeply. He felt that it was a public recognition for all that he had been trying to do in the first four years of the war, and an acknowledgment of the worth of the Division. Furthermore it settled his personal future once and for all: 2 NZEF was now to stay in the Mediterranean theatre for the rest of the war, and he was invited to stay on with them as its commander. He asked for nothing better.

Freyberg left Auckland on the morning of 10 July 1943 – the day the Allies landed in Sicily – and was seen off by Peter Fraser and a large gathering. The importance of his visit was commented upon by the Prime Minister when he said how valuable their discussions had been:

> They related largely to the work of the Division and its future role, and by those talks the War Cabinet had been able to form a more complete picture of what had been done and what work the Division would be likely to undertake in the future . . . the enthusiastic welcomes extended to General Freyberg indicated the regard in which he was held by all the people . . . it was abundantly evident that they all had the same confidence in General Freyberg as had the members of the War Cabinet and every member of both branches of the Legislature.[3]

Freyberg had been invited to visit Australia, and on arrival was given a private dinner in Sydney by several of the Australian generals who had served in the Middle East. Next day he flew to Canberra to stay with the Governor-General Lord Gowrie, whose son Patrick had recently died

[442]

of wounds in Libya. The following day General Blamey gave a luncheon for him at the Athenaeum Club. That afternoon he saw John Curtin the Prime Minister, and addressed the Australian Cabinet. On 13 July he flew to Brisbane where he called on General MacArthur, the American C-in-C, who was very friendly. In the evening he made a radio broadcast to the people of Australia over the national network, and his journey back across the Pacific began in the early hours of 14 July.[2]

At Washington, which he reached on Friday, 16 July, he was met again by Geoffrey Cox. Freyberg's appointment to see President Roosevelt had to be cancelled because the latter was away from the White House that weekend. Instead he had a meeting with Field Marshal Dill (head of the British Military Mission) and General McCreery in the afternoon, and in the evening the American Chief of Army Staff, General Marshall, came to his hotel, the Shoreham. Next day Freyberg left by train for New York, where he spent three days of relaxation after his gruelling schedule. He stayed with the celebrated Mrs Otto Kahn, universally known as Mrs OK, whom he had previously met in Cairo.[2]

The journey back to England started from Baltimore at midnight on 20 July. Freyberg wore plain clothes and became 'Mr Bertie Fisher' because the aircraft was routed through Foynes in neutral southern Ireland. Freyberg spent five days in England, his time being divided almost equally between his public and his private life. Now that the decision had been taken about the future of the New Zealand Division, he was able to start making definite plans for its employment. He spent a morning at the War Office where he had a discussion with the CIGS, and made arrangements to meet General Alexander in Sicily at the end of the month. He called on Churchill at Downing Street at 11.30 p.m. on 26 July and spent two hours with him; and on 27 July was received in audience at Buckingham Palace by King George VI, who formally conferred upon him his two knighthoods, the KCB and the KBE, awarded in 1942.[3]

One personal item of military news gave Freyberg particular pleasure. The Army No. 1 Selection Board at a meeting on 6 July 1943 had recommended 'that Major-General (temporary Lieutenant-General) Sir Bernard Freyberg, should be restored to the Active List of the Regular Army with effect from that date, and with seniority from 2 November 1939'. This was approved by the Secretary of State on 8 July. To take back on to the Active List of the Regular Army a General Officer who had been retired six years before was almost unprecedented. When he wrote to tell me about it he commented, 'It is also an admission that they were completely wrong to invalid me out when they did.'[3]

During this visit Freyberg also saw his stepson Guy McLaren, just repatriated from an Italian hospital; and met for the first time Nancy, soon to be married to his other stepson, Martin. But the visit marked his last meetings with the McKennas. He twice visited his brother-in-law Reginald in hospital, who at the age of eighty was awaiting a major operation, from which he did not recover. Nor did Reggie's much loved wife Pamela, Barbara's sister, long survive her husband.

Freyberg left England on the evening of 27 July, and arrived at Algiers next morning. He called on General Eisenhower and had lunch in his American–British HQ mess. He then flew to Malta, and stayed that night with Field Marshal Gort at Government House; and the next day, 29 July, he went to Sicily to discuss with Generals Alexander and Montgomery the arrangements for the move of the New Zealand Division from Egypt to Italy. On 30 July he flew from Sicily back to Algiers, where he caught the American daily courier plane to Cairo. He had been away from the Division for seven memorable weeks.

The Diary for 1 August reads. 'Out to Maadi picking up the threads.' The Division was now in the middle of its reorganisation, and Freyberg spent the next three days finding out what had been happening during his absence. He also had a conference for all commanding officers when he outlined the programme for the move to Italy.[2]

Cairo was particularly hot and sticky that August, and having set all the necessary wheels in motion Freyberg and his wife thought longingly of the cool and peace of the Levant. To Barbara's surprise and delight Bernard suddenly decided to take a week off, and she hardly had time to pack before they were on an Egyptian Misra plane heading for the Lebanon. They landed at Lydda, and after driving through Haifa and Beirut took the familiar hill road to the Victoria Hotel at Air Gohella, just below the Cedars of Lebanon. They returned to Cairo on 10 August.

On 21 August Freyberg telegraphed Fraser about his recent visit to London:

As you know I saw Prime Minister and CIGS on way back from NZ. I also saw heads of Intelligence Services. Great spirit of optimism prevails in highest quarters ...

I feel optimism to great extent is justified. This winter is likely to see great change in Axis position but forecast of future is difficult because there are so many uncertain factors. Germany is to all intents fighting on two fronts, a

[444]

situation she has always tried to avoid. Although she has 289 fighting divisions on order of battle, there is every indication that she has not men to maintain them. She has few reserves in depots in rear and some of the fighting divisions on the Russian front are reported to be 40 per cent below strength.[4a]

This signal was sent two days after the conquest of Sicily was completed on 19 August, and at the beginning of the protracted negotiations with, and frequent changes of plan by, Marshal Badaglio over the unconditional surrender of the Italian armed forces. But the major problem which confronted the Italians, and the Allies too, of course, was the presence in southern Italy of substantial German forces. The Italians knew the Germans' military capabilities only too well and were extremely nervous about what the latter would do when they discovered the extent of the Italian duplicity.

It had been intended to announce the Italian surrender at the beginning of September to coincide with the start of the Allied invasion of the toe of Italy, which went ahead on 3 September as planned; but the main invasion at Salerno, and the announcement of the capitulation, had to be put off until 9 September, all of which helps to explain the somewhat disjointed operations that followed.

The landing from Sicily by the Eighth Army across the Straits of Messina met little opposition and made good progress. But the main assault at Salerno by the US Fifth Army – which consisted of the British X Corps and the American VI Corps – was soon in serious trouble, and after suffering heavy casualties only just avoided being thrown back into the sea. In the south-east of Italy things went rather better. The Royal Navy landed 1 Airborne Division at Taranto on 9 September virtually unopposed, and a fortnight later Bari was occupied. By the end of September the cluster of strategically important airfields at Foggia had likewise come into Allied possession, as had the major port of Naples. So, by the time the New Zealand Division was ready to move across from Egypt, the whole of southern Italy from Termoli on the Adriatic to the river Volterno on the west coast was in Allied hands.

For the six weeks from the middle of August to the end of September 1943 the Division had been fully occupied with an intensive period of training. On 18 August Freyberg went to Suez to meet 10 Reinforcements from New Zealand, who had come to fill the gaps left under the Ruapehu scheme. He was as determined as ever that the men should be toughened up and made physically fit and battleworthy.[3] On 28 August he wired to the Minister of Defence in New Zealand:

Upon whole all goes well but there are obvious weaknesses at present. Many officers and NCOs and some thousands of men from last reinforcement drafts have not of course seen action and infantry are undoubtedly short of experienced company commanders. Experience has shown that unbattleworthy troops suffer much higher percentage casualties than experienced units. In present state of Division training is of greatest importance and we have been forced to go back to most elementary stages before we can tackle full scale divisional exercises.[4b]

Ten days later he reported:

Meanwhile we are concentrating at Burg-el-Arab. 50 per cent of Division still marching from Cairo arrive here during next two days. It has been obvious that the hot summer and living at Maadi have made men soft and this hardening process was most necessary preparation before facing ordeal of winter campaign in Europe.[4c]

Finally on 6 October 1943 Freyberg sent his last signal from Egypt as the Division was moving to transit camp to embark for Italy:

I made the training progressively severe to fit [the men] for the obvious battles which will be the common lot of all troops that are in position to fight the Germans during winter. We followed up three months intensive training with one hundred mile march from Cairo to Burg-el-Arab and divisional exercise complete with newly joined Armoured Brigade. I consider that the Division is now as fit as we can make it to take the Field.[4d]

The New Zealand Division of 22,000 men sailed from Alexandria to Taranto in two convoys on 6 and 19 October 1943, and arrived in Italy three days later. In all 4,600 vehicles, tanks and guns were moved to Italy in four separate lifts, the last of which left Egypt in early November. The Division moved first to a staging area at Altamura, west of Bari, where many of the units married up with their vehicles and equipment. Then they went on to an assembly area at Lucera to the north-west of Foggia. By 20 November the Division was concentrated, ready to participate in operations.[3]

26

The Sangro and the Cassino Battles

The campaign in Italy throughout 1943–5 was adversely affected by disagreement between the Allies about their objectives. After the Italians had capitulated in September 1943, and the port of Naples and the airfields at Foggia had been occupied by the Allies, the Americans seemed to regard the war in Italy as no longer of very great importance. They wanted resources to be concentrated on, and top priority given to the cross-Channel invasion of France, the 'second front'.

Churchill and the British Chiefs of Staff recognised the overriding importance of the ultimate cross-Channel invasion, but they wished to exploit success in the Mediterranean, and wanted to pin down the maximum number of German troops in Italy. This could only be done by attacking. There were disagreements between them about the limits to which the campaign in Italy could be pushed – with Churchill periodically enamoured of an exploitation following German collapse which could even take Alexander's armies to the Danube with incalculable political benefits – but there was no dissent from the view that the Italian campaign was making an essential contribution to victory. The Americans were more sceptical.

Churchill's disagreement with the Americans, because of his (generally unsupported) vision of an ultimate march northwards by the armies of Italy, was not only about strategy, it was even more about the kind of Europe that they wished to see when the war was over, whether western influences prevailed or Communist ones. The Americans aimed to defeat the Germans first, then to concentrate on the war with Japan. They had no wish to become involved in what they regarded as local European quarrels. For instance, they pointedly distanced themselves from Churchill's endeavours to sustain the democratic forces in Greece after the German withdrawal in the late autumn of 1944. As usual, Churchill sensed the shape of things to come long before most people.

When Freyberg visited Eighth Army HQ in Sicily in late July he had discussed possible operational roles for the New Zealand Division with Alexander and Montgomery. His next visit was in early October, as the Division was beginning its move from Egypt, by which time Army HQ was in southern Italy. The front was fluid, there was still a relatively small number of German divisions in Italy, and enemy policy appeared to be to withdraw gradually to the line of the Apennines north of Florence, where defensive positions were being prepared.

After the Eighth Army reached Termoli at the beginning of October, Montgomery devised a plan to make a quick dash for Rome by switching his forces from the Adriatic coast across the Abruzzi mountains to Avezzano, and then on to the Roman plains on the western side of the Italian peninsula. There appeared to be just enough time before the weather broke, and in a letter dated 10 November to the Vice-CIGS General 'Simbo' Simpson, Montgomery outlined his ideas for the employment of the New Zealand Division in such an operation:

> 2 NZ Div (directly under my command) will advance on the left rear of 8 Ind. Div . . . it will then turn left-handed and operate on the axis Popoli–Avezzano, and get in behind the German divisions facing 5 Army. These German divisions will either have to come out of it and retire hurriedly, or be cut off. In any case I hope to accompany the NZ Division into Rome !! It is a very powerful Division; 20,000 men and 170 tanks; it will take a bit of stopping.[1a]

But Montgomery's optimism was ill-founded. The Italian east coast ports were too small to handle quickly the large tonnages required by an army. There was also a shortage of transport companies to bring supplies from further afield, while the requirements to stock up the Foggia airfields with fuel and ammunition for the American bomber offensive against Germany could only be achieved at the expense of the army. At the beginning of October the stock of petrol for the Eighth Army was down to 21 tons. In comparison, that of X Corps on the west coast, supplied from Naples, was 6,000 tons.[1b]

More ominously, early in October, on the advice of Field Marshal Kesselring, Hitler changed his mind about his Italian strategy. Till then he had intended to withdraw his forces from central Italy and hold only northern Italy. Now he ordered them to fight as far south as possible. The line selected, the 'Winterstellung', ran behind the river

Sangro on the Adriatic side, across the mountainous spine of Italy to the mouth of the Garigliano on the west. The steep mountains and swift rivers made this position, several miles in depth, very strong.

Montgomery soon became aware of the change of tactics for, far from retreating behind a plethora of demolitions, the Germans were starting to counter-attack, almost driving the Eighth Army out of Termoli on 5 October. By 22 October the Germans were moving reinforcements into the theatre: they now had eleven divisions in the south and twelve in the north, a total of 23 divisions in Italy.[1c]

The administrative difficulties and the stiffening German resistance caused a delay which put back the date of the British attack. By this time too the winter weather had arrived. These three factors proved fatal to the forthcoming offensive, operation 'Encroach'.

At the end of October the Eighth Army began operations to clear enemy troops from the hills between the rivers Trigno and Sangro, which formed the eastern flank of the 'Winterstellung'. By 8 November the Eighth Army had squared up to the Sangro, its patrols were across the river and reconnoitring the main German positions to the north.

Montgomery's plan was to launch his attack across the Sangro on 20 November. As the wintry weather made an attack through the central mountains impossible he opted for a 'heavy blow on the Adriatic side':

All I want is good weather. I have gone all out for surprise; and have concentrated such strength on my right flank that given fine weather, and dry ground underfoot, I will hit the Bosche a crack that will be heard all over Italy. I have lined up three divisions on my right: 78 Div, 8 Ind Div, 2 NZ Div, with 400 tanks and the whole of my air power . . . If I can then get Freyberg's party to Popoli and on to Avezzano, then Rome should fall to the 5th Army.[1d]

But there were several disturbing factors. On 10 November the chief artillery officer of V Corps and his GSO2 had been taken prisoner while on reconnaissance, and their marked maps and papers made it clear to the Germans that some action was brewing in the coastal sector. The weather had broken the day before and a continuous heavy deluge set in, severely hampering all preparatory movements for the battle. The Sangro and the Trigno rivers rose alarmingly as the mountain rains swirled seawards. The rains continued on 17 and 18

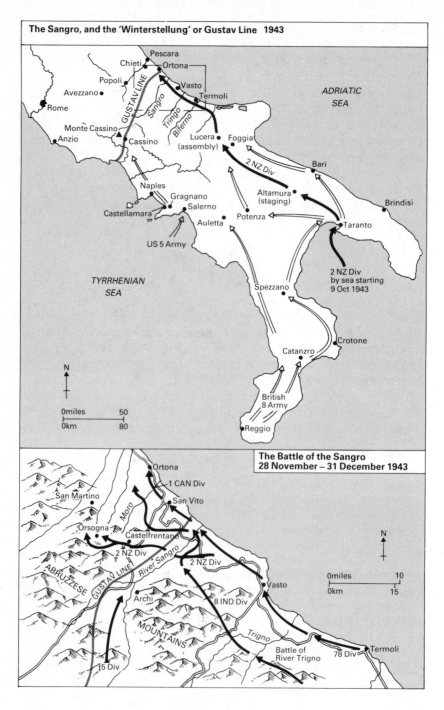

The Sangro, and the 'Winterstellung' or Gustav Line 1943

The Battle of the Sangro
28 November – 31 December 1943

November, but the 19th was a fine day. On 20 November very heavy rain started again at 0500 hours and carried on all morning. Montgomery postponed the operation, first to 23 November and then to 28 November.[1e]

By 20 November the New Zealand Division had taken over a sector of the front on the river Sangro, where the rain was turning the countryside into a sea of mud; but at last on 28 November conditions moderated sufficiently for the New Zealand Division to attack. At first it went surprisingly well. The Sangro was crossed in strength and in sufficient depth to allow bridge-building to start. Soon tanks and supporting arms were on the far bank and pushing northwards. At this point Montgomery sent a handwritten letter to Freyberg:

> My dear Bernard
> 1.   My LO [liaison officer] brought me back your news; I do not think you will have any difficulty at all in getting Archi.
> 2.   Your activities are making the Germans think that my main attack is on your thrust line; this is of course exactly what we want.
> 3.   There are very definite indications that he is pulling 16 Panzer out to refit, it has had a very good beating up. So it will probably pull out from in front of you – if it can disengage. We know it needs a rest badly.
> He would have to replace 16 Panzer Div by something, and the most obvious thing to do would be to take Hermann Goering Div, which has been resting south of Rome and is probably now not too bad, and put it in to relieve 16 Panzer.
> 4.   In any case when 5 Corps attack they should have no difficulty in smashing through – especially in view of para 2 above.
> 5.   Your operations have been quite splendid and have been conducted with all your usual energy and 'drive'. Push on 100% up your axis towards Chieti.[2]

There were two telephone conversations between them on 1 and 2 December. In the first Freyberg said he hoped to go through to Chieti, and Montgomery stated that he thought the enemy was pulling out and the way to Pescara was open. In the second Freyberg reported:

> We advanced last night and took Castelfrentano capturing about 100 prisoners. We are on to the cross-roads and moving to clear up the roads beyond Castelfrentano. 6 Brigade is now moving to Orsogna, will then be directed on San Martino. We are all set now with food and communications to move night and day.[2]

General Montgomery responded: 'That's the stuff. You will be able to hit him for six.'

For the next two days it seemed the offensive was still going satisfactorily. But on 4 December heavy rain caused the Sangro to rise 8 feet, and next day all the bridges were under water or washed away. Then the three German divisions opposite the Eighth Army – 65 Division, 90 Panzer Grenadier Division, and 26 Panzer Division – were reinforced by three more. By this time it was obvious there was no possibility of any breakthrough to Rome. The combination of the late start, the strong enemy resistance and above all the atrocious weather in mountainous country, all combined to frustrate what had at first seemed a feasible operation. Although the New Zealand Division struggled on to the outskirts of Orsogna in the second half of December, and Ortona on the coast actually fell to the Canadians on 28 December, stalemate had now set in.

Rain and mud had turned to snow and ice. The New Zealand Division spent Christmas 1943 in miserable conditions. There was little in prospect on the military side except for a long, hard slog up the Italian peninsula. It was Freyberg's fifth Christmas away from home, and in his message of seasonal goodwill to the NZ Division he said he 'hoped that it would be the last for us all'. But the next Christmas found the Division still in Italy, still near the mountains and the Adriatic, and still living in conditions of cold, rain and mud.[2]

The end of 1943 brought changes among the senior ranks of the Eighth Army. Montgomery, selected to command the British armies in England for the Normandy landings, left Italy, taking with him a number of experienced staff officers including General de Guingand. The new Eighth Army Commander was to be General Oliver Leese. At Army HQ on 30 December Montgomery addressed all the officers and men of his staff, and took his leave of his principal commanders, including Freyberg, who had called for three cheers at the end of Montgomery's speech.

Montgomery recognised that the New Zealand Division was being misemployed in the Abruzzi mountains, for in his final report to the CIGS on 28 December 1943 he stated: 'I believe 2 NZ Div under Freyberg would be better employed in Western Europe than Italy. It is a motorised division, highly trained in mobile battle; its full capabilities cannot be properly exploited in Italy.'[1f]

In a signal to his Minister of Defence in New Zealand Freyberg reported his last conversation with Montgomery:

When I was saying goodbye to him he made it clear that he would like to have your Division under his command for the [second front] campaign. I said immediately that I was not empowered to discuss questions of higher policy such as future employment in another theatre of war, this being matter for British and New Zealand Governments. This telegram is merely to report conversation so that if you are approached officially you will be aware of what has taken place. As shipping difficulties are great it is not likely the question will be raised.[3a]

As 1943 turned to 1944 the weather conditions grew even worse. Freyberg reported to his government that they had not experienced anything like it since Greece;[3b] and in a letter dated 2 January 1944 to his wife, who had arrived in Italy to help set up the NZ Club in Bari, he said, 'Here we are well under snow. On New Year's night there was a blizzard when we had a foot of snow. Conditions were for a little while quite Arctic.' In the same letter he mentioned that the following day the first batch of men would be going on leave to Bari, and that he hoped that it would go well and smoothly as far as the club was concerned. Unfortunately reports soon started to come back from the town of misbehaviour and fights caused by excessive drinking. New Zealanders at that stage, unaccustomed to drinking wine, tended to treat it as beer. Freyberg blamed himself for not having established wine bars at the Bari club, where drinking could be supervised and to some extent controlled.[2]

The ending of the offensive in the Adriatic coastal sector led to a regrouping of Allied forces. The first weeks of January 1944 saw preparations being made for operation 'Shingle', the landing at Anzio on the west coast of Italy south of Rome, and for further offensive action on the Fifth Army front to link up with the beachhead. The change of plan required the relief of the New Zealand Division in the Orsogna area by 4 Indian Division. This started on 13 January, took about a week to carry out, and was followed by the NZ Division moving across the mountain divide to the western side some 20 miles behind the front line. Their destination and assembly area was the wooded valley of the Volturno river on the downward slopes of the Matese mountains near the walled village of Alife from which, it was hoped, they could take part in the pursuit of German forces after the landings at Anzio.

The assault force chosen for operation 'Shingle' at Anzio was US VI Corps, comprising 1 British Division and 3 US Division. At that time I was serving with 5 Battalion, Grenadier Guards which was part of 1 British Division and we were stationed at Gragnano, south of Naples in the Castellamare area. As NZ Divisional HQ was one of the first units to move to the Alife district I was able to visit my father at his new headquarters on the night of 16–17 January. We did not see each other again for nearly five months and much was to happen to us both.

Early on 22 January 1944 VI Corps landed at Anzio, virtually unopposed. Even so the commander of VI Corps, the American General John Lucas, largely as a result of unhappy experiences during the Salerno landings four months before, spent the first few days consolidating the Anzio beachhead instead of pressing inland with all speed. By the time he was ready to move forward at the end of the month it was too late. General Westphal, now Kesselring's Chief of Staff, recorded:

> At the moment of the landing south of Rome, apart from certain coastal batteries standing by, there were only two battalions [available]. There was nothing else in the neighbourhood which could be thrown against the enemy on that same day. The road to Rome was open. No one could have stopped a bold advance-guard entering the Holy City. The breathtaking situation continued for the first two days after the landing.[4]

The Germans, however, reacted very quickly, and gathered together enough troops to seal off any further Allied advance. Indeed the British and American troops found that their main task during February and March was to prevent themselves being driven back into the Mediterranean. Churchill's comment on the Anzio landings says all that is needed: 'I had hoped that we were hurling a wild cat on to the shore, but all we had got was a stranded whale.'[4]

What made this outcome all the more disappointing was that Anzio provided exactly the role for which Freyberg had been training his force in the summer of 1943. In his report to the New Zealand Minister of Defence on 28 August 1943 he had stated: 'Our training programme therefore for September and October is to prepare Division for (1) any operation that may be demanded of a mobile division; (2) outflanking movements by sea.'[3c] Anzio was the one place in southern Italy where the New Zealand Division could have been employed with maximum effect. From the point of view of timing the dates fitted perfectly, with the Division and its equipment complete in Italy by the second half of November 1943 and the Anzio landings due to take place some seven weeks later. There were excellent embarkation ports at Naples and Castellamare, a relatively short sea journey, and good disembarkation facilities at Anzio and Nettuno.

The country south of Rome was ideally suited for an armoured motorised force, with its rolling open farmland leading gently upwards towards the Alban hills. The New Zealand Division with its armour and 20,000 troops could indeed have acted as Churchill's 'wild cat' let loose on the enemy's open and undefended flank. The Armoured

Brigade would have had a field day among the enemy's lines of communications in the initial absence of organised resistance; and the powerful Allied air forces would have been available to attack very vulnerable targets in open country when the inevitable German counter-attacks were mounted.

In Freyberg's view a great opportunity was missed in not using the New Zealand Division at Anzio. In the minutes of a conference held at NZ Divisional HQ on 30 January 1944 he was asked why so little had been done by the US VI Corps to expand the bridgehead after the landings. Freyberg replied that had the NZ Division been there by then, 'I think we would have been in Rome.'[2]

The planning of operations in Italy in December 1943 to January 1944 lacked overall direction and drive. It coincided with the change-over of senior commanders in the Mediterranean; and also with the period when Churchill, the instigator of the Anzio landings, was seriously ill at Carthage. No one appeared to have a grip on the military situation or had the foresight to match the commanders and troops with the tasks in hand. It made little sense to send the New Zealand Division with its 170 tanks and 4,500 vehicles into the Abruzzi mountains in the depth of winter, when other infantry divisions were available. And it made even less sense to send infantry divisions to Anzio when the highly mobile New Zealand Division, trained to operate in such conditions, was to hand. And if the mountains near the Adriatic were unsuitable, how much more so was the bottleneck at Cassino, where the Division was to be hemmed in on all sides by natural obstacles.

The German Gustav Line, part of the 'Winterstellung' on the western side of Italy, was based on holding the high ground to the north and west of the Rapido–Garigliano river. The key and centrepiece of the position was Monte Cassino, on the crest of which stood the massive Benedictine monastery. On 23 December 1943 the German Tenth Army passed on to 14 Panzer Korps the Führer's order that 'Monte Cassino is to be included in the defence line and to be fortified'.[5a]

Cassino was reckoned to be one of the strongest defensive positions in the Italian peninsula, endowed by nature as a fortress against any movement from south to north. The high ground gave unimpeded observation for many miles to the south, and anyone approaching from that direction could almost always be seen in daylight. The Rapido river in the valley beneath the Abbey was in itself a considerable obstacle, especially when swollen with storm water, while the ground and the many streams between the monastery and the sea usually became flooded and waterlogged in winter. The mountainous hinterland to the east and north of Cassino was full of high ridges and deep ravines, which were virtually impassable to tracked and wheeled vehicles and could only be traversed slowly on foot or with mules. Most of the main communications on the western side of the Apennines, except for the road and rail links on the coast, passed within sight of Monte Cassino. It dominated the whole area.

When the New Zealand Division made its move across from the Adriatic front in mid-January 1944, the intention was that it would stand by to take up its traditional 'pursuit' role. The plan was based on certain assumptions. The landings at Anzio by the American–British VI Corps were expected to outflank the German 'Winterstellung' and force the enemy to withdraw from the Cassino front. At the same time the American II Corps was to clear the way through into the Liri valley, and thus open a route for the New Zealand Corps – consisting of 2 New Zealand, 4 Indian and later 78 British Divisions – to link up with the Anzio landings and press on towards Rome.[2]

That events were not going according to plan was evident as early as 23 January, when the Diary records Freyberg's incomprehension as to why the troops in the Anzio bridgehead were not moving swiftly inland. Although the initial landings on 22 January appeared to have gained complete surprise and encountered little opposition, the Germans not only succeeded in halting the Allied advance by the end of January but by the second week of February they had gone over to the offensive, and by the end of the third week of February the American and British troops were fighting hard to maintain the bridgehead.

The Germans, after their initial swift response, were known to be contemplating withdrawing troops from the Cassino area to try and crush the bridgehead at Anzio. To prevent this was an additional and urgent reason for the assault on Cassino to be mounted in February.[2]

On 30 January Freyberg was sent for by General Alexander. In what proved to be a fateful interview, Alexander intimated that, in view of what was happening, or more accurately what was not happening, it would be necessary to ask the New Zealand Corps to take over from the Americans the task of breaking through the German 'Winterstellung' at Cassino, as well as to carry out exploitation beyond it. The Americans, having suffered heavy casualties, had conceded that they had failed to achieve their objectives, and felt that they were unlikely to be able to do so in the immediate future.[2]

At this point Freyberg asked the Commander-in-Chief whether, if he refused to carry out the operation, another Division would be detailed to do so? He was told 'yes'.[5b] In these circumstances, as had happened before, Freyberg felt he could not pick and choose which operations the New Zealand Division would participate in, however much he disliked the situation. Freyberg agreed with the view that:

> on its military merits alone no competent soldier would have chosen to assault Cassino in February/March 1944. He would have looked askance at the very notion of trying to carry by storm the strongest fortress in Europe in the dead of winter by a single corps unsupported by diversionary operations.[5b]

Yet this was what Alexander was now asking Freyberg and the New Zealand Corps to do. It was the failure to exploit the initial success of the Anzio landings – which had led to the dangerous German counter-attacks, and to the Allies nearly being forced back into the sea – that necessitated the attacks at Cassino in February and March to prevent further enemy troops being transferred from there to the bridgehead. And because its flanks were impassable in mid-winter, there was no alternative to trying to capture Cassino town and the Monte Cassino feature itself if a breakthrough into the Liri valley was to be achieved. Nor should it be forgotten that it was the Germans who were primarily responsible for precipitating the destruction of the Abbey, by incorporating the monastery into the centre of their positions at Monte Cassino, which they proceeded to defend whatever it cost. As Freyberg said at the time and afterwards, 'no one wanted to bomb the Abbey',[*] but it was the only way of eliminating the German defences, if the attack was to have any chance of success.[6]

There were four phases in the battle for Cassino. During the first, which lasted to the end of January 1944, the American II Corps closed up to the main features of the Monte Cassino position. The second phase started in early February when the New Zealand Corps took over. During this period 4 Indian Division tried to outflank and capture the monastery from the high ground to the north and east, while the New Zealand Division attacked Cassino itself. It was during this operation that the Abbey was bombed. The third phase began in the middle of March, when the New Zealand Division again tried to capture the town of Cassino and cross the Rapido river into the Liri valley. In the final phase in May 1944, the offensive near the coastal sector eventually succeeded in outflanking the Monte Cassino

---

[*] See page 536 for Freyberg's considered view written in 1950.

position, breaking through the German 'Winterstellung', and opening up the road to Rome.[2]

On 3 February 1944 the New Zealand Corps came into being with Freyberg as Corps Commander under the US General Mark Clark's Fifth Army. For its first battle at Cassino it fought as a binary corps consisting of 2 NZ Division and 4 Indian Division – as at its second battle. The Corps staff was improvised, with Brigadier Ray Queree becoming BGS, and Lieutenant-Colonel Thornton taking over as GSO1 of the New Zealand Division. Major-General Kippenberger was on 11 February appointed acting commander of the NZ Division. Major-General Tuker was theoretically in command of 4 Indian Division, but because he fell ill his CRA, Brigadier Dimoline, on 6 February, became the operational commander. Meanwhile, on the same day as the New Zealand Corps came into being the Germans made their first counterattack at Anzio.

Freyberg had not served in close association with the Americans before. His relations with General Mark Clark, were correct, but formal rather than close, and marked by reservations on both sides. Clark was a young general, who had been promoted very quickly and had little battle experience. He had a reputation for being somewhat impetuous and brash, and he did not seem to inspire much warmth even among his own troops. Freyberg's relations with Clark's Chief of Staff, Major-General Gruenther, on the other hand, were on a completely different footing. Freyberg recognised in Al Gruenther a through-and-through professional soldier, and their relationship remained warm and cordial even during the very difficult two months ahead. After the war Freyberg was not in the least surprised by Gruenther's climb right up the military ladder to become Supreme Allied Commander Europe.

On 6 February the New Zealand Corps began to take over from the US II Corps. In the mountainous country to the north of Monte Cassino the US 34 Division had, to its credit, penetrated to within a few hundred yards of the monastery on the northern slopes, and, the day before it handed over on 11 February, it made one last attempt to capture the fortress. This failed. That evening Gruenther spoke to Freyberg on the telephone, 'The torch is now thrown to you,' he said. 'We have had many torches thrown to us,' Freyberg commented later, in the full realization that the latest would not be the lightest.[5c]

So the 'Winterstellung' had to be attacked now, in the depth of winter, but both flanks of the great centrepiece were already impassable. In the north, the Americans had failed to subdue the German positions in the Monte Cairo and Monte Castellone areas, while the country between Cassino and the sea was waterlogged throughout February and March. Later, in May, when the ground had dried out, it was used as the springboard from which the fourth phase of the Cassino battle was launched. But this option was not available earlier. When Churchill visited the New Zealand Division near Florence in the summer of 1944 he asked Freyberg why he had chosen to strike at the strongest part of the German defences at Cassino. Freyberg's answer was 'because there was no alternative'.[2] With both flanks impassable, the only way forward into the Liri valley and the road to Anzio and Rome required the prior occupation of the town of Cassino and Monastery Hill.

The main advantage possessed by the Allies in the depth of winter at Cassino – some would say the only one they had – was their over-whelming superiority in firepower. There were no fewer than thirty-six regiments of artillery available, from 25-pounder field guns to 8-inch howitzers, for which there was no shortage of ammunition. The main problem was to find the space on the ground in which to deploy these 900 guns. It was the same problem for the air forces. There were three medium bomber groups located in Sardinia, and a further three in the Naples area. In the airfield complex at Foggia there were no fewer than ten heavy bomber groups, each of several squadrons. All these aircraft were within a few minutes flying time of the land battlefield, and with a bomb capacity of thousands rather than hundreds of tons; but they could not be used when the Italian weather closed in over the soggy base airfields or the target areas. This was a major drawback.[2]

In the February attempt to break the German 'Winterstellung' the plan was for 4 Indian Division to take over from the Americans in the Monte Castellone area, while the New Zealand Division advanced towards Cassino and crossed the Rapido river into the Liri valley. The Indians, with their North-West Frontier background, seemed the obvious troops to send into the hills, while the New Zealanders with their tanks tackled the lower ground. The problem was that there was insufficient space in the Cassino area in which to deploy at any one time more than a fraction of the troops that were available.

The geographical constraints at Monte Cassino not only prevented the Allies from making proper use of their superiority in firepower and mobility; it resulted also in their being unable to exploit this advantage in areas where the enemy was strong, such as in the Liri valley, whilst it led to overkill elsewhere as at the town of Cassino. In addition, there was the problem of the abbey of Monte Cassino itself.

Monte Cassino had been the site of religious foundations for many centuries. The Benedictine Abbey had been started in the sixth

[459]

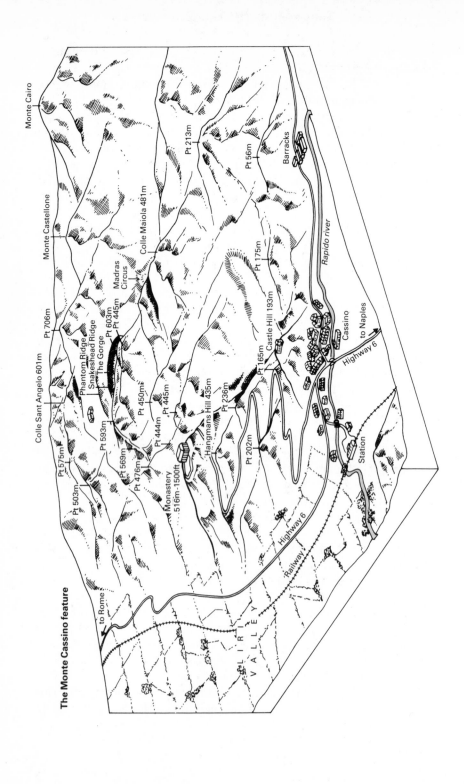

The Monte Cassino feature

Monte Cairo

Monte Castellone

Colle Sant Angelo 601m

Pt 706m

Pt 575m

Pt 503m

Phantom Ridge
Snakeshead Ridge
The Gorge

Pt 603m
Pt 445m

Colle Maiola 481m

Madras
Circus

Pt 213m

Pt 56m

Barracks

Pt 175m

Pt 593m

Pt 569m

Pt 476m

Pt 450m

Pt 444m

Pt 445m

Castle Hill 193m

Pt 165m

Cassino

to Naples

Highway 6

Monastery
516m-1500ft

Hangmans Hill 435m

Pt 236m

Pt 202m

Station

Rapido river

Highway 6

Railway

to Rome

L I R I   V A L L E Y

century, and during its long and chequered history had endured many sackings and plunderings, as well as repeated rebuildings. The resulting structure, with buildings dating from the sixteenth century, was massive, its walls many feet thick. It normally housed art treasures and ancient manuscripts of great historical importance, but the Germans had insisted that these should be evacuated to the Vatican in Rome. As the Allies approached, the Germans also ordered that the monks should leave the Abbey; some did, but the abbot and a number of refugees stayed on.

The Germans had constructed concrete and reinforced steel dugouts and pillboxes all over Monastery Hill, so that the Abbey was no longer an isolated sanctuary but formed the middle of the German front-line defences. This meant that it was in the line of fire, and as the abbot, Gregorio Diamare, later told Pope Pius XII: 'Each side lobbed shells at each other over the hill. The gunners had not meant to hit the monastery but sometimes their aim was poor. This had been happening since January. No one was killed. But the place was half-ruined.'[7] More was to come, for if it was intended to capture the Monte Cassino feature, as the high command's orders required, then the whole area had to be regarded as a military objective, and that objective had to be subjected to intensive bombing in order to overcome enemy resistance. These reasons impelled the ailing General Tuker, commander of 4 Indian Division, to request, in two long letters to Freyberg on 12 February, that the Monte Cassino feature, including the Abbey, should be subjected to heavy bombing. The bombing of the Abbey had been under discussion for some days. 4 Indian Division had the unenviable task of attacking positions which several other well-trained troops had previously found to be nearly impregnable. Their commander felt that it was essential to ask for all the firepower that was available to be brought to bear on the German positions. Freyberg agreed with Tuker's reasons for requesting the operation, which he passed on to the Army and Army Group Commanders. However, Freyberg made it clear at the time, and after the war, that Tuker was not responsible for ordering the bombing of the monastery.[2]

The first bombing of Monte Cassino took place at 9.30 a.m. on 15 February. In a subsequent Report Freyberg related how the ground attacks by 4 Indian Division and the New Zealand Division came to a halt in the next few days through a mixture of appalling weather, flooding, lack of space in which to deploy, and extremely accurate fire directed from observation posts on Monastery Hill. 4 Indian Division had needed to move quickly if they were to make the maximum advantage of the effect of the bombing, but for a number of reasons they were unable to do so. The Maori Battalion won a bridgehead over the Rapido river on 17–18 February at great cost, and were hoping to get a bridge across, but at dawn work on it had to be abandoned because of heavy aimed fire. This bridgehead was lost when the Germans counter-attacked with tanks from the Liri valley.

The Germans were too battle-wise to construe their success of 18 February as any sort of augury of victory, but they welcomed the respite as an opportunity to strengthen their defences, and they moved into the ruins of the Abbey.[5d]

Freyberg had been under no illusion about the prospects of the operation:

> We never thought that the attack could succeed, and long before the attack was launched, when asked by General Gruenther as to the chances of success, I said 'fifty-fifty'. He said 'Not more than that?' I said 'No'. I then told him that if I saw we had failed and had a thousand casualties, I would stop. This caused consternation among the Americans.[8]

This was written in 1955, eleven years after the event. Although Freyberg had rated the chances of success as no more than fifty-fifty, John White, his PA, remembers how at the time he was less definite that there was no chance of the attack succeeding, although he was always pessimistic. The person who did later attempt to alter the record was Mark Clark, who claimed that he had had to acquiesce in the decision to bomb the monastery because of Freyberg's insistence. Freyberg's recollections in 1955 were different:

> Mark Clark was shifty and wanted it both ways. It was he who decided to use the heavy bombers. I made a definite point at one of the Conferences that I did not like the operation, it had the elements of a failure and an expensive one.[8]

Freyberg himself always accepted his share of the responsibility in asking for the bombing. But in the final resort the decision had to be taken by General Alexander, and he supported Freyberg. That remarkable priest, Father Dolly Brookes, who was the Padre of 1 Battalion, Irish Guards, paid a visit to the area of Cassino with General Alexander shortly after the bombing:

> Alex took me in his open staff car with his ADC and we called at General Freyberg's headquarters on our way to the front. The latter dissuaded us from continuing in so conspicuous a vehicle and provided a Jeep instead. We proceeded to the slopes of Monte Trocchio which faces Monte Cassino

[462]

and there sat down and ate our packed luncheon. We were in full view of the enemy, though well out of rifle shot range, and Alex was wearing his General's red-banded cap and red 'tabs', but fortunately the enemy OPs did not decide to send any shells our way. As we gazed at the ruined monastery Alex told me that giving the order to bomb the abbey had been the most difficult decision he had ever had to make, but that he had finally decided that men's lives must come before stones however holy.[9]

This decision was in accordance with General Eisenhower's directive of 29 December 1943: 'If we have to choose between destroying a famous building and sacrificing our own men, then our men's lives count infinitely more and the buildings must go.'[5d]

What can no longer be sustained in the light of recent knowledge is the argument put forward for many years by those who consider the bombing of the monastery was unnecessary because the Germans never made any military use of the Abbey and its grounds. In *Britain and the Vatican during the Second World War* Professor Owen Chadwick gives details of an interview which took place in the Vatican on 20 February 1944 between Abbot Diamare of Monte Cassino and Domenico Tardini, Pro-Secretary of State at the Vatican (later Cardinal Secretary of State).[7] In the course of the discussion, which took place under conditions of secrecy, the abbot enumerated the many violations of the monastery grounds that the German military forces had committed, and said he had protested about them, and had been ignored. Yet in public the same abbot had denounced the Allies for bombing the Abbey and denied that the Germans had made any military use of it. The actual wording of the abbot's statement is not without interest, because the Germans were quick to give it wide publicity for propaganda purposes:

> The statement given out by the Abbot of MONTE CASSINO after the destruction of the Monastery by ANGLO-AMERICAN aircraft on 15 February 1944.
>
> 'I testify that the whole truth is that in the precinct of this holy monastery of CASSINO there have never been German soldiers. There were only for a certain time three police with the sole task of carrying out an inspection of the neutral zone which was established around the Monastery, but these were withdrawn about 20 days ago.
>
> Monte Cassino 15 February 1944.
>
> GREGORIO DIAMARE
>
> Rev. Bishop and Abbot
> Montepore.[2]

On 22 February, at Anzio, which was still under considerable German pressure, General Lucas was replaced by General Truscott. Then at Cassino, on 25 February, old opponents of the New Zealanders, 1 Parachute Division relieved 90 Panzer Grenadier Division, and the new commander of the Cassino front was Lieutenant-General Richard Heidrich. Heidrich had fought against the New Zealanders in Crete as commander of 3 Parachute Regiment, and was known to be a strict disciplinarian and an ambitious soldier. He had one of the élite formations in the German Army made up of 13,000 volunteers, who were physically and mentally tough and trained to perfection. They were excellently equipped particularly with light automatic weapons and anti-tank guns. The parachutists' steadiness in action was renowned. They at once set to work to construct dugouts inside the houses at Cassino town, and to strengthen the cellars with concrete. The defences were deepened by siting heavy machine-guns and anti-tank guns well behind the front line, and these were further strengthened by new positions on the Monte Cassino feature. Reserves of supplies were built up forward in case Route 6 should be cut behind them.[5e]

The Allies had hoped shortly to be able to resume their attacks, as soon as the ground and air conditions were suitable; and orders to this effect were issued on 21 February. But bad weather caused one postponement after another, which was unnerving for the participating troops, and bad for morale generally.

It was during this period, on 24 February, that Freyberg received disturbing personal news from London. It came in a civilian telegram from Martin McLaren and reported that he had been notified officially, as a result of routine casualty returns from Italy, that I had been reported missing at the Anzio beachhead.

Shortly after this, Freyberg had an unexpected meeting on Route 6 with Brigadier Jim Burrows, the commander of 5 NZ Brigade. Burrows recorded what occurred in his autobiography *Pathway among Men*:

> One day while I was still making myself familiar with the ground we were holding, I was walking very carefully along the side of Route 6, the road that led straight to Cassino. The enemy at the Cassino end could easily see movement along the road and with field glasses could probably see in detail more than was good for anyone careless enough to stay long in view. I had been as far forward as I wanted to go and was moving back along a ditch in the shadow of a hedge when I was horrified to see General Freyberg, general's red hat and all, walking by himself along the road towards me. I

immediately came out to meet him but I doubt if he saw me until I was very close and spoke to him. I knew from past experience that he gave little thought to his personal safety; on the other hand, he did not do silly things. Moreover, he was almost always accompanied by his aide. So to walk like this, in full view of anyone with good field glasses, seemed to me to be most unlike him.

I said, 'I think, sir, we should move off the road'.

To my surprise he made no objection and we walked to the shadow of the hedge and eventually back to where his driver was waiting anxiously with his car.

Later I heard that on this morning he had received news that his son Paul was missing at Anzio.[10]

A story about Freyberg, which had a wide currency about this time, also illustrated his occasional forgetfulness of his own safety. It was later adapted by Dan Davin, then an Intelligence Officer at NZ Divisional Headquarters, and published under the title 'The General and the Nightingale'. The essence of it has the General telling his Jeep driver, Alec, to stop out in the open, 'under all those guns, a sitting shot,' as Alec narrates. The General says, 'Was that a nightingale I heard?' His ADC, as anxious to move on as Alec, says, 'I think it was a blackbird, sir.' 'Nonsense, Harry, nonsense,' the General says. 'I know a nightingale when I hear one.' So they all listen and, sure enough, they hear it now. 'There you are, Harry,' said the General. 'I told you so. Didn't I, G1? Drive on, Alec,' adds the General. And they were halfway up the Terelle staircase road before Alec remembered to change down.[11]

On 2 March came the grievous news that General Kippenberger, after stepping on a mine, had had to have both his feet amputated. Freyberg was deeply upset, both for personal and military reasons. General 'Kip', who was commanding the New Zealand Division at the time, was one of the most experienced and able officers that 2 NZEF produced in the Second World War. His wounding happened at a critical moment in the battle when his expertise was most needed, and he was greatly missed in the days to come.[2]

Then, on 10 March, Freyberg received a signal from London telling him that I was in the Vatican. At least he knew I was alive and safe, but he had no idea what had happened to me.

Not until the middle of March did the weather moderate sufficiently to permit a resumption of operations at Cassino, but the final New Zealand Corps plan of attack on 15 March did not differ materially from the orders issued on 21 February. As the Official NZ History explains:

[465]

'Before dawn on D-day the Indian and New Zealand troops would
withdraw to a safety line 1,000 yards from Cassino. The air bombardment
of the town would begin at 8.30 a.m. and last until noon. Ten groups of
heavy bombers and six groups of medium, nearly 500 aircraft in all, would
drop more than 1,000 tons of 1,000-pound high-explosive bombs on a
target measuring about 1,400 yards by 400. The attack would be delivered
by relays of medium, heavy, and medium bombers, in that order, rising to a
crescendo as midday approached.

Zero hour for the ground troops to advance was fixed for midday. At that
time 6 Brigade was to move at the deliberate rate of 100 yards in 10 minutes
to capture Point 193 and the whole of the town north of Route 6. It was to be
preceded by a creeping barrage fired by the artillery, escorted by the tanks
of 19 Armoured Regiment.[5e]

Artillery support was planned on a scale to eclipse all precedent in
the history of New Zealanders. Nearly 900 guns were available, and
Freyberg calculated that in all a quarter of a million shells would be
fired weighing between 3,000 and 4,000 tons. If the enemy could be
blasted into submission, this was the plan to do it. As the Official New
Zealand History recounts:

Though it was fine on the corps front, the weather forecast on 13 March
was bad. On the 14th the indications had improved, and at 10.30 that night
Fifth Army confirmed that the operation would begin next day. The
long-awaited code-word BRADMAN was circulated through the corps.
Those who affected sporting language speculated on the state of the wicket;
and the historically minded noted that the morrow was the Ides of March.[5f]

Freyberg watched the opening of the air bombardment from his
command post at Cervaro, in the company of Generals Alexander,
Clark and Eaker (commanding US air forces). The town of Cassino
was momentarily lit with the flame of detonation, and then became
shrouded in smoke and dust, which soon hid it from observation. The
bombers followed wave on wave, the medium in tight formations, the
heavies more raggedly. Freyberg wrote, 'none who saw it will forget the
terrible one-sidedness of the spectacle'. Fifty per cent of the bombs fell
on Cassino, but many were widely scattered, causing considerable
casualties both to Allied troops and Italian civilians.[5g]

At midday the artillery took up the bombardment. 'As displays of
destructive majesty, there was little to choose between the clean sweep
of silver wings as the earth erupted beneath them and the stabbing
flashes and rippling fortissimo of drumfire from the massed artillery,'
the Official NZ History noted.[5h] Under this umbrella the assaulting

infantry of 25 Battalion approached the town at a brisk pace. But where they hoped to find no life, rifle and machine-gun fire soon started up. The German parachutists crawled out of their dugouts, cellars and concrete shelters and opened up on the advancing New Zealanders. 'Now that they had their enemy at close quarters on ground they knew and had prepared, the terms of combat had turned dramatically in their favour.'

New Zealand tanks were unable to get through the rubble, and bulldozers which tried to clear a path lost their drivers. In the face of the fanatical defence by the German parachutists the New Zealand attack slowed down and then petered out. In Alexander's opinion no other troops in the German Army could have endured such a hammering, and then fought back so hard.[5h]

As the first day of the battle came to an end the commander of 14 Panzer Korps, General von Senger und Etterlin, told his Tenth Army Commander, Colonel-General von Vietinghoff, 'Rain would be even better than air support.' By that time rain was indeed pouring on Cassino.[5i] For the next five days the battle continued in the rubble of Cassino town and on Castle Hill, below the monastery, where New Zealand and Indian troops made some progress, but not enough to be decisive. Once again the overwhelming Allied firepower and superiority of forces could not be brought to bear on enemy targets. As Freyberg wrote subsequently, 'The approach was a bottleneck restricted by massive mountains on the west, and by the Rapido river on the east. Only one battalion could be deployed at a time, a factor which was a great handicap to our operations.'[3d]

Among Freyberg's papers of this period are daily casualty returns, covered by his scribbled arithmetic. Before 15 March New Zealand casualties at Cassino stood at just over 500; on 16 March they were 638; on 17 March 719; on 18 March they had reached 807; and on 19 March 922. On 20 March 1944 they reached 998, which was Freyberg's signal for calling off the battle. The casualties in the Indian Division were even higher.

On 23 March Freyberg held a conference with all the senior officers of the Corps, and they agreed that there was no point in going on. General Alexander arrived on the morning of 24 March and after discussions in Freyberg's caravan he accepted that they had come to the end of that particular phase in the battle for Cassino.[2]

After the March attack at Cassino there was a seven-week period of reorganisation and redeployment. The headquarters of the Eighth Army was brought over from the Adriatic front and became responsible for the area north of the Liri river. The Polish Corps of two divisions took over the Cassino front, while the New Zealand Division sidestepped to the north and moved into the mountains. On 4 April Freyberg wrote to his wife, 'We are moving out to a quieter sector in the course of a few days.' On 15 April he wrote, 'We arrived here in the forward area after a good trip over the mountains. We are in a new HQ 2,000 feet up. Our front is a long one and a lot of our time will be taken up with travelling.' The new sector was almost equidistant between the Adriatic and Tyrrenhian seas.

Meanwhile in the area immediately inland from the Mediterranean, a force of seven divisions (four French and three American) was assembled under the US Fifth Army for the next offensive: the fourth attempt to break the 'Winterstellung'. By the beginning of May the ground had dried out, and on 11 May the Fifth and Eighth armies began their offensive on a broad front. There were only four German divisions between Cassino and the sea, and these were attacked by thirteen Allied divisions. In conditions where greater mobility was possible their numerical superiority soon began to tell, and significant gains were made in the enemy defensive positions. The Polish divisions carried out a series of gallant attacks at Cassino itself, where they suffered heavy losses at the hands of the well-entrenched defenders. But the Cassino fortifications were at long last being outflanked, and eventually the Germans had no choice but to withdraw. The Official New Zealand History tells eloquently how the end of the battle came about:

> It is no disparagement of the Poles' splendid bravery to say that it availed little until success elsewhere threatened the defenders of Monte Cassino with encirclement. Only then, on the morning of 18 May, did the Polish flag and the Union Jack fly above the dusty ruins of the abbey.

'So at last,' the official historian N. C. Phillips added, 'though the great fortress fell, it was never conquered.'[5j]

(Above) The Tripoli parade, 4 February 1943. Churchill takes the salute with Generals Leese, Alexander, Freyberg, Brooke (CIGS), and Montgomery. *(Above right)* Churchill has a private word with Freyberg. *(Below)* Relaxation – as Generals Leese, Freyberg and Montgomery enjoy a Kiwi concert party with their men

(Top) Freyberg in his light tank with his ADC, 1943 *(Imperial War Museum). (Above left)* The end in Africa as Freyberg takes the surrender of Marshal Messe, Commander of the Axis Forces since the departure of Rommel; and *(left)* of Major-General von Liebenstein, Commander of 164 Light Division, 25 May 1943

(Top) In Italy, before the Sangro battle, Freyberg confers with the CIGS, General Sir Alan Brooke. *(Middle and below)* With the Americans, Freyberg got on less well with the 5 Army Commander, General Mark Clark than he did with his Chief of Staff, General Al Gruenther who, after the war, became Supreme Allied Commander Europe

(*Above*) Peter Fraser, Prime Minister of New Zealand, visits the NZ Division south of Rome, May 1944. (*Middle*) Freyberg with his Intelligence officers, Dan Davin and Geoffrey Cox (*right*). (*Below*) After the battle of Florence, Freyberg meets with Churchill and General Sir Harold Alexander, C-in-C, Italy, on 24 August 1944 (*Turnbull Library*)

The final phase of the war for
Freyberg was in Trieste where he
met with hostility from the Yugoslav
4 Army Commander. In the picture
(above left) Trieste is in the distance
and in the middle ground is
Miramare Castle where 2NZ
Division had its headquarters
although Freyberg still lived in his
caravan *(right)* which housed his
communications. *(Left)* An end-of-
war photograph, taken in April 1945
by George Kaye on the eve of the
final offensive in Italy

(Above) Freyberg being welcomed to New Zealand as Governor-General in 1946. The boys lining the route to Government House were from his old school, Wellington College. *(Below)* An official visit by the Governor-General to Niue in the Cook Islands, July 1948. HMNZS *Bellona* is in the background

(Right) The Governor-General with the new Prime Minister, Sydney Holland, 1949. *(Below)* The Opening of Parliament, 1951

(*Above*) The Garter ceremony. Lord
Freyberg, as Deputy Constable and
Lieutenant-Governor of Windsor
Castle, leads the procession to St
George's Chapel on 18 June 1956.
In the background, to the right of the
Gate Towers, is Norman Tower.
(*Right*) Bust of General Freyberg,
VC, by Oscar Nemon. It was
presented to Freyberg by the New
Zealand community in London at the
Guildhall on 26 July 1962, and is now
in New Zealand House

The Advance to Florence and the Lombardy Plain

On Anzac day 1944 Freyberg wrote to his wife, 'We are all well here and enjoying our mountain home, but I feel very much cut off.' There follow several references to myself, in particular wondering whether Barbara had had any news.

I had been taken prisoner on the Anzio beachhead on 7–8 February when my Grenadier company was surrounded in a night attack by the German 4 Parachute Division. I managed to escape on the afternoon of 9 February and went into hiding with some Italian refugees who were sheltering from Allied bombing. One of the Italians was an elderly man who had returned to his own country after a long stay in America. He spoke English fluently, so my language problems were solved. He was also a person of ideas and initiative who had many local contacts, so when I asked him whether he thought I had any chance of getting into the Vatican City – which was neutral territory – he said he would make inquiries. After a few days he returned and told me that there was little prospect of my getting into the Vatican directly from the streets of Rome, because of the high wall which surrounded it. Furthermore the entrances to the Vatican were closely guarded by carabinieri, who had strict orders to turn away escaped prisoners. But there was a back door which might be worth investigating. The Lateran Treaty of 1928, which governed the relationship between Italy and the Vatican State, was still in force. Under its provisions extra-territorial rights applied not only to the Vatican City itself but to various other buildings owned by the Vatican; that is, all such buildings had the same rights and duties under international law as for neutral Switzerland. One of these was the Pope's summer residence at Castel Gondolfo.

Castel Gondolfo is situated in the Alban hills only a few miles from where we were hiding. The outer walls of the estate bordered on one of the main routes south from Rome to the Cassino battlefield, known as the Appian Way or Route 7. A few days earlier the RAF/US Air Force had attacked German convoys using this road. Some of the bombs, missing their targets, had flattened sections of the walls surrounding the Castel Gondolfo estate. There appeared to be nothing to stop anyone climbing over the rubble and, once inside, claiming asylum under the international law which gave escaped prisoners the right of internment in a neutral country.

My helper said he would guide me to Albano, the nearest town to Castel Gondolfo, but that I must follow him at a distance and if I was picked up or got into trouble he would have no option but to disappear. I told him he must do nothing to compromise himself further. By this time I had discarded my uniform and acquired a ragged civilian coat and trousers. We duly walked, well apart, to Albano, which was swarming with German soldiers, and eventually reached Castel Gondolfo. My guide gave me a final farewell wave, and was gone. I clambered through a gap in the wall into the grounds of Castel Gondolfo, and once inside asked to be taken to the Chief Administrator to whom I disclosed my British Army identity, and asked for asylum. I was treated with correctness and courtesy, and in due course my status was confirmed by the papal authorities in Rome. I was then able to communicate with the British Minister at the Vatican, Sir d'Arcy Osborne.

My presence at Castel Gondolfo was an obvious embarrassment to my involuntary hosts, who had no facilities for my continued presence there. After some time they suggested that I should be transferred to the Vatican itself where suitable accommodation existed, but the difficulty was how to arrange transport through German-controlled territory between the Alban hills and Rome. Eventually they decided I should travel in the weekly delivery lorry that plied between Castel Gondolfo and the Vatican with consignments of vegetables. When the time came to leave I found that a small cavity had been made in the centre of the vehicle which was otherwise piled high with sacks of potatoes and crates of garden produce, and this niche was further hidden by being lined with thick sacking. There was a heartstopping moment when we reached the German road block on the outskirts of Rome and the doors at the back of the vehicle were thrown open. But the search was perfunctory, and soon we were on our way again. Thus I made my entry into the Eternal City.

My father, of course, could know nothing about any of this. The first information he had that I was alive came in the signal dated 10 March 1944 from Brigadier Keith Park, the New Zealand liaison officer in London. The Foreign Office had received a signal from the British Minister to say that I was in the Vatican. My father was advised to keep the news of my whereabouts quiet, for fear of causing embarrassment to the Vatican authorities over their interpretation of international law; and I remained inside the Vatican City until Rome was freed by Allied forces some three months later.

Freyberg's letters to Barbara in May 1944 are full of plans for the New Zealand Prime Minister's forthcoming visit to the Division, and for a future club in Rome. After a good deal of jockeying for position with other nationalities, one of the big hotels – the Quirinale – was eventually secured as the New Zealand Forces Club.

The fall of Cassino on 18 May opened the way for the advance by the Division through the mountains, to keep pace with the Allied offensive along the coastal plain. The axis of advance was through Atina, Sora and eventually Avezzano, which, ironically, had been the NZ Division's objective in Montgomery's attempt to capture Rome from the Adriatic side in November 1943. This advance was slow and ponderous. The Germans retired at their own pace behind a large number of demolitions, and in the narrow valleys there was little room for manoeuvre or opportunity for deploying the Division. Freyberg's orders to his brigade commanders were to keep the enemy moving, but not to get embroiled with a strong German rearguard. 5 NZ Brigade reached Atina on 27 May, and on 31 May 28 Battalion occupied Sora, which then became the headquarters of the New Zealand Division. The leading troops pushed on to the final objective Avezzano, which was reached on 10 June.[1a]

Peter Fraser, accompanied by the Chief of the NZ General Staff, Lieutenant-General Sir Edward Puttick, arrived at Caserta on 26 May and was met by Freyberg. The Prime Minister spent a week with the Division and visited all its formations. This included one morning at Cassino observing the battlefield and the ruins of the Abbey, and another occasion when he followed the line of march of the Division in the Atina and Sora areas.

Meanwhile on 5 June 1944 Rome fell to the Americans. My father sent his Intelligence Officer Geoffrey Cox (now back with the division) to collect me from the Vatican, and the next morning, 6 June, we set out

[471]

for Sora. We gave a lift to two fellow escapers, John Syms of the Seaforth Highlanders and Colin Leslie of the Irish Guards, and on the way south called in at tactical headquarters of the Eighth Army to find out about our future. The Army Commander General Oliver Leese was told of our arrival, and we trooped into his caravan still dressed in plain clothes to tell our stories. The other two, who had escaped much earlier than myself, were ordered back to England. I was given the choice of going home or rejoining my battalion in Italy after a month's leave, and chose the latter.

Geoffrey Cox and I reached HQ New Zealand Division at Sora soon after breakfast next morning, 7 June, and I was reunited with my father. I had often wondered how he had reacted to my being 'put in the bag'. While I was in the Vatican I had written an account of my adventures, running to over 100 pages, which I gave to him when I arrived. He read it and was wholly sympathetic, indeed he wrote to my mother from Sora on 11 June 1944:

> By the time you get this you will have Paul with you. I was enormously impressed with his written account and more so with my conversation with him. He had a most difficult job, and the way he managed to get away and into the Vatican was very greatly to his credit.

When my month's leave was over I returned to 5 Battalion Grenadiers, and for the rest of 1944 the battalion was part of 24 Guards Brigade under command of 6 South African Armoured Division. When 5 Battalion was eventually disbanded early in 1945 because of shortage of reinforcements I was transferred to 3 Battalion, Grenadier Guards, a lorried infantry unit in the British 6 Armoured Division. From time to time both formations fought alongside the New Zealand Division, so my father and I had many opportunities to see each other during the last year of the war.

After the capture of Avezzano the New Zealand Division went into a rest area at Arce. Freyberg was told by Oliver Leese on 16 June that he did not see a role for the New Zealanders for a month, because of the difficulty of maintaining more than a limited number of troops in the forward areas.[1b] As well as doing a certain amount of training, full advantage was taken of getting the maximum number of troops away sightseeing in Rome, and bathing at Sorrento, Amalfi, the Isle of Ischia and elsewhere. Such a period of military unemployment was too good to last, and it came to an abrupt end three weeks later with an unexpected and immediate call to action.

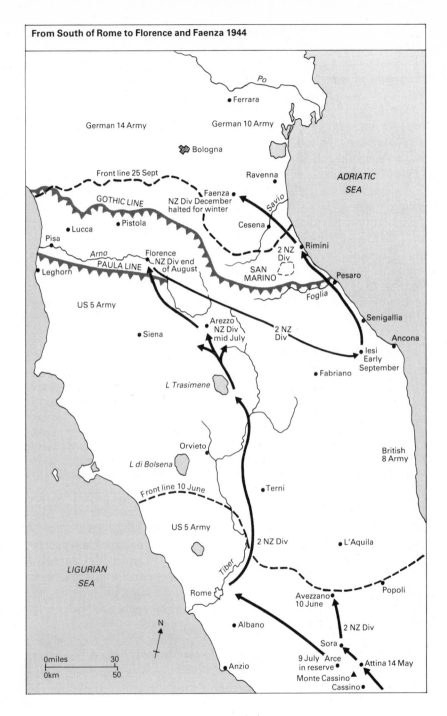

From South of Rome to Florence and Faenza 1944

Po

• Ferrara

German 14 Army   German 10 Army

🖐 Bologna

Front line 25 Sept   Ravenna   *ADRIATIC*
                                                        SEA
GOTHIC LINE   Faenza •
                     NZ Div December
                     halted for winter   Cesena •   Savio

• Lucca   • Pistola

Pisa •   2 NZ   Rimini •
        Arno   Florence   Div
Leghorn • PAULA LINE • NZ Div end   Pesaro •
                        of August   SAN
                                    MARINO   *Foglia*

US 5 Army   Arezzo •
                                  NZ Div   2 NZ   Senigallia •
                  • Siena   mid July   Div   Ancona •

                                                    • Iesi
                    L Trasimene   Early
                                                      September
                                       • Fabriano

                    Orvieto •
L di Bolsena   British
                                                          8 Army

        Front line 10 June   • Terni

                    US 5 Army

                              2 NZ Div   • L'Aquila

LIGURIAN   *Tiber*
SEA
        Rome ⟍   Avezzano •   Popoli •
                                  10 June

        N   • Albano   2 NZ Div

                                     Sora •
0miles   30   9 July Arce   Attina 14 May •
0km   50   • Anzio in reserve •
                              Monte Cassino ▲
                                Cassino •

[473]

The New Zealand Division started to leave Arce on 9 July and moved through Rome to a concentration area to the west of Lake Trasimene about 200 miles to the north. They were first involved in mid-July in a series of skirmishes in the area of Monte Lignano, immediately south of Arezzo.

On 16 July 1944 my father wrote to say that he was near to where I was serving with 24 Guards Brigade, and that he would come and see me shortly. He ended his letter in a characteristic way: 'I am glad you are back again with all your friends. Don't grieve too much about your losses. War is such a silly business and the cost has to be put up with.'

On occasions I used to hear how officers outside the NZ Division reacted when they came across Freyberg in the field. One such encounter occurred at this time south of Arezzo when two companies of 7 Battalion Rifle Brigade came briefly under the command of the NZ Division. Sir Charles Mott-Radclyffe, one of the company commanders, described many years later how he had had difficulty in finding his way to the position he was to take up in the mountains. Freyberg met him by chance on the way and took him to his headquarters to have tea and scones:

> General Freyberg quickly made me forget the difference in rank between a lieutenant-general and a major. We conversed about every conceivable subject, including the Greek campaign, in which he had played so prominent a part, though one would not have thought so from the way in which he referred to it. He then took me half-way up the mountain track in his jeep, pointed out on the ground the exact position which my company was to occupy and came up the following morning to see how we had fared during the night. Other generals of less distinction and achievement were apt to treat incompetent company commanders in a very different way.[2]

In the second half of July the Division closed up to the river Arno prior to the capture of Florence. The Germans attempted to hold a position on high ground 10 miles to the south of the city, known as the Paula Line, and a series of engagements by 6 South African and 8 Indian Divisions as well as the New Zealanders was required to push them back. By 4 August 5 NZ Brigade had fought its way into the southern outskirts of Florence; but it was to be some time before the whole town was cleared of the enemy.

Freyberg took a prominent part in organising these attacks, which were against the New Zealanders' old foes, the German I Parachute Division. He was determined to exploit the great superiority in Allied firepower, and to keep casualties in the Division as low as possible by

[474]

saturating enemy defences with massive artillery bombardments. The GSO1 Colonel Thornton remembers Freyberg saying to him that the war was not going to be won in their locality, and that it was too nearly over to justify a lot of additional NZ casualties. Of course, the landings in Normandy had opened the 'second front' on 6 June 1944, and by now the Allies had broken out of the bridgehead; indeed Paris fell on 24 August.

The Official NZ History records that the expenditure of ammunition in the Division at this time was very high. More than 100,000 rounds of 25-pounder ammunition were used in the three days 29–31 July as well as large quantities of other calibres.[1c] Freyberg told XIII Corps, 'No ammunition, no attack.' It was a refrain that was to be repeated many times during the rest of the war in Italy. When anxious senior commanders, alarmed by dwindling stocks of ammunition, pleaded with Freyberg to moderate his consumption, he would ask them whether shells were likely to be suitable adornments on their mantelpieces after the war. His concluding remark to them was always the same, 'No ammunition – no fight!'

While the New Zealand Division was approaching Florence, Freyberg gave an order that completely startled the New Zealand official war artist, Peter McIntyre. He said: 'McIntyre, go to Rome and paint the Pope.' On Freyberg's initiative the New Zealand government had been persuaded to establish the position of an 'Official War Artist to the 2 NZEF'. Freyberg had spotted Peter McIntyre's talents as a painter while the latter was working in the drawing office of Divisional Headquarters, and promoted him to the post in the spring of 1941. As a result there are now many hundreds of pictures and drawings of the Second World War in museums and galleries in New Zealand, including a number of Freyberg himself, both portraits and in action. McIntyre duly went to Rome and was granted a private audience with Pope Pius XII during which he made several drawings.[3]

August 1944 saw the beginning of the regrouping in Italy prior to the attempt to break through the Etruscan Apennines north of Florence into the Lombardy Plain beyond Bologna; and it was precisely when the mountain-trained French Corps of four divisions was most needed in Italy that, on 15 August 1944, they and an equivalent number of American troops were landed in the south of France against negligible opposition. Southern France would have fallen anyway as a result of the overrunning of northern France, rendering operation 'Dragoon' (or 'Anvil' as it was first called) completely unnecessary; and, as Field Marshal Alexander wrote subsequently, its effect on the Italian campaign was disastrous: 'The Allied Armies in full pursuit of a beaten enemy were called off from the chase, Kesselring was given a breathing space to reorganise his scattered forces, and I was left with insufficient strength to break through the barrier of the Apennines.'[4]

At the request of the Greek government, 3 Greek Mountain Brigade was placed under the aegis of the New Zealand Division. Ever since the dark days of Greece and Crete in 1941, Freyberg and the New Zealanders had had very warm feelings for the Greeks, and this feeling was evidently reciprocated. On a number of occasions the New Zealanders had helped the Greeks with their military training, and on 17 August Freyberg flew to Taranto to inspect the brigade and was much impressed by their bearing.[1d] The brigade took part in some of the preliminary fighting in and around Rimini, but on 18 October they returned to their homeland when it was liberated from the Germans.

On 24 August Churchill again visited the New Zealand Division, driving past units drawn up by the road to Freyberg's headquarters mess, where all brigade commanders, commanding officers and senior staff officers were assembled to have lunch with the Prime Minister. Brigadier Burrows has left his impressions of the occasion:

> The morning had been hot and the roads along which the Prime Minister had travelled were winding and dusty. At first he sat slumped in his chair, looking hot and tired. After a moment General Freyberg said, 'Sir, it is hot in here. Let me remove your jacket.'
>
> He went behind the Prime Minister, helped him off with his jacket and hung it on the back of his chair. The Prime Minister of England, with his trousers held up with a pair of black braces, made a very interesting sight for New Zealanders.
>
> After a bowl of toheroa* soup, Mr Churchill was clearly much revived and one of his first questions, addressed to me, was 'Why did the soldiers give me a better welcome the second time they saw me?'
>
> I said 'Because they do not cheer very well to orders, sir, and the second time they cheered of their own accord.'
>
> General Freyberg was always a perfect host and soon he had brought us all into the conversation. Mr Churchill asked us in turn about the battle front and we were all surprised how easy it was to talk to him.
>
> Quite soon he rose to his feet and in his black braces and with glass upraised he said, 'I am going to give you a toast. To your great Division.'[5]

The Prime Minister's toast was recorded by John White:

> I cannot leave without raising my glass to you, my dear Bernard, and the gallant New Zealand Division whose name is honoured and cherished

* A New Zealand shellfish. The soup is now a rare NZ delicacy since the toheroa is in danger of becoming extinct.

among the Nations. Its career and record is one that will live not only in the history of New Zealand but in the history of the British Empire as an example of duty, valour and honour. For four and half years you have been in the forefront of the battle. I myself have visited you four times – in theatres of war – in England in 1940, in the desert at Alamein, at Tripoli and now in Italy. Everything is going well and I hope it will not be long before you can rest on your laurels and return to your beautiful country. I wish you all the very best of luck. I drink to the New Zealand Division. Although you haven't anything to drink, drink to me with your hearts.[6]

This visit came at the end of the Division's stay in the Florence area. The Eighth Army had already begun its sideways redeployment in the direction of the Adriatic coast, prior to the forthcoming offensive towards the flat country of the Romagna – the great plain that opens out beyond Rimini and stretches for over 100 miles to the Alps. The New Zealand Division followed the other formations during the last week of August, and after a journey of 220 miles reached their new concentration area at Iesi, about 15 miles inland from the port of Ancona on the Adriatic. For the time being their role was to be held in the Eighth Army Reserve.[1d]

The Eighth Army's offensive started on 25 August in the coastal strip by the Adriatic, south of Rimini. The aim was to make a breakthrough into the Lombardy Plain. The Germans, taken by surprise, were bounced out of their defensive positions behind the Foglia river at the eastern end of the Gothic Line, which stretched right across Italy. Freyberg kept in close touch with, and paid frequent visits to Eighth Army HQ even though the roads were very congested. On 29 August it took seven and a half hours to get there and back, since General Leese's tactical HQ was situated well forward. Thereafter Freyberg took to the air, and did the return trip in a small Auster aircraft known as a 'Whizzer'. The weather conditions on 3 September, unfortunately, were unfavourable with high winds, and according to the Diary, 'When landing at Tac Army Strip GOC's plane tipped and GOC was wounded on the right side below his ribs by a piece of the wing which broke through the side of the plane.'

After the accident, although shaken, Freyberg was able to walk and was perfectly lucid. He was taken by ambulance to No. 1 NZ General Hospital at Senigallia and operated on that afternoon. It was found that the wound was a deep one penetrating the abdomen, but that no vital organs had been touched. Freyberg's condition after the operation was 'satisfactory', but he was likely to be out of action for six or eight weeks.

The question immediately arose, who would command the Division in his absence? This was a delicate matter, since the person Freyberg

[477]

recommended to the New Zealand government as his temporary successor was Brigadier Steve Weir, commander of artillery, and not the most senior officer available. The most senior was Brigadier Inglis, commander of 4 NZ Armoured Brigade, who had commanded the Division in the summer of 1942 when Freyberg had last been incapacitated. Inglis did not take kindly to being passed over, and the Diary records that some fairly tense scenes took place round Freyberg's hospital bed in the days immediately after his injury. When the New Zealand government accepted Freyberg's recommendation and confirmed Weir in the appointment Inglis asked to be relieved of the command of his brigade, and eventually returned to New Zealand.

Freyberg thought Weir was the most balanced and sensible of the New Zealand senior officers available, and his choice was vindicated by events. He did such an excellent job in command of the Division in Freyberg's absence that, on the latter's return to duty, Weir was given command of the British 46 Division, where he proved to be both effective and popular.

After being notified of my father's accident I went to see him immediately. He was in considerable discomfort but adamant that his condition did not justify Barbara – who was now back in London helping to start the New Zealand Forces Club there – coming out to see him. However it was obvious that there would have to be a considerable period of rest and convalescence. Meanwhile a large number of messages of sympathy arrived, including one from Winston Churchill congratulating Freyberg on his nineteenth wound! When it was announced on 7 September that the general had had a second operation the Greek Brigade sent a signal saying, 'With exceptional joy received the news of the General's health progress. Long live our divisional commander.'[7]

Freyberg responded well to treatment. On 28 September he wrote to me, 'I am now up and about. The stitches are out and the wound is healed. I have been swimming for the last three days, and I walked about three miles on the beach today.' And on 8 October: 'A line to say that I am taking over the Division again in about three or four days. We shall then be in for a bit and then out for a rest.'

While Freyberg was away from the battlefield the Eighth Army had made its initial penetration of the Gothic Line – which followed the line of the Apennines from Pisa in the west to Rimini – but thereafter it encountered increasingly stubborn German resistance. It did not reach Rimini until 21 September, and only then was it possible for the Army to deploy into the Romagna.

But a double disillusionment awaited the Eighth Army when eventually they reached the great plain. The intention had been to move forward along Route 9 to Bologna, and along Route 16 to Ravenna and then Ferrara. But the weather broke on 20 September, and heavy rain turned the area into a quagmire. Although the Po valley was flat it was extremely unfavourable country for armour. In fact the Romagna was basically still a swamp, whose major watercourses had been canalised between floodbanks rising in places 40 feet above the plain. Thirteen rivers and many more small streams flowed from the Apennines into the Adriatic at right angles to the army advancing on Bologna and Ravenna. These river floodbanks were an effective anti-tank obstacle, and when the rivers were in spate after heavy rains in the mountains they were unfordable as well. The civilian bridges were mostly confined to the main roads but these were almost invariably destroyed by the enemy as they retreated. Thus as the summer turned into autumn any hope there may have been for a resumption of quick-moving mobile operations was dashed.[1e]

The New Zealand Division under Weir had participated in several operations during September and October, and had cleared the area between the Uso and Fiumicino rivers, one of which was probably the Rubicon of classical history (although its exact identification is disputed). Progress during this period was very slow, determined by the pace at which the infantry could advance.

On 14 October Freyberg took command of the New Zealand Division again. While in hospital he had had the time to think about how he wanted to reorganise the Division, and there were several new factors to be taken into account. The first was that by the autumn of 1944 it was clear that the hitherto expected and hoped-for German collapse was not going to happen before the end of the year, either in north-west Europe, on the Russian front or in Italy, and that the war would continue well into 1945. Second, the enemy's equipment was in the process of changing. There were fewer German aircraft and tanks, and therefore less need for Allied anti-aircraft and anti-tank guns. Also, in the slow, hard slog up the Italian peninsula, the highly mobile NZ Divisional Cavalry had had few opportunities to carry out its traditional role. What was needed above all was more infantry.

Another problem Freyberg faced was the need to replace the old hands with new blood. The original Ruapehu leave scheme had not been an unqualified success. After three months leave in New Zealand the veterans had been expected to return to the Division, but many had claimed exemption on personal grounds; and those who did come back were thoroughly unsettled by their time at home. Undoubtedly this had contributed to a lowering of morale and discipline that became apparent in the summer of 1944. Freyberg felt that it was unrealistic to expect troops to continue to be exemplary soldiers after more than three years on active service. He thought they should be replaced and honourably returned home having done their duty.

The two major considerations in reorganising the Division, therefore, were the need to replace at least half the personnel – those who had served for three years or more – and to increase the number of infantry battalions in place of units whose operational roles were no longer required.

During the second half of October and November there were a large number of signals between Freyberg and the New Zealand government about the measures necessary to implement the new policy. It was decided to return the veterans to New Zealand early in 1945 and to absorb new drafts as soon as possible afterwards, so that the Division would be ready to take the field for the new and hopefully the final offensive in Italy in the early spring.[8]

Freyberg took a great deal of trouble to explain the reasons for the changes to those affected by them. For example, he knew that the 'Div Cav' would not be pleased to lose their scout cars and be converted to infantry, so he made a special point of going in person to explain to them why the reorganisation was necessary. As a result of having the reasons fully spelt out, the changes were accepted by the men, and implemented without further argument.

The end result of the reorganisation was the disbandment of several units and the conversion of others to infantry. The Division would shortly have three infantry brigades, each with three infantry battalions and a regiment of tanks, as well as the normal complement of artillery, engineer and other supporting units. In its final shape it was probably as well-balanced and well-found a division as it had ever been in the Second World War. However, much retraining was needed before the Division was fit to take the field in an offensive role, and this was to be given priority in the coming months. The changes involved absorbing over 10,000 reinforcements to replace the same number of men returning home.

The 5 Canadian Armoured Division relieved the New Zealanders on the Savio river near Cesena between 22 and 25 October, and the latter went back to a rest area in the Fabriano–Camerino region to the south-west of Ancona. Freyberg took the opportunity of being out of the line to spend two weeks in the Middle East, arriving in Cairo on 31 October. The officer commanding the New Zealand troops in Egypt was Brigadier Gentry, one of the most experienced officers both as a commander and as a staff officer, and who was shortly to be selected as

Commander 9 NZ Infantry Brigade, the newly raised third infantry brigade of the division.[1f]

Freyberg took a postponed convalescent leave and went to stay for a few days with his old friends Sir Edward and Lady Spears in the Lebanon. He returned to Cairo much refreshed, and after a further week spent there in a fairly leisurely fashion, he was back with the Division in Italy by the middle of November, well before it was due to return to the line after its month's rest.

It is clear from appreciations written at this time that the main objective of the Allies was to tie down the twenty-nine German-controlled divisions still in Italy, to prevent them being transferred to the Russian front or to the west, where the German Ardennes offensive was about to start. But Alexander and General McCreery, the new Eighth Army Commander, still hoped it would be possible also to make further progress into 'The Plain' during a late autumn offensive, before winter conditions brought active operations to a halt, and Bologna was set as their final objective. The Fifth Army too had been on the move in November on either side of the Florence–Bologna road, but it was unable to make much progress in the mountains. The main part of this operation therefore was an attack in 'The Plain' with Route 9 forming the axis of advance.

The New Zealand Division started to go back into the line on 24 November, relieving 4 British Division which had been operating in the area between the Montone and Lamone rivers to the north of Route 9. This relief was completed on the night of 26–7 November. Freyberg's Diary records: 'We are to push until the weather breaks – then close down for the winter'.[1g]

The fighting on the outskirts of Faenza during the first three weeks of December was confusing. Some of the best German formations – including 26 Panzer, 90 Light and 29 Panzer Grenadier Divisions – disputed each defensive position and counter-attacked whenever possible. Faenza was eventually captured, and the enemy was eliminated east of the Senio river; but the NZ Division was unable to get a permanent foothold on the west bank. On 30 December Field Marshal Alexander decided to abandon the offensive. The New Zealand Division therefore halted on the Senio river, and spent the next three and a half months making preparations for the spring offensive.

On the night of 26–7 December 1944 Freyberg's caravan was parked inside the garage of a house in the Divisional HQ compound near Faenza. The Germans carried out several air attacks that night, and one bomb went through the roof of the house, penetrated a floor and the outside wall, and came to rest on the roadway near where

Freyberg was sleeping.[1h] In a letter to his wife on 22 January he confirmed a report that had reached her: 'A very large bomb dropped on top of my building. It landed 20 feet from where I was in my caravan. It did not go off. It was a huge 1,200 lb one, so we were lucky.' Early in the New Year he was still telling the story with relish. After describing the arrival and passage of the bomb he would pause, half cover his mouth with the back of his hand, and exclaim, 'It was a dud!'

The New Zealand Division remained deployed on the Senio river during January and February 1945. Operationally it was a quiet time, with the Allies temporarily on the defensive during the worst of the winter weather; and the Germans in no condition to undertake anything except minor engagements. For Freyberg and his staff, however, it was a very busy period. They were implementing the 'Tongariro' scheme, as the new replacement arrangements were called. There was no question of anyone coming back to the Division this time, and those who departed under this scheme knew they were leaving for good. They comprised not only the original members of the NZ Division but the next three Reinforcement Groups as well. Only a few remained who had been overseas for more than three years, and these were mostly senior commanders and certain specialists.

Freyberg was wholeheartedly in favour of these changes, but these replacements had only left New Zealand in January 1945; and so there was less than three months in which to transport them to Italy, absorb them into the Division, train them, and be ready for the spring offensive. Over half of the New Zealand Division that eventually crossed the River Senio on 9 April 1945 had never been in action before, but this proved to be an advantage. The rejuvenated force found its feet in a matter of days and the remaining 'old hands' were quick to acknowledge that the Division had once again regained its old bounce and vitality.

The slack period in the line in January and February allowed Freyberg to greet a number of visitors. Among the first was General Barrowclough who had given up command of 3 New Zealand Division in the Pacific, recently disbanded for manpower reasons. A considerable number of its more experienced officers and NCOs were sent to Italy as Tongariro replacements, and proved to be of great value to 2 Division in Italy.

Just before the Division left for the front line Freyberg entertained Sir Patrick Duff, the British High Commissioner Designate to New Zealand. Sir Patrick had had an eventful career, having served with 29 Division in Gallipoli and then been Private Secretary to successive British Prime Ministers for the ten years 1923–33. Freyberg wrote to his wife on 4 March, 'he has made an excellent impression'. The feeling was evidently mutual, because in Dunedin on 21 September 1945 Sir Patrick had this to say about the Division:

It was an eye opener for me when I spent a couple of nights and a day in the line in Italy, just on the eve of the last push . . .

Brigadier Gentry took me one afternoon to hear him brief his officers. His brigade was in reserve and was to push through the first wave after the initial attack. We sat on some forms grouped in a small semi-circle in a field of young clover just outside a farmhouse, against the haystacks of which tanks and trucks nestled neatly camouflaged. Every now and again one of our guns behind us would bark. But everything was ominously still that day. The Brigadier explained to his officers the general plan. There was a blackboard and some maps on it: and the Intelligence Officer explained the situation – where resistance must be expected, what obstacles would be met. Tasks were allotted. Questions were asked.

I looked at that circle of eager young faces. I never saw a younger crowd of Field Officers, many wearing decorations for gallantry. They had seen many actions in many a setting. Here they were again on the eve of battle. As I looked at them I thought of Shakespeare's lines:

> I do not think that braver gentlemen,
> More active-valiant or more valiant-young,
> More daring or more bold, are now alive
> To grace this latter age with noble deeds.[7]

The new 9 NZ Infantry Brigade had come into being on 20 January 1945. All three of its battalions joined the brigade in the next fortnight, although they were not made up to full strength until the second half of March.[1f]

A characteristic letter reached Freyberg towards the end of February from Montgomery at tactical headquarters 21 Army Group. It was accompanied by two photographs, each signed 'B. L. Montgomery, Field Marshal'.

My dear Bernard

I hope all goes well with you.

I am reminded of you by having just seen one Barrowclough – a Major-General of yours who is visiting this theatre.

He tells me you may be the next Governor-General of New Zealand. I shall most certainly come and stay with you in one of your many residences.

[483]

You may like the enclosed photographs. They were taken on a cold day in the Ardennes during the German break-in battle in those parts. I am dressed as Colonel Commandant of the Parachute Regiment. Though I doubt if any of my predecessors had ever dressed like that!!!

Good luck to you.[7]

Now that it was the policy for men who had served overseas for more than three years to return to New Zealand, Freyberg did not feel it right to expect his own staff, who had served him for so long and so devotedly, to remain with him any longer. This meant the parting of the ways for his ADC Jack Griffiths, and for John White, his Personal Assistant since January 1940, who had run Freyberg's private office in a most exemplary way through all the campaigns. John White wrote to me on 27 February, 'It was *very* hard to leave the General.' My father was equally sorry. He wrote to Barbara, 'John went two days ago. He was sad and I am very sorry to lose him. However I am lucky to have kept him for five years.'

Jack Griffiths, a former All-Black, had been Freyberg's ADC since before the Greek campaign. He had been a splendid guardian to him throughout the lean years in Crete and the Western Desert, and had nursed him in the period immediately after he was wounded at Minqar Qaim. Jack's unfailing cheerfulness and tact had helped to make the headquarters of the Division a very friendly place, and visitors were always made to feel welcome.

In a letter to Barbara on 4 February Freyberg wrote:

We are at present carrying out another stage of the replacement scheme. It is sad saying goodbye to a lot of people but I am sure the decision was the right one. I have been looking at the men on parade and many of them show signs of battle-weariness. The Tongariro scheme has also taken my batman and my confidential clerk so there is a clean sweep.

The New Zealand Division was relieved on the Senio by the Polish 5 Kresorva Division between 4 and 6 March, and went back to the pleasant surroundings of the Fabriano region, well inland from the port of Ancona. An early visitor during this period was General Kippenberger, making his first return to the Division since his injuries at Cassino. It was an emotional occasion at which Kip took the salute at a ceremonial parade held in his honour on 19 March.

A German document captured early in 1945 contained an enemy appreciation of the situation and views about Allied troops on the Eighth Army front. These appeared in an Intelligence Summary of 278 Division, stating that 'the Allies will make every effort to break through in the Bologna sector, and we can expect fresh attacks from the crack NZ Division and Canadian Forces for this purpose'. The summary goes on:

> The New Zealanders, most of whom volunteered for service in Europe out of sense of adventure, are trained and led by General Freyberg, a dangerous opponent. They are specialist in night fighting, they fight on a wide front and their method of attack resembles the German method. The New Zealanders have learnt to follow closely under the heavy artillery barrages which they use; by this means they are able to take their opponents off their guard and gain their objectives without heavy losses.[7]

The move back to the Senio, a drive of some 130 miles, began on the evening of 30 March. The New Zealand Division took over a sector of the line from 78 British Division, and the relief was complete by 2 April.[1i] A momentous month lay ahead.

28

One More River . . . and the Dash to Trieste

By April 1945 Freyberg's subordinate commanders were all very experienced. Two of his three Infantry Brigade commanders were regular soldiers – Brigadier Gentry with 9 NZ Brigade, and Brigadier Parkinson with 6 NZ Brigade – and the third, Brigadier Bonifant of 5 Brigade, a stock auctioneer by profession who had risen from troop leader in the Divisional Cavalry, was a natural soldier. The Commander of Artillery, Brigadier Queree, was also a regular soldier and had been Freyberg's principal Staff Officer from before Alamein to after Cassino.

Colonel Hanson the engineer commander was one of the leading engineers in New Zealand in civilian life, and had already made the NZ Engineers one of the best-trained specialist corps in the army; but their expertise in bridge-building and road-making, among other skills, was about to be tested as never before. Brigadier Campbell, the armoured commander and a former civil servant, was to become a Regular later, following a successful and much decorated war. Completing Freyberg's team were Bill Gilbert, principal staff officer of the Division and still in his twenties; and Geoffrey Cox, senior Intelligence officer – a Rhodes scholar and already an accomplished journalist, who after the war was to carve out for himself a distinguished career in Independent Television.

It was Geoffrey Cox who later wrote one of the best descriptions of the New Zealand Division in action in Italy, in *The Road to Trieste*,

[486]

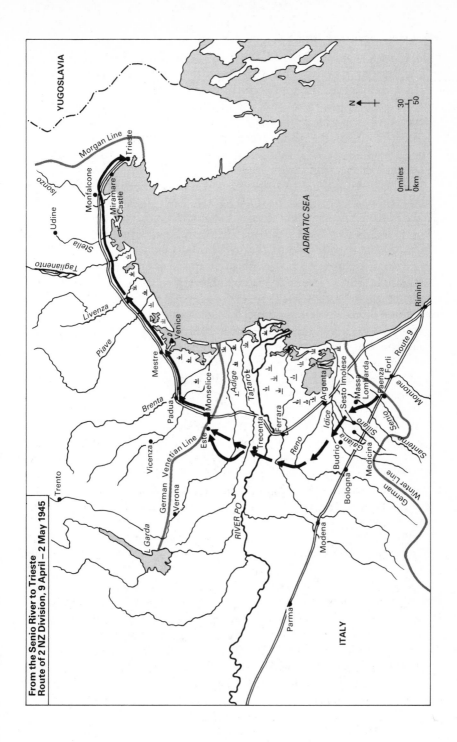

From the Senio River to Trieste
Route of 2 NZ Division, 9 April – 2 May 1945

YUGOSLAVIA

Isonzo
Udine
Tagliamento
Stella
Monfalcone
Morgan Line
Trieste
Miramare
Castle
Livenza
Piave
Venice
Mestre
Brenta
Padua
Monselice
Este
Adige
Vicenza
German Venetian Line
Trento
Verona
L. Garda
RIVER PO
Trecenta
Tartaro
Ferrara
Reno
Idice
Argenta
Sesto Imolese
Massa
Lombarda
Budrio
Gaiana
Medicina
Bologna
Modena
Parma
Santerno
Senio
Sillaro
Faenza
Forlì
Montone
Route 9
German Winter Line
Rimini
ADRIATIC SEA

ITALY

N

0 miles   30
0 km   50

published in 1947. This book contains a thoughtful analysis of some of the factors that made the Division so successful at this period. In his view there was nothing unusual about the divisional 'Cabinet', as he called the ruling hierarchy, or its conferences or 'Order Groups', where it conducted the business of the day. Where it differed from other divisions was in the more informal nature of these meetings. British 'O' (Order) Groups were usually strictly formal affairs, where the Divisional General laid down policy and gave out orders without comment or interruption.

In the New Zealand Division there was much more open discussion about how things should be done, as General Thornton describes on pages 410–11 above. This often led to arguments between the principal commanders and Staff Officers. British officers attending New Zealand 'O' Groups for the first time were often taken aback at some of the frank things that were said, with their apparent challenges to military orthodoxy. But it was a procedure that suited New Zealanders, and enabled them to say what they felt and let off steam without impairing agreement on the decisions that were subsequently arrived at. Freyberg relished the cut and thrust of these arguments, yet there was never any question but that, in the final resort, he had the last word. His experience and authority were such that there was no danger of things getting out of hand; and once his decision on any matter was announced, it was accepted by all concerned.

While Alexander's main object during the winter of 1944 had been to prevent the twenty-nine enemy divisions in Italy being diverted elsewhere, his aim in the spring of 1945 was the destruction of the German forces in Italy. The New Zealand Division's role was to participate in the elimination of the German Tenth Army facing the British Eighth Army in the Lombardy Plain and in occupation of the rest of northern Italy.

The military problem was how to deal with the German divisions entrenched behind a series of river lines, of which there were six major ones south of the river Po, running across Route 9 and barring the approaches to the Po itself. From south to north these rivers were the Senio, the Santerno, the Sillaro, the Gaiana, the Idice and the Reno, and in varying degrees they all presented the attacker with the same problem: high flood-banks with a tank-proof ditch in between, and an enemy well dug in behind the far bank, with an armoured counter-attack force in the rear ready to seal off any penetrations.

The difficulties that faced the New Zealand Division in the centre of the line – with the Polish Corps on its left flank and 8 and 10 Indian

Divisions on the right – was how to breach each river line and get tanks and anti-tank guns forward in time to support the leading infantry and deal with the counter-attacks. It was a problem that Freyberg and his commanders had been studying very carefully since they first reached the area of the Senio in November 1944. Geoffrey Cox particularly remembered a remark the General had made during one of the planning conferences: 'If we can catch them often enough on a set line, and pound them like hell, they will break. There is not a unit in the world can be caught three times under a proper barrage and stay battleworthy.'[1a] He spoke with the voice, Cox commented, not of the Second World War, but of the one before – that of Passchendaele and the Somme. However much the Allies had suffered from the enemy's air superiority in the early years of the war, their infantry never had to endure such concentrated and devastating artillery fire as the enemy troops encountered in Italy in the final month of the war.[1b]

The solution eventually arrived at was to subject the enemy defensive position to intensive artillery fire and then, just before the infantry assault, to hose the far bank with burning oil from flame-throwers mounted on the chassis of tanks. Provided the infantry attacks were successful, the next phase was to bridge the ditch and stop banks so that tanks and support weapons could marry up with the infantry beyond the river obstacle before they were counter-attacked. This was often a race against time, with the engineers struggling in the dark to complete their bridges before first light. To facilitate bridge-building, massed searchlights were often deployed some miles to the rear, and when reflected off clouds, lit up the front lines clearly, and facilitated movement.

Freyberg and his staff were faced with a particularly tricky problem over the Senio and Santerno lines. The Santerno was a much more formidable obstacle than the Senio, and had been strongly fortified; Freyberg was worried that the Germans would hold the Senio until the last moment and then withdraw to the Santerno, leaving the whole attack schedule to be repeated a second time after a prodigious expenditure of wasted ammunition. Such an obvious tactic had also occurred to the German commanders, who made full arrangements to do just that; but the situation was saved by Hitler who refused to allow a yard of territory to be given up voluntarily, and to the chagrin of his generals they were ordered to fight with their full strength on the Senio river. Freyberg did not know this, of course, and was concerned that the enemy had thinned out or had gone altogether. On the eve of the attack he said to Geoffrey Cox, 'Don't forget – we won't get those quarter of a million shells back if we fire them into an empty bank.'[1c]

D-day was 9 April, and H-hour 1920 hours. Before the appointed time heavy attacks had been made from the air by the strategic bombers in conjunction with the tactical air force, and then, precisely on time, the artillery barrage began, to be followed, just as the infantry went forward, by evil-looking red streaks from the flame-throwers. By eight o'clock that evening all four assaulting battalions were over the Senio, and forming up for the attack beyond it. Meanwhile the bridge-building had started. The number of prisoners began to mount and eventually reached 600. Soon it became clear that the Germans had been manning the Senio at full strength.

At the morning conference next day Parkinson and Bonifant, leading 6 and 5 Brigades respectively, confirmed that they had captured their objectives, and that all the tanks and supporting weapons were over the Senio. The engineers had done a magnificent job, and by dawn on 10 April six bridges had been completed. German counter-attacks in the NZ sector had fizzled out, and already the main problem was that the Allied troops on the flanks were way behind the New Zealanders. Geoffrey Cox recorded a conversation with Freyberg that morning:

'How heavy are his minefields on the Santerno?' said the General suddenly.
'As heavy as these [on the Senio] if not heavier. This was to have been his main line.'
'And the Sillaro?'
'There are fields there, too – but thinner.'
The General was silent for a moment. 'It cannot last for ever, this mined area of his. Soon we shall outrun his minefields, then we will outrun his demolitions, and then we will be able to go like hell.'[1d]

The next river line, the Santerno, was very nearly gate-crashed in the early hours of 11 April – that is, four New Zealand battalions were on to the river line before it could be properly manned by the enemy. A dogfight developed in the afternoon with some German Tiger tanks, but these were severely harassed by 'cabrank' aircraft. This was the system, developed towards the end of the war, whereby a number of fighter bombers were stacked on call awaiting targets. When these appeared in the form of Tiger tanks, or important headquarters moving into new positions, the cabrank pilots were given the map reference over the air and engaged the targets within a few minutes.

After by-passing Massa Lombarda on 12 April with 5 and 6 Brigades, Freyberg was determined to press on to the Sillaro river line, which was reached two days later. 'Push on, push on as hard as you can, Ike,' he said to Parkinson. 'He's not far from busting.'[1e] By this time 9

Brigade had been brought into line opposite Sesto Imolese, and 12
Lancers had joined the Division and were covering the northern flanks.

The divisional attack on the Sillaro river line was planned for 14–15
April but had to be postponed for twenty-four hours because the
artillery arrangements could not be completed in time. The attack duly
went in on 15–16 April with 6 Brigade on the right and 9 Brigade on the
left against new opponents. The old German 98 Division had been
virtually destroyed on the Senio and Santerno rivers, and the New
Zealanders now faced a weak 278 Division in the north and 26 Panzer
and 4 Parachute Divisions further south. These latter formations were
among the best troops the Germans had in the plains, but nothing was
now left in reserve.

At 6 a.m. on 16 April the Division was able to report a satisfactory
situation to XIII Corps. The attack had made its objective, more than
260 Germans had been taken prisoner and some eight enemy tanks had
been knocked out or captured. Four bridges had been put over the
Sillaro river, and the armour and supporting arms were with the
infantry.

A captured enemy map showed, in Freyberg's words, 'that the Boche
knew where we were and put the whole of his tank battalion opposite
us. I think we are now through the heavy mine belt. Our objective now
is to destroy as many of his tanks as possible. It will then be comparatively easy.'[2a] At the 'O' Group at 5 p.m. on 16 April Freyberg was very
optimistic:

> I think we are pushing him back and forcing him to withdraw along Route 9
> as the Poles have not taken many prisoners. He is on the verge of a very big
> decision about going back. I think if he does not do it in two or three days, it
> will be too late. The Staff estimate it will take him three weeks to get out of
> the hills in the west [that is, in the Apennines opposite the American Fifth
> Army]. He will hold at every obstacle on the front to gain time for that. Most
> people think he has left it too late.[2b]

Meanwhile 43 Gurkha Lorried Infantry Brigade had taken
Medicina, and was placed under the command of the New Zealand
Division. They came up on the left of 9 NZ Brigade. This enabled
Freyberg to maintain the momentum of the advance with two brigades,
while resting the other two. He said at this stage, a week after the start
of the battle: 'There is one point – we are getting tired. It is essential
that the reserve brigades and the reserve battalions are out of the battle.
We will be going on for another five days.'[2c]

During the night of 16–17 April and the next day the NZ Division moved steadily forward towards the next big river, the Idice. But before they got there they bumped unexpectedly into a solid line of the German Parachute force, who were dug in behind the Gaiana river. It soon became obvious that nothing short of a major set-piece attack was going to dislodge them. Geoffrey Cox relates how Freyberg interrogated him closely on the enemy layout:

> Were we sure the parachutists were there in strength? Yes, we had identifications from six full battalions, in the line or in reserve – two battalions of 12th Para Regiment, two of 10th Para Regiment, one of 4th Para and one of 11th Para Regiment. Tanks? Yes. The few remaining Tigers had been moved off our front, but his half-dozen Panthers were still opposite us.
>
> Would the enemy be sure to stand and fight on the Gaiana? There was every sign that he would. He had now committed all his reserves, and was fighting hard on every front in Italy. 90th Panzer Grenadier Division was fully committed, partly towards the west coast, partly south of Bologna. 29th PG Division, which started to leave for the Western front, had been recalled to try and plug the Argenta Gap [one of the routes to the river Po on the Ravenna–Ferrara road]. A breakthrough anywhere would threaten all his fronts.
>
> 'Very well, then,' said the General. 'We will break him here.'[1f]

The reports from the Brigades confirmed that the Gaiana Line was strongly held by the enemy. The river banks were low enough to ensure that flame-throwers could reach the far bank without difficulty; as Brigadier Gentry remarked, 'The situation is most suitable for flaming.' A full-scale attack was arranged to go in at 2100 hours that night, and the main difficulty was to find room for all the artillery regiments that were to participate. There were nine field regiments and three medium regiments ready to fire 100,000 rounds of ammunition. As Freyberg remarked with satisfaction, 'They're worried sick at Corps and Army that we're going to shoot off all their ammunition tonight. So we are. But we are the only ones in position and ready to do so, so why shouldn't we?'[1g]

Geoffrey Cox describes the beginning of the battle:

> 2130 hours. The barrage opened with a roar on right and left ... The flashes lit and flared like a hundred thunderstorms. The trees around us changed from lumps of soft, slumberous darkness to shapes of green and yellow. The whole western sky was alive with bursting shells.
>
> It looked appalling, far far worse than the Senio. It moved the General to a rare moral judgement about the enemy. 'I hate these paratroopers,' he said suddenly, 'they represent all that is worst in the whole Nazi system.'

At ten o'clock the flame-throwers went in. Their spurts of flame, red under the lightning flashes, showed again, again, again. All along the line of the river they glared, red and ugly. The black smoke mounted up into the stars. The assault was on.[1h]

The parachutists fought back hard. The prisoners who came back were confused and dazed, but there were less than 200 of them. It was only next morning in daylight that the full extent of the German casualties became apparent. 'Few battlefields in this war can have presented the picture of carnage which the banks of the Gaiana showed that day, this spectacle of Germans killed by the barrage, or caught crouching in their holes by the flame-throwers.'[1h]

Many years later Geoffrey Cox gave his considered view of the Gaiana battle to the author:

In the history of the Italian campaign, the battle of the Gaiana River line of April 18/19 is not by itself of major significance . . . But in the story of 2 New Zealand Division, and in that of Bernard Freyberg, it *has* a major significance. The attack on the German positions along the Gaiana was the last set-piece attack, mounted with full scale artillery support, according to a carefully predetermined plan, which the Division was to launch. For General Freyberg it was to be the last occasion upon which he would conduct such a battle, the last opportunity for him to exercise what was his most outstanding military skill, that of planning, preparing and pressing home an attack which utilised to the full against a formidable enemy the weapons of modern war, and which utilised equally to the full the training and experience of the troops under his command, and their ability and courage. His other great skill, that of swiftness and dash in a breakthrough, would still have a final opportunity in the race for Trieste. But for the General, and the men of the force de frappe which he and events had forged into a great fighting formation, recognised as such by ally and foe alike, the Gaiana battle of the night of 18/19 April was the end of an epoch.[1n]

The battle of the Gaiana was one of the most remarkable that Freyberg ever fought. It is also one of the least known. The New Zealand Division's battles against the German parachutists in Crete and at Cassino attracted world-wide attention because of their setting and results. But no one can doubt that, in the end, Freyberg and his Division had their revenge, and that on the Gaiana river they more than settled old scores with the Parachute Korps. Little was heard about the Gaiana battle even at the time, because of the spectacular events that were happening in north-west Europe and on the Russian front in the second half of April 1945.

In Italy too the news was exciting. Early on 21 April troops of Polish 3

Carpathian Division had entered Bologna from the south-west, and later that day they were joined by 34 and 91 US Divisions from the south. The Americans were quick to fan out into the Lombardy Plain once German resistance crumbled, and soon they were threatening, and then occupying towns as far apart as Milan, Bergamo, Brescia, Verona and Vicenza.

After crossing the Gaiana 9 NZ Brigade and the Gurkhas had pressed on towards Budrio. On 19 April they were relieved by 5 and 6 NZ Brigades in their vehicles, led by the armoured cars of 12 Lancers. They met no opposition on the Idice river and on 22 April joined up with the Americans at Castel Maggiore. The following day the Division turned north and advanced towards the Reno river on two separate but parallel roads. They crossed the Reno on 23 April, and by the next day the New Zealand Division had reached the river Po.

Meanwhile the 6 Armoured Division (in which I was serving) had also reached the river Po via the Argenta Gap, and the two divisions were side by side for a short time, waiting for bridging to catch up before the crossing could be started. I took advantage of the lull to pay a brief visit to my father's headquarters, where an 'O' Group was assembling. I had recently been awarded the Military Cross and was wearing the ribbon for the first time. There had been no opportunity to tell my father, so he knew nothing about it. When he first noticed the ribbon, instead of congratulating me quietly as I had expected, he insisted on drawing it to the attention of other members of the 'O' Group, to my acute embarrassment

5 and 6 NZ Brigades were ordered to cross the Po the next morning, 25 April, and found negligible opposition. It was the thirtieth anniversary of Anzac day, there were blue skies, a warm sun, and the crossing was more like a regatta than a military operation.[2d] Once the Division was established on the north bank the armoured cars of 12 Lancers hurried on to take over the lead from the infantry. They surprised and dispersed a German rearguard at Trecenta, and by nightfall had secured a bridge over the nearby Tartaro river.[2e]

Next morning 5 and 6 NZ Brigade continued the advance to the line of the Adige river. As usual Freyberg was all for pressing on: 'I think if we don't stop the enemy won't be able to fight again.'[2e] At the 'O' Group conference on the afternoon of 26 April he ordered 9 NZ Brigade and the Gurkhas to take over the running from 5 and 6 NZ Brigades as soon as a bridgehead had been established over the Adige, which was nearly as wide an obstacle as the Po. At this stage the main expectation was that the Germans would attempt to re-establish their defensive position on their 'Venetian Line', which had been strongly fortified. It ran to the south of Padua and Venice from Chioggia on the Adriatic to the Alps through Monselice and Este.

Originally the plan was to assault across the Adige at 2300 hours under an artillery barrage, but later, when it appeared the enemy was withdrawing, 5 and 6 NZ Brigades went over without artillery support, and established themselves on the far bank without difficulty. Heavy rain delayed bridge-building, and the 400-foot Class 9 bridge being thrown across was not ready for some time.

Freyberg had ordered that the armoured cars of 12 Lancers were to be given first priority to cross and were to 'push out on a very wide front and carry on right up to the Venetian Line. I don't think we will be able to gatecrash it . . . this delay with the bridge may allow the Hun to get troops into the line.'[2f]

In the meantime the Division was getting ready for a mobile role. There was sufficient transport to carry all three brigades in vehicles, and three days' rations, petrol and ammunition were distributed, so that units were independent of supply constraints, as they had been in the desert. The Division was champing to go and, as Geoffrey Cox wrote, 'no one champed with more vigour than the General. The infantry commander who had thought in terms of massive barrages had dropped away now; in his place there appeared the cavalry commander who was going to push on at the utmost speed!' Geoffrey Cox next analysed the qualities and characteristics of Freyberg, the fighting general, particularly in the context of the current campaign:

The General throughout this campaign – as throughout all actions so far as we could remember – had always been the most optimistic, the most aggressive, the most anxious to seize the initiative and smash hard. 'He's gone – he's bust – he's shooting off his dumps.' These sayings of his had become bywords among his officers, as he would urge the leading briga-diers to press on, on. They were in part, I believe, an instinctive expression of the natural belligerency of the man, of his great physical and mental aggressiveness and energy, and in part a carefully calculated policy. Freyberg knew that his task as a commander was to maintain the constant dynamic which any force must have. So he called continually for every possible effort, pointed out every optimistic feature in the situation. His brigadiers and his staff knew this, and worked their views in with it, distinguishing between those statements which the general made as adjur-ations and those which were definite orders. 'Press on at full speed, press on,' he would say. 'Give them no rest.' At times his staff and commanders would try to put the brakes on to this eagerness by pointing out reasons why it would not be possible. If the reasons were factual he would listen; if they were opinions he would listen too, but would be unconvinced.[1i]

On the morning of 28 April Freyberg had to decide whether to race towards the Venetian Line and try to break through with mobile columns, or whether to shape up to the line and put in a set-piece attack.[2g] The enemy still appeared to have troops to occupy the line, but the situation was unclear. Geoffrey Cox relates what happened when, at one o'clock, he turned on his wireless for the BBC news:

> The Russian and American forces had linked up in Germany. The partisans in Milan were rumoured to have captured Mussolini. General Dittmar, the German military spokesman, had surrendered and described the situation as hopeless. Then the telephone rang. Ian Whigham, the G2 Intelligence of XIII Corps was on the line. 'The Yanks say they are through the Venetian Line and north of Vicenza.' I started across to the General with this news, when the phone went again. It was the artillery IO. 'The air op. reports that the Este Bridge is intact and that the armoured cars of the 12th Lancers are almost on it.'
>
> This time I sprinted to the General's caravan. He was already in his jeep, with his ADC climbing in the back holding the General's revolver belt and steel helmet. He had the news direct from the CRA. 'I'm off to Este,' he said. 'Whips out!' He drove off down the narrow track towards the gateway. The next time I saw him, twelve hours later, we were in the outskirts of Padua, well behind the remnants of the Germany Army on this front.[1i]

The XIII Corps under General Sir John Harding had been ordered to get to Trieste as quickly as possible. The object was to forestall any takeover of Venezia Giulia by the Yugoslavs, and to open up the port of Trieste for British troops moving into Austria. There were only sufficient supplies and transport to maintain one division forward to carry out this task. In spite of the fact that it had been in continuous action since 9 April, the New Zealand Division was the obvious one to be chosen. It was already centrally positioned, and was a fully mobile, well-balanced force of all arms. Freyberg used to describe his three New Zealand Brigades at this period as 'my three little Panzer Divisions'. The operation required was the kind at which the Division had always excelled, but which it had not previously been given any opportunity to carry out in Italy. Now, at long last, the New Zealand Division was again in its element.

The 9 NZ Brigade had taken over the running, having passed through 5 and 6 NZ Brigades on the banks of the Adige river. In front of them 12 Lancers were making spectacular advances. By nightfall on 28 April they had penetrated the Venetian Line and reached Este and Monselice, followed hard by the infantry. Early in the morning of 29

April 9 NZ Brigade was on the outskirts of Padua, fighting a German detachment at Ponte di Brenta on the Mestre road, and taking 230 prisoners. A further 200 prisoners were rounded up shortly afterwards by 27 NZ Battalion, opening up the road to Mestre, from where a detachment was sent into Venice. In the meantime 12 Lancers were despatched down Route 14 to try and prevent the bridge over the river Piave from being destroyed.

New Zealand troops were the first Allied soldiers to enter Venice, at about 4 p.m. on 29 April. Freyberg sent a company of 22 Battalion under Colonel Thodey to secure the Danieli Hotel as a club for the Division. In later years many inaccurate stories circulated about this incident, but the correct version of what happened appears in the Official History, quoting Freyberg himself, who wrote:

> We were allotted the Excelsior Hotel as a Club in Rome and when we arrived there we found Americans with a mounted Guard, who told us to buzz off, and they occupied the hotel themselves for a Club. When we were going up on the way to Trieste, we heard that the Americans were coming up the road, and on their lorries had placards with Danieli Hotel. We were not going to have a repetition of what had happened in Rome, and I sent a Company of the 22 Battalion to occupy the Danieli Hotel, and made Colonel Thodey personally responsible to me that he kept the Americans out.[2h]

On 30 April, after a detour due to rebuilding the bridge over the river Piave, the New Zealand Division set out to cover the 100 miles to Trieste. The order of march was 12 Lancers, Freyberg's tactical headquarters, 9 Brigade, Main Divisional HQ, the Engineers, 6 Brigade, the Gun Group and 5 Brigade. The ease with which the New Zealand Division had passed through the Venetian Line demonstrated how complete had been the enemy's defeat in the Po valley. They no longer had sufficient cohesion to fight organised delaying actions on any of the main river lines of north-eastern Italy, although individual pockets of Germans mounted the occasional forays against soft targets on the line of march. Freyberg held his last 'O' Group of the war on 1 May, at which he reported that a bridge had been secured by 12 Lancers over the Tagliamento river. The next bridge over the Stella river had been blown, but a way round had been found over an inland bridge at Rivignano.[2i]

At this stage Freyberg became aware of the limited amount of petrol available, and the need to conserve what there was if the Division was to reach Trieste. He could see the large number of captured German vehicles that had been pressed into unauthorised use by individuals in the Division. He said to the Provost Marshal, 'We have to be careful about petrol. For that reason all captured enemy vehicles must be left behind. Take those vehicles out of the columns at once.' Geoffrey Cox describes how this was done:

> So the Provost stood at the roadhead and diverted to one side the captured vehicles, till there were dozens of them lined up, while their indignant drivers and passengers, reduced once again to the back of their regulation three-tonners, ran, cursing and holding their gear, to climb on to the nearest passing vehicle.[1m]

At 1430 hours on 1 May 1945 the 12 Lancers reached the intact bridge over the Isonzo river.[2m] The Isonzo marked the most westerly point claimed by the Yugoslavs in their dispute over Italian territory. At an earlier stage in the war an agreement had been made between Alexander and Tito to share the facilities at Trieste in order to sustain the war against the Germans as and when it reached that part of Europe. However, now that the war was virtually over, the Yugoslavs intended to occupy the whole area of Trieste and its hinterland themselves, and to present the Allies with a *fait accompli*. In order to do so, however, they had to keep Allied forces out, and here they miscalculated. In the last week of April the Yugoslavs were fighting the Germans on the outskirts of Trieste. The Allied forces were still south of the river Po, nearly 200 miles away, and there appeared to be no possibility that they could appear on the Isonzo until well after the Yugoslavs had occupied the whole Trieste region.

There were no Yugoslav officers on the Isonzo bridge when 12 Lancers arrived, so Freyberg ordered their advance to continue. They went on to Monfalcone, when Freyberg joined them at 1730 hours and made his first contact with two senior Yugoslav officers. By this time 9 NZ Brigade was occupying high ground just beyond the town. The Yugoslavs agreed to the New Zealanders staying in and around Monfalcone, and arrangements were made for Freyberg to meet the Yugoslav Fourth Army Commander at 7.30 p.m. The Yugoslav general did not keep the appointment, however, and Freyberg concluded that the Yugoslavs were bluffing about how far they had advanced. He sent a message to XIII Corps Commander, Harding, at 11 p.m., stating that he was now expecting to meet the Yugoslav commander at 8.30 a.m.[3]

When the Yugoslav Army Commander did not arrive next morning, Freyberg gave the order to advance, and 9 NZ Brigade set off for Trieste shortly after 0830 hours on 2 May, headed by 'A' Squadron of 12 Lancers and supported by tanks of 19 and 20 NZ Armoured

Regiments.[2n] They met with a certain amount of German opposition on the way, which had to be dealt with first, so it was not until 1600 hours that the leading New Zealand troops entered Trieste, closely followed by Brigadier Gentry and Freyberg.[2p] They found a chaotic situation there, with large crowds of wildly cheering Italians, a force of sullen Yugoslav soldiers and a considerable number of Germans, some of whom were still armed and defiant. 9 NZ Brigade set up its headquarters in Trieste in the Grande Albergo della Citta, while Divisional Headquarters took over Mirimare Castle on the coast 5 miles to the north-west of Trieste. Later that day the unconditional surrender of all Geman forces in Italy was signed at Caserta.

In his last campaign Freyberg had been able over three weeks to keep up the momentum of the advance for over 250 miles in which the Division took almost double their own number of prisoners. This was achieved at a cost of fewer than 250 New Zealanders killed in action.

There is a curious parallel between the way in which Freyberg spent the last day of both the First and the Second World Wars. In the Great War he had headed the cavalry charge of the 7 Dragoon Guards that seized the bridges over the river Dendre at Lessines just before the arnistice came into force. For this action he was awarded a second bar to his DSO. For the advance on Trieste, Freyberg was awarded a third bar to his DSO. He was also made a Commander of the Legion of Merit by the Americans, and the citation was signed by the President of the United States at the White House on the 17 August 1945.[4]

[499]

29

Cold War and Peace

Freyberg and the New Zealand Division were to stay in Trieste for nearly three months. For the first few weeks it was a time of very considerable tension and uncertainty, caused by the hostility of the Yugoslav high command. Freyberg had his first taste of the Yugoslavs' attitude when General Drapsin, Commander of the Yugoslav Fourth Army, came to visit him at his headquarters at Miramare on the evening of 4 May 1945, presumably at the instigation of Marshal Tito:

> His attitude came as a shock. He was offensive and truculent. His opening remarks were: 'I tell you categorically to get back behind the Isonzo River. If you don't, I won't be responsible for what happens.'
> That was not the tone or language of a friend or ally. He greatly mistook our character if he thought that it would influence our actions in the slightest way. I answered with firmness: 'After that remark, General, I hold you directly responsible for what happens.'[1]

Drapsin could hardly have chosen a worse moment to utter threats. At the time the New Zealand Division, over 30,000 men, consisted of four infantry brigades, an armoured brigade of 150 tanks, and more artillery than could easily be deployed. The Yugoslav Army was still basically organised as a guerrilla force, and was mostly clothed and equipped with captured German material. Its transport was mainly horse-drawn. One of the British liaison officers attached to the Yugoslavs told Freyberg that the only language the Yugoslav commanders understood was force.

After his disturbing encounter with Drapsin Freyberg wasted no

[500]

more time on discussion. He prepared a plan based on the assumption that the Yugoslavs might try to eject the New Zealand and British troops forcibly. As Trieste would not easily be defended against a Yugoslav attack because of its long eastern perimeter, he arranged for the withdrawal of 9 NZ Brigade from the town and the taking up of defensive positions on high ground south-east of Monfalcone. All necessary reconnaissances and other preparations were carried out so that the new deployment could be put into effect within a few hours, but no actual movement of troops took place.

Meanwhile the uneasy stalemate in Trieste continued, with the two opposing centres of power trying to administer the same area. Freyberg found himself in the middle of the first 'cold war' type of clash between East and West. For example, the Yugoslavs started to make arbitrary arrests in Trieste, on the grounds that the people concerned were Fascists. They disappeared, and in certain cases were never seen again. Civic and church leaders would then appeal to Freyberg for protection. The population of Trieste, mainly Italian, was understandably apprehensive.

Within a few days the problem had been taken to the highest level. Peter Fraser, the New Zealand Premier, was in San Francisco for the conference to set up the United Nations, so there had to be a triangular exchange of views between Wellington, Trieste and San Francisco to establish New Zealand's policy, as well as frequent consultation with London and Washington. Freyberg was greatly impressed by Fraser's attitude, which is summed up in his signal of 14 May from San Francisco to Wellington:

I have received a message from Mr Churchill regarding the implications of Tito's occupation of Trieste, and he has sent me copies of the messages exchanged between President Truman and himself . . . In my own mind, there is no doubt that these acts of encroachment, for the purpose of snatching territory by force of arms before a peace conference can meet and adjust territorial claims, are just that form of aggression against which the United Nations have fought for over five and a half years and are still fighting, and which, if unchecked, will nullify and destroy all that has been won. In that case, the heavy sacrifices of New Zealand, as well as of the United Nations generally, will be in vain. In my opinion, therefore, Tito or any other similar aggressor Allied or otherwise – must be halted at the earliest possible stage. You will see from the telegrams that Field Marshal Alexander is asking what part of his present troops will be at his disposal in the event of action which might develop into hostilities against Yugoslavia's deliberate aggression.

I do not see how we can do otherwise than agree to authorise the

[501]

Commander-in-Chief to use our Division, which is actually on the spot, in the hope and belief that a firm stand now against Tito in this particular instance will not only deter him from taking similar action in other neighbouring territories but will prevent an extension of such dangerous and inadmissible actions, which clearly must lead either again to war in the future or to further disastrous concessions on our part.[2a]

Fortunately both Truman and Churchill were of one mind in resisting Yugoslav aggression. Truman wrote:

I have come to the conclusion that we must decide now whether we should uphold the fundamental principles of territorial settlement by orderly process against force, intimidation, or blackmail. The problem is essentially one of deciding whether our two countries are going to permit our allies to engage in uncontrolled land-grabbing or tactics which are all too reminiscent of those of Hitler and Japan.[2a]

He went on to suggest that the United Kingdom and the United States should insist that 'Field Marshal Alexander should obtain complete and exclusive control of Trieste and Pola, the line of communication through Gorizia and Monfalcone, and an area sufficiently to the east of this line to permit proper administrative control'.[2a]

Churchill replied:

I agree with every word you say and will work with all my strength on the line you propose . . . If [the situation] is handled firmly before our strength is dispersed, Europe may be saved another bloodbath. Otherwise the whole fruits of our victory may be cast away and none of the purposes of World Organisation to prevent territorial aggression and future wars will be attained.[2a]

He detailed the eighteen divisions available to Alexander in the event of hostilities against Yugoslavia, adding that he would need to obtain permission from the New Zealand and South African governments for the use of their two divisions.

Freyberg's letters to his wife resumed after a gap of five weeks on 13 May 1945:

I have not been able to settle down to any private letters for a long time now. Today, even, I am in the middle of cables and calculations for the New Zealand Government. I fully expect a message to fly out to New Zealand for consultations. But that can wait until it happens. As you can gather the situation in this part of the world is tricky so that for the moment I am tied here, even from going away for the night. I have seen quite a bit of Paul who is fit and well and is much encouraged by his MC, which needless to say has given me a great deal of satisfaction.[1]

The 6 Armoured Division in which I was serving had ended up in southern Austria, and my battalion was billeted in houses on the southern shores of the Wörther See. In May it was a very agreeable place in which to be stationed, and our only troubles were also being caused by the Yugoslavs, who had invaded southern Carinthia just as they had Trieste.

Freyberg's last operational headquarters of the war, at Miramare Castle, was situated about 5 miles from the centre of Trieste, in a setting of great beauty, being on the tip of a small peninsula jutting out into the Adriatic. From its battlements Freyberg could see the city of Trieste, with ships moving into and out of the harbour and docks. To the north-east were the mountains of Venezia Giulia whose summits in early May were still covered in snow, while in the far distance to the north-west were the massive outlines of the Alps. The sea breezes ensured that, even in summer, the climate was not unduly hot.

Miramare had been built 100 years before for the Archduke Maximilian of Austria. In 1864 he had set sail from the little jetty beneath the castle walls for Mexico, where he was proclaimed Emperor; but his short and troubled reign ended in 1867 with his execution by a republican firing squad. For that reason Miramare was thought to be unlucky, and it was alleged that because of this Freyberg would not sleep in the castle but continued to use his caravan parked in its grounds.

Freyberg had a reputation – not entirely unjustified – for being superstitious. It had begun at Shorncliffe in 1930 when one day he saw the new moon through glass, and returned home to find that I had fallen off my pony and broken my collarbone. Ever afterwards he took endless trouble to avoid seeing a new moon through glass. It was an innocent and harmless eccentricity but sometimes it led to absurd situations. For example, in Wellington after the war his Vice-Regal party was *en route* from Government House to the theatre to see Laurence Olivier and Vivien Leigh in *The School for Scandal*; half-way there Freyberg suddenly remembered that there was a new moon, so he stopped the car in the centre of the city, and all of us, in full evening regalia, the ladies in long dresses and white gloves, had to get out and look for it. It was in the middle of the evening rush hour and the streets were thronged. What the good citizens must have thought when the

[503]

party, having eventually found the new moon, bowed and curtsied to it seven times, was mercifully not reported to us.

But superstition was not the reason why Freyberg avoided the grand rooms of the Miramare Castle. The explanation was that communications with his subordinate commanders by telephone and wireless were all conveniently to hand in his caravan. There was also a distinct possibility in the first weeks in Trieste that, if the Yugoslavs had resorted to force, Divisional Headquarters might have had to leave Miramare in a hurry. By the time the threat passed Freyberg was sufficiently well established not to want to make any changes.

On 16 May Freyberg produced a long 'Appreciation of the Situation'[2b] for his government in which he drew attention to a 'situation not only fraught with political complications but even the risk of armed conflict with the Yugoslav Army'; and in view of the feelings of the NZ Prime Minister and his Cabinet, he agreed that full operational control of the Division be given to Field Marshal Alexander. This was duly approved.

Four days later on 20 May Freyberg was addressing his Prime Minister again:

> There are the makings of trouble both here and in Austria. The Yugoslavs have moved a large force into and around Trieste and Gorizia. We are now following suit. I want the New Zealand Government to know the fact that we are sitting at the point of greatest tension and that fighting may break out.[3a]

But this proved to be the darkest moment of the crisis, and in the last days of May and the first ones of June Freyberg's letters home reveal the beginning of a lightening of the atmosphere, so that he even felt free to leave his headquarters for a couple of days to attend a victory party in Austria.

The Yugoslavs had been made to realise by representations at the highest level in Washington and London that their attempts to bluff the Allied forces out of Trieste and Carinthia had failed, and the only options left to them were to use force or back down. Evidently they had done their military homework and decided to abandon their attempt to annex the province, while saving face as much as possible. On 9 June the Yugoslav government signed an agreement accepting the Allies' requirement for the withdrawal of Yugoslav troops and administration west of the Morgan Line (named after Alexander's Chief of Staff Lieutenant-General W. D. Morgan, who negotiated the new arrangements with his Yugoslav opposite number), which was drawn so that the whole of Trieste came under Allied jurisdiction. They were also to withdraw from Austria. These arrangements were due to come into force by 12 June, when the Allied military government would move in and take over control. The Yugoslav Army began to leave Trieste on 11 June, and had evacuated the city and its immediate hinterland by the morning of 12 June amid scenes of rejoicing by the Italian population, and to the relief of Freyberg and the New Zealand Division.[3b]

The Trieste 'problem' lingered on for many years in the council chambers of the United Nations, and in the national Parliaments of the West. What was never in doubt, however, was that in the conflict between East and West during the next decades, possession of the territory in question was worth nine-tenths of any argument. The Berlin blockade, which came three years later, was another example of the same phenomenon. Had the New Zealand Division not moved with such speed in the final offensive in Italy, the Yugoslav Army would have had enough time to complete its subjugation of the territory east of the Isonzo river before the Allied armies arrived there, and Trieste would have disappeared behind the Iron Curtain.

In May and June 1945 Freyberg also had some domestic problems to deal with. He had been adopted as the prospective Conservative parliamentary candidate for the Spelthorne Division of Middlesex in 1938. At the beginning of the war he had offered to resign, since he could no longer give any time to the constituency. His Spelthorne Selection Committee saw no reason to accept his resignation and asked him to continue. The agent of the association, Mr Lowles, had kept in touch with him throughout the war, and always discouraged further suggestions of resignation which Freyberg voiced from time to time. Now, however, the issue could be postponed no longer.

The Conservative/Labour/Liberal coalition fell apart in England soon after victory in Europe, and Churchill called a General Election at the end of May to be held on 5 July. Since Freyberg could not leave Trieste in the middle of the crisis with Yugoslavia, Lowles offered to fight the election for him in his absence. But Freyberg felt that this would be an unsuitable and unworkable arrangement, and insisted that his resignation must now be accepted.

On 25 May Freyberg wrote to his wife: 'About Spelthorne – I am certain that the decision was the correct one. I can't get away from here at the present difficult time. I feel very tired mentally and would be much better if I had a good rest, and could not face another job in my present condition.' He had been away from England for over five years and felt he was out of touch with people's feelings; he told me also on

[505]

one occasion that after achieving victory as a member of a united team he would find going back to party politics very difficult. He never regretted his decision to stand down.

Freyberg was not surprised by the election results, which were announced on 26 July, three weeks after the votes were cast, in order to allow time for the Services' ballot boxes to be brought back to Britain. In a private and personal signal to Fraser on 15 August 1945 he analysed what he considered to be the main reasons for Churchill's defeat at the polls. By this time it was generally accepted that it was the Services' vote that had produced the Labour landslide:

> I attribute the root cause of dissatisfaction in the British Army mostly to their failure to have a fair system of replacement of battle-weary fighting troops.
>
> During the final stages of North African Campaign and heavy fighting in Italy it was apparent that the morale of the Army as a whole was deteriorating. An examination of statistics showed that when formations had been two years overseas there was a sharp increase of sickness and crime, particularly absence without leave and desertion on the eve of a battle. This fact was known to us and also to the War Office. 'Ruapehu' and 'Tongariro' leave schemes helped us through 1943 and early 1944, while our replacement scheme was a complete corrective and enabled us to complete the war in good shape. Nevertheless, as you know, there was an anxious time during 1944 at the time of your visit.
>
> On the other hand the steps taken by the British Government to relieve men with long service caused dissatisfaction because they were inadequate and what was fatal they were unfair between the various theatres of war. In Italy desertion became very frequent and in fact so grave that in one British Division in 1944 there were nearly 1,000 cases of desertion and serious AWOL. In comparison, for the whole 2 NZEF, a force nearly double the strength of a Division, we had 73 cases of desertion or serious AWOL up to the end of 1944 or five years' service overseas.
>
> There were further factors which caused dissatisfaction. The British soldier came into close contact with Dominion and American troops and found by comparison that their conditions of service were appreciably better than his own. This was apparent not only in the matter of replacement but also those of pay, medical services and particularly of welfare.
>
> There was no excuse for bad welfare as it is a most important and relatively inexpensive service. Until a later stage in the European War British welfare was deplorable. Their set-up was bad, they had no central fund, welfare was linked up to NAAFI, an excellent trading organisation, but interested mainly in making profits as a trader from its sales and not understanding the needs or scope of welfare. In the final year British welfare improved but the damage had been done.
>
> It is difficult to say when the turn against the Government came. I believe

COLD WAR AND PEACE

that after two years overseas the men became critical. It was obvious to most
of us in Italy that the British soldier was going to vote against the
Government.[4]

In Freyberg's former prospective constituency of Spelthorne a
Conservative majority of 16,000 in 1935 was turned into a Labour
majority of over 8,000 in 1945. This was the only occasion in which
Spelthorne voted Labour in the fifty years between 1935 and 1987. In
the New Zealand General Elections of 1943 and 1946 the Labour
government was returned to power on both occasions.

During the final week of July 1945, 56 Division relieved the New
Zealand Division in Trieste and the last NZ troops left there on 31
July.[3c] Just before the change-over a parade was held in St Mark's
Square in Venice, when General Mark Clark, now the Commander
of 15 Army Group, invested a number of British officers with
American decorations, and Freyberg received his Legion of Merit.
The recipients were lined up at the corner of the Doge's Palace facing
out over the Canale di San Marco and looking towards the church of
San Giorgio Maggiore.

Also in July Freyberg received a private letter from his Prime
Minister, written in his own hand, in answer to one of condolence he
had written to Peter Fraser on the death of his wife. Most of it was about
Mrs Fraser, but two paragraphs concerned their wartime relationship:

> Your writing me as a friend was most acceptable. It made your letter feel
> warmer. Our official relationship, which has been so trustful on both sides,
> has been a very important factor in the success of New Zealand's war effort.
>
> Never once did I hesitate to accept and support your point of view in
> reference to the Division, and never once was my confidence misplaced.
> We could have had no better Commander of our Expeditionary Force and
> never was a Commander more thoroughly and completely trusted. That
> trust has certainly developed into a close personal friendship which I will
> always value.

Having been away for the whole of the Second World War the
Freybergs were keen now to spend at least a year in England to
rearrange their personal affairs, which had of necessity been neglected
for six years. They were aware that Marshal of the RAF Lord Newall's
five-year term of office at Government House, New Zealand was soon
due to expire and there had been much press speculation that, after his
war service, Freyberg was a strong candidate to be his successor. Now,
late in July in Trieste, Freyberg signalled to his wife in London: 'Blow

has fallen. Have just been handed telegram from S of S [Addison] asking whether I will accept Governor-Generalship New Zealand. Expect to fly UK approximately 1st August to discuss matter with you and others'.

Freyberg had several pressing reasons to visit London, besides his desire to talk over the offer of the Governor-Generalship with his family. At the time it was difficult to get firm indications when transport would become available to take troops home to New Zealand, because of the shipping needs of the war in the Far East. Also the New Zealand government had asked for Freyberg's advice about what military contribution they ought to offer for the war against Japan. There had already been discussions over several months about the size of the New Zealand effort, and where it should be deployed. For a time it was thought that it might be used in south-east Asia, or in conjunction with the Australian forces in the South Pacific. Towards the end, however, there was a proposal to send a mixed Empire force with American equipment to fight under General MacArthur's command in operations against mainland Japan. Freyberg believed that this might be a better solution because it would enable a New Zealand force, of whatever size, 'to get clear of jungle fighting and ... be used in our traditional role together with all our guns and heavy equipment'.[3d]

But nothing had been decided when Freyberg and his GSO1, Colonel Gilbert, left Italy for England by air on 30 July. By a coincidence I was due to arrive in England forty-eight hours later, my battalion having been flown back from Foggia in Italy in heavy bombers. The 1 Guards Brigade had been nominated to be part of the Empire force that was to train in America *en route* for Japan, and this was to be the first leg of our journey there. My mother's diary lists the highlights of this period as seen by us all in London:

Monday, 30 July
Bernard arrived at Clarendon Place soon after 7, looking so sunburned and amazingly well and young. It is a miracle to have him home. We had such a happy dinner with Martin and Nancy.

Wednesday, 1 August
Bernard and I had dinner together and a lovely evening of talk. To my great joy, Paul rang up at 9.30 p.m. from Peterborough where he had just landed. It was such a thrill to hear his voice. He has to look after his men for the next two days, and will come to London on leave, he hopes, in 48 hours.

Tuesday, 7 August
Bernard and I listened to the news with the amazing story of the Atomic Bomb which, it seems, is an absolutely revolutionary discovery – greater

than any previous scientific stride forward. The world now waits to see the reactions of the Japs after one bomb has been dropped on one of their cities.

Thursday, 9 August
War news looks promising – Russia came in this morning and is into Manchuria. The Americans have dropped another Atom Bomb on Nagasaki – one would think the sponge must go up soon.

Friday, 10 August
I went to Thomas for my hair appointment, and heard from Mrs Thomas that the Japs had come to terms. It does not seem confirmed and we are all inclined to be a bit incredulous. However, on emerging, Paul met me and we found the streets of the West End were a snowstorm of torn up fragments of paper – a queer demonstration of joy.

Saturday, 11 August
The Jap news is still not completely confirmed, but there seems little doubt that the Japs have chucked it.

Thursday, 14 August
The news of the Jap surrender is still not confirmed, and there still appears to be heavy fighting and bombing.

Later
At midnight the longed-for news came at last – an announcement by Mr Attlee from Downing Street that the Japs had surrendered and we are at Peace.

Freyberg stayed on in England for the rest of August. He had been asked to remain by Peter Fraser in the hope that he might be able to speed up the repatriation of the Division to New Zealand. However, the sudden end of the war had thrown all previous transport arrangements into the melting pot, and it was to take several weeks before a new shipping plot emerged.

There was little discussion within the family about the offer of the Governor-Generalship of New Zealand. The conjunction of events – Bernard's standing down at Spelthorne, the General Election, and now the end of the war with Japan – all within a few short weeks of each other, seemed to be an almost pre-ordained sequence, pointing to the acceptance of the appointment. Only my mother had reservations. The family had been scattered to the winds for the last six years and now, just when there was the prospect of being reunited again, the new appointment would ensure a further separation for a minimum of five more years. Meanwhile many of the problems at home were still unresolved, and it was obvious that, by the time they were next back in England in the 1950s, the world would be a very different place.

The announcement of the Governor-Generalship was to be made on 5 September, and Freyberg deliberately arranged to be out of England by that date. I had hired a small car for some leave, and at 5 a.m. on Sunday, 2 September I drove my parents and Colonel Gilbert from Munstead to Blackbushe aerodrome on Hartford Bridge Flats, where my father and Gilbert boarded a plane for Naples. My father's appointment was welcomed both in New Zealand and England, and he and my mother had very heavy postbags over the next few weeks.

After leaving Trieste at the end of July the New Zealand Division spent the rest of the summer in the Lake Trasimene area, where Freyberg joined them on his return from England. One of the first things he then started to plan was a return visit to Crete. The object was to hold a memorial service in the New Zealand Cemetery, and to make a gesture of thanks to the Cretan people for their steadfastness in the battle and the help they had given to New Zealand soldiers who were left behind.

The Royal Navy made the cruiser HMS *Ajax* available to transport a party of 100 NZ veterans of the Crete campaign from Naples to Suda Bay and back for a three-day visit between 29 September and 2 October. *Ajax*, one of the ships which had evacuated the New Zealanders from Greece and Crete in 1941, was accompanied by the destroyer HMS *Marne*. Some 10,000 local Cretans attended the service, and afterwards their hospitality and kindness to the representatives of the Division knew no bounds. The Greek Prime Minister and the Greek Army and Navy sent high-ranking representatives, and the whole visit was a most moving occasion, as Freyberg emphasised in the numerous speeches he made in the towns and villages where fighting had been most intense. The gesture received wide publicity and favourable comments in Greece.

Peter McIntyre, in his book *The Painted Years*, recalled how the visit finished:

> At the end, Freyberg gave a stag party on the *Ajax* for the Cretan leaders, brigands, and guerrillas who had carried on the resistance against the Germans. Baggy-trousered, knife-armed, bearded Cretans arrived on the quarter-deck; their brigand costumes were offset by the white of the Navy and the khaki of the Army against the array of flags under the awnings. It was a splendid scene.
>
> The Navy served a powerful rum punch which the brigands, by polite Cretan custom, tossed off in one gulp. The sailors as quickly refilled the glasses until it was toss-and-refill like a hard-worked pump. The scene

[510]

warmed and the noise of voices rose as the rum, the battles refought, and the desperate moments relived, stirred the warriors into high animation. Then the Maoris amongst us enlivened proceedings further by stripping to the waist and putting on a tremendous stamping haka that shook the deck. This was too much for the brigands. Fiercely afire with Navy rum, they leapt into the fray brandishing their long knives, leaping and yelling.

It was like the Hades scene from Faust when I noticed, in the middle of it all, Freyberg, his face blandly unconcerned, saying in that voice of his, 'Have we any more sandwiches?'[5]

Freyberg went back to England on 19 October to participate in two ceremonies. The first Alamein reunion took place at Claridges on 23 October 1945 when 180 guests sat down to dinner. Alan Moorehead wrote a description of the evening next day in the *Daily Express*, in which he said that he had never before seen so many generals together in one place. Monty of course made the main speech and sat at the head of the table with Churchill on his right, and Freyberg on his left. Churchill, dressed as a Colonel of 4 Hussars, his old regiment, had just been given the campaign medals by the King in recognition of his visits to the front, so he was wearing five rows of medal ribbons and was as pleased as Punch.

The following afternoon we all drove down to Oxford for the Convocation ceremonies next day, when the university's honorary degrees were to be conferred. Appropriately enough it was held on St Crispin's day, the anniversary of Agincourt. Freyberg stayed the night with the President of Trinity College. At the main luncheon party at All Souls on 25 October Freyberg sat next to his old friend from the Royal Naval Division, A. P. Herbert, by then Sir Alan Herbert, MP, Member for Oxford University. When lunch was over they assembled in the Codrington Library at All Souls prior to moving across to the Sheldonian Theatre where the degrees were to be bestowed. When they arrived there General Mark Clark murmured to Freyberg, 'This is worse than Cassino!' Among the other military to be honoured were General Eisenhower, Field Marshals Alanbrooke and Montgomery, Admiral of the Fleet Sir John Tovey and Marshal of the RAF Sir Arthur Tedder.

When the time came to present Freyberg (all the presentations were in Latin) the Public Orator could not resist making a pun adapted from the famous line of Horace which translates as, 'The mountain labours and a mouse is born.' So when he said, ' *"Monte" ubi parturiente, Libys sua fata novat "Mus"*,' a very audible chuckle went up from the packed ranks of the academic audience. I had to wait until the next day to see

[511]

the English translation in the papers before I understood the joke: 'A mountain was in labour – and the Desert Rat reborn.'

Freyberg returned to Italy on 29 October for what was to be the final stage in the winding up of the Division. By this time the New Zealand government had decided to participate in the occupation of Japan, and to provide a Brigade Group of some 4,000 men. This became known as 'J' Force, composed of those who had arrived in the Mediterranean in the most recent reinforcement drafts. It was to be commanded by Brigadier Keith Stewart and, after a period of reorganisation, re-equipment and training, left Italy for Japan early in 1946.[3e]

The return of the rest of the Division to New Zealand took longer than anticipated because of the acute shortage of shipping, so that on average only one large ship carrying 4,000 men was made available each month. At the end of the war with Japan there had still been some 22,000 New Zealand soldiers overseas, which had been reduced by about half at the end of October, excluding 'J' Force. At this rate it was unlikely that the last of them would depart from Europe until the New Year.[3f]

Freyberg instituted a leave scheme whereby 105 soldiers a day left Italy in army vehicles and stopped at a series of transit camps *en route* until they reached England, where they stayed in New Zealand clubs in London for a fortnight. The journey took a week each way. The scheme proved to be popular and kept the men occupied; and by the time the trip was over the next ship was usually available to take them home.

It had been arranged that Freyberg should give up command of 2 NZEF on 22 November 1945. The date was chosen because it was the sixth anniversary of his appointment in 1939.[3f] He began his round of goodbyes by flying to Egypt during the first week of November. On 9 November an impressive memorial service was held at El Alamein attended by some 400 men and women of all ranks including nearly all the senior officers of the Division, and representatives from other services and British troops in Egypt. Messages were received from the senior commanders in the battle, and Freyberg sent signals to all the formations that had taken part, saying he had placed wreaths on their memorials.

He held a party in the New Zealand Club in Cairo to thank all the voluntary workers for all they had done over the years for the welfare of the Division. Peter Fraser had agreed to sign an official letter of thanks in the name of the government of New Zealand embossed with the coat of arms of New Zealand and the fernleaf emblem of the Division, for sending to the voluntary workers and others elsewhere who had also helped, as a gesture of appreciation. Freyberg also paid a final visit to Maadi, where an obelisk was shortly to be erected recording that, between 1940 and 1946, 76,000 members of 2 NZEF had passed through the camp and trained there.

On Freyberg's return to Italy he made a farewell tour of the dwindling number of troops of the Division, now housed in winter accommodation in Florence and Siena. On 16 November he handed over command of 2 NZEF to Major-General W. G. Stevens, who had long been its Chief Administrative Officer. That evening his remaining senior officers and staff officers gave a farewell dinner in his honour at the New Zealand Club at the Hotel Baglione in Florence.

On Tuesday, 20 November 1945 my father came back to England from the Division for the last time. My mother and I went to Charing Cross station at 6.30 that evening to meet the boat train and to drive him and his luggage back to Clarendon Place. All the members of our family had by then assembled, and we all had dinner together for the first time for nearly seven years. My father had finally returned from the wars for good.

30

Governor-General of New Zealand – I

One of the first things that Freyberg tried to do on returning home was to make arrangements for the journey to New Zealand, but with the continuing shortage of shipping it was not until early April 1946 that the date of sailing was confirmed. The voyage was to be in the New Zealand Shipping Company vessel *Ruahine*, due to leave London's Albert Docks on 3 May 1946.

After six years a number of problems had accumulated on the home front, as previously mentioned, but the Freybergs realised there would not be enough time to tackle most of them and make all the necessary arrangements for leaving England for at least five more years. The major problems were the future of their two houses, and these were resolved by marking time: a tenant was found to rent Clarendon Place for five years, while the Surrey County Council agreed to continue to use Munstead House as a children's nursery for the same length of time.

The next problem to settle was their personal staff. The Governor-General's establishment called for a Comptroller responsible for the day-to-day running of Government House, two ADCs, and a lady-in-waiting. Freyberg was determined to make his staff a tri-service one, so, having chosen Major Neville Wigram from the Grenadiers as his Comptroller, he appointed as ADCs David Loram and Michael Cole of the Royal Navy and the RAF respectively. The usual arrangement was for this team to do a tour of two and a half years, and then change over to a second team at half-time. An old friend of Barbara's, Rosemary Eley, was to come as her lady-in-waiting.

Freyberg's personal position also required adjustment. He was on the Active List of the British Regular Army as a Lieutenant-General, and had been given leave pending retirement. This was eventually promulgated in the *London Gazette* on 10 September 1946, in a statement that added that he had 'No reserve liability'. Thus he finally left the army at the age of fifty-seven, nine years after being invalided out the first time.

At the beginning of February 1946 the Freybergs went to Scotland for the launch of the motor vessel the *Port Wellington* at John Brown's shipyard on the Clyde. Barbara named the ship, a 15,000-ton refrigerator vessel for use on the run between New Zealand and Britain, which also had accommodation for 24 passengers. Peter McIntyre was commissioned by Barbara to produce an oil painting of the port of Wellington, which occupied a prominent place on board throughout her working life. When the ship was broken up in the early 1970s the picture was returned to the family.

After the launch the Freybergs went to stay with General Sir Charles and Lady Fergusson at Maybole in Ayrshire. Sir Charles had been Governor-General of New Zealand in 1924–30,* and Bernard took the opportunity to learn all he could about his new appointment. In the following weeks he visited other former Australasian Governors-General, such as Lord Bledisloe and Lord Gowrie.

One major problem was what clothes to take to New Zealand. After years of wartime austerity cupboards in England were bare, and new outfits required much thought and many fittings. The basic furniture at Government House was provided, but the occupants were expected to bring their own pictures, silver, china, glass, rugs, and so on. A further question was what was needed in the way of cars. All forms of transport were at a premium in New Zealand, and the existing Government House cars were apparently on their last legs. New vehicles would have to come from England when manufacture restarted. An important-looking limousine for ceremonial occasions was an obvious necessity, but several ordinary vehicles for use on less public occasions were also required. It was some time before these needs could be met.

On 5 March one of the ancient city guilds, the Worshipful Company of Stationers and Newspapermakers, admitted Freyberg as a freeman of the Company and of the City of London. Two days later, on 7

---

* As had his father before him, and as his son Bernard Fergusson, later Lord Ballantrae, was after him.

March, the Freybergs went to Buckingham Palace to have lunch with the King and Queen prior to going to New Zealand as their Representatives. Barbara described the occasion in her diary:

We went to the front entrance of Buckingham Palace and had a few minutes in Tommy Lascelles' [Private Secretary to the King] room and were then taken to an ante-room upstairs for another short wait – Just before 1.30 p.m. Bernard was summoned but I waited on for another short time and then I was brought in too. The King was alone with Bernard and dressed as an Admiral of the Fleet – He had just presented Bernard with his GCMG, his KCB, his KBE, and the Bar to the DSO. He said he had never given so many awards to one man at an Investiture before. Then the Queen came in dressed in pale blue, with the two Princesses – Princess Elizabeth in lime green and Princess Margaret in grey. We went into lunch and had delicious food – gnocchi, poussins, apple meringue. Afterwards Bernard stayed behind with the King, and I had a few minutes with the Queen after the Princesses and their corgis had gone. She was very sweet and asked me to write to her about NZ, when we had been there about six months. They gave us some lovely photographs in plain silver frames. They were so simple and so kind and we really enjoyed it.

Thursday, 4 April was typical of the busy time at this period. The Freybergs drove to Marlborough House to call on Queen Mary. They were impressed by how beautifully she was dressed even for a private audience, and how easy she was to talk to. She gave them a signed photograph of herself in her Coronation robes. Then there was a rush to Waterloo Station to say goodbye to the Alexanders on the first stage of their journey to Canada, where Field Marshal Viscount Alexander had been appointed Governor-General. In the evening they went to the Albert Hall for the Victoria League Concert, and were invited to sit in the Royal Box with the Queen.

And so, relentlessly, the final days rushed by and soon it was time to pack and say goodbye to close friends and family. The departure took place at Liverpool Street Station in the early afternoon of Friday, 3 May, when a large number of friends and relations came to see them off. Lord Pakenham was present, and represented the King; Lord Addison, Dominion Affairs Secretary, represented the British government; while William Jordan represented the New Zealand government. Martin, Nancy and I travelled with my parents for the short train journey to the Albert Docks, and went on board the *Ruahine*, where we eventually said our goodbyes.

[516]

The sea journey to New Zealand took just over six weeks. The *Ruahine* was an old ship and somewhat slow, but after the hectic life the Freybergs had been leading in their last weeks in London the enforced rest and leisure were most welcome, particularly during the first few days at sea. On 18 May the ship called at Curaçao to take on oil and three days later she arrived at the entrance to the Panama Canal. Most of 21 May was spent watching the ship negotiate the locks on her way between the Caribbean and the Pacific, and at six that evening she anchored off Balboa. Here the party found quite a reception committee including the British Minister, Mr Irving, and the Commander of the US Forces in the Canal Zone, General Crittenberger, whom Freyberg had met in Italy.

The days that followed at sea were uneventful. The ship was still in the tropics in the area of the doldrums, and it was hot and sticky. However, gradually the climate became cooler and the skies greyer. The last port of call was the Pitcairn Islands which they reached on 3 June, where the *Ruahine* anchored in the approaches; the islanders came out in boats and clambered on board to sell their wares including their beautifully designed stamps, which were used to adorn letters home.

As the ship approached New Zealand the weather became rough, wet and chilly. The ship had been due to arrive in Wellington on the morning of Saturday, 15 June but, owing to the storm, she was late and Bernard and Barbara were unable to go through the arrival ceremonies until after the weekend. None the less Barbara was delighted with her first impression of New Zealand:

We watched the lovely panorama unfold, with the mountains of the South Island snow-capped and ghostlike and the headlands round Wellington dark and grey – The moon rose and when we slipped into the huge harbour, it was a fairyland of lights and sparkling reflections and complete stillness and great beauty. I finished my letters, and went out at intervals to marvel at the beauty of the harbour with its lights in the full moonlight, and above all at the stillness in this reputedly windy place.

Monday, 17 June 1946 turned out to be a fine sunny day with no wind. Peter Fraser the Prime Minister and the Cabinet came on board at 9.15 a.m. to welcome the new Governor-General and his wife to New Zealand. Soon afterwards the Freybergs left the ship and drove to the war memorial to lay a wreath, and then departed for a first glimpse of their new home. As they passed the entrance lodge to Government House they found the drive lined with boys from Wellington College,

[517]

Bernard's old school – an imaginative gesture which he much appreciated. Then at midday they left for Parliament Buildings for the swearing-in ceremony, with large crowds, a guard of honour from all three services, a fly-past by the New Zealand Air Force, and the oath administered by Sir Michael Myers, the Chief Justice. The day concluded with a civic reception in the evening in the Town Hall.

The years that followed were among the happiest of Bernard Freyberg's life. After the stresses and strains of the battlefield, Government House proved to be a very pleasant and agreeable existence. It provided moreover the kind of life that Bernard particularly enjoyed: a formal position as the King's Representative, the requirement to undertake a great deal of entertaining, a duty to visit every part of the country and to be seen by as many of its citizens as possible, and most important of all, to do so in the company of Barbara, from whom he was never again separated for any length of time.

From the outset it was clear that the Freybergs were going to provide a rather different style of Governor-Generalship to any of the earlier ones. Most Governors-General had arrived from England having met few people in New Zealand before, and it took them time to become well known. The Freybergs had no such problem. Tens of thousands of New Zealanders had served overseas in the war, the majority with the New Zealand Division, and Freyberg was a household name in the country. His wife was also well known for her five years with the New Zealand Overseas Clubs. There was hardly anywhere in New Zealand which did not have a veteran of the war, and this provided the Freybergs with immediate contacts wherever they went.

There was another element in Freyberg's favour. Although he was not native born, he was a New Zealander by upbringing. This gave him an insight into the psychology of New Zealanders which no previous Governor-General had possessed. The time was to come when only New Zealanders would be considered for the viceregal appointment, so Bernard was the forerunner, with his links in two nations.

Freyberg was fortunate too in being in office during a relatively tranquil period of the country's history. After the war the predominant thought with most New Zealanders was to get back to, and on with, their civilian occupations. The immediate post-war world was crying out for the primary products of meat, dairy products and related

[518]

commodities that were New Zealand's main exports – more indeed than could be produced, for rationing in England continued throughout Bernard and Barbara's time at Government House. The result was that New Zealand achieved full employment and a standard of living that had not been enjoyed before.

It was the usual custom for incoming Governors-General to pay an early visit to all four of the main cities of New Zealand. So on 18 June the Freybergs boarded a special railway coach to visit Auckland. They were both delighted by the convenience and comfort of having a coach at their disposal, and were to use it constantly. It was indeed a much needed adjunct to Government House, enabling them to receive mayors and distinguished local dignitaries while they were on tour, and dispense modest hospitality in the small sitting- and dining-room.

Their arrival in Auckland followed a pattern that was to become familiar over the next years. A drive from the station in the early morning to the Grand Hotel was followed by breakfast. An hour later came the official call by the Mayor and Mayoress, followed by a wreath-laying ceremony at the Cenotaph, and a visit to the Returned Services Association. After lunch with the mayor and town clerk, a visit to Auckland Hospital lasted most of the afternoon. A quick change and dinner at the hotel was followed by a civic reception at the Town Hall and a number of speeches to a large audience. Next day was less formal with drives to Mount Eden and other places of interest, a visit to a naval establishment, a luncheon engagement with councillors and prominent citizens, before the Freybergs finally returned to the train for the night journey back to Wellington.

Some ten days later they went to the South Island. In those days a comfortable overnight ferry ran between Wellington and Lyttelton. Otherwise the routine followed a similar pattern to the visit to Auckland, with an early morning drive over the Cashmere Hills to Christchurch. Three days later, it was time to take the train for Dunedin and a similar mixture of formal and informal receptions. One variation in the South Island was that there were many more train stops at small towns and villages, to enable people to meet the viceregal party. The arrival back at Government House on 7 July marked the end of the opening phase of Freyberg's time as Governor-General. The rest of 1946 was devoted to domestic matters and to learning the ropes of life in and around Wellington.

Government House was an unpretentious building of no great architectural merit externally, set in a pleasant suburb not far from the centre of Wellington. Inside it was comfortable and well found, with commodious accommodation. The main downstairs drawing-rooms were large and well appointed for entertaining. Both Their Excellencies had their own sitting-rooms, as did the members of the staff. The ADCs' room was hung with photographs of former occupants, mostly in uniform, which inevitably became known as 'The Rogues Gallery'. There was also a big ballroom which was in frequent use for functions such as investitures, Christmas and children's parties, debutantes' balls and concerts. Upstairs there were numerous bedrooms for the staff, and to accommodate the regular flow of visitors. Appropriately the first guest to stay with the Freybergs was General Sir Andrew Russell who had commanded 1 New Zealand Division in the Great War.

The day-to-day running of Government House was in the hands of the Comptroller, Neville Wigram. Neville, the son of Lord Wigram, Private Secretary to George V, had several connections with New Zealand including an aunt, Lady Wigram. She was the widow of Sir Henry Wigram, a pioneer of aviation in New Zealand who gave his name to Wigram aerodrome, just outside Christchurch. Neville and his vivacious wife Poppy, with their two young daughters – shortly to be joined by a New Zealand-born son – occupied a comfortable bungalow in the grounds. Neville was soon to need all his background experience of regal and viceregal establishments to cope with a series of domestic dramas which took place behind the scenes in the first few weeks of the new regime.

The Official Secretary at Government House was Dave Fouhy. His main task was to act as the link between Ministers, government departments and the Governor-General. Freyberg soon found that Dave was shrewd and a good judge of character. He had a country bungalow on the coast north of Wellington, and whenever the Freybergs wanted to get away from Government House for any reason – usually to give the staff time off – they would repair to Dave's cottage. Dave was also an enthusiastic follower of the turf, and could be counted on to produce remunerative tips whenever his employers went to the races, which they did often. He had too a well-developed sense of fun and of the ridiculous and was a born raconteur. Those who had the pleasure of listening to his after-dinner reminiscences about the peculiarities of some of the previous occupants of Government House are unlikely ever to forget them. Alas for posterity, he was far too discreet ever to put pen to paper.

The two ADCs, David Loram and Michael Cole, were treated as sons of the house. Whenever Freyberg went on an official visit one of them always accompanied him. They were good at mixing with the younger generation of New Zealanders and giving informal cocktail

[520]

parties at Government House at which Freyberg and Barbara happened to 'look in' for short periods.

David Loram, with his extrovert and breezy naval manner, was reputed to have left behind several sad hearts when he returned to England. Later he became an equerry to the Queen; and he was one of the two officers on Freyberg's staff who ended up at the top of the Royal Navy, his last appointment being Deputy Supreme Allied Commander Atlantic. By contrast, Michael Cole appeared shy and diffident on first acquaintance, and only later did it became apparent how much his manner concealed. He was a person of charm and intelligence, and had an excellent war record, winning the DFC. He was determined, after his tour in New Zealand, to go back to the RAF and make it his career. Tragically he was killed in 1953 while piloting a fighter aircraft from Canada to England, a victim of horizon blindness, a condition sometimes encountered after a long and tiring solo flight.

Barbara had known the Eley family for many years, and when she was looking for a lady-in-waiting had thought that Rosemary might like to come for a couple of years. In the event Rosemary stayed for all six years. She was always beautifully turned out and looked the part to perfection. While in New Zealand she developed her considerable talent as a painter; during quiet periods she would disappear to remote places like Tahiti, and return with attractive scenes in oil and water-colour.

There were also a considerable number of honorary ADCs who would come in from time to time to help with the big occasions. Prominent among these were Jim Vogel, son of a former NZ Prime Minister, and Heathcote Helmore, one of New Zealand's best known architects, who had once been in Lutyens's drawing office. Heathcote lived in Christchurch, and his local knowledge was of particular value during the centenary celebrations in 1950. Laura Mappin, as an honorary lady-in-waiting, performed a similar function in Auckland, but here of course there was already an established Government House dating back before 1865 when Auckland had been the seat of government.

Lastly there was Mr Kitney, the Government House butler. Kitney was an ex-Chief Petty Officer in the Royal Navy and a great character, as well as being an extremely hard worker. He filled the role to perfection with a gravitas, dignity and sense of humour that was hardly ever ruffled.

During the last weeks of November 1946 a General Election took place. Traditionally the start of the campaign was the signal for Government House to put up the shutters and for the Governor-

General to make himself scarce, to leave the stage clear for the politicians. Bernard and Barbara decided on this occasion to disappear to a small lodge on the shores of Lake Okataina. The object was to take the waters and baths at the spa at nearby Rotorua, and to combine this with fishing expeditions at Lake Taupo. The baths were a great success, the fishing rather less so, and they spent a fortnight there until the end of November. When the election results came in, Peter Fraser and the Labour government were returned to office, as had been expected.

The first days of December were spent on an official visit to the west coast of the South Island, including calls at Westport, Greymouth, Kumara and Hokitika. The tour ended at Invercargill where an investiture was held on the evening of 10 December, followed the next day by an Agricultural and Pony Show. During the second half of December the main events were a large children's party at Government House just before Christmas, a reception for the household on Christmas Eve, and on the day itself church in the morning followed by dinner with their personal staff.

Enough has already been said about Bernard and Barbara's first six months in office to give some idea of what the Governor-General's life was like – a mixture of official engagements centred on Government House, a lot of travelling about the country, visiting factories and new enterprises, entertaining and being entertained by recognised societies and movements, and playing host to the increasing number of overseas visitors who began to arrive in New Zealand from 1947 onwards.

Before the war the Diplomatic Corps in Wellington had been confined to a small number of representatives from the other Dominions and a few of the Pacific powers. Now, as a result of the war and the increase in trade, there were many more legations and missions, all of which had to be received, entertained and visited back. Most of this was a pleasure since they were a lively and well-informed community, and several friendships endured long after the Freybergs left New Zealand. Among these were Roden and Helen Cutler, and Patrick and Meg Duff, respectively the Australian and British High Commissioners; and the Scottens – the American Minister and his wife.

Visitors from England began to come in earnest early in 1947 and continued almost without a break for the rest of the Freybergs' time. Among the first were General Sir Noel and Lady Beresford-Pierce whose ship, the *Wanganella*, impaled itself on a reef outside Wellington Harbour. Another of its passengers was Lord Nuffield, who so impressed the Freybergs by his gaiety, vigour and quickness, that he could have passed for fifty when his actual age was seventy.

[522]

Early in February 1947 Bernard, Barbara, Michael Cole and Rosemary Eley spent five days walking the famous Milford Track. Milford Sound is in the south-western corner of the South Island, on the edge of the Southern Alps, and the walk is considered to be among the most beautiful in the world. Its length, about 50 miles through canyons and gorges, and over Mackinnon Pass, 3,400 feet high, is broken up into sections of about ten miles with small hotels at each end, and, in the 1940s, fairly simple huts in between. The country is wild as well as very beautiful, with rare birds, flowers and ferns that are found nowhere else in New Zealand, or indeed in the world. Much of its interior was still marked 'unexplored' on the maps. The Sutherland Falls, with three successive drops totalling just over 2,000 feet, was particularly spectacular. In 1947 the walk was in a rough condition since avalanches had destroyed some of the steeper parts of the track, and no maintenance had been done during the war years. However the weather was sunny, and the party ended up fishing from boats in Milford Sound, where they caught forty 'blue cod' weighing between five and ten pounds each. These fish, when smoked, taste like delicate haddock.

Early March brought the move of Government House from Wellington to Auckland. The Freybergs found it cosy, with a very sympathetic atmosphere and, as Barbara confided to her diary, 'the absence of wind is such a rest'. March in New Zealand is summer and the time for outdoor pursuits, including sailing in Waitemata Harbour and big game-fishing in the Hauraki Gulf, where Michael Cole caught the record striped marlin, and was awarded the 'Silver Fish' of the season.

During the next months the Freybergs attended a number of Maori functions. Bernard's regard for the Maoris had been enhanced by the magnificent record of the Maori Battalion in the Second World War. Their reputation as a warrior race had developed from the Maori wars of the previous century, where their frequent acts of chivalry and sense of humour had won the respect of their opponents. On 29 March many thousands gathered at Ngaruawahia – the historic Maori site at the confluence of the Waikato and Waipa rivers – to greet the Governor-General. His party embarked in one of the great war canoes, with a hundred paddlers, which conveyed them to Ngaruawahia Pa for the welcoming ceremonies.

Early April saw the arrival of Lord and Lady Bledisloe – the first time a previous Governor-General had returned to the country. The Bledisloes had a special place in New Zealand hearts for two reasons. First, they farmed extensively in England, and therefore talked the farmer's language to the farming community of New Zealand. Second, they had realised the importance of the Waitangi Treaty House in the Bay of Islands, where the sovereignty of New Zealand had been ceded to the British Crown, and had had the generosity to purchase it and present the house and its surrounding land to the nation.

The date of Anzac day was of special significance in 1947 as the occasion of the unveiling by the Governor-General of the plaques commemorating the Second World War on the Auckland Cenotaph, in the presence of large congregations at the dawn and morning services.

On 14 June 1947 the Freybergs celebrated their silver wedding. They were on their way back to Wellington after their three months in Auckland, and marked the occasion by spending a long weekend at the Waitomo Caves Hotel, of which Barbara wrote:

> The first part [of our visit] was fine architectural caves with a few frightening chasms and some dramatic corners. But the Glow-Worm Grotto is really wonderful – something out of this world. There must be no noise or their little lights go out, so one slips silently in 'Charon's boat', which steers into the darkness, and there one is suddenly in a world of dim, cold, still light, with myriads of the tiny stars burning blue above one – like the thickest part of the Milky Way and then much more so – patinas of dim silver rather than of bright gold . . . Rosemary said to me that it felt to her as our last journey out of this world must be – without life or emotion and full of cold beauty completely impersonal. We all came out feeling stirred and with far-off thoughts hard to express.

Charon, of course, was the boatman of the ancient Greeks who ferried the souls of the dead across the river Styx to the Elysian Fields.

The Freybergs' return to Wellington was timed for the opening of Parliament on 25 June, when it took place with a pageantry not seen in New Zealand since before the war. The Royal New Zealand Air Force provided a full Guard of Honour and its band. The NZ Chiefs of Staff took part in the parade, and the Governor-General read the Speech from the Throne outlining the government's legislative programme for the coming session.

The next visitor of note was none other than Field Marshal Viscount Montgomery, who arrived on 16 July 1947 on an official visit as Chief of the Imperial General Staff. On the first night there was a dinner party of thirty to meet him, including the Prime Minister, the political world, and the NZ Chiefs of Staff. Next morning Monty held a large press conference in Government House with correspondents from all over New Zealand. On the third night there was an all-male dinner to meet the principal officers of 2 NZEF, followed by a large reception afterwards. He departed on the fourth day to make a tour of the South Island, when Freyberg saw him off at the aerodrome, having much enjoyed his visit.

The Secretary of State for Dominion Affairs and Leader of the House of Lords, Lord Addison, followed with his wife and stayed for a week. They were particularly friendly and appreciative guests. In October the irrepressible Randolph Churchill arrived for a lecture tour. In private at Government House he was full of bonhomie and courtly manners with a fund of amusing stories. In public he made a number of controversial remarks, among other things criticising the New Zealand licensing laws, a subject always guaranteed to stir up a hornet's nest in the press.

Part of the Governor-General's duties was to visit all the smaller towns and country areas at least once during his term of office. Between 10 and 14 September it was the turn of Gisborne in Poverty Bay and Ruatoria, 80 kilometres further north. A month later the itinerary included visits to Napier, Hastings, Havelock North and Wairoa; and on 31 October an official visit to Levin where Freyberg had lived for eighteen months in 1912–13.

In mid-November he and Barbara travelled over to the South Island again to open the Agricultural Show at Christchurch, and then across to the West Coast and on to the Franz Joseph Hotel, with expeditions to the Fox and Franz Joseph glaciers. At the end of the month they were back in the North Island and again in Rotorua for a few days, before setting out for another strenuous round of official visits to New Plymouth, Stratford, Eltham and Hawera in the second week of December. After that it was home to Government House for Christmas, where they were joined by their old friends Oliver and Margaret Leese, and Andrew and Margaret Thorne, Neville Wigram's parents-in-law.

On 20 November, when the Freybergs had been in Christchurch, they had listened with particular interest to the wireless broadcast from Westminster Abbey of the marriage of Princess Elizabeth to the Duke of Edinburgh. Only six weeks earlier, on 7 October, Princess Elizabeth had written to Barbara from Balmoral in her own hand:

Dear Lady Freyberg
I am so very sorry to have been so long in answering your letter of July 3rd, which I received when I was already up here.

The trouble was the photographs of The Trooping the Colour, which were taken specially, have taken a very long time being enlarged and mounted, and it is only now that they have arrived.

I do hope that you will like the one that I have chosen for you and Sir

Bernard. The horse is an old hunter called Tommy, who has now been given to me, and he only had a month's training as a charger! He was rather frightened by the people cheering, but he was perfect on parade, and coming back up the Mall behind the band – he had done that many times before, and I think he really enjoyed the music!

My uniform was great fun to invent, and we are hoping very much that, next year, everyone will be in blue, but it seems rather a forlorn hope just at the moment!

I met your youngest son not very long ago in London, when I saw the few Grenadiers that are stationed there – the 1st Battalion.

I am hoping very much that an official version of my broadcast will be published for schools and youth organisations, but nowadays everything takes ages to do and it will probably be produced later on.

Yours very sincerely
Elizabeth.

Three major excursions were scheduled for 1948. Early in the year Government House was to move to Dunedin to participate in Otago Province's centenary celebrations. In July the Governor-General would pay an official visit to the Pacific Island Dependencies of New Zealand; and towards the end of the year the Freybergs were to visit Australia as guests of the Federal and State governments – the first New Zealand Governor-General to do so while in office.

The Dunedin celebrations, which took place in February and March, were the first of several centenaries that were commemorated during Freyberg's term of office. He made a point of participating as fully as possible in all the planned programmes. In Dunedin a Victorian mansion, 'Corstorphine', was loaned by the Sidey family (whose son Murray Sidey had been ADC to Bernard during the last months of the Italian campaign) for six weeks as a temporary Government House, and here he and Barbara gave a large garden party on 16 March.

Dunedin, of course, was a settlement founded directly from Scotland, and there were many reminders of this in the 'Early Settlers Exhibition' and the 'Picture Exhibition', which included some fine paintings by Frith, McEvoy, Richard Wilson and Raeburn. An ex-Lord Provost of Edinburgh, Sir John Falconer, was one of the principal guests. The highlight of the centenary celebrations was the re-enactment of the arrival of the first ship from Scotland, the *John Wickliffe*, and they watched a display of the arrival of the first settlers.

The object of the Governor-General's visit to the Pacific Islands in July was to register New Zealand's interest in the welfare and well-being of the inhabitants of the islands, which in some cases were in remote and almost inaccessible places. The larger islands such as those of Fiji, Tonga and Samoa were independent and self-governing, but they still had close links with New Zealand, which assisted them over education, health and trade. Most of the smaller islands and communities were looked after by Resident Agents.

On 29 June the Freybergs and their staff left Auckland in a Sunderland flying boat, and arrived at Suva after a six-hour flight. Freyberg inspected a very smart guard of honour of Fijian soldiers at Government House, Fiji, before being received by the Governor and his wife, Sir Brian and Lady Freeston. Visits followed to the Fijian forces and to the Royal New Zealand Air Force at Laucals Bay.

On 2 July the party embarked for Tonga in the cruiser HMNZS *Bellona*, arriving the next day, when they were met by the British Consul and the Premier Mr Tungi and his ministers. They were then driven to the Palace of Queen Salote. The Queen had organised 'a Tonga Feast' at her 'Queen's House' on a lagoon, where Bernard and Barbara sat on each side of her, and ate with their fingers from a large range of dishes brought to them by her girls.

From Tonga it was a two-day journey by sea to Rarotonga (which Bernard had visited over thirty years earlier), followed in quick succession by visits, some for only half a day, to Mangaia, Mauke, Atiu, Aitutaki and Niue in the Cook Islands. At Rarotonga they went ashore and stayed the night with the Commissioner, after a parade of ex-servicemen, Boys Brigade and Girl Guides in the morning, a garden party in the afternoon, and a ball in the evening. Some of the smaller islands had formidable outer reefs, and there was considerable difficulty in getting ashore. Once in shallow waters the party was often transferred from the *Bellona's* boats to open litters manned by up to thirty islanders, to bring them to the 'marae' or meeting house.

On 13 July they anchored off Apia in Samoa. Their launch was escorted across the harbour by four great native rowing boats, and at the pier to greet them was the Chief Minister, the Council and Legislative assembly and a large group of leading citizens. A 19-gun salute was fired from a nearby wharf. They stayed with the High Commissioner Colonel Voelcker, at Vailima, near to where Robert Louis Stevenson had lived, and as Barbara wrote, were much struck by their 'beautiful drive through endless gardens and charming Samoan thatched houses – all so bright and fresh. Vailima is *lovely*. Such a glorious view of the sea across the trees.'

[527]

Wherever they went the Freybergs were particularly interested in the local industries and the plantations of the NZ Government Estates producing cocoa, rubber, bananas and cattle, desiccated coconut and copra. Their final days were spent visiting the three Tokelau Islands of Fakaofo, Atafu and Nukunono, after which they enjoyed three days at sea on the way back to Fiji.

At this time I was travelling to Australia on board the MV *Orontes*. Since 1947 I had been commanding a Grenadier Company in Palestine but the ending of the British Mandate in the middle of 1948 enabled me to take some leave to visit New Zealand. I flew the final leg from Sydney to Auckland to arrive in Wellington on 26 July, four days after my parents had returned from their Islands tour.

My visit was well timed in other ways too, for the next few weeks was a comparatively slack period at Government House. The first outside engagement I attended was in early August, when we flew in the Dove aircraft from Paraparaumu airfield near Wellington to RNZAF Station Wigram. On the return flight we gave a lift to Marie Rambert, whose touring Ballet Company had given a great fillip to the New Zealand artistic world. She was an old friend of my mother's, who reminded her how before the war she used to do the most beautiful cartwheels. Whereupon Marie Rambert, who had celebrated her sixtieth birthday the previous February, took off her jewellery and proceeded to do a series of impeccable cartwheels down the main corridor of Government House! She later recorded the occasion in her memoirs *Quicksilver*:

> In Wellington I spent a weekend at Government House as guest of that delightful pair Sir Bernard and Lady Freyberg, and did cartwheels all along an endless passage. When some years later I visited them in Windsor Castle, Lord Freyberg, as he was by then, asked me jokingly whether I still did cartwheels. I said I did and he became quite alarmed and begged me to desist.[1]

On 8 September Sir Keith Murdoch and his seventeen-year-old son Rupert came to stay for two days. Keith Murdoch, a Press 'magnate', had visited Gallipoli briefly as a journalist thirty-two years before, when he had written a report of the conditions he had seen. This so shocked the authorities in London that it had been one of the factors that eventually led to the decision to evacuate the peninsula.[2] Barbara noted in her diary: 'In the evening we had home dinner with Sir Keith Murdoch and his nice boy Rupert – such a friendly, pleasant type. I have enjoyed meeting them both.'

On 24 September David Loram left Government House to return to England, but as his replacement was not immediately available Michael Cole soon found himself overloaded with work and asked me to help out. I agreed, although neither my father nor I thought it suitable for a son to be ADC to his father except as a very temporary stop-gap.

My first venture in this new capacity was an official visit to Palmerston North, Feilding, Marton and Wanganui, starting on 4 October at the Agricultural School at Feilding. We then went to the train to change for an Investiture at Palmerston North, where over sixty people were to be decorated. The first call next day was to the Marton High School, followed by a gathering of ten other schools including the High Town Girls School. After that there was a civic reception, and visits to the Returned Services Association, the Red Cross, St John Ambulance, the Cadets, Guides and Scouts. Then to Wanganui Collegiate for lunch and speeches, followed by a tree-planting ceremony, visits to two orphanages and to an old people's home. After that it was back to the train to change for another Investiture, at Wanganui this time. On the train back to Wellington that night my mother wrote: 'It has been fun to have Paul with us, who now sees what it means to play at being the Royal Family.'

During the first half of October the touring Old Vic Company performed three plays: *The School for Scandal*, *The Skin of our Teeth* (by Thornton Wilder) and *Richard III*, all starring Vivien Leigh and Laurence Olivier. They were superb productions which caused great excitement, and during the weekend of 9–11 October the Oliviers came to stay at Government House, where they proved to be easy and pleasant guests.

My second, and final, stand-in took place from 18 to 21 October on an official visit to Tauranga, Te Puke, Whakatane and Opotiki, in the Bay of Plenty. This time we flew there and back in the Dove, and stayed at two hotels at Tauranga and Whakatane. The programme was much on the same lines as for my previous visit, except that time there were more Maori functions. The coastline with huge pohutukawa trees coming right down to the sea near Opotiki, and great stretches of open sandy beaches near Mount Maunganui, was particularly memorable. During my final three weeks in New Zealand the routine at Government House ticked away smoothly, with Michael Cole back in the saddle as sole ADC, and preparing for the forthcoming tour of Australia.

Half-way across the Tasman sea we heard on the flying boat's radio of the birth of Princess Elizabeth's first child, Prince Charles. It was a

[529]

good excuse to open a bottle of champagne, to toast both the new arrival and our forthcoming tour. At Sydney we found that my father was being accorded the full ceremonial treatment with a guard of honour and a reception committee headed by the Governor of New South Wales General Sir John Northcote, and the Australian Minister for the Army, Hon. C. Chambers, who introduced Major Walshe, our liaison officer during the tour. The Australian government also provided an aircraft from the VIP flight of 86 Transport Squadron RAAF to be permanently on call, which was just as well if we were to carry out the formidable programme in the time allotted.

The aircraft was put to immediate use that same afternoon by flying our party from Sydney to Canberra, the federal capital, where another guard of honour and the Australian Prime Minister, J. B. Chifley, were there to welcome my father. Our party stayed with the Governor-General and Mrs McKell at Government House.

Next day was a full one, with a motor tour of Canberra and a visit to the magnificent war memorial in the morning, followed by a diplomatic reception later in the afternoon at the NZ Legation, and an all-male dinner with Ministers, the Speaker, the President of the Senate and Party leaders.

After a further day in Canberra we started on the first visit to the six Australian states. These each have separate Governors and Government Houses as well as their own Parliaments dealing with all matters except Foreign Affairs, Defence, and Taxation, which are reserved to the federal government. Our first two visits were to New South Wales and Queensland, where the Governors – General Northcote in Sydney, and General Laverack in Brisbane – had both been wartime colleagues of Freyberg. They had arranged extensive programmes, intermingling ex-Service organisations with visits to some of the more interesting industrial companies, such as the Broken Hill Proprietary at Newcastle.

Freyberg wanted to meet Australian servicemen who had served under his command in 1941, and was particularly anxious to see men of the two Australian brigades who had fought in Crete, especially those who had been at Retimo. He was especially glad of a long talk with General Campbell, who had held out for so long at Retimo, and who afterwards, like most of his garrison, spent four years as a prisoner of war.

Victoria was our next port of call, but Government House was in the hands of builders preparing it for the royal visit, so we stayed at the Hotel Windsor in Melbourne. The Governor, Sir Winston Dugan, gave an afternoon party for the Freybergs in the grounds of Government House, and they stayed with Dick and Maie Casey, old friends from Cairo days. The next stop was Adelaide, South Australia, where General Sir Willoughby Norrie was Governor. After two days there I had to leave to catch a ship at Fremantle to return to my battalion, now stationed in North Africa, but my parents' tour continued to the remaining Government Houses, where their hosts were Sir James Mitchell in Perth, and Admiral Sir Hugh Binnie in Hobart. My father took the salute at the graduation parade at the Royal Military College at Duntroon on 14 December, after which they left for Tasmania, where they stayed for three days. On 20 December they were back in Wellington, and the end of 1948 brought Freyberg's term of office to the half-way mark.

Governor-General of New Zealand – II

Although there had been many royal visits to Australasia in earlier years, no reigning monarch had ever set foot in New Zealand. When, therefore, it was announced in March 1948 that King George VI and Queen Elizabeth would make a visit in 1949, the news was greeted with enthusiasm.

Much of the second half of the Freybergs' time in New Zealand was taken up with the details of the royal visit. The suites of rooms intended for royal occupation at Government House, both in Wellington and in Auckland, were completely refurbished; new Spode china depicting the flora, ferns and birds special to New Zealand was designed and produced for their use, and a set of 38 dining-room chairs was commissioned, each one embroidered by local volunteers with the place name and emblem of one of the main towns of the country.

Planning began early in 1948. First to arrive was Air Commodore Fielden, Captain of the King's Flight, who came on a reconnaissance of the airfields to be used during the visit. He was followed by Brigadier Norman Gwatkin, from the Lord Chamberlain's Office, to work out details of the itinerary with Government House, the local authorities and the mayors. These arrangements had reached an advanced stage when, on 23 November, came an announcement that the royal visit had had to be postponed because of George VI's illness. The Freybergs heard the news over the wireless while they were still in Australia, and apart from their concern about the King's health, they shared the general sense of anti-climax that inevitably followed long months of preparation.

Because of the postponement, 1949 was the least eventful year of Freyberg's period of office. Neville Wigram and Michael Cole followed David Loram back to England at the beginning of May, and were replaced by Squadron Leader Peter Clapham as Comptroller, and Flight Lieutenant David Robert and Lieutenant Gordon Tait, RN, as aides-de-camp. Gordon Tait was the second of Freyberg's ADCs to have a distinguished naval career, in which he ended up as Second Sea Lord.

Freyberg was asked to give the inaugural address at the Law Societies' Conference in Auckland which began on 30 April 1949. He told the conference about a legal case in Egypt early in the Second World War in which he had been involved as the Confirming Officer:

> Take the simple case of arresting a man who is 'under the influence'. If private soldiers are sent to apprehend him and he resists, even with violence, it is resisting arrest – a simple crime, punished summarily. But, if the Sergeant or the Officer of the Guard in his zeal tried to arrest the man, and he is struck, it is a very serious offence – striking a superior officer when on active service – for which he must be tried by court martial, and punished, if found guilty, by imprisonment.
>
> I will give you an actual case. When we arrived in Egypt, I was handed the reports of several courts martial and asked to confirm their findings. The first one I looked at was a serious case, which concerned a man who was found guilty of striking a superior officer while on active service. I straightaway examined the man's documents – his conduct sheet and attestation papers. He was a professional man, married, with two children. According to his conduct sheet, his character was exemplary; further, he was a volunteer, with only three months' service. The men from his home town gave him an excellent character. I have always held that nothing discredits a Service more than this sort of thing. It is no recommendation for the Army if it turns a good man into a bad one.
>
> When I went closely into the case, the facts that were disclosed were these. The man's unit was on board ship coming up the Red Sea in convoy. The temperature was 108° in the shade, and tempers were getting short. For some quite unimportant lapse the man was placed under arrest and marched before his Commanding Officer. He had never been under arrest before, and he resented the whole incident so much that he lost his temper with his Commanding Officer. The Commanding Officer should have said: 'March this man out until he calms down.' The man was a very nice fellow, and would have been ashamed of himself when he regained his temper. He would have been admonished, and all would have been well. But not at all. The Commanding Officer decided to reason with him, and it went something like this:

COMMANDING OFFICER: But did you not join to fight for your King and your country?
PRISONER: — the King and — the country.

The Commanding Officer then had no option but to punish him for a most improper remark. The man was given detention and marched away to the cells by the Provost Sergeant. When they came to the companionway, he got the order, 'Keep to the right,' and he, of course, immediately kept to the left. When he got to the bottom of the ladder, the Provost Sergeant said: 'Now go back and come down properly.' By this time, the prisoner was seeing red, and answered him in the vernacular. The sergeant placed hands on him, and the prisoner struck the blow.[1]

Freyberg commented:

The proceedings were naturally quashed. But that case was a godsend. It enabled me to make everyone laugh at a big conference of Commanding Officers, and at the same time teach the vital lesson that a superior officer must always keep away from anyone who has had too much to drink or who has lost his temper.[1]

A curious episode happened at this time concerning General Mark Clark, the commander of the US Fifth Army at Cassino. Freyberg had been in the habit of sending Christmas cards from New Zealand to his wartime friends and associates, and his 1948 card produced this reply from Clark:

Now, when are you coming to see us? You know you would have a warm welcome. Alexander is coming down in the spring to my Headquarters in San Francisco. I will take him to Fort Ord near Monterey, where the Fourth Division is in training; then to Fort Lewis in the State of Washington to receive a review of our Second Division. We would love to do the same thing for you, and then some day I'll come over and pay you a visit.[2]

Freyberg, never slow to respond to a friendly gesture, answered by return of post:

My wife and I would be delighted for you and your wife and daughters to come down here to New Zealand and we would do the best we could to make your stay a memorable one. Not many soldiers to see but lots of your old friends who served under you, like Gentry, Hanson, Kippenberger, etc., and if you decide seriously to come I would then put it up to the New Zealand Government and I am certain Mr Fraser would send you an official invitation to come as guest of the country. They would give you a tour round.[2]

[534]

This invitation produced another warm letter from Mark Clark, dated 14 April 1949, in which he indicated interest in visiting New Zealand, and suggested that some time in the autumn would be a possible date for him. Freyberg had to reply to Clark that the autumn of 1949 was not a suitable date because it coincided with the New Zealand General Election, but that he would be very welcome at any time after that. He heard from Mark Clark again in a letter written on 14 December 1949, in answer to that year's Christmas card, saying how greatly he appreciated the further invitation to visit New Zealand. The correspondence then lapsed, but Mark Clark's invitation to visit New Zealand remained open.

In view of this friendly background, Freyberg was astonished when, on 18 October 1950, without a word of warning, a sensational story was circulated in the New York news bulletins 'that United States General Mark Clark placed the blame for bombing the historic Monte Cassino monastery in February 1944 on the Commander of the New Zealand troops, Lieutenant-General Freyberg'.[2]

The detailed attack on Freyberg was contained in General Clark's book *Calculated Risk*, which was about to be published, in which he attempted to disown any responsibility for ordering the bombing of the monastery, which he attributed entirely to Freyberg's insistence. General Kippenberger, who had been commanding the New Zealand Division at the time, pointed out that 'it was very uncommon for a commander who had to admit that he acquiesced in a course of action of which he did not approve, to attempt afterwards to throw the responsibility on to a subordinate'.[2] The incident attracted much publicity in view of the circumstances and the personalities involved. Freyberg decided that it would be more dignified not to reply publicly, and especially not from Government House. But in private he said what he thought to some of those who had been involved in the original decision. One of these was General Tuker, who commanded 4 Indian Division at Cassino and had written a long personal letter to Freyberg on 19 October 1950 which ended: 'In my opinion, Alexander, Clark, you and I are all responsible for the bombing or bombardment of the Monastery. Why try to lie about it?'[2]

Winston Churchill also mentioned the subject to Freyberg in a letter from Chartwell dated 21 October 1950. After discussing an unconnected matter he ended, 'Clark has not behaved too well about Cassino. I am sure you need not worry – if you could, Yours ever, Winston.'[2] Freyberg never heard from Mark Clark again, and the incident confirmed him in his original opinion – that Mark Clark was not to be trusted.

Freyberg spent much of his spare time in New Zealand, and later at Windsor, over the war histories. The official New Zealand histories were being written by a team of authors under the overall supervision of General Sir Howard Kippenberger, and during this period Freyberg participated in the task of producing a full account of the various campaigns, correcting errors in the versions sent to him, and suggesting additions. In fact, only two months before Clark's charge was made public, he had written a considered view of his own on the bombing of the Cassino Abbey by way of comment on a draft report on the battle produced by the Historical Section of the British Cabinet Office:

There seems to be a certain conflict of opinion between the various interests as to whether the Abbey itself was occupied or not by the Germans. That is, apart from the real question which is, was it defended? If any soldier is denying a dominating feature to the enemy, that feature, and especially the dominating part, becomes a military objective, the defence or capture of which must be left to the Commanders in charge of the operations. Nobody could object to the Monte Cassino Abbey feature being occupied by the Germans. It was a dominating feature; without it the line of defence would go, and with it, Rome. How they held it, and held it they did, matters not whether they put actual troops in or in front of the Abbey. I should say that they did not actually have men and weapons in the building, because the Germans knew that in our position they, the Germans or any other force of any nation, would be bound to attack the dominating feature or risk failure.

Further, if the Monte Cassino Abbey were attacked, the [centre] of the shoot would be the Abbey; therefore it is probable that except for observation purposes, the Abbey buildings were not put into a state of defence. Nobody wants to sit on an obvious target.

I notice that Mark Clark (the Commanding General of the 5th US Army) in some recent public announcement in Rome, declared that he had never believed in the bombing and had been against it. I cannot say what anybody's inner thoughts are – I can only record his outward reactions. I know that he had not made up his mind when we took over the line from the US II Corps.

When I discussed the question with him at the outset I could see that he had given the question a good deal of consideration. No one wanted to bomb the Abbey. I made a suggestion, which brought forth ridicule from Mark Clark. I suggested at the outset to drop a token bomb, to show what lay in store for the defenders, and to get them to clear the refugees out. I suggested that it should be dropped from a fighter bomber. Mark Clark poured ridicule on this, and said that nothing would do but to bring in the heavy Fortresses with delayed action 1,000-pound bombs. He had obviously been considering it deeply. The decision to bomb Monte Cassino in my opinion was the only one if it was decided to attack the Monte Cassino Abbey feature.[2]

The year 1949 began with several return visits from Australia including one from the Governor of South Australia, Sir Willoughby and Lady Norrie. Lord Rowallan, the Chief Scout, stayed at Government House for several days, as did Harald Peake, Vice-Chairman of Lloyds Bank. Two other welcome guests were Anthony Eden and his Parliamentary Private Secretary, Commander Allan Noble, who stayed for five days. Barbara recounted in her diary for 12 February: 'We had a fascinating evening, as Mr Eden recounted stories of how he dined with Hitler, Mussolini and Stalin – we all listened open-mouthed. He is a *very* good storyteller and his memories and talk are as good as any I have ever heard.'

After such close personal contact, the Freybergs were much distressed when, three weeks afterwards, they heard in a letter from England that Anthony Eden and his wife had parted. At the end of the year they got a poignant solo Christmas card on which was written, 'With very best wishes and enduring memories of the wonderful kindness you both showed me, from Anthony.'

Freyberg took a great deal of pleasure as Governor-General in keeping in touch – or in many cases resuming contact – with old friends. This applied not only to the many colleagues from the Second World War, but also to those he had known in his youth. He made a particular point of inviting to Government House, or meeting when on tour in the country, his contemporaries and masters from Wellington College, his coaches and companions from his swimming days, and those he had known from his time at Levin and Morrinsville. For example his contemporary, Dick Hegglum, wrote to the author on 16 January 1964: 'Tiny Freyberg never forgot his old friends. Whether it be a viceregal visit or private holiday, Tiny was Tiny, the same carefree youth that sailed the Viking and swam so effortlessly in the old Te Aro Baths.' Another friend and one of his swimming coaches, W. T. Churchward, wrote: 'Whilst he was Governor-General I frequently met him and called him "General". Whenever he came to Blenheim or passed through, he would always see me and still called me by my Christian name.'

The Freybergs moved to Auckland in mid-March and remained there until the first week in June. By this time their lives had developed into a settled routine of public engagements in and around Government House interspersed with tours and visits further afield – in August 1949 to Christchurch, and in October to Dunedin. The second of the three General Elections during my father's tour of office took place in November 1949, and he wrote a series of letters to keep me in touch with developments:

9 October 1949
We are now getting close to the General Election in about seven weeks time. I am writing an appreciation for the King, and I am still uncertain what I shall say. I can't see the National Party having a large majority. If they win it will be because the people, after fourteen years, feel that a change would be for the good.

16 October
This is the last week of this Parliament, as on the 21st, Friday next, it dissolves, and they go to the country. We have Syd Holland [Leader of the Opposition the National Party] to supper tonight. Both sides seem to be equally confident of having a majority. I think it will be very close. I hope that it will not be a dead heat. I hope that whoever gets in will have a clear majority.

23 October – Alamein Day
Parliament dissolved on the 21st, and the PM [Fraser, leader of the Labour party] comes to dine here tonight before he goes off to Auckland to start his Election tour.

9 November
We are now busy with the General Election which will be very close. Nobody can say which party will win. We go away to the Bay of Plenty on Monday the 14th for the rest of the month. We come back on Election Day 30th Nov. We shall be living in our railway coach in the fishing area, and it will be a nice quiet and cheap holiday for us.[2]

The holiday provided a much needed change of scene. Their two railway carriages were parked in a siding at the end of the line at Taneatua near Opotiki, 'in a nice quiet corner surrounded by a green hill and meadows all round, with long green grass and birds singing in little bushes'. They were within easy distance of Rotorua and its surrounding fishing lakes, and also of Ohope beach near Whakatane. The rumbles of the election only reached them through the wireless, and the days were mainly spent out of doors, fishing or on the beach, to the understandable exclusion of letters.

They drove back to Wellington on 30 November, in time to hear the election results as they started to come in. To many people's surprise the outcome was not all that close, and the Labour government was decisively defeated by 46 seats to 34, a majority of 12 in a House of Representatives of 80. My father's letters resumed:

[538]

9 December 1949
The actual result came as a blow to Mr Fraser, but he took it well. We had a leave-taking this week at Government House. We had a sad Executive Council with the whole Cabinet, and I made them an affectionate speech in which I referred to our intimate association for ten years and Mr Fraser replied in a similar vein from the heart. I am very fond of them all; they have been good friends. Then I sent for the New Prime Minister Mr Holland, and it all starts over again.[2]

The change of government took place amicably and without recrimination. Freyberg's relationship with Peter Fraser had always been warm and friendly. Their wartime association had generated a bond of mutual trust that had withstood many hard knocks on the battlefield and difficult decisions in the council chambers. These problems increased the regard in which each held the other, and in peacetime the association had mellowed into personal friendship. The Freybergs were very conscious of Fraser's loneliness following the death of his wife in 1945, and it became almost a ritual that he and other members of his family came to supper at Government House every Sunday evening when they were both in Wellington.

Peter Fraser did not long survive the election. On 2 October 1950 he suffered a stroke and was taken to Lewisham Hospital in Wellington. On 8 October my father visited him and wrote to me that Fraser was not very well. On 12 November he wrote again:

Poor Mr Fraser is very ill. I flew back to Wellington on Sunday and I go to see him again next Sunday. I am very fond of the old boy. He has been a good friend to us both over a period of years. We shall be sad if he dies, which I feel is very likely.

His fears were realised a month later when Peter Fraser died on 12 December 1950, aged sixty-six. The King asked Freyberg to represent him at the funeral in St John's Presbyterian Church in Wellington on 15 December 1950. He flew up from Christchurch, where he had been participating in the centenary celebrations, and after the service he followed Fraser's coffin to Karori for the interment, in the same cemetery where his own parents lay buried.

The first major event of the new decade was the Fourth British Empire Games which took place in Auckland in early February 1950. In order to participate fully in all the ceremonies and associated events, the household moved from Wellington to Auckland in mid-December immediately after the new government had been sworn in. On 2 February the Freybergs gave a garden party for 1,100 guests.

The Governor-General opened the Empire Games at Eden Park on Saturday, 4 February. There were twelve national teams – from the UK, the other three main dominions (which still included South Africa), and from smaller countries such as Ceylon and Fiji. They all paraded past the saluting base in bright sunshine, watched by a capacity crowd of 40,000. The Chairman of the Organising Committee was Arthur Porritt, later Lord Porritt and the first native-born Governor-General of New Zealand (1967–72). The competitions lasted for a week and comprised the full range of athletic contests, as well as fencing, track cycling, rowing, water polo and swimming.

The Freybergs remained on in Auckland for the rest of February and most of March. Towards the end of that month they spent nearly a week in the Bay of Islands in the far north, and then slowly made their way southwards, arriving back in main Government House on 3 April. Lord and Lady Cobham came to stay on 19 April. His family, the Lytteltons, had much to do with the founding of Canterbury Province and the port of Lyttelton took their name; they still had property there. He had been Vice-Captain on the MCC cricket tour of 1935–6, and was to be Governor-General from 1957–62. Thus three out of the four succeeding Governors-General visited the Freybergs at Government House during 1949–50 – the Norries, the Cobhams and the Porritts. The exception was Bernard Fergusson, who was still serving with the British Army in England.

By June 1950 Freyberg had been at Government House for four years, and his five-year appointment was due to end in May 1951. In a letter to me dated 21 June 1950 my father said that he had written to the Prime Minister asking for agreement to his booking his return journey on a ship leaving Wellington in May 1951. He also suggested that, as the next opening of Parliament would be his last, he should make a suitable reference to this in the Speech from the Throne.

Mr Holland's reaction had been to seek an audience, which took place on 16 June. By this time the King's health appeared to have improved, and there seemed a possibility that the royal visit could be re-scheduled for early 1952. Mr Holland suggested therefore that my father's term of office should be extended for a further two years. Although they were flattered to be asked, neither of my parents favoured an extension. They had been away from England since 1939, and problems there were piling up remorselessly. My father felt this as strongly as my mother, and after an extremely happy period of office he was keen not to outstay his welcome. Moreover, on the financial front the expenses at Government House had already cost more than they could afford. Most previous Governors-General had had considerable private means and the time was still to come when all Government House expenses would be defrayed from the public purse.

On the other hand, if the King and Queen were to visit the country at the beginning of the New Zealand summer of 1951–2, it would not give their successors enough time to establish themselves. My parents knew that it took at least a year to organise a smoothly running staff at Government House, capable of undertaking the demands of a royal visit. In the end a compromise was reached, whereby Freyberg agreed to stay on for a further year until the middle of 1952, and he announced the extension in the Speech from the Throne on 28 June 1950. As it turned out, this decision did not take account of the true state of the King's health, but at the time no one was in a position to assess that accurately.

In the second half of June the CIGS, Field Marshal Sir William Slim, of whom Freyberg had a high opinion, stayed at Government House with his entourage. The war in Korea had started, the Commonwealth Division was in the process of being formed, and the CIGS was having discussions with the New Zealand government and General Staff about their participation. The New Zealand contribution for Korea, known as 'K Force', consisted of a Field Regiment of some 1,600 men, plus two frigates – a contribution that was larger in proportion than any other in the Commonwealth – under the overall command of Brigadier R. S. Park. The men were all volunteers and Freyberg went to inspect them on 30 November, when he told them:

> To have to say goodbye to New Zealand troops going overseas is a new role for me to play. If I were younger I would like to be with you, and I would go with a light heart. I know you will be the gainers in the long run.
>
> You are going to a country where fighting will be severe. Time may be short and you should make sure you are absolutely fit. The reputation of New Zealand is in your hands. I wish you God speed and a safe and quick return.[2]

1950 was to end, as it had begun, on a high note. Great efforts were made to mark the hundredth anniversary of the founding of the Settlement of Canterbury in an appropriate way. Its origins were unusual in that it was a colony founded by the Church under the auspices of the Archbishop of Canterbury, with close ties with the College and Cathedral of Christ Church, Oxford.

The Freybergs had spent much time preparing for the centenary celebrations, guided by Heathcote Helmore. They were loaned a large house called 'Daresbury' by the Christchurch City Council as a temporary Government House. It had a beautiful garden, with wide lawns going down to the river Avon, and was very suitable for entertaining. But before starting on the hectic round of events the Freybergs decided to enjoy a week of rest and leisure. A passage on the Wellington ferry *Tamahine* on 27 October took them across the Cook Strait to Queen Charlotte Sound and thence to Picton. It was a journey familiar to Bernard from half a century before, in the days of his sailing boat *Viking*, which, incidentally, he had seen in Wellington harbour on 1 October 1949, still as sound as a bell; but it was an eye-opener to Barbara, who was seeing the beauty of the Sound for the first time.

For the two months from 3 November until they left Christchurch on 3 January 1951, there was no day without some official function, and usually at least two or three engagements. The Freybergs were determined to support the committees organising the celebrations in every way they could. Their activities on Thursday, 9 November gives an example of what was involved. They left Daresbury at 9.45 a.m. for the Royal Show, which the Governor-General opened on arrival with a suitable speech. They then made a tour of the stands, visiting those displaying machinery, handicrafts, flowers and animals of all descriptions. After lunching with the committee, they watched a procession of dairy and beef cattle, followed by a display of jumping, first by children and then by grown-ups. They got back to Government House for tea, when it was nearly time to start changing for the Randolph Ball, one of the highlights of the celebrations. The Christchurch *Press* described their arrival;

> Shortly after 8.30 p.m. when the room was thronged, their Excellencies Sir Bernard and Lady Freyberg and party arrived and were conducted to the viceregal box, which was draped in red, white and blue in the style common in Queen Victoria's reign. His Excellency wore evening dress with orders and decorations. So beautiful and becoming was Lady Freyberg's Victorian gown that the big gathering broke into spontaneous applause as she appeared in the ballroom.[3]

One of those who stayed at Government House was Lord Kilbracken, a great-grandson of John Robert Godley who, with Edward

Gibbon Wakefield, had been largely instrumental in launching the whole Anglican Settlement. During November and early December the Freybergs held two Investitures, one for 250 people, and two receptions at Daresbury, a Government House ball for 400 in the Winter Garden, a garden party for 600, not to mention a large number of lunches and dinners, innumerable smaller functions and various visits to hospitals, schools and local industries. The climax of the celebrations came in the middle of December with the re-enactment of the landing at Lyttelton of the four ships, and the thanksgiving service in Christchurch Cathedral attended by the Archbishop of Canterbury, Dr Geoffrey Fisher.

Centennial day, Saturday, 16 December 1950, started in the morning with the 'arrival' of the *Charlotte Jane* and her sister ships in Lyttelton Harbour, and the disembarkation of the pilgrims to be greeted by the Governor of the day, Sir George Grey, and Mr Godley. Then at 11.15 a.m. there was a service on the wharf conducted by the Archbishop of New Zealand, followed at 12 noon by a banquet for 1,000 people given by the Lyttelton Harbour Board in one of their large stores. In the afternoon the 'Centennial Procession' wended its way through the streets of Lyttelton, watched by large crowds.

The great religious thanksgiving took place on Sunday, 17 December, when the Freybergs went to church four times: in the early morning to Holy Communion, followed by morning service at the Presbyterian Church, and evensong, when Dr Fisher preached for the second time. The main service, however, took place at 3 p.m., when 1,500 people were packed inside the cathedral as if it were the choir, and 20,000 were seated in the Cathedral Square, which became the nave. When the moment arrived for the Archbishop's sermon, he delivered it from an open-air pulpit specially built for the occasion by the west door of the cathedral. He based much of his address on the words that his predecessor, Dr J. B. Sumner, had used when he preached to the pilgrims in St Paul's Cathedral, London, a century before, on the eve of their voyage to New Zealand.

The Archbishop and Mrs Fisher stayed with the Freybergs. My mother's letter to me dated 17 December 1950 records: 'they couldn't be nicer – he has infectiously high spirits and general enjoyment, besides the great ability to produce the right word at the right moment'. After discussing the morning and afternoon events in Port Lyttelton, her letter describes the evening party at Daresbury:

> The general idea was maximum demonstration to the Archbishop and the Church, so we did what we could to infiltrate prominent laity with the clergy

and wives, who were fairly numerous – no fewer than eight bishops, as well as the Archbishop of NZ and archdeacons and canons galore. But we jollied them along with champagne, and the High Commissioners and diplomats added chic and interest. We wound up by a very good group of carol singers on the lawn and little lighted floats looking very pretty drifting down the river.

After all this, the Freybergs' final fortnight in Christchurch was almost an anti-climax, among other reasons because after weeks of sunshine the weather broke. But their efforts to contribute towards the success of the centenary had been appreciated, as shown by the leading article which appeared in the *Christchurch Star Sun* on the day they left, 3 January 1951:

> Among the many who have sought to do honour to Canterbury during its Centennial celebrations none have been more eager and assiduous than his Excellency the Governor-General and Lady Freyberg. There was nothing perfunctory about this visit and no mere compliance with the calls of official duty. The capacity for associating themselves so very intimately with the lives of the people, and of sharing their enthusiasms, their aspirations and their quiet pride in achievement has endeared Sir Bernard and Lady Freyberg to the people.[4]

On 14 February 1951 Freyberg returned to Christchurch Cathedral to give an address in memory of the New Zealand doctors who had been killed in the Second World War. His starting point was the needless loss of life he had seen in the First World War because of inadequate medical facilities, and ignorance about how to treat badly wounded cases. He went on to discuss the many improvements that had come about in the Second World War, and how, as a result, far fewer of the wounded had died unnecessarily. This had also been due to the devotion and skill of doctors and nurses. Freyberg stressed how important it was in maintaining high morale in battle that it should be known throughout the force that, in the event of becoming casualties the best medical facilities would be immediately available. He pointed out that it was equally important to protect the troops from sickness and disease when out of battle, and to see that they were properly looked after when they were off duty. He ended the address: 'We start the second century of our country from the dual angle of courage and efficiency and the requisite toughness of both body and mind, for steadfastness of mind is even more important than mere toughness of body.'[5]

Government House reopened again in Auckland three days later, and the usual procession of visitors recommenced. Among the first was Sir John Anderson and his wife Ava (later Lord and Lady Waverley) and a few days later there followed the Governor of the Bank of England, C. F. Cobbold, and his wife Lady Hermione.

The Cobbolds were still staying with my parents when I arrived for my second visit to New Zealand at the beginning of March 1951. At that time I was serving as a staff officer at Headquarters 4 Guards Brigade, stationed in Germany near Düsseldorf. I had just sat the Staff College exams, and had saved up a year's ration of leave to take consecutively. When I first visited New Zealand in 1948 the normal way of travelling was still by sea. Three years later the normal method was by air.

I arrived at the height of the New Zealand summer, and when my parents were much preoccupied with arrangements for the royal visit, which was now planned for early in 1952. Because of the extension of Freyberg's term of office it had again been necessary to change over their personal staff. Paddy Jeffreys of the Irish Guards arrived as the new Comptroller, with Sandy Leven (Earl of Leven and Melville) of the Coldstreams and Dickie Howson of the Royal Navy as the replacement ADCs.

For some time there had been suggestions that a peerage should be offered to Freyberg, and both the past and present Prime Ministers of the United Kingdom and New Zealand, Churchill and Attlee, Fraser and Holland, had agreed that the appropriate moment would be towards the end of his time as Governor-General. Clement Attlee had written on 2 May 1951:

> It would give me much pleasure to include your name in the list of recommendations which I shall submit to the King for the Birthday Honours. I have it in mind to recommend that the dignity of a Barony of the United Kingdom be conferred upon you, and I hope you will allow me to do so.
>
> When Mr Holland was over here in January, I took the opportunity of mentioning this proposal to him and he warmly concurred.
>
> Perhaps you will be so good as to let me have your reply by telegram.[2]

The King's Birthday Honours List in 1951 was published on 7 June, and a long correspondence then ensued with Garter King of Arms about how Freyberg's title was to be promulgated. In the end it was agreed that it should be 'of Wellington, New Zealand and of Munstead in the County of Surrey'. On 11 October he received a telegram from His Majesty's Private Secretary saying 'The King has approved the warrant for your Peerage'.[2] My father chose a pair of salamanders as supporters for his coat of arms, which included a heraldic version of the Southern Cross. The College of Arms added a pun for the superscription on its base by including the words 'New Zeal and Honour'.

The result of my staff college examination came through on 20 June, and to my surprise I found that I had passed. The most satisfying aspect from my point of view was the pleasure it gave my parents, and particularly my father. Subsequently I was selected to attend the 1952 course at Camberley, which meant I would be in England when my parents returned from New Zealand.

On Friday, 13 July 1951 Freyberg received a considerable shock. Without any warning he was asked by Sydney Holland to dissolve Parliament. The National government had been in power for only eighteen months, and in the ordinary course of events there was a year and a half before another election was due. There was, of course, a major political calculation behind the request for the dissolution. For several years there had been recurring strikes and trouble on the waterfront and in the docks, with which the previous Labour government had not succeeded in dealing effectively, and this was reckoned to be one of the reasons for their defeat in the 1949 General Election. The National government faced the same problem on taking office, but they took a firmer line by bringing in outside labour, including servicemen, to work in the docks. After several months this had broken the striking dockers' monopoly.

The Labour Opposition put down a motion of no confidence over the government's 'Fascist handling of the strike', and consequently the Prime Minister decided to appeal to the country. Once again my father wrote a series of letters on the subject:

14 July
Syd Holland decided to force an election on the issue of the strike. It will be held in the course of the next six weeks. I believe that the date of the election may be 1st, 8th or 15th of September. Both sides think that they are going to win. I don't know how it will go, but I think that the Government should get back comfortably.

29 July
We have been busy the last few days with the Dissolution of Parliament which took place last Friday (27th). So now we have no Government until after the 1st of September. By all the known form the Government should get back again, but with a reduced majority ... They are faced with a General Election in any case in 1952, so that they would, if they win, have

[546]

another three years instead of only one. They calculate that their shares stand high at the moment. But in a year with the cost of living rising they figure it out that they would lose a large number of the marginal seats. I believe that they are right, provided that they are able to fight the election upon the strike as an issue. If the cost of living becomes one of the election issues then anything may happen. As you realise, I am not entitled to any opinion on this subject.

3 August
Mr Nash (Labour) has been making a lot of bricks and is busy throwing them at Mr Holland. It is early days yet to predict what will happen. The Press here is pro Mr Holland or rather the National Party. We naturally keep out, and will favour the party that gets in irrespective of who they are. I find it hard to believe that in such a short time the solid New Zealand public will alter much.

2 September
New Zealand went to the Polls yesterday and the Count is still in progress. The Government has been returned with much the same number of seats.[2]

The New Zealand election came a few weeks before the election in Britain at the end of October, when Churchill was returned to power with a small majority. The Freybergs' old friends William and Lesley Jowitt had stayed with them for a short time in early September in the middle of an official visit to Australasia in his capacity as Lord Chancellor. He foretold what was likely to happen in England with remarkable accuracy, and frankly admitted that several of the recent British Acts of Parliament, such as the Town and Country Planning and the Steel Bill, were unworkable. For a senior Labour Minister he was remarkably frank about his party's shortcomings, and reminded my parents of their pre-war joke that his only concession to socialism had been to paint his Rolls-Royce red.

In the second half of September 1951 the sad news came through that the King's health had again suffered a relapse, and he was to undergo a serious operation. This coincided with the opening of the new Parliament in Wellington on 26 September, when in the Speech from the Throne the Governor-General expressed the deep sympathy of the New Zealand people, and their hope that His Majesty's condition would soon respond to medical treatment. The last weeks of 1951 were a period of uncertainty. Even if the King's operation had been a complete success, any visit by him before the onset of the New Zealand winter was now ruled out. As 1951 came to an end the Freybergs could only sit back and await developments.

Princess Elizabeth and the Duke of Edinburgh had left England shortly after the King's operation for a six weeks tour of Canada and the United States. The suggestion that they should come to Australasia in place of the King and Queen had to wait until their return, and it was not until the beginning of 1952 that a new plan was devised. The proposals were that the Princess and the Duke should leave London by air on 31 January, spend a week in Kenya, and depart from Mombasa in the liner *Gothic* on 7 February. After spending another week in the new Dominion of Ceylon, between 14 and 21 February, they were due to arrive at Fremantle on 1 March to begin their tour of Australia. After that was over, the *Gothic* was to arrive in Wellington on 7 May. This date was not ideal because the New Zealand summer would be over by the time they got there. Also, on this timetable, the Freybergs had only two months in which to pack up and say their goodbyes after the royal visitors had departed in early June and before they themselves were due to leave for England in August.

For the third time the Freybergs started to plan for a royal visit, but now, because Princess Elizabeth and the Duke of Edinburgh were young and energetic, there appeared to be no obvious reason why it should not go ahead.

The Freybergs spent their last Christmas in New Zealand in Wellington. The staff of Government House moved to Auckland in the last days of January 1952, and the Freybergs took up residence there on 2 February. My mother wrote to me shortly after her arrival that 'Brigadier Sir Norman Gwatkin [Deputy Comptroller, Royal Household] has arrived in Wellington and will be with us here next week, to put some finishing touches to the plans, which are beginning to take more definite and detailed shape.'

On 5 February my father departed for Waitangi for the annual meeting of the Treaty House Board and the anniversary of the assumption of British sovereignty in New Zealand in 1840. He returned by car to Government House in Auckland at 7 p.m. next day, 6 February. My mother's diary records: 'Just as we were getting into bed – I was getting up from saying my prayers – there was a loud knock on our door by Rosemary Eley and Paddy Jeffreys who had just had a telephone call from the papers to say that the King was dead.'

Freyberg left for Wellington next morning, 7 February, so as to be in touch with Ministers about the arrangements for the accession of the new sovereign. He read the lesson at the memorial service for King George VI on 10 February. Next day Freyberg read the Proclamation of the Accession of Queen Elizabeth II from the steps of Parliament Buildings. He did so dressed in the same scarlet tunic that he had worn as a Grenadier thirty years before, which still fitted him perfectly.

When all the ceremonies in the capital were over, the Freybergs returned to Auckland, and decided to remain there for their normal length of time until the end of March. Their subsequent moves depended on the nomination of their successors and the arrangements for the change-over. The newspapers had been full of gossip, not only about who was likely to succeed them, but also about other appointments that the Freybergs might be invited to fill after leaving New Zealand. In succession they were tipped to follow the Alexanders in Canada, to go to Malaya (in the appointment filled by General Templer), and to become the new Governor-General of Australia. As each new kite was flown my mother pointed out to me that none of them took any account of the realities of the situation, or of their personal inclinations (invariably their lack of any), or the fact that by then they were too old to start such new ventures. The Prime Minister, Sydney Holland, was in England at the time of the King's death, and had had an audience at Buckingham Palace only a few days before it happened. One of his main objects was to take soundings about who was available and acceptable to succeed as Governor-General.

General 'Pug' Ismay, Secretary of State, Commonwealth Relations Office, wrote to Freyberg on 8 February:

> I have very much enjoyed meeting your Prime Minister and have had several long talks with him. Your ears must have burnt on these occasions as he has quite made up his mind that New Zealand will never get a pair like you and your lady at Government House again.
>
> Your Prime Minister has been throwing an eye over various possibilities but he had not made up his mind definitely when he left for Paris last week. I shall see him on his return journey and strongly advise him to try Willoughby. If he does not move quickly I imagine that Australia may grab him to succeed [Governor-General] McKell.[2]

General Sir Willoughby Norrie was still Governor of South Australia. He was regarded by Freyberg, Buckingham Palace and the Commonwealth Relations Office as the most suitable of the choices available, not least because he had a very sensible and agreeable wife. His many years experience as Governor in Adelaide had well prepared him for what was required as Governor-General, and he was immediately available. The announcement of his appointment was made on 13 March 1952. This decision cleared the way for the final arrangements of Freyberg's period of office. He decided to stick to the timetable which would have been followed had the royal visit taken place, and to leave New Zealand in August 1952. On 15 March it was announced that the Freybergs would return to England on the liner *Rangitane*, due to depart from Wellington on 9 August. In the meantime the Norries were to leave South Australia for England, and arrive in New Zealand in November. As the Coronation was due to take place in June 1953, the first possible date for a royal visit to Australasia could not be before November 1953 to March 1954, which would give the Norries plenty of time to find their feet before it took place.

For the next two and a half months life reverted to the normal routine. At the end of March the Freybergs left Government House, Auckland for the last time, and by 6 April they were back in Wellington for the final lap. June was set aside for farewell visits. During the first week, the Freybergs went to towns in the South Island including, of course, Dunedin and Christchurch, but also to Invercargill, Timaru, Greymouth and Nelson. During the second week, back in the North Island, it was the turn of Auckland, Hamilton, Rotorua and Napier, while during the third week Gisborne, Palmerston North, Wanganui and New Plymouth were all visited. They were touched by the warmth of their reception and by the expressions of genuine regret that they were leaving.

One of the last matters that Freyberg dealt with while he was at Government House concerned the Severn Wildfowl Trust at Slimbridge, Gloucestershire, which was trying to preserve some of the world's most unusual species of geese and duck in England, in case of disaster in the wild state. The Trust was particularly anxious to obtain specimens of the rare species of New Zealand Brown Duck and Blue Duck, and Freyberg was able to effect suitable introductions for this purpose. The Director of the Trust was Peter Scott, and Freyberg ended his letter to him: 'It is, indeed, many years since we met – I think 1922 or 1923 when you came into Barrie's in Adelphi Terrace with your Mother, leading a goat. I don't think you were very old then.'

The Freybergs had to return to Wellington on 25 June for the first opening of Parliament of the new reign. It had been intended to have a considerable ceremonial to mark the occasion, which was also the hundredth anniversary of constitutional government in New Zealand, which had likewise taken place under a young Queen. However, it was such a stormy and wild day that the guard of honour and most of the outside pageantry had to be cancelled.

Two days later, on 27 June, the tenth anniversary of the battle of Minqar Qaim, 175 officers of the New Zealand Division of the rank of Lieutenant-Colonel and above were asked to Government House for a buffet dinner and dancing. They had subscribed to a presentation to the Freybergs prior to their departure. It took the form of a portrait of

Bernard by Peter McIntyre and a Spode dinner service embossed with Bernard's and Barbara's monogram. In return they were each given a signed photograph of Bernard and Barbara in silver frames.

The month of July was one of the busiest of the Freybergs' six years at Government House. On 3 July Freyberg went to the Victoria University of Wellington, to be given the honorary degree of Doctor of Laws. The Chancellors and Vice-Chancellors of the six University Collegers and an impressive number of deans and dons had all assembled in their gowns. The *New Zealand Evening Post* reported his speech, saying that Freyberg:

> emphasised the great need today to train men and women not merely as scholars, but also to become leaders who could hold together and build on to the fabric of national life.
>
> Robustness was one of the great attributes of leadership [Lord Freyberg said]. The qualities of leadership were products of the mind and body and not the prerogative of any one class or type. They were found in Servicemen who were trained and promoted because they had shown powers of leadership.[6]

The next evening, 4 July the Freybergs gave a dinner party for the Cabinet and Executive Council and their wives. On 9 and 16 July Freyberg had meetings of the Executive Council and on 17 July there was a presentation by Members of Parliament at Government House for the 'Address in Reply'. On 22 July the Freybergs both went for a farewell visit to Wellington College, where Freyberg inspected a guard of honour of the Cadet Corps and presented a portrait of himself in oils to the school.

There was a special Rugby match on 26 July in the Governor-General's honour at Athletic Park – New Zealand versus the Maoris. The Freybergs shook hands with both teams beforehand, and following an exciting game there was an enthusiastic public demonstration. By this time news of their farewell receptions had begun to percolate back to England, for *The Times* reported:

> Lord Freyberg, VC, the Governor-General, and Lady Freyberg have, during recent weeks, had abundant evidence of the high esteem and warm affection which they have won from all classes of people in their six-year term of office. A remarkable spontaneous demonstration of their popularity was given on Saturday at a Rugby football match between New Zealand and Maori teams which had been arranged as a Rugby farewell. At the end of the game a crowd of about 30,000 people streamed across the Athletic Park, Wellington, to the front of the Governor-General's box and sang 'Auld

Lang Syne' and the New Zealand farewell song 'Now is the Hour'. Their Excellencies joined hands and joined in the singing, and were then cheered with enthusiasm.[7]

On Sunday, 3 August the Freybergs attended St Luke's Church, Wadestown, where Freyberg unveiled the beautiful war memorial window, which had been made in London and was described as being 'like a jewel'. A week later they attended their last Sunday Service at St Paul's Pro-Cathedral, when the Dean, who had a puckish sense of fun, solemnly intoned the words of the 8th Psalm which begins: 'O Lord our Governor, how excellent is thy name in all the world'.

Freyberg was charged by the Queen to hand over to the government a presentation copy of the Diary of Captain James Cook's Second Voyage to Australasia (13 July 1772 to 29 July 1775). The original had been given by Captain Cook to George III at Bristol. In 1937 the late King had donated it to the National Maritime Museum at Greenwich, but knowing what a particular interest it had for New Zealand, he had ordered that a facsimile volume be made, which first George VI, and then Princess Elizabeth had been intending to hand over had either of their visits taken place. The ceremony took place in the Turnbull Library during the morning of 13 August, when Freyberg gave the volume to Mr Harper, the Under-Secretary of Internal Affairs, and to the Librarian for safekeeping.[8]

On 13 August a state luncheon was held by the Government and Opposition to say goodbye to the Freybergs, which was attended by 300 guests representing every sphere of public life in New Zealand. In his speech the Prime Minister said that the luncheon had been held to do three things – to honour a great man, to record their gratitude to him and to her Excellency for what they had done for New Zealand, and to express cordial good wishes for the future. The Leader of the Opposition, Walter Nash, said that the Labour government in office between 1935 and 1949 was never more proud of any decision than that of appointing Lord Freyberg to his post as commander of the New Zealand Forces.[9]

In his reply the Governor-General expressed his thanks to all concerned, and then said, as reported in *The Dominion*,

'In laying down this task it makes me happy to think I have the goodwill and affection of the Government and Opposition.' Lady Freyberg and he had endeavoured to see as much of New Zealand and of all sections of the people as they could, but they still felt acutely that they had not done many things they would have wished to have done.

[552]

'New Zealanders are the most practical and resourceful people I have been associated with,' said his Excellency. Those qualities were most important, and had enabled New Zealand to develop in 100 years from a primitive beginning to the stage it had reached today. That development, and the qualities necessary, had come about through environment and necessity.

'I shall think of New Zealand and pray for her people always. Good luck and Godspeed. To the Maori people I say *kia ora katoa*.'[9]

On their last evening the Freybergs attended a farewell reception in the Town Hall, with speeches by Mr Holland, Mr Nash and the Governor-General, which were broadcast live on radio. Freyberg said he had served New Zealand almost continuously for thirteen years in the field and as Governor-General. 'I did the best I could for New Zealand in what have been the most important years of my life.' After the reception the Freybergs stood for almost an hour shaking hands with people who had waited to make a personal farewell.[10]

The best description of their departure on 15 August is given in Barbara's diary:

A day of experience of once in a lifetime. Least of all could I ever have believed that it could have happened to me. We got up and looked out on the stormy skies of the last few days and then, as we dressed, the miracle seemed to happen – the clouds lifted and the sun came out. (B. had asked the Archbishop to do what he could about it and Lady O'Leary had turned on the RCs.) We had a hour or so after breakfast for final jobs and goodbyes and at 11.20, we got into a fairy-story Daimler meant for the Queen – dark blue with red lines and an entire plastic roof so that it looked like an open car plus! Sergeant Morton drove us. When we got to the gates of GH (the gardeners had lined up and waved near the house), we found a solid crowd all along the road – St Mark's schoolchildren all out with flags and as we went on, there were crowds the whole way, shouting and cheering, from windows and balconies and on the street front all the schools in groups. We saw a good few friends on the way but it was the most incredible experience, and down such a long route – Kent Terrace, Courtenay Place, Manners Street, Willis Street, Lambton Quay, past the War Memorial and so to the Dock Gates.

When the Freybergs reached the docks they found a guard of honour of 400 men from the Returned Services Association under the command of Major-General Sir Howard Kippenberger, together with further contingents of 100 each from the Boy Scouts, the Girl Guides and Wellington College. After these had been inspected, they turned to greet the Mayor of Wellington, members of the Harbour Board,

Bernard's brothers Cuthbert and Claud, the Cabinet and wives, some MPs, the Leader of the Opposition and finally the Prime Minister, who were drawn up on the quayside in the Harbour Board shed waiting to say goodbye.

Barbara, who had been touched by the sight of so many old friends and Tuis in the guard of honour, then described how they:

> went through with the Hollands and McAlisters [Head of the Civil Service] to another Military Guard. It was a big moment to see B. in uniform inspecting NZ troops, probably for the last time. Beyond the open square there was a huge crowd, along the wharf and up on cranes, buildings and ships, and the PM called for three cheers and started off a frenzy of shouting and waving. Then we met Mr Marchington by the gangway and he took us on board and the twenty-one gun salute started off from Point Jerningham. We went to an upper deck and B. saluted as the Air Force Band on the Quay played 'God Save' first six bars for him for the last time, followed by 'Auld Lang Syne'. After that, I believe they played 'Now is the Hour' as the *Rangitane* pulled out from the Wharf, but the band was drowned by the chorus of sirens and hooters from every ship in the Harbour. The cheers and waving went on and on as we began to turn and then a squadron of Vampires came flying down in beautiful formation. They came round and over four or five times as we went on towards the Heads.

The Freybergs stayed on the bridge for the next hour. After she left the Wellington docks, the ship passed through the great landlocked harbour of Port Nicholson to the Heads, and then sailed into the waters of the Cook Strait. Eighteen years later, in 1970, Barbara was to return by herself for a final visit, but Bernard would never again see the land of his youth and his adoption. As the *Rangitane* crossed the three-mile limit into international waters, his Governor-General's flag was lowered from the masthead for the last time, and New Zealand faded slowly from his sight.

32

Windsor

When they reached England on 17 September 1952 nearly all the passengers, including their two ADCs, disembarked at Southampton; but the Freybergs, Rosemary Eley and Paddy Jeffreys remained on board for a further twenty-four hours, going ashore next day in the London Docks. They had brought such a mountain of luggage back with them that it was a necessity to unload the ship as near to home as possible. That evening the whole family was reunited again for dinner at Clarendon Place for the first time since their last meeting together in 1945 at the end of the war. Five days later Harry and Christabel Aberconway gave a 'Welcome Home' party at their North Audley Street house. The occasion took the form of a musical evening followed by supper, to which Bernard and Barbara's special friends were invited. It was a heart-warming occasion and it helped Bernard and Barbara to pick up the threads of their English life from where they had left off in 1939.

The major problem which my parents faced on their return dated back to 1937, when Lady Jekyll had died leaving her Munstead property to my mother. My parents had twice delayed making a long-term decision whether to sell Munstead or Clarendon Place, first because of the war, and then when my father went to New Zealand. But his year's extension had caused further problems – no maintenance had been carried out on either property for thirteen years. Clarendon Place proved to be unlettable when it came back on the family's hands in 1951, and the Surrey County Council had by then indicated that they would be giving up their occupation of Munstead in 1952.

As an interim measure my parents decided to do a certain amount of internal renovation at Clarendon Place in order to make it more habitable. It fell to me to supervise the work as far as I could, initially from Germany, and then later from the staff college at Camberley. During the first half of 1952 it looked increasingly likely, therefore, that Clarendon would again become the family's home and, since we could not afford to run both, that Munstead would have to be sold.

However a totally unexpected event altered the situation. While he was still in New Zealand my father had received the following letter from Sir Alan Lascelles, the Queen's Private Secretary:

> The Queen has instructed me to make tentative enquiry whether, after your return to England, you would care to accept the post of Deputy Constable and Lieutenant-Governor of Windsor Castle, now held by Lord Gowrie, and to occupy the Norman Tower.
>
> Gowrie proposes to vacate both the office and the house towards the end of this year. The office carries no salary with it, but the house (which is fully furnished) and garden involve the occupant in no direct financial obligation, though he is generally expected to do a certain amount of mild entertaining.
>
> I will not go into further detail, because the general idea may not commend itself to Barbara and you; in any case, I expect you would like to have a look at Norman Tower before committing yourself.
>
> For the present, would you merely let me know if you would like your name to be considered pending your return to England.[1]

My father replied that he was glad that there was no immediate hurry for a decision. However, he added, 'Barbara and I would like our names to be considered pending our return to England.' After my parents had re-established themselves at Clarendon Place, one of their first visits, on 26 September, was to Norman Tower.

The offices of Constable and Deputy Constable of Windsor Castle are among the oldest in the kingdom, and can be traced back to William the Conqueror. The recent occupants had been ex-Governors-General, and the Earl of Athlone, brother to Queen Mary, sometime Governor-General of both Canada and South Africa, was the Constable of Windsor Castle at the time. His was an honorific appointment as a member of the Royal Family, and he did not reside in the castle. In 1952 the Deputy Constable and Lieutenant-Governor was the Earl of Gowrie, VC, who had been Governor-General of Australia.

In her diary following our first visit my mother wrote: 'We spent a fascinating morning looking round that romantic house – it is brimming with charm and interest – divine views, fascinating rooms and the garden is enchanting. But it is wonderfully inconvenient and difficult as a modern residence!'

Originally the Tower had formed part of the Keep of the Castle and in the Civil War it was used to house Royalist prisoners. Its layout was rambling and disjointed. The kitchen was below ground in what had once been not so much a basement as a dungeon. Hardly any two rooms were on the same level, and everything had to be carried up an uneven central staircase, with passageways leading off it at irregular intervals. My parents felt that the only way of running the place satisfactorily was by installing a lift, to connect the various parts of the house – especially the kitchen with the dining-room. Because of the difficulties they remained undecided for several months whether to accept the appointment at Windsor.

On 17 October they went to Buckingham Palace for their 'signing off' as Her Majesty's Representatives in New Zealand. My mother wrote in her diary:

I got dressed and put on my little brown suit with the short coat and velvet collar and my pheasant feather hat and with Bernard in his morning suit off we went, first to St James's Palace, where Bernard had an appointment with Sir Terence Nugent to find out more about the Norman Tower. I waited and wrote letters in the car meanwhile.

When he emerged, we went together to Buckingham Palace where he was to see the Queen first on his own and I prepared to wait in the car again, but I was quickly extracted by a charming equerry, Major Milbank, and taken in to the same big ground-floor room where Bernard was also waiting, with windows to the garden and terrace. The lady-in-waiting, Lady Palmer, came down and also a young airman, Peter Townsend, Sir Piers Leigh and General Browning. Presently, Bernard was summoned and after another ten minutes or so I was taken in to a big sitting-room, where the Queen and Prince Philip were alone. They gave us some sherry and were most kind and friendly – so sweet and natural and charming in the way they talked. Luncheon was in quite a small dining-room, where we had delicious lunch of egg cutlets, poussins and chocolate soufflé. They both talked away and could not have been nicer. The Queen looked enchanting – so slim and such an exquisite complexion. She was dressed in a leaf-brown taffeta dress and followed about by two corgis – one fat and elderly and one a puppy. Prince Philip talked interestingly at lunch and his scientific interests seem to be engrossing him more and more. We stayed for a few minutes after lunch and then went off after a very enjoyable occasion.

The Alamein Reunion in 1952 was another special occasion, being the first one held after Churchill was again Prime Minister, and which

Field Marshal Viscount Alexander and my father had attended after returning from Canada and New Zealand respectively. It took place at the Empress Hall and, after an impressive military pageant there were speeches first by Monty, then Alexander, followed by General Ridgway, Supreme Allied Commander Europe (SACEUR). My father had the somewhat daunting task of speaking last after Churchill, but he did so very successfully, and later the party repaired to 10 Downing Street for supper. 'It was a great evening and Clemmie and Winston were angelic!' my mother wrote.

On Wednesday, 29 October my father took his seat in the House of Lords. He gave a lunch party beforehand for members of the family, and for his two sponsors and their wives. He was introduced by his old friends Lord Burnham and Lord Balfour of Burleigh, and his procession into the Chamber of the House was headed by the Earl Marshal and the Lord Great Chamberlain – a rare occurrence. When it was over the House gave the low buzz that is their Lordships' way of indicating approval of a new member. My father took his seat on the cross benches, as was then the custom for former Governors-General.

My father attended the House of Lords often during the rest of his life, but at the beginning he made a particular point of doing so whenever the House met so as to learn its procedures, and to get to know as many of his fellow peers as possible. He kept a special pocket notebook in which he recorded the names of all the politically active peers, their party allegiances, and what they looked like.

1952 was the last of the 'watershed years' of Freyberg's life. It covered his final months in New Zealand, his emotional farewell and his re-establishment in England. But there was one final pleasure in store for him. In the New Year Honours Barbara was awarded the Dame Grand Cross of the Order of the British Empire. It was included in the New Zealand list at the instigation of Sydney Holland, the Prime Minister, 'in recognition of her services to New Zealand'. The award of his wife's GBE produced an almost bigger response from friends in England and New Zealand than had his peerage. That too gave my father great pleasure and he went with Barbara to Buckingham Palace on 10 February 1953 for her investiture.

Early in 1953 the Gowries gave notice that they wished to leave Norman Tower as soon as a successor had been nominated. Little maintenance had been possible at Norman Tower during the war or in the immediate post-war years, but on receiving assurances that the house would be properly renovated before they moved in – including,

[558]

as he thought, the installation of a lift – Freyberg indicated that he would be honoured to accept the appointment of Deputy Constable and Lieutenant-Governor of Windsor Castle. He and Gowrie agreed that the change-over should be at the end of February, and his Instrument of Appointment, dated 1 March 1953, was issued by Lord Athlone, signed by the Queen, and took immediate effect.[1] A public announcement was made at the same time.

Freyberg found himself involved almost immediately in the day-to-day activities of the appointment. One of his first duties was to show Marshal Tito over the State Apartments on 20 March.[1] It was a curious encounter. They had never met before, but Freyberg had been largely responsible for thwarting Tito's attempt to take over the city of Trieste eight years before. Nothing, however, was said. Freyberg was also present at the funeral of Queen Mary which took place in St George's Chapel on 31 March.[1]

A few days after the Gowries had left Windsor Castle I accompanied my parents on their first visit to Norman Tower on their own. Now that the house was stripped of all furniture and furnishings it became even more obvious just how antiquated its facilities were, and what a major task it was going to be to make the place into a home. But much more upsetting was the news brought by the Clerk of Works at the Castle that, owing to recent economies, it would not be possible to install a lift.

We drove back to London in gloomy silence. Eventually my mother said that, without a lift, she did not see how it was going to be possible to run the house. My father was equally downcast: he said that, if it had been made plain to him beforehand that a lift would not be forthcoming he would not have accepted the appointment. However, he pointed out, it would be hard to unscramble the arrangement now that it had been announced publicly, and with the Coronation only two months away.

As a member of the Queen's Household, Freyberg participated in all the main ceremonies of the Coronation. He and my mother went to Westminster Abbey on 2 June, suitably attired in their ermine robes and barons' coronets, and attended the state banquet at Buckingham Palace on the evening of 3 June. They were at the gala performance of Benjamin Britten's opera *Gloriana* at Covent Garden on 8 June, and on 15 June Bernard, 'in a blazer and yachting cap and Barbara in a nice little navy number', caught Train No. 15 from Waterloo to Portsmouth to attend the Spithead Review of the Fleet. They were accommodated on board the liner *Orcades*, which followed the Queen's ship *Surprise* through the lines of warships in the review that afternoon. In the evening they watched the whole fleet 'light up' on the Queen's signal, and the display of fireworks that followed. Sydney Holland invited

[559]

them to join his launch for a visit to HMNZS *Black Prince*, and they did not get to bed until 3 a.m.

After nearly three weeks of almost non-stop activities it was a relief, in the last week of June, to return to a more normal style of existence. But life was not all sunlight at this time. Eddie Marsh, who had befriended Bernard in the early days of the First World War, died in his sleep early in January at the age of eighty. On 23 May Harry Aberconway died – he had always been unfailingly kind to Barbara, his brother's widow, and on her remarriage, to Bernard. Also Michael Cole, Bernard's former ADC, was killed in a flying accident early in April. In Bernard's view he had had all the qualities necessary to take him to the top of the Royal Air Force.

But the loss that affected the family most closely was the death of Muriel Tolley. 'Milly' had been personal maid to my mother ever since my parents' marriage. She went with my mother to the Middle East and Italy during the war, and had been with my parents throughout their time in New Zealand. There were few days in their married lives when Milly had not been around, and the whole family was devoted to her. When she died on 3 June, the day after the Coronation, her sudden and unexpected demise left a large gap in all our lives.

In July my father returned to the attack over the lift at Norman Tower by offering to pay half its cost. Undoubtedly a lot of discreet arm-twisting went on behind the scenes, but in the end it was agreed that a lift would be installed, and it proved to be the key to running a difficult house, not just for my parents, but for their successors too.

My parents remained in England that summer having spent every one since 1939 abroad. On Battle of Britain Sunday, 20 September 1953, Freyberg was asked to unveil the memorial window in Lincoln Cathedral to the New Zealand airmen who had died in the Second World War while serving with the RAF. Lincoln was an appropriate site for the memorial since many of the bomber squadrons had been based nearby, and as their aircraft crossed the coast and set out over the North Sea, one of their last views in the twilight was of the great cathedral towering over the Lincolnshire countryside.

A large gathering of RAF officers assembled for the ceremony, headed by the Commander-in-Chief Bomber Command, Air Marshal G. H. Mills. Freyberg reminded the congregation in his address that out of a population of about 1,600,000 in 1939, 135,000 New Zealanders had served overseas in the forces, of whom 11,000 lost their lives and twice as many were wounded. Of the 11,000 New Zealanders who served in the RAF in Europe 3,318 gave their lives:

I also like to think that the names of these New Zealanders are now recorded not only on the memorials in their own home towns, but also here in the calm peace of this lovely Cathedral, where generations to come of young British people will linger here at this memorial, read their names and honour their memory.[1]

That month work began on renovating Norman Tower, but it was obviously going to take a long time, and in the meantime Bernard and Barbara remained contentedly at Clarendon Place. On 21 December the whole family went to Clydebank to watch Barbara launch the 11,000-ton refrigerated cargo liner *Essex*, which had been built by John Brown's for the NZ Shipping Company for the run between New Zealand and England. We were also taken on a tour of the new Royal Yacht *Britannia*, being fitted out in their yard nearby.

As 1953 drew to its close, the Queen began the much postponed royal visit to New Zealand, and Freyberg was asked by the *Daily Telegraph* to write an article, which appeared just as the first visit of a reigning sovereign to New Zealand started.[2] On Christmas Eve 1953, however, there was a rail disaster at Tangiwai in the North Island, when 151 people lost their lives, and this inevitably overshadowed the start of the royal tour. In London Freyberg represented the Queen at the memorial service in Westminster Abbey.

On 17 March 1954 Freyberg took part in a defence debate in the House of Lords. After discussing the conduct of future wars in an age dominated by atom and hydrogen bombs, he concentrated on two aspects – the military relationship between the British and Dominion forces, and, especially, the command and control of operations:

The more one reads the contemporary histories, the more one realises that not only policy but now strategy is in the hands of the political leaders. Only the training and movement of troops on the battlefield remain in the hands of generals. That was obvious in Crete. Every decision that was taken had to be referred to Whitehall – and rightly so, because they had the whole picture. The information that I was getting came direct from the War Office Intelligence room. It was accurate intelligence – nobody has been better served than we were. The decisions could be taken just as well in Whitehall as they could by the Commander-in-Chief. It is the speed and perfection of modern communications that have made these changes inevitable. None the less, this change is accompanied by grave dangers, the principal one being that few political leaders are trained to take military decisions. Hitler was a case in point. Hitler's handling of his army in Russia had as much to do with his defeat as did the Russian generals.[3]

Freyberg was asked by the NZ government to represent New Zealand at the unveiling by the Queen of the 'Malta Memorial', which had been built by the Imperial War Graves Commission to commemorate 2,301 airmen who gave their lives over the Mediterranean in the Second World War and have no known graves. He and Barbara flew out from England on Saturday, 1 May with Sir Thomas White, the Australian High Commissioner in London, and stayed with the Governor of Malta, Sir Gerald Creasy, at St Anton Palace. On Monday, 3 May they went early to Valetta to watch the newly commissioned royal yacht *Britannia* approaching harbour escorted on either side by two long lines of warships of the Mediterranean Fleet. Later that morning the fine memorial in travertine marble was unveiled by the Queen in the presence of the airmen's relatives, who came from all over the world.[1]

The Garter Investiture on 14 June 1954 was the first time in the new reign that the full ceremonial was performed – in 1952 the Court had still been in mourning, and in 1953 the Investiture coincided with the Coronation. The Freybergs were bidden to the Garter luncheon in the Waterloo Chamber where the assembled company, seventy strong, sat at a single table stretching the length of that large room, and ate off gold plates with solid gold knives, forks and spoons. Afterwards Freyberg led the Garter procession headed by the Military Knights of Windsor and the Heralds of the College of Arms, which wended its way past the Moat Garden and down the hill in Lower Ward, to St George's Chapel. The star attraction, of course, was the newly knighted *Sir Winston Churchill, KG*, who beamed in acknowledgment of the cheers from the large crowds.

After a whole year spent in making alterations and renovations, Norman Tower was eventually ready for occupation in September 1954. During the course of that summer my father had managed to sell Clarendon Place to the Government of Ceylon, and in mid-September we were offered the tenancy of 88 Whitelands House, a small flat on the eighth floor of a big block in the King's Road. Finally, the Munstead problem was solved as far as my parents were concerned, by handing the property over to me.

I arrived back from the Canal Zone of Egypt to take up a staff appointment at the Headquarters London District, in time to participate in the change-over from our old home to the new one. Furniture vans removed the contents of Clarendon Place to Windsor Castle, and on 30 September my father handed over the keys of No. 7, which had served as a very happy home for us all for over thirty years, to the purchasers. That weekend my parents stayed with Lord and Lady

Burnham at Hall Barn, Beaconsfield, and on 7 October 1954 they slept in Norman Tower for the first time. Shortly afterwards they also moved into the Whitelands House flat.

My parents' main base, of course, was at Windsor where they soon got involved in the sort of activities expected of them. My father was asked to be a Trustee of the Princess Christian Nursing Home, to be a Vice-President of the Windsor Horse Show, to sit on various committees and take part in numerous local events, some of which were connected with the town of Windsor. The castle community was a thriving one, containing as it did the Dean, canons and clergy of the 'Royal Peculiar', the Military Knights of Windsor, members of the army garrison based on Victoria Barracks, as well as the large civilian element. When the Queen's Private Secretary had written that the occupant of Norman Tower was 'expected to do a certain amount of mild entertaining', it was a considerable understatement.

The London flat was a much needed adjunct. My father had many activities that took him to London, where some functions often went on until late in the evening. The M4 motorway to Windsor had yet to be built, and the old route was winding and slow. In addition to attendance at the House of Lords, my father was on the board of several companies in the City, such as the National Bank of New Zealand and Australian Mutual Provident (AMP). He also resumed attending First World War Association meetings and dinners, which he had not been able to do for thirteen years; and when he turned up at the Royal Naval Division and 29 Division Association get-togethers as if he had never been away, he was given an enthusiastic welcome. A round robin letter was handed to him at the end of the 1954 dinner of the RND Association signed by a number of his old comrades, which said: 'Greetings and good wishes from those old Hoods present at the reunion, who were so glad to see their old leader who has inspired them in the past and still commands their loyalty and admiration.'

The unveiling of the Alamein memorial by Field Marshal Viscount Montgomery took place at El Alamein in Egypt on Sunday, 24 October 1954; and Freyberg was asked to represent New Zealand. The Imperial War Graves Commission had spent the twelve years since the battle concentrating the graves of some 7,300 men of all three services within the cemetery, and building the Memorial Cloister. In a signal to the New Zealand Prime Minister Freyberg reported:

> The Memorial is most impressive and beautiful. The Cloister 270 feet long is being built against the escarpment that forms the background of the battlefield cemetery. Within its shady arcades are the names of 12,000

officers and men of the land and air forces of the Commonwealth who have no known graves.

The Service of dedication and remembrance took place at noon from the roof of the Cloister under a cloudless sky and blazing sun. The Memorial was unveiled by Field Marshal Montgomery and the dedication was pronounced by Bishop Johnston, Bishop in Egypt, well known to so many during the war when he was Archdeacon of All Saints Cathedral in Cairo. The guards of honour were formed up in front of the cloisters and by a coincidence, the New Zealand contingent, the largest from any Commonwealth country except Great Britain, stood to the north and overlooking the New Zealand section of the cemetery which, alas, contains some 1,200 graves, amongst them those of ten Battalion Commanders, and including Colonel Te Whiti Love, the first Maori to command the Maori Battalion. The smartness and size of our guard, wearing their well-known New Zealand Hats, was greatly appreciated.

While I was standing by our Guard with Sir Thomas White, the High Commissioner for Australia in the United Kingdom, Field Marshal Montgomery said to us, 'But for the New Zealanders this victory would not have been possible.'[4]

The Prime Minister of New Zealand, Sydney Holland, replied:

Your graphic descriptions of the beauty of the Memorial and its setting, and your sensitive and personal account of the dignity of the Ceremony, conveyed to us, even at this distance, a sense of direct participation. The sad and proud memories which I know the occasion must have evoked in your mind, we in New Zealand fully shared.[4]

On 30 November 1954 Freyberg was asked to participate in a BBC Television tribute to the Prime Minister, Sir Winston Churchill, on his eightieth birthday. The programme was compered by his wartime Chief of Staff, General 'Pug' Ismay, and included many of his special friends such as Bernard Baruch, the American banker, Field Marshal Viscount Alexander, and Violet Bonham Carter. Freyberg said:

A Happy Birthday, dear Winston, from your wartime friends in the Armed Forces, and particularly from the men and women of the Second New Zealand Expeditionary Force, whom you visited so frequently on the battlefields, often at times of special difficulty, when your encouragement meant so much.

Looking back into the past, do you realise it is now over forty years since you befriended a young New Zealander and sent him into the Naval Division. I was happy there – I got to know many of your young friends. Four of the most remarkable young men were my Platoon Commanders in the Gallipoli Campaign – Patrick Shaw-Stewart, Charles Lister, Arthur Asquith and Rupert Brooke. You knew them all.

Although this is my personal greeting to you, I do know what is passing through the minds of my comrades in-arms in New Zealand, including the Maoris. They would wish to join their warm-hearted birthday greetings with my own.

We salute you with veneration and deep affection.[5]

The head of the television film unit subsequently wrote to Freyberg: 'Our producer in Downing Street reports that the moment the New Zealand sheep were seen crossing over the hill the Prime Minister smiled and said "Bernard" and that this was one of the sections he particularly enjoyed.'[5]

The remainder of 1954 was spent settling in at Norman Tower. On 20 December my parents gave a house-warming party, and on Christmas Eve there was the traditional carol service at St George's Chapel with one of the Nine Lessons being read by the Deputy Constable. This was followed by mulled wine at Norman Tower for relatives and friends, and became a regular feature at every Christmas.

From 1955 onwards my father lived in a settled home in the same place, for the first time for fifteen years. During the six war years he had been continually on the move and his six years in New Zealand were similar, with Government House constantly moving between the main cities, and his frequent visits to smaller places.

Inevitably, my father's lifestyle slowed down. Moving in accordance with the requirements of the moment had become a way of life with him as with most soldiers. But the additional leisure that the change in tempo brought was not always welcomed by him. Although there was enough to keep him occupied for most of the time, with his directorships, the demands of the Windsor jobs and attendance at the House of Lords, there were moments when time seemed to stand still, and my father longed again for the more active life that he had been used to. My mother wrote of a holiday that year: 'Our rest and cure are being bliss for me – while I would say that Daddy is enjoying it as much as he enjoys any holiday – peaceful toleration rather than active pleasure.'

1956 brought two particular events – the centenary of the Institution of the Victoria Cross, and the long drawn-out Suez Crisis. During its first 100 years there had been comparatively few gatherings of holders of the Victoria Cross, and the only one of any size was the dinner the Prince of Wales gave in 1929 in the House of Lords. Now, on 26 June 1956, Freyberg was in command of the parade in Hyde Park when 297

VCs were present. The weather was perfect, a cloudless June day, with full guards of honour from the three services as a backcloth, and the VCs drawn up in front of them. The Queen arrived at 11.30 a.m. in an open landau drawn by four grey horses, to be greeted by a royal salute and the National Anthem. She was then conducted by Freyberg through the lines of the VCs, when she spoke to a large number of the able-bodied, and to every one of those in wheelchairs. The parade concluded with the VCs marching past the royal dais led by Freyberg.

There followed a government reception in Westminster Hall, a service of thanksgiving in Westminster Abbey, and a Victoria Cross Centenary Exhibition at Marlborough House. Freyberg also entertained the ten New Zealand VCs on several occasions privately. But perhaps his most daunting moment was in making the principal speech at the Victoria Cross dinner. His opening words, however, generated laughter:

> I have spoken in my time, at a great number of public dinners, and I have proposed toasts on almost every subject under the sun, and when I say that tonight I speak with 'considerable embarrassment', I mean that I feel probably as uncomfortable as you do, because it is not our national habit to invite men to dinner in order to tell them how brave they are. But I will assume that whatever 'small deed of arms', as the Knights of old used to call it, stands to the credit of each one of you, you perpetrated it from motives of self-preservation, or because you happened to notice that someone on the staff was watching and admiring you![1]

1957 brought the loss of several friends. Lord Athlone, the Constable of Windsor Castle, died in January and was given a full military funeral. Later in the year came the death of Lord Jowitt. But undoubtedly the one most mourned by my father was General Sir Howard Kippenberger, 'Kip', greatly valued as a personal friend as well as a military colleague. Freyberg admired his lack of complaints or self-pity despite the almost continual pain from his wounds. During the six years of the Second World War my father made many friends in the Division, but Kip was the one nearest to him. There were remarkable similarities between Kip and Oc Asquith, Freyberg's closest friend in the Great War. Both were quiet and reserved, both had cores of steel and inflexible determination. Neither was a Regular, but they adapted to soldiering as to the manner born and became brilliant military leaders. Both were happily married with contented family lives, and both died well before their time.

My father's devotion to Kip was recorded in the address he gave at the memorial service for him in London on 21 May 1957.[1] That their regard for each other was mutual is to be seen from letters that Kip wrote to my father. One of these was written on 9 September 1953 on board the ship taking him and his wife back to New Zealand from a visit to England, and from his last meeting with my father:

> I enlisted in 1939 and someone said he envied me the prospects of getting to know this chap Freyberg. You interviewed me briefly at Burnham and said that no doubt we would see a lot more of each other. And so it proved. Once you told me, and I heard it with pride, that our lives had been bound together in this war as yours with Arthur Asquith in the First. All the long hard wonderful years, disaster and triumph, griefs and joys, high endeavour and selfless service, and the years since of unbroken friendship.
>
> It is very possible that we will not meet again. I found it bitterly hard to part. In one way it doesn't matter. The links were forged in a hot fire.
>
> I would like you to know, I suppose you do know, that I served you with satisfaction and pride and with complete loyalty. Our years of service together have meant much in my life. Often, when I have been tempted to do or say something petty or ungenerous I have remembered my commander's example and refrained. I think better of myself that I earned your friendship and trust. Now the great days are over but it was a wonderful thing to have lived through them.[1]

On 21 March 1959 my father reached his three score years and ten. Considering the battering he had received in two world wars, his mind and body were in remarkably good shape. Compared with the recurrent bouts of illness he had had after the Great War, he had suffered very little following the second. But his seventieth birthday marked the beginning of a decline in his health – although at first it was so gradual as to be almost imperceptible.

Early October was the timing of the 1959 General Election, and on 8 October my parents went to the *Daily Telegraph* evening party to hear the results as they came in. My half-brother Martin McLaren, Bernard's stepson, was contesting Bristol North-West as the Conservative candidate, and to their pleasure and delight converted a Labour majority of 1,655 into a Conservative majority of 1,919.

That spring I became engaged to Ivry Guild, who came from a Huguenot family – the Chevalliers – who had lived in Jersey and Suffolk since the family escaped from Paris on the night of the St

[567]

Bartholomew massacre in 1572. My father arranged for us to have an evening party in St James's Palace three days beforehand, and the wedding took place in the little church of St Mary of Grace at Aspall, near to Ivry's home at Aspall Hall, on 23 July. There was a full family turnout, and my father was particularly interested in the link with Kitchener, whose mother had been a Chevallier from the same Aspall Hall – indeed he took as his title 'Lord Kitchener of Khartoum and of Aspall in Suffolk'. There is a memorial plaque to him in the church.

My father had been asked to represent the New Zealand government at the unveiling of the Athens memorial to the soldiers of the Commonwealth. My parents linked up at London Airport with Ray Queree, one of my father's NZ Staff Officers, and they flew to Greece on 9 May 1961 with over 100 other representatives including many old friends such as General Allan Adair and Admiral Baillie-Grohman. Next day they were taken to the beautifully laid out memorial at Phaleron on the coast south of Athens, where the unveiling ceremony was performed by the Duke of Gloucester in the presence of the King and Queen of Greece. Afterwards my parents were entertained to lunch at the Royal Palace of Athens, where Queen Frederika of the Hellenes spoke very warmly to Bernard about his care of the Greek royal family in Crete twenty years before. On the following day they were visited in their hotel by a delegation from the Athens Town Council headed by the mayor, who formally presented Bernard with the gold medal of the City of Athens and a diploma naming him a Hero of Crete.[1]

The battalion in which I was then serving was sent in early May 1961 to the British Cameroons where families were not allowed. My wife was then having our first child, and she went to stay with my parents at Windsor for the final three months. My father was normally a rather intermittent correspondent, and only put pen to paper when in the mood or when he had something particular to say. But during the summer of 1961 he wrote to me every week without fail, and in every letter he mentioned how much he was enjoying Ivry's company. Apart from my mother, he had spent most of his life in male company and, never having had a sister or a daughter, he found that a daughter-in-law was very much to his liking. He made a writing desk available for her in his 'Prison Room' study, and they spent many hours in each other's company. Ivry became devoted to him, and loved his good manners, his kindness and his gentleness. Like all happy relationships it suited them both, and gave to each an experience they had not enjoyed before.

When I returned to England in mid-September 1961 I found that my father's health had lost some ground, but to outward appearances at least he seemed to be reasonably well. My mother warned me later in the year, however, that there had been some disquieting developments, and the long-term prognosis was not good. The first symptoms were a very mild form of Parkinson's Disease – the biblical 'palsy'. It worried my father greatly not to be in full control of his physical faculties, and on one occasion he gave up alcohol for three months. In truth the Parkinson element appeared so late in his life that it was never to matter much, unlike another element.

The medical explanation for his condition was simple. He was suffering from the hardening of the arteries of the brain, so that the normal flow of blood to nourish his brain was just not getting through, and this was having a debilitating effect on his mind. Needless to say my mother took him to all the leading experts, and I remember early in 1963 going with his Windsor general practitioner, Dr May, to see a Harley Street specialist in this field, the day after my father had visited him. The verdict could not have been bleaker. There was no cure for his condition, and nothing could be done to alleviate it. His state of mind could only get progressively worse, until it ended in death, but there was no telling how long this might take. My mother and I agreed not to tell my father of this forecast, as it would deprive him of hope, but from little remarks he made from time to time I believe he had already sensed what was happening. My father had been a fighter all his life, and he was determined to battle on to the end. The only thing his family could do was to give him all the love and support that was in their power.

For some time the New Zealand community in London had been discussing making some form of gesture to my father, and had formed a committee for the purpose, headed by Sir Arthur Porritt. After consultation with the family it was decided to commission a bust of my father, and to present it at a public ceremony in the City. Oscar Nemon was chosen to make a head and shoulder sculpture, which was ultimately cast in bronze; and on 25 July 1962 'An evening in honour of Lieutenant-General The Lord Freyberg' was held in the Guildhall. There was a large English–New Zealand audience to hear a programme of music, a tribute by Sir Arthur Porritt, the presentation of the sculpture by the New Zealand High Commissioner, and the reply by Freyberg.

My mother and I were somewhat apprehensive about the last item in view of my father's state of health, but we worried unnecessarily. When the moment came he discarded a long, rambling address that he had prepared, and instead rose to the occasion by making a short but very effective speech which began:

[569]

There are moments which come to us in life when words fail to express the thoughts and the emotions in our hearts. This is indeed such a moment for me. My New Zealand friends have given me such a moving demonstration this evening of their friendship that I am at a loss in trying to tell them what this occasion has meant for me.

And ended:

To all those who have joined in planning what is for me and for my wife such a very great occasion, I cannot attempt adequately to express my deep appreciation and gratitude, and can only say very simply and very sincerely, thank you with all my heart. You have made me feel very proud, but even more, very humble.[1]

The occasion was a great success. My father and his family were able afterwards to meet the many friends who had come, and to admire the fine Nemon bust which was presented to New Zealand House in London, where it occupies a prominent position to this day.

Freyberg saw Churchill for the last time in the Middlesex Hospital later in 1962, where the latter had been admitted for an injury to his leg. He visited his old friend twice, and each time Winston gave him one of his enormous cigars, which the family still treasures. Freyberg told the RND Officers' Association dinner at the House of Commons on 17 November 1962: 'I have seen Sir Winston twice since his accident and have had an opportunity of talking over our Royal Naval Division days. I am hoping to visit him again shortly, when I shall be able to give him an account of our Reunion.'

The new year of 1963 found my father increasingly frail, but still with an iron determination to keep going. He attended all the fortnightly board meetings of Australian Mutual Provident and the New Zealand Bank and was present at his local Windsor activities during the first three months of 1963.

It was difficult even for his family to know how much he was taking in, as sometimes he would come out with some surprisingly shrewd remarks that showed that he had understood more of what was going on than we had thought. On Anzac day he attended his last military function with the 29 Division Association, forming up on the Horse Guards Parade in his bowler hat, with rolled umbrella and the Red Triangle Divisional Sign temporarily stitched on his coat sleeve, and then marching down Whitehall with the contingent to the Cenotaph to lay wreaths to commemorate the fallen at Gallipoli. Two days later he presided at the 29 Division dinner at the Cavalry Club. On 9 May we all went to New Zealand House for its official opening by the Queen, and on 11 May my parents had lunch and spent the afternoon at the Windsor Horse Show.

The next major occasion was the Garter ceremony on Monday, 17 June. My father was not well enough to lead the procession as he had previously done, but he was determined to attend the service. I was asked to go as his escort, and we both put on our scarlet tunics, medals and regalia. My mother had ordered an imposing Rolls-Royce to convey us in appropriate style to St George's Chapel. However my father cancelled this part of the arrangements, on grounds of needless expense, and said that he was quite capable of walking the 400 yards to the chapel. He put on his white plumed cocked hat, and I my bearskin, and clutching our swords we duly marched down the processional route, lined with Household troops, to our pews in the choir. When the service was over, we returned to Norman Tower the same way.

Lord Alanbrooke had died on the day of the Garter service. On 26 June his coffin was brought to St George's Chapel for a funeral service appropriate for a Field Marshal and Knight of the Garter. My father attended, sitting in his choir stall. A fortnight later there was another funeral in St George's Chapel – this time his own.

Our second daughter, Venetia, had been born on 28 May at the Princess Christian Nursing Home, and after the Garter Ceremony I drove her and Ivry back to Munstead. On Sunday, 23 June my parents came over for lunch. My mother's diary records: 'Bernard in a happier mood than I have known for weeks – admired the view and the house, and was full of smiles and bonhomie.' He was still bright and light-hearted when he arrived at Munstead, so much so that I could scarcely believe my eyes and ears – he was just like the Bernard of old. After he died I remembered Shakespeare's words in *Romeo and Juliet*:

> How oft when men are at the point of death
> Have they been merry! Which their keepers call
> A lightning before death.

The last of several thousands of letters my father sent me over a period of forty years was written two days before he died:

My dear Paul
I would so like to help towards all the expense you had for Nursing Home etc. over Venetia, so do let me know how much it all came to as soon as you can.
  With much love
                              Daddy.[1]

[571]

I asked my mother later whether she had suggested to my father that he should write it. She told me she had no knowledge of the letter until I showed it to her, and that it was entirely his own doing.

The last day of my father's life is well documented. My mother's diary for 4 July 1963 begins:

> As I write this I am writing the end of the biggest chapter of my life. We started a normal day in the flat. Bernard had breakfast and seemed rather cheerful, and dressed himself painstakingly but with his usual willpower. I saw him off with Bert to drive him to his Bank Board.

Bert was a freelance London chauffeur who often drove my parents. Sir Patrick Duff, a fellow director at the Bank of New Zealand, takes up the account in a letter written to my mother the following day:

> Bernard had quite a bit of interest and enjoyment at the Bank yesterday. There were two meetings – the Board and the Annual General Meeting, and there were consequently more people about. He had a small glass of sherry, which we recently discovered that he liked, and he was recommending me to try it before lunch. I sat next to him at lunch – we were about 14 in all. He asked me if there were any speeches. As Arnold was taking him to the House of Lords, I left a bit before him. But I heard from Geoffrey Davies this morning that all went according to plan up to the time when he got to the House of Lords.[1]

My father listened to Parliamentary Questions and the first part of the Second Reading Debate on the Peerage Bill that followed. My mother collected him at about 4.30 p.m. to drive him back to Windsor. Neither of them knew at this time that their great friend Lord Burnham had died that morning. My parents arrived an hour later at Norman Tower at the same time as Miss Lock, who used to give my father massage. My mother's diary continued:

> Bernard said that he would like to have massage. I went into his room a few minutes after they had started and he was complaining about what he thought was cramp in his leg, but it soon became obvious that he was very ill as he started to moan and breathe with gasps. I rang up Dr May who arrived within half an hour. All the time Bernard was getting worse and never spoke or regained consciousness. Dr May warned me that he thought it was the end.

Dr May wrote subsequently: 'On 4 July 1963 I received an emergency call to Windsor Castle at 6.30 p.m. and found that Lord Freyberg had collapsed with a ruptured abdominal aorta. I arranged for him to be admitted to the King Edward VII Hospital at Windsor.'

What had happened was that my father's old Gallipoli stomach wound had opened up. Dr May and my mother travelled with him in the ambulance to the hospital.

I had had a normal day at HQ London District, returning to Munstead by train at about 8 p.m., and telephoned Norman Tower as soon as I got home. My mother had just arrived back there from hospital to collect some necessities. She told me what had happened, and repeated Dr May's warning. Ivry and I collected as many flowers as we could, and I set off by car for Windsor arriving at the hospital at about 10 p.m. I was asked to wait in an anteroom until the ward sister came to collect me. On the way up the broad main staircase of the hospital she told me quietly that my father had died an hour before. I was reunited with my mother and together we went into my father's room. The strained and troubled look on his face had gone, and he looked young again and at peace.

The evening before his funeral on 10 July, his coffin was brought to St George's Chapel and lay there for the night draped with the Union Jack and the New Zealand flag. A bearer party from his old regiment carried his coffin out of the chapel to the music of Handel's 'Toll for the Brave', and as the hearse left, the Windsor Castle Guard turned out and presented arms.

Sir Patrick Duff described the final journey:

Two or three hours later a small party, about 20, of the General's and Lady Freyberg's nearest relatives and a few most privileged friends set out from Norman Tower to the spot, some 35 miles away, to which the young Colonel Freyberg, VC, in the full flush of his fame after the First World War, had led his bride-to-be, with a small bevy of friends including Sir J. M. Barrie and Arthur Asquith to be married in St Martha's Church on St Martha's Hill.

They had chosen this to be their burial ground.

It was deep in the country. Towards the journey's end, the lanes grew narrower and the hill steeper until cars could go no further. The party then went onwards on foot. The way lay uphill, at first through oaks making in places a tunnel of deep shade over the track, with sand deep and loose underfoot. Further up there were stands of pines, the ground covered with pine needles and criss-crossed with their gnarled roots.

This track was the ancient Pilgrims' Way by which pilgrims went from Winchester to Canterbury. One of the party at least, a little out of breath and slipping on the pine needles could not help smiling to think how like the General it was to lead us by so exciting and arduous a route. We emerged at length on to the bare summit where the coffin (which had gone up before) draped with the Union Jack and New Zealand flag lay beside the grave.

Hard by was the little Church of St Martha where a church has stood from the earliest days of Christianity in Britain. The hill looked down over far green distances, towards the north of London in one direction, towards the Channel in another.

Many wreaths had come up with the coffin – prominent was a noble one from the Government of New Zealand and another tiny one 'To our darling grandfather' from Colonel Paul Freyberg's two little children.

We went into the little church where the Vicar said a few prayers: thence only a step outside to the graveside. There was a salver heaped with fresh rose petals: Lady Freyberg, with one last lingering gesture, let a handful of petals flutter down upon the coffin and the rest of the small party did likewise.[1]

My father had stayed in harness to the very end as he had been determined to do, and he died after a full and busy day. His life had been one of adventure and action in many parts of the world, but eventually he returned home to lie in the quiet English churchyard of St Martha's, less than twenty miles from where he was born nearly three-quarters of a century before.

Epilogue

Whenever he was called upon to give a toast, my father used to say, 'Here's Luck!' And in his later years he often remarked to me that he had been very lucky in life. This was true. He had survived ten years of fighting in the First and Second World Wars, enduring a large number of wounds, near-misses and accidents of all kinds, and he could not have done so without a greater measure of good luck than is allowed to most people.

He was lucky too in other ways. He was at the right place at the right time at the beginning of both wars. It was by chance and not by design that he arrived in London in August 1914 at the moment when the Royal Naval Division was being formed. Again, in 1939, it was a matter of luck for him that New Zealand did not have an officer of the right age and experience to lead their Expeditionary Force. And it was through good fortune or luck that in the middle of the First World War he met the lady who was later to become his wife and share his life for more than forty years.

In many ways this last was the most important. By temperament my parents were ideally suited to each other, and their marriage was an extremely happy one. This was as apparent to those outside the family as it was to those within: after my father died Sir Owen Morshead, the Librarian at Windsor Castle, wrote a tribute in *The Times* which ended: 'His past of which he seldom spoke was the pride of all but himself. His modest bearing, his generosity of mind, and the perfection of his married life, these were his true honours'.

Marriage gave my father a stability and self-confidence that were to become two of his main characteristics. He was able to give his whole attention to his profession secure in the knowledge that he had the full support and love of his wife, and a happy home to return to whatever happened. It was a factor of inestimable value, which enabled him to survive the two major disasters of his career – being invalided out of the Army in 1937, and the Crete defeat in 1941.

[575]

His being retired from the Army was the more traumatic mishap of the two. My father had been a keen and ambitious soldier until then, so that to be compulsorily retired on grounds that he was physically unfit was a devastating blow. That he was able, in his mid-forties, to build a new career and way of life was a tribute both to his own zest for living and to Barbara. Her advice was always sensible and wise, and throughout their marriage my father took more notice of her views than those of anyone else.

Crete – involving a military defeat at the hands of the enemy – was a different kind of setback. My father was in no way responsible for the background in which the reverse took place, but again he showed his determination not to be beaten and, in the two years that followed, he led one of the most successful of all the Western Desert formations. My father's perseverance, vitality and determination during these two years calls to mind President Calvin Coolidge's dictum:

> Nothing in the world can take the place of persistence. Talent will not; nothing is more common than unsuccessful men with talent. Genius will not; unrewarded genius is almost a proverb. Education will not: the world is full of educated derelicts. Persistence and determination alone are omnipotent.

There was one other important ingredient in my father's general approach to soldiering, and indeed to most other things in his life – common sense. It made him as concerned with his soldiers' well-being off the battlefield as well as on it, and his approach and ideas on the subject were ahead of his time. He had seen much unnecessary suffering and loss of life through lack and misuse of medical resources in the First World War; therefore in the Second he gave high priority to the provision of first-class facilities and modern techniques. He instituted the founding of suitable clubs and amenities, where his soldiers could spend their leaves and leisure. And over matters of discipline he introduced a code of conduct suitable for non-regular soldiers, and trusted to the good sense of the vast majority of his troops to abide by its spirit.

All these factors contributed to the high morale of his troops during the first four years of the Second World War, but the New Zealand Division went through a difficult period during the summer of 1944. For the only time in the war there was a slackening of discipline and morale. Some blamed the malaise on the frustrations resulting from the Cassino battles but my father realised that the cause went deeper. He had never forgotten that he commanded a force of civilian soldiers taken from their normal occupations, and serving thousands of miles from home; and he recognised that the basic problem was that the men had been asked to serve in the field for too long. As soon as it was evident that the war was going to last well into 1945, my father proposed to the New Zealand government that all those who had been overseas for more than three years should return to New Zealand for good, having done their duty, and be replaced by new drafts. This was accepted by the government, and his proposals were implemented. There was no further trouble. His percipience was not recognised at the time, but his foresight was vindicated by the remarkable performance of the Division in its final offensive which, in three weeks, took it the 250 miles from the banks of the Senio River to the city of Trieste.

After all the storms and tribulations of the war years, the afternoon and evening of my father's life were golden. His six years as Governor-General of New Zealand were very happy ones and gave him the opportunity to display leadership qualities in a civilian setting, which did not necessarily follow from his military training and background. With his good manners and innate charm he had a 'classlessness' about him which, allied to a natural sympathy for the underdog, seemed to put people at their ease.

My father had been brought up in the vigorous but straight-laced atmosphere of New Zealand at the turn of the last century. His honesty and truthfulness, for example, were instilled into him at school. The importance of physical fitness was another lesson he learnt in his early years. His sense of humour was of the robust rather than the subtle variety, but he had the ability to laugh at himself and to tell jokes at his own expense. For example, soon after the end of the Second World War my father and General Steve Weir were travelling by train in uniform to Leicester to watch a rugby match between the New Zealand and British Army teams. Two cockneys were on the same train, and stared goggle-eyed at the two generals when they made their way to the restaurant-car. 'Did you see him?' said one to the other. 'Did you see him and all his ribbons? My God, he must have been careful.'

Many stories have been told of my father's intrepidity. Early in 1917 Major R. C. Foot, commanding D/310 Battery, Royal Artillery, had been ordered to report to the Hood Battalion headquarters. When Foot got to the usual site for a battalion headquarters in the third line of trenches, he found simply an arrow pointing forward; in the second line he found the same. Battalion headquarters was in a dugout in the front line. It was after dark by now – nearly time for dinner. After the meal, Freyberg asked his adjutant to wake him in forty minutes, pushed aside what lay on the mess table in front of him, dropped his head on his forearms and fell asleep at once. Forty minutes later the adjutant touched his elbow: he was instantly wide awake. 'Come on, Gunner,' he said to Foot, 'let's go for a walk.' He took Foot through the British wire, and through the German wire, to lie for some time under the German parapet, listening to the German soldiers chatting. Foot commented later: 'His enormous vitality was infectious to men both older and younger than himself, and as a leader in battle he had no peer'.

His soldiers in the Second World War loved the fact that, even as a general whose first concern was to defeat the enemy, my father never lost his personal interest in them and their well-being. They were aware that he was a soldier's soldier intent on creating a team to achieve a common aim, and that he still led from the front.

I had a happy relationship with my father all my life. He was invariably understanding and tolerant of my failings, and was determined that the difficult relationship he had had with his own father should not be perpetuated into another generation. At the same time living under his roof was not always easy. The problem was not so much being the son of a well-known father but in making the adjustments necessary to cope with his personality which was stronger than that of any other person I have ever known. Not that he was domineering or inconsiderate – in fact he was very much the reverse. Many people have commented on how gentle and kind he was in his dealings with individuals. For him nearly everything with which he was associated had a very strong *personal* flavour. He was never interested in abstract theory, or with events with which he was no longer associated. Once the personal link had gone, his interest declined or disappeared.

At the same time he had a quality that is difficult to define or analyse accurately, but which nevertheless played a large part in his achievement. I am not alone in finding it hard to define this quality. A one-time head chaplain of the New Zealand Division, Rev. Jim McKenzie, wrote, as recorded by Jim Burrows in *Pathway among Men*:

> Perhaps more than any man I have known [he] made me ponder over the elements of greatness. What is it that makes one man so eminent, so much above, and so powerful over his fellows? I don't know. But in him it was a combination of endowments immediately felt but impossible to analyse and explain. Few men can hold high office humbly and use great power justly. He was one of the few. In him power did not corrupt.

My father was born without family influence, or wealth. What he accomplished came as a result of his own effort, whether it was being a champion swimmer, commanding troops, winning the Victoria Cross, or being Governor-General. He had his reverses as well as successes, but was basically unmoved by either. Kipling's famous lines, 'If you can meet with Triumph and Disaster / And treat those two impostors just the same', might have been written with Bernard Freyberg in mind.

APPENDIXES

APPENDIX I

A Note on Unpublished Sources

After my father died in July 1963 I wrote to some twenty-five of his friends for information about his life in New Zealand between 1891 and 1914. I had a kind and generous response varying from a single anecdote scribbled in pencil on half a sheet of paper to a careful account of the Freyberg family, typewritten on twenty foolscap pages, from a doctor who had lived in the same street as the Freybergs in Wellington. All these contemporaries are now dead, but they have left behind a record of what life was like in New Zealand at the turn of the century.

There was another invaluable source of information. When it came to correspondence my mother was one of nature's magpies – she never threw anything away. When I started on research for this book I found a dozen trunks in the cellar of our family home at Munstead, each containing hundreds of letters and documents, and some of which had not been opened since my mother's Edwardian youth. The contents were bewildering in their range and variety: hotel bills from Alexandria, Madrid and St Moritz; and handwritten letters from H. H. Asquith, James Barrie, Winston Churchill and other well-known figures. And, of course, from my father.

The letters from my father to my mother began in 1917, when there were eleven of them; in 1918 they rose to twenty-one; for 1919, 1920 and 1921 there are eighty-eight, ninety-four and sixty-nine respectively; and in 1922 sixty-nine, up to 14 June when Bernard and Barbara were married. All are preserved in their original envelopes just as he wrote them. A large number more were written after my parents were married, whenever they were separated, and particularly during the Second World War. These letters give a vivid account of my father's life and what he was doing at any given moment.

My mother also kept a personal diary. She began it in 1902 when she was fifteen, but there are gaps between 1914 and 1930 when she had young children to look after, although she later remedied the omissions by recounting stories of the houses she had lived in during those years. From 1930 until her death in September 1973 she wrote a day-by-day record, which covers my father's life in the 1930s, the Second World War, their time at Government House in New Zealand, and my father's final decade at Windsor.

Thus my father's life is well documented from his arrival in New Zealand on 1 December 1891 until his death on 4 July 1963. There was one exception, however: the period from his leaving New Zealand on 27 March 1914 until his arrival in Liverpool on 24 August 1914. Even his family had little idea what happened to him during those five months – a period about which he was always very reserved. Then one day in 1976, as related in Chapter 3, a packet arrived at Munstead containing a number of his letters written while he was in America in 1914, plus a scrapbook. These documents were sent to the family from the estate of Miss Queenie Penboss.

My father called the account of his experiences in the First World War 'A Linesman in Picardy', which was written at the persuasion of Sir James Barrie but never published. My mother kept a First World War scrapbook, compiled after they were married, which incorporates many letters that were sent to him after he won the VC on the Ancre in 1916 and press cuttings about his exploits. It was the first of many: there are fourteen scrapbooks for the period 1919–39, seven for 1939–45, twelve of Government House, New Zealand 1946–52, and five of Windsor 1953–63.

As mentioned in the Introduction, my father started work on his memoirs of the Second World War, but he never got beyond Crete. He covered the months from September 1939–September 1940 under the provisional title 'Historical Review'; and the Greek campaign under 'The New Zealand Division in Greece, 1941'.

He wrote his first 'Report on the Battle for Crete' for the New Zealand Minister of Defence while he was still in Egypt in the second half of 1941. After the war, while he was Governor-General of New Zealand, he added a number of chapters or sections about different aspects of the Greek and Crete campaigns, and he wrote more when he was at Windsor Castle. In all, his notes run to several hundred pages. He contemplated publishing his version of events, but always came up against the security problem, since ULTRA remained classified during his lifetime.

My father's accounts of the battles in North Africa and Italy from June 1941 to the end of the war in May 1945 were usually written shortly after the events themselves, and produced as special reports, or long signals to the Minister of Defence in New Zealand. Most of these were made available to the official NZ historians, but some of the more sensitive documents were withheld as the persons concerned were then still alive. These are released now for the first time.

Family Tree

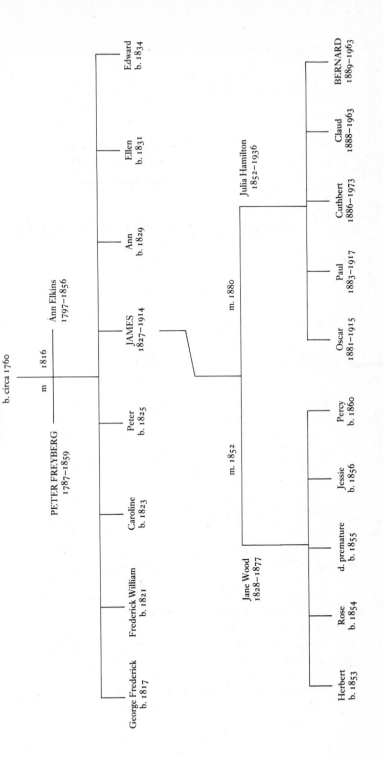

IVAN PETROVITCH FREYBERG
b. circa 1760

PETER FREYBERG
1787–1859

m 1816

Ann Elkins
1797–1856

George Frederick
b. 1817

Frederick William
b. 1821

Caroline
b. 1823

Peter
b. 1825

JAMES
1827–1914

Ann
b. 1829

Ellen
b. 1831

Edward
b. 1834

Jane Wood
1828–1877

m. 1852

Herbert
b. 1853

Rose
b. 1854

d. premature
b. 1855

Jessie
b. 1856

Percy
b. 1860

Julia Hamilton
1852–1936

m. 1880

Oscar
1881–1915

Paul
1883–1917

Cuthbert
1886–1973

Claud
1888–1963

BERNARD
1889–1963

APPENDIX III

Bernard Freyberg's Swimming Medals

SILVER	1900		25 yds	Under 12
SILVER	1900		25 yds	Under 12
SILVER	BLANK			
SILVER	1900		25 yds	Under 13
SILVER	1901		Plunge	
GOLD	1902		50 yds	
GOLD	1904/5	NZASA*	100 yds	
GOLD	1904/5	NZASA	440 yds	
GOLD	1906	NZASA	100 yds	
GOLD	1906	NZASA	200 yds	
GOLD	1906	NEW ZEALAND†	100 yds	
SILVER	1906	NEW ZEALAND	200 yds	
SILVER	1906	NEW ZEALAND	220 yds	
GOLD	1906	NEW ZEALAND	440 yds	
GOLD	1906	NEW ZEALAND	880 yds	
GOLD	1906	NEW ZEALAND	1 mile	
GOLD	1907	NZASA	220 yds	
GOLD	1908	NZASA	440 yds	
SILVER	1909	NZASA	440 yds	
GOLD	1910	NZASA	100 yds	
SILVER	1910	NZASA	220 yds	
GOLD	1910	NEW ZEALAND	100 yds	
GOLD	1911	NZASA	440 yds	

*NZASA   New Zealand Amateur Swimming Association
†NEW ZEALAND   Championship

APPENDIX IV

Notes and Sources

Note to the Reader. The full details of any book are only given on its first mention in these Notes. Thereafter the reference is abbreviated.

Chapter 1: The Family Background (pages 7–10)

1 Family Tree of Homagius, *Neues Allgemeines Deutschen Adels Lexicon.* 1861; *Dictionnaire Historique et Biographique de la Suisse.* 1926.
2 The history of the Freyberg suit of armour is described in full in the catalogue of the Wallace Collection.
3 The drawings of the Milan coat of arms remained in England with James Freyberg's first family.
4 USSR History Institute, letter of 28 June 1983.
5 E. Amburger, *Geschichte der Behördeorganisation Russlands von Peter des Grossen bis 1917* (Leiden, 1966).
6 *Horowhenua Chronicle* (NZ), 6 February 1914.
7 Freyberg Papers. Ann Elkins died on 21 August 1856, aged 59, and Peter on 28 March 1859, aged 72. They were both buried in a family grave in Brompton Cemetery, as were some of their children.
8 *Burke's Peerage*, 1956.
9 Letter from Captain Geoffrey Freyberg, RN, 30 September 1963, which mentions a house built in Folkestone by James Freyberg, known locally as 'Freyberg's Folly'. Nothing more is known.
10 *New Zealand Times*, Wednesday, 2 December 1891. 'Aorangi' means 'cloud in the sky' or 'cloud piercer' and is the Maori name for Mount Cook.

Note. It has not proved possible to follow the English branch of the Freyberg family back to Switzerland in a direct line, for two reasons: first the fire in 1901 in the Freyberg house in Hawker Street, Wellington, which destroyed nearly all the family records; second, the two generations of Freybergs preceding those who came to England after the end of the Napoleonic wars in 1815 lived in Russia, and only very limited access has so far been possible to late eighteenth- and early nineteenth-century records in Soviet hands.

Chapter 2: New Zealand (pages 11–26)

1 Reminiscences of the Freyberg family by Dr Macdonald Wilson sent to author, 1963.
2 Letters from Dick Hegglum, January 1964 ff.
3 Harry Hardham, art. in *Sea Spray* magazine, vol. I, No. 4, 15 March 1946, pp. 10–11.
4 Sir James Elliott, *Firth of Wellington* (Whitcombe & Tombs, 1937).
5 Letter from Dr J. S. Monro, 14 March 1968.
6 Obituary by W. T. Churchward, Bernard Freyberg's swimming coach, in NZ *Marlborough Express*, 9 July 1963.
7 Statistics supplied by George Kaye, 18 May 1983 ff.
8 Anthony Alpers, *Katherine Mansfield* (Jonathan Cape, 1954. Revised and reissued 1980).
9 Katherine Mansfield, *The Scholarship*. Written 1917–18. The full story appears in *Undiscovered Country: The New Zealand Stories of Katherine Mansfield* (Longman, 1974).
10 Freyberg Papers.
11 *NZ Dental Journal*, vol. 85, Nos 379–380, January–April 1989.
12 Letter from Sir Vincent Meredith, 15 November 1963.
13 Researches by Brigadier J. Ferris Fuller, 1989.
14 *Horowhenua Chronicle*, 27 March 1914.
15 Letters from Mrs Lesbia Paine (née Wilson), 28 June 1975 ff. See Note 5, Chapter 3.
16 Doreen Brown and Evan H. Williams, *NZ Amateur Swimming Association – A Short History* (1965), p. 17.
17 Letter from Sir Stephen Allen, 8 December 1963.
18 NZ Military Forces File D2/545, vol. 2 of 1912.
19 Letter and notes from J. O. C. Neill, 11 February 1968.

Chapter 3: A Price on his Head? (pages 27–34)

1 Bermuda newspaper article, March 1976.

2   *Wellingtonian*, vol. 30, No. 2.
3   Letter from Bernard Freyberg to Barbara McLaren, 16 January 1918.
4   Jim Tuck, *Pancho Villa and John Reed* (University of Arizona Press, 1984), pp. 56, 98–102.
5   Lesbia Paine was the daughter of Helen Wilson of Levin, NZ, who wrote *The First Eighty Years* in which Bernard is mentioned several times.
6   Violet Bonham Carter, *Winston Churchill As I Knew Him* (Eyre & Spottiswoode and Collins, 1965), pp. 410–12.
7   Diary of Sergeant A. E. M. Rhind, HQ 1 NZ Division.
8   *The Letters of Rupert Brooke*, ed. Geoffrey Keynes (Faber, 1968), p. 645. 'Beb' Asquith may have been with the RND for a short time.
9   Patrick O'Hea, *Reminiscences of the Mexican Revolution* (Sphere, 1981), pp. 156–7.
10 NZ Military Forces File g2/545, vol. 2 of 1914.
11 Shipping Registers in London Guildhall Library.

Chapter 4: The Royal Naval Division and the 'Argonauts' (pages 35–52)

1   Martin Gilbert, *Winston S. Churchill* vol. III, *1914–1916* (Heinemann, 1971), pp. 111–12, 47.
2   Philip Magnus, *Kitchener* (Murray, 1958), p. 304.
3   Alan Hercus, *Freyberg* (A. H. & A. W. Reed, 1946), p. 17.
4   Richardson's report to NZ government, August 1914. Official NZ Papers.
5   Winston S. Churchill, *The Second World War*, vol. III, *The Grand Alliance* (Cassell, 1950), p. 242.
6   Witnessed by Surgeon W. J. McCracken, doctor of Hood Bn, RND, and told to the author at Windsor in September 1963.
7   Bonham Carter, *Winston Churchill As I Knew Him*, pp. 362–5, 408–12.
8   Freyberg Papers.
9   Peter Singleton-Gates, *General Lord Freyberg, VC* (Michael Joseph, 1963), p. 30.
10 Letters and postcard from the Penboss package; see Chapter 3.
11 Backhouse diaries given by his widow to the RND Association, who allowed the author unrestricted use of them. Now in the Imperial War Museum.
12 Douglas Jerrold, *The Royal Naval Division* (Hutchinson, 1923), ch. 2.
13 Dispatches of Field Marshal Sir John French, October 1914.
14 Christopher Hassall, *Edward Marsh, Patron of the Arts: A Biography* (Longman, 1959), pp. 300, 364.

15 The Coutts ledgers give a record of what Freyberg was doing over the next few years, when this was not otherwise known.
16 Address by Freyberg at Arthur Asquith's funeral, August 1939.
17 Douglas Jerrold, *Georgian Adventure* (Collins, 1938), p. 201.
18 Obituary of F. S. Kelly, *Eton College Chronicle*, 7 December 1916.
19 *Gallipoli 1915*, an anthology collected by Lady Monica Salmond (née Grenfell) and printed privately.
20 *Letters of Rupert Brooke*, ed. Keynes, pp. 534, 563, 635, 638, 645–6, 653, 670, 685, 688.
21 Christopher Hassall, *Biography of Rupert Brooke* (Faber, 1964), pp. 475, 487, 488, 499, 511–13.
22 Obituary, *The Times*, 1 January 1918; *Eton College Chronicle*.
23 Ronald Knox, *Life of Patrick Shaw-Stewart* (Collins, 1920).
24 Geoffrey Cox, *The Road to Trieste* (Heinemann, 1947), p. 30.
25 Freyberg's account of Rupert Brooke's burial, *Daily Telegraph*, 23 June 1961.

Chapter 5: Gallipoli (pages 53–74)

1 Backhouse diary.
2 Interview with General Sir George Richardson (ex-AQMG, RND), in *NZ Herald* in 1931.
3 Brigadier-General C. F. Aspinall-Oglander, *The Official History 'Gallipoli'* (Heinemann, 1929), vol. I, pp. 164–6.
4 Joseph Murray, *Call to Arms* (Kimber, 1980). Also private letters.
5 Robert Rhodes James, *Gallipoli* (Batsford, 1965), pp. 3–13, 71, 77–9, 84, 101–2, 120, 183.
6 Jerrold, *Royal Naval Division*, pp. 72–95, 130–8, 149–67.
7 Dan van der Vat, *The Ship that Changed the World* (Hodder, 1985), pp. 183 ff.
8 Sherman Miles, 'Notes on the Dardanelles campaign', *US Coastal Artillery Journal*, lxi–lxii (1924–5).
9 Field Marshal Lord Birdwood, *Khaki and Gown: An Autobiography* (Ward, Lock, 1941), p. 252.
10 A memorial oration, given in 1951, for New Zealand doctors killed on active service. Printed in *NZ Medical Journal*, vol. LI No. 276, July 1951.
11 Christopher Hassall, *Edward Marsh*, p. 359.
12 Bonham Carter, *Winston Churchill As I Knew Him*, pp. 408–12.
13 Figures supplied by Commonwealth War Graves Commission, PUR 12/2 (F68), 19 September 1984.

14 Charles Lister, *Letters and Recollections*, with a memoir by his father, Lord Ribblesdale (Fisher Unwin, 1917).
15 Bernard Freyberg, 'Why we failed at Gallipoli', *Sunday Times*, 29 April 1956.
16 General Sir Ian Hamilton, *The Commander*, ed. Anthony Farrar-Hockley (Hollis & Carter, 1957).
17 Lt.-Col. C. O. Head, *A Glance at Gallipoli* (Eyre & Spottiswoode, 1931), ch. 9.

Chapter 6: The Somme and the Battle of the Ancre (pages 75–96)

1 Jerrold, *Royal Naval Division*, pp. 185–9, 205. The Salonika army was a British and French expeditionary force intended to aid Serbia, but it established a new 'Macedonian Front' from which an eventual Balkan campaign could be launched.
2 Joseph Murray's diary and letters.
3 Freyberg Papers.
4 Recollections of Miss Julia McRae, and Coutts ledgers.
5 Barbara related this story at the dinner of the RND Association at the House of Commons, 13 November 1965, on the anniversary of the battle of the Ancre, at which she and Violet Bonham Carter were guests of honour.
6 Recollections of Surgeon W. J. McCracken, 1963.
7 *Lady Cynthia Asquith's Diaries 1915–18* (Hutchinson, 1968), p. 160. The Introduction is unsigned and the editor not named.
8 Jerrold, *Georgian Adventure*, p. 158.
9 Letter from Dr McCracken to Barbara Freyberg, 10 September 1963.
10 Murray, *Call to Arms*, pp. 120–1.
11 Letter from Lionel 'Cardy' Montague to his mother, 20 November 1916.
12 Correspondence with Mrs Greaves, 1983–4.
13 Lyn Macdonald, *Somme* (Michael Joseph, 1983), p. 336.
14 *The Times*, 23 November 1916.
15 Letter from Violet Bonham Carter to Barbara Freyberg, 8 July 1963.
16 *London Gazette*, 15 December 1916.
17 Letter from J. P. Firth, 16 December 1916.
18 *The Story of the 29th Division*, ed. Captain Stair Gillon (Nelson, 1925), p. 90.

Chapter 7: The Hindenburg Line and Passchendaele (pages 97–117)

1 Denis Mackail, *The Story of JMB* (Peter Davies, 1941), pp. 451, 499–500.

2   *Lady Cynthia Asquith's Diaries 1915–18*, pp. 257, 268, 295–7, 350–1, 374–93. The portrait of Freyberg by Ambrose McEvoy is now in the Imperial War Museum.

3   Letter to Barbara McLaren, 23 February 1917. Freyberg Papers.

4   Letter from Surgeon McCracken, 10 August 1963. Freyberg Papers.

5   Letter from Patrick Shaw-Stewart, Christmas 1916. Freyberg Papers.

6   Letter from Charles Howard to Freyberg, 16 September 1960. Freyberg Papers.

7   One day while Freyberg was convalescing from his wounds a small parcel arrived at his bedside. It contained a platinum fob watch of considerable value, but with no indication where it came from. He asked a number of friends and acquaintances whom he thought might have sent it, but they all denied doing so. He never found out who sent it but Lady Desborough, a prominent society hostess, was thought to have been the likely donor.

8   Letter from Royal Archives, Windsor Castle, 5 August 1983.

9   'Exceptional measures to achieve surprise with seven divisions – the massing of 324 tanks on ground favourable to armour and employment of 1003 guns without prior registration by new method of surveying. Results – complete success of Cambrai battle.' From *Byng of Vimy: General and Governor-General* by Jeffrey Williams (Leo Cooper, 1983).

Chapter 8: 88 Brigade: Bailleul, Last Ypres and Lessines (pages 118–139)

1   Robert Rhodes James, *Gallipoli*, p. 307.

2   Previously unpublished letters from Sir James Barrie to Freyberg. Freyberg Papers.

3   Letter from General Sir Aylmer Hunter-Weston to Freyberg, 29 January 1918. Freyberg Papers.

4   *Official History: France and Belgium, 1918*, vol. II (Macmillan, 1935), p. 512.

5   Memorandum by General Nicholson, GOC 34 Division. Freyberg Papers.

6   Figures from 'The Military Effort', Official Statistics 1918.

7   Letter to Barbara McLaren from A. Asquith, War Office, 27 June 1918.

8   Gillon, *Story of the 29th Division*, pp. 198–227.

9   *Official History: France and Belgium, 1918*, vol. III (Macmillan, 1935), p. 320.

10   Supplement to *London Gazette*, 1 February 1919.

11   Supplement to *London Gazette*, 4 October 1919.

12   Singleton-Gates, *General Lord Freyberg, VC.*

Chapter 9: Return to England (pages 140–152)

1 Freyberg Papers, including his bank statements; and Barbara McLaren's letters to her mother 1919–21.
2 *London Gazette*, 5 March 1919.
3 Staff College, Camberley, Records.
4 Mary Motley, *Morning Glory* (Longman, 1961), pp. 18–19.
5 Cynthia Asquith, *Portrait of Barrie* (Barrie, 1954), pp. 103–4. pp. 103–4.
6 Letter from General Sir Allan Adair to the author, 27 June 1984.
7 *Letters and Journals of Sir Alan Lascelles* (Hamish Hamilton, 1986), pp. 332–3.
8 Denis Mackail, *The Story of JMB*, pp. 552–3.
9 *Letters of J. M. Barrie*, ed. Viola Meynell (Peter Davies, 1942), pp. 146, 176, 190.
10 Churchill *Second World War*, vol. III, p. 242.
11 *The Wellingtonian*, vol. 30 No. 2, November 1921.
12 Barrie's address on 'Courage', given at St Andrews University, 3 May 1922 (Edinburgh University Press, 1922).

Chapter 10: A New Family (pages 153–157)

1 *The Letters of Edwin Lutyens to his wife, Lady Emily*, ed. Clayre Percy and Jane Ridley (Collins, 1985), p. 428.

Chapter 11: Only Five Hundred Yards Short (pages 158–166)

1 Freyberg Papers.
2 *Household Brigade Magazine*, 1926.
3 *Handbook of the Channel Swimming Association*, ed. W. Floyd (1956).
4 BCF's copy of official confidential reports.

Chapter 12: Unit Administration and Half-Pay (pages 167–179)

1 Letter from Sergeant Frank Worsman to Barbara Freyberg, May 1964.
2 Barbara's diary.
3 *A Study of Unit Administration* (Gale and Polden, 1933).
4 Freyberg Papers.
5 *The Times*, 20 June 1934.

6 Letter from J. M. Barrie to Barbara Freyberg, 16 November 1934.
7 Diana Hopkinson, *The Incense Tree* (Routledge, 1968), p. 118.
8 Letter to the author from General Sir James Marshall-Cornwall, 5 July 1977.

Chapter 13: Change of Direction (pages 180–199)

1 Army List, 1935.
2 BCF personal medical documents. Freyberg kept records of his medical problems in his personal papers, which have been used for this chapter.
3 Letter from Sir James Barrie, 12 June 1937. Scrapbook.
4 Other Freyberg Papers.
5 Sir Roderick Jones, *A Life in Reuters* (Hodder, 1950).
6 BCF's letters to his son Paul Freyberg, 21 and 26 September 1939.
7 Barbara's diary for October 1939.

Chapter 14: Commander of 2 New Zealand Expeditionary Force (pages 200–219)

1 *Official History of New Zealand in the Second World War 1939–45*, Documents relating to New Zealand's participation in the Second World War, vol. I, 1949, Signals, 27–40 (War History Branch, Department of Internal Affairs, Wellington, 1949).
2 Major-General W. G. Stevens, *Freyberg VC: The Man* (Reed, 1965), pp. 14–18, 37.
3 Freyberg Papers.
4 Letter dated 12 February 1940 to Freyberg from Major-General Sir John Duigan, Chief of NZ General Staff.
5 *Egyptian Mail*, 14 February 1940; and British newspapers.
6 Memorial address, *NZ Medical Journal*, vol. L No. 275, April 1951.
7 *Official History NZ*: Documents, vol. I, Signals 77–84.

Chapter 15: 'If you are not careful you will lose Egypt' (pages 220–237)

1 Freyberg's 'Historical Review', September 1939 to September 1940, pp. 1–82.
2 Other Freyberg Papers.
3 John Hetherington, *Blamey* (F. W. Cheshire, 1954), pp. 111, 121.

Chapter 16: The Campaign in Greece (pages 238–262)

1 'The New Zealand Division in Greece', historical account (unpublished) written by Freyberg, 1941.
2 *Official History NZ*: W. G. McClymont, *To Greece* (1959).
3 Sir Charles Mott-Radclyffe, *Foreign Body in the Eye* (Leo Cooper, 1975), pp. 55–87. Mott-Radclyffe was later Member of Parliament for Windsor for twenty-eight years. In 1936 he had served in the British Legation in Athens before moving to Rome. In November 1940 he returned to Greece as a captain in the Rifle Brigade and GSO 3 to General Gambier-Parry, Head of the British Military Mission to Greece during the war between Italy and Greece in Albania. He knew most of the Greek and British personalities involved, and from the headquarters of the Military Mission in Athens he was admirably placed to observe events. He also had access to the diaries of Colonel Jasper Blunt, RA (the British Military Attaché).
4 John Baynes, *The Forgotten Victor: General Sir Richard O'Connor* (Brassey's, 1989), pp. 108, 123.
5 Brigadier C. N. Barclay, *Against Great Odds* (Blake & Mackenzie, 1955), pp. 64–74.
6 Churchill, *Second World War*, vol. III: (a) p. 58; (b) p. 90; (c) p. 309; (d) p. 95.
7 Admiral of the Fleet Viscount Cunningham, *A Sailor's Odyssey* (Hutchinson, 1951), p. 315.
8 Christopher Buckley, Greece and Crete 1941 (HMSO, 1952), pp. 309–10.
9 Other Freyberg Papers.
10 *Official History NZ*: Documents, vol. I (1949), p. 257.
11 Gavin Long, *Greece, Crete and Syria*, vol. II of *Australia in the War of 1939–45* (Series 1, Army) (Australian War Memorial, 1953), pp. 182–3, 143.
12 Joint Planning Staff paper on Greece, 8 January 1941.
13 John Masefield, *The Nine Day Wonder* (Heinemann, 1941).

Chapter 17: Crete – The Prelude (pages 263–289)

1 Cunningham, *A Sailor's Odyssey*: (a) p. 232; (b) pp. 282–3; (c) p. 358.
2 Report of the Inter-Services Committee on Crete chaired by Brigadier G. Salisbury-Jones, 2 July 1941; tells in detail the story of the army's participation in Crete.

[595]

3   Churchill, *Second World War*, vol. III: (a): p. 239; (b) p. 201; (c) pp. 239–40; (d) pp. 308–9; (e) p. 240; (f) pp. 241–2.

4   Freyberg Papers.

5   WO 106/3240 Cipher 64174, 30 April 1941. PRO.

6   Anthony Cave Brown, *The Life of Sir Stewart Menzies* (Michael Joseph, 1988), pp. 338–40.

7   Some of these messages the author later found in the Orange Leonard (OL) series, PRO, Kew.

8   AIR 40/2323. PRO Kew.

9   Report on battle of Crete by Freyberg to NZ Minister of Defence.

10 HQ CREFORCE 5/23, 29 April 1941. Freyberg Papers.

11 WO 106/Cipher 644141 (MI 14), 29 April 1941. PRO.

12 JIC (41) 181, 27 April 1941. PRO.

13 I. McD. G. Stewart, *The Struggle for Crete* (Oxford University Press, 1966), pp. 103, 127–8.

14 Letter from Major-General Sir Digby Raeburn to the author, 29 November 1981.

15 WO 201/61. PRO.

16 Martin Gilbert, *'Finest Hour': Winston S. Churchill, 1939–41* (Heinemann, 1983), pp. 1085–6.

17 PREM 3/109 No. 119, 12 May 1941. PRO.

18 Letter to the author dated 29 August 1982 from Group Captain G. Francis, Commanding 230 Sunderland Flying Boat Squadron RAF.

19 Letter from Professor Sir Harry Hinsley to the author dated 17 December 1981.

20 30 Blenheim Squadron Records AIR 27/344. PRO.

21 Engagement Diary for 1941. Freyberg Papers.

22 The Dorman-Smith Papers deposited in the John Rylands University Library, Manchester.

23 The five officers mentioned in Wavell's letter were either on Freyberg's staff or his subordinate commanders. Barbara Freyberg at this time was on board ship rounding the Cape and due at Suez in mid-June 1941. Paul was flown from Crete to Cairo on 7 May 1941.

24 . This appreciation is reproduced from Freyberg's own copy, brought out of Crete with his personal papers.

25 PREM 3/109. PRO Kew.

26 *The Political Diary of Hugh Dalton, 1940–45*, ed. Ben Pimlott (Jonathan Cape, 1986).

27 *Official History NZ*: Dan Davin, *Crete* (1953), pp. 59–60; 45.

28 Letter from Major-General Sir Guy Salisbury-Jones to the author, 2 July 1983.

Chapter 18: Crete – The Battle (pages 290–312)

Most of the narrative and excerpts in this chapter are from the many hundred pages of Freyberg's notes, so as to give a shortened and consecutive account of the battle as far as possible in his words. Two of the most comprehensive published accounts are those in Notes 1 and 2.

1   *Official History NZ*: Dan Davin, *Crete*. Davin's book drew much on Freyberg's papers.
2   Stewart, *The Struggle for Crete*: (2a) p. 92; (2b) pp. 206, 208–9; (2c) p. 318; (2d) pp. 319–20; (2e) p. 208. See Note 13, Chapter 17.
3   Report on the Battle for Crete by Freyberg to the New Zealand Minister of Defence, 1941.
4   Freyberg's unpublished narratives and papers.
5   Cunningham, *A Sailor's Odyssey*, pp. 375–6, 372–90.
6   From a memorandum handed to the author by Major-General Sir Guy Salisbury-Jones on 4 February 1982. In May 1941 he was the British liaison officer with the Greeks and attached to HQ Creforce.
7   Report of the Inter-Services Committee on Crete, chaired by Brigadier G. Salisbury-Jones, 2 July 1941. PRO Kew WO 201/99.
8   Report dated 18 July 1941 from Colonel Selwyn Kenrick, acting ADMS HQ CREFORCE, usually ADMS 2 NZ Division.

Chapter 19: Crete – The Inquiry and the Aftermath (pages 313–335)

1   Freyberg's unpublished narratives.
2   Report of the Inter-Services Committee on Crete chaired by Brigadier G. Salisbury-Jones, 2 July 1941.
3   Letter to Sir Guy Salisbury-Jones from Major-General Sir Robert Laycock, 21 November 1959.
4   Letter from Lord Ballantrae to Sir Alister McIntosh, 16 September 1977.
5   PRO Kew WO 201/2652 678/10, 4 February 1947.
6   PRO Kew WO 201/2652, 26 September 1941.
7   PRO Kew WO 193/970.
8   Stewart, *The Struggle for Crete*, pp. 120, 476.
9   PRO PREM 3/109.
10 Martin Gilbert, *'Finest Hour': Winston S. Churchill 1939–1941*, pp. 1110–15.
11 Letter from Michael King (biographer of Peter Fraser) to the author, 11 December 1982.

12 John McLeod, *Myth and Reality* (Reed Methuen, 1986), pp. 175, 177.
13 *Official History NZ*: W. G. McClymont, *To Greece*, pp. 489–90.
14 *Official History NZ*: Documents, vol. I, No. 447.
15 James Thorn, *Peter Fraser* (Odhams, 1952), p. 196.
16 Major-General Sir John Kennedy, *The Business of War* (Hutchinson, 1957), p. 160.
17 WO 216/125 Cipher 85190, 20 August 1941.
18 WO 216/125 Cipher 11519, 21 August 1941.
19 WO 216/125 Cipher 11931, 27 August 1941.
20 WO 216/125 Cipher C5/28, 2 September 1941.
21 From Land Forces Greece to War Office, 15 March 1946.
22 Long, *Greece, Crete and Syria*, p. 316.
23 Enemy Documents Section (EDS): EDS/Apprec/1/Supp III, paras 22, 23; and associated documents.
24 War Cabinet (41) 44th Conclusions, Minute 2, pp. 85–7.
25 PRO PREM file for 1941, p. 58.
26 *Hansard*, House of Commons, 10 June 1941, cols 147–8.
27 Churchill, *Second World War*, vol. III, p. 268.

Chapter 20: The Relief of Tobruk (pages 336–361)

The three official histories of the 1941 battles to relieve Tobruk by Playfair (British), Agar-Hamilton (South African) and Murphy (New Zealand), are admirably written and describe the action in great detail, but for that very reason they are somewhat indigestible for the ordinary reader. Only Field Marshal Lord Carver's two accounts 'Tobruk' and 'Dilemmas of the Desert War' are in a form that is easily understood by laymen.

1 Churchill, *Second World War*, vol. III, pp. 304, 307.
2 Peter Coates, *Of Generals and Gardens* (Weidenfeld, 1976), p. 104.
3 *Official History NZ*: W. E. Murphy, *The Relief of Tobruk* (War History Branch, 1961), pp. 1–29, 41, 108, 307–8, 352, 368, 414–15, 464, 524.
4 Freyberg Papers.
5 Major-General Sir Howard Kippenberger, *Infantry Brigadier* (Oxford University Press, 1949), pp. 81–3.
6 Sir Geoffrey Cox, *A Tale of Two Battles* (Kimber, 1987), pp. 151, 179–80, 182–3.
7 Narrative and Lessons of NZ Division in Cyrenaica, HQ NZ Division in the Field, 4 January 1942.
8 Letter dated 28 September 1950 from Brigadier Latham, Historical

Section, Cabinet Office, London to General Kippenberger, NZ War
History Branch.

Chapter 21: The Lebanon and Minqar Qaim (pages 362–382)

1 Freyberg Papers.
2 *Official History NZ:* J. L. Scoullar, *The Battle for Egypt.* (War History
   Branch, 1955): (a) p. 5; (b) p. 14; (c) pp. 22–3; (d) pp. 34–6; (e) pp. 50, 52,
   56; (f) p. 66; (g) pp. 69, 74; (i) pp. 97–9; (k) pp. 113–15; (m) ch. 32; (n)
   pp. 382–5.
3 Hetherington, *Blamey*, pp. 118–24.
4 Field Marshal Lord Carver, *Dilemmas of the Desert War* (Batsford, 1986),
   pp. 54–61.
5 *Official History NZ:* Documents, Vol. II (1951), Signals 119–129,
   pp. 90–7.
6 Field Marshal Erich von Manstein, *Lost Victories* (Methuen, 1958), p.
   275.
7 Kippenberger, *Infantry Brigadier*, pp. 127–8.
8 Letter from Freyberg in hospital in Egypt to his son in England, July
   1942.
9 *The Rommel Papers*, ed. B. H. Liddell-Hart (Collins, 1953), pp. 238, 240.
10 *The Times*, 3 July 1942.
11 Stevens, *Freyberg, VC*, p. 90.
12 Churchill, *Second World War*, vol. IV, *The Hinge of Fate* (Cassell, 1951),
   p. 382.

Chapter 22: The Battles of Alam Halfa and Alamein (pages 383–408)

1 Official History NZ: Ronald Walker, *Alam Halfa and Alamein* (1967): (a)
   pp. 22–4; (b) p. 7; (c) pp. 93–5; (d) p. 176; (e) p. 195; (f) pp. 211–12.
2 Nigel Hamilton, *Monty: The Making of a General, 1887–1942* (Hamish
   Hamilton, 1981): (a) pp. 620–1; (b) pp. 676–83; (c) pp. 692–3; (d) p.
   700; (e) p. 642; (g) p. 642; (h) p. 748; (j) p. 789; (m) pp. 800–1; (n) p. 804;
   (p) p. 812; (r) p. 817; (s) pp. 827–30; (t) p. 831.
3 Alan Moorehead, *Montgomery* (Hamish Hamilton, 1946), p. 123.
4 Freyberg Papers.
5 Harold Macmillan, *Winds of Change 1914–1939* (Macmillan, 1966),
   pp. 92–4.
6 Churchill, *Second World War*, vol IV, p. 464.
7 Stevens, *Freyberg, VC*, p. 67.

8   Signal P132, 3 November 1942, for Minister of Defence from Freyberg. *Official History NZ:* Documents, vol II, p. 126.
9   B. L. Montgomery, *Alamein and the Desert War*, ed. Derek Jewell (Sphere, 1967), pp. 75–6.
10   Kippenberger, *Infantry Brigadier*, p. 228.

Chapter 23: The Salamander of the British Empire (pages 409–421)

1   Personal communication to author from Lieutenant-General Sir Leonard Thornton.
2   *Official History NZ:* Major-General W. G. Stevens, *Bardia to Enfidaville* (War History Branch, 1962): (a) p. 2; (b) pp. 5–6; (c) pp. 13–14; (d) p. 25; (e) p. 84; (f) pp. 88–94; (g) p. 98; (h) pp. 100–7.
3   Freyberg Papers.
4   Earl of Rocksavage, *A Day's March Nearer Home* (Bumpus, 1947), p. 156.
5   *The Times*, 28 January 1943.

Chapter 24: The Last of the Desert (pages 422–435)

1   *Official History NZ:* Stevens, *Bardia to Enfidaville.* (a) pp. 122–32; (b) p. 199; (c) pp. 251–80; (d) p. 355; (e) p. 386.
2   Nigel Hamilton, *Monty: Master of the Battlefield 1942–1944*, vol. II (Hamish Hamilton, 1983): (a) p. 143; (b) pp. 144–5; (c) p. 170; (d) p. 183.
3   Freyberg Papers.
4   General Sir Charles Richardson, *Send for Freddie: The Story of Montgomery's Chief of Staff, Major-General Sir Francis de Guingand, KBE, CB, DSO* (Kimber, 1987) p. 117.
5   *Official History NZ:* Documents, vol. II; (a) pp. 171–3 (10 March 1943); (b) p. 192 and n.
6   *Hansard*, 30 March 1943.
7   Churchill, *Second World War*, vol. IV, pp. 846, 851.
8   Alan Moorehead, *The End in Africa* (Hamish Hamilton, 1943), pp. 209–10.

Chapter 25: Europe or the Pacific? (pages 436–446)

1   *Official History NZ:* N. C. Phillips, *Italy*, vol. I, *The Sangro to Cassino* (War History Branch, 1957): (a) p. 26; (b) pp. 29–30.
2   New Zealand Division Diary kept by John White.
3   Freyberg Papers.

4 *Official History NZ*: Documents, vol. II: (a) p. 263; (b) p. 266; (c) p. 268; (d) p. 271.

Chapter 26: The Sangro and the Cassino Battles (pages 447–468)

1 Hamilton, *Monty*, vol. II, 1942–44: (a) p. 445; (b) p. 433; (c) p. 438; (d) p. 446; (e) pp. 449–50; (f) p. 477.
2 Freyberg Papers.
3 Freyberg's personal signals to New Zealand: (a) P189, 4 January 1944; (b) P191, 11 January 1944; (c) P172, 28 August 1943; (d) P203, 4 April 1944.
4 Churchill, *Second World War*, vol. V, *Closing the Ring*, quoting General Westphal's 'Heer in Fesseln', pp. 426, 432.
5 *Official History NZ*, Phillips, *Italy*, vol. I, *The Sangro to Cassino*: (a) p. 204; (b) p. 342; (c) p. 193; (d) p. 261; (e) p. 262–3; (f) p. 266; (g) pp. 267–8; (h) p. 269; (i) p. 279; (j) p. 337.
6 Letter from Freyberg to Kippenberger, 11 August 1950. NZ Histories Archives. After the war Freyberg wrote his considered view of the bombing of the abbey on 15 February 1944. This was put in a letter to the New Zealand military historian on 11 August 1950, when Freyberg was asked to comment on a draft report of the battle produced by the British Historical Section of the Cabinet Office. See p. 536.
7 Owen Chadwick, *Britain and the Vatican during the Second World War* (Cambridge University Press, 1986), pp. 278–84.
8 Letters from Freyberg to Kippenberger, 3 January and 16 December 1955. NZ Histories Archives.
9 *Father Dolly: The Memoirs of the Rt Revd Don Brookes* (Henry Melland, 1983), p. 155.
10 J. T. Burrows, *Pathway Among Men* (Whitcombe & Tombs, 1974), pp. 181–2.
11 Dan Davin, 'The General and the Nightingale' in *The Gorse Blooms Pale* (Nicholson & Watson, 1947), pp. 190–8.

Chapter 27: The Advance to Florence and the Lombardy Plain (pages 469–485)

1 *Official History NZ:* Robin Kay, *Italy*, vol. II, *From Cassino to Trieste*: (War History Branch, 1967): (a) pp. 55–85; (b) p. 92; (c) p. 169; (d) p. 215; (e) p. 228; (f) p. 387; (g) p. 292; (h) p. 346; (i) p. 405.
2 Letter from Sir Charles Mott-Radclyffe after Freyberg's death, in *Windsor and Eton Express*, July 1963.

3   Peter McIntyre, *The Painted Years* (Reed, 1962), pp. 77–85.
4   Field Marshal Alexander's Dispatches, in 'The Allied Armies in Italy', *London Gazette*, 6 June 1960, p. 2930.
5   Burrows, *Pathway Among Men*, pp. 198–9.
6   Contained in letter from Major J. C. White, HQ 2 NZ Div., to Lady Freyberg in London, 15 September 1944.
7   Freyberg Papers. Montgomery letter dated 20 February 1945.
8   *Official History NZ:* Documents, vol. II, pp. 364–78.

Chapter 28: One more river . . . and the dash to Trieste (pages 486–499)

1   Cox: *The Road to Trieste*: (a) p. 83; (b) p. 83; (c) p. 60; (d) pp. 92–3; (e) p. 108; (f) pp. 126–7; (g) p. 129; (h) pp. 130–1; (i) pp. 161–3; (m) p. 187; (n) Memorandum from Sir Geoffrey Cox to the author, 29 August 1988.
2   *Official History NZ: Italy*, vol. II: (a) p. 460; (b) p. 462; (c) p. 463; (d) p. 506; (e) p. 509; (f) p. 513; (g) p. 516; (h) pp. 525–6 including Freyberg letter dated 2 July 1955; (i) p. 532–3; (m) p. 535; (n) p. 536–7; (p) p. 541–2.
3   Freyberg Papers.
4   Citation for Legion of Merit Degree of Commander:

Lieutenant General Sir Bernard C. Freyberg, V.C., K.C.B., K.B.E., C.M.G., D.S.O., New Zealand Expeditionary Force, performed outstanding services as commander of 2 New Zealand Division in Italy from 1 April to 2 May 1945. His division played a vital part in breaching the German defense line on the Senio River. So skillful was his movement of troops that the Germans were allowed no respite in their rapid retreat, and at no time was contact lost with the enemy. When the Germans withdrew across the Po River, the New Zealanders were the first British Eighth Army formation to secure a bridgehead over that river and to pursue the fleeing enemy northward. The 2NZ Division was the first to reach and breach the Adige Line, and climaxed its glorious campaign by entering and capturing Trieste on the day that hostilities ceased in the Italian theater. A large measure of the credit for these great accomplishments belongs to General Freyberg for his keen foresight and sound tactical planning of the attack, for his expert handling of his troops and for his ability to meet and cope with unforeseen problems that arose in the heat and stress of battle. His accomplishments and those of 2 New Zealand Division constituted a great contribution to the success of the 15th Army Group in northern Italy.

(sgd) HARRY TRUMAN

Chapter 29: Cold War and Peace (pages 500–513)

1 Freyberg Papers.
2 *Official History NZ*: Documents, vol. II: (a) pp. 415–16 and 415 n; (b) pp. 419–21; (c) pp. 444–8.
3 *Official History NZ: Italy*, vol. II: (a) p. 562; (b) p. 565; (c) pp. 570–1; (d) pp. 575–7; (e) pp. 577–8; (f) pp. 578–82.
4 ML2256, 15 August 1945, TOPSEC and personal for Prime Minister from Freyberg.
5 McIntyre, *Painted Years*, p. 85.

Chapter 30: Governor-General of New Zealand – I (pages 514–531)

The principal sources for this chapter and the following chapter are: (a) Official Government House records 1946–1952; (b) Lady Freyberg's personal diaries 1946–1952; (c) Her scrapbooks for the period; (d) Contemporary letters and papers.
1 Marie Rambert, *Quicksilver* (Macmillan, 1972), p. 186.
2 Moorehead, *Gallipoli*, pp. 107–112.

Chapter 31: Governor-General of New Zealand – II (pages 532–554)

1 *New Zealand Law Journal*, 7 June 1949, pp. 103 ff.
2 Freyberg Papers.
3 Christchurch *Press*, 10 November 1950.
4 Christchurch *Star Sun*, 3 January 1951.
5 *New Zealand Medical Journal*, vol. L, No. 275 (April 1951).
6 New Zealand *Evening Post*, 4 July 1952.
7 *The Times*, 30 July 1952.
8 *The Times*, 14 August 1952.
9 *The Dominion*, 14 August 1952.
10 *The Times*, 16 August 1952.

Chapter 32: Windsor (pages 555–574)

1 Freyberg Papers.
2 *Daily Telegraph*, December 1953.
3 *Hansard*, HL, 17 March 1954, pp. 474–5.
4 *New Zealand News*, London, 9 November 1954.
5 BBC transcript and letter, 3 December 1954.

APPENDIX V

Abbreviations used

(including foreign words, technical terms and names given to special operations)

AA = anti-aircraft

ACROBAT = Planned continuation of CRUSADER to capture Tripolitania. Also known as GRADUATE.

ACV = Armoured Command Vehicle

ADC = aide-de-camp

ADMS = Assistant Director of Medical Services

ADS = Advanced Dressing Station

AIF = Australian Imperial Force

ANVIL (later DRAGOON) = Code-name for Allied landing in southern France

ANZAC = Australian and New Zealand Army Corps

AOC = Air Officer Commanding

(A)QMG = (Assistant) Quartermaster-General

AT = anti-tank

BARBAROSSA = German invasion of Russia, 22 June 1941

Battery = two, three or four troops of guns

BATTLEAXE = British offensive of 15–17 June 1941 on the Egyptian–Libyan frontier

Bde = Brigade

BEF = British Expeditionary Force

BERESFORD = 8 Army operation, 3–4 Sept 1942 against flank of Rommel's advance to Alam Halfa

BGS = Brigadier, General Staff (chief staff officer at Corps or Army)

Bir = well or cistern (pl. Abiar)
Blenheim = British twin-engined bomber
Bn = Battalion
Bofors = Automatic 40 mm light anti-aircraft gun of Swedish design
Box = All-round defensive position for battalion, brigade or division in static operations
Bren = Standard British light machine-gun
Bren-carrier = Light armoured tracked vehicle intended to carry bren gun, but also used for reconnaissance, etc.
BSA = Birmingham Small Arms Company
BTE = British Troops in Egypt

CB = Companion of the Order of the Bath
CCS = Casualty Clearing Station
CGS = Chief of the General Staff
CIGS = Chief of the Imperial General Staff
C-in-C = Commander-in-Chief
CO = Commanding Officer
Commando = unit, or member of such, trained for amphibious raids on enemy territory
Corps = number of divisions under a lieutenant-general or major-general
COS = Chief of Staff
coy = company (in infantry, three platoons; otherwise three or four sections)
CPO = Chief Petty Officer
CRA = Commander, Royal Artillery (of division)
CRE = Commander, Royal Engineers (of division)
Creforce = British and Dominion Troops in Crete
Crumbling = Minor operation to improve local situation
CRUSADER = Code-name for British offensive resulting in relief of Tobruk (November–December 1941)
Crusader = British Cruiser tank Mark VI, in Crusader campaign

DA = Deputy Adjutant
D-Day etc = Starting date of an operation
detachment = unit of troops or ships separated and sent on a special mission
Div = Division (number of brigades under a major-general)
DMO = Director of Military Operations
DMS = Director of Medical Services
DSC = Distinguished Service Cross

DSO = Distinguished Service Order

Echelon = First, Second, Third, three main contingents of 2NZEF in
  order of embarkation
EDS = Enemy Documents Section
ENCROACH = Operation on the Sangro, November 1943

Fd = Field
FDL = Forward defended locality
FE = Forward Everywhere (medical grading)
Fifth Column(ist) = Subversive group working for Axis powers (mem-
  ber of the same)
Fire-eater = 8 Army operation to capture Tripoli, January 1943
FSDs = Forward Supply Depots

Gabr = tomb
Gasr = fort, or hill that resembles one
GBE = Grand Cross of the British Empire
GCB = Grand Commander of the Order of the Bath
GCMG = Knight Grand Cross of the Order of St Michael and St
  George
(G)HQ = (General) Headquarters
GOC(-in-c) = General Officer Commanding (-in-Chief)
GSO (1, 2, 3) = General Staff Officer (Class 1, 2, 3). Also G1, etc.
Gp = Group (Battalion or Brigade) force of all arms
Grant = American M3 medium (Lee) tank

HAC = Honourable Artillery Company
H-hour = Time of launch of operation
HMAS = His Majesty's Australian Ship
HMNZS = His Majesty's New Zealand Ship
HMS = His Majesty's Ship
Honey = Nickname for General Stuart tank (American M3)
HQ = Headquarters

I tank (Infantry tank) = heavily-armoured slow tank, either Mark II
  (Matilda) or Mark III (Valentine), designed to support infantry
  attacks
IO = Intelligence Officer

JIC = Joint Intelligence Committee
Jock column = usually a field battery, two infantry companies, anti-

tank troop, etc., on an independent mission (after Brig. 'Jock' Campbell)

JU52 = Junkers 52, the Luftwaffe's main transport plane

KBE = Knight Commander of the British Empire
KCB = Knight Commander of the Order of the Bath

Lee = American M3 (Grant) tank with 75mm, 37mm guns
LMG = Light machine-gun
LO = Liaison Officer
LRDG = Long Range Desert Group
Luftwaffe = German Air Force

M13/40 = Chief Italian medium tank
MA = Military Assistant
Mark (I, II, etc) = designation of production type, especially of tanks
Marsa, mersa = fort, anchorage
Matilda = see I tank – the only British tank to serve through the war
MC = Military Cross
MDS = Medical Dressing Station
ME(F) = Middle East (Forces)
MMG = Medium machine-gun
MNBDO = Mobile Naval Base Defence Organisation
MO = Medical Officer

NAAFI = Navy, Army, and Air Force Institute
NCO = Non-commissioned officer
NZEF = New Zealand Expeditionary Force

'O' group = Orders group
OC = Officer Commanding (squadron, battery, company)
OCTU = Officer Cadet Training Unit
OKW = Oberkommando der Wehrmacht (Supreme Command of the German Armed Forces)
OP = Observation Post
Ops = Operations; or staff branch dealing with them

PA = Personal Assistant
Panther = German medium tank with 75mm gun
Panzer = German tank or armoured unit
Platoon = Approx 30 men in three sections, under a junior officer
POW = Prisoner of War

PRO = Public Records Office

'Q' Branch = Supply services
QMG = Quartermaster-General

RAMC = Royal Army Medical Corps
RAOC = Royal Army Ordnance Corps
RASC = Royal Army Service Corps
recce = Reconnaissance; reconnoitre
regt = Regiment
Reinforcements (4th, 5th, etc) = Successive contingents of 2NZEF
    after Third Echelon
RMS = Royal Mail Ship
RND = Royal Naval Division
RNVR = Royal Naval Volunteer Reserve
R/T = radio-telephony (wireless transmission of speech)

SAA = Small arms ammunition
section = smallest army formation; 8–10 men under NCO
Sherman = American M4 medium tank, with 75mm gun; the princi-
    pal battle tank of the British and US Armies in Second World War.
Sidi = saint, or marabout
Sommernachtstraum = German reconnaissance into Egypt, 14–16
    September 1941
spandau = Nickname for standard German light and medium
    machine-gun
SS = steam ship
Stuart (General) = American M3 light cruiser tank
Stuka = Junkers 87 dive-bomber

TA = Territorial Army
Tac HQ = Tactical headquarters
Tiger = German heavy tank with 88mm gun
Trigh = track

2NZDiv = Second New Zealand Division
2NZEF = Second New Zealand Expeditionary Force

'U' info = Ultra information

Valentine = see I tank; Mark III
VC = Victoria Cross

ABBREVIATIONS USED

'W' force = Expeditionary force sent to Greece, April 1941
wadi = watercourse, usually dry
WWSA = Women's War Service Auxiliary

For readers who may not be readily conversant with army terms and formations, it may be helpful to explain that, from the smallest units upwards, there are normally:

3 sections (8–10 persons each) in 1 platoon (25–32 each)
3 platoons in 1 company (100–120 each)
3 or 4 companies in 1 battalion (600–1,000 each)
3 battalions in 1 brigade (4,000–8,000 each)
3 brigades in 1 division (10,000–20,000 each)

This is a basic guide rather than a watertight organisation, and above a division there are Army Corps, Armies, and Army Groups; but these vary so much in composition that it can be misleading to define them. Of course, as formations get larger there are more ancillary staff to account for, and specialist units as well.

Index

Charles, Prince of Wales, 529
Charlotte Jane (ship), 543
Cheape, Brig., 137
Cherry Tree Avenue (Surrey), 184, 191
Cherwell, Frederick Lindemann, Viscount, 224
Chifley, J. B., 530
Christchurch (New Zealand), 542–4
Churchill, Clementine, 48, 176
Churchill, Lady Gwendolyn, 146
Churchill, Randolph, 525
Churchill, (Sir) Winston: and ULTRA in Crete, 4;
 and Royal Naval Division, 35–7, 42, 45, 49,
 77; meets BCF in Great War, 37, 42; resigns
 after Gallipoli disaster, 64; BCF entertains,
 98, 176–7; visits BCF in France, 107, 167;
 and BCF's wounds, 147; at Gallipoli memorial
 ceremony, 161; congratulates BCF on
 promotion to major-general, 176; friendship,
 177, 188; and war threat, 195; supports BCF's
 wartime appointment, 201; becomes Prime
 Minister, 218; BCF visits in war, 224–5, 228;
 and BCF's views on Middle East situation,
 225–6, 228; and defence of Egypt, 228–9;
 visits New Zealand forces, 230; keeps New
 Zealand forces in Britain, 230–1; BCF's
 relations with, 234; and Wavell, 234, 241, 285;
 and Greek campaign, 243, 256; on Rommel's
 successes, 249; and defence of Crete, 264,
 333–4; and BCF's command in Crete, 276,
 280; and battle for Crete, 279, 285, 307, 335;
 and use of ULTRA intelligence, 279–81,
 285–6; calls for inquiries on Crete, 314,
 320–1; Inglis reports to, 319–20, 322;
 criticises BCF, 320; reconciliation with BCF,
 334, 381; presses Auchinleck to attack, 339;
 praises New Zealanders for Minqar Qaim
 action, 378–9; loses confidence in Auchinleck,
 381; at 1942 Cairo conference, 381–2; visits
 8th Army, 386–7, 415; praises BCF and New
 Zealanders, 387; at Tripoli victory parade,
 420–1; calls BCF a salamander, 420–1; and
 BCF's dual command at Mareth, 430; and
 BCF's position and promotion to Corps,
 431–3; gives priority to Europe, 438; supports
 campaign in Italy, 447; and post-war European
 settlement, 447–8; disappointment over Anzio,
 454; illness in Carthage, 455; questions BCF
 on Cassino attack, 459; visits New Zealand
 Division in Italy, 476; and BCF's plane
 accident injury, 478; and Yugoslavs in Trieste,
 501–2; 1945 Election defeat, 506; at Alamein
 reunions, 511, 557–8; on bombing of Monte
 Cassino, 535; 1951 Election success, 547;
 receives Garter, 562; 80th birthday tributes,
 564; BCF visits in hospital, 570
Churchward, W. T., 17, 537
Citerne (France), 78
Clapham, S/Ldr. Peter, 533
Clarendon Place (London): Freybergs' home in,
 158, 165, 175–6, 194; move from in war, 196;
 rented during BCF's absence in New Zealand,
 514; renovated on return, 555–6; life at, 561;
 sold, 562

Clark, Alan: *The Fall of Crete*, 4
Clark, Gen. Mark: commands US 5th Army, 458;
 and bombing of Monte Cassino, 462, 466,
 535–6; in Italy, 507, 511; BCF invites to New
 Zealand, 534–5; blames BCF for Monte
 Cassino bombing, 535–6; *Calculated Risk*, 535
Clifton, Brig. George, 259, 355, 369, 392
Coates, Peter, 336
Cobbold, C. F. and Lady Hermione, 545
Cobham, Charles John Lyttelton, 10th Viscount
 and Elizabeth, Lady, 540
Colchester (Essex), 206
Cole, Michael, 514, 520–1, 523, 529, 533; killed,
 560
Condé, Gen., 204
Conservative Party (British), 189–90
Constable, Lt. c.c., 87
Constantine's Bay, Cornwall, 196
Cook, Capt. James: Diary, 552
Coolidge, Calvin, 576
Cooper, Alfred Duff, 195
Cooper, Sir Gilbert, 28
Corbett, Gen. T. W., 375, 386
Coronation, 1953, 559
Cory, Sir John, 160
Cotton, Dr T. F. 182–3, 186
Courtauld, Samuel, 176
Courtrai (Belgium), 136
Coutts Bank, 42
Cox, (Sir) Geoffrey: produces troop newspaper,
 273; in relief of Tobruk, 346, 348, 355; on
 captured German general, 356–7; BCF meets
 in USA, 439, 443; in Italy, 471, 486, 489–90,
 492–3, 495–6, 498; and BCF's character,
 577; *The Road to Trieste*, 48, 486–7; *A Tale of
 Two Battles*, 346
Crawford-Stewart, Col., 67
Creasy, Sir Gerald, 562
Crèche, La (France), 125
CREFORCE: headquarters, 268–70
Cresswell, Lt. T. E., 84
Crete: Allied forces in Greece evacuated to, 257–8,
 262–3, 265; as British base, 263–4; as
 battlefield, 264–5; defence plans and strategy,
 266–8, 270–3, 275, 333–4; ULTRA and,
 276–82, 284–9, 320, 324–5, 333, 335;
 German plans for, 283–4, 330–1; Courts of
 Inquiry on, 287–8, 314–21; Allied troops and
 equipment in, 290–2; hospital and medical
 facilities, 291–2, 310; supply difficulties, 292;
 Greeks in, 293; weak air defences, 293–4;
 German airborne attacks on, 297–301, 305–7,
 331; casualties, 302, 306–7, 312, 329–31,
 334; defeat in, 308–9; evacuation, 309–12;
 Commons emergency debate on, 333; effects
 of campaign, 333–5; BCF visits in 1945, 510
Crete News, 275
Crittenberger, Gen. Willis D., 517
Crusader, Operation, 344–5, 347–60, 410
Cunningham, General Alan, 342–4, 349, 384
Cunningham, Admiral Sir Andrew: and Greek
 campaign, 244; and defence of Crete, 263,
 267, 272–3, 296; and ULTRA in Matapan

Norrie, Gen. Willoughby: experience, 343; commands XXX Corps, 344; and Operation Crusader, 349, 359; and disposition of New Zealand Division, 373; resignation, 384; in Australia, 531; visits New Zealand, 537; succeeds BCF as Governor-General, 549–50
Northcote, Gen. Sir John, 530
Nuffield, William Morris, Viscount, 522
Nugent, Sir Terence, 557
Nye, Gen. Archibald, 370

Ocean, HMS, 59
O'Connor, Gen. Sir Richard: rank, 188; in Egypt and Libya, 236, 240; on Wilson, 247; captured, 249, 336, 384
O'Hea, Patrick: Reminiscences of the Mexican Revolution, 31–2
OL 302 (Orange Leonard; intelligence documents, Crete), 276, 282
Olivier, Laurence, 529
Olympia, SS, 76
Orion, HMS, 39, 295
Osborne, Sir d'Arcy, 470
Osborne, Lt.-Gen. Edmund Archibald, 142
Ostler, Mr Justice, 212
Otago University, Dunedin, 20, 22
Ottley, Bruce, 176

Pacific: campaign in, 437
Pacific Islands Dependencies, 526–8
Paget, Gen. Sir Bernard, 230
Paine, Lesbia (née Wilson), 22, 30
Pakenham, Francis Aungier Pakenham, 1st Baron (later 7th Earl of Longford), 516
Palairet, Sir Michael, 243–4, 266, 293
Pangalos, Gen., 255
Papagos, Field Marshal A., 242
Paris Conference (1916), 93
Paris, Gen. Sir Archibald, 41, 52, 59, 76, 95, 160
Park, Brigadier Keith, 471, 541
Parkinson, Brig. G. B., 486, 490
Parminter, Brig. Reginald, 439
Passchendaele see Ypres, Third Battle of
Patton, Gen. George, 422
Paulus, Gen. Friedrich von, 330
Peake, Harald, 537
Pearl Harbor, 332, 360
Peart, Col. J. N., 392
Pelly, Captain, 222
'Pelorus Jack' (dolphin), 16
Penboss, Lucinda, 28–9, 33, 38
Penboss, Queenie, 27–8, 33–4, 38, 42
Perth, HMAS, 258, 295
Peter, Prince of Greece, 369
Philip, Prince, Duke of Edinburgh, 525, 547–8, 557
Phillips, N. C., 468
Pickerill, Professor H. P., 22
Pienaar, Gen. D. H., 357–8
Piraeus (Greece), 246, 254
Pirbright Camp (Surrey), 145
Pius XII, Pope, 461, 475
Platt, Gen. Sir William, 142

Plumer, Gen. Sir Herbert, 124–5, 133, 139
Po river (Italy), 494
Poland, 196
  Polish Forces
  Corps, 468, 488
  3 Carpathian Division, 493–4
  5 Kresorva Division, 484
  Brigade, 249
Poperinghe, 122
Porritt, Sir Arthur (later Lord), 540, 569
Port Wellington, MV, 515
Presidency and Assam District (India), 180–1, 188
Prince of Wales, HMS, 360
Pugilist, Operation, 425
Puttick, Lt.-Gen. Sir Edward: in Egypt, 232; and Greek campaign, 239; in evacuation from Greece, 257, 260; promoted to command New Zealand Division, 270; in defence of Crete, 287, 303–4, 308; relations with BCF, 303; evidence to Crete Inquiry, 324; made Chief of General Staff, 368; in Italy with Fraser, 471

Qattara Depression, 389–90
Queen Elizabeth, RMS, 195
Queree, Brigadier Ray, 458, 486, 568
Quilter, Lady, 73
Quilter, Lt.-Col. Arnold, 38, 41, 49, 51–2, 54, 64, 67, 76
Quinan, Gen. Sir Edward, 370

Rackham, Brig. B. B., 73
Radcliffe, Gen. Sir Percy, 175
Raeburn, Maj.-Gen. Sir Digby, 278
Rambert, Marie, 528
Ramillies, HMS, 212–13
Ramsden, Gen. W. H. C., 384
Ravelsburg Ridge, 126–7
Ravenstein, Maj.-Gen. Johann von, 356–7
Rawlinson, Gen. Sir Henry, 39, 133, 140
Reno river (Italy), 494
Renton, Gen. J. M. L., 384
Repulse, HMS, 360
Retimo (Crete), 283, 289, 297–9, 302–3, 306, 308–9
Rhind, A. E. M., 31
Ribbentrop, Joachim von, 193–4
Ribblesdale, Thomas Lister, 4th Baron, 76
Richardson, Lt.-Gen. Charles: Send for Freddie, 425, 427
Richardson, Maj. George S., 21, 36–7
Riddell-Webster, General Sir Thomas Sheridan, 142
Ridgway, Gen. Matthew, 558
Ritchie, Lt.-Gen. Neil, 343, 349, 363, 373–5, 384
Robert, F/Lt. David, 533
Roberts, Field Marshal Frederick Sleigh Roberts, 1st Earl, 70
Robinson, William, 154
Rocksavage, George Hugh Cholmondeley, Earl of: A Day's March Nearer Home, 415
Rome, 471
Rommel, Gen. Erwin: arrives in North Africa, 241; captures Benghazi, 249; ULTRA intelligence

266; on defence of Crete, 267–8, 285; and BCF's knowledge and use of ULTRA intelligence, 268, 278, 281–2, 284–6; and inquiries into Crete, 288, 315–16, 318, 320–1; and air attacks on Navy, 295; messages from BCF in Crete, 299, 307, 311; orders BCF out of Crete, 312; BCF visits after Crete, 313; moves to India, 316; row with BCF, 321–2; replaced as Middle East Commander, 322, 338, 384; Fraser consults over BCF, 327–8; calls off Operation Battleaxe, 338; recommends knighthood for BCF, 361; at 1942 Cairo conference, 381
Wavell, Eugénie Marie, Viscountess, 313
Weir, General Steve, 369, 478, 577
Weldon, Lt.-Col., 136
Wellington (New Zealand), 11–15, 18–19, 149; *see also* Victoria University
Wellington College, 14–16, 19, 149, 517, 551
Wellington, Arthur Wellesley, 1st Duke of, 139
Wemyss, Gabriel, 116
Wemyss, Adm. Sir Rosslyn, 63
Wenlock, Lord and Lady (parents of Irene Lawley), 131
Western Desert Court of Inquiry (1942), 375
Westminster, Hugh Richard Arthur Grosvenor, 2nd Duke of ('Bendor'), 165
Westmoreland, Col., 127
Weston, Maj.-Gen. C. E., 264, 266–7, 269–70, 275, 282, 312 & n
Westphal, Gen. Siegfried, 351, 353, 454
Whigham, Ian, 496
Whigham, Gen. Sir R., 166
White, Gen. Sir Brudenell, 68, 208
White, (Sir) John: appointed BCF's Personal Assistant, 212; in Greece, 250; in Crete, 275; leaves for Egypt, 311–12; keeps GOC's Diary, 343, 357; and Relief of Tobruk, 357; on Freyberg in Minqar Qaim action, 377; injured in car crash, 393; at Tripoli parade, 420; collects BCF in Cairo, 423; and Axis surrender in Tunisia, 435; 1943 visit to New Zealand, 439–40; on battle for Cassino, 462; on Churchill's visit, 476; leaves service, 484

White, Sir Thomas, 562
Whitelands House (Chelsea), 562–3
Wieltje (Flanders), 119
Wigram, Sir Henry and Lady, 520
Wigram, Maj. Neville, 514, 520, 533
Wigram, Poppy, 520
Wilder, Brig. N. P., 358, 362
Wilder's Gap (Tunisia), 424
Williams, Gen. G. C., 142
Willink, Henry, 190
Wilson, Admiral of the Fleet Sir Arthur, 71
Wilson, Helen, 24
Wilson, Field Marshal Henry Maitland, 1st Baron ('Jumbo'): at Camberley, 142; rank, 188; and disposal of New Zealand troops in Egypt, 234–5; commands expeditionary force in Greece, 236, 238, 241, 247, 250, 255; qualities, 247; and evacuation of Greece, 257, 259, 261; at conference in Crete, 266; and ULTRA, 269; and Crete strategy, 270; receives ULTRA intelligence, 281; commands Ninth Army in Lebanon, 368; at 1942 Cairo conference, 381
Wilson, Dr Macdonald, 11–12, 14, 18
Wimberley, Gen. D. N., 419
Windsor: BCF's appointment as Deputy Constable and occupation of Norman Tower, 556–7, 563; Victoria Barracks, 163
Winnezeele (Flanders), 119
Women's War Services Auxiliary (WWSA; NZ), 215
Woolwich, 149, 158, 160
Worsman, Sergeant, 167
Wryneck, HMS, 295

York, HMS, 245, 295
Ypres, Third Battle of (Passchendaele), 110–12, 122; Last Battle of, 133
Yugoslavia: and Greek campaign, 241–3; invaded, 249; claims on Trieste, 497–-502, 504; withdraws from Trieste, 504–5
Yule, Arthur L., 21, 23–4

Zaafran (Libya), 359
Zacatecas (Mexico), 31–2